X WINDOW SYSTEM

C Library and Protocol Reference

X WINDOW SYSTEM

C Library and Protocol Reference

Robert W. Scheifler   James Gettys   Ron Newman

With Al Mento and Al Wojtas

 Digital Press

Printed in the United States of America.

9 8 7 6 5 4 3 2

Order number EY-6737E-DP

Design: David Ford
Manuscript editor: Christie Williams
Production coordinator: Editorial Inc.
Index: Howard Burrows and Rosemary Simpson
Compositor: Black Dot Graphics
Printer: Murray Printing Company

DEC, DECnet, the Digital logo, ULTRIX, MicroVAX II, VAX, VAX-11, VAXstation, VAXstation II/GPX, VAX/VMS, VMS are trademarks of Digital Equipment Corporation.

IBM, Personal Computer AT, Personal Computer RT are trademarks of International Business Machines Corporation.

MS-DOS is a trademark of Microsoft Corporation.

PostScript is a trademark of Adobe Systems Inc.

UNIX is a trademark of AT&T Bell Laboratories.

X Window System is a trademark of The Massachusetts Institute of Technology.

Library of Congress Cataloging in Publication Data

Scheifler, Robert W., 1954-
  X window system.

  Includes index.
  1. X Window System (Computer system) 2. C (Computer program language) I. Gettys, James, 1953–
II. Newman, Ron, 1957-   . III. Title.
QA76.76.W56S34 1988   005.4'3   88-30869
ISBN 1-55558-012-2

Contents

Chapter 6. Graphics Functions 118

Acknowledgments

Xlib—C Library X Interface

The design and implementation of the first ten versions of X were primarily the work of three individuals: Robert Scheifler of the MIT Laboratory for Computer Science, Jim Gettys of Digital Equipment Corporation, and Ron Newman of MIT, while at MIT/Project Athena. X version 11, however, is the result of the efforts of dozens of individuals at almost as many locations and organizations. At the risk of offending some of the players by exclusion, we would like to acknowledge some of the people who deserve special credit and recognition. Our apologies to anyone inadvertently overlooked.

First our thanks goes to Phil Karlton and Scott McGregor, both of Digital, for their considerable contributions to the specification of the version 11 protocol. Digital employees Susan Augebranndt, Raymond Drewry, Todd Newman (all members of WSE), and Phil Karlton (of WSL) worked long and hard to produce the sample server implementation.

Next, our thanks goes to Ralph Swick (MIT/Project Athena and Digital) who kept it all together for us. He handled literally thousands of requests from people everywhere and saved the sanity of at least one of us. His calm good cheer was a foundation on which we could build.

Our thanks also go to Todd Brunhoff (Tektronix) who was "loaned" to MIT/Project Athena at exactly the right moment to provide very capable and much-needed assistance during the alpha and beta releases. He was responsible for the successful integration of sources from multiple sites; we would not have had a release without him.

Our thanks also go to Al Mento and Al Wojtas of Digital's ULTRIX Documentation Group. With good humor and cheer, they took a rough draft and made it an infinitely better and more useful document. The work they have done will help many everywhere. We also would like to thank Hal Murray (Digital SRC) and Peter George (Digital VMS) who contributed much by proofreading the early drafts of this document.

Our thanks also go to Jeff Dike (Digital UEG), Tom Benson, Jackie Granfield, and Vince Orgovan (Digital VMS), who helped with the library utilities implementation; to Hania Gajewska (Digital UEG-WSL) who, along with Ellis Cohen (CMU and Siemens), was instrumental in the semantic design of the window manager properties; to Dave Rosenthal (Sun Microsystems) who also contributed to the protocol and provided the sample generic color frame buffer device-dependent code; and to Tim Greenwood (Digital IECG) for his help in understanding international keyboards and for providing the KeySyms in Appendix E.

The alpha and beta test participants deserve special recognition and thanks as well. It is significant that the bug reports (and many fixes) during alpha and beta test came almost exclusively from just a few of the alpha testers, mostly hardware vendors working on product implementations of X. The continued public contribution of vendors and universities is certainly to the benefit of the entire X community.

Our special thanks must go to Sam Fuller, Vice-President of Corporate Research at Digital, who has remained committed to the widest public availability of X and who made it possible to greatly supplement MIT's resources with the Digital staff in order to make version 11 a reality. Many of the people mentioned here are part of the Western Software Laboratory (Digital UEG-WSL) of the ULTRIX Engineering group and work for Smokey Wallace, who has been vital to the project's success. Others not mentioned here worked on the toolkit and are acknowledged in the X Toolkit documentation.

Of course, we must particularly thank Paul Asente, formerly of Stanford University and now of Digital UEG-WSL, who wrote W, the predecessor to X, and Brian Reid, formerly of Stanford University and now of Digital WRL, who had much to do with W's design.

Finally, our thanks go to MIT, Digital Equipment Corporation, and IBM for providing the environment where it could happen.

X Window System Protocol

The primary contributors to the X11 protocol are: Dave Carver (Digital HPW); Branko Gerovac (Digital HPW); Jim Gettys (Digital SRC); Phil Karlton (Digital WSL); Scott McGregor (Digital SSG); Ram Rao (Digital UEG); David Rosenthal (Sun Microsystems); and Dave Winchell (Digital UEG).

The implementors of initial server who provided useful input are: Susan Angebranndt (Digital WSL); Raymond Drewry (Digital); and Todd Newman (Digital).

The invited reviewers who provided useful input are: Andrew Cherenson (Berkeley); Burns Fisher (Digital VMS); Dan Garfinkel (HP); Leo Hourvitz (Next); Brock Krizan (HP); David Laidlaw (Stellar); Dave Mellinger (Interleaf); Ron Newman (MIT); John Ousterhout (Berkeley); Andrew Palay (ITC CMU); Ralph Swick (MIT/Project Athena and Digital); Craig Taylor (Sun Microsystems); and Jeffery Vroom (Stellar).

Thanks go to Al Mento of Digital's UEG Documentation Group for formatting this document.

This document does not attempt to provide the rationale or pragmatics required to fully understand the protocol or to place it in perspective within a complete system.

The protocol contains many management mechanisms that are not intended for normal applications. Not all mechanisms are needed to build a particular user interface. It is important to keep in mind that the protocol is intended to provide mechanism, not policy.

Robert W. Scheifler

Laboratory for Computer Science
Massachusetts Institute of Technology

Jim Gettys

Systems Research Center
Digital Equipment Corporation

Ron Newman

Project Athena
Massachusetts Institute of Technology

September 1988

Introduction

The X Window System, or X, is a network-transparent window system. With X, you can run multiple applications simultaneously in windows, generating text and graphics in monochrome or color on a bitmap display. Network transparency means that you can use application programs that are running on other machines scattered throughout the network, as if they were running on your machine. Because X permits applications to be device independent, applications need not be rewritten, recompiled, or even relinked to work with new display hardware.

X provides facilities for generating multifont text and two-dimensional graphics (such as points, lines, arcs, and polygons) in a hierarchy of rectangular windows. Every window can be thought of as a "virtual screen" and can contain subwindows within it, to an arbitrary depth. Windows can overlap each other like stacks of papers on a desk and can be moved, resized, and restacked dynamically. Windows are inexpensive resources; applications using several hundred subwindows are common. For example, windows are often used to implement individual user interface components such as scroll bars, menus, buttons, and so forth.

Although you may think of yourself as a client of the system, in network terms, the application programs you run are called clients and they use the network services of the window system. A program running on the machine with your display provides these services and so is called the X server. The X server acts as an intermediary between you and the applications, handling output from the clients to the display and forwarding your input (entered with a keyboard or mouse) to the appropriate clients for processing.

Clients and servers use some form of interprocess communication to exchange information. The syntax and semantics of this conversation are defined by a communication protocol. This protocol is the foundation of the X Window System and is presented in Part II of this book. Clients use the protocol to send requests to the server to create and manipulate windows, to generate text and graphics, to control input from the user, and to communicate with other clients. The server uses the protocol to send information back to the client in response to various requests and to forward keyboard and other user input on to the appropriate clients.

Because a network roundtrip is an expensive operation relative to basic request execution, the protocol is primarily asynchronous, and data can be in transit in both directions (client to server and server to client) simultaneously. After generating a request, a client typically does not wait for the server to execute the request before generating a new request. Instead, the client generates a stream of requests that are eventually received by the server and executed. The server does not acknowledge receipt of a request and, in most cases, does not acknowledge execution of a request. (This is possible because the underlying transport being used is reliable.)

The protocol is designed explicitly to minimize the need to query the window system for information. Clients should not depend on the server to obtain information that the clients initially supplied. In addition, clients do not poll for input by sending requests to the server. Instead, clients use requests to register interest in various events, and the server sends event notifications asynchronously. Asynchronous operation may be one of the most significant differences between X and other window systems with which you may be familiar.

For the best performance, when the client and the server reside on the same machine, communication between them often is implemented using shared memory. When the client and the server reside on different machines, communication can take place over any network transport layer that provides reliable, in-order delivery of data in both directions (usually called a reliable duplex byte stream). For example, TCP (in the Internet protocol family) and DECnet streams are two commonly used transport layers. To support distributed computing in a heterogeneous environment, the communication protocol is designed to be independent of the operating system, programming language, and processor hardware. Thus, you can use a single display to run applications written in multiple languages under multiple operating systems on multiple hardware architectures simultaneously.

Although X is fundamentally defined by a network protocol, most application programmers do not want to think about bits, bytes, and message formats. Therefore, X has an interface library. This library provides a familiar procedural interface that masks the details of the protocol encoding and transport interactions and automatically handles the buffering of requests for efficient transport to the server, much as the C standard I/O library buffers output to minimize system calls. The library also provides various utility functions that are not directly related to the protocol but that are nevertheless important in building applications. The exact interface for this library differs for each programming language. Xlib is the library for the C programming language and is presented in Part I of this book.

The accompanying figure shows a block diagram of a complete X environment. Each X server controls one or more screens, a keyboard, and a pointing device (typically a mouse) with one or more buttons on it. There can be many X servers; often there is one for every workstation on the network. Applications can run on any machine, even those without X servers. An application might communicate with multiple servers simultaneously (for example, to support computer conferencing between individuals in different locations). Multiple applications can be active at the same time on a single server.

In X, many facilities that are built into other window systems are provided by client libraries. You will not find specifications for things like menus, scroll bars, and dialog boxes; nor will you find the interpretation of particular key and button sequences in this book. The protocol and Xlib avoid mandating such policy decisions as much as possible. You can view the protocol and Xlib as a construction kit providing a rich set of mechanisms that can implement a variety of user interface policies. Toolkits (providing menus, scroll bars, dialog boxes, and so on), higher-level graphics libraries (which might transform abstract object descriptions into graphics requests, for example), and user interface management systems (UIMS) can all be implemented on top of Xlib. Although Xlib provides the foundation, the expectation is that applications will be written using these higher-level facilities in conjunction with the facilities of Xlib, rather than solely on the "bare bones" of Xlib.

You can think of the total user interface as having two primary compo-

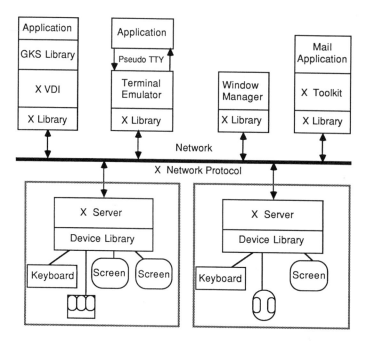

Figure 1. X window system block diagram

nents: the interaction with the user that is logically internal to an application (for example, typing text into a text editor or changing a cell's contents in a spreadsheet) and the interaction that is logically external to an application (for example, moving or resizing an application window or turning an application window into an icon). The external user interface is built into many other window systems, but this is not the case with X. The X protocol does not define an external user interface at all. Rather, the protocol provides mechanisms with which a variety of external user interfaces can be built. These mechanisms are designed so that a single client, called a window manager, can provide the external user interface independent of all of the other clients.

A window manager can automatically:

- Provide title bars, borders, and other window decorations for each application
- Provide a uniform means of moving and resizing windows

- Enforce a strict window layout policy if it desires (for example, "tiling" the screen so that application windows never overlap)
- Provide uniform icons for applications
- Provide a uniform interface for switching the keyboard between applications

With a suitable set of conventions, you can construct applications that are insensitive to the external user interface provided by a window manager but that run unmodified in multiple environments and still behave properly.

Because the protocol can deal with such a broad spectrum of user interfaces, no single program, toolkit, UIMS, or window manager is likely to use all of the facilities the protocol and Xlib provide. Do not be concerned if you do not understand why some facility exists; it may support a user interface style with which you are not familiar.

Principles

Early in the development of X, we argued about what should and should not be implemented in the server. For example, we did not know if menus or terminal emulators could be implemented in the client with adequate performance or whether "rubber banding" (dynamically stretching a simple figure in response to movement of the pointing device) would be acceptable when performed across a network. Experimentation during the first months showed us that more was possible than we had first believed.

These observations hardened into the following principles, which guided us through the early X design:

- Do not add new functionality unless an implementor cannot complete a real application without it.
- It is as important to decide what a system is not, as to decide what it is. Do not serve all the world's needs, but make the system extensible so that additional needs can be met in an upwardly compatible fashion.
- The only thing worse than generalizing from one example is generalizing from no examples at all.
- If a problem is not completely understood, it is probably best to provide no solution at all.
- If you can get 90 percent of the desired effect for 10 percent of the work, use the simpler solution.

- Isolate complexity as much as possible.

- Provide mechanism rather than policy. In particular, place user interface policy in the client's hands.

The first principle kept the wish list under control. Just because someone wanted something in the server, we did not feel obligated to add it. This kept us focused on the important issues that made real applications work. This principle was a somewhat more difficult touchstone to use during the design of the present version of X, given its significantly larger audience. We modified the principle to be "know of some real application that will require it."

At each iteration of the X design, there was always more to do than time allowed. We therefore focused on mechanisms with the broadest applicability and for which consensus in the group could easily be achieved. For example, we focused on two-dimensional graphics, explicitly deferring three-dimensional graphics.

At the same time, to avoid obsolescence, we designed the present version of X to be extensible at both the protocol and library interfaces and without requiring incompatible changes to existing applications. Examples of extensions we had in mind were additional graphics models (such as PHIGS and PostScript), real-time video, and general programmability in the server. (We view programmability as simply one example of an extension, not as the sole mechanism for extensibility; mere programmability does not give you support for video or high-performance support for graphics.)

During the design and implementation process, we generally suspected that any problems were just the tips of large icebergs. Expending effort to solve an immediate problem without first trying to generalize the problem is usually a mistake; a few related examples often make a whole class of problems obvious. This is not to say that we ignored the first instance of a problem; often there were adequate solutions using existing mechanisms.

We attempted to avoid solutions to problems we did not fully understand. For example, the preliminary design for the present version of X supported multiple input devices (more than just a single keyboard and mouse). As we worked through the design, we realized it had flaws that would take significant time and experimentation to correct. As a result, we removed this support from the system, knowing that correct support could be added later through the extension mechanism.

We also tried to avoid winning a complexity merit badge. If we could get most of what we needed with less complexity than a complete solution would require, we were willing to compromise our goals. Only history will decide if these tradeoffs were successful. Much of the existing complexity is a result of providing support for external window management; most programmers need not be concerned with this, particularly those using an X toolkit. We expected that toolkits would hide various forms of tedium from the programmer. For example, a program that displays "Hello World" with configurable colors and font and obeys window management conventions is about 150 lines of code when written using only the facilities of Xlib; an equivalent program written using a toolkit can have fewer than a dozen lines of code. Thus, it is important to keep in mind that Xlib is only one layer in a complete X programming environment.

Isolation of complexity is necessary in large systems. A system in which every component is intimately related to every other becomes difficult to change as circumstances change. We therefore attempted to build as much as possible into client programs, introducing only the minimum mechanisms required in the server.

Deciding what a system is not is as important as deciding what it is. For example, at various times people urged that remote execution and general interclient remote procedure call be integral parts of X. They felt there were no established standards in these areas, and they wanted X to be a self-contained environment. As is often the case, solving the immediate problem by adding to the existing framework rather than by integrating into a larger framework is less work, but the result is not satisfactory for long. The X protocol is correctly viewed as just one component in an overall distributed systems architecture, not as the complete architecture by itself.

User interface design is difficult and currently quite diverse. Although global user interface standards might someday be possible, we believed it prudent to promote the cooperative coexistence of a variety of user interface styles and to support diverse user communities and ongoing research activities. By separating window management functions from the server and from normal applications and by layering user interface policy in higher-level libraries on top of Xlib, we allowed for experimentation without forcing all users to be guinea pigs. As a result, many existing user interfaces have been imported into the X environment. Having a "pick one or roll your own" policy instead of a "love it or leave it" one has drawbacks; the applications developer must choose a user interface style and user community. You should remember, however, that Xlib and the protocol is not an end but a foundation.

History

X was born of necessity in 1984. Bob Scheifler was working at MIT's Laboratory for Computer Science (LCS) on a distributed system called Argus and was in need of a decent display environment for debugging multiple distributed processes. Jim Gettys, a Digital engineer, was assigned to MIT's Project Athena, an undergraduate education program sponsored by Digital and IBM that would ultimately populate the campus with thousands of workstations.

Neither Digital nor IBM had a workstation product with a bitmap display in 1984. The closest thing available from Digital was a VS100 display attached to a VAX. Both Athena and LCS had VAX-11/750s, and Athena was in the process of acquiring about 70 VS100s. VS100s were in field test at the time, and the firmware for them was unreliable. Athena loaned one of the first VS100s to LCS in exchange for cooperative work on the software. Our immediate goal was clear: We needed to build a window system environment running under UNIX on VS100s for ourselves and the groups we worked for. We had little thought of anything beyond these goals, but wondered where to begin. Little software was available elsewhere that was not encumbered by license or portability.

Paul Asente and Brian Reid, then both at Stanford University, had developed a prototype window system called W to run under Stanford's V operating system. W used a network protocol and supported "dumb terminal" windows and "transparent graphics" windows with display lists maintained in the server. In the summer of 1983, Paul Asente and Chris Kent, summer students at Digital's Western Research Laboratory, ported W to the VS100 under UNIX. They were kind enough to give us a copy.

The V system has reasonably fast synchronous remote procedure call, and W in the V environment was designed with a synchronous protocol. The port to UNIX retained the synchronous communication even though communication in UNIX was easily five times slower than in V. The combination of prototype VS100s with unreliable firmware and W using slow communication was not encouraging, to say the least; one could easily type faster than the terminal window could echo characters.

In May of 1984, we received reliable VS100 hardware and firmware. That summer, Bob replaced the synchronous protocol of W with an asynchronous protocol and replaced the display lists with immediate mode graphics. The result was sufficiently different from W that continuing to call it W was inappropriate and would cause confusion, as W was in some limited use at Athena. With no particular thought about the name, and because the familial resemblance to W was still strong at that date, Bob called the result X. Much later, when the name became a serious issue, X had already stuck and was used by too many people to permit a change.

Development was rapid during the next eight months. The first terminal emulator (VT52) and window manager were written in the CLU programming language, the language of choice in the research group where Bob worked. Bob continued development of the server and the protocol, which went from version 1 to version 6 during this period (the version number was incremented each time an incompatible change was made). Mark Vandevoorde at Athena wrote a new VT100 terminal emulator in C, and Jim Gettys worked on Xlib and the UNIX support for starting the window system. Late in 1984, we received faster VS100 firmware, causing the first round of performance analysis and optimization. Within a few weeks, we were again hardware limited, but we had a much better understanding of performance issues.

By early 1985, many people inside Digital were using X, and plans were underway for the first Digital UNIX workstation product, which was based on the MicroVAX-II. At the time, support for UNIX in Digital was limited, and there was no chance of getting any other window system except X on Digital hardware. Other systems were either highly nonportable or were unavailable because of licensing problems (this was the case with Andrew). X was the logical candidate. We had ported X version 6 to the QVSS display on the MicroVAX. Ron Newman joined Project Athena at this time and worked on documenting Xlib, already in its third major revision.

We redesigned X to support color during the second quarter of 1985, with Digital's eventual VAXstation-II/GPX as the intended target. Although MIT had licensed version 6 to a few outside groups for a brief time at nominal charge, a key decision was made in the summer of 1985 not to license future versions of X. Instead, it would be available to anyone at the cost of production. In September of 1985, version 9 of X was made publicly available, and the field test of the VAXstation-II/GPX began. During that fall, Brown University and MIT started porting X to the IBM RT/PC, which was in field test at those universities. A problem with reading unaligned data on the RT forced an incompatible change to the protocol; this was the only difference between version 9 and version 10.

During the fall, the first significant outside contributions of code to X started to appear from several universities and from Digital. In January of 1986, Digital announced the VAXstation-II/GPX, which was the first commercial X implementation. Release 3 of X (X10R3) was available in February and was a major watershed in X development. Although we were happy to see a major corporation incorporate X into its product line, we knew the design was limited to the taste and needs of a small group of people. It could solve just the problems we faced, and its hardware origins were still obvious in key aspects of the design. We knew version 10 had inherent limitations that would force major redesign within a few years, although it was certainly adequate for developing many interesting applications.

Over the next few months, a strange phenomenon occurred. Many other corporations, such as Hewlett-Packard, were basing products on version 10, and groups at universities and elsewhere were porting X to other displays and systems, including Apollo Computer and Sun Microsystems workstations. The server was even ported to the IBM PC/AT. Somewhat later, Hewlett-Packard contributed their toolkit to the MIT distribution.

We tired of hearing comments such as "We like X, but there is this one thing you ought to change." People were already declaring it a "standard," which was, to our thinking, premature. Before long, however, we were confronted with a fundamental decision about X's future. We seriously considered doing nothing; after all, X did almost everything we needed it to, and what it did not do could be added without difficulty. Unfortunately, this would leave many people using an inadequate platform for their work. In the long run, X would either die because of its inadequacies, or it would spawn wildly incompatible variations. Alternatively, based on feedback from users and developers, we could undertake a second major redesign of X.

Although we were willing to do the design work, we knew that the resulting design would be ambitious and would require much more implementation work than our meager resources at MIT would permit. Fortunately, Digital's Western Software Laboratory (DECWSL) was between projects. This group had the required expertise, including people who had contributed to pioneering Xerox window systems. More importantly, these people were intimately familiar with X. Smokey Wallace, DECWSL's manager, and Jim Gettys proposed the implementation of version 11, which would then be given back to MIT for public distribution without a license. Digital management quickly approved the proposal.

We started intensive protocol design in May of 1986. No proprietary information was used in the design process. Key contributors included Phil Karlton and Scott McGregor of Digital. Dave Rosenthal of Sun Microsystems was invited to join Digital engineers in the design team, and Bob Scheifler acted as the chief architect. At the first design meeting, we decided it was not feasible to design a protocol that would be upwardly compatible with version 10 and still provide the functionality essential for the range of display hardware that had to be supported. With some reluctance, we abandoned compatibility with version 10 (although Todd Brunhoff of Tektronix has since shown that one can build a reasonable "compatibility server" to display version 10 applications on a version 11 server).

We carried out most of the actual design work using the electronic mail facilities of the DARPA Internet, which connects hundreds of networks around the country, including MIT's campus network and Digital's engineering network. The entire group held only three day-long meetings during the design process. During these meetings we reached a consensus on issues we could not resolve by mail. Even with group members on opposite coasts, responses to most design issues were only a few minutes away. A printed copy of all the messages exchanged during this time would be a stack of paper several feet high. Without electronic mail, the design simply would not have been possible.

Once we completed a preliminary protocol design, we invited people from other companies and universities to review the specification. By August, we had a design ready for public review, which was again carried out using electronic mail, courtesy of the Internet. Design of the sample server implementation started at this time. Phil Karlton and Susan Angebranndt of DECWSL designed and implemented the device-independent parts of the server, and

Raymond Drewry and Todd Newman implemented the portable, machine-independent graphics library. Jim Gettys acted as the Xlib architect and with Ron Newman at MIT worked on the redesign and implementation of the X library. Many other contributions came from DECWSL as well, such as rewriting version 10 clients and the Xt toolkit intrinsics (another story in itself).

During the fall of 1986, Digital decided to base its entire desktop workstation strategy for ULTRIX, VMS, and MS-DOS on X. Although this was gratifying to us, it also meant we had even more people to talk to. This resulted in some delay, but also in a better design in the end. Ralph Swick of Digital joined Project Athena during this period and played a vital role thoughout version 11's development. The last version 10 release was made available in December of 1986.

In January of 1987, about 250 people attended the first X technical conference, which was held at MIT. During the conference, eleven major computer hardware and software vendors announced their support for X version 11 at an unprecedented press conference.

Alpha test of version 11 started in February of 1987, and beta testing started three months later at over 100 sites. Server back-ends and other code contributions came from Apollo, Digital, Hewlett-Packard, IBM, Sun, and the University of California at Berkeley. Tektronix loaned Todd Brunhoff to MIT to help coordinate testing and integration, which was a godsend to us all. Texas Instruments provided an implementation of a Common LISP interface library, based on an interface specification by Bob Scheifler. We made the first release of version 11 (V11R1) available on September 15, 1987.

At this point, MIT was thinking of getting out of the mainstream X development, but at a meeting in June 1987, nine major computer companies made it clear that they would like MIT to remain firmly in control of X. Over the next few months, a proposal was put together to create the MIT X Consortium, an open organization funded by the participants and with a charter of supporting and controlling the development and evolution of the system. The MIT X Consortium was created in January 1988, with Bob Scheifler as its director. The X Consortium hosted the second annual X conference in January, with approximately 900 people in attendance. The second release of version 11 was available March 1, 1988. At the present time, the X Consortium consists of over 30 organizations, including almost all major US computer vendors and many international vendors.

The Structure of This Book

This book consists of two parts: Part I is a reference manual for the C Language X Interface library, also known as Xlib; and Part II is the X protocol specification. The MIT X Consortium consider both the protocol and Xlib as standards, with Xlib being the exclusive interface to the protocol for the C programming language.

Part I consists of ten chapters. The first chapter provides a basic overview and establishes conventions used throughout the book. Chapter 2 deals with opening and closing connections and obtaining basic information about the connected display. Chapters 3 and 4 explain how to create and manipulate windows. Graphics capabilities are presented in chapters 5 and 6. Chapters 7 and 9 describe window manager functions and data, and chapter 8 explains events and event-handling functions. Finally, a variety of utility functions for keyboard input, command line parsing, region arithmetic, and resource management are presented in chapter 10.

Part II is a concise, precise specification of the X protocol semantics. The protocol specification is independent of any particular programming language, and as such, is an appropriate starting point for creating interface libraries for other programming languages. C programmers will prefer the Xlib reference to the protocol descriptions, although the protocol's alternate description may clarify points of confusion.

The glossary provides definitions of the terminology used elsewhere in the book. The book also includes a number of appendixes:

- Appendix A provides cross-reference information between protocol requests and library functions.
- Appendix B provides the available predefined cursor shapes.
- Appendix C provides information required to extend the X library.
- Appendix D provides information about functions that may be available to ease conversion of version 10 code to version 11.
- Appendix E provides the predefined keyboard symbol (KEYSYM) encodings.
- Appendix F provides the bit and byte description of the X protocol.

Part I. XLib—C Library X Interface

James Gettys   Robert W. Scheifler   Ron Newman

Chapter 1

Introduction to Xlib

The X Window System is a network-transparent window system that was designed at MIT. It runs under 4.3BSD UNIX, ULTRIX-32, many other UNIX variants, VAX/VMS, MS/DOS, as well as several other operating systems.

X display servers run on computers with either monochrome or color bitmap display hardware. The server distributes user input to and accepts output requests from various client programs located either on the same machine or elsewhere in the network. Xlib is a C subroutine library that application programs (clients) use to interface with the window system by means of a stream connection. Although a client usually runs on the same machine as the X server it is talking to, this need not be the case.

Xlib − C Language X Interface is a reference guide to the low-level C language interface to the X Window System protocol. It is neither a tutorial nor a user's guide to programming the X Window System. Rather, it provides a detailed description of each function in the library as well as a discussion of the related background information. *Xlib − C Language X Interface* assumes a basic understanding of a graphics window system and of the C programming language. Other higher-level abstractions (for example, those provided by the toolkits for X) are built on top of the Xlib library. For further information about these higher-level libraries, see the appropriate toolkit documentation. The *X Window System Protocol* provides the definitive word on the behavior of X. Although additional information appears here, the protocol document is the ruling document.

To provide an introduction to X programming, this chapter discusses:

- Overview of the X Window System
- Errors
- Naming and argument conventions
- Programming considerations
- Conventions used in this document

1.1   Overview of the X Window System

Some of the terms used in this book are unique to X, and other terms that are common to other window systems have different meanings in X. You may find it helpful to refer to the glossary, which is located at the end of the book.

The X Window System supports one or more screens containing overlapping windows or subwindows. A screen is a physical monitor and hardware, which can be either color or black and white. There can be multiple screens for each display or workstation. A single X server can provide display services for any number of screens. A set of screens for a single user with one keyboard and one pointer (usually a mouse) is called a display.

All the windows in an X server are arranged in strict hierarchies. At the top of each hierarchy is a root window, which covers each of the display screens. Each root window is partially or completely covered by child windows. All windows, except for root windows, have parents. There is usually at least one window for each application program. Child windows may in turn have their own children. In this way, an application program can create an arbitrarily deep tree on each screen. X provides graphics, text, and raster operations for windows.

A child window can be larger than its parent. That is, part or all of the child window can extend beyond the boundaries of the parent, but all output to a window is clipped by its parent. If several children of a window have overlapping locations, one of the children is considered to be on top of or raised over the others thus obscuring them. Output to areas covered by other windows is suppressed by the window system unless the window has backing store. If a window is obscured by a second window, the second window obscures only those ancestors of the second window, which are also ancestors of the first window.

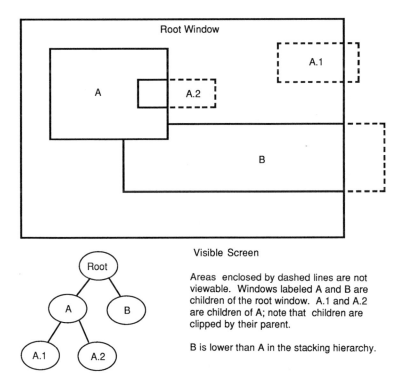

Figure 1.1. Window hierarchy

A window has a border zero or more pixels in width, which can be any pattern (pixmap) or solid color you like. A window usually but not always has a background pattern, which will be repainted by the window system when uncovered. Each window has its own coordinate system. Child windows obscure their parents unless the child windows (of the same depth) have no background, and graphic operations in the parent window usually are clipped by the children.

X does not guarantee to preserve the contents of windows. When part or all of a window is hidden and then brought back onto the screen, its contents may be lost. The server then sends the client program an Expose event to notify it that part or all of the window needs to be repainted. Programs must be prepared to regenerate the contents of windows on demand.

X also provides off-screen storage of graphics objects, called pixmaps. Single plane (depth 1) pixmaps are sometimes referred to as bitmaps. Pixmaps can be used in most graphics functions interchangeably with windows and are used in various graphics operations to define patterns or tiles. Windows and pixmaps together are referred to as drawables.

Most of the functions in Xlib just add requests to an output buffer. These requests later execute asynchronously on the X server. Functions that return values of information stored in the server do not return (that is, they block) until an explicit reply is received or an error occurs. You can provide an error handler, which will be called when the error is reported.

If a client does not want a request to execute asynchronously, it can follow the request with a call to XSync, which blocks until all previously buffered asynchronous events have been sent and acted on. As an important side effect, the output buffer in Xlib is always flushed by a call to any function that returns a value from the server or waits for input.

Many Xlib functions will return an integer resource ID, which allows you to refer to objects stored on the X server. These can be of type Window, Font, Pixmap, Colormap, Cursor, and GContext, as defined in the file <X11/X.h>.[1] These resources are created by requests and are destroyed (or freed) by requests or when connections are closed. Most of these resources are potentially sharable between applications, and in fact, windows are manipulated explicitly by window manager programs. Fonts and cursors are shared automatically across multiple screens. Fonts are loaded and unloaded as needed and are shared by multiple clients. Fonts are often cached in the server. Xlib provides no support for sharing graphics contexts between applications.

Client programs are informed of events. Events may either be side effects of a request (for example, restacking windows generates Expose events) or completely asynchronous (for example, from the keyboard). A client program asks to be informed of events. Because other applications can send events to your application, programs must be prepared to handle (or ignore) events of all types.

Input events (for example, a key pressed or the pointer moved) arrive asynchronously from the server and are queued until they are requested by an explicit call (for example, XNextEvent or XWindowEvent). In addition, some library functions (for example, XRaiseWindow) generate Expose and

---

[1] The <> has the meaning defined by the # include statement of the C compiler and is a file relative to a well-known directory. On UNIX-based systems, this is **/usr/include**.

ConfigureRequest events. These events also arrive asynchronously, but the client may wish to explicitly wait for them by calling XSync after calling a function that can cause the server to generate events.

1.2   Errors

Some functions return Status, an integer error indication. If the function fails, it returns a zero. If the function returns a status of zero, it has not updated the return arguments. Because C does not provide multiple return values, many functions must return their results by writing into client-passed storage. By default, errors are handled either by a standard library function or by one that you provide. Functions that return pointers to strings return NULL pointers if the string does not exist.

The X server reports protocol errors at the time that it detects them. If more than one error could be generated for a given request, the server can report any of them.

Because Xlib usually does not transmit requests to the server immediately (that is, it buffers them), errors can be reported much later than they actually occur. For debugging purposes, however, Xlib provides a mechanism for forcing synchronous behavior (see section 8.12.1). When synchronization is enabled, errors are reported as they are generated.

When Xlib detects an error, it calls an error handler, which your program can provide. If you do not provide an error handler, the error is printed, and your program terminates.

1.3   Naming and Argument Conventions within Xlib

Xlib follows a number of conventions for the naming and syntax of the functions. Given that you remember what information the function requires, these conventions are intended to make the syntax of the functions more predictable.

The major naming conventions are:

• To differentiate the X symbols from the other symbols, the library uses mixed case for external symbols. It leaves lowercase for variables and all uppercase for user macros, as per existing convention.

• All Xlib functions begin with a capital X.

• The beginnings of all function names and symbols are capitalized.

- All user-visible data structures begin with a capital X. More generally, anything that a user might dereference begins with a capital X.

- Macros and other symbols do not begin with a capital X. To distinguish them from all user symbols, each word in the macro is capitalized.

- All elements of or variables in a data structure are in lowercase. Compound words, where needed, are constructed with underscores (_).

- The display argument, where used, is always first in the argument list.

- All resource objects, where used, occur at the beginning of the argument list immediately after the display argument.

- When a graphics context is present together with another type of resource (most commonly, a drawable), the graphics context occurs in the argument list after the other resource. Drawables outrank all other resources.

- Source arguments always precede the destination arguments in the argument list.

- The x argument always precedes the y argument in the argument list.

- The width argument always precedes the height argument in the argument list.

- Where the x, y, width, and height arguments are used together, the x and y arguments always precede the width and height arguments.

- Where a mask is accompanied with a structure, the mask always precedes the pointer to the structure in the argument list.

1.4   Programming Considerations

The major programming considerations are:

- Keyboards are the greatest variable between different manufacturers' workstations. If you want your program to be portable, you should be particularly conservative here.

- Many display systems have limited amounts of off-screen memory. If you can, you should minimize use of pixmaps and backing store.

- The user should have control of his screen real estate. Therefore, you should write your applications to react to window management rather than presume control of the entire screen. What you do inside of your top-level window, however, is up to your application. For further information, see chapter 9.

- Coordinates and sizes in X are actually 16-bit quantities. They usually are declared as an "int" in the interface (int is 16 bits on some machines). Values larger than 16 bits are truncated silently. Sizes (width and height) are unsigned quantities. This decision was taken to minimize the bandwidth required for a given level of performance.

1.5   Conventions Used in Xlib – C Language X Interface

This document uses the following conventions:

- Global symbols in *Xlib – C Language X Interface* are printed in `this special font`. These can be either function names, symbols defined in include files, or structure names. Arguments are printed in *italics*.

- Each function is introduced by a general discussion that distinguishes it from other functions. The function declaration itself follows, and each argument is specifically explained. General discussion of the function, if any is required, follows the arguments. Where applicable, the last paragraph of the explanation lists the possible Xlib error codes that the function can generate. For a complete discussion of the Xlib error codes, see section 8.12.2.

- To eliminate any ambiguity between those arguments that you pass and those that a function returns to you, the explanations for all arguments that you pass start with the word *specifies* or, in the case of multiple arguments, the word *specify*. The explanations for all arguments that are returned to you start with the word *returns* or, in the case of multiple arguments, the word *return*. The explanations for all arguments that you can pass and are returned start with the words *specifies and returns*.

- Any pointer to a structure that is used to return a value is designated as such by the *_return* suffix as part of its name. All other pointers passed to these functions are used for reading only. A few arguments use pointers to structures that are used for both input and output and are indicated by using the *_in_out* suffix.

- Xlib defines the Boolean values of `True` and `False`.

Chapter 2

Display Functions

Before your program can use a display, you must establish a connection to the X server. Once you have established a connection, you then can use the Xlib macros and functions discussed in this chapter to return information about the display. This chapter discusses how to:

- Open (connect to) the display
- Obtain information about the display, image format, and screen
- Free client-created data
- Close (disconnect from) a display

The chapter concludes with a general discussion of what occurs when the connection to the X server is closed.

2.1   Opening the Display

To open a connection to the X server that controls a display, use XOpenDisplay.

Display *XOpenDisplay(*display_name*)
        char **display_name*;

display_name   Specifies the hardware display name, which determines the display and communications domain to be used. On a UNIX-based system, if the display_name is NULL, it defaults to the value of the DISPLAY environment variable.

On UNIX-based systems, the display name or DISPLAY environment variable is a string in the format:

hostname:number.screen_number

hostname   Specifies the name of the host machine on which the display is physically attached. You follow the hostname with either a single colon (:) or a double colon (::).

number   Specifies the number of the display server on that host machine. You may optionally follow this display number with a period (.). A single CPU can have more than one display. Multiple displays are usually numbered starting with zero.

screen_number   Specifies the screen to be used on that server. Multiple screens can be controlled by a single X server. The screen_number sets an internal variable that can be accessed by using the DefaultScreen macro or the XDefaultScreen function if you are using languages other than C (see section 2.2.1).

For example, the following would specify screen 2 of display 0 on the machine named mit-athena:

mit-athena:0.2

The XOpenDisplay function returns a Display structure that serves as the connection to the X server and that contains all the information about that X server. XOpenDisplay connects your application to the X server through TCP, UNIX domain, or DECnet communications protocols. If the hostname is a host machine name and a single colon (:) separates the hostname and display number, XOpenDisplay connects using TCP streams. If the hostname is *unix* and a single colon (:) separates it from the display number, XOpenDisplay connects using UNIX domain IPC streams. If the hostname is not specified, Xlib uses whatever it believes is the fastest transport. If the hostname is a host machine name and a double colon (::) separates the hostname and display number, XOpenDisplay connects using DECnet. A single X server can support any or all of these transport mechanisms simultaneously. A particular Xlib implementation can support many more of these transport mechanisms.

If successful, XOpenDisplay returns a pointer to a Display structure, which is defined in <X11/Xlib.h>. If XOpenDisplay does not succeed, it returns NULL. After a successful call to XOpenDisplay, all of the screens in the display can be used by the client. The screen number specified in the display_name argument is returned by the `DefaultScreen` macro (or the `XDefaultScreen` function). You can access elements of the `Display` and `Screen` structures only by using the information macros or functions. For information about using macros and functions to obtain information from the `Display` structure, see section 2.2.1

X servers may implement various types of access control mechanisms (see section 7.11).

2.2   Obtaining Information about the Display, Image Formats, or Screens

The Xlib library provides a number of useful macros and corresponding functions that return data from the `Display` structure. The macros are used for C programming, and their corresponding function equivalents are for other language bindings. This section discusses the:

• Display macros

• Image format macros

• Screen macros

All other members of the `Display` structure (that is, those for which no macros are defined) are private to Xlib and must not be used. Applications must never directly modify or inspect these private members of the `Display` structure.

Note   The `XDisplayWidth`, `XDisplayHeight`, `XDisplayCells`, `XDisplay-Planes`, `XDisplayWidthMM`, and `XDisplayHeightMM` functions in the next sections are misnamed. These functions really should be named Screen*whatever* and XScreen*whatever*, not Display*whatever* or XDisplay-*whatever*. Our apologies for the resulting confusion.

2.2.1   Display Macros

Applications should not directly modify any part of the `Display` and `Screen` structures. The members should be considered read-only, although they may change as the result of other operations on the display.

The following lists the C language macros, their corresponding function equivalents that are for other language bindings, and what data they both can return.

AllPlanes()

unsigned long XAllPlanes()

Both return a value with all bits set to 1 suitable for use in a plane argument to a procedure.

Both `BlackPixel` and `WhitePixel` can be used in implementing a monochrome application. These pixel values are for permanently allocated entries in the default colormap. The actual RGB (red, green, and blue) values are settable on some screens and, in any case, may not actually be black or white. The names are intended to convey the expected relative intensity of the colors.

BlackPixel(*display, screen_number*)

unsigned long XBlackPixel(*display, screen_number*)
    Display **display*;
    int *screen_number*;

Both return the black pixel value for the specified screen.

WhitePixel(*display, screen_number*)

unsigned long XWhitePixel(*display, screen_number*)
    Display **display*;
    int *screen_number*;

Both return the white pixel value for the specified screen.

ConnectionNumber(*display*)

int XConnectionNumber(*display*)
    Display **display*;

Both return a connection number for the specified display. On a UNIX-based system, this is the file descriptor of the connection.

DefaultColormap(*display, screen_number*)

Colormap XDefaultColormap(*display, screen_number*)
    Display **display*;
    int *screen_number*;

Both return the default colormap ID for allocation on the specified screen. Most routine allocations of color should be made out of this colormap.

DefaultDepth(*display, screen_number*)

int XDefaultDepth(*display, screen_number*)
    Display **display*;
    int *screen_number*;

Both return the depth (number of planes) of the default root window for the specified screen. Other depths may also be supported on this screen (see XMatchVisualInfo).

DefaultGC(*display, screen_number*)

GC XDefaultGC(*display, screen_number*)
    Display **display*;
    int *screen_number*;

Both return the default graphics context for the root window of the specified screen. This GC is created for the convenience of simple applications and contains the default GC components with the foreground and background pixel values initialized to the black and white pixels for the screen, respectively. You can modify its contents freely because it is not used in any Xlib function. This GC should never be freed.

DefaultRootWindow(*display*)

Window XDefaultRootWindow(*display*)
    Display **display*;

Both return the root window for the default screen.

DefaultScreenOfDisplay(*display*)

Screen *XDefaultScreenOfDisplay(*display*)
    Display **display*;

Both return a pointer to the default screen.

ScreenOfDisplay(*display, screen_number*)

Screen *XScreenOfDisplay(*display, screen_number*)

Display **display*;
int *screen_number*;

Both return a pointer to the indicated screen.

DefaultScreen(*display*)

int XDefaultScreen(*display*)
    Display **display*;

Both return the default screen number referenced by the XOpenDisplay
function. This macro or function should be used to retrieve the screen number in applications that will use only a single screen.

DefaultVisual(*display, screen_number*)

Visual *XDefaultVisual(*display, screen_number*)
    Display **display*;
    int *screen_number*;

Both return the default visual type for the specified screen. For further information about visual types, see section 3.1.

DisplayCells(*display, screen_number*)

int XDisplayCells(*display, screen_number*)
    Display **display*;
    int *screen_number*;

Both return the number of entries in the default colormap.

DisplayPlanes(*display, screen_number*)

int XDisplayPlanes(*display, screen_number*)
    Display **display*;
    int *screen_number*;

Both return the depth of the root window of the specified screen. For an explanation of depth, see the glossary.

DisplayString(*display*)

char *XDisplayString(*display*)
    Display **display*;

Both return the string that was passed to XOpenDisplay when the current display was opened. On UNIX-based systems, if the passed string was NULL, these return the value of the DISPLAY environment variable when the current display was opened. These are useful to applications that invoke the fork system call and want to open a new connection to the same display from the child process as well as for printing error messages.

LastKnownRequestProcessed(*display*)

unsigned long XLastKnownRequestProcessed(*display*)
    Display **display*;

Both extract the full serial number of the last request known by Xlib to have been processed by the X server. Xlib automatically sets this number when replies, events, and errors are received.

NextRequest(*display*)

unsigned long XNextRequest(*display*)
    Display **display*;

Both extract the full serial number that is to be used for the next request. Serial numbers are maintained separately for each display connection.

ProtocolVersion(*display*)

int XProtocolVersion(*display*)
    Display **display*;

Both return the major version number (11) of the X protocol associated with the connected display.

ProtocolRevision(*display*)

int XProtocolRevision(*display*)
    Display **display*;

Both return the minor protocol revision number of the X server.

QLength(*display*)

int XQLength(*display*)
    Display **display*;

Both return the length of the event queue for the connected display. Note that there may be more events that have not been read into the queue yet (see XEventsQueued).

RootWindow(*display, screen_number*)

Window XRootWindow(*display, screen_number*)
    Display *display;
    int *screen_number*;

Both return the root window. These are useful with functions that need a drawable of a particular screen and for creating top-level windows.

ScreenCount(*display*)

int XScreenCount(*display*)
    Display *display;

Both return the number of available screens.

ServerVendor(*display*)

char *XServerVendor(*display*)
    Display *display;

Both return a pointer to a null-terminated string that provides some identification of the owner of the X server implementation.

VendorRelease(*display*)

int XVendorRelease(*display*)
    Display *display;

Both return a number related to a vendor's release of the X server.

2.2.2 Image Format Macros

Applications are required to present data to the X server in a format that the server demands. To help simplify applications, most of the work required to convert the data is provided by Xlib (see sections 6.7 and 10.9).

The following lists the C language macros, their corresponding function equivalents that are for other language bindings, and what data they both return for the specified server and screen. These are often used by toolkits as well as by simple applications.

ImageByteOrder(*display*)

int XImageByteOrder(*display*)
    Display **display*;

Both specify the required byte order for images for each scanline unit in XY
format (bitmap) or for each pixel value in Z format. The macro or function
can return either `LSBFirst` or `MSBFirst`.

BitmapUnit(*display*)

int XBitmapUnit(*display*)
    Display **display*;

Both return the size of a bitmap's scanline unit in bits. The scanline is calculated in multiples of this value.

BitmapBitOrder(*display*)

int XBitmapBitOrder(*display*)
    Display **display*;

Within each bitmap unit, the left-most bit in the bitmap as displayed on the
screen is either the least-significant or most-significant bit in the unit. This
macro or function can return `LSBFirst` or `MSBFirst`.

BitmapPad(*display*)

int XBitmapPad(*display*)
    Display **display*;

Each scanline must be padded to a multiple of bits returned by this macro or
function.

DisplayHeight(*display*, *screen_number*)

int XDisplayHeight(*display*, *screen_number*)
    Display **display*;
    int *screen_number*;

Both return an integer that describes the height of the screen in pixels.

DisplayHeightMM(*display*, *screen_number*)

int XDisplayHeightMM(*display*, *screen_number*)

Display *display*;
int *screen_number*;

Both return the height of the specified screen in millimeters.

DisplayWidth(*display, screen_number*)

int XDisplayWidth(*display, screen_number*)
Display *display*;
int *screen_number*;

Both return the width of the screen in pixels.

DisplayWidthMM(*display, screen_number*)

int XDisplayWidthMM(*display, screen_number*)
Display *display*;
int *screen_number*;

Both return the width of the specified screen in millimeters.

2.2.3 Screen Information Macros

The following lists the C language macros, their corresponding function equivalents that are for other language bindings, and what data they both can return. These macros or functions all take a pointer to the appropriate screen structure.

BlackPixelOfScreen(*screen*)

unsigned long XBlackPixelOfScreen(*screen*)
Screen *screen*;

Both return the black pixel value of the specified screen.

WhitePixelOfScreen(*screen*)

unsigned long XWhitePixelOfScreen(*screen*)
Screen *screen*;

Both return the white pixel value of the specified screen.

CellsOfScreen(*screen*)

int XCellsOfScreen(*screen*)
Screen *screen*;

Both return the number of colormap cells in the default colormap of the specified screen.

DefaultColormapOfScreen(*screen*)

Colormap XDefaultColormapOfScreen(*screen*)
    Screen **screen*;

Both return the default colormap of the specified screen.

DefaultDepthOfScreen(*screen*)

int XDefaultDepthOfScreen(*screen*)
    Screen **screen*;

Both return the depth of the root window.

DefaultGCOfScreen(*screen*)

GC XDefaultGCOfScreen(*screen*)
    Screen **screen*;

Both return a default graphics context (GC) of the specified screen, which has the same depth as the root window of the screen. The GC must never be freed.

DefaultVisualOfScreen(*screen*)

Visual *XDefaultVisualOfScreen(*screen*)
    Screen **screen*;

Both return the default visual of the specified screen. For information on visual types, see section 3.1.

DoesBackingStore(*screen*)

int XDoesBackingStore(*screen*)
    Screen **screen*;

Both return a value indicating whether the screen supports backing stores. The value returned can be one of `WhenMapped`, `NotUseful`, or `Always` (see section 3.2.4).

DoesSaveUnders(*screen*)

Bool XDoesSaveUnders(*screen*)
    Screen *_screen_;

Both return a Boolean value indicating whether the screen supports save unders. If `True`, the screen supports save unders. If `False`, the screen does not support save unders (see section 3.2.5).

DisplayOfScreen(*screen*)

Display *XDisplayOfScreen(*screen*)
    Screen *_screen_;

Both return the display of the specified screen.

EventMaskOfScreen(*screen*)

long XEventMaskOfScreen(*screen*)
    Screen *_screen_;

Both return the event mask of the root window for the specified screen at connection setup time.

WidthOfScreen(*screen*)

int XWidthOfScreen(*screen*)
    Screen *_screen_;

Both return the width of the specified screen in pixels.

HeightOfScreen(*screen*)

int XHeightOfScreen(*screen*)
    Screen *_screen_;

Both return the height of the specified screen in pixels.

WidthMMOfScreen(*screen*)

int XWidthMMOfScreen(*screen*)
    Screen *_screen_;

Both return the width of the specified screen in millimeters.

HeightMMOfScreen(*screen*)

int XHeightMMOfScreen(*screen*)
    Screen **screen*;

Both return the height of the specified screen in millimeters.

MaxCmapsOfScreen(*screen*)

int XMaxCmapsOfScreen(*screen*)
    Screen **screen*;

Both return the maximum number of installed colormaps supported by the specified screen (see section 7.3).

MinCmapsOfScreen(*screen*)

int XMinCmapsOfScreen(*screen*)
    Screen **screen*;

Both return the minimum number of installed colormaps supported by the specified screen (see section 7.3).

PlanesOfScreen(*screen*)

int XPlanesOfScreen(*screen*)
    Screen **screen*;

Both return the depth of the root window.

RootWindowOfScreen(*screen*)

Window XRootWindowOfScreen(*screen*)
    Screen **screen*;

Both return the root window of the specified screen.

2.3   Generating a NoOperation Protocol Request

To execute a `NoOperation` protocol request, use `XNoOp`.

XNoOp(*display*)
    Display **display*;
display   Specifies the connection to the X server.

The XNoOp function sends a NoOperation protocol request to the X server, thereby exercising the connection.

2.4   Freeing Client-Created Data

To free any in-memory data that was created by an Xlib function, use XFree.

XFree(*data*)
    char **data*;
data   Specifies a pointer to the data that is to be freed.

The XFree function is a general-purpose Xlib routine that frees the specified data. You must use it to free any objects that were allocated by Xlib.

2.5   Closing the Display

To close a display or disconnect from the X server, use XCloseDisplay.

XCloseDisplay(*display*)
    Display **display*;
display   Specifies the connection to the X server.

The XCloseDisplay function closes the connection to the X server for the display specified in the Display structure and destroys all windows, resource IDs (Window, Font, Pixmap, Colormap, Cursor, and GContext), or other resources that the client has created on this display, unless the close-down mode of the resource has been changed (see XSetCloseDown-Mode). Therefore, these windows, resource IDs, and other resources should never be referenced again or an error will be generated. Before exiting, you should call XCloseDisplay explicitly so that any pending errors are reported as XCloseDisplay performs a final XSync operation.

XCloseDisplay can generate a BadGC error.

2.6   X Server Connection Close Operations

When the X server's connection to a client is closed either by an explicit call to XCloseDisplay or by a process that exits, the X server performs the following automatic operations:

- It disowns all selections owned by the client (see XSetSelectionOwner).

- It performs an `XUngrabPointer` and `XUngrabKeyboard` if the client has actively grabbed the pointer or the keyboard.

- It performs an `XUngrabServer` if the client has grabbed the server.

- It releases all passive grabs made by the client.

- It marks all resources (including colormap entries) allocated by the client either as permanent or temporary, depending on whether the close-down mode is `RetainPermanent` or `RetainTemporary`. However, this does not prevent other client applications from explicitly destroying the resources (see `XSetCloseDownMode`).

When the close-down mode is `DestroyAll`, the X server destroys all of a client's resources as follows:

- It examines each window in the client's save-set to determine if it is an inferior (subwindow) of a window created by the client. (The save-set is a list of other clients' windows, which are referred to as save-set windows.) If so, the X server reparents the save-set window to the closest ancestor so that the save-set window is not an inferior of a window created by the client The reparenting leaves unchanged the absolute coordinates (with respect to the root window) of the upper-left outer corner of the save-set window.

- It performs a `MapWindow` request on the save-set window if the save-set window is unmapped. The X server does this even if the save-set window was not an inferior of a window created by the client.

- It destroys all windows created by the client.

- It performs the appropriate free request on each nonwindow resource created by the client in the server (for example, `Font`, `Pixmap`, `Cursor`, `Colormap`, and `GContext`).

- It frees all colors and colormap entries allocated by a client application.

Additional processing occurs when the last connection to the X server closes. An X server goes through a cycle of having no connections and having some connections. When the last connection to the X server closes as a result of a connection closing with the close_mode of `DestroyAll`, the X server does the following:

- It resets its state as if it had just been started. The X server begins by destroying all lingering resources from clients that have terminated in `RetainPermanent` or `RetainTemporary` mode.

- It deletes all but the predefined atom identifiers.

- It deletes all properties on all root windows (see chapter 4).

- It resets all device maps and attributes (for example, key click, bell volume, and acceleration) as well as the access control list.

- It restores the standard root tiles and cursors.

- It restores the default font path.

- It restores the input focus to state `PointerRoot`.

However, the X server does not reset if you close a connection with a close-down mode set to `RetainPermanent` or `RetainTemporary`.

Chapter 3

Window Functions

In the X Window System, a window is a rectangular area on the screen that lets you view graphic output. Client applications can display overlapping and nested windows on one or more screens that are driven by X servers on one or more machines. Clients who want to create windows must first connect their program to the X server by calling `XOpenDisplay`. This chapter begins with a discussion of visual types and window attributes. The chapter continues with a discussion of the Xlib functions you can use to:

- Create windows
- Destroy windows
- Map windows
- Unmap windows
- Configure windows
- Change the stacking order
- Change window attributes
- Translate window coordinates

This chapter also identifies the window actions that may generate events.

Note that it is vital that your application conform to the established conventions for communicating with window managers for it to work well with the various window managers in use (see section 9.1). Toolkits generally adhere to these conventions for you, relieving you of the burden. Toolkits also often supersede many functions in this chapter with versions of their own. Refer to the documentation for the toolkit you are using for more information.

3.1   Visual Types

On some display hardware, it may be possible to deal with color resources in more than one way. For example, you may be able to deal with a screen of either 12-bit depth with arbitrary mapping of pixel to color (pseudo-color) or 24-bit depth with 8 bits of the pixel dedicated to each of red, green, and blue. These different ways of dealing with the visual aspects of the screen are called visuals. For each screen of the display, there may be a list of valid visual types supported at different depths of the screen. Because default windows and visual types are defined for each screen, most simple applications need not deal with this complexity. Xlib provides macros and functions that return the default root window, the default depth of the default root window, and the default visual type (see section 2.2.1 and `XMatchVisualInfo`).

Xlib uses a `Visual` structure that contains information about the possible color mapping. The members of this structure pertinent to this discussion are class, red_mask, green_mask, blue_mask, bits_per_rgb, and map_entries. The class member specifies one of the possible visual classes of the screen and can be `StaticGray`, `StaticColor`, `TrueColor`, `GrayScale`, `PseudoColor`, or `DirectColor`.

The following concepts may serve to make the explanation of visual types clearer. The screen can be color or grayscale, can have a colormap that is writable or read-only, and can also have a colormap whose indices are decomposed into separate RGB pieces, provided one is not on a grayscale screen. This leads to the following diagram:

	Color		GrayScale	
	R/O	R/W	R/O	R/W
Undecomposed Colormap	Static Color	Pseudo Color	Static Gray	Gray Scale
Decomposed Colormap	True Color	Direct Color		

Conceptually, as each pixel is read out of video memory for display on the screen, it goes through a look-up stage by indexing into a colormap. Colormaps can be manipulated arbitrarily on some hardware, in limited ways on other hardware, and not at all on other hardware. The visual types affect the colormap and the RGB values in the following ways:

- For PseudoColor, a pixel value indexes a colormap to produce independent RGB values, and the RGB values can be changed dynamically.

- GrayScale is treated the same way as PseudoColor except that the primary that drives the screen is undefined. Thus, the client should always store the same value for red, green, and blue in the colormaps.

- For DirectColor, a pixel value is decomposed into separate RGB subfields, and each subfield separately indexes the colormap for the corresponding value. The RGB values can be changed dynamically.

- TrueColor is treated the same way as DirectColor except that the colormap has predefined, read-only RGB values. These RGB values are server-dependent but provide linear or near-linear ramps in each primary.

- StaticColor is treated the same way as PseudoColor except that the colormap has predefined, read-only, server-dependent RGB values.

- StaticGray is treated the same way as StaticColor except that the RGB values are equal for any single pixel value, thus resulting in shades of gray. StaticGray with a two-entry colormap can be thought of as monochrome.

The red_mask, green_mask, and blue_mask members are only defined for DirectColor and TrueColor. Each has one contiguous set of bits with no intersections. The bits_per_rgb member specifies the log base 2 of the

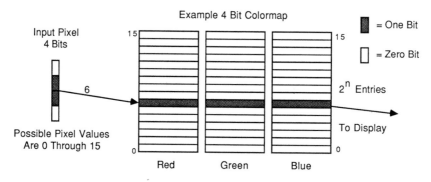

Figure 3.1. Pseudo color, gray scale, static color or static gray

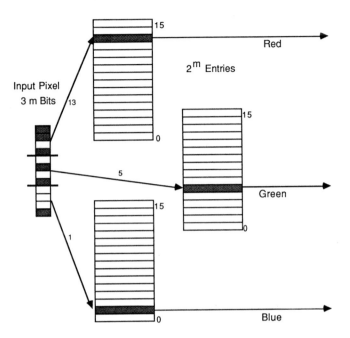

Example 3 x 4 Colormap (12 Bits/Pixel)

Figure 3.2. Direct color

number of distinct color values (individually) of red, green, and blue. Actual RGB values are unsigned 16-bit numbers. The map_entries member defines the number of available colormap entries in a newly created colormap. For `DirectColor` and `TrueColor`, this is the size of an individual pixel subfield.

To obtain the visual ID from a `Visual`, use `XVisualIDFromVisual`.

VisualID XVisualIDFrom Visual (*visual*)
    Visual **visual*;
visual   Specifies the visual type.

The `XVisualIDFromVisual` function returns the visual ID for the specified visual type.

3.2   Window Attributes

All InputOutput windows have a border width of zero or more pixels, an optional background, an event suppression mask (which suppresses propagation of events from children), and a property list (see section 4.2). The window border and background can be a solid color or a pattern, called a tile. All windows except the root have a parent and are clipped by their parent. If a window is stacked on top of another window, it obscures that other window for the purpose of input. If a window has a background (almost all do), it obscures the other window for purposes of output. Attempts to output to the obscured area do nothing, and no input events (for example, pointer motion) are generated for the obscured area.

Windows also have associated property lists (see section 4.2).

Both InputOutput and InputOnly windows have the following common attributes, which are the only attributes of an InputOnly window:

- win-gravity
- event-mask
- do-not-propagate-mask
- override-redirect
- cursor

If you specify any other attributes for an InputOnly window, a BadMatch error results.

InputOnly windows are used for controlling input events in situations where InputOutput windows are unnecessary. InputOnly windows are invisible; can only be used to control such things as cursors, input event generation, and grabbing; and cannot be used in any graphics requests. Note that InputOnly windows cannot have InputOutput windows as inferiors.

Windows have borders of a programmable width and pattern as well as a background pattern or tile. Pixel values can be used for solid colors. The background and border pixmaps can be destroyed immediately after creating the window if no further explicit references to them are to be made. The pattern can either be relative to the parent or absolute. If Parent-Relative, the parent's background is used.

When windows are first created, they are not visible (not mapped) on the screen. Any output to a window that is not visible on the screen and that does not have backing store will be discarded. An application may wish to create a window long before it is mapped to the screen. When a window is eventually mapped to the screen (using `XMapWindow`), the X server generates an `Expose` event for the window if backing store has not been maintained.

A window manager can override your choice of size, border width, and position for a top-level window. Your program must be prepared to use the actual size and position of the top window. It is not acceptable for a client application to resize itself unless in direct response to a human command to do so. Instead, either your program should use the space given to it, or if the space is too small for any useful work, your program might ask the user to resize the window. The border of your top-level window is considered fair game for window managers.

To set an attribute of a window, set the appropriate member of the `XSetWindowAttributes` structure and OR in the corresponding value bitmask in your subsequent calls to `XCreateWindow` and `XChange-WindowAttributes`, or use one of the other convenience functions that set the appropriate attribute. The symbols for the value mask bits and the `XSetWindowAttributes` structure are:

```
/* Window attribute value mask bits */
#define CWBackPixmap         (1L<<0)
#define CWBackPixel          (1L<<1)
#define CWBorderPixmap       (1L<<2)
#define CWBorderPixel        (1L<<3)
#define CWBitGravity         (1L<<4)
#define CWWinGravity         (1L<<5)
#define CWBackingStore       (1L<<6)
#define CWBackingPlanes      (1L<<7)
#define CWBackingPixel       (1L<<8)
#define CWOverrideRedirect   (1L<<9)
#define CWSaveUnder          (1L<<10)
#define CWEventMask          (1L<<11)
#define CWDontPropagate      (1L<<12)
#define CWColormap           (1L<<13)
#define CWCursor             (1L<<14)
```

```
/* Values */
typedef struct {
      Pixmap background_pixmap;            /* background, None, or
                                              ParentRelative */
      unsigned long background_pixel;      /* background pixel */
      Pixmap border_pixmap;                /* border of the window or
                                              CopyFromParent */
      unsigned long border_pixel;          /* border pixel value */
      int bit_gravity;                     /* one of bit gravity values */
      int win_gravity;                     /* one of the window gravity values */
      int backing_store;                   /* NotUseful, WhenMapped,
                                              Always */
      unsigned long backing_planes;        /* planes to be preserved if possible */
      unsigned long backing_pixel;         /* value to use in restoring planes */
      Bool save_under;                     /* should bits under be saved?
                                              (popups) */
      long event_mask;                     /* set of events that should be saved */
      long do_not_propagate_mask;          /* set of events that should not
                                              propagate */
      Bool override_redirect;              /* boolean value for override_redirect */
      Colormap colormap;                   /* color map to be associated with
                                              window */
      Cursor cursor;                       /* cursor to be displayed (or None) */
} XSetWindowAttributes;
```

The following lists the defaults for each window attribute and indicates whether the attribute is applicable to InputOutput and InputOnly windows:

Attribute	Default	InputOutput	InputOnly
background-pixmap	None	Yes	No
background-pixel	Undefined	Yes	No
border-pixmap	CopyFromParent	Yes	No
border-pixel	Undefined	Yes	No
bit-gravity	ForgetGravity	Yes	No
win-gravity	NorthWestGravity	Yes	Yes
backing-store	NotUseful	Yes	No
backing-planes	All ones	Yes	No
backing-pixel	zero	Yes	No
save-under	False	Yes	No

Attribute	Default	InputOutput	InputOnly
event-mask	empty set	Yes	Yes
do-not-propagate-mask	empty set	Yes	Yes
override-redirect	`False`	Yes	Yes
colormap	`CopyFromParent`	Yes	No
cursor	`None`	Yes	Yes

3.2.1 Background Attribute

Only `InputOutput` windows can have a background. You can set the background of an `InputOutput` window by using a pixel or a pixmap.

The background-pixmap attribute of a window specifies the pixmap to be used for a window's background. This pixmap can be of any size, although some sizes may be faster than others. The background-pixel attribute of a window specifies a pixel value used to paint a window's background in a single color.

You can set the background-pixmap to a pixmap, `None` (default), or `ParentRelative`. You can set the background-pixel of a window to any pixel value (no default). If you specify a background-pixel, it overrides either the default background-pixmap or any value you may have set in the background-pixmap. A pixmap of an undefined size that is filled with the background-pixel is used for the background. Range checking is not performed on the background pixel; it simply is truncated to the appropriate number of bits.

If you set the background-pixmap, it overrides the default. The background-pixmap and the window must have the same depth, or a `BadMatch` error results. If you set background-pixmap to `None,` the window has no defined background. If you set the background-pixmap to `ParentRelative`:

- The parent window's background-pixmap is used. The child window, however, must have the same depth as its parent, or a `BadMatch` error results.

- If the parent window has a background-pixmap of `None`, the window also has a background-pixmap of `None.`

- A copy of the parent window's background-pixmap is not made. The parent's background-pixmap is examined each time the child window's background-pixmap is required.

- The background tile origin always aligns with the parent window's background tile origin. If the background-pixmap is not `ParentRelative`, the background tile origin is the child window's origin.

Setting a new background, whether by setting background-pixmap or background-pixel, overrides any previous background. The background-pixmap can be freed immediately if no further explicit reference is made to it (the X server will keep a copy to use when needed). If you later draw into the pixmap used for the background, what happens is undefined because the X implementation is free to make a copy of the pixmap or to use the same pixmap.

When no valid contents are available for regions of a window and either the regions are visible or the server is maintaining backing store, the server automatically tiles the regions with the window's background unless the window has a background of `None`. If the background is `None`, the previous screen contents from other windows of the same depth as the window are simply left in place as long as the contents come from the parent of the window or an inferior of the parent. Otherwise, the initial contents of the exposed regions are undefined. `Expose` events are then generated for the regions, even if the background-pixmap is `None` (see chapter 8).

3.2.2   Border Attribute

Only `InputOutput` windows can have a border. You can set the border of an `InputOutput` window by using a pixel or a pixmap.

The border-pixmap attribute of a window specifies the pixmap to be used for a window's border. The border-pixel attribute of a window specifies a pixmap of undefined size filled with that pixel be used for a window's border. Range checking is not performed on the background pixel; it simply is truncated to the appropriate number of bits. The border tile origin is always the same as the background tile origin.

You can also set the border-pixmap to a pixmap of any size (some may be faster than others) or to `CopyFromParent` (default). You can set the border-pixel to any pixel value (no default).

If you set a border-pixmap, it overrides the default. The border-pixmap and the window must have the same depth, or a `BadMatch` error results. If you set the border-pixmap to `CopyFromParent`, the parent window's border-pixmap is copied. Subsequent changes to the parent window's border attribute do not affect the child window. However, the child window must have the same depth as the parent window, or a `BadMatch` error results.

The border-pixmap can be freed immediately if no further explicit reference is made to it. If you later draw into the pixmap used for the border, what happens is undefined because the X implementation is free either to make a copy of the pixmap or to use the same pixmap. If you specify a border-pixel, it overrides either the default border-pixmap or any value you may have set in the border-pixmap. All pixels in the window's border will be set to the border-pixel. Setting a new border, whether by setting border-pixel or by setting border-pixmap, overrides any previous border.

Output to a window is always clipped to the inside of the window. Therefore, graphics operations never affect the window border.

3.2.3 Gravity Attributes

The bit gravity of a window defines which region of the window should be retained when an `InputOutput` window is resized. The default value for the bit-gravity attribute is `ForgetGravity`. The window gravity of a window allows you to define how the `InputOutput` or `InputOnly` window should be repositioned if its parent is resized. The default value for the win-gravity attribute is `NorthWestGravity`.

If the inside width or height of a window is not changed and if the window is moved or its border is changed, then the contents of the window are not lost but move with the window. Changing the inside width or height of the window causes its contents to be moved or lost (depending on the bit-gravity of the window) and causes children to be reconfigured (depending on their win-gravity). For a change of width and height, the (x, y) pairs are defined:

Gravity Direction	*Coordinates*
`NorthWestGravity`	(0, 0)
`NorthGravity`	(Width/2, 0)
`NorthEastGravity`	(Width, 0)
`WestGravity`	(0, Height/2)
`CenterGravity`	(Width/2, Height/2)
`EastGravity`	(Width, Height/2)
`SouthWestGravity`	(0, Height)
`SouthGravity`	(Width/2, Height)
`SouthEastGravity`	(Width, Height)

When a window with one of these bit-gravity values is resized, the corresponding pair defines the change in position of each pixel in the window. When a window with one of these win-gravities has its parent window resized, the corresponding pair defines the change in position of the window within the parent. When a window is so repositioned, a `GravityNotify` event is generated (see chapter 8).

A bit-gravity of `StaticGravity` indicates that the contents or origin should not move relative to the origin of the root window. If the change in size of the window is coupled with a change in position (x, y), then for bit-gravity the change in position of each pixel is $(-x, -y)$, and for win-gravity the change in position of a child when its parent is so resized is $(-x, -y)$. Note that `StaticGravity` still only takes effect when the width or height of the window is changed, not when the window is moved.

A bit-gravity of `ForgetGravity` indicates that the window's contents are always discarded after a size change, even if a backing store or save under has been requested. The window is tiled with its background and zero or more `Expose` events are generated. If no background is defined, the existing screen contents are not altered. Some X servers may also ignore the specified bit-gravity and always generate `Expose` events.

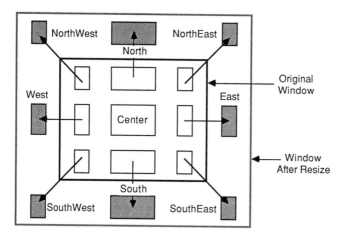

Figure 3.3.   Window gravity

A win-gravity of `UnmapGravity` is like `NorthWestGravity` (the window is not moved), except the child is also unmapped when the parent is resized, and an `UnmapNotify` event is generated.

3.2.4 Backing Store Attribute

Some implementations of the X server may choose to maintain the contents of `InputOutput` windows. If the X server maintains the contents of a window, the off-screen saved pixels are known as backing store. The backing store advises the X server on what to do with the contents of a window. The backing-store attribute can be set to `NotUseful` (default), `WhenMapped`, or `Always`.

A backing-store attribute of `NotUseful` advises the X server that maintaining contents is unnecessary, although some X implementations may still choose to maintain contents and, therefore, not generate `Expose` events. A backing-store attribute of `WhenMapped` advises the X server that maintaining contents of obscured regions when the window is mapped would be beneficial. In this case, the server may generate an `Expose` event when the window is created. A backing-store attribute of `Always` advises the X server that maintaining contents even when the window is unmapped would be beneficial. Even if the window is larger than its parent, this is a request to the X server to maintain complete contents, not just the region within the parent window boundaries. While the X server maintains the window's contents, `Expose` events normally are not generated, but the X server may stop maintaining contents at any time.

When the contents of obscured regions of a window are being maintained, regions obscured by noninferior windows are included in the destination of graphics requests (and source, when the window is the source). However, regions obscured by inferior windows are not included.

3.2.5 Save Under Flag

Some server implementations may preserve contents of `InputOutput` windows under other `InputOutput` windows. This is not the same as preserving the contents of a window for you. You may get better visual appeal if transient windows (for example, pop-up menus) request that the system preserve the screen contents under them, so the temporarily obscured applications do not have to repaint.

You can set the save-under flag to `True` or `False` (default). If save-under is `True`, the X server is advised that, when this window is mapped, saving the contents of windows it obscures would be beneficial.

3.2.6   Backing Planes and Backing Pixel Attributes

You can set backing planes to indicate (with bits set to 1) which bit planes of an `InputOutput` window hold dynamic data that must be preserved in backing store and during save unders. The default value for the backing-planes attribute is all bits set to 1. You can set backing pixel to specify what bits to use in planes not covered by backing planes. The default value for the backing-pixel attribute is all bits set to 0. The X server is free to save only the specified bit planes in the backing store or the save under and is free to re-generate the remaining planes with the specified pixel value. Any extraneous bits in these values (that is, those bits beyond the specified depth of the window) may be simply ignored. If you request backing store or save unders, you should use these members to minimize the amount of off-screen memory required to store your window.

3.2.7   Event Mask and Do Not Propagate Mask Attributes

The event mask defines which events the client is interested in for this `InputOutput` or `InputOnly` window (or, for some event types, inferiors of that window). The do-not-propagate-mask attribute defines which events should not be propagated to ancestor windows when no client has the event type selected in this `InputOutput` or `InputOnly` window. Both masks are the bitwise inclusive OR of one or more of the valid event mask bits. You can specify that no maskable events are reported by setting `NoEventMask` (default).

3.2.8   Override Redirect Flag

To control window placement or to add decoration, a window manager often needs to intercept (redirect) any map or configure request. Pop-up windows, however, often need to be mapped without a window manager getting in the way. To control whether an `InputOutput` or `InputOnly` window is to ignore these structure control facilities, use the override-redirect flag.

The override-redirect flag specifies whether map and configure requests on this window should override a `SubstructureRedirectMask` on the parent. You can set the override-redirect flag to `True` or `False` (default). Window managers use this information to avoid tampering with pop-up windows (see also chapter 9).

3.2.9 Colormap Attribute

The colormap attribute specifies which colormap best reflects the true colors of the `InputOutput` window. The colormap must have the same visual type as the window, or a `BadMatch` error results. X servers capable of supporting multiple hardware colormaps can use this information, and window manager can use it for calls to `XInstallColormap`. You can set the colormap attribute to a colormap or to `CopyFromParent` (default).

If you set the colormap to `CopyFromParent`, the parent window's colormap is copied and used by its child. However, the child window must have the same visual type as the parent, or a `BadMatch` error results. The parent window must not have a colormap of `None`, or a `BadMatch` error results. The colormap is copied by sharing the colormap object between the child and parent, not by making a complete copy of the colormap contents. Subsequent changes to the parent window's colormap attribute do not affect the child window.

3.2.10 Cursor Attribute

The cursor attribute specifies which cursor is to be used when the pointer is in the `InputOutput` or `InputOnly` window. You can set the cursor to a cursor or `None` (default).

If you set the cursor to `None`, the parent's cursor is used when the pointer is in the `InputOutput` or `InputOnly` window, and any change in the parent's cursor will cause an immediate change in the displayed cursor. By calling `XFreeCursor`, the cursor can be freed immediately as long as no further explicit reference to it is made.

3.3 Creating Windows

Xlib provides basic ways for creating windows, and toolkits often supply higher-level functions specifically for creating and placing top-level windows, which are discussed in the appropriate toolkit documentation. If you do not use a toolkit, however, you must provide some standard information or hints for the window manager by using the Xlib predefined property functions (see chapter 9).

If you use Xlib to create your own top-level windows (direct children of the root window), you must observe the following rules so that all applications interact reasonably across the different styles of window management:

- You must never fight with the window manager for the size or placement of your top-level window.

- You must be able to deal with whatever size window you get, even if this means that your application just prints a message like "Please make me bigger" in its window.

- You should only attempt to resize or move top-level windows in direct response to a user request. If a request to change the size of a top-level window fails, you must be prepared to live with what you get. You are free to resize or move the children of top-level windows as necessary. (Toolkits often have facilities for automatic relayout.)

- If you do not use a toolkit that automatically sets standard window properties, you should set these properties for top-level windows before mapping them.

XCreateWindow is the more general function that allows you to set specific window attributes when you create a window. XCreateSimpleWindow creates a window that inherits its attributes from its parent window.

The X server acts as if InputOnly windows do not exist for the purposes of graphics requests, exposure processing, and VisibilityNotify events. An InputOnly window cannot be used as a drawable (that is, as a source or destination for graphics requests). InputOnly and Input-Output windows act identically in other respects (properties, grabs, input control, and so on). Extension packages can define other classes of windows.

To create an unmapped window and set its window attributes, use XCreateWindow.

Window XCreateWindow(*display, parent, x, y, width, height, border_width, depth, class, visual, valuemask, attributes*)
      Display *display*;
      Window *parent*;
      int *x, y*;

    unsigned int *width, height*;
    unsigned int *border_width*;
    int *depth*;
    unsigned int *class*;
    Visual **visual*
    unsigned long *valuemask*;
    XSetWindowAttributes **attributes*;

display	Specifies the connection to the X server.
parent	Specifies the parent window.
x	
y	Specify the x and y coordinates, which are the top-left outside corner of the created window's borders and are relative to the inside of the parent window's borders.
width	
height	Specify the width and height, which are the created window's inside dimensions and do not include the created window's borders. The dimensions must be nonzero, or a `BadValue` error results.
border_width	Specifies the width of the created window's border in pixels.
depth	Specifies the window's depth. A depth of `CopyFromParent` means the depth is taken from the parent.
class	Specifies the created window's class. You can pass `InputOutput`, `InputOnly`, or `CopyFromParent`. A class of `CopyFromParent` means the class is taken from the parent.
visual	Specifies the visual type. A visual of `CopyFromParent` means the visual type is taken from the parent.
valuemask	Specifies which window attributes are defined in the attributes argument. This mask is the bitwise inclusive OR of the valid attribute mask bits. If valuemask is zero, the attributes are ignored and are not referenced.
attributes	Specifies the structure from which the values (as specified by the value mask) are to be taken. The value mask should have the appropriate bits set to indicate which attributes have been set in the structure.

The `XCreateWindow` function creates an unmapped subwindow for a specified parent window, returns the window ID of the created window, and causes the X server to generate a `CreateNotify` event. The created window is placed on top in the stacking order with respect to siblings.

The border_width for an `InputOnly` window must be zero, or a `BadMatch` error results. For class `InputOutput`, the visual type and depth must be a combination supported for the screen, or a `BadMatch` error results. The depth need not be the same as the parent, but the parent must not

be a window of class `InputOnly`, or a `BadMatch` error results. For an
`InputOnly` window, the depth must be zero, and the visual must be one
supported by the screen. If either condition is not met, a `BadMatch` error
results. The parent window, however, may have any depth and class. If you
specify any invalid window attribute for a window, a `BadMatch` error results.

The created window is not yet displayed (mapped) on the user's display.
To display the window, call `XMapWindow`. The new window initially uses the
same cursor as its parent. A new cursor can be defined for the new window
by calling `XDefineCursor`. The window will not be visible on the screen
unless it and all of its ancestors are mapped and it is not obscured by any of
its ancestors.

`XCreateWindow` can generate `BadAlloc`, `BadColor`, `BadCursor`,
`BadMatch`, `BadPixmap`, `BadValue`, and `BadWindow` errors.

To create an unmapped `InputOutput` subwindow of a given parent window, use `XCreateSimpleWindow`.

Window XCreateSimpleWindow(*display, parent, x, y, width, height, border_width,*
border, background)

    Display **display*;
    Window *parent*;
    int *x, y*;
    unsigned int *width, height*;
    unsigned int *border_width*;
    unsigned long *border*;
    unsigned long *background*;

display	Specifies the connection to the X server.
parent	Specifies the parent window.
x	
y	Specify the x and y coordinates, which are the top-left outside corner of the new window's borders and are relative to the inside of the parent window's borders.
width	
height	Specify the width and height, which are the created window's inside dimensions and do not include the created window's borders. The dimensions must be nonzero, or a `BadValue` error results.
border_width	Specifies the width of the created window's border in pixels.
border	Specifies the border pixel value of the window.
background	Specifies the background pixel value of the window.

The XCreateSimpleWindow function creates an unmapped Input-Output subwindow for a specified parent window, returns the window ID of the created window, and causes the X server to generate a CreateNotify event. The created window is placed on top in the stacking order with respect to siblings. Any part of the window that extends outside its parent window is clipped. The border_width for an InputOnly window must be zero, or a BadMatch error results. XCreateSimpleWindow inherits its depth, class, and visual from its parent. All other window attributes, except background and border, have their default values.

XCreateSimpleWindow can generate BadAlloc, BadMatch, BadValue, and BadWindow errors.

3.4 Destroying Windows

Xlib provides functions that you can use to destroy a window or destroy all subwindows of a window.

To destroy a window and all of its subwindows, use XDestroyWindow.

XDestroyWindow(*display, w*)
    Display **display*;
    Window *w*;
display   Specifies the connection to the X server.
w   Specifies the window.

The XDestroyWindow function destroys the specified window as well as all of its subwindows and causes the X server to generate a DestroyNotify event for each window. The window should never be referenced again. If the window specified by the w argument is mapped, it is unmapped automatically. The ordering of the DestroyNotify events is such that for any given window being destroyed, DestroyNotify is generated on any inferiors of the window before being generated on the window itself. The ordering among siblings and across subhierarchies is not otherwise constrained. If the window you specified is a root window, no windows are destroyed. Destroying a mapped window will generate Expose events on other windows that were obscured by the window being destroyed.

XDestroyWindow can generate a BadWindow error.

To destroy all subwindows of a specified window, use XDestroy-
Subwindows.

XDestroySubwindows(*display, w*)
     Display *display*;
     Window *w*;
display   Specifies the connection to the X server.
w   Specifies the window.

The XDestroySubwindows function destroys all inferior windows of the
specified window, in bottom-to-top stacking order. It causes the X server to
generate a DestroyNotify event for each window. If any mapped
subwindows were actually destroyed, XDestroySubwindows causes the X
server to generate Expose events on the specified window. This is much
more efficient than deleting many windows one at a time because much of
the work need be performed only once for all of the windows, rather than
for each window. The subwindows should never be referenced again.
     XDestroySubwindows can generate a BadWindow error.

3.5   Mapping Windows

A window is considered mapped if an XMapWindow call has been made on
it. It may not be visible on the screen for one of the following reasons:

- It is obscured by another opaque window.
- One of its ancestors is not mapped.
- It is entirely clipped by an ancestor.

Expose events are generated for the window when part or all of it becomes
visible on the screen. A client receives the Expose events only if it has asked
for them. Windows retain their position in the stacking order when they are
unmapped.
     A window manager may want to control the placement of subwindows. If
SubstructureRedirectMask has been selected by a window manager on
a parent window (usually a root window), a map request initiated by other
clients on a child window is not performed, and the window manager is sent
a MapRequest event. However, if the override-redirect flag on the child
had been set to True (usually only on pop-up menus), the map request is
performed.

A tiling window manager might decide to reposition and resize other clients' windows and then decide to map the window to its final location. A window manager that wants to provide decoration might reparent the child into a frame first. For further information, see section 3.2.8 and chapter 8. Only a single client at a time can select for `SubstructureRedirectMask`.

Similarly, a single client can select for `ResizeRedirectMask` on a parent window. Then, any attempt to resize the window by another client is suppressed, and the client receives a `ResizeRequest` event.

To map a given window, use `XMapWindow`.

XMapWindow(*display, w*)
    Display **display*;
    Window *w*;
display   Specifies the connection to the X server.
w   Specifies the window.

The `XMapWindow` function maps the window and all of its subwindows that have had map requests. Mapping a window that has an unmapped ancestor does not display the window but marks it as eligible for display when the ancestor becomes mapped. Such a window is called unviewable. When all its ancestors are mapped, the window becomes viewable and will be visible on the screen if it is not obscured by another window. This function has no effect if the window is already mapped.

If the override-redirect of the window is `False` and if some other client has selected `SubstructureRedirectMask` on the parent window, then the X server generates a `MapRequest` event, and the `XMapWindow` function does not map the window. Otherwise, the window is mapped, and the X server generates a `MapNotify` event.

If the window becomes viewable and no earlier contents for it are remembered, the X server tiles the window with its background. If the window's background is undefined, the existing screen contents are not altered, and the X server generates zero or more `Expose` events. If backing-store was maintained while the window was unmapped, no `Expose` events are generated. If backing-store will now be maintained, a full-window exposure is always generated. Otherwise, only visible regions may be reported. Similar tiling and exposure take place for any newly viewable inferiors.

If the window is an `InputOutput` window, `XMapWindow` generates `Expose` events on each `InputOutput` window that it causes to be displayed. If the client maps and paints the window and if the client begins processing events, the window is painted twice. To avoid this, first ask for `Expose` events and then map the window, so the client processes input events as usual. The event list will include `Expose` for each window that has appeared on the screen. The client's normal response to an `Expose` event should be to repaint the window. This method usually leads to simpler programs and to proper interaction with window managers.

`XMapWindow` can generate a `BadWindow` error.

To map and raise a window, use `XMapRaised`.

XMapRaised(*display, w*)
     Display **display*;
     Window *w*;
display   Specifies the connection to the X server.
w   Specifies the window.

The `XMapRaised` function essentially is similar to `XMapWindow` in that it maps the window and all of its subwindows that have had map requests. However, it also raises the specified window to the top of the stack. For additional information, see `XMapWindow`.

`XMapRaised` can generate multiple `BadWindow` errors.

To map all subwindows for a specified window, use `XMapSubwindows`.

XMapSubwindows(*display, w*)
     Display **display*;
     Window *w*;
display   Specifies the connection to the X server.
w   Specifies the window.

The `XMapSubwindows` function maps all subwindows for a specified window in top-to-bottom stacking order. The X server generates `Expose` events on each newly displayed window. This may be much more efficient than mapping many windows one at a time because the server needs to perform much of the work only once, for all of the windows, rather than for each window.

XMapSubwindows can generate a BadWindow error.

3.6   Unmapping Windows

Xlib provides functions that you can use to unmap a window or all subwindows.

To unmap a window, use XUnmapWindow.

XUnmapWindow(*display, w*)
    Display **display*;
    Window *w*;
display   Specifies the connection to the X server.
w   Specifies the window.

The XUnmapWindow function unmaps the specified window and causes the X server to generate an UnmapNotify event. If the specified window is already unmapped, XUnmapWindow has no effect. Normal exposure processing on formerly obscured windows is performed. Any child window will no longer be visible until another map call is made on the parent. In other words, the subwindows are still mapped but are not visible until the parent is mapped. Unmapping a window will generate Expose events on windows that were formerly obscured by it.

XUnmapWindow can generate a BadWindow error.

To unmap all subwindows for a specified window, use XUnmap-Subwindows.

XUnmapSubwindows(*display, w*)
    Display **display*;
    Window *w*;
display   Specifies the connection to the X server.
w   Specifies the window.

The XUnmapSubwindows function unmaps all subwindows for the specified window in bottom-to-top stacking order. It causes the X server to generate an UnmapNotify event on each subwindow and Expose events on formerly obscured windows. Using this function is much more efficient than unmapping multiple windows one at a time because the server needs to perform much of the work only once, for all of the windows, rather than for each window.

XUnmapSubwindows can generate a BadWindow error.

3.7   Configuring Windows

Xlib provides functions that you can use to move a window, resize a window, move and resize a window, or change a window's border width. To change one of these parameters, set the appropriate member of the XWindowChanges structure and OR in the corresponding value mask in subsequent calls to XConfigureWindow. The symbols for the value mask bits and the XWindowChanges structure are:

```
/* Configure window value mask bits */
#define CWX            (1<<0)
#define CWY            (1<<1)
#define CWWidth        (1<<2)
#define CWHeight       (1<<3)
#define CWBorderWidth  (1<<4)
#define CWSibling      (1<<5)
#define CWStackMode    (1<<6)
/* Values */
typedef struct {
     int x, y;
     int width, height;
     int border_width;
     Window sibling;
     int stack_mode;
} XWindowChanges;
```

The x and y members are used to set the window's x and y coordinates, which are relative to the parent's origin and indicate the position of the upper-left outer corner of the window. The width and height members are used to set the inside size of the window, not including the border, and must be nonzero, or a BadValue error results. Attempts to configure a root window have no effect.

The border_width member is used to set the width of the border in pixels. Note that setting just the border width leaves the outer-left corner of the window in a fixed position but moves the absolute position of the window's origin. If you attempt to set the border-width attribute of an `InputOnly` window nonzero, a `BadMatch` error results.

The sibling member is used to set the sibling window for stacking operations. The stack_mode member is used to set how the window is to be restacked and can be set to `Above`, `Below`, `TopIf`, `BottomIf`, or `Opposite`.

If the override-redirect flag of the window is `False` and if some other client has selected `SubstructureRedirectMask` on the parent, the X server generates a `ConfigureRequest` event, and no further processing is performed. Otherwise, if some other client has selected `Resize-RedirectMask` on the window and the inside width or height of the window is being changed, a `ResizeRequest` event is generated, and the current inside width and height are used instead. Note that the override-redirect flag of the window has no effect on `ResizeRedirectMask` and that `SubstructureRedirectMask` on the parent has precedence over `ResizeRedirectMask` on the window.

When the geometry of the window is changed as specified, the window is restacked among siblings, and a `ConfigureNotify` event is generated if the state of the window actually changes. `GravityNotify` events are generated after `ConfigureNotify` events. If the inside width or height of the window has actually changed, children of the window are affected as specified.

If a window's size actually changes, the window's subwindows move according to their window gravity. Depending on the window's bit gravity, the contents of the window also may be moved (see section 3.2.3).

If regions of the window were obscured but now are not, exposure processing is performed on these formerly obscured windows, including the window itself and its inferiors. As a result of increasing the width or height, exposure processing is also performed on any new regions of the window and any regions where window contents are lost.

The restack check (specifically, the computation for `BottomIf`, `TopIf`, and `Opposite`) is performed with respect to the window's final size and position (as controlled by the other arguments of the request), not its initial position. If a sibling is specified without a stack_mode, a `BadMatch` error results.

If a sibling and a stack_mode are specified, the window is restacked as follows:

Above	The window is placed just above the sibling.
Below	The window is placed just below the sibling.
TopIf	If the sibling occludes the window, the window is placed at the top of the stack.
BottomIf	If the window occludes the sibling, the window is placed at the bottom of the stack.
Opposite	If the sibling occludes the window, the window is placed at the top of the stack. If the window occludes the sibling, the window is placed at the bottom of the stack.

If a stack_mode is specified but no sibling is specified, the window is restacked as follows:

Above	The window is placed at the top of the stack.
Below	The window is placed at the bottom of the stack.
TopIf	If any sibling occludes the window, the window is placed at the top of the stack.
BottomIf	If the window occludes any sibling, the window is placed at the bottom of the stack.
Opposite	If any sibling occludes the window, the window is placed at the top of the stack. If the window occludes any sibling, the window is placed at the bottom of the stack.

Attempts to configure a root window have no effect.

To configure a window's size, location, stacking, or border, use XConfigureWindow.

XConfigureWindow(*display, w, value_mask, values*)
    Display **display*;
    Window *w*;
    unsigned int *value_mask*;
    XWindowChanges **values*;

display	Specifies the connection to the X server.
w	Specifies the window to be reconfigured.
value_mask	Specifies which values are to be set using information in the values structure. This mask is the bitwise inclusive OR of the valid configure window values bits.
values	Specifies a pointer to the XWindowChanges structure.

The XConfigureWindow function uses the values specified in the XWindowChanges structure to reconfigure a window's size, position, border, and stacking order. Values not specified are taken from the existing geometry of the window.

If a sibling is specified without a stack_mode or if the window is not actually a sibling, a BadMatch error results. Note that the computations for BottomIf, TopIf, and Opposite are performed with respect to the window's final geometry (as controlled by the other arguments passed to XConfigureWindow), not its initial geometry. Any backing store contents of the window, its inferiors, and other newly visible windows are either discarded or changed to reflect the current screen contents (depending on the implementation).

XConfigureWindow can generate BadMatch, BadValue, and BadWindow errors.

To move a window without changing its size, use XMoveWindow.

XMoveWindow(*display, w, x, y*)
    Display **display*;
    Window *w*;
    int *x, y*;

display	Specifies the connection to the X server.
w	Specifies the window to be moved.
x	
y	Specify the x and y coordinates, which define the new location of the top-left pixel of the window's border or the window itself if it has no border.

The XMoveWindow function moves the specified window to the specified x and y coordinates, but it does not change the window's size, raise the window, or change the mapping state of the window. Moving a mapped window may or may not lose the window's contents depending on if the window is obscured by nonchildren and if no backing store exists. If the contents of the window are lost, the X server generates Expose events. Moving a mapped window generates Expose events on any formerly obscured windows.

If the override-redirect flag of the window is False and some other client has selected SubstructureRedirectMask on the parent, the X server generates a ConfigureRequest event, and no further processing is performed. Otherwise, the window is moved.

XMoveWindow can generate a BadWindow error.

To change a window's size without changing the upper-left coordinate, use XResizeWindow.

XResizeWindow(*display, w, width, height*)
    Display **display*;
    Window *w*;
    unsigned int *width, height*;

display   Specifies the connection to the X server.

w   Specifies the window.

width

height   Specify the width and height, which are the interior dimensions of the window after the call completes.

The XResizeWindow function changes the inside dimensions of the specified window, not including its borders. This function does not change the window's upper-left coordinate or the origin and does not restack the window. Changing the size of a mapped window may lose its contents and generate Expose events. If a mapped window is made smaller, changing its size generates Expose events on windows that the mapped window formerly obscured.

If the override-redirect flag of the window is False and some other client has selected SubstructureRedirectMask on the parent, the X server generates a ConfigureRequest event, and no further processing is performed. If either width or height is zero, a BadValue error results.

XResizeWindow can generate BadValue and BadWindow errors.

To change the size and location of a window, use XMoveResize-Window.

XMoveResizeWindow(*display, w, x, y, width, height*)
    Display **display*;
    Window *w*;
    int *x, y*;
    unsigned int *width, height*;

display   Specifies the connection to the X server.

w   Specifies the window to be reconfigured.

x

y   Specify the x and y coordinates, which define the new position of the window relative to its parent.

width

height   Specify the width and height, which define the interior size of the window.

The XMoveResizeWindow function changes the size and location of the specified window without raising it. Moving and resizing a mapped window may generate an Expose event on the window. Depending on the new size and location parameters, moving and resizing a window may generate Expose events on windows that the window formerly obscured.

If the override-redirect flag of the window is False and some other client has selected SubstructureRedirectMask on the parent, the X server generates a ConfigureRequest event, and no further processing is performed. Otherwise, the window size and location are changed.

XMoveResizeWindow can generate BadValue and BadWindow errors.

To change the border width of a given window, use XSetWindowBorderWidth.

XSetWindowBorderWidth(*display, w, width*)
    Display *display;
    Window *w*;
    unsigned int *width*;

display   Specifies the connection to the X server.
w   Specifies the window.
width   Specifies the width of the window border.

The XSetWindowBorderWidth function sets the specified window's border width to the specified width.

XSetWindowBorderWidth can generate a BadWindow error.

3.8   Changing Window Stacking Order

Xlib provides functions that you can use to raise, lower, circulate, or restack windows.

To raise a window so that no sibling window obscures it, use XRaiseWindow.

XRaiseWindow(*display, w*)
    Display *display;
    Window *w*;

display   Specifies the connection to the X server.
w   Specifies the window.

The `XRaiseWindow` function raises the specified window to the top of the stack so that no sibling window obscures it. If the windows are regarded as overlapping sheets of paper stacked on a desk, then raising a window is analogous to moving the sheet to the top of the stack but leaving its x and y location on the desk constant. Raising a mapped window may generate `Expose` events for the window and any mapped subwindows that were formerly obscured.

If the override-redirect attribute of the window is `False` and some other client has selected `SubstructureRedirectMask` on the parent, the X server generates a `ConfigureRequest` event, and no processing is performed. Otherwise, the window is raised.

`XRaiseWindow` can generate a `BadWindow` error.

To lower a window so that it does not obscure any sibling windows, use `XLowerWindow`.

XLowerWindow(*display*, *w*)
    Display **display*;
    Window *w*;
display   Specifies the connection to the X server.
w   Specifies the window.

The `XLowerWindow` function lowers the specified window to the bottom of the stack so that it does not obscure any sibling windows. If the windows are regarded as overlapping sheets of paper stacked on a desk, then lowering a window is analogous to moving the sheet to the bottom of the stack but leaving its x and y location on the desk constant. Lowering a mapped window will generate `Expose` events on any windows it formerly obscured.

If the override-redirect attribute of the window is `False` and some other client has selected `SubstructureRedirectMask` on the parent, the X server generates a `ConfigureRequest` event, and no processing is performed. Otherwise, the window is lowered to the bottom of the stack.

`XLowerWindow` can generate a `BadWindow` error.

To circulate a subwindow up or down, use `XCirculateSubwindows`.

XCirculateSubwindows(*display, w, direction*)
    Display **display*;
    Window *w*;
    int *direction*;

display	Specifies the connection to the X server.
w	Specifies the window.
direction	Specifies the direction (up or down) that you want to circulate the window. You can pass `RaiseLowest` or `LowerHighest`.

The `XCirculateSubwindows` function circulates children of the specified window in the specified direction. If you specify `RaiseLowest`, `XCirculateSubwindows` raises the lowest mapped child (if any) that is occluded by another child to the top of the stack. If you specify `LowerHighest`, `XCirculateSubwindows` lowers the highest mapped child (if any) that occludes another child to the bottom of the stack. Exposure processing is then performed on formerly obscured windows. If some other client has selected `SubstructureRedirectMask` on the window, the X server generates a `CirculateRequest` event, and no further processing is performed. If a child is actually restacked, the X server generates a `CirculateNotify` event.

    `XCirculateSubwindows` can generate `BadValue` and `BadWindow` errors.

To raise the lowest mapped child of a window that is partially or completely occluded by another child, use `XCirculateSubwindowsUp`.

XCirculateSubwindowsUp(*display, w*)
    Display **display*;
    Window *w*;

display	Specifies the connection to the X server.
w	Specifies the window.

The `XCirculateSubwindowsUp` function raises the lowest mapped child of the specified window that is partially or completely occluded by another child. Completely unobscured children are not affected. This is a convenience function equivalent to `XCirculateSubwindows` with `RaiseLowest` specified.

    `XCirculateSubwindowsUp` can generate a `BadWindow` error.

To lower the highest mapped child of a window that partially or completely occludes another child, use XCirculateSubwindowsDown.

XCirculateSubwindowsDown(*display, w*)
    Display **display*;
    Window *w*;
display   Specifies the connection to the X server.
w   Specifies the window.

The XCirculateSubwindowsDown function lowers the highest mapped child of the specified window that partially or completely occludes another child. Completely unobscured children are not affected. This is a convenience function equivalent to XCirculateSubwindows with Lower-Highest specified.

XCirculateSubwindowsDown can generate a BadWindow error.

To restack a set of windows from top to bottom, use XRestack-Windows.

XRestackWindows(*display, windows, nwindows*);
    Display **display*;
    Window *windows*[];
    int *nwindows*;
display   Specifies the connection to the X server.
windows   Specifies an array containing the windows to be restacked.
nwindows   Specifies the number of windows to be restacked.

The XRestackWindows function restacks the windows in the order specified, from top to bottom. The stacking order of the first window in the windows array is unaffected, but the other windows in the array are stacked underneath the first window, in the order of the array. The stacking order of the other windows is not affected. For each window in the window array that is not a child of the specified window, a BadMatch error results.

If the override-redirect attribute of a window is False and some other client has selected SubstructureRedirectMask on the parent, the X server generates ConfigureRequest events for each window whose override-redirect flag is not set, and no further processing is performed. Otherwise, the windows will be restacked in top to bottom order.

XRestackWindows can generate a BadWindow error.

3.9   Changing Window Attributes

Xlib provides functions that you can use to set window attributes.
`XChangeWindowAttributes` is the more general function that allows
you to set one or more window attributes provided by the
`XSetWindowAttributes` structure. The other functions described in this
section allow you to set one specific window attribute, such as a window's
background.

To change one or more attributes for a given window, use
`XChangeWindowAttributes`.

XChangeWindowAttributes(*display, w, valuemask, attributes*)
    Display **display*;
    Window *w*;
    unsigned long *valuemask*;
    XSetWindowAttributes **attributes*;

display	Specifies the connection to the X server.
w	Specifies the window.
valuemask	Specifies which window attributes are defined in the attributes argument. This mask is the bitwise inclusive OR of the valid attribute mask bits. If valuemask is zero, the attributes are ignored and are not referenced. The values and restrictions are the same as for `XCreateWindow`.
attributes	Specifies the structure from which the values (as specified by the value mask) are to be taken. The value mask should have the appropriate bits set to indicate which attributes have been set in the structure (see section 3.2).

Depending on the valuemask, the `XChangeWindowAttributes` function
uses the window attributes in the `XSetWindowAttributes` structure to
change the specified window attributes. Changing the background does not
cause the window contents to be changed. To repaint the window and its
background, use `XClearWindow`. Setting the border or changing the background such that the border tile origin changes causes the border to
be repainted. Changing the background of a root window to `None` or
`ParentRelative` restores the default background pixmap. Changing the
border of a root window to `CopyFromParent` restores the default border
pixmap. Changing the win-gravity does not affect the current position
of the window. Changing the backing-store of an obscured window to
`WhenMapped` or `Always`, or changing the backing-planes, backing-pixel, or

save-under of a mapped window may have no immediate effect. Changing the colormap of a window (that is, defining a new map, not changing the contents of the existing map) generates a `ColormapNotify` event. Changing the colormap of a visible window may have no immediate effect on the screen because the map may not be installed (see `XInstallColormap`). Changing the cursor of a root window to `None` restores the default cursor. Whenever possible, you are encouraged to share colormaps.

Multiple clients can select input on the same window. Their event masks are maintained separately. When an event is generated, it is reported to all interested clients. However, only one client at a time can select for `SubstructureRedirectMask`, `ResizeRedirectMask`, and `ButtonPressMask`. If a client attempts to select any of these event masks and some other client has already selected one, a `BadAccess` error results. There is only one do-not-propagate-mask for a window, not one per client.

`XChangeWindowAttributes` can generate `BadAccess`, `BadColor`, `BadCursor`, `BadMatch`, `BadPixmap`, `BadValue`, and `BadWindow` errors.

To set the background of a window to a given pixel, use `XSetWindowBackground`.

XSetWindowBackground(*display, w, background_pixel*)
    Display *display;
    Window *w*;
    unsigned long *background_pixel*;

display	Specifies the connection to the X server.
w	Specifies the window.
background_pixel	Specifies the pixel that is to be used for the background.

The `XSetWindowBackground` function sets the background of the window to the specified pixel value. Changing the background does not cause the window contents to be changed. `XSetWindowBackground` uses a pixmap of undefined size filled with the pixel value you passed. If you try to change the background of an `InputOnly` window, a `BadMatch` error results.

`XSetWindowBackground` can generate `BadMatch` and `BadWindow` errors.

To set the background of a window to a given pixmap, use `XSetWindowBackgroundPixmap`.

XSetWindowBackgroundPixmap(*display, w, background_pixmap*)
 Display **display*;
 Window *w*;
 Pixmap *background_pixmap*;

display	Specifies the connection to the X server.
w	Specifies the window.
background_pixmap	Specifies the background pixmap, `ParentRelative`, or `None`.

The `XSetWindowBackgroundPixmap` function sets the background pixmap of the window to the specified pixmap. The background pixmap can immediately be freed if no further explicit references to it are to be made. If `ParentRelative` is specified, the background pixmap of the window's parent is used, or on the root window, the default background is restored. If you try to change the background of an `InputOnly` window, a `BadMatch` error results. If the background is set to `None`, the window has no defined background.

   `XSetWindowBackgroundPixmap` can generate `BadMatch`, `Bad-Pixmap,` and `BadWindow errors.`

Note   `XSetWindowBackground` and `XSetWindowBackgroundPixmap` do not change the current contents of the window.

   To change and repaint a window's border to a given pixel, use `XSetWindowBorder.`

XSetWindowBorder(*display, w, border_pixel*)
 Display **display*;
 Window *w*;
 unsigned long *border_pixel*;

display	Specifies the connection to the X server.
w	Specifies the window.
border_pixel	Specifies the entry in the colormap.

The `XSetWindowBorder` function sets the border of the window to the pixel value you specify. If you attempt to perform this on an `InputOnly` window, a `BadMatch` error results.

   `XSetWindowBorder` can generate `BadMatch` and `BadWindow` errors.

To change and repaint the border tile of a given window, use
`XSetWindowBorderPixmap`.

XSetWindowBorderPixmap(*display, w, border_pixmap*)
    Display **display*;
    Window *w*;
    Pixmap *border_pixmap*;

display	Specifies the connection to the X server.
w	Specifies the window.
border_pixmap	Specifies the border pixmap or `CopyFromParent`.

The `XSetWindowBorderPixmap` function sets the border pixmap of the
window to the pixmap you specify. The border pixmap can be freed immediately if no further explicit references to it are to be made. If you specify
`CopyFromParent`, a copy of the parent window's border pixmap is used. If
you attempt to perform this on an `InputOnly` window, a `BadMatch` error
results.

    `XSetWindowBorderPixmap` can generate `BadMatch`, `BadPixmap`, and
`BadWindow` errors.

3.10   Translating Window Coordinates

Applications, mostly window managers, often need to perform a coordinate
transformation from the coordinate space of one window to another window or need to determine which subwindow a coordinate lies in.
`XTranslateCoordinates` fulfills these needs (and avoids any race conditions) by asking the X server to perform this operation.

Bool XTranslateCoordinates (*display, src_w, dest_w, src_x, src_y, dest_x_return,*
                                  dest_y_return, child_return)
    Display **display*;
    Window *src_w, dest_w*;
    int *src_x, src_y*;
    int **dest_x_return, *dest_y_return*;
    Window **child_return*;

display	Specifies the connection to the X server.
src_w	Specifies the source window.
dest_w	Specifies the destination window.
src_x	
src_y	Specify the x and y coordinates within the source window.

dest_x_return
dest_y_return   Return the x and y coordinates within the destination window.
child_return   Returns the child if the coordinates are contained in a mapped child of the destination window.

The XTranslateCoordinates function takes the src_x and src_y coordinates relative to the source window's origin and returns these coordinates to dest_x_return and dest_y_return relative to the destination window's origin. If XTranslateCoordinates returns zero, src_w and dest_w are on different screens, and dest_x_return and dest_y_return are zero. If the coordinates are contained in a mapped child of dest_w, that child is returned to child_return. Otherwise, child_return is set to None.

XTranslateCoordinates can generate a BadWindow error.

Chapter 4

Window Information Functions

After you connect the display to the X server and create a window, you can use the Xlib window information functions to:

- Obtain information about a window
- Manipulate property lists
- Obtain and change window properties
- Manipulate selections

4.1 Obtaining Window Information

Xlib provides functions that you can use to obtain information about the window tree, the window's current attributes, the window's current geometry, or the current pointer coordinates. Because they are most frequently used by window managers, these functions all return a status to indicate whether the window still exists.

To obtain the parent, a list of children, and number of children for a given window, use XQueryTree.

Status XQueryTree(*display, w, root_return, parent_return, children_return,*
　　　　　　　　　　nchildren_return)
　　Display **display*;
　　Window *w*;
　　Window **root_return*;
　　Window **parent_return*;

Window **children_return*;
unsigned int *nchildren_return*;

display	Specifies the connection to the X server.
w	Specifies the window whose list of children, root, parent, and number of children you want to obtain.
root_return	Returns the root window.
parent_return	Returns the parent window.
children_return	Returns a pointer to the list of children.
nchildren_return	Returns the number of children.

The XQueryTree function returns the root ID, the parent window ID, a pointer to the list of children windows, and the number of children in the list for the specified window. The children are listed in current stacking order, from bottommost (first) to topmost (last). XQueryTree returns zero if it fails and nonzero if it succeeds. To free this list when it is no longer needed, use XFree.

To obtain the current attributes of a given window, use XGetWindow-Attributes.

Status XGetWindowAttributes(*display, w, window_attributes_return*)
Display **display*;
Window *w*;
XWindowAttributes **window_attributes_return*;

display	Specifies the connection to the X server.
w	Specifies the window whose current attributes you want to obtain.
window_attributes_return	Returns the specified window's attributes in the XWindowAttributes structure.

The XGetWindowAttributes function returns the current attributes for the specified window to an XWindowAttributes structure.

```
typedef struct {
    int x, y;                    /* location of window */
    int width, height;           /* width and height of window */
    int border_width;            /* border width of window */
    int depth;                   /* depth of window */
    Visual *visual;              /* the associated visual structure */
    Window root;                 /* root of screen containing window */
    int class;                   /* InputOutput, InputOnly*/
```

```
int bit_gravity;              /* one of the bit gravity values */
int win_gravity;              /* one of the window gravity values */
int backing_store;            /* NotUseful, WhenMapped, Always */
unsigned long backing_planes; /* planes to be preserved if possible */
unsigned long backing_pixel;  /* value to be used when restoring planes */
Bool save_under;              /* boolean, should bits under be saved? */
Colormap colormap;            /* color map to be associated with window */
Bool map_installed;           /* boolean, is color map currently
                                 installed*/
int map_state;                /* IsUnmapped, IsUnviewable,
                                 IsViewable */
long all_event_masks;         /* set of events all people have interest in*/
long your_event_mask;         /* my event mask */
long do_not_propagate_mask;   /* set of events that should not propagate */
Bool override_redirect;       /* boolean value for override-redirect */
Screen *screen                /* back pointer to correct screen */
} XWindowAtrributes;
```

The x and y members are set to the upper-left outer corner relative to the parent window's origin. The width and height members are set to the inside size of the window, not including the border. The border_width member is set to the window's border width in pixels. The depth member is set to the depth of the window (that is, bits per pixel for the object). The visual member is a pointer to the screen's associated Visual structure. The root member is set to the root window of the screen containing the window. The class member is set to the window's class and can be either InputOutput or InputOnly.

The bit_gravity member is set to the window's bit gravity and can be one of the following:

```
ForgetGravity         EastGravity
NorthWestGravity      SouthWestGravity
NorthGravity          SouthGravity
NorthEastGravity      SouthEastGravity
WestGravity           StaticGravity
CenterGravity
```

The win_gravity member is set to the window's window gravity and can be one of the following:

```
UnmapGravity          EastGravity
NorthWestGravity      SouthWestGravity
```

```
NorthGravity          SouthGravity
NorthEastGravity      SouthEastGravity
WestGravity           StaticGravity
CenterGravity
```

For additional information on gravity, see section 3.3.

The backing_store member is set to indicate how the X server should maintain the contents of a window and can be WhenMapped, Always, or NotUseful. The backing_planes member is set to indicate (with bits set to 1) which bit planes of the window hold dynamic data that must be preserved in backing_stores and during save_unders. The backing_pixel member is set to indicate what values to use for planes not set in backing_planes.

The save_under member is set to True or False. The colormap member is set to the colormap for the specified window and can be a colormap ID or None. The map_installed member is set to indicate whether the colormap is currently installed and can be True or False. The map_state member is set to indicate the state of the window and can be IsUnmapped, IsUnviewable, or IsViewable. IsUnviewable is used if the window is mapped but some ancestor is unmapped.

The all_event_masks member is set to the bitwise inclusive OR of all event masks selected on the window by all clients. The your_event_mask member is set to the bitwise inclusive OR of all event masks selected by the querying client. The do_not_propagate_mask member is set to the bitwise inclusive OR of the set of events that should not propagate.

The override_redirect member is set to indicate whether this window overrides structure control facilities and can be True or False. Window manager clients should ignore the window if this member is True.

The screen member is set to a screen pointer that gives you a back pointer to the correct screen. This makes it easier to obtain the screen information without having to loop over the root window fields to see which field matches.

XGetWindowAttributes can generate BadDrawable and BadWindow errors.

To obtain the current geometry of a given drawable, use XGet-Geometry.

Status XGetGeometry(*display, d, root_return, x_return, y_return, width_return,*
                                height_return, border_width_return, depth_return)
    Display **display*;
    Drawable *d*;
    Window **root_return*;
    int **x_return, *y_return*;
    unsigned int **width_return, *height_return*;
    unsigned int **border_width_return*;
    unsigned int **depth_return*;

display	Specifies the connection to the X server.
d	Specifies the drawable, which can be a window or a pixmap.
root_return	Returns the root window.
x_return	
y_return	Return the x and y coordinates that define the location of the drawable. For a window, these coordinates specify the upper-left outer corner relative to its parent's origin. For pixmaps, these coordinates are always zero.
width_return	
height_return	Return the drawable's dimensions (width and height). For a window, these dimensions specify the inside size, not including the border.
border_width_return	Returns the border width in pixels. If the drawable is a pixmap, it returns zero.
depth_return	Returns the depth of the drawable (bits per pixel for the object).

The XGetGeometry function returns the root window and the current geometry of the drawable. The geometry of the drawable includes the x and y coordinates, width and height, border width, and depth. These are described in the argument list. It is legal to pass to this function a window whose class is InputOnly.

To obtain the root window the pointer is currently on and the pointer coordinates relative to the root's origin, use XQueryPointer.

Bool XQueryPointer(*display, w, root_return, child_return, root_x_return,*
                                root_y_return, win_x_return, win_y_return, mask_return)
    Display **display*;
    Window *w*;
    Window **root_return, *child_return*;
    int **root_x_return, *root_y_return;*

int *win_x_return*, *win_y_return*;
unsigned int *mask_return*;

display	Specifies the connection to the X server.
w	Specifies the window.
root_return	Returns the root window that the pointer is in.
child_return	Returns the child window that the pointer is located in, if any.
root_x_return	
root_y_return	Return the pointer coordinates relative to the root window's origin.
win_x_return	
win_y_return	Return the pointer coordinates relative to the specified window.
mask_return	Returns the current state of the modifier keys and pointer buttons.

The XQueryPointer function returns the root window the pointer is logically on and the pointer coordinates relative to the root window's origin. If XQueryPointer returns False, the pointer is not on the same screen as the specified window, and XQueryPointer returns None to child_return and zero to win_x_return and win_y_return. If XQueryPointer returns True, the pointer coordinates returned to win_x_return and win_y_return are relative to the origin of the specified window. In this case, XQueryPointer returns the child that contains the pointer, if any, or else None to child_return.

XQueryPointer returns the current logical state of the keyboard buttons and the modifier keys in mask_return. It sets mask_return to the bitwise inclusive OR of one or more of the button or modifier key bitmasks to match the current state of the mouse buttons and the modifier keys.

Note that the logical state of a device (as seen through Xlib) may lag the physical state if device event processing is frozen (see section 7.4).

XQueryPointer can generate a BadWindow error.

4.2 Properties and Atoms

A property is a collection of named, typed data. The window system has a set of predefined properties (for example, the name of a window, size hints, and so on), and users can define any other arbitrary information and associate it with windows. Each property has a name, which is an ISO Latin-1 string. For each named property, a unique identifier (atom) is associated with it. A property also has a type, for example, string or integer. These types are also indicated using atoms, so arbitrary new types can be defined. Data of only one type may be associated with a single property name. Clients can store and retrieve properties associated with windows. For efficiency reasons, an atom is used rather than a character string. XInternAtom can be used to obtain the atom for property names.

A property is also stored in one of several possible formats. The X server can store the information as 8-bit quantities, 16-bit quantities, or 32-bit quantities. This permits the X server to present the data in the byte order that the client expects.

Note   If you define further properties of complex type, you must encode and decode them yourself. These functions must be carefully written if they are to be portable. For further information about how to write a library extension, see appendix C.

The type of a property is defined by an atom, which allows for arbitrary extension in this type scheme.

Certain property names are predefined in the server for commonly used functions. The atoms for these properties are defined in <X11/Xatom.h>. To avoid name clashes with user symbols, the #define name for each atom has the XA_ prefix. For definitions of these properties, see section 4.3. For an explanation of the functions that let you get and set much of the information stored in these predefined properties, see chapter 9.

You can use properties to communicate other information between applications. The functions described in this section let you define new properties and get the unique atom IDs in your applications.

Although any particular atom can have some client interpretation within each of the name spaces, atoms occur in five distinct name spaces within the protocol:

- Selections
- Property names
- Property types
- Font properties
- Type of a ClientMessage event (none are built into the X server)

The built-in selection property names are:

PRIMARY
SECONDARY

The built-in property names are:

CUT_BUFFER0   RGB_RED_MAP
CUT_BUFFER1   RESOURCE_MANAGER
CUT_BUFFER2   WM_CLASS
CUT_BUFFER3   WM_CLIENT_MACHINE
CUT_BUFFER4   WM_COMMAND
CUT_BUFFER5   WM_HINTS
CUT_BUFFER6   WM_ICON_NAME
CUT_BUFFER7   WM_ICON_SIZE
RGB_BEST_MAP   WM_NAME
RGB_BLUE_MAP   WM_NORMAL_HINTS
RGB_DEFAULT_MAP   WM_ZOOM_HINTS
RGB_GRAY_MAP   WM_TRANSIENT_FOR
RGB_GREEN_MAP

The built-in property types are:

ARC   PIXMAP
ATOM   POINT
BITMAP   RGB_COLOR_MAP
CARDINAL   RECTANGLE
COLORMAP   STRING
CURSOR   VISUALID
DRAWABLE   WINDOW
FONT   WM_HINTS
INTEGER   WM_SIZE_HINTS

The built-in font property names are:

MIN_SPACE   STRIKEOUT_DESCENT
NORM_SPACE   STRIKEOUT_ASCENT
MAX_SPACE   ITALIC_ANGLE
END_SPACE   X_HEIGHT
SUPERSCRIPT_X   QUAD_WIDTH
SUPERSCRIPT_Y   WEIGHT
SUBSCRIPT_X   POINT_SIZE

SUBSCRIPT_Y	RESOLUTION
UNDERLINE_POSITION	COPYRIGHT
UNDERLINE_THICKNESS	NOTICE
FONT_NAME	FAMILY_NAME
FULL_NAME	CAP_HEIGHT

For further information about font properties, see section 6.5.

To return an atom for a given name, use XInternAtom.

Atom XInternAtom(*display, atom_name, only_if_exists*)
    Display **display*;
    char **atom_name*;
    Bool *only_if_exists;*

display   Specifies the connection to the X server.
atom_name   Specifies the name associated with the atom you want returned.
only_if_exists Specifies a Boolean value that indicates whether XInternAtom
                 creates the atom.

The XInternAtom function returns the atom identifier associated with the specified atom_name string. If only_if_exists is False, the atom is created if it does not exist. Therefore, XInternAtom can return None. You should use a null-terminated ISO Latin-1 string for atom_name. Case matters; the strings *thing, Thing,* and *thinG* all designate different atoms. The atom will remain defined even after the client's connection closes. It will become undefined only when the last connection to the X server closes.

    XInternAtom can generate BadAlloc and BadValue errors.

To return a name for a given atom identifier, use XGetAtomName.

char *XGetAtomName(*display, atom*)
    Display **display*;
    Atom *atom;*

display Specifies the connection to the X server.
atom   Specifies the atom for the property name you want returned.

The XGetAtomName function returns the name associated with the specified atom. To free the resulting string, call XFree.

    XGetAtomName can generate a BadAtom error.

4.3   Obtaining and Changing Window Properties

You can attach a property list to every window. Each property has a name, a type, and a value (see section 4.2). The value is an array of 8-bit, 16-bit, or 32-bit quantities, whose interpretation is left to the clients.

Xlib provides functions that you can use to obtain, change, update, or interchange window properties. In addition, Xlib provides other utility functions for predefined property operations (see chapter 9).

To obtain the type, format, and value of a property of a given window, use XGetWindowProperty.

```
int XGetWindowProperty(display, w, property, long_offset, long_length, delete, req_type,
                       actual_type_return, actual_format_return, nitems_return,
                       bytes_after_return, prop_return)
```
Display *display;
Window w;
Atom property;
long long_offset, long_length;
Bool delete;
Atom req_type;
Atom *actual_type_return;
int *actual_format_return;
unsigned long *nitems_return;
unsigned long *bytes_after_return;
unsigned char **prop_return;

display	Specifies the connection to the X server.
w	Specifies the window whose property you want to obtain.
property	Specifies the property name.
long_offset	Specifies the offset in the specified property (in 32-bit quantities) where the data is to be retrieved.
long_length	Specifies the length in 32-bit multiples of the data to be retrieved.
delete	Specifies a Boolean value that determines whether the property is deleted.
req_type	Specifies the atom identifier associated with the property type or AnyPropertyType.
actual_type_return	Returns the atom identifier that defines the actual type of the property.
actual_format_return	Returns the actual format of the property.
nitems_return	Returns the actual number of 8-bit, 16-bit, or 32-bit items stored in the prop_return data.

bytes_after_return   Returns the number of bytes remaining to be read in the property if a partial read was performed.

prop_return   Returns a pointer to the data in the specified format.

The XGetWindowProperty function returns the actual type of the property; the actual format of the property; the number of 8-bit, 16-bit, or 32-bit items transferred; the number of bytes remaining to be read in the property; and a pointer to the data actually returned. XGetWindowProperty sets the return arguments as follows:

- If the specified property does not exist for the specified window, XGetWindowProperty returns None to actual_type_return and the value zero to actual_format_return and bytes_after_return. The nitems_return argument is empty. In this case, the delete argument is ignored.

- If the specified property exists but its type does not match the specified type, XGetWindowProperty returns the actual property type to actual_type_return, the actual property format (never zero) to actual_format_return, and the property length in bytes (even if the actual_format_return is 16 or 32) to bytes_after_return. It also ignores the delete argument. The nitems_return argument is empty.

- If the specified property exists and either you assign AnyPropertyType to the req_type argument or the specified type matches the actual property type, XGetWindowProperty returns the actual property type to actual_type_return and the actual property format (never zero) to actual_format_return. It also returns a value to bytes_after_return and nitems_return, by defining the following values:

$$N = \text{actual length of the stored property in bytes}$$
$$\text{(even if the format is 16 or 32)}$$
$$I = 4 * \text{long\_offset}$$
$$T = N - I$$
$$L = \text{MINIMUM}(T, 4 * \text{long\_length})$$
$$A = N - (I + L)$$

The returned value starts at byte index I in the property (indexing from zero), and its length in bytes is L. If the value for long_offset causes L to be negative, a BadValue error results. The value of bytes_after_return is A, giving the number of trailing unread bytes in the stored property.

XGetWindowProperty always allocates one extra byte in prop_return (even if the property is zero length) and sets it to ASCII null so that simple properties consisting of characters do not have to be copied into yet another string before use. If delete is True and bytes_after_retrun is zero, XGetWindowProperty deletes the property from the window and generates a PropertyNotify event on the window.

The function returns Success if it executes successfully. To free the resulting data, use XFree.

XGetWindowProperty can generate BadAtom, BadValue, and Bad-Window errors.

To obtain a given window's property list, use XListProperties.

Atom *XListProperties(*display, w, num_prop_return*)
  Display *display*;
  Window *w*;
  int *num_prop_return*;
  display   Specifies the connection to the X server.
  w   Specifies the window whose property list you want to obtain.
  num_prop_return   Returns the length of the properties array.

The XListProperties function returns a pointer to an array of atom properties that are defined for the specified window or returns NULL if no properties were found. To free the memory allocated by this function, use XFree.

XListProperties can generate a BadWindow error.

To change a property of a given window, use XChangeProperty.

XChangeProperty(*display, w, property, type, format, mode, data, nelements*)
  Display *display*;
  Window *w*;
  Atom *property, type*;
  int *format*;
  int *mode*;
  unsigned char **data*;
  int *nelements*;
  display   Specifies the connection to the X server.
  w   Specifies the window whose property you want to change.
  property   Specifies the property name.
  type   Specifies the type of the property. The X server does not interpret the type but simply passes it back to an application that later calls XGetWindowProperty.

format	Specifies whether the data should be viewed as a list of 8-bit, 16-bit, or 32-bit quantities. Possible values are 8, 16, and 32. This information allows the X server to correctly perform byte-swap operations as necessary. If the format is 16-bit or 32-bit, you must explicitly cast your data pointer to a (char *) in the call to `XChangeProperty`.
mode	Specifies the mode of the operation. You can pass `PropModeReplace`, `PropModePrepend`, or `PropModeAppend`.
data	Specifies the property data.
nelements	Specifies the number of elements of the specified data format.

The `XChangeProperty` function alters the property for the specified window and causes the X server to generate a `PropertyNotify` event on that window. `XChangeProperty` performs the following:

- If mode is `PropModeReplace`, `XChangeProperty` discards the previous property value and stores the new data.

- If mode is `PropModePrepend` or `PropModeAppend`, `XChangeProperty` inserts the specified data before the beginning of the existing data or onto the end of the existing data, respectively. The type and format must match the existing property value, or a `BadMatch` error results. If the property is undefined, it is treated as defined with the correct type and format with zero-length data.

The lifetime of a property is not tied to the storing client. Properties remain until explicitly deleted, until the window is destroyed, or until the server resets. For a discussion of what happens when the connection to the X server is closed, see section 2.5. The maximum size of a property is server dependent and can vary dynamically depending on the amount of memory the server has available. (If there is insufficient space, a `BadAlloc` error results.)

   `XChangeProperty` can generate `BadAlloc`, `BadAtom`, `BadMatch`, `BadValue`, and `BadWindow` errors.

   To rotate a window's property list, use `XRotateWindowProperties`.

XRotateWindowProperties(*display, w, properties, num_prop, npositions*)
    Display **display*;
    Window *w*;
    Atom *properties*[];
    int *num_prop*;
    int *npositions*;

display	Specifies the connection to the X server.
w	Specifies the window.

properties Specifies the array of properties that are to be rotated.

num_prop Specifies the length of the properties array.

npositions Specifies the rotation amount.

The XRotateWindowProperties function allows you to rotate properties on a window and causes the X server to generate PropertyNotify events. If the property names in the properties array are viewed as being numbered starting from zero and if there are num_prop property names in the list, then the value associated with property name I becomes the value associated with property name (I + npositions) mod N for all I from zero to N − 1. The effect is to rotate the states by npositions places around the virtual ring of property names (right for positive npositions, left for negative npositions). If npositions mod N is nonzero, the X server generates a PropertyNotify event for each property in the order that they are listed in the array. If an atom occurs more than once in the list or no property with that name is defined for the window, a BadMatch error results. If a BadAtom or BadMatch error results, no properties are changed.

XRotateWindowProperties can generate BadAtom, BadMatch, and BadWindow errors.

To delete a property on a given window, use XDeleteProperty.

XDeleteProperty(*display, w, property*)
    Display **display*;
    Window *w*;
    Atom *property*;

display Specifies the connection to the X server.

w Specifies the window whose property you want to delete.

property Specifies the property name.

The XDeleteProperty function deletes the specified property only if the property was defined on the specified window and causes the X server to generate a PropertyNotify event on the window unless the property does not exist.

XDeleteProperty can generate BadAtom and BadWindow errors.

4.4 Selections

Selections are one method used by applications to exchange data. By using the property mechanism, applications can exchange data of arbitrary types and can negotiate the type of the data. A selection can be thought of as an indirect property with a dynamic type. That is, rather than having the property stored in the X server, the property is maintained by some client (the owner). A selection is global in nature (considered to belong to the user but be maintained by clients) rather than being private to a particular window subhierarchy or a particular set of clients.

Xlib provides functions that you can use to set, get, or request conversion of selections. This allows applications to implement the notion of current selection, which requires that notification be sent to applications when they no longer own the selection. Applications that support selection often highlight the current selection and so must be informed when another application has acquired the selection so that they can unhighlight the selection.

When a client asks for the contents of a selection, it specifies a selection target type. This target type can be used to control the transmitted representation of the contents. For example, if the selection is "the last thing the user clicked on" and that is currently an image, then the target type might specify whether the contents of the image should be sent in XY format or Z format.

The target type can also be used to control the class of contents transmitted, for example, asking for the "looks" (fonts, line spacing, indentation, and so forth) of a paragraph selection, not the text of the paragraph. The target type can also be used for other purposes. The protocol does not constrain the semantics.

To set the selection owner, use `XSetSelectionOwner`.

XSetSelectionOwner(*display, selection, owner, time*)
      Display **display*;
      Atom *selection*;
      Window *owner*;
      Time *time*;

display	Specifies the connection to the X server.
selection	Specifies the selection atom.
owner	Specifies the owner of the specified selection atom. You can pass a window or `None`.
time	Specifies the time. You can pass either a timestamp or `CurrentTime`.

The `XSetSelectionOwner` function changes the owner and last-change time for the specified selection and has no effect if the specified time is earlier than the current last-change time of the specified selection or is later than the current X server time. Otherwise, the last-change time is set to the specified time, with `CurrentTime` replaced by the current server time. If the owner window is specified as `None`, then the owner of the selection becomes `None` (that is, no owner). Otherwise, the owner of the selection becomes the client executing the request.

If the new owner (whether a client or `None`) is not the same as the current owner of the selection and the current owner is not `None`, the current owner is sent a `SelectionClear` event. If the client that is the owner of a selection is later terminated (that is, its connection is closed) or if the owner window it has specified in the request is later destroyed, the owner of the selection automatically reverts to `None`, but the last-change time is not affected. The selection atom is uninterpreted by the X server. `XGetSelectionOwner` returns the owner window, which is reported in `SelectionRequest` and `SelectionClear` events. Selections are global to the X server.

`XSetSelectionOwner` can generate `BadAtom` and `BadWindow` errors.

To return the selection owner, use `XGetSelectionOwner`.

Window XGetSelectionOwner(*display, selection*)
    Display *display;
    Atom *selection*;
display   Specifies the connection to the X server.
selection   Specifies the selection atom whose owner you want returned.

The `XGetSelectionOwner` function returns the window ID associated with the window that currently owns the specified selection. If no selection was specified, the function returns the constant `None`. If `None` is returned, there is no owner for the selection.

`XGetSelectionOwner` can generate a `BadAtom` error.

To request conversion of a selection, use `XConvertSelection`.

XConvertSelection(*display, selection, target, property, requestor, time*)
    Display *display;
    Atom *selection, target*;
    Atom *property*;
    Window *requestor*;
    Time *time*;

display   Specifies the connection to the X server.
selection   Specifies the selection atom.
target   Specifies the target atom.
property   Specifies the property name. You also can pass None.
requestor   Specifies the requestor.
time   Specifies the time. You can pass either a timestamp or CurrentTime.

XConvertSelection requests that the specified selection be converted to the specified target type:

- If the specified selection has an owner, the X server sends a SelectionRequest event to that owner.

- If no owner for the specified selection exists, the X server generates a SelectionNotify event to the requestor with property None.

In either event, the arguments are passed on unchanged. There are two predefined selection atoms: PRIMARY and SECONDARY.

XConvertSelection can generate BadAtom and BadWindow errors.

Chapter 5

Graphics Resource Functions

After you connect your program to the X server by calling XOpenDisplay, you can use the Xlib graphics resource functions to:

- Create, copy, and destroy colormaps
- Allocate, modify, and free color cells
- Read entries in a colormap
- Create and free pixmaps
- Create, copy, change, and destroy graphics contexts

A number of resources are used when performing graphics operations in X. Most information about performing graphics (for example, foreground color, background color, line style, and so on) are stored in resources called graphics contexts (GC). Most graphics operations (see chapter 6) take a GC as an argument. Although in theory it is possible to share GCs between applications, it is expected that applications will use their own GCs when performing operations. Sharing of GCs is highly discouraged because the library may cache GC state.

Each X window always has an associated colormap that provides a level of indirection between pixel values and colors displayed on the screen. Many of the hardware displays built today have a single colormap, so the primitives are written to encourage sharing of colormap entries between applications. Because colormaps are associated with windows, X will support displays with multiple colormaps and, indeed, different types of colormaps. If there are not sufficient colormap resources in the display, some windows may not be displayed in their true colors. A client or window manager can control which windows are displayed in their true colors if more than one colormap is required for the color resources the applications are using.

Off-screen memory or pixmaps are often used to define frequently used images for later use in graphics operations. Pixmaps are also used to define tiles or patterns for use as window backgrounds, borders, or cursors. A single bit-plane pixmap is sometimes referred to as a bitmap.

Note that some screens have very limited off-screen memory. Therefore, you should regard off-screen memory as a precious resource.

Graphics operations can be performed to either windows or pixmaps, which collectively are called drawables. Each drawable exists on a single screen and can only be used on that screen. GCs can also only be used with drawables of matching screens and depths.

5.1   Colormap Functions

Xlib provides functions that you can use to manipulate a colormap. This section discusses how to:

• Create, copy, and destroy a colormap

• Allocate, modify, and free color cells

• Read entries in a colormap

The following functions manipulate the representation of color on the screen. For each possible value that a pixel can take in a window, there is a color cell in the colormap. For example, if a window is 4 bits deep, pixel values 0 through 15 are defined. A colormap is a collection of color cells. A color cell consists of a triple of red, green, and blue. As each pixel is read out of display memory, its value is taken and looked up in the colormap. The values of the cell determine what color is displayed on the screen. On a multiplane display with a black-and-white monitor (with grayscale but not color), these values can be combined to determine the brightness on the screen.

Screens always have a default colormap, and programs typically allocate cells out of this colormap. You should not write applications that monopolize color resources. On a screen that either cannot load the colormap or cannot have a fully independent colormap, only certain kinds of allocations may work. Depending on the hardware, one or more colormaps may be resident (installed) at one time. To install a colormap, use `XInstallColormap`. The `DefaultColormap` macro returns the default colormap. The `DefaultVisual` macro returns the default visual type for the specified screen. Colormaps are local to a particular screen. Possible visual types are `StaticGray`, `GrayScale`, `StaticColor`, `PseudoColor`, `True-Color`, or `DirectColor` (see section 3.1).

The functions discussed in this section operate on an `XColor` structure, which contains:

```
typedef struct {
        unsigned long pixel;                /* pixel value */
        unsigned short red, green, blue;    /* rgb values */
        char flags;                         /* DoRed, DoGreen, DoBlue */
        char pad;
} XColor;
```

The red, green, and blue values are scaled between 0 and 65535. On full in a color is a value of 65535 independent of the number of bits actually used in the display hardware. Half brightness in a color is a value of 32767, and off is 0. This representation gives uniform results for color values across different screens. In some functions, the flags member controls which of the red, green, and blue members is used and can be one or more of `DoRed`, `DoGreen`, and `DoBlue`.

The introduction of color changes the view a programmer should take when dealing with a bitmap display. For example, when printing text, you write a pixel value, which is defined as a specific color, rather than setting or clearing bits. Hardware will impose limits (the number of significant bits, for example) on these values. Typically, one allocates color cells or sets of color cells. If read-only, the pixel values for these colors can be shared among multiple applications, and the RGB values of the cell cannot be changed. If read/write, they are exclusively owned by the program, and the color cell associated with the pixel value may be changed at will.

5.1.1   Creating, Copying, and Destroying Colormaps

To create a colormap for a screen, use `XCreateColormap`.

Colormap XCreateColormap(*display, w, visual, alloc*)
    Display **display*;
    Window *w*;
    Visual **visual*;
    int *alloc*;

display   Specifies the connection to the X server.
w   Specifies the window on whose screen you want to create a colormap.
visual   Specifies a pointer to a visual type supported on the screen. If the visual type is not one supported by the screen, a `BadMatch` error results.
alloc   Specifies the colormap entries to be allocated. You can pass `AllocNone` or `AllocAll`.

The `XCreateColormap` function creates a colormap of the specified visual type for the screen on which the specified window resides and returns the colormap ID associated with it. Note that the specified window is only used to determine the screen.

The initial values of the colormap entries are undefined for the visual classes `GrayScale`, `PseudoColor`, and `DirectColor`. For `Static-Gray`, `StaticColor`, and `TrueColor`, the entries have defined values, but those values are specific to the visual and are not defined by X. For `StaticGray`, StaticColor, and `TrueColor`, alloc must be `AllocNone`, or a `BadMatch` error results. For the other visual classes, if alloc is `AllocNone`, the colormap initially has no allocated entries, and clients can allocate them. For information about the visual types, see section 3.1.

If alloc is `AllocAll`, the entire colormap is allocated writable. The initial values of all allocated entries are undefined. For `GrayScale` and `PseudoColor`, the effect is as if an `XAllocColorCells` call returned all pixel values from zero to N − 1, where N is the colormap entries value in the specified visual. For `DirectColor`, the effect is as if an `XAlloc-ColorPlanes` call returned a pixel value of zero and red_mask, green_mask, and blue_mask values containing the same bits as the corresponding masks in the specified visual. However, in all cases, none of these entries can be freed by using `XFreeColors`.

`XCreateColormap` can generate `BadAlloc`, `BadMatch`, `BadValue`, and `BadWindow` errors.

To create a new colormap when the allocation out of a previously shared colormap has failed because of resource exhaustion, use XCopy-ColormapAndFree.

Colormap XCopyColormapAndFree(*display, colormap*)
    Display **display*;
    Colormap *colormap*;
display   Specifies the connection to the X server.
colormap   Specifies the colormap.

The XCopyColormapAndFree function creates a colormap of the same visual type and for the same screen as the specified colormap and returns the new colormap ID. It also moves all of the client's existing allocation from the specified colormap to the new colormap with their color values intact and their read-only or writable characteristics intact and frees those entries in the specified colormap. Color values in other entries in the new colormap are undefined. If the specified colormap was created by the client with alloc set to AllocAll, the new colormap is also created with AllocAll, all color values for all entries are copied from the specified colormap, and then all entries in the specified colormap are freed. If the specified colormap was not created by the client with AllocAll, the allocations to be moved are all those pixels and planes that have been allocated by the client using XAllocColor, XAllocNamedColor, XAllocColorCells, or XAlloc-ColorPlanes and that have not been freed since they were allocated.

    XCopyColormapAndFree can generate BadAlloc and BadColor errors.

To set the colormap of a given window, use XSetWindowColormap.

XSetWindowColormap(*display, w, colormap*)
    Display **display*;
    Window *w*;
    Colormap *colormap*;
display   Specifies the connection to the X server.
w   Specifies the window.
colormap   Specifies the colormap.

The XSetWindowColormap function sets the specified colormap of the specified window. The colormap must have the same visual type as the window, or a BadMatch error results.

XSetWindowColormap can generate BadColor, BadMatch, and BadWindow errors.

To destroy a colormap, use XFreeColormap.

XFreeColormap(*display, colormap*)
    Display **display*;
    Colormap *colormap*;

display   Specifies the connection to the X server.
colormap Specifies the colormap that you want to destroy.

The XFreeColormap function deletes the association between the colormap resource ID and the colormap and frees the colormap storage. However, this function has no effect on the default colormap for a screen. If the specified colormap is an installed map for a screen, it is uninstalled (see XUninstallColormap). If the specified colormap is defined as the colormap for a window (by XCreateWindow, XSetWindowColormap, or XChangeWindowAttributes), XFreeColormap changes the colormap associated with the window to None and generates a ColormapNotify event. X does not define the colors displayed for a window with a colormap of None.

XFreeColormap can generate a BadColor error.

5.1.2   Allocating, Modifying, and Freeing Color Cells

There are two ways of allocating color cells: explicitly as read-only entries by pixel value or read/write, where you can allocate a number of color cells and planes simultaneously. The read/write cells you allocate do not have defined colors until set with XStoreColor or XStoreColors.

To determine the color names, the X server uses a color database. Although you can change the values in a read/write color cell that is allocated by another application, this is considered "antisocial" behavior.

To allocate a read-only color cell, use XAllocColor.

Status XAllocColor(*display, colormap, screen_in_out*)
    Display **display*;
    Colormap *colormap*;
    XColor **screen_in_out*;

> *display*   Specifies the connection to the X server.
> *colormap*   Specifies the colormap.
> *screen_in_out* Specifies and returns the values actually used in the colormap.

The XAllocColor function allocates a read-only colormap entry corresponding to the closest RGB values supported by the hardware. XAllocColor returns the pixel value of the color closest to the specified RGB elements supported by the hardware and returns the RGB values actually used. The corresponding colormap cell is read-only. In addition, XAllocColor returns nonzero if it succeeded or zero if it failed. Read-only colormap cells are shared among clients. When the last client deallocates a shared cell, it is deallocated. XAllocColor does not use or affect the flags in the XColor structure.

XAllocColor can generate a BadColor error.

To allocate a read-only color cell by name and return the closest color supported by the hardware, use XAllocNamedColor.

Status XAllocNamedColor(*display, colormap, color_name, screen_def_return,*
                                      exact_def_return)
    Display **display*;
    Colormap *colormap*;
    char **color_name;*
    XColor **screen_def_return, * exact_def_return*;

> *display*   Specifies the connection to the X server.
> *colormap*   Specifies the colormap.
> *color_name*   Specifies the color name string (for example, red) whose color definition structure you want returned.
> *screen_def_return* Returns the closest RGB values provided by the hardware.
> *exact_def_return*   Returns the exact RGB values.

The XAllocNamedColor function looks up the named color with respect to the screen that is associated with the specified colormap. It returns both the exact database definition and the closest color supported by the screen. The allocated color cell is read-only. You should use the ISO Latin-1 encoding; uppercase and lowercase do not matter.

XAllocNamedColor can generate a BadColor error.

To look up the name of a color, use XLookupColor.

Status XLookupColor(*display, colormap, color_name, exact_def_return,*
                    screen_def_return)
    Display *display*;
    Colormap *colormap*;
    char *color_name*;
    XColor *exact_def_return, *screen_def_return*;

display	Specifies the connection to the X server.
colormap	Specifies the colormap.
color_name	Specifies the color name string (for example, red) whose color definition structure you want returned.
exact_def_return	Returns the exact RGB values.
screen_def_return	Returns the closest RGB values provided by the hardware.

The XLookupColor function looks up the string name of a color with respect to the screen associated with the specified colormap. It returns both
the exact color values and the closest values provided by the screen with respect to the visual type of the specified colormap. You should use the ISO
Latin-1 encoding; uppercase and lowercase do not matter. XLookupColor
returns nonzero if the name existed in the color database or zero if it did not
exist.

To allocate read/write color cell and color plane combinations for a
PseudoColor model, use XAllocColorCells.

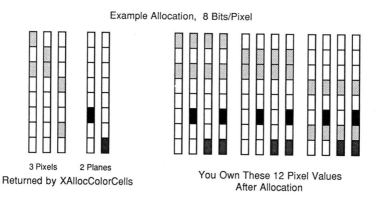

Example Allocation, 8 Bits/Pixel

3 Pixels   2 Planes
Returned by XAllocColorCells

You Own These 12 Pixel Values
After Allocation

Figure 5.1. Request of 3 cells and two planes

Status XAllocColorCells(*display, colormap, contig, plane_masks_return, nplanes,*
pixels_return, npixels)

Display **display;*
Colormap *colormap;*
Bool *contig;*
unsigned long *plane_masks_return*[];
unsigned int *nplanes*;
unsigned long *pixels_return*[];
unsigned int *npixels*;

display	Specifies the connection to the X server.
colormap	Specifies the colormap.
contig	Specifies a Boolean value that indicates whether the planes must be contiguous.
plane_mask_return	Returns an array of plane masks.
nplanes	Specifies the number of plane masks that are to be returned in the plane masks array.
pixels_return	Returns an array of pixel values.
npixels	Specifies the number of pixel values that are to be returned in the pixels_return array.

The `XAllocColorCells` function allocates read/write color cells. The number of colors must be positive and the number of planes nonnegative, or a `BadValue` error results. If ncolors and nplanes are requested, then ncolors pixels and nplane plane masks are returned. No mask will have any bits set to 1 in common with any other mask or with any of the pixels. By ORing together each pixel with zero or more masks, ncolors * $2^{nplanes}$ distinct pixels can be produced. All of these are allocated writable by the request. For `GrayScale` or `PseudoColor`, each mask has exactly one bit set to 1. For `DirectColor`, each has exactly three bits set to 1. If contig is `True` and if all masks are ORed together, a single contiguous set of bits set to 1 will be formed for `GrayScale` or `PseudoColor` and three contiguous sets of bits set to 1 (one within each pixel subfield) for `DirectColor`. The RGB values of the allocated entries are undefined. `XAllocColorCells` returns nonzero if it succeeded or zero if it failed.

`XAllocColorCells` can generate `BadColor` and `BadValue` errors.

To allocate read/write color resources for a `DirectColor` model, use `XAllocColorPlanes`.

Status XAllocColorPlanes(*display, colormap, contig, pixels_return, ncolors, nreds,*
                         ngreens, nblues, rmask_return, gmask_return, bmask_return)
　　　　Display **display*;
　　　　Colormap *colormap*;
　　　　Bool *contig*;
　　　　unsigned long *pixels_return*[];
　　　　int *ncolors*;
　　　　int *nreds, ngreens, nblues*;
　　　　unsigned long **rmask_return, *gmask_return, *bmask_return*;

display	Specifies the connection to the X server.
colormap	Specifies the colormap.
contig	Specifies a Boolean value that indicates whether the planes must be contiguous.
pixels_return	Returns an array of pixel values. `XAllocColorPlanes` returns the pixel values in this array.
ncolors	Specifies the number of pixel values that are to be returned in the pixels_return array.
nreds	
ngreens	
nblues	Specify the number of red, green, and blue planes. The value you pass must be nonnegative.
rmask_return	
gmask_return	
bmask_return	Return bit masks for the red, green, and blue planes.

The specified ncolors must be positive; and nreds, ngreens, and nblues must be nonnegative, or a `BadValue` error results. If ncolors colors, nreds reds, ngreens greens, and nblues blues are requested, ncolors pixels are returned; and the masks have nreds, ngreens, and nblues bits set to 1, respectively. If contig is `True`, each mask will have a contiguous set of bits set to 1. No mask will have any bits set to 1 in common with any other mask or with any of the pixels. For `DirectColor`, each mask will lie within the corresponding pixel subfield. By ORing together subsets of masks with each pixel value, ncolors * $2^{(nreds\ +ngreens\ +\ nblues)}$ distinct pixel values can be produced. All of these are allocated by the request. However, in the colormap, there are only ncolors * 2^{nreds} independent red entries, ncolors * $2^{ngreens}$ independent green entries, and ncolors * 2^{nblues} independent blue entries. This is true even for `PseudoColor`. When the colormap entry of a pixel value is changed (using `XStoreColors`, `XStoreColor`, or `XStoreNamedColor`), the pixel is decomposed according to the masks, and the corresponding independent entries are updated. XAllocColorPlanes returns nonzero if it succeeded or zero if it failed.

XAllocColorPlanes can generate BadColor and BadValue errors.

To store RGB values into colormap cells, use XStoreColors.

XStoreColors(*display, colormap, color, ncolors*)
    Display *display;
    Colormap *colormap*;
    XColor *color*[];
    int *ncolors*;

display   Specifies the connection to the X server.
colormap   Specifies the colormap.
color   Specifies an array of color definition structures to be stored.
ncolors   Specifies the number of XColor structures in the color definition array.

The XStoreColors function changes the colormap entries of the pixel values specified in the pixel members of the XColor structures. You specify which color components are to be changed by setting DoRed, DoGreen, and/or DoBlue in the flags member of the XColor structures. If the colormap is an installed map for its screen, the changes are visible immediately. XStoreColors changes the specified pixels if they are allocated writable in the colormap by any client, even if one or more pixels generates an error. If a specified pixel is not a valid index into the colormap, a BadValue error results. If a specified pixel either is unallocated or is allocated read-only, a BadAccess error results. If more than one pixel is in error, the one that gets reported is arbitrary.

XStoreColors can generate BadAccess, BadColor, and BadValue errors.

To store an RGB value in a single colormap cell, use XStoreColor.

XStoreColor(*display, colormap, color*)
    Display *display;
    Colormap *colormap*;
    XColor *color;

display   Specifies the connection to the X server.
colormap   Specifies the colormap.
color   Specifies the pixel and RGB values.

The XStoreColor function changes the colormap entry of the pixel value specified in the pixel member of the XColor structure. You specified this value in the pixel member of the XColor structure. This pixel value must be a read/write cell and a valid index into the colormap. If a specified pixel is not a valid index into the colormap, a BadValue error results. XStoreColor also changes the red, green, and/or blue color components. You specify which color components are to be changed by setting DoRed, DoGreen, and/or DoBlue in the flags member of the XColor structure. If the colormap is an installed map for its screen, the changes are visible immediately.

XStoreColor can generate BadAccess, BadColor, and BadValue errors.

To set the color of a pixel to a named color, use XStoreNamedColor.

XStoreNamedColor(*display, colormap, color, pixel, flags*)
    Display **display*;
    Colormap *colormap*;
    char **color*;
    unsigned long *pixel*;
    int *flags*;

display	Specifies the connection to the X server.
colormap	Specifies the colormap.
color	Specifies the color name string (for example, red).
pixel	Specifies the entry in the colormap.
flags	Specifies which red, green, and blue components are set.

The XStoreNamedColor function looks up the named color with respect to the screen associated with the colormap and stores the result in the specified colormap. The pixel argument determines the entry in the colormap. The flags argument determines which of the red, green, and blue components are set. You can set this member to the bitwise inclusive OR of the bits DoRed, DoGreen, and DoBlue. If the specified pixel is not a valid index into the colormap, a BadValue error results. If the specified pixel either is unallocated or is allocated read-only, a BadAccess error results. You should use the ISO Latin-1 encoding; uppercase and lowercase do not matter.

XStoreNamedColor can generate BadAccess, BadColor, BadName, and BadValue errors.

To free colormap cells, use XFreeColors.

XFreeColors(*display, colormap, pixels, npixels, planes*)
    Display **display*;
    Colormap *colormap*;
    unsigned long *pixels[]*;
    int *npixels*;
    unsigned long *planes*;

display	Specifies the connection to the X server.
colormap	Specifies the colormap.
pixels	Specifies an array of pixel values that map to the cells in the specified colormap.
npixels	Specifies the number of pixels.
planes	Specifies the planes you want to free.

The XFreeColors function frees the cells represented by pixels whose values are in the pixels array. The planes argument should not have any bits set to 1 in common with any of the pixels. The set of all pixels is produced by ORing together subsets of the planes'argument with the pixels. The request frees all of these pixels that were allocated by the client (using XAlloc-Color, XAllocNamedColor, XAllocColorCells, and XAllocColor-Planes). Note that freeing an individual pixel obtained from XAllocColorPlanes may not actually allow it to be reused until all of its related pixels are also freed.

All specified pixels that are allocated by the client in the colormap are freed, even if one or more pixels produce an error. If a specified pixel is not a valid index into the colormap, a BadValue error results. If a specified pixel is not allocated by the client (that is, is unallocated or is only allocated by another client), a BadAccess error results. If more than one pixel is in error, the one that gets reported is arbitrary.

XFreeColors can generate BadAccess, BadColor, and BadValue errors.

5.1.3 Reading Entries in a Colormap

The XQueryColor and XQueryColors functions return the RGB values stored in the specified colormap for the pixel value you pass in the pixel member of the XColor structure(s). The values returned for an unallocated entry are undefined. These functions also set the flags member in the XColor structure to all three colors. If a pixel is not a valid index into the specified colormap, a BadValue error results. If more than one pixel is in error, the one that gets reported is arbitrary.

To query the RGB values of a single specified pixel value, use XQueryColor.

XQueryColor(*display, colormap, def_in_out*)
    Display **display*;
    Colormap *colormap*;
    XColor **def_in_out*;

display   Specifies the connection to the X server.
colormap   Specifies the colormap.
def_in_out Specifies and returns the RGB values for the pixel specified in the structure.

The XQueryColor function returns the RGB values for each pixel in the XColor structures and sets the DoRed, DoGreen, and DoBlue flags.
    XQueryColor can generate BadColor and BadValue errors.

To query the RGB values of an array of pixels stored in color structures, use XQueryColors.

XQueryColors(*display, colormap, defs_in_out, ncolors*)
    Display **display*;
    Colormap *colormap*;
    XColor *defs_in_out*[];
    int *ncolors*;

display   Specifies the connection to the X server.
colormap   Specifies the colormap.
defs_in_out Specifies and returns an array of color definition structures for the pixel specified in the structure.
ncolors   Specifies the number of XColor structures in the color definition array.

The XQueryColors function returns the RGB values for each pixel in the XColor structures and sets the DoRed, DoGreen, and DoBlue flags.
    XQueryColors can generate BadColor and BadValue errors.

5.2   Creating and Freeing Pixmaps

Pixmaps can only be used on the screen on which they were created. Pixmaps are off-screen resources that are used for various operations, for example, defining cursors as tiling patterns or as the source for certain raster operations. Most graphics requests can operate either on a window or on a pixmap. A bitmap is a single bit-plane pixmap.

To create a pixmap of a given size, use `XCreatePixmap`.

Pixmap XCreatePixmap(*display, d, width, height, depth*)
        Display *display;
        Drawable *d*;
        unsigned int *width, height*;
        unsigned int *depth*;

display	Specifies the connection to the X server.
d	Specifies which screen the pixmap is created on.
width	
height	Specify the width and height, which define the dimensions of the pixmap.
depth	Specifies the depth of the pixmap.

The `XCreatePixmap` function creates a pixmap of the width, height, and depth you specified and returns a pixmap ID that identifies it. It is valid to pass an `InputOnly` window to the drawable argument. The width and height arguments must be nonzero, or a `BadValue` error results. The depth argument must be one of the depths supported by the screen of the specified drawable, or a `BadValue` error results.

The server uses the drawable argument to determine on which screen to create the pixmap. The pixmap can be used only on this screen and only with other drawables of the same depth (see `XCopyPlane` for an exception to this rule). The initial contents of the pixmap are undefined.

`XCreatePixmap` can generate `BadAlloc`, `BadDrawable`, and `BadValue` errors.

To free all storage associated with a specified pixmap, use `XFreePixmap`.

XFreePixmap(*display, pixmap*)
        Display *display;
        Pixmap *pixmap*;

display   Specifies the connection to the X server.
pixmap   Specifies the pixmap.

The `XFreePixmap` function first deletes the association between the pixmap ID and the pixmap. Then, the X server frees the pixmap storage when there are no references to it. The pixmap should never be referenced again.

`XFreePixmap` can generate a `BadPixmap` error.

5.3   Manipulating Graphics Context/State

Most attributes of graphics operations are stored in Graphic Contexts (GCs). These include line width, line style, plane mask, foreground, background, tile, stipple, clipping region, end style, join style, and so on. Graphics operations (for example, drawing lines) use these values to determine the actual drawing operation. Extensions to X may add additional components to GCs. The contents of a GC are private to Xlib.

Xlib implements a write-back cache for all elements of a GC that are not resource IDs to allow Xlib to implement the transparent coalescing of changes to GCs. For example, a call to `XSetForeground` of a GC followed by a call to `XSetLineAttributes` results in only a single-change GC protocol request to the server. GCs are neither expected nor encouraged to be shared between client applications, so this write-back caching should present no problems. Applications cannot share GCs without external synchronization. Therefore, sharing GCs between applications is highly discouraged.

To set an attribute of a GC, set the appropriate member of the `XGCValues` structure and OR in the corresponding value bitmask in your subsequent calls to `XCreateGC`. The symbols for the value mask bits and the `XGCValues` structure are:

```
/* GC attribute value mask bits */
#define GCFunction              (1L<<0)
#define GCPlaneMask             (1L<<1)
#define GCForeground            (1L<<2)
#define GCBackground            (1L<<3)
#define GCLineWidth             (1L<<4)
#define GCLineStyle             (1L<<5)
#define GCCapStyle              (1L<<6)
#define GCJoinStyle             (1L<<7)
#define GCFillStyle             (1L<<8)
```

```
#define GCFillRule              (1L<<9)
#define GCTile                  (1L<<10)
#define GCStipple               (1L<<11)
#define GCTileStipXOrigin       (1L<<12)
#define GCTileStipYOrigin       (1L<<13)
#define GCFont                  (1L<<14)
#define GCSubwindowMode         (1L<<15)
#define GCGraphicsExposures     (1L<<16)
#define GCClipXOrigin           (1L<<17)
#define GCClipYOrigin           (1L<<18)
#define GCClipMask              (1L<<19)
#define GCDashOffset            (1L<<20)
#define GCDashList              (1L<<21)
#define GCArcMode               (1L<<22)
/* Values */
typedef struct {
    int function;                    /* logical operation */
    unsigned long plane_mask;        /* plane mask */
    unsigned long foreground;        /* foreground pixel */
    unsigned long background;        /* background pixel */
    int line_width;                  /* line width (in pixels) */
    int line_style;                  /* LineSolid, LineOnOffDash,
                                        LineDoubleDash */
    int cap_style;                   /* CapNotLast, CapButt, CapRound,
                                        CapProjecting */
    int join_style;                  /* JoinMiter, JoinRound,
                                        JoinBevel*/
    int fill_style;                  /* FillSolid, FillTiled,
                                        FillStippled,
                                        FillOpaqueStippled*/
    int fill_rule;                   /* EvenOddRule, WindingRule */
    int arc_mode;                    /* ArcChord, ArcPieSlice */
    Pixmap tile;                     /* tile pixmap for tiling operations */
    Pixmap stipple;                  /* stipple 1 plane pixmap for stippling */
    int ts_x_origin;                 /* offset for tile or stipple operations */
    int ts_y_origin;
    Font font;                       /* default text font for text operations */
    int subwindow_mode;              /* ClipByChildren,
                                        IncludeInferiors */
    Bool graphics_exposures;         /* boolean, should exposures be
                                        generated */
```

```
    int clip_x_origin;                  /* origin for clipping */
    int clip_y_origin;
    Pixmap clip_mask;                   /* bitmap clipping; other calls for rects */
    int dash_offset;                    /* patterned/dashed line information */
    char dashes;
} XGCValues;
```

The default GC values are:

Component	Default
function	GXcopy
plane_mask	All ones
foreground	0
background	1
line_width	0
line_style	LineSolid
cap_style	CapButt
join_style	JoinMiter
fill_style	FillSolid
fill_rule	EvenOddRule
arc_mode	ArcPieSlice
tile	Pixmap of unspecified size filled with foreground pixel (that is, client specified pixel if any, else 0) (subsequent changes to foreground do not affect this pixmap)
stipple	Pixmap of unspecified size filled with ones
ts_x_origin	0
ts_y_origin	0
font	<implementation dependent>
subwindow_mode	ClipByChildren
graphics_exposures	True
clip_x_origin	0
clip_y_origin	0
clip_mask	None
dash_offset	0
dashes	4 (that is, the list [4, 4])

Note that foreground and background are not set to any values likely to be useful in a window.

The function attributes of a GC are used when you update a section of a drawable (the destination) with bits from somewhere else (the source). The function in a GC defines how the new destination bits are to be computed from the source bits and the old destination bits. GXcopy is typically the most useful because it will work on a color display, but special applications may use other functions, particularly in concert with particular planes of a color display. The 16 GC functions, defined in <X11/X.h>, are:

Function Name	Hex Code	Operation
GXclear	0x0	0
GXand	0x1	src AND dst
GXandReverse	0x2	src AND NOT dst
GXcopy	0x3	src
GXandInverted	0x4	(NOT src) AND dst
GXnoop	0x5	dst
GXxor	0x6	src XOR dst
GXor	0x7	src OR dst
GXnor	0x8	(NOT src) AND (NOT dst)
GXequiv	0x9	(NOT src) XOR dst
GXinvert	0xa	NOT dst
GXorReverse	0xb	src OR (NOT dst)
GXcopyInverted	0xc	NOT src
GXorInverted	0xd	(NOT src) OR dst
GXnand	0xe	(NOT src) OR (NOT dst)
GXset	0xf	1

Many graphics operations depend on either pixel values or planes in a GC. The planes attribute is of type long, and it specifies which planes of the destination are to be modified, one bit per plane. A monochrome display has only one plane and will be the least-significant bit of the word. As planes are added to the display hardware, they will occupy more significant bits in the plane mask.

In graphics operations, given a source and destination pixel, the result is computed bitwise on corresponding bits of the pixels. That is, a Boolean operation is performed in each bit plane. The plane_mask restricts the operation to a subset of planes. A macro constant AllPlanes can be used to refer to all planes of the screen simultaneously. The result is computed by the following:

((src FUNC dst) AND plane-mask) OR (dst AND (NOT plane-mask))

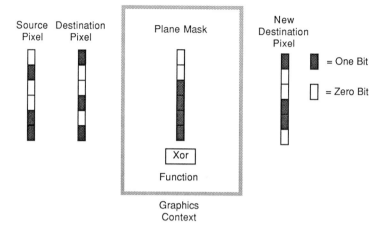

Figure 5.2. Example graphics operation using function and plane mask (4 bits/pixel)

Range checking is not performed on the values for foreground, background, or plane_mask. They are simply truncated to the appropriate number of bits. The line-width is measured in pixels and either can be greater than or equal to one (wide line) or can be the special value zero (thin line).

Wide lines are drawn centered on the path described by the graphics request. Unless otherwise specified by the join-style or cap-style, the bounding box of a wide line with endpoints [x1, y1], [x2, y2] and width w is a rectangle with vertices at the following real coordinates:

$$[x1 - (w*sn/2), y1 + (w*cs/2)], [x1 + (w*sn/2), y1 - (w*cs/2)],$$
$$[x2 - (w*sn/2), y2 + (w*cs/2)], [x2 + (w*sn/2), y2 - (w*cs/2)]$$

Here sn is the sine of the angle of the line, and cs is the cosine of the angle of the line. A pixel is part of the line and so is drawn if the center of the pixel is fully inside the bounding box (which is viewed as having infinitely thin edges). If the center of the pixel is exactly on the bounding box, it is part of the line if and only if the interior is immediately to its right (x increasing direction). Pixels with centers on a horizontal edge are a special case and are part of the line if and only if the interior or the boundary is immediately below (y increasing direction) and the interior or the boundary is immediately to the right (x increasing direction).

Thin lines (zero line-width) are one-pixel-wide lines drawn using an unspecified, device-dependent algorithm. There are only two constraints on this algorithm.

1. If a line is drawn unclipped from [xl,yl] to [x2,y2] and if another line is drawn unclipped from [xl + dx,yl + dy] to [x2 + dx,y2 + dy], a point [x,y] is touched by drawing the first line if and only if the point [x + dx,y + dy] is touched by drawing the second line.
2. The effective set of points comprising a line cannot be affected by clipping. That is, a point is touched in a clipped line if and only if the point lies inside the clipping region and the point would be touched by the line when drawn unclipped.

A wide line drawn from [x1,y1] to [x2,y2] always draws the same pixels as a wide line drawn from [x2,y2] to [x1,y1], not counting cap-style and join-style. It is recommended that this property be true for thin lines, but this is not required. A line-width of zero may differ from a line-width of one in which pixels are drawn. This permits the use of many manufacturers' line drawing hardware, which may run many times faster than the more precisely specified wide lines.

In general, drawing a thin line will be faster than drawing a wide line of width one. However, because of their different drawing algorithms, thin lines may not mix well aesthetically with wide lines. If it is desirable to obtain precise and uniform results across all displays, a client should always use a line-width of one rather than a line-width of zero.

The line-style defines which sections of a line are drawn:

LineSolid	The full path of the line is drawn.
LineDoubleDash	The full path of the line is drawn, but the even dashes are filled differently than the odd dashes (see fill-style) with CapButt style used where even and odd dashes meet.
LineOnOffDash	Only the even dashes are drawn, and cap-style applies to all internal ends of the individual dashes, except CapNotLast is treated as CapButt.

The cap-style defines how the endpoints of a path are drawn:

CapNotLast	This is equivalent to CapButt except that for a line-width of zero the final end-point is not drawn.
CapButt	The line is square at the endpoint (perpendicular to the slope of the line) with no projection beyond.

CapRound	The line has a circular arc with the diameter equal to the line-width, centered on the endpoint. (This is equivalent to CapButt for line-width of zero.)
CapProjecting	The line is square at the end, but the path continues beyond the endpoint for a distance equal to half the line-width. (This is equivalent to CapButt for line-width of zero.)

The join-style defines how corners are drawn for wide lines:

JoinMiter	The outer edges of two lines extend to meet at an angle. However, if the angle is less than 11 degrees, then a JoinBevel join-style is used instead.
JoinRound	The corner is a circular arc with the diameter equal to the line-width, centered on the joinpoint.
JoinBevel	The corner has CapButt endpoint styles with the triangular notch filled.

For a line with coincident endpoints (x1 = x2, y1 = y2), when the cap-style is applied to both endpoints, the semantics depends on the line-width and the cap-style:

CapNotLast	thin	The results are device-dependent, but the desired effect is that nothing is drawn.
CapButt	thin	The results are device-dependent, but the

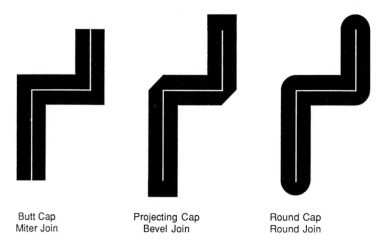

Butt Cap   Projecting Cap   Round Cap
Miter Join   Bevel Join   Round Join

Figure 5.3.   Wide line cap and join styles

		desired effect is that a single pixel is drawn.
CapRound	thin	The results are the same as for CapButt/thin.
CapProjecting	thin	The results are the same as for Butt/thin.
CapButt	wide	Nothing is drawn.
CapRound	wide	The closed path is a circle, centered at the endpoint, and with the diameter equal to the line-width.
CapProjecting	wide	The closed path is a square, aligned with the coordinate axes, centered at the endpoint, and with the sides equal to the line-width.

For a line with coincident endpoints (x1 = x2, y1 = y2), when the join-style is applied at one or both endpoints, the effect is as if the line was removed from the overall path. However, if the total path consists of or is reduced to a single point joined with itself, the effect is the same as when the cap-style is applied at both endpoints.

The tile/stipple and clip origins are interpreted relative to the origin of whatever destination drawable is specified in a graphics request. The tile pixmap must have the same root and depth as the GC, or a BadMatch error results. The stipple pixmap must have depth one and must have the same root as the GC, or a BadMatch error results. For stipple operations where the fill-style is FillStippled but not FillOpaqueStippled, the stipple pattern is tiled in a single plane and acts as an additional clip mask to be ANDed with the clip-mask. Although some sizes may be faster to use than others, any size pixmap can be used for tiling or stippling.

The fill-style defines the contents of the source for line, text, and fill requests. For all text and fill requests (for example, XDrawText, XDraw-Text16, XFillRectangle, XFillPolygon, and XFillArc); for line requests with line-style LineSolid (for example, XDrawLine, XDraw-Segments, XDrawRectangle, XDrawArc); and for the even dashes for line requests with line-style LineOnOffDash or LineDoubleDash, the following apply:

FillSolid	Foreground
FillTiled	Tile

| FillOpaqueStippled | A tile with the same width and height as stipple, but with background everywhere stipple has a zero and with foreground everywhere stipple has a one |
| FillStippled | Foreground masked by stipple |

When drawing lines with line-style LineDoubleDash, the odd dashes are controlled by the fill-style in the following manner:

FillSolid	Background
FillTiled	Same as for even dashes
FillOpaqueStippled	Same as for even dashes
FillStippled	Background masked by stipple

Storing a pixmap in a GC might or might not result in a copy being made. If the pixmap is later used as the destination for a graphics request, the change might or might not be reflected in the GC. If the pixmap is used simultaneously in a graphics request both as a destination and as a tile or stipple, the results are undefined.

For optimum performance, you should draw as much as possible with the same GC (without changing its components). The costs of changing GC components relative to using different GCs depend upon the display hardware and the server implementation. It is quite likely that some amount of GC information will be cached in display hardware and that such hardware can only cache a small number of GCs.

The dashes value is actually a simplified form of the more general patterns that can be set with XSetDashes. Specifying a value of N is equivalent to specifying the two-element list [N, N] in XSetDashes. The value must be nonzero, or a BadValue error results.

The clip-mask restricts writes to the destination drawable. If the clip-mask is set to a pixmap, it must have depth one and have the same root as the GC, or a BadMatch error results. If clip-mask is set to None, the pixels are always drawn regardless of the clip origin. The clip-mask also can be set by calling the XSetClipRectangles or XSetRegion functions. Only pixels where the clip-mask has a bit set to 1 are drawn. Pixels are not drawn outside the area covered by the clip-mask or where the clip-mask has a bit set to 0. The clip-mask affects all graphics requests. The clip-mask does not clip sources. The clip-mask origin is interpreted relative to the origin of whatever destination drawable is specified in a graphics request.

You can set the subwindow-mode to `ClipByChildren` or `Include-Inferiors`. For `ClipByChildren`, both source and destination windows are additionally clipped by all viewable `InputOutput` children. For `IncludeInferiors`, neither source nor destination window is clipped by inferiors. This will result in including subwindow contents in the source and drawing through subwindow boundaries of the destination. The use of `IncludeInferiors` on a window of one depth with mapped inferiors of differing depth is not illegal, but the semantics are undefined by the core protocol.

The fill-rule defines what pixels are inside (drawn) for paths given in `XFillPolygon` requests and can be set to `EvenOddRule` or `Winding-Rule`. For `EvenOddRule`, a point is inside if an infinite ray with the point as origin crosses the path an odd number of times. For `WindingRule`, a point is inside if an infinite ray with the point as origin crosses an unequal number of clockwise and counterclockwise directed path segments. A clockwise directed path segment is one that crosses the ray from left to right as observed from the point. A counterclockwise segment is one that crosses the ray from right to left as observed from the point. The case where a directed line segment is coincident with the ray is uninteresting because you can simply choose a different ray that is not coincident with a segment.

For both `EvenOddRule` and `WindingRule`, a point is infinitely small, and the path is an infinitely thin line. A pixel is inside if the center point of the pixel is inside and the center point is not on the boundary. If the center point is on the boundary, the pixel is inside if and only if the polygon interior is immediately to its right (x increasing direction). Pixels with centers on a horizontal edge are a special case and are inside if and only if the polygon interior is immediately below (y increasing direction).

Polygon Before Fill   Even Odd Rule   Winding Rule

Figure 5.4. Fill rule

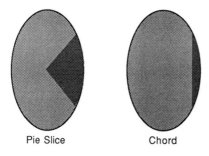

Pie Slice   Chord

Figure 5.5.   Arc mode

The arc-mode controls filling in the XFillArcs function and can be set to ArcPieSlice or ArcChord. For ArcPieSlice, the arcs are pie-slice filled. For ArcChord, the arcs are chord filled.

The graphics-exposure flag controls GraphicsExpose event generation for XCopyArea and XCopyPlane requests (and any similar requests defined by extensions).

To create a new GC that is usable on a given screen with a depth of drawable, use XCreateGC.

GC XCreateGC(*display, d, valuemask, values*)
    Display **display*;
    Drawable *d*;
    unsigned long *valuemask*;
    XGCValues **values*;

display	Specifies the connection to the X server.
d	Specifies the drawable.
valuemask	Specifies which components in the GC are to be set using the information in the specified values structure. This argument is the bitwise inclusive OR of one or more of the valid GC component mask bits.
values	Specifies any values as specified by the valuemask.

The XCreateGC function creates a graphics context and returns a GC. The GC can be used with any destination drawable having the same root and depth as the specified drawable. Use with other drawables results in a BadMatch error.

XCreateGC can generate BadAlloc, BadDrawable, BadFont, BadMatch, BadPixmap, and BadValue errors.

To copy components from a source GC to a destination GC, use `XCopyGC`.

XCopyGC(*display, src, valuemask, dest*)
    Display **display*;
    GC *src, dest*;
    unsigned long *valuemask*;
display   Specifies the connection to the X server.
src   Specifies the components of the source GC.
valuemask   Specifies which components in the GC are to be copied to the destination GC. This argument is the bitwise inclusive OR of one or more of the valid GC component mask bits.
dest   Specifies the destination GC.

The `XCopyGC` function copies the specified components from the source GC to the destination GC. The source and destination GCs must have the same root and depth, or a `BadMatch` error results. The valuemask specifies which component to copy, as for `XCreateGC`.

    `XCopyGC` can generate `BadAlloc`, `BadGC`, and `BadMatch` errors.

To change the components in a given GC, use `XChangeGC`.

XChangeGC(*display, gc, valuemask, values*)
    Display **display*;
    GC *gc*;
    unsigned long *valuemask*;
    XGCValues **values*;
display   Specifies the connection to the X server.
gc   Specifies the GC.
valuemask   Specifies which components in the GC are to be changed using information in the specified values structure. This argument is the bitwise inclusive OR of one or more of the valid GC component mask bits.
values   Specifies any values as specified by the valuemask.

The `XChangeGC` function changes the components specified by valuemask for the specified GC. The values argument contains the values to be set. The values and restrictions are the same as for `XCreateGC`. Changing the clip-mask overrides any previous `XSetClipRectangles` request on the context. Changing the dash-offset or dash-list overrides any previous `XSetDashes` request on the context. The order in which components are verified and altered is server-dependent. If an error is generated, a subset of the components may have been altered.

XChangeGC can generate BadAlloc, BadFont, BadGC, BadMatch, BadPixmap, and BadValue errors.

To free a given GC, use XFreeGC.

XFreeGC(*display, gc*)
    Display **display*;
    GC *gc*;
display   Specifies the connection to the X server.
gc   Specifies the GC.

The XFreeGC function destroys the specified graphics context as well as all the associated storage that was created by Xlib.

XFreeGC can generate a BadGC error.

To obtain the GContext resource ID for a given GC, use XGContextFromGC.

GContext XGContextFromGC(*gc*)
    GC *gc*;
gc   Specifies the GC for which you want the resource ID.

5.4   Using GC Convenience Routines

This section discusses how to set the:

- Foreground, background, plane mask, or function components
- Line attributes and dashes components
- Fill style and fill rule components
- Fill tile and stipple components
- Font component
- Clip region component
- Arc mode, subwindow mode, and graphics exposure components

5.4.1   Setting the Foreground, Background, Function, or Plane Mask

To set the foreground, background, plane mask, and function components for a given GC, use XSetState.

XSetState(*display, gc, foreground, background, function, plane_mask*)
    Display **display*;
    GC *gc*;
    unsigned long *foreground, background*;
    int *function*;
    unsigned long *plane_mask*;

display	Specifies the connection to the X server.
gc	Specifies the GC.
foreground	Specifies the foreground you want to set for the specified GC.
background	Specifies the background you want to set for the specified GC.
function	Specifies the function you want to set for the specified GC.
plane_mask	Specifies the plane mask.

XSetState can generate BadAlloc, BadGC, and BadValue errors.

To set the foreground of a given GC, use XSetForeground.

XSetForeground(*display, gc, foreground*)
    Display **display*;
    GC *gc*;
    unsigned long *foreground*;

display	Specifies the connection to the X server.
gc	Specifies the GC.
foreground	Specifies the foreground you want to set for the specified GC.

XSetForeground can generate BadAlloc and BadGC errors.

To set the background of a given GC, use XSetBackground.

XSetBackground(*display, gc, background*)
    Display **display*;
    GC *gc*;
    unsigned long *background*;

display	Specifies the connection to the X server.
gc	Specifies the GC.
background	Specifies the background you want to set for the specified GC.

XSetBackground can generate BadAlloc and BadGC errors.

To set the display function in a given GC, use XSetFunction.

XSetFunction(*display, gc, function*)
    Display **display*;

    GC *gc*;
    int *function*;
display   Specifies the connection to the X server.
gc   Specifies the GC.
function   Specifies the function you want to set for the specified GC.

XSetFunction can generate BadAlloc, BadGC, and BadValue errors.

To set the plane mask of a given GC, use XSetPlaneMask.

XSetPlaneMask(*display, gc, plane_mask*)
    Display **display*;
    GC *gc*;
    unsigned long *plane_mask*;
display   Specifies the connection to the X server.
gc   Specifies the GC.
plane_mask   Specifies the plane mask.

XSetPlaneMask can generate BadAlloc and BadGC errors.

5.4.2   Setting the Line Attributes and Dashes

To set the line drawing components of a given GC, use XSetLine-Attributes.

XSetLineAttributes(*display, gc, line_width, line_style, cap_style, join_style*)
    Display **display*;
    GC *gc*;
    unsigned int *line_width*;
    int *line_style*;
    int *cap_style*;
    int *join_style*;
display   Specifies the connection to the X server.
gc   Specifies the GC.
line_width   Specifies the line-width you want to set for the specified GC.
line_style   Specifies the line-style you want to set for the specified GC. You can
                pass LineSolid, LineOnOffDash, or LineDoubleDash.
cap_style   Specifies the line-style and cap-style you want to set for the specified
                GC. You can pass CapNotLast, CapButt, CapRound, or
                CapProjecting.
join_style   Specifies the line join-style you want to set for the specified GC. You
                can pass JoinMiter, JoinRound, or JoinBevel.

`XSetLineAttributes` can generate `BadAlloc`, `BadGC`, and `BadValue` errors.

To set the dash-offset and dash-list for dashed line styles of a given GC, use `XSetDashes`.

XSetDashes(*display, gc, dash_offset, dash_list, n*)
    Display *display;
    GC *gc*;
    int *dash_offset*;
    char *dash_list*[];
    int *n*;

display	Specifies the connection to the X server.
gc	Specifies the GC.
dash_offset	Specifies the phase of the pattern for the dashed line-style you want to set for the specified GC.
dash_list	Specifies the dash-list for the dashed line-style you want to set for the specified GC.
n	Specifies the number of elements in dash_list.

The `XSetDashes` function sets the dash-offset and dash-list attributes for dashed line styles in the specified GC. There must be at least one element in the specified dash_list, or a `BadValue` error results. The initial and alternating elements (second, fourth, and so on) of the dash_list are the even dashes, and the others are the odd dashes. Each element specifies a dash length in pixels. All of the elements must be nonzero, or a `BadValue` error results. Specifying an odd-length list is equivalent to specifying the same list concatenated with itself to produce an even-length list.

The dash-offset defines the phase of the pattern, specifying how many

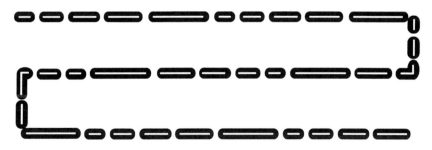

Figure 5.6. Dashes: 20 50 40 50 60 50 80 50 160 50

pixels into the dash-list the pattern should actually begin in any single graphics request. Dashing is continuous through path elements combined with a join-style but is reset to the dash-offset each time a cap-style is applied at a line endpoint.

The unit of measure for dashes is the same for the ordinary coordinate system. Ideally, a dash length is measured along the slope of the line, but implementations are only required to match this ideal for horizontal and vertical lines. Failing the ideal semantics, it is suggested that the length be measured along the major axis of the line. The major axis is defined as the x axis for lines drawn at an angle of between -45 and $+45$ degrees or between 315 and 225 degrees from the x axis. For all other lines, the major axis is the y axis.

XSetDashes can generate BadAlloc, BadGC, and BadValue errors.

5.4.3   Setting the Fill Style and Fill Rule

To set the fill-style of a given GC, use XSetFillStyle.

XSetFillStyle(*display, gc, fill_style*)
    Display **display*;
    GC *gc*;
    int *fill_style*;
display   Specifies the connection to the X server.
gc   Specifies the GC.
fill_style   Specifies the fill-style you want to set for the specified GC. You can pass
    FillSolid, FillTiled, FillStippled, or FillOpaqueStippled.

XSetFillStyle can generate BadAlloc, BadGC, and BadValue errors.

To set the fill-rule of a given GC, use XSetFillRule.

XSetFillRule(*display, gc, fill_rule*)
    Display **display*;
    GC *gc*;
    int *fill_rule*;
display   Specifies the connection to the X server.
gc   Specifies the GC.
fill_rule   Specifies the fill-rule you want to set for the specified GC. You can pass
    EvenOddRule or WindingRule.

XSetFillRule can generate BadAlloc, BadGC, and BadValue errors.

5.4.4 Setting the Fill Tile and Stipple

Some displays have hardware support for tiling or stippling with patterns of specific sizes. Tiling and stippling operations that restrict themselves to those specific sizes run much faster than such operations with arbitrary size patterns. Xlib provides functions that you can use to determine the best size, tile, or stipple for the display as well as to set the tile or stipple shape and the tile or stipple origin.

To obtain the best size of a tile, stipple, or cursor, use XQuery-BestSize.

Status XQueryBestSize(*display, class, which_screen, width, height, width_return,*
                       height_return)
    Display **display*;
    int *class*;
    Drawable *which_screen*;
    unsigned int *width, height*;
    unsigned int **width_return, *height_return*;

display	Specifies the connection to the X server.
class	Specifies the class that you are interested in. You can pass TileShape, CursorShape, or StippleShape.
which_screen	Specifies any drawable on the screen.
width	
height	Specify the width and height.
width_return	
height_return	Return the width and height of the object best supported by the display hardware.

The XQueryBestSize function returns the best or closest size to the specified size. For CursorShape, this is the largest size that can be fully displayed on the screen specified by which_screen. For TileShape, this is the size that can be tiled fastest. For StippleShape, this is the size that can be stippled fastest. For CursorShape, the drawable indicates the desired screen. For TileShape and StippleShape, the drawable indicates the screen and possibly the window class and depth. An InputOnly window cannot be used as the drawable for TileShape or StippleShape, or a BadMatch error results.

XQueryBestSize can generate BadDrawable, BadMatch, and BadValue errors.

To obtain the best fill tile shape, use `XQueryBestTile`.

Status XQueryBestTile(*display, which_screen, width, height, width_return,*
                            height_return)
　　　Display **display*;
　　　Drawable *which_screen*;
　　　unsigned int *width, height*;
　　　unsigned int **width_return, *height_return*;
display　　　　Specifies the connection to the X server.
which_screen　Specifies any drawable on the screen.
width
height　　　　Specify the width and height.
width_return
height_return　Return the width and height of the object best supported by the
　　　　　　　display hardware.

The `XQueryBestTile` function returns the best or closest size, that is, the size that can be tiled fastest on the screen specified by which_screen. The drawable indicates the screen and possibly the window class and depth. If an `InputOnly` window is used as the drawable, a `BadMatch` error results.

`XQueryBestTile` can generate `BadDrawable` and `BadMatch` errors.

To obtain the best stipple shape, use `XQueryBestStipple`.

Status XQueryBestStipple(*display, which_screen, width, height, width_return,*
                            height_return)
　　　Display **display*;
　　　Drawable *which_screen*;
　　　unsigned int *width, height*;
　　　unsigned int **width_return, *height_return*;
display　　　　Specifies the connection to the X server.
which_screen　Specifies any drawable on the screen.
width
height　　　　Specify the width and height.
width_return
height_return　Return the width and height of the object best supported by the
　　　　　　　display hardware.

The `XQueryBestStipple` function returns the best or closest size, that is, the size that can be stippled fastest on the screen specified by which_screen. The drawable indicates the screen and possibly the window class and depth. If an `InputOnly` window is used as the drawable, a `BadMatch` error results.

`XQueryBestStipple` can generate `BadDrawable` and `BadMatch` errors.

To set the fill tile of a given GC, use `XSetTile`.

XSetTile(*display, gc, tile*)
    Display *display;
    GC *gc*;
    Pixmap *tile*;
display   Specifies the connection to the X server.
gc   Specifies the GC.
tile   Specifies the fill tile you want to set for the specified GC.

The tile and GC must have the same depth, or a `BadMatch` error results.
   `XSetTile` can generate `BadAlloc`, `BadGC`, `BadMatch`, and `Bad-Pixmap` errors.

To set the stipple of a given GC, use `XSetStipple`.

XSetStipple(*display, gc, stipple*)
    Display *display;
    GC *gc*;
    Pixmap *stipple*;
display   Specifies the connection to the X server.
gc   Specifies the GC.
stipple Specifies the stipple you want to set for the specified GC.

The stipple and GC must have the same depth, or a `BadMatch` error results.
   `XSetStipple` can generate `BadAlloc`, `BadGC`, `BadMatch`, and `Bad-Pixmap` errors.

To set the tile or stipple origin of a given GC, use `XSetTSOrigin`.

XSetTSOrigin(*display, gc, ts_x_origin, ts_y_origin*)
    Display *display;
    GC *gc*;
    int *ts_x_origin, ts_y_origin*;
display   Specifies the connection to the X server.
gc   Specifies the GC.
ts_x_origin
ts_y_origin   Specify the x and y coordinates of the tile and stipple origin.

When graphics requests call for tiling or stippling, the parent's origin will be interpreted relative to whatever destination drawable is specified in the graphics request.

XSetTSOrigin can generate BadAlloc and BadGC error.

5.4.5   Setting the Current Font

To set the current font of a given GC, use XSetFont.

XSetFont(*display, gc, font*)
    Display *display*;
    GC *gc*;
    Font *font*;
display   Specifies the connection to the X server.
gc   Specifies the GC.
font   Specifies the font.

XSetFont can generate BadAlloc, BadFont, and BadGC errors.

5.4.6   Setting the Clip Region

Xlib provides functions that you can use to set the clip-origin and the clip-mask or set the clip-mask to a list of rectangles.

To set the clip-origin of a given GC, use XSetClipOrigin.

XSetClipOrigin(*display, gc, clip_x_origin, clip_y_origin*)
    Display *display*;
    GC *gc*;
    int *clip_x_origin, clip_y_origin*;
display   Specifies the connection to the X server.
gc   Specifies the GC.
clip_x_origin
clip_y_origin   Specify the x and y coordinates of the clip-mask origin.

The clip-mask origin is interpreted relative to the origin of whatever destination drawable is specified in the graphics request.

XSetClipOrigin can generate BadAlloc and BadGC errors.

To set the clip-mask of a given GC to the specified pixmap, use XSetClipMask.

XSetClipMask(*display, gc, pixmap*)
    Display **display*;
    GC *gc*;
    Pixmap *pixmap*;
display   Specifies the connection to the X server.
gc   Specifies the GC.
pixmap   Specifies the pixmap or None.

If the clip-mask is set to `None`, the pixels are are always drawn (regardless of the clip-origin).

    `XSetClipMask` can generate `BadAlloc`, `BadGC`, `BadMatch`, and `BadValue` errors.

To set the clip-mask of a given GC to the specified list of rectangles, use `XSetClipRectangles`.

XSetClipRectangles(*display, gc, clip_x_origin, clip_y_origin, rectangles, n, ordering*)
    Display **display*;
    GC *gc*;
    int *clip_x_origin, clip_y_origin*;
    XRectangle *rectangles*[];
    int *n*;
    int *ordering*;
display   Specifies the connection to the X server.
gc   Specifies the GC.
clip_x_origin
clip_y_origin   Specify the x and y coordinates of the clip-mask origin.
rectangles   Specifies an array of rectangles that define the clip-mask.
n   Specifies the number of rectangles.
ordering   Specifies the ordering relations on the rectangles. You can pass `Unsorted`, `YSorted`, `YXSorted`, or `YXBanded`.

The `XSetClipRectangles` function changes the clip-mask in the specified graphics context to the specified list of rectangles and sets the clip origin. The output is clipped to remain contained within the rectangles. The clip-origin is interpreted relative to the origin of whatever destination drawable is specified in a graphics request. The rectangle coordinates are interpreted relative to the clip-origin. The rectangles should be nonintersecting, or the graphics results will be undefined. Note that the list of rectangles can be empty, which effectively disables output. This is the opposite of passing

None as the clip-mask in XCreateGC, XChangeGC, and XSet-ClipMask.

If known by the client, ordering relations on the rectangles can be specified with the ordering argument. This may provide faster operation by the server. If an incorrect ordering is specified, the X server may generate a BadMatch error, but it is not required to do so. If no error is generated, the graphics results are undefined. Unsorted means the rectangles are in arbitrary order. YSorted means that the rectangles are nondecreasing in their Y origin. YXSorted additionally constrains YSorted order in that all rectangles with an equal Y origin are nondecreasing in their X origin. YXBanded additionally constrains YXSorted by requiring that, for every possible Y scanline, all rectangles that include that scanline have an identical Y origins and Y extents.

XSetClipRectangles can generate BadAlloc, BadGC, BadMatch, and BadValue errors.

Xlib provides a set of basic functions for performing region arithmetic. For information about these functions, see chapter 10.

5.4.7   Setting the Arc Mode, Subwindow Mode, and Graphics Exposure

To set the arc mode of a given GC, use XSetArcMode.

```
XSetArcMode(display, gc, arc_mode)
    Display *display;
    GC gc;
    int arc_mode;
```

display	Specifies the connection to the X server.
gc	Specifies the GC.
arc_mode	Specifies the arc mode. You can pass ArcChord or ArcPieSlice.

XSetArcMode can generate BadAlloc, BadGC, and BadValue errors.

To set the subwindow mode of a given GC, use XSetSubwindowMode.

```
XSetSubwindowMode(display, gc, subwindow_mode)
    Display *display;
    GC gc;
    int subwindow_mode;
```

display	Specifies the connection to the X server.
gc	Specifies the GC.
subwindow_mode	Specifies the subwindow mode. You can pass `ClipByChildren` or `IncludeInferiors`.

`XSetSubwindowMode` can generate `BadAlloc`, `BadGC`, and `BadValue` errors.

To set the graphics-exposures flag of a given GC, use `XSet-GraphicsExposures`.

XSetGraphicsExposures(*display, gc, graphics_exposures*)
    Display *display;
    GC *gc*;
    Bool *graphics_exposures*;

display	Specifies the connection to the X server.
gc	Specifies the GC.
graphics_exposures	Specifies a Boolean value that indicates whether you want `GraphicsExpose` and `NoExpose` events to be reported when calling `XCopyArea` and `XCopyPlane` with this GC.

`XSetGraphicsExposures` can generate `BadAlloc`, `BadGC`, and `BadValue` errors.

Chapter 6

Graphics Functions

Once you have connected the display to the X server, you can use the Xlib graphics functions to:

- Clear and copy areas
- Draw points, lines, rectangles, and arcs
- Fill areas
- Manipulate fonts
- Draw text
- Transfer images between clients and the server
- Manipulate cursors

If the same drawable and GC is used for each call, Xlib batches back-to-back calls to `XDrawPoint`, `XDrawLine`, `XDrawRectangle`, `XFillArc`, and `XFillRectangle`. Note that this reduces the total number of requests sent to the server.

6.1 Clearing Areas

Xlib provides functions that you can use to clear an area or the entire window. Because pixmaps do not have defined backgrounds, they cannot be filled by using the functions described in this section. Instead, to accomplish an analogous operation on a pixmap, you should use `XFillRectangle`, which sets the pixmap to a known value.

To clear a rectangular area of a given window, use `XClearArea`.

XClearArea(*display, w, x, y, width, height, exposures*)
    Display **display*;
    Window *w*;
    int *x, y*;
    unsigned int *width, height;*
    Bool *exposures*;

display	Specifies the connection to the X server.
w	Specifies the window.
x	
y	Specify the x and y coordinates, which are relative to the origin of the window and specify the upper-left corner of the rectangle.
width	
height	Specify the width and height, which are the dimensions of the rectangle.
exposures	Specifies a Boolean value that indicates if `Expose` events are to be generated.

The `XClearArea` function paints a rectangular area in the specified window according to the specified dimensions with the window's background pixel or pixmap. The subwindow-mode effectively is `ClipByChildren`. If width is zero, it is replaced with the current width of the window minus x. If height is zero, it is replaced with the current height of the window minus y. If the window has a defined background tile, the rectangle clipped by any children is filled with this tile. If the window has background `None`, the contents of the window are not changed. In either case, if exposures is `True`, one or more `Expose` events are generated for regions of the rectangle that are either visible or are being retained in a backing store. If you specify a window whose class is `InputOnly`, a `BadMatch` error results.

    `XClearArea` can generate `BadMatch`, `BadValue`, and `BadWindow` errors.

To clear the entire area in a given window, use `XClearWindow`.

XClearWindow(*display, w*)
    Display **display*;
    Window *w*;

display	Specifies the connection to the X server.
w	Specifies the window.

The `XClearWindow` function clears the entire area in the specified window and is equivalent to `XClearArea` (display, w, 0, 0, 0, 0, `False`). If the window has a defined background tile, the rectangle is tiled with a plane-mask of all ones and `GXcopy` function. If the window has background `None`, the contents of the window are not changed. If you specify a window whose class is `InputOnly`, a `BadMatch` error results.

`XClearWindow` can generate `BadMatch` and `BadWindow` errors.

6.2   Copying Areas

Xlib provides functions that you can use to copy an area or a bit plane.

To copy an area between drawables of the same root and depth, use `XCopyArea`.

XCopyArea(*display, src, dest, gc, src_x, src_y, width, height, dest_x, dest_y*)
    Display **display*;
    Drawable *src, dest*;
    GC *gc*;
    int *src_x, src_y*;
    unsigned int *width, height*;
    int *dest_x, dest_y*;

display	Specifies the connection to the X server.
src	
dest	Specify the source and destination rectangles to be combined.
gc	Specifies the GC.
src_x	
src_y	Specify the x and y coordinates, which are relative to the origin of the source rectangle and specify its upper-left corner.
width	
height	Specify the width and height, which are the dimensions of both the source and destination rectangles.
dest_x	
dest_y	Specify the x and y coordinates, which are relative to the origin of the destination rectangle and specify its upper-left corner.

The `XCopyArea` function combines the specified rectangle of src with the specified rectangle of dest. The drawables must have the same root and depth, or a `BadMatch` error results.

If regions of the source rectangle are obscured and have not been retained in backing store or if regions outside the boundaries of the source drawable are specified, those regions are not copied. Instead, the following occurs on all corresponding destination regions that are either visible or are retained in backing store. If the destination is a window with a background other than `None`, corresponding regions of the destination are tiled with that background (with plane-mask of all ones and `GXcopy` function). Regardless of tiling or whether the destination is a window or a pixmap, if graphics-exposures is `True`, then `GraphicsExpose` events for all corresponding destination regions are generated. If graphics-exposures is `True` but no `GraphicsExpose` events are generated, a `NoExpose` event is generated. Note that by default graphics-exposures is `True` in new GCs.

This function uses these GC components: function, plane-mask, subwindow-mode, graphics-exposures, clip-x-origin, clip-y-origin, and clip-mask.

`XCopyArea` can generate `BadDrawable`, `BadGC`, and `BadMatch` errors.

To copy a single bit plane of a given drawable, use `XCopyPlane`.

XCopyPlane(*display, src, dest, gc, src_x, src_y, width, height, dest_x, dest_y, plane*)
 Display **display*;
 Drawable *src, dest*;
 GC *gc*;
 int *src_x, src_y*;
 unsigned int *width, height*;
 int *dest_x, dest_y*;
 unsigned long *plane*;

display	Specifies the connection to the X server.
src	
dest	Specify the source and destination rectangles to be combined.
gc	Specifies the GC.
src_x	
src_y	Specify the x and y coordinates, which are relative to the origin of the source rectangle and specify its upper-left corner.
width	
height	Specify the width and height, which are the dimensions of both the source and destination rectangles.
dest_x	
dest_y	Specify the x and y coordinates, which are relative to the origin of the destination rectangle and specify its upper-left corner.
plane	Specifies the bit plane. You must set exactly one bit to 1.

The XCopyPlane function uses a single bit plane of the specified source rectangle combined with the specified GC to modify the specified rectangle of dest. The drawables must have the same root but need not have the same depth. If the drawables do not have the same root, a BadMatch error results. If plane does not have exactly one bit set to 1 and the value of plane must be less that 2^n, where n is the depth of src, a BadValue error results.

Effectively, XCopyPlane forms a pixmap of the same depth as the rectangle of dest and with a size specified by the source region. It uses the foreground/background pixels in the GC (foreground everywhere the bit plane in src contains a bit set to 1, background everywhere the bit plane in src contains a bit set to 0) and the equivalent of a CopyArea protocol request is performed with all the same exposure semantics. This can also be thought of as using the specified region of the source bit plane as a stipple with a fill-style of FillOpaqueStippled for filling a rectangular area of the destination.

This function uses these GC components: function, plane-mask, foreground, background, subwindow-mode, graphics-exposures, clip-x-origin, clip-y-origin, and clip-mask.

XCopyPlane can generate BadDrawable, BadGC, BadMatch, and BadValue errors.

6.3   Drawing Points, Lines, Rectangles, and Arcs

Xlib provides functions that you can use to draw:

- A single point or multiple points
- A single line or multiple lines
- A single rectangle or multiple rectangles
- A single arc or multiple arcs

Some of the functions described in the following sections use these structures:

```
typedef struct {
    short x1, y1, x2, y2;
} XSegment;
```

```
typedef struct {
    short x, y;
} XPoint;

typedef struct {
    short x, y;
    unsigned short width, height;
} XRectangle;

typedef struct {
    short x, y;
    unsigned short width, height;
    short angle1, angle2;      /* Degrees * 64 */
} XArc;
```

All x and y members are signed integers. The width and height members are 16-bit unsigned integers. You should be careful not to generate coordinates and sizes out of the 16-bit ranges, because the protocol only has 16-bit fields for these values.

6.3.1   Drawing Single and Multiple Points

To draw a single point in a given drawable, use XDrawPoint.

XDrawPoint(*display, d, gc, x, y*)
    Display **display*;
    Drawable *d*;
    GC *gc*;
    int *x, y*;

display Specifies the connection to the X server.
d   Specifies the drawable.
gc   Specifies the GC.
x
y   Specify the x and y coordinates where you want the point drawn.

To draw multiple points in a given drawable, use XDrawPoints.

XDrawPoints(*display, d, gc, points, npoints, mode*)
    Display **display*;
    Drawable *d*;
    GC *gc*;
    XPoint **points*;

```
    int npoints;
    int mode;
```

display   Specifies the connection to the X server.
d   Specifies the drawable.
gc   Specifies the GC.
points   Specifies a pointer to an array of points.
npoints   Specifies the number of points in the array.
mode   Specifies the coordinate mode. You can pass CoordModeOrigin or
           CoordModePrevious.

The XDrawPoint function uses the foreground pixel and function components of the GC to draw a single point into the specified drawable; XDrawPoints draws multiple points this way. CoordModeOrigin treats all coordinates as relative to the origin, and CoordModePrevious treats all coordinates after the first as relative to the previous point. XDrawPoints draws the points in the order listed in the array.

Both functions use these GC components: function, plane-mask, foreground, subwindow-mode, clip-x-origin, clip-y-origin, and clip-mask.

XDrawPoint can generate BadDrawable, BadGC, and BadMatch errors. XDrawPoints can generate BadDrawable, BadGC, BadMatch, and BadValue errors.

6.3.2   Drawing Single and Multiple Lines

To draw a single line between two points in a given drawable, use XDrawLine.

```
XDrawLine(display, d, gc, x1, y1, x2, y2)
    Display *display;
    Drawable d;
    GC gc;
    int x1, y1, x2, y2;
```

display   Specifies the connection to the X server.
d   Specifies the drawable.
gc   Specifies the GC.
x1
y1
x2
y2   Specify the points (x1, y1) and (x2, y2) to be connected.

To draw multiple lines in a given drawable, use `XDrawLines`.

XDrawLines(*display, d, gc, points, npoints, mode*)
    Display **display*;
    Drawable *d*;
    GC *gc*;
    XPoint **points*;
    int *npoints*;
    int *mode*;

display	Specifies the connection to the X server.
d	Specifies the drawable.
gc	Specifies the GC.
points	Specifies a pointer to an array of points.
npoints	Specifies the number of points in the array.
mode	Specifies the coordinate mode. You can pass `CoordModeOrigin` or `CoordModePrevious`.

To draw multiple, unconnected lines in a given drawable, use `XDrawSegments`.

XDrawSegments(*display, d, gc, segments, nsegments*)
    Display **display*;
    Drawable *d*;
    GC *gc*;
    XSegment **segments*;
    int *nsegments*;

display	Specifies the connection to the X server.
d	Specifies the drawable.
gc	Specifies the GC.
segments	Specifies a pointer to an array of segments.
nsegments	Specifies the number of segments in the array.

The `XDrawLine` function uses the components of the specified GC to draw a line between the specified set of points (x1, y1) and (x2, y2). It does not perform joining at coincident endpoints. For any given line, `XDrawLine` does not draw a pixel more than once. If lines intersect, the intersecting pixels are drawn multiple times.

The `XDrawLines` function uses the components of the specified GC to draw npoints − 1 lines between each pair of points (point[i], point[i + 1]) in the array of `XPoint` structures. It draws the lines in the order listed in the array. The lines join correctly at all intermediate points, and if the first and last points coincide, the first and last lines also join correctly. For any given line, XDrawLines does not draw a pixel more than once. If thin (zero line-width) lines intersect, the intersecting pixels are drawn multiple times. If wide lines intersect, the intersecting pixels are drawn only once, as though the entire PolyLine protocol request were a single, filled shape. CoordModeOrigin treats all coordinates as relative to the origin, and CoordModePrevious treats all coordinates after the first as relative to the previous point.

The XDrawSegments function draws multiple, unconnected lines. For each segment, XDrawSegments draws a line between (x1, y1) and (x2, y2). It draws the lines in the order listed in the array of XSegment structures and does not perform joining at coincident endpoints. For any given line, XDrawSegments does not draw a pixel more than once. If lines intersect, the intersecting pixels are drawn multiple times.

All three functions use these GC components: function, plane-mask, line-width, line-style, cap-style, fill-style, subwindow-mode, clip-x-origin, clip-y-origin, and clip-mask. The XDrawLines function also uses the join-style GC component. All three functions also use these GC mode-dependent components: foreground, background, tile, stipple, tile-stipple-x-origin, tile-stipple-y-origin, dash-offset, and dash-list.

XDrawLine, XDrawLines, and XDrawSegments can generate Bad-Drawable, BadGC, and BadMatch errors. XDrawLines also can generate BadValue errors.

6.3.3   Drawing Single and Multiple Rectangles

To draw the outline of a single rectangle in a given drawable, use XDrawRectangle.

XDrawRectangle(*display, d, gc, x, y, width, height*)
    Display **display*;
    Drawable *d*;
    GC *gc*;
    int *x, y*;
    unsigned int *width, height*;

display   Specifies the connection to the X server.
d   Specifies the drawable.
gc   Specifies the GC.

x

y   Specify the x and y coordinates, which specify the upper-left corner of the rectangle.

width

height   Specify the width and height, which specify the dimensions of the rectangle.

To draw the outline of multiple rectangles in a given drawable, use `XDrawRectangles`.

XDrawRectangles(*display, d, gc, rectangles, nrectangles*)
    Display **display*;
    Drawable *d*;
    GC *gc*;
    XRectangle *rectangles*[];
    int *nrectangles*;

display   Specifies the connection to the X server.

d   Specifies the drawable.

gc   Specifies the GC.

rectangles Specifies a pointer to an array of rectangles.

nrectangles Specifies the number of rectangles in the array.

The `XDrawRectangle` and `XDrawRectangles` functions draw the outlines of the specified rectangle or rectangles as if a five-point `PolyLine` protocol request were specified for each rectangle:

$$[x,y] \; [x+width,y] \; [x+width,y+height] \; [x,y+height] \; [x,y]$$

For the specified rectangle or rectangles, these functions do not draw a pixel more than once. `XDrawRectangles` draws the rectangles in the order listed in the array. If rectangles intersect, the intersecting pixels are drawn multiple times.

Both functions use these GC components: function, plane-mask, line-width, line-style, join-style, fill-style, subwindow-mode, clip-x-origin, clip-y-origin, and clip-mask. They also use these GC mode-dependent components: foreground, background, tile, stipple, tile-stipple-x-origin, tile-stipple-y-origin, dash-offset, and dash-list.

`XDrawRectangle` and `XDrawRectangles` can generate `BadDrawable`, `BadGC`, and `BadMatch` errors.

6.3.4   Drawing Single and Multiple Arcs

To draw a single arc in a given drawable, use XDrawArc.

XDrawArc(*display, d, gc, x, y, width, height, angle1, angle2*)
    Display **display*;
    Drawable *d*;
    GC *gc*;
    int *x, y*;
    unsigned int *width, height*;
    int *angle1, angle2*;

display	Specifies the connection to the X server.
d	Specifies the drawable.
gc	Specifies the GC.
x	
y	Specify the x and y coordinates, which are relative to the origin of the drawable and specify the upper-left corner of the bounding rectangle.
width	
height	Specify the width and height, which are the major and minor axes of the arc.
angle1	Specifies the start of the arc relative to the three-o'clock position from the center, in units of degrees * 64.
angle2	Specifies the path and extent of the arc relative to the start of the arc, in units of degrees * 64.

To draw multiple arcs in a given drawable, use XDrawArcs.

XDrawArcs(*display, d, gc, arcs, narcs*)
    Display **display*;
    Drawable *d*;
    GC *gc*;
    XArc **arcs*;
    int *narcs*;

display	Specifies the connection to the X server.
d	Specifies the drawable.
gc	Specifies the GC.
arcs	Specifies a pointer to an array of arcs.
narcs	Specifies the number of arcs in the array.

XDrawArc draws a single circular or elliptical arc, and XDrawArcs draws multiple circular or elliptical arcs. Each arc is specified by a rectangle and two angles. The center of the circle or ellipse is the center of the rectangle, and the major and minor axes are specified by the width and height. Positive angles indicate counterclockwise motion, and negative angles indicate clockwise motion. If the magnitude of angle2 is greater than 360 degrees, XDrawArc or XDrawArcs truncates it to 360 degrees.

For an arc specified as [*x, y, width, height, angle1, angle2*], the origin of the major and minor axes is at $\left[x+\dfrac{width}{2},\ y+\dfrac{height}{2}\right]$, and the infinitely thin path describing the entire circle or ellipse intersects the horizontal axis at $\left[x,\ y+\dfrac{height}{2}\right]$ and $\left[x+width,\ y+\dfrac{height}{2}\right]$ and intersects the vertical axis at $\left[x+\dfrac{width}{2},\ y\right]$ and $\left[x+\dfrac{width}{2},\ y+height\right]$. These coordinates can be fractional and so are not truncated to discrete coordinates. The path should be defined by the ideal mathematical path. For a wide line with line-width lw, the bounding outlines for filling are given by the two infinitely thin paths consisting of all points whose perpendicular distance from the path of the circle/ellipse is equal to lw/2 (which may be a fractional value). The cap-style and join-style are applied the same as for a line corresponding to the tangent of the circle/ellipse at the endpoint.

For an arc specified as [*x, y, width, height, angle1, angle2*], the angles must be specified in the effectively skewed coordinate system of the ellipse (for a circle, the angles and coordinate systems are identical). The relationship between these angles and angles expressed in the normal coordinate system of the screen (as measured with a protractor) is as follows:

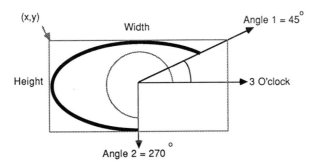

Figure 6.1.   XDrawArc (DPY, W, GC, width, height, 45*64, 270*64)

$$\text{skewed-angle} = \text{atan}\left[\tan(\text{normal-angle})*\frac{width}{height}\right] + adjust$$

The skewed-angle and normal-angle are expressed in radians (rather than in degrees scaled by 64) in the range $[0, 2\pi]$ and where atan returns a value in the range $\left[-\frac{\pi}{2}, \frac{\pi}{2}\right]$ and adjust is:

0	for normal-angle in the range $\left[0, \dfrac{\pi}{2}\right]$
π	for normal-angle in the range $\left[\dfrac{\pi}{2}, \dfrac{3\pi}{2}\right]$
2π	for normal-angle in the range $\left[\dfrac{3\pi}{2}, 2\pi\right]$

For any given arc, XDrawArc and XDrawArcs do not draw a pixel more than once. If two arcs join correctly and if the line-width is greater than zero and the arcs intersect, XDrawArc and XDrawArcs do not draw a pixel more than once. Otherwise, the intersecting pixels of intersecting arcs are drawn multiple times. Specifying an arc with one endpoint and a clockwise extent draws the same pixels as specifying the other endpoint and an equivalent counterclockwise extent, except as it affects joins.

If the last point in one arc coincides with the first point in the following arc, the two arcs will join correctly. If the first point in the first arc coincides with the last point in the last arc, the two arcs will join correctly. By specifying one axis to be zero, a horizontal or vertical line can be drawn. Angles are computed based solely on the coordinate system and ignore the aspect ratio.

Both functions use these GC components: function, plane-mask, line-width, line-style, cap-style, join-style, fill-style, subwindow-mode, clip-x-origin, clip-y-origin, and clip-mask. They also use these GC mode-dependent components: foreground, background, tile, stipple, tile-stipple-x-origin, tile-stipple-y-origin, dash-offset, and dash-list.

XDrawArc and XDrawArcs can generate BadDrawable, BadGC, and BadMatch errors.

6.4 Filling Areas

Xlib provides functions that you can use to fill:

- A single rectangle or multiple rectangles
- A single polygon
- A single arc or multiple arcs

6.4.1 Filling Single and Multiple Rectangles

To fill a single rectangular area in a given drawable, use XFill-Rectangle.

XFillRectangle(*display, d, gc, x, y, width, height*)
    Display **display*;
    Drawable *d*;
    GC *gc*;
    int *x, y*;
    unsigned int *width, height*;

display	Specifies the connection to the X server.
d	Specifies the drawable.
gc	Specifies the GC.
x	
y	Specify the x and y coordinates, which are relative to the origin of the drawable and specify the upper-left corner of the rectangle.
width	
height	Specify the width and height, which are the dimensions of the rectangle to be filled.

To fill multiple rectangular areas in a given drawable, use XFill-Rectangles.

XFillRectangles(*display, d, gc, rectangles, nrectangles*)
    Display **display*;
    Drawable *d*;
    GC *gc*;
    XRectangle **rectangles*;
    int *nrectangles*;

display	Specifies the connection to the X server.
d	Specifies the drawable.
gc	Specifies the GC.
rectangles	Specifies a pointer to an array of rectangles.
nrectangles	Specifies the number of rectangles in the array.

The XFillRectangle and XFillRectangles functions fill the specified rectangle or rectangles as if a four-point FillPolygon protocol request were specified for each rectangle:

$$[x,y]\ [x+\text{width},y]\ [x+\text{width},y+\text{height}]\ [x,y+\text{height}]$$

Each function uses the x and y coordinates, width and height dimensions, and GC you specify.

XFillRectangles fills the rectangles in the order listed in the array. For any given rectangle, XFillRectangle and XFillRectangles do not draw a pixel more than once. If rectangles intersect, the intersecting pixels are drawn multiple times.

Both functions use these GC components: function, plane-mask, fill-style, subwindow-mode, clip-x-origin, clip-y-origin, and clip-mask. They also use these GC mode-dependent components: foreground, background, tile, stipple, tile-stipple-x-origin, and tile-stipple-y-origin.

XFillRectangle and XFillRectangles can generate Bad-Drawable, BadGC, and BadMatch errors.

6.4.2   Filling a Single Polygon

To fill a polygon area in a given drawable, use XFillPolygon.

XFillPolygon(*display, d, gc, points, npoints, shape, mode*)
    Display **display*;
    Drawable *d*;
    GC *gc*;
    XPoint **points*;
    int *npoints*;
    int *shape*;
    int *mode*;

display	Specifies the connection to the X server.
d	Specifies the drawable.
gc	Specifies the GC.
points	Specifies a pointer to an array of points.
npoints	Specifies the number of points in the array.
shape	Specifies a shape that helps the server to improve performance. You can pass Complex, Convex, or Nonconvex.
mode	Specifies the coordinate mode. You can pass CoordModeOrigin or CoordModePrevious.

XFillPolygon fills the region closed by the specified path. The path is closed automatically if the last point in the list does not coincide with the first point. XFillPolygon does not draw a pixel of the region more than once. CoordModeOrigin treats all coordinates as relative to the origin, and CoordModePrevious treats all coordinates after the first as relative to the previous point.

Depending on the specified shape, the following occurs:

- If shape is Complex, the path may self-intersect.
- If shape is Convex, the path is wholly convex. If known by the client, specifying Convex can improve performance. If you specify Convex for a path that is not convex, the graphics results are undefined.
- If shape is Nonconvex, the path does not self-intersect, but the shape is not wholly convex. If known by the client, specifying Nonconvex instead of Complex may improve performance. If you specify Nonconvex for a self-intersecting path, the graphics results are undefined.

The fill-rule of the GC controls the filling behavior of self-intersecting polygons.

This function uses these GC components: function, plane-mask, fill-style, fill-rule, subwindow-mode, clip-x-origin, clip-y-origin, and clip-mask. It also uses these GC mode-dependent components: foreground, background, tile, stipple, tile-stipple-x-origin, and tile-stipple-y-origin.

XFillPolygon can generate BadDrawable, BadGC, BadMatch, and BadValue errors.

6.4.3   Filling Single and Multiple Arcs

To fill a single arc in a given drawable, use XFillArc.

XFillArc(*display, d, gc, x, y, width, height, angle1, angle2*)
    Display **display*;
    Drawable *d*;
    GC *gc*;
    int *x, y*;
    unsigned int *width, height*;
    int *angle1, angle2*;
display   Specifies the connection to the X server.
d   Specifies the drawable.
gc   Specifies the GC.

x

y   Specify the x and y coordinates, which are relative to the origin of the drawable and specify the upper-left corner of the bounding rectangle.

width

height   Specify the width and height, which are the major and minor axes of the arc.

angle1   Specifies the start of the arc relative to the three-o'clock position from the center, in units of degrees * 64.

angle2   Specifies the path and extent of the arc relative to the start of the arc, in units of degrees * 64.

To fill multiple arcs in a given drawable, use `XFillArcs`.

XFillArcs(*display, d, gc, arcs, narcs*)
    Display **display*;
    Drawable *d*;
    GC *gc*;
    XArc **arcs*;
    int *narcs*;

display   Specifies the connection to the X server.

d   Specifies the drawable.

gc   Specifies the GC.

arcs   Specifies a pointer to an array of arcs.

narcs   Specifies the number of arcs in the array.

For each arc, `XFillArc` or `XFillArcs` fills the region closed by the infinitely thin path described by the specified arc and, depending on the arc-mode specified in the GC, one or two line segments. For `ArcChord`, the single line segment joining the endpoints of the arc is used. For `ArcPieSlice`, the two line segments joining the endpoints of the arc with the center point are used. `XFillArcs` fills the arcs in the order listed in the array. For any given arc, `XFillArc` and `XFillArcs` do not draw a pixel more than once. If regions intersect, the intersecting pixels are drawn multiple times.

Both functions use these GC components: function, plane-mask, fill-style, arc-mode, subwindow-mode, clip-x-origin, clip-y-origin, and clip-mask. They also use these GC mode-dependent components: foreground, background, tile, stipple, tile-stipple-x-origin, and tile-stipple-y-origin.

`XFillArc` and `XFillArcs` can generate `BadDrawable`, `BadGC`, and `BadMatch` errors.

6.5   Font Metrics

A font is a graphical description of a set of characters that are used to increase efficiency whenever a set of small, similar sized patterns are repeatedly used.

This section discusses how to:

- Load and free fonts
- Obtain and free font names
- Set and retrieve the font search path
- Compute character string sizes
- Return logical extents
- Query character string sizes

The X server loads fonts whenever a program requests a new font. The server can cache fonts for quick lookup. Fonts are global across all screens in a server. Several levels are possible when dealing with fonts. Most applications simply use `XLoadQueryFont` to load a font and query the font metrics.

Characters in fonts are regarded as masks. Except for image text requests, the only pixels modified are those in which bits are set to 1 in the character.

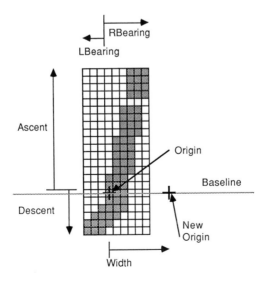

Figure 6.2. XCharStruct components

This means that it makes sense to draw text using stipples or tiles (for example, many menus gray-out unusable entries).

The XFontStruct structure contains all of the information for the font and consists of the font-specific information as well as a pointer to an array of XCharStruct structures for the characters contained in the font. The XFontStruct, XFontProp, and XCharStruct structures contain:

```
typedef struct {
    short lbearing;                 /* origin to left edge of raster */
    short rbearing;                 /* origin to right edge of raster */
    short width;                    /* advance to next char's origin */
    short ascent;                   /* baseline to top edge of raster */
    short descent;                  /* baseline to bottom edge of raster */
    unsigned short attributes;      /* per char flags (not predefined) */
} XCharStruct;

typedef struct {
    Atom name;
    unsigned long card32;
} XFontProp;

typedef struct {                    /* normal 16 bit characters are two bytes */
    unsigned char byte1;
    unsigned char byte2;
} XChar2b;

typedef struct {
    XExtData *ext_data;             /* hook for extension to hang data */
    Font fid;                       /* Font id for this font */
    unsigned direction;             /* hint about the direction font is painted */
    unsigned min_char_or_byte2;     /* first character */
    unsigned max_char_or_byte2;     /* last character */
    unsigned min_byte1;             /* first row that exists */
    unsigned max_byte1;             /* last row that exists */
    Bool all_chars_exist;           /* flag if all characters have nonzero size */
    unsigned default_char;          /* char to print for undefined character */
    int n_properties;               /* how many properties there are */
    XFontProp *properties;          /* pointer to array of additional
                                       properties */

    XCharStruct min_bounds;         /* minimum bounds over all existing
                                       char */

    XCharStruct max_bounds;         /* maximum bounds over all existing
                                       char */
```

XCharStruct *per_char;	/* first_char to last_char information */
int ascent;	/* logical extent above baseline for spacing */
int descent;	/* logical descent below baseline for spacing */

} XFontStruct;

X supports single byte/character, two bytes/character matrix, and 16-bit character text operations. Note that any of these forms can be used with a font, but a single byte/character text request can only specify a single byte (that is, the first row of a 2-byte font). You should view 2-byte fonts as a two-dimensional matrix of defined characters: byte1 specifies the range of defined rows and byte2 defines the range of defined columns of the font. Single byte/character fonts have one row defined, and the byte2 range specified in the structure defines a range of characters.

The bounding box of a character is defined by the XCharStruct of that character. When characters are absent from a font, the default_char is used. When fonts have all characters of the same size, only the information in the XFontStruct min and max bounds are used.

The members of the XFontStruct have the following semantics:

- The direction member can be either FontLeftToRight or FontRightToLeft. It is just a hint as to whether most XCharStruct elements have a positive (FontLeftToRight) or a negative (FontRightToLeft) character width metric. The core protocol defines no support for vertical text.

- If the min_byte1 and max_byte1 members are both zero, min_char_or_byte2 specifies the linear character index corresponding to the first element of the per_char array, and max_char_or_byte2 specifies the linear character index of the last element.

  If either min_byte1 or max_byte1 are nonzero, both min_char_or_byte2 and max_char_or_byte2 are less than 256, and the 2-byte character index values corresponding to the per_char array element N (counting from 0) are:

$$byte1 = N/D + min\_byte1$$
$$byte2 = N\backslash D + min\_char\_or\_byte2$$

where:

$$D = max\_char\_or\_byte2 - min\_char\_or\_byte2 + 1$$
$$/ = integer\ division$$
$$\backslash = integer\ modulus$$

- If the per_char pointer is NULL, all glyphs between the first and last character indexes inclusive have the same information, as given by both min_bounds and max_bounds.

- If all_chars_exist is True, all characters in the per_char array have nonzero bounding boxes.

- The default_char member specifies the character that will be used when an undefined or nonexistent character is printed. The default_char is a 16-bit character (not a 2-byte character). For a font using 2-byte matrix format, the default_char has byte1 in the most-significant byte and byte2 in the least-significant byte. If the default_char itself specifies an undefined or nonexistent character, no printing is performed for an undefined or nonexistent character.

- The min_bounds and max_bounds members contain the most extreme values of each individual XCharStruct component over all elements of this array (and ignore nonexistent characters). The bounding box of the font (the smallest rectangle enclosing the shape obtained by superimposing all of the characters at the same origin [x,y]) has its upper-left coordinate at:

$$[x + min\_bounds.lbearing, y - max\_bounds.ascent]$$

Its width is:

$$max\_bounds.rbearing - min\_bounds.lbearing$$

Its height is:

$$max\_bounds.ascent + max\_bounds.descent$$

- The ascent member is the logical extent of the font above the baseline that is used for determining line spacing. Specific characters may extend beyond this.

- The descent member is the logical extent of the font at or below the baseline that is used for determining line spacing. Specific characters may extend beyond this.

- If the baseline is at Y-coordinate y, the logical extent of the font is inclusive between the Y-coordinate values $(y - font.ascent)$ and $(y + font.descent - 1)$. Typically, the minimum interline spacing between rows of text is given by ascent + descent.

For a character origin at [x,y], the bounding box of a character (that is, the smallest rectangle that encloses the character's shape) described in terms of XCharStruct components is a rectangle with its upper-left corner at:

$$[x + lbearing, y - ascent]$$

Its width is:

$$rbearing - lbearing$$

Its height is:

$$ascent + descent$$

The origin for the next character is defined to be:

$$[x + width, y]$$

The lbearing member defines the extent of the left edge of the character ink from the origin. The rbearing member defines the extent of the right edge of the character ink from the origin. The ascent member defines the extent of the top edge of the character ink from the origin. The descent member defines the extent of the bottom edge of the character ink from the origin. The width member defines the logical width of the character.

Note that the baseline (the y position of the character origin) is logically viewed as being the scanline just below nondescending characters. When descent is zero, only pixels with Y-coordinates less than y are drawn, and the origin is logically viewed as being coincident with the left edge of a nonkerned character. When lbearing is zero, no pixels with X-coordinate less than x are drawn. Any of the `XCharStruct` metric members could be negative. If the width is negative, the next character will be placed to the left of the current origin.

The X protocol does not define the interpretation of the attributes member in the `XCharStruct` structure. A nonexistent character is represented with all members of its `XCharStruct` set to zero.

A font is not guaranteed to have any properties. The interpretation of the property value (for example, long or unsigned long) must be derived from *a priori* knowledge of the property. When possible, fonts should have at least the properties listed in the following table. With atom names, uppercase and lowercase matter. The following built-in property atoms can be found in `<X11/Xatom.h>`:

Property Name	Type	Description
MIN_SPACE	unsigned	The minimum interword spacing, in pixels.
NORM_SPACE	unsigned	The normal interword spacing, in pixels.
MAX_SPACE	unsigned	The maximum interword spacing, in pixels.
END_SPACE	unsigned	The additional spacing at the end of sentences, in pixels.
SUPERSCRIPT_X SUPERSCRIPT_Y	int	Offset from the character origin where superscripts should begin, in pixels. If the origin is at [x,y], then superscripts should begin at [x + SUPERSCRIPT_X, y − SUPERSCRIPT_Y].
SUBSCRIPT_X SUBSCRIPT_Y	int	Offset from the character origin where subscripts should begin, in pixels. If the origin is at [x,y], then subscripts should begin at [x + SUPERSCRIPT_X, y + SUPERSCRIPT_Y].
UNDERLINE_POSITION	int	Y offset from the baseline to the top of an underline, in pixels. If the baseline is Y-coordinate y, then the top of the underline is at (y + UNDERLINE_POSITION).
UNDERLINE_THICKNESS	unsigned	Thickness of the underline, in pixels.
STRIKEOUT_ASCENT STRIKEOUT_DESCENT	int	Vertical extents for boxing or voiding characters, in pixels. If the baseline is at Y-coordinate y, then the top of the strikeout box is at (y − STRIKEOUT_ASCENT), and the height of the box is (STRIKEOUT_ASCENT + STRIKEOUT_DESCENT).
ITALIC_ANGLE	int	The angle of the dominant staffs of characters in the font, in degrees scaled by 64, relative to the three-o'clock position from

Property Name	Type	Description
		the character origin, with positive indicating counterclockwise motion (as in XDrawArc).
X_HEIGHT	int	1 ex as in TeX, but expressed in units of pixels. Often the height of lowercase x.
QUAD_WIDTH	int	1 em as in TeX, but expressed in units of pixels. Often the width of the digits 0–9.
CAP_HEIGHT	int	Y offset from the baseline to the top of the capital letters, ignoring accents, in pixels. If the baseline is at Y-coordinate y, then the top of the capitals is at (y − CAP_HEIGHT).
WEIGHT	unsigned	The weight or boldness of the font, expressed as a value between 0 and 1000.
POINT_SIZE	unsigned	The point size of this font at the ideal resolution, expressed in 1/10 points.
RESOLUTION	unsigned	The number of pixels per point, expressed in 1/100, at which this font was created.

6.5.1 Loading and Freeing Fonts

Xlib provides functions that you can use to load fonts, get font information, unload fonts, and free font information. A few font functions use a GContext resource ID or a font ID interchangeably.

To load a given font, use XLoadFont.

Font XLoadFont(*display, name*)
    Display *display;
    char *name;
display   Specifies the connection to the X server.
name   Specifies the name of the font, which is a null-terminated string.

The XLoadFont function loads the specified font and returns its associated font ID. The name should be ISO Latin-1 encoding; uppercase and lower-case do not matter. If XLoadFont was unsuccessful at loading the specified font, a BadName error results. Fonts are not associated with a particular screen and can be stored as a component of any GC. When the font is no longer needed, call XUnloadFont.

XLoadFont can generate BadAlloc and BadName errors.

To return information about an available font, use XQueryFont.

XFontStruct *XQueryFont(*display, font_ID*)
    Display *display*;
    XID *font_ID*;
display   Specifies the connection to the X server.
font_ID   Specifies the font ID or the GContext ID.

The XQueryFont function returns a pointer to the XFontStruct structure, which contains information associated with the font. You can query a font or the font stored in a GC. The font ID stored in the XFontStruct structure will be the GContext ID, and you need to be careful when using this ID in other functions (see XGContextFromGC). To free this data, use XFreeFontInfo.

To perform a XLoadFont and XQueryFont in a single operation, use XLoadQueryFont.

XFontStruct *XLoadQueryFont(*display, name*)
    Display *display*;
    char *name*;
display   Specifies the connection to the X server.
name   Specifies the name of the font, which is a null-terminated string.

The XLoadQueryFont function provides the most common way for accessing a font. XLoadQueryFont both opens (loads) the specified font and returns a pointer to the appropriate XFontStruct structure. If the font does not exist, XLoadQueryFont returns NULL.

XLoadQueryFont can generate a BadAlloc error.

To unload the font and free the storage used by the font structure that was allocated by XQueryFont or XLoadQueryFont, use XFreeFont.

XFreeFont(*display, font_struct*)
    Display **display*;
    XFontStruct **font_struct*;
display   Specifies the connection to the X server.
font_struct   Specifies the storage associated with the font.

The XFreeFont function deletes the association between the font resource ID and the specified font and frees the XFontStruct structure. The font itself will be freed when no other resource references it. The data and the font should not be referenced again.
    XFreeFont can generate a BadFont error.

To return a given font property, use XGetFontProperty.

Bool XGetFontProperty(*font_struct, atom, value_return*)
    XFontStruct **font_struct*;
    Atom *atom*;
    unsigned long **value_return*;
font_struct   Specifies the storage associated with the font.
atom   Specifies the atom for the property name you want returned.
value_return   Returns the value of the font property.

Given the atom for that property, the XGetFontProperty function returns the value of the specified font property. XGetFontProperty also returns False if the property was not defined or True if it was defined. A set of predefined atoms exists for font properties, which can be found in <X11/Xatom.h>. This set contains the standard properties associated with a font. Although it is not guaranteed, it is likely that the predefined font properties will be present.

To unload a font that was loaded by XLoadFont, use XUnloadFont.

XUnloadFont(*display, font*)
    Display **display*;
    Font *font*;
display   Specifies the connection to the X server.
font   Specifies the font.

The XUnloadFont function deletes the association between the font re-source ID and the specified font. The font itself will be freed when no other resource references it. The font should not be referenced again.

XUnloadFont can generate a BadFont error.

6.5.2   Obtaining and Freeing Font Names and Information

You obtain font names and information by matching a wildcard specification when querying a font type for a list of available sizes and so on.

To return a list of the available font names, use XListFonts.

```
char **XListFonts(display, pattern, maxnames, actual_count_return)
    Display *display;
    char *pattern;
    int maxnames;
    int *actual_count_return;
```

display	Specifies the connection to the X server.
pattern	Specifies the null-terminated pattern string that can contain wildcard characters.
maxnames	Specifies the maximum number of names to be returned.
actual_count_return	Returns the actual number of font names.

The XListFonts function returns an array of available font names (as con-trolled by the font search path; see XSetFontPath) that match the string you passed to the pattern argument. The string should be ISO Latin-1; uppercase and lowercase do not matter. Each string is terminated by an ASCII null. The pattern string can contain any characters, but each asterisk (*) is a wildcard for any number of characters, and each question mark (?) is a wildcard for a single character. The client should call XFreeFontNames when finished with the result to free the memory.

To free a font name array, use XFreeFontNames.

```
XFreeFontNames(list)
    char *list[];
```

list	Specifies the array of strings you want to free.

The XFreeFontNames function frees the array and strings returned by XListFonts or XListFontsWithInfo.

To obtain the names and information about available fonts, use `XListFontsWithInfo`.

char **XListFontsWithInfo(*display, pattern, maxnames, count_return, info_return*)
    Display *display;
    char *pattern;
    int *maxnames*;
    int *count_return;
    XFontStruct **info_return;

display	Specifies the connection to the X server.
pattern	Specifies the null-terminated pattern string that can contain wildcard characters.
maxnames	Specifies the maximum number of names to be returned.
count_return	Returns the actual number of matched font names.
info_return	Returns a pointer to the font information.

The `XListFontsWithInfo` function returns a list of font names that match the specified pattern and their associated font information. The list of names is limited to size specified by maxnames. The information returned for each font is identical to what `XLoadQueryFont` would return except that the per-character metrics are not returned. The pattern string can contain any characters, but each asterisk (*) is a wildcard for any number of characters, and each question mark (?) is a wildcard for a single character. To free the allocated name array, the client should call `XFreeFontNames`. To free the the font information array, the client should call `XFree-FontInfo`.

To free the font information array, use `XFreeFontInfo`.

XFreeFontInfo(*names, free_info, actual_count*)
    char **names;
    XFontStruct *free_info;
    int *actual_count*;

names	Specifies the list of font names returned by `XListFonts-WithInfo`.
free_info	Specifies the pointer to the font information returned by `XListFontsWithInfo`.
actual_count	Specifies the actual number of matched font names returned by `XListFontsWithInfo`.

6.5.3   Setting and Retrieving the Font Search Path

To set the font search path, use XSetFontPath.

XSetFontPath(*display, directories, ndirs*)
    Display **display*;
    char ***directories*;
    int *ndirs*;
display   Specifies the connection to the X server.
directories   Specifies the directory path used to look for a font. Setting the path to the empty list restores the default path defined for the X server.
ndirs   Specifies the number of directories in the path.

The XSetFontPath function defines the directory search path for font lookup. There is only one search path per X server, not one per client. The interpretation of the strings is operating system dependent, but they are intended to specify directories to be searched in the order listed. Also, the contents of these strings are operating system dependent and are not intended to be used by client applications. Usually, the X server is free to cache font information internally rather than having to read fonts from files. In addition, the X server is guaranteed to flush all cached information about fonts for which there currently are no explicit resource IDs allocated. The meaning of an error from this request is operating system dependent.

XSetFontPath can generate a BadValue error.

To get the current font search path, use XGetFontPath.

char **XGetFontPath(*display, npaths_return*)
    Display **display*;
    int **npaths_return*;
display   Specifies the connection to the X server.
npaths_return   Returns the number of strings in the font path array.

The XGetFontPath function allocates and returns an array of strings containing the search path. When it is no longer needed, the data in the font path should be freed by using XFreeFontPath.

To free data returned by XGetFontPath, use XFreeFontPath.

XFreeFontPath(*list*)
    char ***list*;
list   Specifies the array of strings you want to free.

The `XFreeFontPath` function frees the data allocated by `XGet-FontPath`.

6.5.4 Computing Character String Sizes

Xlib provides functions that you can use to compute the width, the logical extents, and the server information about 8-bit and 2-byte text strings. The width is computed by adding the character widths of all the characters. It does not matter if the font is an 8-bit or 2-byte font. These functions return the sum of the character metrics, in pixels.

To determine the width of an 8-bit character string, use `XTextWidth`.

```
int XTextWidth(font_struct, string, count)
    XFontStruct *font_struct;
    char *string;
    int count;
```

font_struct	Specifies the font used for the width computation.
string	Specifies the character string.
count	Specifies the character count in the specified string.

To determine the width of a 2-byte character string, use `XTextWidth16`.

```
int XTextWidth16(font_struct, string, count)
    XFontStruct *font_struct;
    XChar2b *string;
    int count;
```

font_struct	Specifies the font used for the width computation.
string	Specifies the character string.
count	Specifies the character count in the specified string.

6.5.5 Computing Logical Extents

To compute the bounding box of an 8-bit character string in a given font, use `XTextExtents`.

```
XTextExtents(font_struct, string, nchars, direction_return, font_ascent_return,
              font_descent_return, overall_return)
    XFontStruct *font_struct;
    char *string;
    int nchars;
```

```
        int *direction_return;
        int *font_ascent_return, *font_descent_return;
        XCharStruct *overall_return;
```

font_struct   Specifies a pointer to the XFontStruct structure.

string   Specifies the character string.

nchars   Specifies the number of characters in the character string.

direction_return   Returns the value of the direction hint (FontLeftToRight or FontRightToLeft).

font_ascent_return Returns the font ascent.

font_descent_return Returns the font descent.

overall_return   Returns the overall size in the specified XCharStruct structure.

To compute the bounding box of a 2-byte character string in a given font, use XTextExtents16.

```
XTextExtents16(font_struct, string, nchars, direction_return, font_ascent_return,
                font_descent_return, overall_return)
        XFontStruct *font_struct;
        XChar2b *string;
        int nchars;
        int *direction_return;
        int *font_ascent_return, *font_descent_return;
        XCharStruct *overall_return;
```

font_struct   Specifies a pointer to the XFontStruct structure.

string   Specifies the character string.

nchars   Specifies the number of characters in the character string.

direction_return   Returns the value of the direction hint (FontLeftToRight or FontRightToLeft).

font_ascent_return Returns the font ascent.

font_descent_return Returns the font descent.

overall_return   Returns the overall size in the specified XCharStruct structure.

The XTextExtents and XTextExtents16 functions perform the size computation locally and, thereby, avoid the round-trip overhead of XQuery-TextExtents and XQueryTextExtents16. Both functions return an XCharStruct structure, whose members are set to the values as follows.

The ascent member is set to the maximum of the ascent metrics of all characters in the string. The descent member is set to the maximum of the descent metrics. The width member is set to the sum of the character-width metrics of all characters in the string. For each character in the string, let W be the sum of the character-width metrics of all characters preceding it in the string. Let L be the left-side-bearing metric of the character plus W. Let R be the right-side-bearing metric of the character plus W. The lbearing member is set to the minimum L of all characters in the string. The rbearing member is set to the maximum R.

For fonts defined with linear indexing rather than 2-byte matrix indexing, each XChar2b structure is interpreted as a 16-bit number with byte1 as the most-significant byte. If the font has no defined default character, undefined characters in the string are taken to have all zero metrics.

6.5.6   Querying Character String Sizes

To query the server for the bounding box of an 8-bit character string in a given font, use XQueryTextExtents.

XQueryTextExtents(*display, font_ID, string, nchars, direction_return,*
                            font_ascent_return, font_descent_return, overall_return)
        Display *display;
        XID *font_ID*;
        char *string;
        int *nchars*;
        int *direction_return;
        int **font_ascent_return*, **font_descent_return*;
        XCharStruct *overall_return;

display	Specifies the connection to the X server.
font_ID	Specifies either the font ID or the GContext ID that contains the font.
string	Specifies the character string.
nchars	Specifies the number of characters in the character string.
direction_return	Returns the value of the direction hint (FontLeftToRight or FontRightToLeft).
font_ascent_return	Returns the font ascent.
font_descent_return	Returns the font descent.
overall_return	Returns the overall size in the specified XCharStruct structure.

To query the server for the bounding box of a 2-byte character string in a given font, use XQueryTextExtents16.

XQueryTextExtents16(*display, font_ID, string, nchars, direction_return,*
font_ascent_return, font_descent_return, overall_return)
    Display **display*;
    XID *font_ID*;
    XChar2b **string*;
    int *nchars*;
    int **direction_return*;
    int **font_ascent_return, *font_descent_return*;
    XCharStruct **overall_return*;

display	Specifies the connection to the X server.
font_ID	Specifies either the font ID or the GContext ID that contains the font.
string	Specifies the character string.
nchars	Specifies the number of characters in the character string.
direction_return	Returns the value of the direction hint (FontLeftToRight or FontRightToLeft).
font_ascent_return	Returns the font ascent.
font_descent_return	Returns the font descent.
overall_return	Returns the overall size in the specified XCharStruct structure.

The XQueryTextExtents and XQueryTextExtents16 functions return the bounding box of the specified 8-bit and 16-bit character string in the specified font or the font contained in the specified GC. These functions query the X server and, therefore, suffer the round-trip overhead that is avoided by XTextExtents and XTextExtents16. Both functions return a XCharStruct structure, whose members are set to the values as follows.

The ascent member is set to the maximum of the ascent metrics of all characters in the string. The descent member is set to the maximum of the descent metrics. The width member is set to the sum of the character-width metrics of all characters in the string. For each character in the string, let W be the sum of the character-width metrics of all characters preceding it in the string. Let L be the left-side-bearing metric of the character plus W. Let R be the right-side-bearing metric of the character plus W. The lbearing member is set to the minimum L of all characters in the string. The rbearing member is set to the maximum R.

For fonts defined with linear indexing rather than 2-byte matrix indexing, each XChar2b structure is interpreted as a 16-bit number with byte1 as the most-significant byte. If the font has no defined default character, undefined characters in the string are taken to have all zero metrics.

`XQueryTextExtents` and `XQueryTextExtents16` can generate `Bad-Font` and `BadGC` errors.

6.6   Drawing Text

This section discusses how to draw:

- Complex text
- Text characters
- Image text characters

The fundamental text functions `XDrawText` and `XDrawText16` use the following structures.

```
typedef struct {
     char *chars;      /* pointer to string */
     int nchars;       /* number of characters */
     int delta;        /* delta between strings */
     Font font;        /* Font to print it in, None don't change */
} XTextItem;

typedef struct {
     XChar2b *chars;   /* pointer to two-byte characters */
     int nchars;       /* number of characters */
     int delta;        /* delta between strings */
     Font font;        /* font to print it in, None don't change */
} XTextItem16;
```

If the font member is not `None`, the font is changed before printing and also is stored in the GC. If an error was generated during text drawing, the previous items may have been drawn. The baseline of the characters is drawn starting at the x and y coordinates that you pass in the text drawing functions.

For example, consider the background rectangle drawn by `XDrawImage-String`. If you want the upper-left corner of the background rectangle to be at pixel coordinate (x,y), pass the (x,y + ascent) as the baseline origin coordinates to the text functions. The ascent is the font ascent, as given in the `XFontStruct` structure. If you want the lower-left corner of the background rectangle to be at pixel coordinate (x,y), pass the (x,y − descent + 1) as the baseline origin coordinates to the text functions. The descent is the font descent, as given in the XFontStruct structure.

6.6.1   Drawing Complex Text

To draw 8-bit characters in a given drawable, use XDrawText.

XDrawText(*display, d, gc, x, y, items, nitems*)
>   Display **display*;
>   Drawable *d*;
>   GC *gc*;
>   int *x, y*;
>   XTextItem **items*;
>   int *nitems*;

display	Specifies the connection to the X server.
d	Specifies the drawable.
gc	Specifies the GC.
x	
y	Specify the x and y coordinates, which are relative to the origin of the specified drawable and define the origin of the first character.
items	Specifies a pointer to an array of text items.
nitems	Specifies the number of text items in the array.

To draw 2-byte characters in a given drawable, use XDrawText16.

XDrawText16(*display, d, gc, x, y, items, nitems*)
>   Display **display*;
>   Drawable *d*;
>   GC *gc*;
>   int *x, y*;
>   XTextItem16 **items*;
>   int *nitems*;

display	Specifies the connection to the X server.
d	Specifies the drawable.
gc	Specifies the GC.
x	
y	Specify the x and y coordinates, which are relative to the origin of the specified drawable and define the origin of the first character.
items	Specifies a pointer to an array of text items.
nitems	Specifies the number of text items in the array.

The `XDrawText16` function is similar to `XDrawText` except that it uses 2-byte or 16-bit characters. Both functions allow complex spacing and font shifts between counted strings.

Each text item is processed in turn. A font member other than `None` in an item causes the font to be stored in the GC and used for subsequent text. A text element delta specifies an additional change in the position along the x axis before the string is drawn. The delta is always added to the character origin and is not dependent on any characteristics of the font. Each character image, as defined by the font in the GC, is treated as an additional mask for a fill operation on the drawable. The drawable is modified only where the font character has a bit set to 1. If a text item generates a `BadFont` error, the previous text items may have been drawn.

For fonts defined with linear indexing rather than 2-byte matrix indexing, each `XChar2b` structure is interpreted as a 16-bit number with byte1 as the most-significant byte.

Both functions use these GC components: function, plane-mask, fill-style, font, subwindow-mode, clip-x-origin, clip-y-origin, and clip-mask. They also use these GC mode-dependent components: foreground, background, tile, stipple, tile-stipple-x-origin, and tile-stipple-y-origin.

`XDrawText` and `XDrawText16` can generate `BadDrawable`, `BadFont`, `BadGC`, and `BadMatch` errors.

6.6.2 Drawing Text Characters

To draw 8-bit characters in a given drawable, use `XDrawString`.

XDrawString(*display, d, gc, x, y, string, length*)
    Display **display*;
    Drawable *d*;
    GC *gc*;
    int *x, y*;
    char **string*;
    int *length*;

display	Specifies the connection to the X server.
d	Specifies the drawable.
gc	Specifies the GC.
x	
y	Specify the x and y coordinates, which are relative to the origin of the specified drawable and define the origin of the first character.

string   Specifies the character string.

length   Specifies the number of characters in the string argument.

To draw 2-byte characters in a given drawable, use `XDrawString16`.

XDrawString16(*display, d, gc, x, y, string, length*)
    Display **display*;
    Drawable *d*;
    GC *gc*;
    int *x, y*;
    XChar2b **string*;
    int *length*;

display   Specifies the connection to the X server.

d   Specifies the drawable.

gc   Specifies the GC.

x

y   Specify the x and y coordinates, which are relative to the origin of the specified drawable and define the origin of the first character.

string   Specifies the character string.

length   Specifies the number of characters in the string argument.

Each character image, as defined by the font in the GC, is treated as an additional mask for a fill operation on the drawable. The drawable is modified only where the font character has a bit set to 1. For fonts defined with 2-byte matrix indexing and used with `XDrawString16`, each byte is used as a byte2 with a byte1 of zero.

Both functions use these GC components: function, plane-mask, fill-style, font, subwindow-mode, clip-x-origin, clip-y-origin, and clip-mask. They also use these GC mode-dependent components: foreground, background, tile, stipple, tile-stipple-x-origin, and tile-stipple-y-origin.

`XDrawString` and `XDrawString16` can generate `BadDrawable`, `BadGC`, and `BadMatch` errors.

6.6.3   Drawing Image Text Characters

Some applications, in particular terminal emulators, need to print image text in which both the foreground and background bits of each character are painted. This prevents annoying flicker on many displays.

To draw 8-bit image text characters in a given drawable, use `XDraw-ImageString`.

XDrawImageString(*display, d, gc, x, y, string, length*)
    Display **display*;
    Drawable *d*;
    GC *gc*;
    int *x, y*;
    char **string*;
    int *length*;

display	Specifies the connection to the X server.
d	Specifies the drawable.
gc	Specifies the GC.
x	
y	Specify the x and y coordinates, which are relative to the origin of the specified drawable and define the origin of the first character.
string	Specifies the character string.
length	Specifies the number of characters in the string argument.

To draw 2-byte image text characters in a given drawable, use `XDraw-ImageString16`.

XDrawImageString16(*display, d, gc, x, y, string, length*)
    Display **display*;
    Drawable *d*;
    GC *gc*;
    int *x, y*;
    XChar2b **string*;
    int *length*;

display	Specifies the connection to the X server.
d	Specifies the drawable.
gc	Specifies the GC.
x	
y	Specify the x and y coordinates, which are relative to the origin of the specified drawable and define the origin of the first character.
string	Specifies the character string.
length	Specifies the number of characters in the string argument.

The `XDrawImageString16` function is similar to `XDrawImageString` except that it uses 2-byte or 16-bit characters. Both functions also use both the foreground and background pixels of the GC in the destination.

The effect is first to fill a destination rectangle with the background pixel defined in the GC and then to paint the text with the foreground pixel. The upper-left corner of the filled rectangle is at:

$$[x, y - \text{font-ascent}]$$

The width is:

$$\text{overall-width}$$

The height is:

$$\text{font-ascent} + \text{font-descent}$$

The overall-width, font-ascent, and font-descent are as would be returned by XQueryTextExtents using gc and string. The function and fill-style defined in the GC are ignored for these functions. The effective function is GXcopy, and the effective fill-style is FillSolid.

For fonts defined with 2-byte matrix indexing and used with XDraw-ImageString, each byte is used as a byte2 with a byte1 of zero.

Both functions use these GC components: plane-mask, foreground, background, font, subwindow-mode, clip-x-origin, clip-y-origin, and clip-mask.

XDrawImageString and XDrawImageString16 can generate Bad-Drawable, BadGC, and BadMatch errors.

6.7   Transferring Images between Client and Server

Xlib provides functions that you can use to transfer images between a client and the server. Because the server may require diverse data formats, Xlib provides an image object that fully describes the data in memory and that provides for basic operations on that data. You should reference the data through the image object rather than referencing the data directly. However, some implementations of the Xlib library may efficiently deal with frequently used data formats by replacing functions in the procedure vector with special case functions. Supported operations include destroying the image, getting a pixel, storing a pixel, extracting a subimage of an image, and adding a constant to an image (see chapter 10).

All the image manipulation functions discussed in this section make use of the XImage data structure, which describes an image as it exists in the client's memory.

```
typedef struct _XImage {
    int width, height;              /* size of image */
    int xoffset;                    /* number of pixels offset in X direction */
    int format;                     /* XYBitmap, XYPixmap, ZPixmap *
    char *data;                     /* pointer to image data */
    int byte_order;                 /* data byte order, LSBFirst, MSBFirst */
    int bitmap_unit;                /* quant, of scanline 8,16, 32 */
    int bitmap_bit_order;           /* LSBFirst, MSBFirst */
    int bitmap_pad;                 /* 8, 16, 32 either XYPixmap or ZPixmap */
    int depth;                      /* depth of image */
    int bytes_per_line;             /* accelerator to next scanline */
    int bits_per_pixel;             /* bits per pixel (ZPixmap) */
    unsigned long red_mask;         /* bits in z arrangement */
    unsigned long green_mask;
    unsigned long blue_mask;
    char *obdata;                   /* hook for the object routines to hang on */
    struct funcs {                  /* image manipulation routines */
        struct _XImage *(*create_image)();
        int (*destroy_image)();
        unsigned long (*get_pixel)();
        int (*put_pixel)();
        struct _XImage *(*sub_image)();
        int (*add_pixel)();
    } f;
} XImage;
```

You may request that some of the members (for example, height, width, and xoffset) be changed when the image is sent to the server. That is, you may send a subset of the image. Other members (for example, byte_order, bitmap_unit, and so forth) are characteristics of both the image and the server. If these members differ between the image and the server, XPutImage makes the appropriate conversions. The first byte of the first scanline of plane n is located at the address

$$(data + (n * height * bytes\_per\_line)).$$

To combine an image in memory with a rectangle of a drawable on the display use XPutImage.

XPutImage(*display, d, gc, image, src_x, src_y, dest_x, dest_y, width, height*)
    Display **display*;
    Drawable *d*;

GC *gc*;

XImage *image*;

int *src_x, src_y*;

int *dest_x, dest_y*;

unsigned int *width, height*;

display	Specifies the connection to the X server.
d	Specifies the drawable.
gc	Specifies the GC.
image	Specifies the image you want combined with the rectangle.
src_x	Specifies the offset in X from the left edge of the image defined by the `XImage` data structure.
src_y	Specifies the offset in Y from the top edge of the image defined by the `XImage` data structure.
dest_x	
dest_y	Specify the x and y coordinates, which are relative to the origin of the drawable and are the coordinates of the subimage.
width	
height	Specify the width and height of the subimage, which define the dimensions of the rectangle.

The `XPutImage` function combines an image in memory with a rectangle of the specified drawable. If `XYBitmap` format is used, the depth must be one, or a `BadMatch` error results. The foreground pixel in the GC defines the source for the one bits in the image, and the background pixel defines the source for the zero bits. For `XYPixmap` and `ZPixmap`, the depth must match the depth of the drawable, or a `BadMatch` error results. The section of the image defined by the src_x, src_y, width, and height arguments is drawn on the specified part of the drawable.

This function uses these GC components: function, plane-mask, subwindow-mode, clip-x-origin, clip-y-origin, and clip-mask. It also uses these GC mode-dependent components: foreground and background.

`XPutImage` can generate `BadDrawable`, `BadGC`, `BadMatch`, and `BadValue` errors.

To return the contents of a rectangle in a given drawable on the display, use `XGetImage`. This function specifically supports rudimentary screen dumps.

XImage *XGetImage(*display, d, x, y, width, height, plane_mask, format*)
    Display **display*;
    Drawable *d*;
    int *x, y*;
    unsigned int *width, height*;
    long *plane_mask*;
    int *format*;

display	Specifies the connection to the X server.
d	Specifies the drawable.
x	
y	Specify the x and y coordinates, which are relative to the origin of the drawable and define the upper-left corner of the rectangle.
width	
height	Specify the width and height of the subimage, which define the dimensions of the rectangle.
plane_mask	Specifies the plane mask.
format	Specifies the format for the image. You can pass `XYPixmap` or `ZPixmap`.

The `XGetImage` function returns a pointer to an `XImage` structure. This structure provides you with the contents of the specified rectangle of the drawable in the format you specify. If the format argument is `XYPixmap`, the image contains only the bit planes you passed to the plane_mask argument. If the plane_mask argument only requests a subset of the planes of the display, the depth of the returned image will be the number of planes requested. If the format argument is `ZPixmap`, `XGetImage` returns as zero the bits in all planes not specified in the plane_mask argument. The function performs no range checking on the values in plane_mask and ignores extraneous bits.

`XGetImage` returns the depth of the image to the depth member of the `XImage` structure. The depth of the image is as specified when the drawable was created, except when getting a subset of the planes in `XYPixmap` format, when the depth is given by the number of bits set to 1 in plane_mask.

If the drawable is a pixmap, the given rectangle must be wholly contained within the pixmap, or a `BadMatch` error results. If the drawable is a window, the window must be viewable, and it must be the case that if there were no inferiors or overlapping windows, the specified rectangle of the window would be fully visible on the screen and wholly contained within the outside edges of the window, or a `BadMatch` error results. Note that the borders of the window can be included and read with this request. If the window has backing-store, the backing-store contents are returned for regions of the window that are obscured by noninferior windows. If the window does not have backing-store, the returned contents of such obscured regions are undefined. The returned contents of visible regions of inferiors of a different depth than the specified window's depth are also undefined. The pointer cursor image is not included in the returned contents.

`XGetImage` can generate `BadDrawable`, `BadMatch`, and `BadValue` errors.

To copy the contents of a rectangle on the display to a location within a preexisting image structure, use `XGetSubImage`.

XImage *XGetSubImage(*display, d, x, y, width, height, plane_mask, format, dest_image, dest_x, dest_y*)

Display *_display_;
Drawable _d_;
int _x, y_;
unsigned int _width, height_;
unsigned long _plane_mask_;
int _format_;
XImage *_dest_image_;
int _dest_x, dest_y_;

display	Specifies the connection to the X server.
_d_	Specifies the drawable.
_x_	
_y_	Specify the x and y coordinates, which are relative to the origin of the drawable and define the upper-left corner of the rectangle.
width	
height	Specify the width and height of the subimage, which define the dimensions of the rectangle.
_plane_mask_	Specifies the plane mask.
format	Specifies the format for the image. You can pass `XYPixmap` or `ZPixmap`.
_dest_image_	Specifies the destination image.
_dest_x_	
_dest_y_	Specify the x and y coordinates, which are relative to the origin of the destination rectangle, specify its upper-left corner, and determine where the subimage is placed in the destination image.

The XGetSubImage function updates dest_image structure with the specified subimage in the same manner as XGetImage. If the format argument is XYPixmap, the image contains only the bit planes you passed to the plane_mask argument. If the format argument is ZPixmap, XGetSubImage returns as zero the bits in all planes not specified in the plane_mask argument. The function performs no range checking on the values in plane_mask and ignores extraneous bits. As a convenience, XGetSubImage returns a pointer to the same XImage structure specified by dest_image.

The depth of the destination XImage structure must be the same as that of the drawable. If the specified subimage does not fit at the specified location on the destination image, the right and bottom edges are clipped. If the drawable is a pixmap, the given rectangle must be wholly contained within the pixmap, or a BadMatch error results. If the drawable is a window, the window must be viewable, and it must be the case that if there were no inferiors or overlapping windows, the specified rectangle of the window would be fully visible on the screen and wholly contained within the outside edges of the window, or a BadMatch error results. If the window has backing-store, then the backing-store contents are returned for regions of the window that are obscured by noninferior windows. If the window does not have backing-store, the returned contents of such obscured regions are undefined. The returned contents of visible regions of inferiors of a different depth than the specified window's depth are also undefined.

XGetSubImage can generate BadDrawable, BadGC, BadMatch, and BadValue errors.

6.8   Cursors

This section discusses how to:

- Create a cursor
- Change or destroy a cursor
- Define the cursor for a window

Each window can have a different cursor defined for it. Whenever the pointer is in a visible window, it is set to the cursor defined for that window. If no cursor was defined for that window, the cursor is the one defined for the parent window.

From X's perspective, a cursor consists of a cursor source, mask, colors, and a hotspot. The mask pixmap determines the shape of the cursor and must be a depth of one. The source pixmap must have a depth of one, and the colors determine the colors of the source. The hotspot defines the point on the cursor that is reported when a pointer event occurs. There may be limitations imposed by the hardware on cursors as to size and whether a mask is implemented. XQueryBestCursor can be used to find out what sizes are possible. It is intended that most standard cursors will be stored as a special font.

6.8.1   Creating a Cursor

Xlib provides functions that you can use to create a font, bitmap, or glyph cursor.

To create a cursor from a standard font, use XCreateFontCursor.

```
#include <X11/cursorfont.h>
Cursor XCreateFontCursor(display, shape)
      Display *display;
      unsigned int shape;
```
display   Specifies the connection to the X server.
shape   Specifies the shape of the cursor.

X provides a set of standard cursor shapes in a special font named cursor. Applications are encouraged to use this interface for their cursors because the font can be customized for the individual display type. The shape argument specifies which glyph of the standard fonts to use.

The hotspot comes from the information stored in the cursor font. The initial colors of a cursor are a black foreground and a white background (see XRecolorCursor). For further information about cursor shapes, see appendix B.

XCreateFontCursor can generate BadAlloc and BadValue errors.

To create a cursor from two bitmaps, use XCreatePixmapCursor.

```
Cursor XCreatePixmapCursor(display, source, mask, foreground_color,
                           background_color, x, y)
      Display *display;
      Pixmap source;
```

> Pixmap *mask*;
> XColor **foreground_color*;
> XColor **background_color*;
> unsigned int *x, y*;

display	Specifies the connection to the X server.
source	Specifies the shape of the source cursor.
mask	Specifies the cursor's source bits to be displayed or None.
foreground_color	Specifies the RGB values for the foreground of the source.
background_color	Specifies the RGB values for the background of the source.
x	
y	Specify the x and y coordinates, which indicate the hotspot relative to the source's origin.

The XCreatePixmapCursor function creates a cursor and returns the cursor ID associated with it. The foreground and background RGB values must be specified using foreground_color and background_color, even if the X server only has a StaticGray or GrayScale screen. The foreground color is used for the pixels set to 1 in the source, and the background color is used for the pixels set to 0. Both source and mask, if specified, must have depth one (or a BadMatch error results) but can have any root. The mask argument defines the shape of the cursor. The pixels set to 1 in the mask define which source pixels are displayed, and the pixels set to 0 define which pixels are ignored. If no mask is given, all pixels of the source are displayed. The mask, if present, must be the same size as the pixmap defined by the source argument, or a BadMatch error results. The hotspot must be a point within the source, or a BadMatch error results.

The components of the cursor can be transformed arbitrarily to meet display limitations. The pixmaps can be freed immediately if no further explicit references to them are to be made. Subsequent drawing in the source or mask pixmap has an undefined effect on the cursor. The X server might or might not make a copy of the pixmap.

XCreatePixmapCursor can generate BadAlloc and BadPixmap errors.

To create a cursor from font glyphs, use XCreateGlyphCursor.

Cursor XCreateGlyphCursor(*display, source_font, mask_font, source_char, mask_char,*
                                              foreground_color, background_color)

> Display **display*;
> Font *source_font, mask_font*;

```
        unsigned int source_char, mask_char;
        XColor *foreground_color;
        XColor *background_color;
```

display	Specifies the connection to the X server.
source_font	Specifies the font for the source glyph.
mask_font	Specifies the font for the mask glyph or `None`.
source_char	Specifies the character glyph for the source.
mask_char	Specifies the glyph character for the mask.
foreground_color	Specifies the RGB values for the foreground of the source.
background_color	Specifies the RGB values for the background of the source.

The `XCreateGlyphCursor` function is similar to `XCreatePixmap-Cursor` except that the source and mask bitmaps are obtained from the specified font glyphs. The source_char must be a defined glyph in source_font, or a `BadValue` error results. If mask_font is given, mask_char must be a defined glyph in mask_font, or a `BadValue` error results. The mask_font and character are optional. The origins of the source_char and mask_char (if defined) glyphs are positioned coincidently and define the hotspot. The source_char and mask_char need not have the same bounding box metrics, and there is no restriction on the placement of the hotspot relative to the bounding boxes. If no mask_char is given, all pixels of the source are displayed. You can free the fonts immediately by calling `XFreeFont` if no further explicit references to them are to be made.

For 2-byte matrix fonts, the 16-bit value should be formed with the byte1 member in the most-significant byte and the byte2 member in the least-significant byte.

`XCreateGlyphCursor` can generate `BadAlloc`, `BadFont`, and `Bad-Value` errors.

6.8.2   Changing and Destroying Cursors

Xlib provides functions that you can use to change the cursor color, destroy the cursor, and determine the best cursor size.

To change the color of a given cursor, use `XRecolorCursor`.

```
XRecolorCursor(display, cursor, foreground_color, background_color)
    Display *display;
    Cursor cursor;
    XColor *foreground_color, *background_color;
```

display	Specifies the connection to the X server.
cursor	Specifies the cursor.
foreground_color	Specifies the RGB values for the foreground of the source.
background_color	Specifies the RGB values for the background of the source.

The `XRecolorCursor` function changes the color of the specified cursor, and if the cursor is being displayed on a screen, the change is visible immediately.

`XRecolorCursor` can generate a `BadCursor` error.

To free (destroy) a given cursor, use `XFreeCursor`.

XFreeCursor(*display*, *cursor*)
    Display **display*;
    Cursor *cursor*;

display	Specifies the connection to the X server.
cursor	Specifies the cursor.

The `XFreeCursor` function deletes the association between the cursor resource ID and the specified cursor. The cursor storage is freed when no other resource references it. The specified cursor ID should not be referred to again.

`XFreeCursor` can generate a `BadCursor` error.

To determine useful cursor sizes, use `XQueryBestCursor`.

Status XQueryBestCursor(*display, d, width, height, width_return, height_return*)
    Display **display*;
    Drawable *d*;
    unsigned int *width, height*;
    unsigned int **width_return, *height_return*;

display	Specifies the connection to the X server.
d	Specifies the drawable, which indicates the screen.
width	
height	Specify the width and height of the cursor that you want the size information for.
width_return	
height_return	Return the best width and height that is closest to the specified width and height.

Some displays allow larger cursors than other displays. The XQuery-BestCursor function provides a way to find out what size cursors are actually possible on the display. It returns the largest size that can be displayed. Applications should be prepared to use smaller cursors on displays that cannot support large ones.

XQueryBestCursor can generate a BadDrawable error.

6.8.3   Defining the Cursor

Xlib provides functions that you can use to define or undefine the cursor that should be displayed in a window.

To define which cursor will be used in a window, use XDefineCursor.

XDefineCursor(*display, w, cursor*)
    Display **display*;
    Window *w*;
    Cursor *cursor*;
display   Specifies the connection to the X server.
w   Specifies the window.
cursor   Specifies the cursor that is to be displayed or None.

If a cursor is set, it will be used when the pointer is in the window. If the cursor is None, it is equivalent to XUndefineCursor.

XDefineCursor can generate BadCursor and BadWindow errors.

To undefine the cursor in a given window, use XUndefineCursor.

XUndefineCursor(*display, w*)
    Display **display*;
    Window *w*;
display   Specifies the connection to the X server.
w   Specifies the window.

The XUndefineCursor undoes the effect of a previous XDefineCursor for this window. When the pointer is in the window, the parent's cursor will now be used. On the root window, the default cursor is restored.

XUndefineCursor can generate a BadWindow error.

Chapter 7

Window Manager Functions

Although it is difficult to categorize functions as application only or window manager only, the functions in this chapter are most often used by window managers. It is not expected that these functions will be used by most application programs. You can use the Xlib window manager functions to:

- Change the parent of a window
- Control the lifetime of a window
- Determine resident colormaps
- Grab the pointer
- Grab the keyboard
- Grab the server
- Control event processing
- Manipulate the keyboard and pointer settings
- Control the screen saver
- Control host access

7.1 Changing the Parent of a Window

To change a window's parent to another window on the same screen, use `XReparentWindow`.

XReparentWindow(*display, w, parent, x, y*)
    Display **display*;
    Window *w*;

Window *parent*;
int *x, y*;

display   Specifies the connection to the X server.
w   Specifies the window.
parent   Specifies the parent window.
x
y   Specify the x and y coordinates of the position in the new parent window.

If the specified window is mapped, `XReparentWindow` automatically performs an `UnmapWindow` request on it, removes it from its current position in the hierarchy, and inserts it as the child of the specified parent. The window is placed in the stacking order on top with respect to sibling windows.

After reparenting the specified window, `XReparentWindow` causes the X server to generate a `ReparentNotify` event. The override_redirect member returned in this event is set to the window's corresponding attribute. Window manager clients usually should ignore this window if this member is set to `True`. Finally, if the specified window was originally mapped, the X server automatically performs a `MapWindow` request on it.

The X server performs normal exposure processing on formerly obscured windows. The X server might not generate `Expose` events for regions from the initial `UnmapWindow` request that are immediately obscured by the final `MapWindow` request. A `BadMatch` error results if:

• The new parent window is not on the same screen as the old parent window.

• The new parent window is the specified window or an inferior of the specified window.

• The specified window has a `ParentRelative` background, and the new parent window is not the same depth as the specified window.

`XReparentWindow` can generate `BadMatch` and `BadWindow` errors.

7.2   Controlling the Lifetime of a Window

The save-set of a client is a list of other clients' windows that, if they are inferiors of one of the client's windows at connection close, should not be destroyed and should be remapped if they are unmapped. For further information about close-connection processing, see section 2.6. To allow an application's window to survive when a window manager that has reparented a window fails, Xlib provides the save-set functions that you can use to control the longevity of subwindows that are normally destroyed when the parent is destroyed. For example, a window manager that wants to add decoration to a window by adding a frame might reparent an application's window. When the frame is destroyed, the application's window should not be destroyed but be returned to its previous place in the window hierarchy.

The X server automatically removes windows from the save-set when they are destroyed.

To add or remove a window from the client's save-set, use `XChange-SaveSet`.

XChangeSaveSet(*display, w, change_mode*)
    Display **display*;
    Window *w*;
    int *change_mode*;

display	Specifies the connection to the X server.
w	Specifies the window that you want to add to or delete from the client's save-set.
change_mode	Specifies the mode. You can pass `SetModeInsert` or `SetModeDelete`.

Depending on the specified mode, `XChangeSaveSet` either inserts or deletes the specified window from the client's save-set. The specified window must have been created by some other client, or a `BadMatch` error results.

`XChangeSaveSet` can generate `BadMatch`, `BadValue`, and `BadWindow` errors.

To add a window to the client's save-set, use `XAddToSaveSet`.

XAddToSaveSet(*display, w*)
    Display **display*;
    Window *w*;

display	Specifies the connection to the X server.
w	Specifies the window that you want to add to the client's save-set.

The `XAddToSaveSet` function adds the specified window to the client's save-set. The specified window must have been created by some other client, or a `BadMatch` error results.

`XAddToSaveSet` can generate `BadMatch` and `BadWindow` errors.

To remove a window from the client's save-set, use XRemove-
FromSaveSet.

XRemoveFromSaveSet(*display, w*)
    Display **display*;
    Window *w*;
display   Specifies the connection to the X server.
w   Specifies the window that you want to delete from the client's save-set.

The XRemoveFromSaveSet function removes the specified window from
the client's save-set. The specified window must have been created by some
other client, or a BadMatch error results.

   XRemoveFromSaveSet can generate BadMatch and BadWindow
errors.

7.3   Determining Resident Colormaps

Xlib provides functions that you can use to install a colormap, uninstall a
colormap, and obtain a list of installed colormaps.

   At any time, there is a subset of the installed maps that is viewed as an ordered list and is called the required list. The length of the required list is at
most M, where M is the minimum number of installed colormaps specified
for the screen in the connection setup. The required list is maintained as follows. When a colormap is specified to XInstallColormap, it is added to
the head of the list; the list is truncated at the tail, if necessary, to keep its
length to at most M. When a colormap is specified to XUninstall-
Colormap and it is in the required list, it is removed from the list. A
colormap is not added to the required list when it is implicitly installed by the
X server, and the X server cannot implicitly uninstall a colormap that is in
the required list.

   To install a colormap, use XInstallColormap.

XInstallColormap(*display, colormap*)
    Display **display*;
    Colormap *colormap*;
display   Specifies the connection to the X server.
colormap Specifies the colormap.

The XInstallColormap function installs the specified colormap for its associated screen. All windows associated with this colormap immediately display with true colors. You associated the windows with this colormap when you created them by calling XCreateWindow, XCreateSimpleWindow, XChangeWindowAttributes, or XSetWindowColormap.

If the specified colormap is not already an installed colormap, the X server generates a ColormapNotify event on each window that has that colormap. In addition, for every other colormap that is installed as a result of a call to XInstallColormap, the X server generates a Colormap-Notify event on each window that has that colormap.

XInstallColormap can generate a BadColor error.

To uninstall a colormap, use XUninstallColormap.

XUninstallColormap(*display, colormap*)
    Display **display*;
    Colormap *colormap*;
display   Specifies the connection to the X server.
colormap   Specifies the colormap.

The XUninstallColormap function removes the specified colormap from the required list for its screen. As a result, the specified colormap might be uninstalled, and the X server might implicitly install or uninstall additional colormaps. Which colormaps get installed or uninstalled is server-dependent except that the required list must remain installed.

If the specified colormap becomes uninstalled, the X server generates a ColormapNotify event on each window that has that colormap. In addition, for every other colormap that is installed or uninstalled as a result of a call to XUninstallColormap, the X server generates a Colormap-Notify event on each window that has that colormap.

XUninstallColormap can generate a BadColor error.

To obtain a list of the currently installed colormaps for a given screen, use XListInstalledColormaps.

Colormap *XListInstalledColormaps(*display, w, num_return*)
    Display **display*;
    Window *w*;
    int **num_return*;

display   Specifies the connection to the X server.
w   Specifies the window that determines the screen.
num_return   Returns the number of currently installed colormaps.

The `XListInstalledColormaps` function returns a list of the currently installed colormaps for the screen of the specified window. The order of the colormaps in the list is not significant and is no explicit indication of the required list. When the allocated list is no longer needed, free it by using `XFree`.

   `XListInstalledColormaps` can generate a `BadWindow` error.

7.4   Pointer Grabbing

Xlib provides functions that you can use to control input from the pointer, which usually is a mouse. Window managers most often use these facilities to implement certain styles of user interfaces. Some toolkits also need to use these facilities for special purposes.

   Usually, as soon as keyboard and mouse events occur, the X server delivers them to the appropriate client, which is determined by the window and input focus. The X server provides sufficient control over event delivery to allow window managers to support mouse ahead and various other styles of user interface. Many of these user interfaces depend upon synchronous delivery of events. The delivery of pointer and keyboard events can be controlled independently.

   When mouse buttons or keyboard keys are grabbed, events will be sent to the grabbing client rather than the normal client who would have received the event. If the keyboard or pointer is in asynchronous mode, further mouse and keyboard events will continue to be processed. If the keyboard or pointer is in synchronous mode, no further events are processed until the grabbing client allows them (see `XAllowEvents`). The keyboard or pointer is considered frozen during this interval. The event that triggered the grab can also be replayed.

   Note that the logical state of a device (as seen by client applications) may lag the physical state if device event processing is frozen.

   There are two kinds of grabs: active and passive. An active grab occurs when a single client grabs the keyboard and/or pointer explicitly (see `XGrabPointer` and `XGrabKeyboard`). A passive grab occurs when clients grab a particular keyboard key or pointer button in a window, and the grab will activate when the key or button is actually pressed. Passive grabs are convenient for implementing reliable pop-up menus. For example, you can guarantee that the pop-up is mapped before the up pointer button event occurs by grabbing a button requesting synchronous behavior. The down event will trigger the grab and freeze further processing of pointer events until you have the chance to map the pop-up window. You can then allow further event processing. The up event will then be correctly processed relative to the pop-up window.

For many operations, there are functions that take a time argument. The X server includes a timestamp in various events. One special time, called `CurrentTime`, represents the current server time. The X server maintains the time when the input focus was last changed, when the keyboard was last grabbed, when the pointer was last grabbed, or when a selection was last changed. Your application may be slow reacting to an event. You often need some way to specify that your request should not occur if another application has in the meanwhile taken control of the keyboard, pointer, or selection. By providing the timestamp from the event in the request, you can arrange that the operation not take effect if someone else has performed an operation in the meanwhile.

A timestamp is a time value, expressed in milliseconds. It typically is the time since the last server reset. Timestamp values wrap around (after about 49.7 days). The server, given its current time is represented by timestamp T, always interprets timestamps from clients by treating half of the timestamp space as being later in time than T. One timestamp value, named `CurrentTime`, is never generated by the server. This value is reserved for use in requests to represent the current server time.

For many functions in this section, you pass pointer event mask bits. The valid pointer event mask bits are: `ButtonPressMask`, `ButtonRelease-Mask`, `EnterWindowMask`, `LeaveWindowMask`, `PointerMotion-Mask`, `PointerMotionHintMask`, `Button1MotionMask`, `Button2-MotionMask`, `Button3MotionMask`, `Button4MotionMask`, `Button5-MotionMask`, `ButtonMotionMask`, and `KeyMapStateMask`. For other functions in this section, you pass keymask bits. The valid keymask bits are: `ShiftMask`, `LockMask`, `ControlMask`, `Mod1Mask`, `Mod2Mask`, `Mod3Mask`, `Mod4Mask`, and `Mod5Mask`.

To grab the pointer, use `XGrabPointer`.

```
int XGrabPointer(display, grab_window, owner_events, event_mask, pointer_mode,
                 keyboard_mode, confine_to, cursor, time)
    Display *display;
    Window grab_window;
    Bool owner_events;
    unsigned int event_mask;
    int pointer_mode, keyboard_mode;
    Window confine_to;
    Cursor cursor;
    Time time;
```

display	Specifies the connection to the X server.
grab_window	Specifies the grab window.
owner_events	Specifies a Boolean value that indicates whether the pointer events are to be reported as usual or reported with respect to the grab window if selected by the event mask.
event_mask	Specifies which pointer events are reported to the client. The mask is the bitwise inclusive OR of the valid pointer event mask bits.
pointer_mode	Specifies further processing of pointer events. You can pass `GrabModeSync` or `GrabModeAsync`.
keyboard_mode	Specifies further processing of keyboard events. You can pass `GrabModeSync` or `GrabModeAsync`.
confine_to	Specifies the window to confine the pointer in or `None`.
cursor	Specifies the cursor that is to be displayed during the grab or `None`.
time	Specifies the time. You can pass either a timestamp or `CurrentTime`.

The `XGrabPointer` function actively grabs control of the pointer and returns `GrabSuccess` if the grab was successful. Further pointer events are reported only to the grabbing client. `XGrabPointer` overrides any active pointer grab by this client. If owner_events is `False`, all generated pointer events are reported with respect to grab_window and are reported only if selected by event_mask. If owner_events is `True` and if a generated pointer event would normally be reported to this client, it is reported as usual. Otherwise, the event is reported with respect to the grab_window and is reported only if selected by event_mask. For either value of owner_events, unreported events are discarded.

If the pointer_mode is `GrabModeAsync`, pointer event processing continues as usual. If the pointer is currently frozen by this client, the processing of events for the pointer is resumed. If the pointer_mode is

GrabModeSync, the state of the pointer, as seen by client applications, appears to freeze, and the X server generates no further pointer events until the grabbing client calls XAllowEvents or until the pointer grab is released. Actual pointer changes are not lost while the pointer is frozen; they are simply queued in the server for later processing.

If the keyboard_mode is GrabModeAsync, keyboard event processing is unaffected by activation of the grab. If the keyboard_mode is GrabModeSync, the state of the keyboard, as seen by client applications, appears to freeze, and the X server generates no further keyboard events until the grabbing client calls XAllowEvents or until the pointer grab is released. Actual keyboard changes are not lost while the pointer is frozen; they are simply queued in the server for later processing.

If a cursor is specified, it is displayed regardless of what window the pointer is in. If None is specified, the normal cursor for that window is displayed when the pointer is in grab_window or one of its subwindows; otherwise, the cursor for grab_window is displayed.

If a confine_to window is specified, the pointer is restricted to stay contained in that window. The confine_to window need have no relationship to the grab_window. If the pointer is not initially in the confine_to window, it is warped automatically to the closest edge just before the grab activates and enter/leave events are generated as usual. If the confine_to window is subsequently reconfigured, the pointer is warped automatically, as necessary, to keep it contained in the window.

The time argument allows you to avoid certain circumstances that come up if applications take a long time to respond or if there are long network delays. Consider a situation where you have two applications, both of which normally grab the pointer when clicked on. If both applications specify the timestamp from the event, the second application may wake up faster and successfully grab the pointer before the first application. The first application then will get an indication that the other application grabbed the pointer before its request was processed.

XGrabPointer generates EnterNotify and LeaveNotify events.

Either if grab_window or confine_to window is not viewable or if the confine_to window lies completely outside the boundaries of the root window, XGrabPointer fails and returns GrabNotViewable. If the pointer is actively grabbed by some other client, it fails and returns AlreadyGrabbed. If the pointer is frozen by an active grab of another client, it fails and returns GrabFrozen. If the specified time is earlier than the last-pointer-grab time or later than the current X server time, it fails and returns GrabInvalidTime. Otherwise, the last-pointer-grab time is set to the specified time (CurrentTime is replaced by the current X server time).

XGrabPointer can generate BadCursor, BadValue, and BadWindow errors.

To ungrab the pointer, use XUngrabPointer.

XUngrabPointer(*display, time*)
    Display **display*;
    Time *time*;
display   Specifies the connection to the X server.
time   Specifies the time. You can pass either a timestamp or CurrentTime.

The XUngrabPointer function releases the pointer and any queued events if this client has actively grabbed the pointer from XGrabPointer, XGrabButton, or from a normal button press. XUngrabPointer does not release the pointer if the specified time is earlier than the last-pointer-grab time or is later than the current X server time. It also generates EnterNotify and LeaveNotify events. The X server performs an UngrabPointer request automatically if the event window or confine_to window for an active pointer grab becomes not viewable or if window reconfiguration causes the confine_to window to lie completely outside the boundaries of the root window.

To change an active pointer grab, use XChangeActivePointerGrab.

XChangeActivePointerGrab(*display, event_mask, cursor, time*)
    Display **display*;
    unsigned int *event_mask*;
    Cursor *cursor*;
    Time *time*;
display   Specifies the connection to the X server.
event_mask   Specifies which pointer events are reported to the client. The mask is the bitwise inclusive OR of the valid pointer event mask bits.
cursor   Specifies the cursor that is to be displayed or None.
time   Specifies the time. You can pass either a timestamp or CurrentTime.

The XChangeActivePointerGrab function changes the specified dynamic parameters if the pointer is actively grabbed by the client and if the specified time is no earlier than the last-pointer-grab time and no later than the current X server time. This function has no effect on the passive parameters of a XGrabButton. The interpretation of event_mask and cursor is the same as described in XGrabPointer.

XChangeActivePointerGrab can generate BadCursor and Bad-Value errors.

To grab a pointer button, use XGrabButton.

XGrabButton(*display, button, modifiers, grab_window, owner_events, event_mask,*
            pointer_mode, keyboard_mode, confine_to, cursor)
    Display **display*;
    unsigned int *button*;
    unsigned int *modifiers*;
    Window *grab_window*;
    Bool *owner_events*;
    unsigned int *event_mask*;
    int *pointer_mode, keyboard_mode*;
    Window *confine_to*;
    Cursor *cursor*;

display	Specifies the connection to the X server.
button	Specifies the pointer button that is to be grabbed or AnyButton.
modifiers	Specifies the set of keymasks or AnyModifier. The mask is the bitwise inclusive OR of the valid keymask bits.
grab_window	Specifies the grab window.
owner_events	Specifies a Boolean value that indicates whether the pointer events are to be reported as usual or reported with respect to the grab window if selected by the event mask.
event_mask	Specifies which pointer events are reported to the client. The mask is the bitwise inclusive OR of the valid pointer event mask bits.
pointer_mode	Specifies further processing of pointer events. You can pass GrabModeSync or GrabModeAsync.
keyboard_mode	Specifies further processing of keyboard events. You can pass GrabModeSync or GrabModeAsync.
confine_to	Specifies the window to confine the pointer in or None.
cursor	Specifies the cursor that is to be displayed or None.

The XGrabButton function establishes a passive grab. In the future, the pointer is actively grabbed (as for XGrabPointer), the last-pointer-grab

time is set to the time at which the button was pressed (as transmitted in the
ButtonPress event), and the ButtonPress event is reported if all of the
following conditions are true:

- The pointer is not grabbed, and the specified button is logically pressed when the specified modifier keys are logically down, and no other buttons or modifier keys are logically down.
- The grab_window contains the pointer.
- The confine_to window (if any) is viewable.
- A passive grab on the same button/key combination does not exist on any ancestor of grab_window.

The interpretation of the remaining arguments is as for XGrabPointer.
The active grab is terminated automatically when the logical state of the
pointer has all buttons released (independent of the state of the logical modifier keys).

Note that the logical state of a device (as seen by client applications) may
lag the physical state if device event processing is frozen.

This request overrides all previous grabs by the same client on the
same button/key combinations on the same window. A modifiers of
AnyModifier is equivalent to issuing the grab request for all possible modifier combinations (including the combination of no modifiers). It is not required that all modifiers specified have currently assigned KeyCodes. A button of AnyButton is equivalent to issuing the request for all possible
buttons. Otherwise, it is not required that the specified button currently be
assigned to a physical button.

If some other client has already issued a XGrabButton with the same
button/key combination on the same window, a BadAccess error results.
When using AnyModifier or AnyButton, the request fails completely, and
a BadAccess error results (no grabs are established) if there is a conflicting
grab for any combination. XGrabButton has no effect on an active grab.

XGrabButton can generate BadCursor, BadValue, and BadWindow
errors.

To ungrab a pointer button, use XUngrabButton.

XUngrabButton(*display, button, modifiers, grab_window*)
    Display **display*;
    unsigned int *button*;
    unsigned int *modifiers*;
    Window *grab_window*;

display	Specifies the connection to the X server.
button	Specifies the pointer button that is to be released or `AnyButton`.
modifiers	Specifies the set of keymasks or `AnyModifier`. The mask is the bitwise inclusive OR of the valid keymask bits.
grab_window	Specifies the grab window.

The `XUngrabButton` function releases the passive button/key combination on the specified window if it was grabbed by this client. A modifiers of `AnyModifier` is equivalent to issuing the ungrab request for all possible modifier combinations, including the combination of no modifiers. A button of `AnyButton` is equivalent to issuing the request for all possible buttons. `XUngrabButton` has no effect on an active grab.

   `XUngrabButton` can generate `BadValue` and `BadWindow` errors.

7.5 Keyboard Grabbing

Xlib provides functions that you can use to grab or ungrab the keyboard as well as allow events.

For many functions in this section, you pass keymask bits. The valid keymask bits are: `ShiftMask`, `LockMask`, `ControlMask`, `Mod1Mask`, `Mod2Mask`, `Mod3Mask`, `Mod4Mask`, and `Mod5Mask`.

To grab the keyboard, use `XGrabKeyboard`.

int XGrabKeyboard(*display, grab_window, owner_events, pointer_mode, keyboard_mode,*
              time)
    Display **display*;
    Window *grab_window*;
    Bool *owner_events*;
    int *pointer_mode, keyboard_mode*;
    Time *time*;

display	Specifies the connection to the X server.
grab_window	Specifies the grab window.
owner_events	Specifies a Boolean value that indicates whether the pointer events are to be reported as usual or reported with respect to the grab window if selected by the event mask.

pointer_mode	Specifies further processing of pointer events. You can pass GrabModeSync or GrabModeAsync.
keyboard_mode	Specifies further processing of keyboard events. You can pass GrabModeSync or GrabModeAsync.
time	Specifies the time. You can pass either a timestamp or CurrentTime.

The XGrabKeyboard function actively grabs control of the keyboard and generates FocusIn and FocusOut events. Further key events are reported only to the grabbing client. XGrabKeyboard overrides any active keyboard grab by this client. If owner_events is False, all generated key events are reported with respect to grab_window. If owner_events is True and if a generated key event would normally be reported to this client, it is reported normally; otherwise, the event is reported with respect to the grab_window. Both KeyPress and KeyRelease events are always reported, independent of any event selection made by the client.

If the keyboard_mode argument is GrabModeAsync, keyboard event processing continues as usual. If the keyboard is currently frozen by this client, then processing of keyboard events is resumed. If the keyboard_mode argument is GrabModeSync, the state of the keyboard (as seen by client applications) appears to freeze, and the X server generates no further keyboard events until the grabbing client issues a releasing XAllowEvents call or until the keyboard grab is released. Actual keyboard changes are not lost while the keyboard is frozen; they are simply queued in the server for later processing.

If pointer_mode is GrabModeAsync, pointer event processing is unaffected by activation of the grab. If pointer_mode is GrabModeSync, the state of the pointer (as seen by client applications) appears to freeze, and the X server generates no further pointer events until the grabbing client issues a releasing XAllowEvents call or until the keyboard grab is released. Actual pointer changes are not lost while the pointer is frozen; they are simply queued in the server for later processing.

If the keyboard is actively grabbed by some other client, XGrabKeyboard fails and returns AlreadyGrabbed. If grab_window is not viewable, it fails and returns GrabNotViewable. If the keyboard is frozen by an active grab of another client, it fails and returns GrabFrozen. If the specified time is earlier than the last-keyboard-grab time or later than the current X server time, it fails and returns `GrabInvalidTime`. Otherwise, the last-keyboard-grab time is set to the specified time (`CurrentTime` is replaced by the current X server time).

`XGrabKeyboard` can generate `BadValue` and `BadWindow` errors.

To ungrab the keyboard, use `XUngrabKeyboard`.

XUngrabKeyboard(*display*, *time*)
    Display *display;
    Time *time*;
display   Specifies the connection to the X server.
time   Specifies the time. You can pass either a timestamp or `CurrentTime`.

The `XUngrabKeyboard` function releases the keyboard and any queued events if this client has it actively grabbed from either `XGrabKeyboard` or `XGrabKey`. `XUngrabKeyboard` does not release the keyboard and any queued events if the specified time is earlier than the last-keyboard-grab time or is later than the current X server time. It also generates `FocusIn` and `FocusOut` events. The X server automatically performs an `UngrabKeyboard` request if the event window for an active keyboard grab becomes not viewable.

To passively grab a single key of the keyboard, use `XGrabKey`.

XGrabKey(*display*, *keycode*, *modifiers*, *grab_window*, *owner_events*, *pointer_mode*,
        keyboard_mode)
    Display *display;
    int *keycode*;
    unsigned int *modifiers*;
    Window *grab_window*;
    Bool *owner_events*;
    int *pointer_mode*, *keyboard_mode*;
display   Specifies the connection to the X server.
keycode   Specifies the KeyCode or `AnyKey`.
modifiers   Specifies the set of keymasks or `AnyModifier`. The mask is the bitwise inclusive OR of the valid keymask bits.
grab_window   Specifies the grab window.
owner_events   Specifies a Boolean value that indicates whether the pointer events are to be reported as usual or reported with respect to the grab window if selected by the event mask.

pointer_mode   Specifies further processing of pointer events. You can pass
GrabModeSync or GrabModeAsync.

keyboard_mode   Specifies further processing of keyboard events. You can pass
GrabModeSync or GrabModeAsync.

The XGrabKey function establishes a passive grab on the keyboard. In the
future, the keyboard is actively grabbed (as for XGrabKeyboard), the last-
keyboard-grab time is set to the time at which the key was pressed (as transmitted in the KeyPress event), and the KeyPress event is reported if all of
the following conditions are true:

• The keyboard is not grabbed and the specified key (which can itself be a modifier
key) is logically pressed when the specified modifier keys are logically down, and
no other modifier keys are logically down.

• Either the grab_window is an ancestor of (or is) the focus window, or the
grab_window is a descendant of the focus window and contains the pointer.

• A passive grab on the same key combination does not exist on any ancestor of
grab_window.

The interpretation of the remaining arguments is as for XGrabKeyboard.
The active grab is terminated automatically when the logical state of the keyboard has the specified key released (independent of the logical state of the
modifier keys).

Note that the logical state of a device (as seen by client applications) may
lag the physical state if device event processing is frozen.

A modifiers argument of AnyModifier is equivalent to issuing the request for all possible modifier combinations (including the combination of
no modifiers). It is not required that all modifiers specified have currently
assigned KeyCodes. A keycode argument of AnyKey is equivalent to issuing
the request for all possible KeyCodes. Otherwise, the specified keycode must
be in the range specified by min_keycode and max_keycode in the connection setup, or a BadValue error results.

If some other client has issued a XGrabKey with the same key combination
on the same window, a BadAccess error results. When using Any-
Modifier or AnyKey, the request fails completely, and a BadAccess error
results (no grabs are established) if there is a conflicting grab for any combination.

XGrabKey can generate BadAccess, BadValue, and BadWindow errors.

To ungrab a key, use XUngrabKey.

XUngrabKey(*display, keycode, modifiers, grab_window*)
    Display *display;
    int *keycode*;
    unsigned int *modifiers*;
    Window *grab_window*;

display	Specifies the connection to the X server.
keycode	Specifies the KeyCode or AnyKey.
modifiers	Specifies the set of keymasks or AnyModifier. The mask is the bitwise inclusive OR of the valid keymask bits.
grab_window	Specifies the grab window.

The XUngrabKey function releases the key combination on the specified window if it was grabbed by this client. It has no effect on an active grab. A modifiers of AnyModifier is equivalent to issuing the request for all possible modifier combinations (including the combination of no modifiers). A keycode argument of AnyKey is equivalent to issuing the request for all possible key codes.

XUngrabKey can generate BadValue and BadWindow errors.

To allow further events to be processed when the device has been frozen, use XAllowEvents.

XAllowEvents(*display, event_mode, time*)
    Display *display;
    int *event_mode*;
    Time *time*;

display	Specifies the connection to the X server.
event_mode	Specifies the event mode. You can pass AsyncPointer, SyncPointer, AsyncKeyboard, SyncKeyboard, ReplayPointer, ReplayKeyboard, AsyncBoth, or SyncBoth.
time	Specifies the time. You can pass either a timestamp or CurrentTime.

The XAllowEvents function releases some queued events if the client has caused a device to freeze. It has no effect if the specified time is earlier than the last-grab time of the most recent active grab for the client or if the specified time is later than the current X server time. Depending on the event_mode argument, the following occurs:

AsyncPointer   If the pointer is frozen by the client, pointer event processing continues as usual. If the pointer is frozen twice by the client on behalf of two separate grabs, AsyncPointer thaws for both. AsyncPointer has no effect if the pointer is not frozen by the client, but the pointer need not be grabbed by the client.

SyncPointer   If the pointer is frozen and actively grabbed by the client, pointer event processing continues as usual until the next ButtonPress or ButtonRelease event is reported to the client. At this time, the pointer again appears to freeze. However, if the reported event causes the pointer grab to be released, the pointer does not freeze. SyncPointer has no effect if the pointer is not frozen by the client or if the pointer is not grabbed by the client.

ReplayPointer   If the pointer is actively grabbed by the client and is frozen as the result of an event having been sent to the client (either from the activation of a XGrabButton or from a previous XAllowEvents with mode Sync-Pointer but not from a XGrabPointer), the pointer grab is released and that event is completely reprocessed. This time, however, the function ignores any passive grabs at or above (towards the root of) the grab_window of the grab just released. The request has no effect if the pointer is not grabbed by the client or if the pointer is not frozen as the result of an event.

AsyncKeyboard   If the keyboard is frozen by the client, keyboard event processing continues as usual. If the keyboard is frozen twice by the client on behalf of two separate grabs, AsyncKeyboard thaws for both. AsyncKeyboard has no effect if the keyboard is not frozen by the client, but the keyboard need not be grabbed by the client.

SyncKeyboard   If the keyboard is frozen and actively grabbed by the client, keyboard event processing continues as usual until the next KeyPress or KeyRelease event is reported to the client. At this time, the keyboard again appears to freeze. However, if the reported event causes the keyboard grab to be released, the keyboard does not freeze. SyncKeyboard has no effect if the keyboard is

ReplayKeyboard

not frozen by the client or if the keyboard is not grabbed by the client.

If the keyboard is actively grabbed by the client and is frozen as the result of an event having been sent to the client (either from the activation of a XGrabKey or from a previous XAllowEvents with mode SyncKeyboard but not from a XGrabKeyboard), the keyboard grab is released and that event is completely reprocessed. This time, however, the function ignores any passive grabs at or above (towards the root of) the grab_window of the grab just released. The request has no effect if the keyboard is not grabbed by the client or if the keyboard is not frozen as the result of an event.

SyncBoth

If both pointer and keyboard are frozen by the client, event processing for both devices continues as usual until the next ButtonPress, ButtonRelease, KeyPress, or KeyRelease event is reported to the client for a grabbed device (button event for the pointer, key event for the keyboard), at which time the devices again appear to freeze. However, if the reported event causes the grab to be released, then the devices do not freeze (but if the other device is still grabbed, then a subsequent event for it will still cause both devices to freeze). SyncBoth has no effect unless both pointer and keyboard are frozen by the client. If the pointer or keyboard is frozen twice by the client on behalf of two separate grabs, SyncBoth thaws for both (but a subsequent freeze for SyncBoth will only freeze each device once).

AsyncBoth

If the pointer and the keyboard are frozen by the client, event processing for both devices continues as usual. If a device is frozen twice by the client on behalf of two separate grabs, AsyncBoth thaws for both. AsyncBoth has no effect unless both pointer and keyboard are frozen by the client.

AsyncPointer, SyncPointer, and ReplayPointer have no effect on the processing of keyboard events. AsyncKeyboard, SyncKeyboard, and ReplayKeyboard have no effect on the processing of pointer events. It is possible for both a pointer grab and a keyboard grab (by the same or different clients) to be active simultaneously. If a device is frozen on behalf of either grab, no event processing is performed for the device. It is possible for a single device to be frozen because of both grabs. In this case, the freeze must be released on behalf of both grabs before events can again be processed.

XAllowEvents can generate a BadValue error.

7.6   Server Grabbing

Xlib provides functions that you can use to grab and ungrab the server. These functions can be used to control processing of output on other connections by the window system server. While the server is grabbed, no processing of requests or close downs on any other connection will occur. A client closing its connection automatically ungrabs the server. Although grabbing the server is highly discouraged, it is sometimes necessary.

To grab the server, use XGrabServer.

XGrabServer(*display*)
      Display **display*;
display   Specifies the connection to the X server.

The XGrabServer function disables processing of requests and close downs on all other connections than the one this request arrived on. You should not grab the X server any more than is absolutely necessary.

To ungrab the server, use XUngrabServer.

XUngrabServer(*display*)
      Display **display*;
display   Specifies the connection to the X server.

The XUngrabServer function restarts processing of requests and close downs on other connections. You should avoid grabbing the X server as much as possible.

7.7   Miscellaneous Control Functions

This section discusses how to:

• Control the input focus
• Control the pointer
• Kill clients

7.7.1 Controlling Input Focus

Xlib provides functions that you can use to move the pointer position as well as to set and get the input focus.

To move the pointer to an arbitrary point on the screen, use `XWarpPointer`.

XWarpPointer(*display, src_w, dest_w, src_x, src_y, src_width, src_height, dest_x, dest_y*)
    Display **display*;
    Window *src_w, dest_w*;
    int *src_x, src_y*;
    unsigned int *src_width, src_height*;
    int *dest_x, dest_y*;

display	Specifies the connection to the X server.
src_w	Specifies the source window or `None`.
dest_w	Specifies the destination window or `None`.
src_x	
src_y	
src_width	
src_height	Specify a rectangle in the source window.
dest_x	
dest_y	Specify the x and y coordinates within the destination window.

If dest_w is `None`, `XWarpPointer` moves the pointer by the offsets (dest_x, dest_y) relative to the current position of the pointer. If dest_w is a window, `XWarpPointer` moves the pointer to the offsets (dest_x, dest_y) relative to the origin of dest_w. However, if src_w is a window, the move only takes place if the specified rectangle src_w contains the pointer.

The src_x and src_y coordinates are relative to the origin of src_w. If src_height is zero, it is replaced with the current height of src_w minus src_y. If src_width is zero, it is replaced with the current width of src_w minus src_x.

There is seldom any reason for calling this function. The pointer should normally be left to the user. If you do use this function, however, it generates events just as if the user had instantaneously moved the pointer from one position to another. Note that you cannot use `XWarpPointer` to move the pointer outside the confine_to window of an active pointer grab. An attempt to do so will only move the pointer as far as the closest edge of the confine_to window.

XWarpPointer can generate a BadWindow error.

To set the input focus, use XSetInputFocus.

XSetInputFocus(*display, focus, revert_to, time*)
    Display **display*;
    Window *focus*;
    int *revert_to*;
    Time *time*;

display	Specifies the connection to the X server.
focus	Specifies the window, PointerRoot, or None.
revert_to	Specifies where the input focus reverts to if the window becomes not viewable. You can pass RevertToParent, RevertToPointerRoot, or RevertToNone.
time	Specifies the time. You can pass either a timestamp or CurrentTime.

The XSetInputFocus function changes the input focus and the last-focus-change time. It has no effect if the specified time is earlier than the current last-focus-change time or is later than the current X server time. Otherwise, the last-focus-change time is set to the specified time (CurrentTime is replaced by the current X server time). XSetInputFocus causes the X server to generate FocusIn and FocusOut events.

Depending on the focus argument, the following occurs:

- If focus is None, all keyboard events are discarded until a new focus window is set, and the revert_to argument is ignored.

- If focus is a window, it becomes the keyboard's focus window. If a generated keyboard event would normally be reported to this window or one of its inferiors, the event is reported as usual. Otherwise, the event is reported relative to the focus window.

- If focus is PointerRoot, the focus window is dynamically taken to be the root window of whatever screen the pointer is on at each keyboard event. In this case, the revert_to argument is ignored.

The specified focus window must be viewable at the time XSetInputFocus is called, or a BadMatch error results. If the focus window later becomes not viewable, the X server evaluates the revert_to argument to determine the new focus window as follows:

- If revert_to is RevertToParent, the focus reverts to the parent (or the closest viewable ancestor), and the new revert_to value is taken to be RevertToNone.

- If revert_to is `RevertToPointerRoot` or `RevertToNone`, the focus reverts to `PointerRoot` or `None`, respectively. When the focus reverts, the X server generates `FocusIn` and `FocusOut` events, but the last-focus-change time is not affected.

`XSetInputFocus` can generate `BadMatch`, `BadValue`, and `BadWindow` errors.

To obtain the current input focus, use `XGetInputFocus`.

XGetInputFocus(*display, focus_return, revert_to_return*)
    Display **display*;
    Window **focus_return;*
    int **revert_to_return*;
display   Specifies the connection to the X server.
focus_return   Returns the focus window, `PointerRoot`, or `None`.
revert_to_return Returns the current focus state (`RevertToParent`,
                 `RevertToPointerRoot`, or `RevertToNone`).

The `XGetInputFocus` function returns the focus window and the current focus state.

7.7.2   Killing Clients

Xlib provides functions that you can use to control the lifetime of resources owned by a client or to cause the connection to a client to be destroyed.

To change a client's close-down mode, use `XSetCloseDownMode`.

XSetCloseDownMode(*display, close_mode*)
    Display **display*;
    int *close_mode*;
display   Specifies the connection to the X server.
close_mode Specifies the client close-down mode. You can pass `DestroyAll`,
             `RetainPermanent`, or `RetainTemporary`.

The `XSetCloseDownMode` defines what will happen to the client's resources at connection close. A connection starts in `DestroyAll` mode. For information on what happens to the client's resources when the close_mode argument is `RetainPermanent` or `RetainTemporary`, see section 2.6.
    `XSetCloseDownMode` can generate a `BadValue` error.

To destroy a client, use XKillClient.

XKillClient(*display, resource*)
    Display **display*;
    XID *resource*;
display   Specifies the connection to the X server.
resource   Specifies any resource associated with the client that you want to destroy
          or AllTemporary.

The XKillClient function forces a close-down of the client that created
the resource if a valid resource is specified. If the client has already terminated in either RetainPermanent or RetainTemporary mode, all of the
client's resources are destroyed. If AllTemporary is specified, the resources of all clients that have terminated in RetainTemporary are destroyed (see section 2.6). This permits implementation of window manager
facilities that aid debugging. A client can set its close-down mode to
RetainTemporary. If the client then crashes, its windows would not be destroyed. The programmer can then inspect the application's window tree
and use the window manager to destroy the zombie windows.

    XKillClient can generate a BadValue error.

7.8   Keyboard and Pointer Settings

Xlib provides functions that you can use to change the keyboard control, obtain a list of the auto-repeat keys, turn keyboard auto-repeat on or off, ring
the bell, set or obtain the pointer button or keyboard mapping, and obtain
a bit vector for the keyboard.

    This section discusses the user-preference options of bell, key click,
pointer behavior, and so on. The default values for many of these functions
are determined by command line arguments to the X server and, on UNIX-
based systems, are typically set in the /etc/ttys file. Not all implementations will actually be able to control all of these parameters.

    The XChangeKeyboardControl function changes control of a key-
board and operates on a XKeyboardControl structure:

```
/* Mask bits for ChangeKeyboardControl */
#define KBKeyClickPercent      (1L<<0)
#define KBBellPercent          (1L<<1)
#define KBBellPitch            (1L<<2)
#define KBBellDuration         (1L<<3)
```

```
#define KBLed                (1L<<4)
#define KBLedMode            (1L<<5)
#define KBKey                (1L<<6)
#define KBAutoRepeatMode     (1L<<7)
/* Values */
typedef struct {
    int key_click_percent;
    int bell_percent;
    int bell_pitch;
    int bell_duration;
    int led;
    int led_mode;            /* LedModeOn, LedModeOff */
    int key;
    int auto_repeat_mode;    /* AutoRepeatModeOff, AutoRepeatModeOn,
                                AutoRepeatModeDefault */
} XKeyboardControl;
```

The key_click_percent member sets the volume for key clicks between 0 (off) and 100 (loud) inclusive, if possible. A setting of -1 restores the default. Other negative values generate a `BadValue` error.

The bell_percent sets the base volume for the bell between 0 (off) and 100 (loud) inclusive, if possible. A setting of -1 restores the default. Other negative values generate a `BadValue` error. The bell_pitch member sets the pitch (specified in Hz) of the bell, if possible. A setting of -1 restores the default. Other negative values generate a `BadValue` error. The bell_duration member sets the duration of the bell specified in milliseconds, if possible. A setting of -1 restores the default. Other negative values generate a `BadValue` error.

If both the led_mode and led members are specified, the state of that LED is changed, if possible. The led_mode member can be set to `LedModeOn` or `LedModeOff`. If only led_mode is specified, the state of all LEDs are changed, if possible. At most 32 LEDs numbered from one are supported. No standard interpretation of LEDs is defined. If led is specified without led_mode, a `BadMatch` error results.

If both the auto_repeat_mode and key members are specified, the auto_repeat_mode of that key is changed (according to `AutoRepeat-ModeOn`, `AutoRepeatModeOff`, or `AutoRepeatModeDefault`), if possible. If only auto_repeat_mode is specified, the global auto_repeat_mode for the entire keyboard is changed, if possible, and does not affect the per key settings. If a key is specified without an auto_repeat_mode, a `BadMatch` error results. Each key has an individual mode of whether or not it should auto-repeat and a default setting for that mode. In addition, there is a global mode of whether auto-repeat should be enabled or not and a default setting for that mode. When global mode is `AutoRepeatModeOn`, keys should obey their individual auto-repeat modes. When global mode is `AutoRepeatModeOff`, no keys should auto repeat. An auto-repeating key generates alternating `KeyPress` and `KeyRelease` events. When a key is used as a modifier, it is desirable for the key not to auto-repeat, regardless of its auto-repeat setting.

A bell generator connected with the console but not directly on a keyboard is treated as if it were part of the keyboard. The order in which controls are verified and altered is server-dependent. If an error is generated, a subset of the controls may have been altered.

XChangeKeyboardControl(*display, value_mask, values*)
    Display **display*;
    unsigned long *value_mask*;
    XKeyboardControl **values*;

display	Specifies the connection to the X server.
value_mask	Specifies one value for each bit set to 1 in the mask.
values	Specifies which controls to change. This mask is the bitwise inclusive OR of the valid control mask bits.

The `XChangeKeyboardControl` function controls the keyboard characteristics defined by the `XKeyboardControl` structure. The value_mask argument specifies which values are to be changed.

`XChangeKeyboardControl` can generate `BadMatch` and `BadValue` errors.

To obtain the current control values for the keyboard, use `XGetKeyboardControl`.

```
typedef struct {
        int key_click_percent;
        int bell_percent;
        unsigned int bell_pitch, bell_duration;
        unsigned long led_mask;
```

```
        int global_auto_repeat;
        char auto_repeats[32];
} XKeyboardState;
```

XGetKeyboardControl(*display, values_return*)
        Display **display*;
        XKeyboardState **values_return*;
display   Specifies the connection to the X server.
values_return   Returns the current keyboard controls in the specified
                       XKeyboardState structure.

The XGetKeyboardControl function returns the current control values for the keyboard to the XKeyboardState structure.

For the LEDs, the least-significant bit of led_mask corresponds to LED one, and each bit set to 1 in led_mask indicates an LED that is lit. The global_auto_repeat member can be set to AutoRepeatModeOn or AutoRepeatModeOff. The auto_repeats member is a bit vector. Each bit set to 1 indicates that auto-repeat is enabled for the corresponding key. The vector is represented as 32 bytes. Byte N (from 0) contains the bits for keys 8N to 8N + 7 with the least-significant bit in the byte representing key 8N.

To turn on keyboard auto-repeat, use XAutoRepeatOn.

XAutoRepeatOn(*display*)
        Display **display*;
display   Specifies the connection to the X server.

The XAutoRepeatOn function turns on auto-repeat for the keyboard on the specified display.

To turn off keyboard auto-repeat, use XAutoRepeatOff.

XAutoRepeatOff(*display*)
        Display **display*;
display   Specifies the connection to the X server.

The XAutoRepeatOff function turns off auto-repeat for the keyboard on the specified display.

To ring the bell, use XBell.

XBell(*display, percent*)
    Display **display*;
    int *percent*;
display   Specifies the connection to the X server.
percent   Specifies the volume for the bell, which can range from −100 to 100
        inclusive.

The XBell function rings the bell on the keyboard on the specified display,
if possible. The specified volume is relative to the base volume for the keyboard. If the value for the percent argument is not in the range −100 to 100
inclusive, a BadValue error results. The volume at which the bell rings
when the percent argument is nonnegative is:

$$\text{base} - [(\text{base} * \text{percent}) / 100] + \text{percent}$$

The volume at which the bell rings when the percent argument is negative
is:

$$\text{base} + [(\text{base} * \text{percent}) / 100]$$

To change the base volume of the bell, use XChangeKeyboardControl.
    XBell can generate a BadValue error.

To obtain a bit vector that describes the state of the keyboard, use
XQueryKeymap.

XQueryKeymap(*display, keys_return*)
    Display **display*;
    char *keys_return*[32];
display   Specifies the connection to the X server.
keys_return   Returns an array of bytes that identifies which keys are pressed
            down. Each bit represents one key of the keyboard.

The XQueryKeymap function returns a bit vector for the logical state of the
keyboard, where each bit set to 1 indicates that the corresponding key is currently pressed down. The vector is represented as 32 bytes. Byte N (from 0)
contains the bits for keys 8N to 8N + 7 with the least-significant bit in the
byte representing key 8N.
    Note that the logical state of a device (as seen by client applications) may
lag the physical state if device event processing is frozen.

To set the mapping of the pointer buttons, use XSetPointerMapping.

int XSetPointerMapping(*display, map, nmap*)
    Display **display*;
    unsigned char *map*[];
    int *nmap*;
display   Specifies the connection to the X server.
map   Specifies the mapping list.
nmap   Specifies the number of items in the mapping list.

The XSetPointerMapping function sets the mapping of the pointer. If it succeeds, the X server generates a MappingNotify event, and XSet-PointerMapping returns MappingSuccess. Elements of the list are indexed starting from one. The length of the list must be the same as XGetPointerMapping would return, or a BadValue error results. The index is a core button number, and the element of the list defines the effective number. A zero element disables a button, and elements are not restricted in value by the number of physical buttons. However, no two elements can have the same nonzero value, or a BadValue error results. If any of the buttons to be altered are logically in the down state, XSetPointerMapping returns MappingBusy, and the mapping is not changed.

    XSetPointerMapping can generate a BadValue error.

To get the pointer mapping, use XGetPointerMapping.

int XGetPointerMapping(*display, map_return, nmap*)
    Display **display*;
    unsigned char *map_return*[];
    int *nmap*;
display   Specifies the connection to the X server.
map_return   Returns the mapping list.
nmap   Specifies the number of items in the mapping list.

The XGetPointerMapping function returns the current mapping of the pointer. Elements of the list are indexed starting from one. XGet-PointerMapping returns the number of physical buttons actually on the pointer. The nominal mapping for a pointer is the identity mapping: map[i]=i. The nmap argument specifies the length of the array where the pointer mapping is returned, and only the first nmap elements are returned in map_return.

To control the pointer's interactive feel, use XChangePointer-Control.

XChangePointerControl(*display, do_accel, do_threshold, accel_numerator, accel_denominator, threshold*)

> Display **display*;
> Bool *do_accel, do_threshold*;
> int *accel_numerator, accel_denominator*;
> int *threshold*;

display	Specifies the connection to the X server.
do_accel	Specifies a Boolean value that controls whether the values for the accel_numerator or accel_denominator are used.
do_threshold	Specifies a Boolean value that controls whether the value for the threshold is used.
accel_numerator	Specifies the numerator for the acceleration multiplier.
accel_denominator	Specifies the denominator for the acceleration multiplier.
threshold	Specifies the acceleration threshold.

The XChangePointerControl function defines how the pointing device moves. The acceleration, expressed as a fraction, is a multiplier for movement. For example, specifying 3/1 means the pointer moves three times as fast as normal. The fraction may be rounded arbitrarily by the X server. Acceleration only takes effect if the pointer moves more than threshold pixels at once and only applies to the amount beyond the value in the threshold argument. Setting a value to −1 restores the default. The values of the do_accel and do_threshold arguments must be True for the pointer values to be set, or the parameters are unchanged. Negative values (other than −1) generate a BadValue error, as does a zero value for the accel_denominator argument.

XChangePointerControl can generate a BadValue error.

To get the current pointer parameters, use XGetPointerControl.

XGetPointerControl(*display, accel_numerator_return, accel_denominator_return, threshold_return*)

> Display **display*;
> int **accel_numerator_return, *accel_denominator_return*;

     int *threshold_return*;

display	Specifies the connection to the X server.
accel_numerator_return	Returns the numerator for the acceleration multiplier.
accel_denominator_return	Returns the denominator for the acceleration multiplier.
threshold_return	Returns the acceleration threshold.

The `XGetPointerControl` function returns the pointer's current acceleration multiplier and acceleration threshold.

7.9 Keyboard Encoding

Most applications will find the simple interface `XLookupString`, which performs simple translation of a key event to an ASCII string, most useful. Keyboard-related utilities are discussed in chapter 10. The following section explains how to completely control the bindings of symbols to keys and modifiers.

A KeyCode represents a physical (or logical) key. KeyCodes lie in the inclusive range [8,255]. A KeyCode value carries no intrinsic information, although server implementors may attempt to encode geometry (for example, matrix) information in some fashion so that it can be interpreted in a server-dependent fashion. The mapping between keys and KeyCodes cannot be changed.

A KeySym is an encoding of a symbol on the cap of a key. The set of defined KeySyms include the ISO Latin character sets (1–4), Katakana, Arabic, Cyrillic, Greek, Technical, Special, Publishing, APL, Hebrew, and a special miscellany of keys found on keyboards (Return, Help, Tab, and so on). To the extent possible, these sets are derived from international standards. In areas where no standards exist, some of these sets are derived from Digital Equipment Corporation standards. The list of defined symbols can be found in `<X11/keysymdef.h>`. Unfortunately, some C preprocessors have limits on the number of defined symbols. If you must use KeySyms not in the Latin 1–4, Greek, and miscellaneous classes, you may have to define a symbol for those sets. Most applications usually only include `<X11/keysym.h>`, which defines symbols for ISO Latin 1–4, Greek, and miscellaneous.

A list of KeySyms is associated with each KeyCode. The length of the list can vary with each KeyCode. The list is intended to convey the set of symbols on the corresponding key. By convention, if the list contains a single KeySym and if that KeySym is alphabetic and case distinction is relevant for it, then it should be treated as equivalent to a two-element list of the lowercase and uppercase KeySyms. For example, if the list contains the single KeySym for uppercase *A*, the client should treat it as if it were a pair with lowercase *a* as the first KeySym and uppercase *A* as the second KeySym.

For any KeyCode, the first KeySym in the list should be chosen as the interpretation of a `KeyPress` when no modifier keys are down. The second KeySym in the list normally should be chosen when the Shift modifier is on or when the Lock modifier is on and Lock is interpreted as ShiftLock. When the Lock modifier is on and is interpreted as CapsLock, it is suggested that the Shift modifier first be applied to choose a KeySym. However, if that KeySym is lowercase alphabetic, the corresponding uppercase KeySym should be used instead. Other interpretations of CapsLock are possible; for example, it may be viewed as equivalent to ShiftLock, but only applying when the first KeySym is lowercase alphabetic and the second KeySym is the corresponding uppercase alphabetic. No interpretation of KeySyms beyond the first two in a list is suggested here. No spatial geometry of the symbols on the key is defined by their order in the KeySym list, although a geometry might be defined on a vendor-specific basis. The X server does not use the mapping between KeyCodes and KeySyms. Rather, it stores it merely for reading and writing by clients.

To obtain the legal KeyCodes for a display, use `XDisplayKeycodes`.

```
XDisplayKeycodes(display, min_keycodes_return, max_keycodes_return)
    Display *display;
    int *min_keycodes_return, max_keycodes_return;
```

display	Specifies the connection to the X server.
min_keycodes_return	Returns the minimum number of KeyCodes.
max_keycodes_return	Returns the maximum number of KeyCodes.

The `XDisplayKeycodes` function returns the min-keycodes and max-keycodes supported by the specified display. The minimum number of KeyCodes returned is never less than 8, and the maximum number of KeyCodes returned is never greater than 255. Not all KeyCodes in this range are required to have corresponding keys.

To obtain the symbols for the specified KeyCodes, use
`XGetKeyboardMapping`.

KeySym *XGetKeyboardMapping(*display, first_keycode, keycode_count,*
                                              keysyms_per_keycode_return)

> Display **display*;
> KeyCode *first_keycode*;
> int *keycode_count*;
> int **keysyms_per_keycode_return*;

display	Specifies the connection to the X server.
first_keycode	Specifies the first KeyCode that is to be returned.
keycode_count	Specifies the number of KeyCodes that are to be returned.
keysyms_per_keycode_return	Returns the number of KeySyms per KeyCode.

The `XGetKeyboardMapping` function returns the symbols for the specified number of KeyCodes starting with first_keycode. The value specified in first_keycode must be greater than or equal to min_keycode returned by `XDisplayKeycodes` or a `BadValue` error results. In addition, the following expression must be less than or equal to max_keycode returned by `XDisplayKeycodes`:

$$\text{first\_keycode} + \text{keycode\_count} - 1$$

If this is not the case, a `BadValue` error results. The number of elements in the KeySyms list is:

$$\text{keycode\_count} * \text{keysyms\_per\_keycode\_return}$$

KeySym number N, counting from zero, for KeyCode K has the following index in the list, counting from zero:

$$(\text{K} - \text{first\_code}) * \text{keysyms\_per\_code\_return} + \text{N}$$

The X server arbitrarily chooses the keysyms_per_keycode_return value to be large enough to report all requested symbols. A special KeySym value of `NoSymbol` is used to fill in unused elements for individual KeyCodes. To free the storage returned by `XGetKeyboardMapping`, use `XFree`.

`XGetKeyboardMapping` can generate a `BadValue` error.

To change the keyboard mapping, use `XChangeKeyboardMapping`.

XChangeKeyboardMapping(*display, first_keycode, keysyms_per_keycode, keysyms, num_codes*)

    Display **display*;
    int *first_keycode*;
    int *keysyms_per_keycode*;
    KeySym **keysyms*;
    int *num_codes*;

display	Specifies the connection to the X server.
first_keycode	Specifies the first KeyCode that is to be changed.
keysyms_per_keycode	Specifies the number of KeySyms per KeyCode.
keysyms	Specifies a pointer to an array of KeySyms.
num_codes	Specifies the number of KeyCodes that are to be changed.

The `XChangeKeyboardMapping` function defines the symbols for the specified number of KeyCodes starting with first_keycode. The symbols for KeyCodes outside this range remain unchanged. The number of elements in keysyms must be:

$$num\_codes * keysyms\_per\_keycode$$

The specified first_keycode must be greater than or equal to min_keycode returned by `XDisplayKeycodes`, or a `BadValue` error results. In addition, the following expression must be less than or equal to max_keycode returned by `XDisplayKeycodes`, or a `BadValue` error results:

$$first\_keycode + num\_codes - 1$$

KeySym number N, counting from zero, for KeyCode K has the following index in keysyms, counting from zero:

$$(K - first\_keycode) * keysyms\_per\_keycode + N$$

The specified keysyms_per_keycode can be chosen arbitrarily by the client to be large enough to hold all desired symbols. A special KeySym value of `NoSymbol` should be used to fill in unused elements for individual KeyCodes. It is legal for `NoSymbol` to appear in nontrailing positions of the effective list for a KeyCode. `XChangeKeyboardMapping` generates a `MappingNotify` event.

There is no requirement that the X server interpret this mapping. It is merely stored for reading and writing by clients.

XChangeKeyboardMapping can generate BadAlloc and BadValue errors.

The next four functions make use of the XModifierKeymap data structure, which contains:

```
typedef struct {
    int max_keypermod;      /* This server's max number of keys per
                               modifier */
    KeyCode *modifiermap;   /* An 8 by max_keypermod array of the
                               modifiers */
} XModifierKeymap;
```

To create an XModifierKeymap structure, use XNewModifiermap.

XModifierKeymap *XNewModifiermap(*max_keys_per_mod*)
    int *max_keys_per_mod*;
max_keys_per_mod   Specifies the number of KeyCode entries preallocated to the modifiers in the map.

The XNewModifiermap function returns a pointer to an XModifier-Keymap structure for later use.

To add a new entry to an XModifierKeymap structure, use XInsertModifiermapEntry.

XModifierKeymap *XInsertModifiermapEntry(*modmap, keycode_entry, modifier*)
    XModifierKeymap *modmap*;
    KeyCode *keycode_entry*;
    int *modifier*;
modmap   Specifies a pointer to the XModifierKeymap structure.
keycode_entry   Specifies the KeyCode.
modifier   Specifies the modifier.

The XInsertModifiermapEntry function adds the specified KeyCode to the set that controls the specified modifier and returns the resulting XModifierKeymap structure (expanded as needed).

To delete an entry from an XModifierKeymap structure, use XDeleteModifiermapEntry.

XModifierKeymap *XDeleteModifiermapEntry(*modmap, keycode_entry, modifier*)
    XModifierKeymap *modmap*;
    KeyCode *keycode_entry*;
    int *modifier*;

modmap   Specifies a pointer to the `XModifierKeymap` structure.
keycode_entry Specifies the KeyCode.
modifier   Specifies the modifier.

The `XDeleteModifiermapEntry` function deletes the specified KeyCode from the set that controls the specified modifier and returns a pointer to the resulting `XModifierKeymap` structure.

To destroy an `XModifierKeymap` structure, use `XFreeModifiermap`.

XFreeModifiermap(*modmap*)
    XModifierKeymap *modmap*;
modmap   Specifies a pointer to the `XModifierKeymap` structure.

The `XFreeModifiermap` function frees the specified `XModifierKeymap` structure.

To set the KeyCodes to be used as modifiers, use `XSetModifier-Mapping`.

int XSetModifierMapping(*display, modmap*)
    Display *display*;
    XModifierKeymap *modmap*;
display   Specifies the connection to the X server.
modmap Specifies a pointer to the `XModifierKeymap` structure.

The `XSetModifierMapping` function specifies the KeyCodes of the keys (if any) that are to be used as modifiers. If it succeeds, the X server generates a `MappingNotify` event, and `XSetModifierMapping` returns `Mapping-Success`. X permits at most eight modifier keys. If more than eight are specified in the `XModifierKeymap` structure, a `BadLength` error results.

The modifiermap member of the `XModifierKeymap` structure contains eight sets of max_keypermod KeyCodes, one for each modifier in the order `Shift`, `Lock`, `Control`, `Mod1`, `Mod2`, `Mod3`, `Mod4`, and `Mod5`. Only nonzero KeyCodes have meaning in each set, and zero KeyCodes are ignored. In addition, all of the nonzero KeyCodes must be in the range specified by min_keycode and max_keycode in the `Display` structure, or a

`BadValue` error results. No KeyCode may appear twice in the entire map, or a `BadValue` error results.

An X server can impose restrictions on how modifiers can be changed, for example, if certain keys do not generate up transitions in hardware, if auto-repeat cannot be disabled on certain keys, or if multiple modifier keys are not supported. If some such restriction is violated, the status reply is `MappingFailed`, and none of the modifiers are changed. If the new KeyCodes specified for a modifier differ from those currently defined and any (current or new) keys for that modifier are in the logically down state, `XSetModifierMapping` returns `MappingBusy`, and none of the modifiers is changed.

`XSetModifierMapping` can generate `BadAlloc` and `BadValue` errors.

To obtain the KeyCodes used as modifiers, use `XGetModifierMapping`.

XModifierKeymap *XGetModifierMapping(*display*)
    Display **display*;
display   Specifies the connection to the X server.

The `XGetModifierMapping` function returns a pointer to a newly created `XModifierKeymap` structure that contains the keys being used as modifiers. The structure should be freed after use by calling `XFree-Modifiermap`. If only zero values appear in the set for any modifier, that modifier is disabled.

7.10   Screen Saver Control

Xlib provides functions that you can use to set, force, activate, or reset the screen saver and to obtain the current screen saver values.

To set the screen saver, use `XSetScreenSaver`.

XSetScreenSaver(*display, timeout, interval, prefer_blanking, allow_exposures*)
    Display **display*;
    int *timeout, interval*;
    int *prefer_blanking*;
    int *allow_exposures*;
display   Specifies the connection to the X server.
timeout   Specifies the timeout, in seconds, until the screen saver turns on.

interval	Specifies the interval between screen saver alterations.
prefer_blanking	Specifies how to enable screen blanking. You can pass `DontPreferBlanking`, `PreferBlanking`, or `DefaultBlanking`.
allow_exposures	Specifies the screen save control values. You can pass `DontAllowExposures`, `AllowExposures`, or `DefaultExposures`.

Timeout and interval are specified in seconds. A timeout of 0 disables the screen saver, and a timeout of −1 restores the default. Other negative values generate a `BadValue` error. If the timeout value is nonzero, `XSetScreenSaver` enables the screen saver. An interval of 0 disables the random-pattern motion. If no input from devices (keyboard, mouse, and so on) is generated for the specified number of timeout seconds once the screen saver is enabled, the screen saver is activated.

For each screen, if blanking is preferred and the hardware supports video blanking, the screen simply goes blank. Otherwise, if either exposures are allowed or the screen can be regenerated without sending `Expose` events to clients, the screen is tiled with the root window background tile randomly re-origined each interval minutes. Otherwise, the screens' state does not change, and the screen saver is not activated. The screen saver is deactivated, and all screen states are restored at the next keyboard or pointer input or at the next call to `XForceScreenSaver` with mode `ScreenSaverReset`.

If the server-dependent screen saver method supports periodic change, the interval argument serves as a hint about how long the change period should be, and zero hints that no periodic change should be made. Examples of ways to change the screen include scrambling the colormap periodically, moving an icon image around the screen periodically, or tiling the screen with the root window background tile, randomly re-origined periodically.

`XSetScreenSaver` can generate a `BadValue` error.

To force the screen saver on or off, use `XForceScreenSaver`.

XForceScreenSaver(*display, mode*)
    Display **display*;
    int *mode*;

display	Specifies the connection to the X server.
mode	Specifies the mode that is to be applied. You can pass `ScreenSaverActive` or `ScreenSaverReset`.

If the specified mode is `ScreenSaverActive` and the screen saver currently is deactivated, `XForceScreenSaver` activates the screen saver even if the screen saver had been disabled with a timeout of zero. If the specified mode is `ScreenSaverReset` and the screen saver currently is enabled, `XForceScreenSaver` deactivates the screen saver if it was activated, and the activation timer is reset to its initial state (as if device input had been received).

`XForceScreenSaver` can generate a `BadValue` error.

To activate the screen saver, use `XActivateScreenSaver`.

XActivateScreenSaver(*display*)
    Display *display;
display   Specifies the connection to the X server.

To reset the screen saver, use `XResetScreenSaver`.

XResetScreenSaver(*display*)
    Display *display;
display   Specifies the connection to the X server.

To get the current screen saver values, use `XGetScreenSaver`.

XGetScreenSaver(*display, timeout_return, interval_return, prefer_blanking_return,*
           allow_exposures_return)
    Display *display;
    int *timeout_return, *interval_return;
    int **prefer_blanking_return*;
    int **allow_exposures_return*;

display	Specifies the connection to the X server.
timeout_return	Returns the timeout, in minutes, until the screen saver turns on.
interval_return	Returns the interval between screen saver invocations.
prefer_blanking_return	Returns the current screen blanking preference (`DontPreferBlanking`, `PreferBlanking`, or `DefaultBlanking`).
allow_exposures_return	Returns the current screen save control value (`DontAllowExposures`, `AllowExposures`, or `DefaultExposures`).

7.11   Controlling Host Access

This section discusses how to:

- Add, get, or remove hosts from the access control list
- Change, enable, or disable access

X does not provide any protection on a per-window basis. If you find out the resource ID of a resource, you can manipulate it. To provide some minimal level of protection, however, connections are permitted only from machines you trust. This is adequate on single-user workstations but obviously breaks down on timesharing machines. Although provisions exist in the X protocol for proper connection authentication, the lack of a standard authentication server leaves host-level access control as the only common mechanism.

The initial set of hosts allowed to open connections typically consists of:

- The host the window system is running on.
- On UNIX-based systems, each host listed in the /etc/X?.hosts file. The ? indicates the number of the display. This file should consist of host names separated by newlines. DECnet nodes must terminate in :: to distinguish them from Internet hosts.

If a host is not in the access control list when the access control mechanism is enabled and if the host attempts to establish a connection, the server refuses the connection. To change the access list, the client must reside on the same host as the server and/or must have been granted permission in the initial authorization at connection setup.

Servers also can implement other access control policies in addition to or in place of this host access facility. For further information about other access control implementations, see part B, *X Window System Protocol*.

7.11.1   Adding, Getting, or Removing Hosts

Xlib provides functions that you can use to add, get, or remove hosts from the access control list. All the host access control functions use the XHostAddress structure, which contains:

```
typedef struct {
    int family;          /* for example FamilyInternet */
    int length;          /* length of address, in bytes */
```

```
        char *address;        /* pointer to where to find the address */
} XHostAddress;
```

The family member specifies which protocol address family to use (for example, TCP/IP or DECnet) and can be `FamilyInternet`, `Family-DECnet`, or `FamilyChaos`. The length member specifies the length of the address in bytes. The address member specifies a pointer to the address.

For TCP/IP, the address should be in network byte order. For the DECnet family, the server performs no automatic swapping on the address bytes. A Phase IV address is two bytes long. The first byte contains the least-significant eight bits of the node number. The second byte contains the most-significant two bits of the node number in the least-significant two bits of the byte and the area in the most-significant six bits of the byte.

To add a single host, use `XAddHost`.

```
XAddHost(display, host)
        Display *display;
        XHostAddress *host;
```
display   Specifies the connection to the X server.
host   Specifies the host that is to be added.

The `XAddHost` function adds the specified host to the access control list for that display. The server must be on the same host as the client issuing the command, or a `BadAccess` error results.

`XAddHost` can generate `BadAccess` and `BadValue` errors.

To add multiple hosts at one time, use `XAddHosts`.

```
XAddHosts(display, hosts, num_hosts)
        Display *display;
        XHostAddress *hosts;
        int num_hosts;
```
display   Specifies the connection to the X server.
hosts   Specifies each host that is to be added.
num_hosts   Specifies the number of hosts.

The `XAddHosts` function adds each specified host to the access control list for that display. The server must be on the same host as the client issuing the command, or a `BadAccess` error results.

XAddHosts can generate BadAccess and BadValue errors.

To obtain a host list, use XListHosts.

XHostAddress *XListHosts(*display, nhosts_return, state_return*)
    Display *display*;
    int *nhosts_return*;
    Bool *state_return;*

display   Specifies the connection to the X server.
nhosts_return   Returns the number of hosts currently in the access control list.
state_return   Returns the state of the access control.

The XListHosts function returns the current access control list as well as whether the use of the list at connection setup was enabled or disabled. XListHosts allows a program to find out what machines can make connections. It also returns a pointer to a list of host structures that were allocated by the function. When no longer needed, this memory should be freed by calling XFree.

To remove a single host, use XRemoveHost.

XRemoveHost(*display, host*)
    Display *display*;
    XHostAddress *host*;

display   Specifies the connection to the X server.
host   Specifies the host that is to be removed.

The XRemoveHost function removes the specified host from the access control list for that display. The server must be on the same host as the client process, or a BadAccess error results. If you remove your machine from the access list, you can no longer connect to that server, and this operation cannot be reversed unless you reset the server.

    XRemoveHost can generate BadAccess and BadValue errors.

To remove multiple hosts at one time, use XRemoveHosts.

XRemoveHosts(*display, hosts, num_hosts*)
    Display *display*;
    XHostAddress *hosts*;
    int *num_hosts*;

display   Specifies the connection to the X server.

hosts   Specifies each host that is to be removed.

num_hosts Specifies the number of hosts.

The XRemoveHosts function removes each specified host from the access control list for that display. The X server must be on the same host as the client process, or a BadAccess error results. If you remove your machine from the access list, you can no longer connect to that server, and this operation cannot be reversed unless you reset the server.

XRemoveHosts can generate BadAccess and BadValue errors.

7.11.2 Changing, Enabling, or Disabling Access Control

Xlib provides functions that you can use to enable, disable, or change access control.

For these functions to execute successfully, the client application must reside on the same host as the X server and/or have been given permission in the initial authorization at connection setup.

To change access control, use XSetAccessControl.

XSetAccessControl(*display, mode*)
    Display **display*;
    int *mode*;

display Specifies the connection to the X server.

mode   Specifies the mode. You can pass EnableAccess or DisableAccess.

The XSetAccessControl function either enables or disables the use of the access control list at each connection setup.

XSetAccessControl can generate BadAccess and BadValue errors.

To enable access control, use XEnableAccessControl.

XEnableAccessControl(*display*)
    Display **display*;

display Specifies the connection to the X server.

The XEnableAccessControl function enables the use of the access control list at each connection setup.

XEnableAccessControl can generate a BadAccess error.

To disable access control, use `XDisableAccessControl`.

XDisableAccessControl(*display*)
    Display **display*;
display   Specifies the connection to the X server.

The `XDisableAccessControl` function disables the use of the access control list at each connection setup.

`XDisableAccessControl` can generate a `BadAccess` error.

Chapter 8

Events and Event-Handling Functions

A client application communicates with the X server through the connection you establish with the `XOpenDisplay` function. A client application sends requests to the X server over this connection. These requests are made by the Xlib functions that are called in the client application. Many Xlib functions cause the X server to generate events, and the user's typing or moving the pointer can generate events asynchronously. The X server returns events to the client on the same connection.

This chapter begins with a discussion of the following topics associated with events:

- Event types
- Event structures
- Event mask
- Event processing

It then discusses the Xlib functions you can use to:

- Select events
- Handle the output buffer and the event queue
- Select events from the event queue
- Send and get events
- Handle error events

Note   Some toolkits use their own event-handling functions and do not allow you to interchange these event-handling functions with those in Xlib. For further information, see the documentation supplied with the toolkit.

Most applications simply are event loops: they wait for an event, decide what to do with it, execute some amount of code that results in changes to the display, and then wait for the next event.

8.1   Event Types

An event is data generated asynchronously by the X server as a result of some device activity or as side effects of a request sent by an Xlib function. Device-related events propagate from the source window to ancestor windows until some client application has selected that event type or until the event is explicitly discarded. The X server generally sends an event to a client application only if the client has specifically asked to be informed of that event type, typically by setting the event-mask attribute of the window. The mask can also be set when you create a window or by changing the window's event-mask. You can also mask out events that would propagate to ancestor windows by manipulating the do-not-propagate mask of the window's attributes. However, MappingNotify events are always sent to all clients.

An event type describes a specific event generated by the X server. For each event type, a corresponding constant name is defined in <X11/X.h>, which is used when referring to an event type. The following table lists the event category and its associated event type or types. The processing associated with these events is discussed in section 8.4.

Event Category	Event Type
Keyboard events	KeyPress, KeyRelease
Pointer events	ButtonPress, ButtonRelease, MotionNotify
Window crossing events	EnterNotify, LeaveNotify
Input focus events	FocusIn, FocusOut
Keymap state notification event	KeymapNotify
Exposure events	Expose, GraphicsExpose, NoExpose
Structure control events	CirculateRequest, ConfigureRequest, MapRequest, ResizeRequest

Event Category	Event Type
Window state notification events	`CirculateNotify, ConfigureNotify, CreateNotify, DestroyNotify, GravityNotify, MapNotify, MappingNotify, ReparentNotify, UnmapNotify, VisibilityNotify`
Colormap state notification event	`ColormapNotify`
Client communication events	`ClientMessage, PropertyNotify, SelectionClear, SelectionNotify, SelectionRequest`

8.2 Event Structures

For each event type, a corresponding structure is declared in
`<X11/Xlib.h>`. All the event structures have the following common
members:

```
typedef struct {
    int type;
    unsigned long serial;       /* # of last request processed by server */
    Bool send_event;            /* true if this came from a SendEvent request */
    Display *display;           /* Display the event was read from */
    Window window;
} XAnyEvent;
```

The type member is set to the event type constant name that uniquely identifies it. For example, when the X server reports a `GraphicsExpose` event to
a client application, it sends an `XGraphicsExposeEvent` structure with the
type member set to `GraphicsExpose`. The display member is set to a
pointer to the display the event was read on. The send_event member is set
to `True` if the event came from a `SendEvent` protocol request. The serial
member is set from the serial number reported in the protocol but expanded from the 16-bit least-significant bits to a full 32-bit value. The window member is set to the window that is most useful to toolkit dispatchers.

The X server can send events at any time in the input stream. Xlib stores
any events received while waiting for a reply in an event queue for later use.
Xlib also provides functions that allow you to check events in the event
queue (see section 8.7).

In addition to the individual structures declared for each event type, the XEvent structure is a union of the individual structures declared for each event type. Depending on the type, you should access members of each event by using the XEvent union.

```
typedef union _XEvent {
    int type;                                      /* must not be changed */
    XAnyEvent xany;
    XKeyEvent xkey;
    XButtonEvent xbutton;
    XMotionEvent xmotion;
    XCrossingEvent xcrossing;
    XFocusChangeEvent xfocus;
    XExposeEvent xexpose;
    XGraphicsExposeEvent xgraphicsexpose;
    XNoExposeEvent xnoexpose;
    XVisibilityEvent xvisibility;
    XCreateWindowEvent xcreatewindow;
    XDestroyWindowEvent xdestroywindow;
    XUnmapEvent xunmap;
    XMapEvent xmap;
    XMapRequestEvent xmaprequest;
    XReparentEvent xreparent;
    XConfigureEvent xconfigure;
    XGravityEvent xgravity;
    XResizeRequestEvent xresizerequest;
    XConfigureRequestEvent xconfigurerequest;
    XCirculateEvent xcirculate;
    XCirculateRequestEvent xcirculaterequest;
    XPropertyEvent xproperty;
    XSelectionClearEvent xselectionclear;
    XSelectionRequestEvent xselectionrequest;
    XSelectionEvent xselection;
    XColormapEvent xcolormap;
    XClientMessageEvent xclient;
    XMappingEvent xmapping;
    XErrorEvent xerror;
    XKeymapEvent xkeymap;
    long pad[24];
} XEvent;
```

An XEvent structure's first entry always is the type member, which is set to the event type. The second member always is the serial number of the protocol request that generated the event. The third member always is send_event, which is a Bool that indicates if the event was sent by a different client. The fourth member always is a display, which is the display that the event was read from. Except for keymap events, the fifth member always is a window, which has been carefully selected to be useful to toolkit dispatchers. To avoid breaking toolkits, the order of these first five entries is not to change. Most events also contain a time member, which is the time at which an event occurred. In addition, a pointer to the generic event must be cast before it is used to access any other information in the structure.

8.3   Event Masks

Clients select event reporting of most events relative to a window. To do this, pass an event mask to an Xlib event-handling function that takes an event_mask argument. The bits of the event mask are defined in <X11/X.h>. Each bit in the event mask maps to an event mask name, which describes the event or events you want the X server to return to a client application.

Unless the client has specifically asked for them, most events are not reported to clients when they are generated. Unless the client suppresses them by setting graphics-exposures in the GC to False, GraphicsExpose and NoExpose are reported by default as a result of XCopyPlane and XCopyArea. SelectionClear, SelectionRequest, Selection-Notify, or ClientMessage cannot be masked. Selection related events are only sent to clients cooperating with selections (see section 4.4). When the keyboard or pointer mapping is changed, MappingNotify is always sent to clients.

The following table lists the event mask constants you can pass to the event_mask argument and the circumstances in which you would want to specify the event mask:

Event Mask	Circumstances
NoEventMask	No events wanted
KeyPressMask	Keyboard down events wanted
KeyReleaseMask	Keyboard up events wanted

Event Mask	Circumstances
ButtonPressMask	Pointer button down events wanted
ButtonReleaseMask	Pointer button up events wanted
EnterWindowMask	Pointer window entry events wanted
LeaveWindowMask	Pointer window leave events wanted
PointerMotionMask	Pointer motion events wanted
PointerMotionHintMask	Pointer motion hints wanted
Button1MotionMask	Pointer motion while button 1 down
Button2MotionMask	Pointer motion while button 2 down
Button3MotionMask	Pointer motion while button 3 down
Button4MotionMask	Pointer motion while button 4 down
Button5MotionMask	Pointer motion while button 5 down
ButtonMotionMask	Pointer motion while any button down
KeymapStateMask	Keyboard state wanted at window entry and focus in
ExposureMask	Any exposure wanted
VisibilityChangeMask	Any change in visibility wanted
StructureNotifyMask	Any change in window structure wanted
ResizeRedirectMask	Redirect resize of this window
SubstructureNotifyMask	Substructure notification wanted
SubstructureRedirectMask	Redirect structure requests on children
FocusChangeMask	Any change in input focus wanted
PropertyChangeMask	Any change in property wanted
ColormapChangeMask	Any change in colormap wanted
OwnerGrabButtonMask	Automatic grabs should activate with owner_events set to True

8.4   Event Processing

The event reported to a client application during event processing depends on which event masks you provide as the event-mask attribute for a window. For some event masks, there is a one-to-one correspondence between the event mask constant and the event type constant. For example, if you pass the event mask ButtonPressMask, the X server sends back only ButtonPress events. Most events contain a time member, which is the time at which an event occurred.

In other cases, one event mask constant can map to several event type constants. For example, if you pass the event mask Substructure-NotifyMask, the X server can send back CirculateNotify,

`ConfigureNotify`, `CreateNotify`, `DestroyNotify`, `Gravity-Notify`, `MapNotify`, `ReparentNotify`, or `UnmapNotify` events.

In another case, two event masks can map to one event type. For example, if you pass either `PointerMotionMask` or `ButtonMotionMask`, the X server sends back a `MotionNotify` event.

The table on pages 218 and 219 lists the event mask, its associated event type or types, and the structure name associated with the event type. Some of these structures actually are typedefs to a generic structure that is shared between two event types. Note that N.A. appears in columns for which the information is not applicable.

The sections that follow describe the processing that occurs when you select the different event masks. The sections are organized according to these processing categories:

- Keyboard and pointer events
- Window crossing events
- Input focus events
- Keymap state notification events
- Exposure events
- Window state notification events
- Structure control events
- Colormap state notification events
- Client communication events

8.4.1   Keyboard and Pointer Events

This section discusses:

- Pointer button events
- Keyboard and pointer events

8.4.1.1 Pointer Button Events

The following describes the event processing that occurs when a pointer button press is processed with the pointer in some window w and when no active pointer grab is in progress.

The X server searches the ancestors of w from the root down, looking for a passive grab to activate. If no matching passive grab on the button exists,

Event Mask	Event Type	Structure	Generic Structure
ButtonMotionMask	MotionNotify	XPointerMovedEvent	XMotionEvent
Button1MotionMask			
Button2MotionMask			
Button3MotionMask			
Button4MotionMask			
Button5MotionMask			
ButtonPressMask	ButtonPress	XButtonPressedEvent	XButtonEvent
ButtonReleaseMask	ButtonRelease	XButtonReleasedEvent	XButtonEvent
ColormapChangeMask	ColormapNotify	XColormapEvent	
EnterWindowMask	EnterNotify	XEnterWindowEvent	XCrossingEvent
LeaveWindowMask	LeaveNotify	XLeaveWindowEvent	XCrossingEvent
ExposureMask	Expose	XExposeEvent	
GCGraphicsExposure in GC	GraphicsExpose	XGraphicsExposeEvent	
	NoExpose	XNoExposeEvent	
FocusChangeMask	FocusIn	XFocusInEvent	XFocusChangeEvent
	FocusOut	XFocusOutEvent	XFocusChangeEvent
KeymapStateMask	KeymapNotify	XKeymapEvent	
KeyPressMask	KeyPress	XKeyPressedEvent	XKeyEvent
KeyReleaseMask	KeyRelease	XKeyReleasedEvent	XKeyEvent
OwnerGrabButtonMask	N.A.	N.A.	
PointerMotionMask	MotionNotify	XPointerMovedEvent	XMotionEvent
PointerMotionHintMask	N.A.	N.A.	
PropertyChangeMask	PropertyNotify	XPropertyEvent	
ResizeRedirectMask	ResizeRequest	XResizeRequestEvent	
StructureNotifyMask	CirculateNotify	XCirculateEvent	
	ConfigureNotify	XConfigureEvent	
	DestroyNotify	XDestroyWindowEvent	

Mask	Event	Event Type
SubstructureNotifyMask	GravityNotify	XGravityEvent
	MapNotify	XMapEvent
	ReparentNotify	XReparentEvent
	UnmapNotify	XUnmapEvent
	CirculateNotify	XCirculateEvent
	ConfigureNotify	XConfigureEvent
	CreateNotify	XCreateWindowEvent
	DestroyNotify	XDestroyWindowEvent
	GravityNotify	XGravityEvent
	MapNotify	XMapEvent
	ReparentNotify	XReparentEvent
	UnmapNotify	XUnmapEvent
SubstructureRedirectMask	CirculateRequest	XCirculateRequestEvent
	ConfigureRequest	XConfigureRequestEvent
	MapRequest	XMapRequestEvent
N.A.	ClientMessage	XClientMessageEvent
N.A.	MappingNotify	XMappingEvent
N.A.	SelectionClear	XSelectionClearEvent
N.A.	SelectionNotify	XSelectionEvent
N.A.	SelectionRequest	XSelectionRequestEvent
VisibilityChangeMask	VisibilityNotify	XVisibilityEvent

the X server automatically starts an active grab for the client receiving the event and sets the last-pointer-grab time to the current server time. The effect is essentially equivalent to an XGrabButton with these client passed arguments:

Argument	Value
w	The event window
event_mask	The client's selected pointer events on the event window
pointer_mode	GrabModeAsync
keyboard_mode	GrabModeAsync
owner_events	True, if the client has selected OwnerGrabButtonMask on the event window, otherwise False
confine_to	None
cursor	None

The active grab is automatically terminated when the logical state of the pointer has all buttons released. Clients can modify the active grab by calling XUngrabPointer and XChangeActivePointerGrab.

8.4.1.2 Keyboard and Pointer Events

This section discusses the processing that occurs for the keyboard events KeyPress and KeyRelease and the pointer events ButtonPress, ButtonRelease, and MotionNotify. For information about the keyboard event-handling utilities, see chapter 10.

The X server reports KeyPress or KeyRelease events to clients wanting information about keys that logically change state. Note that these events are generated for all keys, even those mapped to modifier bits. The X server reports ButtonPress or ButtonRelease events to clients wanting information about buttons that logically change state.

The X server reports MotionNotify events to clients wanting information about when the pointer logically moves. The X server generates this event whenever the pointer is moved and the pointer motion begins and ends in the window. The granularity of MotionNotify events is not guaranteed, but a client that selects this event type is guaranteed to receive at least one event when the pointer moves and then rests.

The generation of the logical changes lags the physical changes if device event processing is frozen.

To receive `KeyPress`, `KeyRelease`, `ButtonPress`, and `Button-Release` events, set `KeyPressMask`, `KeyReleaseMask`, `ButtonPressMask`, and `ButtonReleaseMask` bits in the event-mask attribute of the window.

To receive `MotionNotify` events, set one or more of the following event mask bits in the event-mask attribute of the window.

`Button1MotionMask`
`Button2MotionMask`
`Button3MotionMask`
`Button4MotionMask`
`Button5MotionMask`
	The client application receives `MotionNotify` events only when one or more of the specified buttons is pressed.

`ButtonMotionMask`	The client application receives `MotionNotify` events only when at least one button is pressed.
`PointerMotionMask`	The client application receives `MotionNotify` events independent of the state of the pointer buttons.
`PointerMotionHint`	If `PointerMotionHintMask` is selected, the X server is free to send only one `MotionNotify` event (with the is_hint member of the `XPointerMovedEvent` structure set to `NotifyHint`) to client for the event window, until either the key or button state changes, the pointer leaves the event window, or the client calls `XQueryPointer` or `XGetMotionEvents`. The server still may send `MotionNotify` events without is_hint set to `NotifyHint`.

The source of the event is the viewable window that the pointer is in. The window used by the X server to report these events depends on the window's position in the window hierarchy and whether any intervening window prohibits the generation of these events. Starting with the source window, the X server searches up the window hierarchy until it locates the first window specified by a client as having an interest in these events. If one of the intervening windows has its do-not-propagate-mask set to prohibit generation of the event type, the events of those types will be suppressed. Clients can modify the actual window used for reporting by performing active grabs and, in the case of keyboard events, by using the focus window.

The structures for these event types contain:

```
typedef struct {
    int type;                 /* ButtonPress or ButtonRelease */
    unsigned long serial;     /* # of last request processed by server */
    Bool send_event;          /* true if this came from a SendEvent request */
    Display *display;         /* Display the event was read from */
    Window window;            /* "event" window it is reported relative to */
    Window root;              /* root window that the event occurred on */
    Window subwindow;         /* child window */
    Time time;                /* milliseconds */
    int x, y;                 /* pointer x, y coordinates in event window */
    int x_root, y_root;       /* coordinates relative to root */
    unsigned int state;       /* key or button mask */
    unsigned int button;      /* detail */
    Bool same_screen;         /* same screen flag */
} XButtonEvent;
typedef XButtonEvent XButtonPressedEvent;
typedef XButtonEvent XButtonReleasedEvent;

typedef struct {
    int type;                 /* KeyPress or KeyRelease */
    unsigned long serial;     /* # of last request processed by server */
    Bool send_*/ event;       /* true if this came from a SendEvent request */
    Display *display;         /* Display the event was read from */
    Window window;            /* "event" window it is reported relative to */
    Window root;              /* root window that the event occurred on */
    Window subwindow;         /* child window */
    Time time;                /* milliseconds */
    int x, y;                 /* pointer x, y coordinates in event window */
    int x_root, y_root;       /* coordinates relative to root */
    unsigned int state;       /* key or button mask */
    unsigned int keycode;     /* detail */
    Bool same_screen;         /* same screen flag */
} XKeyEvent;
typedef XKeyEvent XKeyPressedEvent;
typedef XKeyEvent XKeyReleasedEvent;

typedef struct {
    int type;                 /* MotionNotify */
    unsigned long serial;     /* # of last request processed by server */
    Bool send_event;          /* true if this came from a SendEvent request */
    Display *display;         /* Display the event was read from */
```

```
    Window window;          /* "event" window reported relative to */
    Window root;            /* root window that the event occurred on */
    Window subwindow;       /* child window */
    Time time;              /* milliseconds */
    int x, y;               /* pointer x, y coordinates in event window */
    int x_root, y_root;     /* coordinates relative to root */
    unsigned int state;     /* key or button mask */
    char is_hint;           /* detail */
    Bool same_screen;       /* same screen flag */
} XMotionEvent;
typedef XMotionEvent XPointerMovedEvent;
```

These structures have the following common members: window, root, subwindow, time, x, y, x_root, y_root, state, and same_screen. The window member is set to the window on which the event was generated and is referred to as the event window. As long as the conditions previously discussed are met, this is the window used by the X server to report the event. The root member is set to the source window's root window. The x_root and y_root members are set to the pointer's coordinates relative to the root window's origin at the time of the event.

The same_screen member is set to indicate whether the event window is on the same screen as the root window and can be either `True` or `False`. If `True`, the event and root windows are on the same screen. If `False`, the event and root windows are not on the same screen.

If the source window is an inferior of the event window, the subwindow member of the structure is set to the child of the event window that is the source member or an ancestor of it. Otherwise, the X server sets the subwindow member to `None`. The time member is set to the time when the event was generated and is expressed in milliseconds.

If the event window is on the same screen as the root window, the x and y members are set to the coordinates relative to the event window's origin. Otherwise, these members are set to zero.

The state member is set to indicate the logical state of the pointer buttons and modifier keys just prior to the event which is the bitwise inclusive OR of one or more of the button or modifier key masks: `Button1Mask`, `Button2Mask`, `Button3Mask`, `Button4Mask`, `Button5Mask`, `Shift-Mask`, `LockMask`, `ControlMask`, `Mod1Mask`, `Mod2Mask`, `Mod3Mask`, `Mod4Mask`, and `Mod5Mask`.

Each of these structures also has a member that indicates the detail. For the XKeyPressedEvent and XKeyReleasedEvent structures, this member is called keycode. It is set to a number that represents a physical key on the keyboard. The keycode is an arbitrary representation for any key on the keyboard (see chapter 7).

For the XButtonPressedEvent and XButtonReleasedEvent structures, this member is called button. It represents the pointer button that changed state and can be the Button1, Button2, Button3, Button4, or Button5 value. For the XPointerMovedEvent structure, this member is called is_hint. It can be set to NotifyNormal or NotifyHint.

8.4.2   Window Entry/Exit Events

This section describes the processing that occurs for the window crossing events EnterNotify and LeaveNotify. If a pointer motion or a window hierarchy change causes the pointer to be in a different window than before, the X server reports EnterNotify or LeaveNotify events to clients who have selected for these events. All EnterNotify and LeaveNotify events caused by a hierarchy change are generated after any hierarchy event (UnmapNotify, MapNotify, ConfigureNotify, GravityNotify, CirculateNotify) caused by that change; however, the X protocol does not constrain the ordering of EnterNotify and LeaveNotify events with respect to FocusOut, VisibilityNotify, and Expose events.

This contrasts with MotionNotify events, which are also generated when the pointer moves but only when the pointer motion begins and ends in a single window. An EnterNotify or LeaveNotify event also can be generated when some client application calls XGrabPointer and XUngrabPointer.

To receive EnterNotify or LeaveNotify events, set the Enter-WindowMask or LeaveWindowMask bits of the event-mask attribute of the window.

The structure for these event types contains:

```
typedef struct {
        int type;                /* EnterNotify or LeaveNotify */
        unsigned long serial;    /* # of last request processed by server */
        Bool send_event;         /* true if this came from a SendEvent request */
        Display *display;        /* Display the event was read from */
        Window window;           /* "event" window reported relative to */
```

```
            Window root;              /* root window that the event occurred on */
            Window subwindow;         /* child window */
            Time time;                /* milliseconds */
            int x, y;                 /* pointer x, y coordinates in event window */
            int x_root, y_root;       /* coordinates relative to root */
            int mode;                 /* NotifyNormal, NotifyGrab,
                                         NotifyUngrab */
            int detail;               /* NotifyAncestor, NotifyVirtual,
                                         NotifyInferior, NotifyNonlinear,
                                         NotifyNonlinearVirtual */
            Bool same_screen;         /* same screen flag */
            Bool focus;               /* boolean focus */
            unsigned int state;       /* key or button mask */
     } XCrossingEvent;
     typedef XCrossingEvent XEnterWindowEvent;
     typedef XCrossingEvent XLeaveWindowEvent;
```

The window member is set to the window on which the `EnterNotify` or `LeaveNotify` event was generated and is referred to as the event window. This is the window used by the X server to report the event, and is relative to the root window on which the event occurred. The root member is set to the root window of the screen on which the event occurred.

For a `LeaveNotify` event, if a child of the event window contains the initial position of the pointer, the subwindow component is set to that child. Otherwise, the X server sets the subwindow member to `None`. For an `EnterNotify` event, if a child of the event window contains the final pointer position, the subwindow component is set to that child or `None`.

The time member is set to the time when the event was generated and is expressed in milliseconds. The x and y members are set to the coordinates of the pointer position in the event window. This position is always the pointer's final position, not its initial position. If the event window is on the same screen as the root window, x and y are the pointer coordinates relative to the event window's origin. Otherwise, x and y are set to zero. The x_root and y_root members are set to the pointer's coordinates relative to the root window's origin at the time of the event.

The same_screen member is set to indicate whether the event window is on the same screen as the root window and can be either `True` or `False`. If `True`, the event and root windows are on the same screen. If `False`, the event and root windows are not on the same screen.

The focus member is set to indicate whether the event window is the focus window or an inferior of the focus window. The X server can set this member to either `True` or `False`. If `True`, the event window is the focus window or an inferior of the focus window. If `False`, the event window is not the focus window or an inferior of the focus window.

The state member is set to indicate the state of the pointer buttons and modifier keys just prior to the event. The X server can set this member to the bitwise inclusive OR of one or more of the button or modifier key masks: `Button1Mask`, `Button2Mask`, `Button3Mask`, `Button4Mask`, `Button5-Mask`, `ShiftMask`, `LockMask`, `ControlMask`, `Mod1Mask`, `Mod2Mask`, `Mod3Mask`, `Mod4Mask`, `Mod5Mask`.

The mode member is set to indicate whether the events are normal events, pseudo-motion events when a grab activates, or pseudo-motion events when a grab deactivates. The X server can set this member to `NotifyNormal`, `NotifyGrab`, or `NotifyUngrab`.

The detail member is set to indicate the notify detail and can be `NotifyAncestor`, `NotifyVirtual`, `NotifyInferior`, `Notify-Nonlinear`, or `NotifyNonlinearVirtual`.

8.4.2.1 Normal Entry/Exit Events

`EnterNotify` and `LeaveNotify` events are generated when the pointer moves from one window to another window. Normal events are identified by `XEnterWindowEvent` or `XLeaveWindowEvent` structures whose mode member is set to `NotifyNormal`.

- When the pointer moves from window A to window B and A is an inferior of B, the X server does the following:
  — It generates a `LeaveNotify` event on window A, with the detail member of the `XLeaveWindowEvent` structure set to `NotifyAncestor`.

  — It generates a `LeaveNotify` event on each window between window A and window B, exclusive, with the detail member of each `XLeaveWindowEvent` structure set to `NotifyVirtual`.

  — It generates an `EnterNotify` event on window B, with the detail member of the `XEnterWindowEvent` structure set to `NotifyInferior`.

- When the pointer moves from window A to window B and B is an inferior of A, the X server does the following:
  — It generates a `LeaveNotify` event on window A, with the detail member of the `XLeaveWindowEvent` structure set to `NotifyInferior`.

— It generates an `EnterNotify` event on each window between window A and window B, exclusive, with the detail member of each `XEnterWindowEvent` structure set to `NotifyVirtual`.

— It generates an `EnterNotify` event on window B, with the detail member of the `XEnterWindowEvent` structure set to `NotifyAncestor`.

- When the pointer moves from window A to window B and window C is their least common ancestor, the X server does the following:
  — It generates a `LeaveNotify` event on window A, with the detail member of the `XLeaveWindowEvent` structure set to `NotifyNonlinear`.

  — It generates a `LeaveNotify` event on each window between window A and window C, exclusive, with the detail member of each `XLeaveWindowEvent` structure set to `NotifyNonlinearVirtual`.

  — It generates an `EnterNotify` event on each window between window C and window B, exclusive, with the detail member of each `XEnterWindowEvent` structure set to `NotifyNonlinearVirtual`.

  — It generates an `EnterNotify` event on window B, with the detail member of the `XEnterWindowEvent` structure set to `NotifyNonlinear`.

- When the pointer moves from window A to window B on different screens, the X server does the following:
  — It generates a `LeaveNotify` event on window A, with the detail member of the `XLeaveWindowEvent` structure set to `NotifyNonlinear`.

  — If window A is not a root window, it generates a `LeaveNotify` event on each window above window A up to and including its root, with the detail member of each `XLeaveWindowEvent` structure set to `NotifyNonlinearVirtual`.

  — If window B is not a root window, it generates an `EnterNotify` event on each window from window B's root down to but not including window B, with the detail member of each `XEnterWindowEvent` structure set to `Notify-NonlinearVirtual`.

  — It generates an `EnterNotify` event on window B, with the detail member of the `XEnterWindowEvent` structure set to `NotifyNonlinear`.

8.4.2.2 Grab and Ungrab Entry/Exit Events

Pseudo-motion mode `EnterNotify` and `LeaveNotify` events are generated when a pointer grab activates or deactivates. Events in which the pointer grab activates are identified by `XEnterWindowEvent` or `XLeave-WindowEvent` structures whose mode member is set to `NotifyGrab`. Events in which the pointer grab deactivates are identified by

XEnterWindowEvent or XLeaveWindowEvent structures whose mode member is set to NotifyUngrab (see XGrabPointer).

- When a pointer grab activates after any initial warp into a confine_to window and before generating any actual ButtonPress event that activates the grab, G is the grab_window for the grab, and P is the window the pointer is in, the X server does the following:
  - It generates EnterNotify and LeaveNotify events (see section 8.4.2.1) with the mode members of the XEnterWindowEvent and XLeaveWindowEvent structures set to NotifyGrab. These events are generated as if the pointer were to suddenly warp from its current position in P to some position in G. However, the pointer does not warp, and the X server uses the pointer position as both the initial and final positions for the events.

- When a pointer grab deactivates after generating any actual ButtonRelease event that deactivates the grab, G is the grab_window for the grab, and P is the window the pointer is in, the X server does the following:
  - It generates EnterNotify and LeaveNotify events (see section 8.4.2.1) with the mode members of the XEnterWindowEvent and XLeaveWindowEvent structures set to NotifyUngrab. These events are generated as if the pointer were to suddenly warp from some position in G to its current position in P. However, the pointer does not warp, and the X server uses the current pointer position as both the initial and final positions for the events.

8.4.3   Input Focus Events

This section describes the processing that occurs for the input focus events FocusIn and FocusOut. The X server can report FocusIn or FocusOut events to clients wanting information about when the input focus changes. The keyboard is always attached to some window (typically, the root window or a top-level window), which is called the focus window. The focus window and the position of the pointer determine the window that receives keyboard input. Clients may need to know when the input focus changes to control highlighting of areas on the screen.

To receive FocusIn or FocusOut events, set the FocusChangeMask bit in the event-mask attribute of the window.

The structure for these event types contains:

```
typedef struct {
    int type;                /* FocusIn or FocusOut */
    unsigned long serial;    /* # of last request processed by server */
    Bool send_event;         /* true if this came from a SendEvent request */
```

```
        Display *display;        /* Display the event was read from */
        Window window;           /* window of event */
        int mode;                /* NotifyNormal, NotifyGrab,
                                    NotifyUngrab */
        int detail;              /* NotifyAncestor, NotifyVirtual,
                                    NotifyInferior, NotifyNonlinear,
                                    NotifyNonlinearVirtual, NotifyPointer,
                                    NotifyPointerRoot, NotifyDetailNone */
} XFocusChangeEvent;
typedef XFocusChangeEvent XFocusInEvent;
typedef XFocusChangeEvent XFocusOutEvent;
```

The window member is set to the window on which the `FocusIn` or `FocusOut` event was generated. This is the window used by the X server to report the event. The mode member is set to indicate whether the focus events are normal focus events, focus events while grabbed, focus events when a grab activates, or focus events when a grab deactivates. The X server can set the mode member to `NotifyNormal`, `NotifyWhileGrabbed`, `NotifyGrab`, or `NotifyUngrab`.

All `FocusOut` events caused by a window unmap are generated after any `UnmapNotify` event; however, the X protocol does not constrain the ordering of `FocusOut` events with respect to generated `EnterNotify`, `LeaveNotify`, `VisibilityNotify`, and `Expose` events.

Depending on the event mode, the detail member is set to indicate the notify detail and can be `NotifyAncestor`, `NotifyVirtual`, `Notify-Inferior`, `NotifyNonlinear`, `NotifyNonlinearVirtual`, `Notify-Pointer`, `NotifyPointerRoot`, or `NotifyDetailNone`.

8.4.3.1 Normal Focus Events and Focus Events While Grabbed

Normal focus events are identified by `XFocusInEvent` or `XFocusOutEvent` structures whose mode member is set to `NotifyNormal`. Focus events while grabbed are identified by `XFocusInEvent` or `XFocusOutEvent` structures whose mode member is set to `NotifyWhileGrabbed`. The X server processes normal focus and focus events while grabbed according to the following:

• When the focus moves from window A to window B, A is an inferior of B, and the pointer is in window P, the X server does the following:

— It generates a `FocusOut` event on window A, with the detail member of the `XFocusOutEvent` structure set to `NotifyAncestor`.

— It generates a `FocusOut` event on each window between window A and window B, exclusive, with the detail member of each `XFocusOutEvent` structure set to `NotifyVirtual`.

— It generates a `FocusIn` event on window B, with the detail member of the `XFocusOutEvent` structure set to `NotifyInferior`.

— If window P is an inferior of window B but window P is not window A or an inferior or ancestor of window A, it generates a `FocusIn` event on each window below window B, down to and including window P, with the detail member of each `XFocusInEvent` structure set to `NotifyPointer`.

• When the focus moves from window A to window B, B is an inferior of A, and the pointer is in window P, the X server does the following:

— If window P is an inferior of window A but P is not an inferior of window B or an ancestor of B, it generates a `FocusOut` event on each window from window P up to but not including window A, with the detail member of each `XFocusOutEvent` structure set to `NotifyPointer`.

— It generates a `FocusOut` event on window A, with the detail member of the `XFocusOutEvent` structure set to `NotifyInferior`.

— It generates a `FocusIn` event on each window between window A and window B, exclusive, with the detail member of each `XFocusInEvent` structure set to `NotifyVirtual`.

— It generates a `FocusIn` event on window B, with the detail member of the `XFocusInEvent` structure set to `NotifyAncestor`.

• When the focus moves from window A to window B, window C is their least common ancestor, and the pointer is in window P, the X server does the following:

— If window P is an inferior of window A, it generates a `FocusOut` event on each window from window P up to but not including window A, with the detail member of the `XFocusOutEvent` structure set to `NotifyPointer`.

— It generates a `FocusOut` event on window A, with the detail member of the `XFocusOutEvent` structure set to `NotifyNonlinear`.

— It generates a `FocusOut` event on each window between window A and window C, exclusive, with the detail member of each `XFocusOutEvent` structure set to `NotifyNonlinearVirtual`.

— It generates a `FocusIn` event on each window between C and B, exclusive, with the detail member of each `XFocusInEvent` structure set to `Notify-NonlinearVirtual`.

- It generates a `FocusIn` event on window B, with the detail member of the `XFocusInEvent` structure set to `NotifyNonlinear`.

- If window P is an inferior of window B, it generates a `FocusIn` event on each window below window B down to and including window P, with the detail member of the `XFocusInEvent` structure set to `NotifyPointer`.

• When the focus moves from window A to window B on different screens and the pointer is in window P, the X server does the following:
  - If window P is an inferior of window A, it generates a `FocusOut` event on each window from window P up to but not including window A, with the detail member of each `XFocusOutEvent` structure set to `NotifyPointer`.

  - It generates a `FocusOut` event on window A, with the detail member of the `XFocusOutEvent` structure set to `NotifyNonlinear`.

  - If window A is not a root window, it generates a `FocusOut` event on each window above window A up to and including its root, with the detail member of each `XFocusOutEvent` structure set to `NotifyNonlinearVirtual`.

  - If window B is not a root window, it generates a `FocusIn` event on each window from window B's root down to but not including window B, with the detail member of each `XFocusInEvent` structure set to `Notify-NonlinearVirtual`.

  - It generates a `FocusIn` event on window B, with the detail member of each `XFocusInEvent` structure set to `NotifyNonlinear`.

  - If window P is an inferior of window B, it generates a `FocusIn` event on each window below window B down to and including window P, with the detail member of each `XFocusInEvent` structure set to `NotifyPointer`.

• When the focus moves from window A to `PointerRoot` (events sent to the window under the pointer) or `None` (discard), and the pointer is in window P, the X server does the following:
  - If window P is an inferior of window A, it generates a `FocusOut` event on each window from window P up to but not including window A, with the detail member of each `XFocusOutEvent` structure set to `NotifyPointer`.

  - It generates a `FocusOut` event on window A, with the detail member of the `XFocusOutEvent` structure set to `NotifyNonlinear`.

  - If window A is not a root window, it generates a `FocusOut` event on each window above window A up to and including its root, with the detail member of each `XFocusOutEvent` structure set to `NotifyNonlinearVirtual`.

  - It generates a `FocusIn` event on the root window of all screens, with the detail member of each `XFocusInEvent` structure set to `NotifyPointerRoot` (or `NotifyDetailNone`).

— If the new focus is `PointerRoot`, it generates a `FocusIn` event on each window from window P's root down to and including window P, with the detail member of each `XFocusInEvent` structure set to `NotifyPointer`.

- When the focus moves from `PointerRoot` (events sent to the window under the pointer) or `None` to window A, and the pointer is in window P, the X server does the following:

  — If the old focus is `PointerRoot`, it generates a `FocusOut` event on each window from window P up to and including window P's root, with the detail member of each `XFocusOutEvent` structure set to `NotifyPointer`.

  — It generates a `FocusOut` event on all root windows, with the detail member of each `XFocusOutEvent` structure set to `NotifyPointerRoot` (or `NotifyDetailNone`).

  — If window A is not a root window, it generates a `FocusIn` event on each window from window A's root down to but not including window A, with the detail member of each `XFocusInEvent` structure set to `NotifyNonlinearVirtual`.

  — It generates a `FocusIn` event on window A, with the detail member of the `XFocusInEvent` structure set to `NotifyNonlinear`.

  — If window P is an inferior of window A, it generates a `FocusIn` event on each window below window A down to and including window P, with the detail member of each `XFocusInEvent` structure set to `NotifyPointer`.

- When the focus moves from `PointerRoot` (events sent to the window under the pointer) to `None` (or vice versa), and the pointer is in window P, the X server does the following:

  — If the old focus is `PointerRoot`, it generates a `FocusOut` event on each window from window P up to and including window P's root, with the detail member of each `XFocusOutEvent` structure set to `NotifyPointer`.

  — It generates a `FocusOut` event on all root windows, with the detail member of each `XFocusOutEvent` structure set to either `NotifyPointerRoot` or `NotifyDetailNone`.

  — It generates a `FocusIn` event on all root windows, with the detail member of each `XFocusInEvent` structure set to `NotifyDetailNone` or `NotifyPointerRoot`.

  — If the new focus is `PointerRoot`, it generates a `FocusIn` event on each window from window P's root down to and including window P, with the detail member of each `XFocusInEvent` structure set to `NotifyPointer`.

8.4.3.2 Focus Events Generated by Grabs

Focus events in which the keyboard grab activates are identified by `XFocusInEvent` or `XFocusOutEvent` structures whose mode member is set to `NotifyGrab`. Focus events in which the keyboard grab deactivates are identified by `XFocusInEvent` or `XFocusOutEvent` structures whose mode member is set to `NotifyUngrab` (see `XGrabKeyboard`).

- When a keyboard grab activates before generating any actual `KeyPress` event that activates the grab, G is the grab_window, and F is the current focus, the X server does the following:
  — It generates `FocusIn` and `FocusOut` events, with the mode members of the `XFocusInEvent` and `XFocusOutEvent` structures set to `NotifyGrab`. These events are generated as if the focus were to change from F to G.

- When a keyboard grab deactivates after generating any actual `KeyRelease` event that deactivates the grab, G is the grab_window, and F is the current focus, the X server does the following:
  — It generates `FocusIn` and `FocusOut` events, with the mode members of the `XFocusInEvent` and `XFocusOutEvent` structures set to `NotifyUngrab`. These events are generated as if the focus were to change from G to F.

8.4.4 Keymap State Notification Events

The X server can report `KeymapNotify` events to clients that want information about changes in their keyboard state.

To receive `KeymapNotify` events, set the `KeymapStateMask` bit in the event-mask attribute of the window. The X server generates this event immediately after every `EnterNotify` and `FocusIn` event.

The structure for this event type contains:

```
/* generated on EnterWindow and FocusIn when KeymapState selected */
typedef struct {
    int type;                  /* KeymapNotify */
    unsigned long serial;      /* # of last request processed by server */
    Bool send_event;           /* true if this came from a SendEvent request */
    Display *display;          /* Display the event was read from */
    Window window;
    char key_vector[32];
} XKeymapEvent;
```

The window member is not used but is present to aid some toolkits. The key_vector member is set to the bit vector of the keyboard. Each bit set to 1 indicates that the corresponding key is currently pressed. The vector is represented as 32 bytes. Byte N (from 0) contains the bits for keys 8N to 8N + 7 with the least-significant bit in the byte representing key 8N.

8.4.5   Exposure Events

The X protocol does not guarantee to preserve the contents of window regions when the windows are obscured or reconfigured. Some implementations may preserve the contents of windows. Other implementations are free to destroy the contents of windows when exposed. X expects client applications to assume the responsibility for restoring the contents of an exposed window region. (An exposed window region describes a formerly obscured window whose region becomes visible.) Therefore, the X server sends Expose events describing the window and the region of the window that has been exposed. A naive client application usually redraws the entire window. A more sophisticated client application redraws only the exposed region.

8.4.5.1   Expose Events

The X server can report Expose events to clients wanting information about when the contents of window regions have been lost. The circumstances in which the X server generates Expose events are not as definite as those for other events. However, the X server never generates Expose events on windows whose class you specified as InputOnly. The X server can generate Expose events when no valid contents are available for regions of a window and either the regions are visible, the regions are viewable and the server is (perhaps newly) maintaining backing store on the window, or the window is not viewable but the server is (perhaps newly) honoring the window's backing-store attribute of Always or WhenMapped. The regions decompose into an (arbitrary) set of rectangles, and an Expose event is generated for each rectangle. For any given window, the X server guarantees to report contiguously all of the regions exposed by some action that causes Expose events, such as raising a window.

To receive Expose events, set the ExposureMask bit in the event-mask attribute of the window.

The structure for this event type contains:

```
typedef struct {
    int type;                    /* Expose */
    unsigned long serial;        /* # of last request processed by server */
    Bool send_event;             /* true if this came from a SendEvent request */
    Display *display;            /* Display the event was read from */
    Window window;
    int x, y;
    int width, height;
    int count;                   /* if nonzero, at least this many more */
} XExposeEvent;
```

The window member is set to the exposed (damaged) window. The x and y members are set to the coordinates relative to the window's origin and indicate the upper-left corner of the rectangle. The width and height members are set to the size (extent) of the rectangle. The count member is set to the number of Expose events that are to follow. If count is zero, no more Expose events follow for this window. However, if count is nonzero, at least that number of Expose events (and possibly more) follow for this window. Simple applications that do not want to optimize redisplay by distinguishing between subareas of its window can just ignore all Expose events with nonzero counts and perform full redisplays on events with zero counts.

8.4.5.2 GraphicsExpose and NoExpose Events

The X server can report GraphicsExpose events to clients wanting information about when a destination region could not be computed during certain graphics requests: XCopyArea or XCopyPlane. The X server generates this event whenever a destination region could not be computed due to an obscured or out-of-bounds source region. In addition, the X server guarantees to report contiguously all of the regions exposed by some graphics request (for example, copying an area of a drawable to a destination drawable).

The X server generates a NoExpose event whenever a graphics request that might produce a GraphicsExpose event does not produce any. In other words, the client is really asking for a GraphicsExpose event but instead receives a NoExpose event.

To receive GraphicsExpose or NoExpose events, you must first set the graphics-exposure attribute of the graphics context to True. You also can set the graphics-expose attribute when creating a graphics context using XCreateGC or by calling XSetGraphicsExposures.

The structures for these event types contain:

```
typedef struct {
    int type;                    /* GraphicsExpose */
    unsigned long serial;        /* # of last request processed by server */
    Bool send_event;             /* true if this came from a SendEvent request */
    Display *display;            /* Display the event was read from */
    Drawable drawable;
    int x, y;
    int width, height;
    int count;                   /* if nonzero, at least this many more */
    int major_code;              /* core is CopyArea or CopyPlane */
    int minor_code;              /* not defined in the core */
} XGraphicsExposeEvent;

typedef struct {
    int type;                    /* NoExpose */
    unsigned long serial;        /* # of last request processed by server */
    Bool send_event;             /* true if this came from a SendEvent request */
    Display *display;            /* Display the event was read from */
    Drawable drawable;
    int major_code;              /* core is CopyArea or CopyPlane */
    int minor_code;              /* not defined in the core */
} XNoExposeEvent;
```

Both structures have these common members: drawable, major_code, and minor_code. The drawable member is set to the drawable of the destination region on which the graphics request was to be performed. The major_code member is set to the graphics request initiated by the client and can be either X_CopyArea or X_CopyPlane. If it is X_CopyArea, a call to XCopyArea initiated the request. If it is X_CopyPlane, a call to XCopyPlane initiated the request. These constants are defined in <X11/Xproto.h>. The minor_code member, like the major_code member, indicates which graphics request was initiated by the client. However, the minor_code member is not defined by the core X protocol and will be zero in these cases, although it may be used by an extension.

The XGraphicsExposeEvent structure has these additional members:

x, y, width, height, and count. The x and y members are set to the coordinates relative to the drawable's origin and indicate the upper-left corner of the rectangle. The width and height members are set to the size (extent) of the rectangle. The count member is set to the number of GraphicsExpose events to follow. If count is zero, no more GraphicsExpose events follow for this window. However, if count is nonzero, at least that number of GraphicsExpose events (and possibly more) are to follow for this window.

8.4.6 Window State Change Events

The following sections discuss:

- CirculateNotify events
- ConfigureNotify events
- CreateNotify events
- DestroyNotify events
- GravityNotify events
- MapNotify events
- MappingNotify events
- ReparentNotify events
- UnmapNotify events
- VisibilityNotify events

8.4.6.1 CirculateNotify Events

The X server can report CirculateNotify events to clients wanting information about when a window changes its position in the stack. The X server generates this event type whenever a window is actually restacked as a result of a client application calling XCirculateSubwindows, XCirculate-SubwindowsUp, or XCirculateSubwindowsDown.

To receive CirculateNotify events, set the StructureNotifyMask bit in the event-mask attribute of the window or the Substructure-NotifyMask bit in the event-mask attribute of the parent window (in which case, circulating any child generates an event).

The structure for this event type contains:

```
typedef struct {
    int type;                 /* CirculateNotify */
    unsigned long serial;     /* # of last request processed by server */
    Bool send_event;          /* true if this came from a SendEvent request */
    Display *display;         /* Display the event was read from */
    Window event;
    Window window;
    int place;                /* PlaceOnTop, PlaceOnBottom */
} XCirculateEvent;
```

The event member is set either to the restacked window or to its parent, depending on whether StructureNofify or SubstructureNotify was
selected. The window member is set to the window that was restacked. The
place member is set to the window's position after the restack occurs
and is either PlaceOnTop or PlaceOnBottom. If it is Place-
OnTop, the window is now on top of all siblings. If it is PlaceOnBottom, the
window is now below all siblings.

8.4.6.2 ConfigureNotify Events

The X server can report ConfigureNotify events to clients wanting information about actual changes to a window's state, such as size, position, border, and stacking order. The X server generates this event type whenever
one of the following configure window requests made by a client application
actually completes:

- A window's size, position, border, and/or stacking order is reconfigured by calling
  XConfigureWindow.

- The window's position in the stacking order is changed by calling XLowerWindow,
  XRaiseWindow, or XRestackWindows.

- A window is moved by calling XMoveWindow.

- A window's size is changed by calling XResizeWindow.

- A window's size and location is changed by calling XMoveResizeWindow.

- A window is mapped and its position in the stacking order is changed by calling
  XMapRaised.

- A window's border width is changed by calling XSetWindowBorderWidth.

To receive `ConfigureNotify` events, set the `StructureNotifyMask`
bit in the event-mask attribute of the window or the `Substructure-
NotifyMask` bit in the event-mask attribute of the parent window (in which
case, configuring any child generates an event).

The structure for this event type contains:

```
typedef struct {
        int type;                    /* ConfigureNotify */
        unsigned long serial;        /* # of last request processed by server */
        Bool send_event;             /* true if this came from a SendEvent request */
        Display *display;            /* Display the event was read from */
        Window event;
        Window window;
        int x, y;
        int width, height;
        int border_width;
        Window above;
        Bool override_redirect;
} XConfigureEvent;
```

The event member is set either to the reconfigured window or to its parent,
depending on whether `StructureNotify` or `SubstructureNotify` was
selected. The window member is set to the window whose size, position, border, and/or stacking order was changed.

The x and y members are set to the coordinates relative to the parent window's origin and indicate the position of the upper-left outside corner of the
window. The width and height members are set to the inside size of the window, not including the border. The border_width member is set to the width
of the window's border, in pixels.

The above member is set to the sibling window and is used for stacking operations. If the X server sets this member to `None`, the window whose state
was changed is on the bottom of the stack with respect to sibling windows.
However, if this member is set to a sibling window, the window whose state
was changed is placed on top of this sibling window.

The override_redirect member is set to the override-redirect attribute of
the window. Window manager clients normally should ignore this window if
the override_redirect member is `True`.

8.4.6.3 CreateNotify Events

The X server can report `CreateNotify` events to clients wanting information about creation of windows. The X server generates this event whenever a client application creates a window by calling `XCreateWindow` or `XCreateSimpleWindow`.

To receive `CreateNotify` events, set the `SubstructureNotifyMask` bit in the event-mask attribute of the window. Creating any children then generates an event.

The structure for the event type contains:

```
typedef struct {
    int type;                    /* CreateNotify */
    unsigned long serial;        /* # of last request processed by server */
    Bool send_event;             /* true if this came from a SendEvent request */
    Display *display;            /* Display the event was read from */
    Window parent;               /* parent of the window */
    Window window;               /* window id of window created */
    int x, y;                    /* window location */
    int width, height;           /* size of window */
    int border_width;            /* border width */
    Bool override_redirect;      /* creation should be overridden */
} XCreateWindowEvent;
```

The parent member is set to the created window's parent. The window member specifies the created window. The x and y members are set to the created window's coordinates relative to the parent window's origin and indicate the position of the upper-left outside corner of the created window. The width and height members are set to the inside size of the created window (not including the border) and are always nonzero. The border_width member is set to the width of the created window's border, in pixels. The override_redirect member is set to the override-redirect attribute of the window. Window manager clients normally should ignore this window if the override_redirect member is `True`.

8.4.6.4 DestroyNotify Events

The X server can report `DestroyNotify` events to clients wanting information about which windows are destroyed. The X server generates this event whenever a client application destroys a window by calling `XDestroy Window` or `XDestroySubwindows`.

The ordering of the `DestroyNotify` events is such that for any given window, `DestroyNotify` is generated on all inferiors of the window before being generated on the window itself. The X protocol does not constrain the ordering among siblings and across subhierarchies.

To receive `DestroyNotify` events, set the `StructureNotifyMask` bit in the event-mask attribute of the window or the `Substructure-NotifyMask` bit in the event-mask attribute of the parent window (in which case, destroying any child generates an event).

The structure for this event type contains:

```
typedef struct {
        int type;                /* DestroyNotify */
        unsigned long serial;    /* # of last request processed by server */
        Bool send_event;         /* true if this came from a SendEvent request */
        Display *display;        /* Display the event was read from */
        Window event;
        Window window;
} XDestroyWindowEvent;
```

The event member is set either to the destroyed window or to its parent, depending on whether `StructureNotify` or `SubstructureNotify` was selected. The window member is set to the window that is destroyed.

8.4.6.5 GravityNotify Events

The X server can report `GravityNotify` events to clients wanting information about when a window is moved because of a change in the size of its parent. The X server generates this event whenever a client application actually moves a child window as a result of resizing its parent by calling `XConfigureWindow`, `XMoveResizeWindow`, or `XResizeWindow`.

To receive `GravityNotify` events, set the `StructureNotifyMask` bit in the event-mask attribute of the window or the `Substructure-NotifyMask` bit in the event-mask attribute of the parent window (in which case, any child that is moved because its parent has been resized generates an event).

The structure for this event type contains:

```
typedef struct {
        int type;                /* GravityNotify */
        unsigned long serial;    /* # of last request processed by server */
```

```
    Bool send_event;        /* true if this came from a SendEvent request */
    Display *display;       /* Display the event was read from */
    Window event;
    Window window;
    int x, y;
} XGravityEvent;
```

The event member is set either to the window that was moved or to its parent, depending on whether StructureNotify or SubstructureNotify was selected. The window member is set to the child window that was moved. The x and y members are set to the coordinates relative to the new parent window's origin and indicate the position of the upper-left outside corner of the window.

8.4.6.6 MapNotify Events

The X server can report MapNotify events to clients wanting information about which windows are mapped. The X server generates this event type whenever a client application changes the window's state from unmapped to mapped by calling XMapWindow, XMapRaised, XMapSubwindows, XReparentWindow, or as a result of save-set processing.

To receive MapNotify events, set the StructureNotifyMask bit in the event-mask attribute of the window or the SubstructureNotifyMask bit in the event-mask attribute of the parent window (in which case, mapping any child generates an event).

The structure for this event type contains:

```
typedef struct {
    int type;               /* MapNotify */
    unsigned long serial;   /* # of last request processed by server */
    Bool send_event;        /* true if this came from a SendEvent request */
    Display *display;       /* Display the event was read from */
    Window event;
    Window window;
    Bool override_redirect; /* boolean, is override set . . .*/
} XMapEvent;
```

The event member is set either to the window that was mapped or to its parent, depending on whether StructureNotify or SubstructureNotify was selected. The window member is set to the window that was mapped. The override_redirect member is set to the override-redirect attribute of the window. Window manager clients normally should ignore this window if the override-redirect attribute is `True`, because these events usually are generated from pop-ups, which override structure control.

8.4.6.7 MappingNotify Events

The X server reports `MappingNotify` events to all clients. There is no mechanism to express disinterest in this event. The X server generates this event type whenever a client application successfully calls:

- `XSetModifierMapping` to indicate which KeyCodes are to be used as modifiers
- `XChangeKeyboardMapping` to change the keyboard mapping
- `XSetPointerMapping` to set the pointer mapping

The structure for this event type contains:

```
typedef struct {
      int type;                 /* MappingNotify */
      unsigned long serial;     /* # of last request processed by server */
      Bool send_event;          /* true if this came from a SendEvent request */
      Display *display;         /* Display the event was read from */
      Window window;            /* unused */
      int request;              /* one of MappingModifier, MappingKeyboard,
                                   MappingPointer */
      int first_keycode;        /* first keycode */
      int count;                /* defines range of change w. first_keycode*/
} XMappingEvent;
```

The request member is set to indicate the kind of mapping change that occurred and can be `MappingModifier`, `MappingKeyboard`, `MappingPointer`. If it is `MappingModifier`, the modifier mapping was changed. If it is `MappingKeyboard`, the keyboard mapping was changed. If it is `MappingPointer`, the pointer button mapping was changed. The first_keycode and count members are set only if the request member was set to `MappingKeyboard`. The number in first_keycode represents the first number in the range of the altered mapping, and count represents the number of keycodes altered.

To update the client application's knowledge of the keyboard, you should call `XRefreshKeyboardMapping`.

8.4.6.8 ReparentNotify Events

The X server can report `ReparentNotify` events to clients wanting information about changing a window's parent. The X server generates this event whenever a client application calls `XReparentWindow` and the window is actually reparented.

To receive `ReparentNotify` events, set the `StructureNotifyMask` bit in the event-mask attribute of the window or the `Substructure-NotifyMask` bit in the event-mask attribute of either the old or the new parent window (in which case, reparenting and child generates an event).

The structure for this event type contains:

```
typedef struct {
    int type;                  /* ReparentNotify */
    unsigned long serial;      /* # of last request processed by server */
    Bool send_event;           /* true if this came from a SendEvent request */
    Display *display;          /* Display the event was read from */
    Window event;
    Window window;
    Window parent;
    int x, y;
    Bool override_redirect;
} XReparentEvent;
```

The event member is set either to the reparented window or to its old or new parent, depending on whether `StructureNotify` or `Substructure-Notify` was selected. The window member is set to the window that was reparented. The parent member is set to the new parent window. The x and y members are set to the reparented window's coordinates relative to the new parent window's origin and define the upper-left outer corner of the reparented window. The override_redirect member is set to the override-redirect attribute of the window specified by the window member. Window manager clients normally should ignore this window if the override_redirect member is `True`.

8.4.6.9 UnmapNotify Events

The X server can report `UnmapNotify` events to clients wanting information about which windows are unmapped. The X server generates this event type whenever a client application changes the window's state from mapped to unmapped.

To receive `UnmapNotify` events, set the `StructureNotifyMask` bit in the event-mask attribute of the window or the `SubstructureNotifyMask` bit in the event-mask attribute of the parent window (in which case, unmapping any child window generates an event).

The structure for this event type contains:

```
typedef struct {
    int type;                /* UnmapNotify */
    unsigned long serial;    /* # of last request processed by server */
    Bool send_event;         /* true if this came from a SendEvent request */
    Display *display;        /* Display the event was read from */
    Window event;
    Window window;
    Bool from_configure;
} XUnmapEvent;
```

The event member is set either to the unmapped window or to its parent, depending on whether `StructureNotify` or `SubstructureNotify` was selected. This is the window used by the X server to report the event. The window member is set to the window that was unmapped. The from_configure member is set to `True` if the event was generated as a result of a resizing of the window's parent when the window itself had a win_gravity of `UnmapGravity`.

8.4.6.10 VisibilityNotify Events

The X server can report `VisibilityNotify` events to clients wanting any change in the visibility of the specified window. A region of a window is visible if someone looking at the screen can actually see it. The X server generates this event whenever the visibility changes state. However, this event is never generated for windows whose class is `InputOnly`.

All `VisibilityNotify` events caused by a hierarchy change are generated after any hierarchy event (`UnmapNotify`, `MapNotify`, `Configure-Notify`, `GravityNotify`, `CirculateNotify`) caused by that change. Any `VisibilityNotify` event on a given window is generated before any `Expose` events on that window, but it is not required that all `VisibilityNotify` events on all windows be generated before all `Expose` events on all windows. The X protocol does not constrain the ordering of

`VisibilityNotify` events with respect to `FocusOut`, `EnterNotify`, and `LeaveNotify` events.

To receive `VisibilityNotify` events, set the `Visibility-ChangeMask` bit in the event-mask attribute of the window.

The structure for this event type contains:

```
typedef struct {
    int type;                   /* VisibilityNotify */
    unsigned long serial;       /* # of last request processed by server */
    Bool send_event;            /* true if this came from a SendEvent request */
    Display *display;           /* Display the event was read from */
    Window window;
    int state;
} XVisibilityEvent;
```

The window member is set to the window whose visibility state changes. The state member is set to the state of the window's visibility and can be `VisibilityUnobscured`, `VisibilityPartiallyObscured`, or `VisibilityFullyObscured`. The X server ignores all of a window's subwindows when determining the visibility state of the window and processes `VisibilityNotify` events according to the following:

• When the window changes state from partially obscured, fully obscured, or not viewable to viewable and completely unobscured, the X server generates the event with the state member of the `XVisibilityEvent` structure set to `Visibility-Unobscured`.

• When the window changes state from viewable and completely unobscured or not viewable to viewable and partially obscured, the X server generates the event with the state member of the `XVisibilityEvent` structure set to `Visibility-PartiallyObscured`.

• When the window changes state from viewable and completely unobscured, viewable and partially obscured, or not viewable to viewable and fully obscured, the X server generates the event with the state member of the `XVisibility-Event` structure set to `VisibilityFullyObscured`.

8.4.7   Structure Control Events

This section discusses:

• `CirculateRequest` events
• `ConfigureRequest` events

- `MapRequest` events

- `ResizeRequest` events

8.4.7.1 CirculateRequest Events

The X server can report `CirculateRequest` events to clients wanting information about when another client initiates a circulate window request on a specified window. The X server generates this event type whenever a client initiates a circulate window request on a window and a subwindow actually needs to be restacked. The client initiates a circulate window request on the window by calling `XCirculateSubwindows`, `XCirculateSubwindows-Up`, or `XCirculateSubwindowsDown`.

To receive `CirculateRequest` events, set the `Substructure-RedirectMask` in the event-mask attribute of the window. Then, in the future, the circulate window request for the specified window is not executed, and thus, any subwindow's position in the stack is not changed. For example, suppose a client application calls `XCirculateSubwindowsUp` to raise a subwindow to the top of the stack. If you had selected `SubstructureRedirectMask` on the window, the X server reports to you a `CirculateRequest` event and does not raise the subwindow to the top of the stack.

The structure for this event type contains:

```
typedef struct {
      int type;                /* CirculateRequest */
      unsigned long serial;    /* # of last request processed by server */
      Bool send_event;         /* true if this came from a SendEvent request */
      Display *display;        /* Display the event was read from */
      Window parent;
      Window window;
      int place;               /* PlaceOnTop, PlaceOnBottom */
} XCirculateRequestEvent;
```

The parent member is set to the parent window. The window member is set to the subwindow to be restacked. The place member is set to what the new position in the stacking order should be and is either `PlaceOnTop` or `PlaceOnBottom`. If it is `PlaceOnTop`, the subwindow should be on top of all siblings. If it is `PlaceOnBottom`, the subwindow should be below all siblings.

8.4.7.2 ConfigureRequest Events

The X server can report ConfigureRequest events to clients wanting information about when a different client initiates a configure window request on any child of a specified window. The configure window request attempts to reconfigure a window's size, position, border, and stacking order. The X server generates this event whenever a different client initiates a configure window request on a window by calling XConfigureWindow, XLower-Window, XRaiseWindow, XMapRaised, XMoveResizeWindow, XMove-Window, XResizeWindow, XRestackWindows, or XSetWindow-BorderWidth.

To receive ConfigureRequest events, set the Substructure-RedirectMask bit in the event-mask attribute of the window. ConfigureRequest events are generated when a ConfigureWindow protocol request is issued on a child window by another client. For example, suppose a client application calls XLowerWindow to lower a window. If you had selected SubstructureRedirectMask on the parent window and if the override-redirect attribute of the window is set to False, the X server reports a ConfigureRequest event to you and does not lower the specified window.

The structure for this event type contains:

```
typedef struct {
        int type;                       /* ConfigureRequest */
        unsigned long serial;           /* # of last request processed by server */
        Bool send_event;                /* true if this came from a SendEvent
                                           request */
        Display *display;               /* Display the event was read from */
        Window parent;
        Window window;
        int x, y;
        int width, height;
        int border_width;
        Window above;
        int detail;                     /* Above, Below, TopIf, BottomIf,
                                           Opposite */
        unsigned long value_mask;
} XConfigureRequestEvent;
```

The parent member is set to the parent window. The window member is set to the window whose size, position, border width, and/or stacking order is to be reconfigured. The value_mask member indicates which components were specified in the ConfigureWindow protocol request. The corresponding values are reported as given in the request. The remaining values are filled in from the current geometry of the window, except in the case of above (sibling) and detail (stack-mode), which are reported as Above and None, respectively, if they are not given in the request.

8.4.7.3 MapRequest Events

The X server can report MapRequest events to clients wanting information about a different client's desire to map windows. A window is considered mapped when a map window request completes. The X server generates this event whenever a different client initiates a map window request on an unmapped window whose override_redirect member is set to False. Clients initiate map window requests by calling XMapWindow, XMapRaised, or XMapSubwindows.

To receive MapRequest events, set the SubstructureRedirectMask bit in the event-mask attribute of the window. This means another client's attempts to map a child window by calling one of the map window request functions is intercepted, and you are sent a MapRequest instead. For example, suppose a client application calls XMapWindow to map a window. If you (usually a window manager) had selected SubstructureRedirectMask on the parent window and if the override-redirect attribute of the window is set to False, the X server reports a MapRequest event to you and does not map the specified window. Thus, this event gives your window manager client the ability to control the placement of subwindows.

The structure for this event type contains:

```
typedef struct {
    int type;                    /* MapRequest */
    unsigned long serial;        /* # of last request processed by server */
    Bool send_event;             /* true if this came from a SendEvent request */
    Display *display;            /* Display the event was read from */
    Window parent;
    Window window;
} XMapRequestEvent;
```

The parent member is set to the parent window. The window member is set to the window to be mapped.

8.4.7.4 ResizeRequest Events

The X server can report `ResizeRequest` events to clients wanting information about another client's attempts to change the size of a window. The X server generates this event whenever some other client attempts to change the size of the specified window by calling `XConfigureWindow`, `XResize-Window`, or `XMoveResizeWindow`.

To receive `ResizeRequest` events, set the `ResizeRedirect` bit in the event-mask attribute of the window. Any attempts to change the size by other clients are then redirected.

The structure for this event type contains:

```
typedef struct {
    int type;                 /* ResizeRequest */
    unsigned long serial;     /* # of last request processed by server */
    Bool send_event;          /* true if this came from a SendEvent request */
    Display *display;         /* Display the event was read from */
    Window window;
    int width, height;
} XResizeRequestEvent;
```

The window member is set to the window whose size another client attempted to change. The width and height members are set to the inside size of the window, excluding the border.

8.4.8   Colormap State Change Events

The X server can report `ColormapNotify` events to clients wanting information about when the colormap changes and when a colormap is installed or uninstalled. The X server generates this event type whenever a client application:

• Changes the colormap member of the `XSetWindowAttributes` structure by calling `XChangeWindowAttributes`, `XFreeColormap`, or `XSetWindow-Colormap`

• Installs or uninstalls the colormap by calling `XInstallColormap` or `XUninstallColormap`

To receive `ColormapNotify` events, set the `ColormapChangeMask` bit in the event-mask attribute of the window.

The structure for this event type contains:

```
typedef struct {
      int type;                    /* ColormapNotify */
      unsigned long serial;        /* # of last request processed by server */
      Bool send_event;             /* true if this came from a SendEvent request */
      Display *display;            /* Display the event was read from */
      Window window;
      Colormap colormap;           /* colormap or None */
      Bool new;
      int state;                   /* ColormapInstalled,
                                      ColormapUninstalled */
} XColormapEvent;
```

The window member is set to the window whose associated colormap is changed, installed, or uninstalled. For a colormap that is changed, installed, or uninstalled, the colormap member is set to the colormap associated with the window. For a colormap that is changed by a call to `XFreeColormap`, the colormap member is set to `None`. The new member is set to indicate whether the colormap for the specified window was changed or installed or uninstalled and can be `True` or `False`. If it is `True`, the colormap was changed. If it is `False`, the colormap was installed or uninstalled. The state member is always set to indicate whether the colormap is installed or uninstalled and can be `ColormapInstalled` or `Colormap-Uninstalled`.

8.4.9 Client Communication Events

This section discusses:

- `ClientMessage` events
- `PropertyNotify` events
- `SelectionClear` events
- `SelectionNotify` events
- `SelectionRequest` events

8.4.9.1 ClientMessage Events

The X server generates `ClientMessage` events only when a client calls the function `XSendEvent`.

The structure for this event type contains:

```
typedef struct {
    int type;                 /* ClientMessage */
    unsigned long serial;     /* # of last request processed by server */
    Bool send_event;          /* true if this came from a SendEvent request */
    Display *display;         /* Display the event was read from */
    Window window;
    Atom message_type;
    int format;
    union {
        char b[20];
        short s[10];
        long l[5];
    } data;
} XClientMessageEvent;
```

The window member is set to the window to which the event was sent. The message_type member is set to an atom that indicates how the data should be interpreted by the receiving client. The format member is set to 8, 16, or 32 and specifies whether the data should be viewed as a list of bytes, shorts, or longs. The data member is a union that contains the members b, s, and l. The b, s, and l members represent data of 20 8-bit values, 10 16-bit values, and 5 32-bit values. Particular message types might not make use of all these values. The X server places no interpretation on the values in the message_type or data members.

8.4.9.2 PropertyNotify Events

The X server can report `PropertyNotify` events to clients wanting information about property changes for a specified window.

To receive `PropertyNotify` events, set the `PropertyChangeMask` bit in the event-mask attribute of the window.

The structure for this event type contains:

```
typedef struct {
    int type;                 /* PropertyNotify */
    unsigned long serial;     /* # of last request processed by server */
```

```
        Bool send_event;        /* true if this came from a SendEvent request */
        Display *display;       /* Display the event was read from */
        Window window;
        Atom atom;
        Time time;
        int state;              /* PropertyNewValue or PropertyDelete */
} XPropertyEvent;
```

The window member is set to the window whose associated property was changed. The atom member is set to the property's atom and indicates which property was changed or desired. The time member is set to the server time when the property was changed. The state member is set to indicate whether the property was changed to a new value or deleted and can be `PropertyNewValue` or `PropertyDelete`. The state member is set to `PropertyNewValue` when a property of the window is changed using `XChangeProperty` or `XRotateWindowProperties` (even when adding zero-length data using `XChangeProperty`) and when replacing all or part of a property with identical data using `XChangeProperty` or `XRotate-WindowProperties`. The state member is set to `Property-Deleted` when a property of the window is deleted using `XDelete-Property` or, if the delete argument is `True`, `XGetWindow-Property`.

8.4.9.3 SelectionClear Events

The X server reports `SelectionClear` events to the current owner of a selection. The X server generates this event type on the window losing ownership of the selection to a new owner. This sequence of events could occur whenever a client calls `XSetSelectionOwner`.

The structure for this event type contains:

```
typedef struct {
        int type;               /* SelectionClear */
        unsigned long serial;   /* # of last request processed by server */
        Bool send_event;        /* true if this came from a SendEvent request */
        Display *display;       /* Display the event was read from */
        Window window;
        Atom selection;
        Time time;
} XSelectionClearEvent;
```

The window member is set to the window losing ownership of the selection. The selection member is set to the selection atom. The time member is set to the last change time recorded for the selection. The owner member is the window that was specified by the current owner in its XSet-SelectionOwner call.

8.4.9.4 SelectionRequest Events

The X server reports SelectionRequest events to the owner of a selection. The X server generates this event whenever a client requests a selection conversion by calling XConvertSelection and the specified selection is owned by a window.

The structure for this event type contains:

```
typedef struct {
        int type;                  /* SelectionRequest */
        unsigned long serial;      /* # of last request processed by server */
        Bool send_event;           /* true if this came from a SendEvent request */
        Display *display;          /* Display the event was read from */
        Window owner;
        Window requestor;
        Atom selection;
        Atom target;
        Atom property;
        Time time;
} XSelectionRequestEvent;
```

The owner member is set to the window owning the selection and is the window that was specified by the current owner in its XSetSelectionOwner call. The requestor member is set to the window requesting the selection. The selection member is set to the atom that names the selection. For example, PRIMARY is used to indicate the primary selection. The target member is set to the atom that indicates the type the selection is desired in. The property member can be a property name or None. The time member is set to the time and is a timestamp or CurrentTime from the ConvertSelection request.

The client who owns the selection should do the following:

• The owner client should convert the selection based on the atom contained in the target member.

- If a property was specified (that is, the property member is set), the owner client should store the result as that property on the requestor window and then send a SelectionNotify event to the requestor by calling XSendEvent with an empty event-mask; that is, the event should be sent to the creator of the requestor window.

- If None is specified as the property, the owner client should choose a property name on the requestor window and then send a SelectionNotify event giving the actual name.

- If the selection cannot be converted as requested, the owner client should send a SelectionNotify event with the property set to None.

8.4.9.5 SelectionNotify Events

This event is generated by the X server in response to a ConvertSelection protocol request when there is no owner for the selection. When there is an owner, it should be generated by the owner of the selection by using XSendEvent. The owner of a selection should send this event to a requestor when a selection has been converted and stored as a property or when a selection conversion could not be performed (which is indicated by setting the property member to None).

If None is specified as the property in the ConvertSelection protocol request, the owner should choose a property name, store the result as that property on the requestor window, and then send a SelectionNotify giving that actual property name.

The structure for this event type contains:

```
typedef struct {
        int type;                /* SelectionNotify */
        unsigned long serial;    /* # of last request processed by server */
        Bool send_event;         /* true if this came from a SendEvent request */
        Display *display;        /* Display the event was read from */
        Window requestor;
        Atom selection;
        Atom target;
        Atom property;           /* atom or None */
        Time time;
} XSelectionEvent;
```

The requestor member is set to the window associated with the requestor of the selection. The selection member is set to the atom that indicates the selection. For example, PRIMARY is used for the primary selection. The target member is set to the atom that indicates the converted type. For example, PIXMAP is used for a pixmap. The property member is set to the atom that indicates which property the result was stored on. If the conversion failed, the property member is set to None. The time member is set to the time the conversion took place and can be a timestamp or CurrentTime.

8.5   Selecting Events

There are two ways to select the events you want reported to your client application. One way is to set the event_mask member of the XSet-WindowAttributes structure when you call XCreateWindow and XChangeWindowAttributes. Another way is to use XSelectInput.

XSelectInput(*display, w, event_mask*)
    Display **display*;
    Window *w*;
    long *event_mask*;
display   Specifies the connection to the X server.
w   Specifies the window whose events you are interested in.
event_mask Specifies the event mask.

The XSelectInput function requests that the X server report the events associated with the specified event mask. Initially, X will not report any of these events. Events are reported relative to a window. If a window is not interested in a device event, it usually propagates to the closest ancestor that is interested, unless the do_not_propagate mask prohibits it.

Setting the event-mask attribute of a window overrides any previous call for the same window but not for other clients. Multiple clients can select for the same events on the same window with the following restrictions:

- Multiple clients can select events on the same window because their event masks are disjoint. When the X server generates an event, it reports it to all interested clients.

- Only one client at a time can select CirculateRequest, ConfigureRequest, or MapRequest events, which are associated with the event mask Substructure-RedirectMask.

- Only one client at a time can select a ResizeRequest event, which is associated with the event mask ResizeRedirectMask.

- Only one client at a time can select a ButtonPress event, which is associated with the event mask ButtonPressMask.

The server reports the event to all interested clients.

XSelectInput can generate a BadWindow error.

8.6   Handling the Output Buffer

The output buffer is an area used by Xlib to store requests. The functions described in this section flush the output buffer if the function would block or not return an event. That is, all requests residing in the output buffer that have not yet been sent are transmitted to the X server. These functions differ in the additional tasks they might perform.

To flush the output buffer, use XFlush.

XFlush(*display*)
        Display **display*;
display   Specifies the connection to the X server.

The XFlush function flushes the output buffer. Most client applications need not use this function because the output buffer is automatically flushed as needed by calls to XPending, XNextEvent, and XWindowEvent. Events generated by the server may be enqueued into the library's event queue.

To flush the output buffer and then wait until all requests have been processed, use XSync.

XSync(*display, discard*)
        Display **display*;
        Bool *discard*;
display   Specifies the connection to the X server.
discard   Specifies a Boolean value that indicates whether XSync discards all
                   events on the event queue.

The XSync function flushes the output buffer and then waits until all requests have been received and processed by the X server. Any errors generated must be handled by the error handler. For each error event received and processed by the X server, XSync calls the client application's error handling routine (see section 8.12.2). Any events generated by the server are enqueued into the library's event queue.

Finally, if you passed False, XSync does not discard the events in the queue. If you passed True, XSync discards all events in the queue, including those events that were on the queue before XSync was called. Client applications seldom need to call XSync.

8.7   Event Queue Management

Xlib maintains an event queue. However, the operating system also may be buffering data in its network connection that is not yet read into the event queue.

To check the number of events in the event queue, use XEvents-Queued.

int XEventsQueued(*display, mode*)
    Display **display*;
    int *mode*;
display   Specifies the connection to the X server.
mode   Specifies the mode. You can pass QueuedAlready, QueuedAfterFlush, or QueuedAfterReading.

If mode is QueuedAlready, XEventsQueued returns the number of events already in the event queue (and never performs a system call). If mode is QueuedAfterFlush, XEventsQueued returns the number of events already in the queue if the number is nonzero. If there are no events in the queue, XEventsQueued flushes the output buffer, attempts to read more events out of the application's connection, and returns the number read. If mode is QueuedAfterReading, XEventsQueued returns the number of events already in the queue if the number is nonzero. If there are no events in the queue, XEventsQueued attempts to read more events out of the application's connection without flushing the output buffer and returns the number read.

XEventsQueued always returns immediately without I/O if there are events already in the queue. XEventsQueued with mode QueuedAfterFlush is identical in behavior to XPending. XEventsQueued with mode QueuedAlready is identical to the XQLength function.

To return the number of events that are pending, use XPending.

int XPending(*display*)
    Display **display*;
display   Specifies the connection to the X server.

The XPending function returns the number of events that have been received from the X server but have not been removed from the event queue. XPending is identical to XEventsQueued with the mode Queued-AfterFlush specified.

8.8 Manipulating the Event Queue

Xlib provides functions that let you manipulate the event queue. The next three sections discuss how to:

- Obtain events, in order, and remove them from the queue
- Peek at events in the queue without removing them
- Obtain events that match the event mask or the arbitrary predicate procedures that you provide

8.8.1 Returning the Next Event

To get the next event and remove it from the queue, use XNextEvent.

XNextEvent(*display, event_return*)
    Display **display*;
    XEvent **event_return*;
display   Specifies the connection to the X server.
event_return   Returns the next event in the queue.

The XNextEvent function copies the first event from the event queue into the specified XEvent structure and then removes it from the queue. If the event queue is empty, XNextEvent flushes the output buffer and blocks until an event is received.

To peek at the event queue, use XPeekEvent.

XPeekEvent(*display, event_return*)
    Display **display*;
    XEvent **event_return*;
display   Specifies the connection to the X server.
event_return   Returns a copy of the matched event's associated structure.

The XPeekEvent function returns the first event from the event queue, but it does not remove the event from the queue. If the queue is empty, XPeekEvent flushes the output buffer and blocks until an event is received.

It then copies the event into the client-supplied XEvent structure without removing it from the event queue.

8.8.2   Selecting Events Using a Predicate Procedure

Each of the functions discussed in this section requires you to pass a predicate procedure that determines if an event matches what you want. Your predicate procedure must decide only if the event is useful and must not call Xlib functions. In particular, a predicate is called from inside the event routine, which must lock data structures so that the event queue is consistent in a multi-threaded environment.

The predicate procedure and its associated arguments are:

Bool (*predicate)(display, event, arg)
    Display *display;
    XEvent *event;
    char *arg;

display   Specifies the connection to the X server.

event   Specifies a pointer to the XEvent structure.

arg   Specifies the argument passed in from the XIfEvent, XCheckIfEvent, or XPeekIfEvent function.

The predicate procedure is called once for each event in the queue until it finds a match. After finding a match, the predicate procedure must return True. If it did not find a match, it must return False.

To check the event queue for a matching event and, if found, remove the event from the queue, use XIfEvent.

XIfEvent(display, event_return, predicate, arg)
    Display *display;
    XEvent *event_return;
    Bool (*predicate)();
    char *arg;

display   Specifies the connection to the X server.

event_return   Returns the matched event's associated structure.

predicate   Specifies the procedure that is to be called to determine if the next event in the queue matches what you want.

arg   Specifies the user-supplied argument that will be passed to the predicate procedure.

The XIfEvent function completes only when the specified predicate procedure returns True for an event, which indicates an event in the queue matches. XIfEvent flushes the output buffer if it blocks waiting for additional events. XIfEvent removes the matching event from the queue and copies the structure into the client-supplied XEvent structure.

To check the event queue for a matching event without blocking, use XCheckIfEvent.

Bool XCheckIfEvent(*display, event_return, predicate, arg*)
    Display **display*;
    XEvent **event_return*;
    Bool (**predicate*)();
    char **arg*;

display	Specifies the connection to the X server.
event_return	Returns a copy of the matched event's associated structure.
predicate	Specifies the procedure that is to be called to determine if the next event in the queue matches what you want.
arg	Specifies the user-supplied argument that will be passed to the predicate procedure.

When the predicate procedure finds a match, XCheckIfEvent copies the matched event into the client-supplied XEvent structure and returns True. (This event is removed from the queue.) If the predicate procedure finds no match, XCheckIfEvent returns False, and the output buffer will have been flushed. All earlier events stored in the queue are not discarded.

To check the event queue for a matching event without removing the event from the queue, use XPeekIfEvent.

XPeekIfEvent(*display, event_return, predicate, arg*)
    Display **display*;
    XEvent **event_return*;
    Bool (**predicate*)();
    char **arg*;

display	Specifies the connection to the X server.
event_return	Returns a copy of the matched event's associated structure.
predicate	Specifies the procedure that is to be called to determine if the next event in the queue matches what you want.
arg	Specifies the user-supplied argument that will be passed to the predicate procedure.

The XPeekIfEvent function returns only when the specified predicate procedure returns True for an event. After the predicate procedure finds a match, XPeekIfEvent copies the matched event into the client-supplied XEvent structure without removing the event from the queue. XPeek-IfEvent flushes the output buffer if it blocks waiting for additional events.

8.8.3   Selecting Events Using a Window or Event Mask

The functions discussed in this section let you select events by window or event types, allowing you to process events out of order.

To remove the next event that matches both a window and an event mask, use XWindowEvent.

XWindowEvent(*display, w, event_mask, event_return*)
    Display **display*;
    Window *w*;
    long *event_mask*;
    XEvent **event_return*;

display	Specifies the connection to the X server.
w	Specifies the window whose events you are interested in.
event_mask	Specifies the event mask.
event_return	Returns the matched event's associated structure.

The XWindowEvent function searches the event queue for an event that matches both the specified window and event mask. When it finds a match, XWindowEvent removes that event from the queue and copies it into the specified XEvent structure. The other events stored in the queue are not discarded. If a matching event is not in the queue, XWindowEvent flushes the output buffer and blocks until one is received.

To remove the next event that matches both a window and an event mask (if any), use XCheckWindowEvent. This function is similar to XWindowEvent except that it never blocks and it returns a Bool indicating if the event was returned.

Bool XCheckWindowEvent(*display, w, event_mask, event_return*)
    Display **display*;
    Window *w*;
    long *event_mask*;
    XEvent **event_return*;

display	Specifies the connection to the X server.
w	Specifies the window whose events you are interested in.
event_mask	Specifies the event mask.
event_return	Returns the matched event's associated structure.

The `XCheckWindowEvent` function searches the event queue and then the events available on the server connection for the first event that matches the specified window and event mask. If it finds a match, `XCheckWindowEvent` removes that event, copies it into the specified `XEvent` structure, and returns `True`. The other events stored in the queue are not discarded. If the event you requested is not available, `XCheckWindowEvent` returns `False`, and the output buffer will have been flushed.

To remove the next event that matches an event mask, use `XMaskEvent`.

XMaskEvent(*display, event_mask, event_return*)
    Display **display*;
    long *event_mask*;
    XEvent **event_return*;

display	Specifies the connection to the X server.
event_mask	Specifies the event mask.
event_return	Returns the matched event's associated structure.

The `XMaskEvent` function searches the event queue for the events associated with the specified mask. When it finds a match, `XMaskEvent` removes that event and copies it into the specified `XEvent` structure. The other events stored in the queue are not discarded. If the event you requested is not in the queue, `XMaskEvent` flushes the output buffer and blocks until one is received.

To return and remove the next event that matches an event mask (if any), use `XCheckMaskEvent`. This function is similar to `XMaskEvent` except that it never blocks and it returns a `Bool` indicating if the event was returned.

Bool XCheckMaskEvent(*display, event_mask, event_return*)
    Display **display*;
    long *event_mask*;
    XEvent **event_return*;

display   Specifies the connection to the X server.
event_mask   Specifies the event mask.
event_return   Returns the matched event's associated structure.

The XCheckMaskEvent function searches the event queue and then any events available on the server connection for the first event that matches the specified mask. If it finds a match, XCheckMaskEvent removes that event, copies it into the specified XEvent structure, and returns True. The other events stored in the queue are not discarded. If the event you requested is not available, XCheckMaskEvent returns False, and the output buffer will have been flushed.

To return and remove the next event in the queue that matches an event type, use XCheckTypedEvent.

Bool XCheckTypedEvent(*display, event_type, event_return*)
    Display *display*;
    int *event_type*;
    XEvent *event_return*;
display   Specifies the connection to the X server.
event_type   Specifies the event type to be compared.
event_return   Returns the matched event's associated structure.

The XCheckTypedEvent function searches the event queue and then any events available on the server connection for the first event that matches the specified type. If it finds a match, XCheckTypedEvent removes that event, copies it into the specified XEvent structure, and returns True. The other events in the queue are not discarded. If the event is not available, XCheckTypedEvent returns False, and the output buffer will have been flushed.

To return and remove the next event in the queue that matches an event type and a window, use XCheckTypedWindowEvent.

Bool XCheckTypedWindowEvent(*display, w, event_type, event_return*)
    Display *display*;
    Window *w*;
    int *event_type*;
    XEvent *event_return*;
display   Specifies the connection to the X server.

w	Specifies the window.
event_type	Specifies the event type to be compared.
event_return	Returns the matched event's associated structure.

The `XCheckTypedWindowEvent` function searches the event queue and then any events available on the server connection for the first event that matches the specified type and window. If it finds a match, `XCheck-TypedWindowEvent` removes the event from the queue, copies it into the specified `XEvent` structure, and returns `True`. The other events in the queue are not discarded. If the event is not available, `XCheck-TypedWindowEvent` returns `False`, and the output buffer will have been flushed.

8.9 Putting an Event Back into the Queue

To push an event back into the event queue, use `XPutBackEvent`.

XPutBackEvent(*display, event*)
    Display **display*;
    XEvent **event*;

display	Specifies the connection to the X server.
event	Specifies a pointer to the event.

The `XPutBackEvent` function pushes an event back onto the head of the display's event queue by copying the event into the queue. This can be useful if you read an event and then decide that you would rather deal with it later. There is no limit to the number of times in succession that you can call `XPutBackEvent`.

8.10 Sending Events to Other Applications

To send an event to a specified window, use `XSendEvent`. This function is often used in selection processing. For example, the owner of a selection should use `XSendEvent` to send a `SelectionNotify` event to a requestor when a selection has been converted and stored as a property.

Status XSendEvent(*display, w, propagate, event_mask, event_send*)
    Display **display*;
    Window *w*;
    Bool *propagate*;
    long *event_mask*;
    XEvent **event_send*;

display	Specifies the connection to the X server.
w	Specifies the window the event is to be sent to, `PointerWindow`, or `InputFocus`.
propagate	Specifies a Boolean value.
event_mask	Specifies the event mask.
event_send	Specifies a pointer to the event that is to be sent.

The `XSendEvent` function identifies the destination window, determines which clients should receive the specified events, and ignores any active grabs. This function requires you to pass an event mask. For a discussion of the valid event mask names, see section 8.3. This function uses the w argument to identify the destination window as follows:

- If w is `PointerWindow`, the destination window is the window that contains the pointer.

- If w is `InputFocus` and if the focus window contains the pointer, the destination window is the window that contains the pointer; otherwise, the destination window is the focus window.

To determine which clients should receive the specified events, `XSendEvent` uses the propagate argument as follows:

- If event_mask is the empty set, the event is sent to the client that created the destination window. If that client no longer exists, no event is sent.

- If propagate is `False`, the event is sent to every client selecting on destination any of the event types in the event_mask argument.

- If propagate is `True` and no clients have selected on destination any of the event types in event-mask, the destination is replaced with the closest ancestor of destination for which some client has selected a type in event-mask and for which no intervening window has that type in its do-not-propagate-mask. If no such window exists or if the window is an ancestor of the focus window and `InputFocus` was originally specified as the destination, the event is not sent to any clients. Otherwise, the event is reported to every client selecting on the final destination any of the types specified in event_mask.

The event in the `XEvent` structure must be one of the core events or one of the events defined by an extension (or a `BadValue` error results) so that the X server can correctly byte-swap the contents as necessary. The contents of the event are otherwise unaltered and unchecked by the X server except to force send_event to `True` in the forwarded event and to set the serial number in the event correctly.

XSendEvent returns zero if the conversion to wire protocol format failed and returns nonzero otherwise.

XSendEvent can generate BadValue and BadWindow errors.

8.11 Getting Pointer Motion History

Some X server implementations will maintain a more complete history of pointer motion than is reported by event notification. The pointer position at each pointer hardware interrupt may be stored in a buffer for later retrieval. This buffer is called the motion history buffer. For example, a few applications, such as paint programs, want to have a precise history of where the pointer traveled. However, this historical information is highly excessive for most applications.

To determine the size of the motion buffer, use XDisplay-MotionBufferSize.

unsigned long XDisplayMotionBufferSize (*display*)
    Display **display*;
display   Specifies the connection to the X server.

The server may retain the recent history of the pointer motion and do so to a finer granularity than is reported by MotionNotify events. The XGetMotionEvents function makes this history available.

To get the motion history for a specified window and time, use XGet-MotionEvents.

XTimeCoord *XGetMotionEvents(*display, w, start, stop, nevents_return*)
    Display **display*;
    Window *w*;
    Time *start, stop*;
    int **nevents_return*;

display	Specifies the connection to the X server.
w	Specifies the window.
start	
stop	Specify the time interval in which the events are returned from the motion history buffer. You can pass a timestamp or CurrentTime.
nevents_return	Returns the number of events from the motion history buffer.

The XGetMotionEvents function returns all events in the motion history buffer that fall between the specified start and stop times, inclusive, and that have coordinates that lie within the specified window (including its borders) at its present placement. If the start time is later than the stop time or if the start time is in the future, no events are returned. If the stop time is in the future, it is equivalent to specifying CurrentTime. The return type for this function is a structure defined as follows:

```
typedef struct {
    Time time;
    short x, y;
} XTimeCoord;
```

The time member is set to the time, in milliseconds. The x and y members are set to the coordinates of the pointer and are reported relative to the origin of the specified window. To free the data returned from this call, use XFree.

XGetMotionEvents can generate a BadWindow error.

8.12   Handling Error Events

Xlib provides functions that you can use to enable or disable synchronization and to use the default error handlers.

8.12.1   Enabling or Disabling Synchronization

When debugging X applications, it often is very convenient to require Xlib to behave synchronously so that errors are reported as they occur. The following function lets you disable or enable synchronous behavior. Note that graphics may occur 30 or more times more slowly when synchronization is enabled. On UNIX-based systems, there is also a global variable _Xdebug that, if set to nonzero before starting a program under a debugger, will force synchronous library behavior.

After completing their work, all Xlib functions that generate protocol requests call what is known as an after function. XSetAfterFunction sets which function is to be called.

```
int (*XSetAfterFunction(display, procedure))()
    Display *display;
    int (*procedure)();
```

display   Specifies the connection to the X server.

procedure   Specifies the function to be called after an Xlib function that generates a protocol request completes it work.

The specified procedure is called with only a display pointer. XSet-AfterFunction returns the previous after function.

To enable or disable synchronization, use XSynchronize.

int (*XSynchronize(*display, onoff*))()
     Display *display*;
     Bool *onoff*;

display   Specifies the connection to the X server.

onoff   Specifies a Boolean value that indicates whether to enable or disable synchronization.

The XSynchronize function returns the previous after function. If onoff is True, XSynchronize turns on synchronous behavior. If onoff is False, XSynchronize turns off synchronous behavior.

8.12.2   Using the Default Error Handlers

There are two default error handlers in Xlib: one to handle typically fatal conditions (for example, the connection to a display server dying because a machine crashed) and one to handle error events from the X server. These error handlers can be changed to user-supplied routines if you prefer your own error handling and can be changed as often as you like. If either function is passed a NULL pointer, it will reinvoke the default handler. The action of the default handlers is to print an explanatory message and exit.

To set the error handler, use XSetErrorHandler.

XSetErrorHandler(*handler*)
     int (*handler*)(Display *, XErrorEvent *)

handler   Specifies the program's supplied error handler.

Xlib generally calls the program's supplied error handler whenever an error is received. It is not called on BadName errors from OpenFont, Lookup-Color, or AllocNamedColor protocol requests or on BadFont errors from a QueryFont protocol request. These errors generally are reflected back to the program through the procedural interface. Because this condition is not assumed to be fatal, it is acceptable for your error handler to return. However, the error handler should not call any functions (directly or indirectly) on the display that will generate protocol requests or that will look for input events.

The XErrorEvent structure contains:

```
typedef struct {
    int type;
    Display *display;              /* Display the event was read from */
    unsigned long serial;         /* serial number of failed request */
    unsigned char error_code;     /* error code of failed request */
    unsigned char request_code;   /* Major op-code of failed request */
    unsigned char minor_code;     /* Minor op-code of failed request */
    XID resourceid;               /* resource id */
} XErrorEvent;
```

The serial member is the number of requests, starting from one, sent over the network connection since it was opened. It is the number that was the value of NextRequest immediately before the failing call was made. The request_code member is a protocol request of the procedure that failed, as defined in <X11/Xproto.h>. The following error codes can be returned by the functions described in this chapter:

Error Code	Description
BadAccess	A client attempts to grab a key/button combination already grabbed by another client.
	A client attempts to free a colormap entry that it had not already allocated.
	A client attempts to store into a read-only or unallocated colormap entry.
	A client attempts to modify the access control list from other than the local (or otherwise authorized) host.
	A client attempts to select an event type that another client has already selected.
BadAlloc	The server fails to allocate the requested resource. Note that the explicit listing of BadAlloc errors in requests only covers allocation errors at a very coarse level and is not intended to (nor can it in practice hope to) cover all cases of a server running out of

Error Code	*Description*
	allocation space in the middle of service. The semantics when a server runs out of allocation space are left unspecified, but a server may generate a BadAlloc error on any request for this reason, and clients should be prepared to receive such errors and handle or discard them.
BadAtom	A value for an atom argument does not name a defined atom.
BadColor	A value for a colormap argument does not name a defined colormap.
BadCursor	A value for a cursor argument does not name a defined cursor.
BadDrawable	A value for a drawable argument does not name a defined window or pixmap.
BadFont	A value for a font argument does not name a defined font (or, in some cases, GContext).
BadGC	A value for a GContext argument does not name a defined GContext.
BadIDChoice	The value chosen for a resource identifier either is not included in the range assigned to the client or is already in use. Under normal circumstances, this cannot occur and should be considered a server or Xlib error.
BadImplementation	The server does not implement some aspect of the request. A server that generates this error for a core request is deficient. As such, this error is not listed for any of the requests, but clients should be prepared to receive such errors and handle or discard them.
BadLength	The length of a request is shorter or longer than that required to contain the arguments. This is an internal Xlib or server error.
	The length of a request exceeds the maximum length accepted by the server.
BadMatch	In a graphics request, the root and depth of the graphics context does not match that of the drawable.
	An InputOnly window is used as a drawable.
	Some argument or pair of arguments has the correct type and range, but it fails to match in some other way required by the request.
	An InputOnly window lacks this attribute.

Error Code	Description
BadName	A font or color of the specified name does not exist.
BadPixmap	A value for a pixmap argument does not name a defined pixmap.
BadRequest	The major or minor opcode does not specify a valid request. This usually is an Xlib or server error.
BadValue	Some numeric value falls outside of the range of values accepted by the request. Unless a specific range is specified for an argument, the full range defined by the argument's type is accepted. Any argument defined as a set of alternatives typically can generate this error (due to the encoding).
BadWindow	A value for a window argument does not name a defined window.

Note   The BadAtom, BadColor, BadCursor, BadDrawable, BadFont, BadGC, BadPixmap, and BadWindow errors are also used when the argument type is extended by a set of fixed alternatives.

To obtain textual descriptions of the specified error code, use XGetErrorText.

XGetErrorText(*display, code, buffer_return, length*)
    Display **display*;
    int *code*;
    char **buffer_return*;
    int *length*;

display	Specifies the connection to the X server.
code	Specifies the error code for which you want to obtain a description.
buffer_return	Returns the error description.
length	Specifies the size of the buffer.

The XGetErrorText function copies a null-terminated string describing the specified error code into the specified buffer. It is recommended that you use this function to obtain an error description because extensions to Xlib may define their own error codes and error strings.

To obtain error messages from the error database, use XGetErrorDatabaseText.

XGetErrorDatabaseText(*display, name, message, default_string, buffer_return, length*)
    Display **display*;
    char **name, *message*;
    char **default_string*;
    char **buffer_return*;
    int *length*;

display	Specifies the connection to the X server.
name	Specifies the name of the application.
message	Specifies the type of the error message.
default_string	Specifies the default error message if none is found in the database.
buffer_return	Returns the error description.
length	Specifies the size of the buffer.

The `XGetErrorDatabaseText` function returns a message (or the default message) from the error message database. Xlib uses this function internally to look up its error messages. On a UNIX-based system, the error message database is /usr/lib/X11/XErrorDB.

The name argument should generally be the name of your application. The message argument should indicate which type of error message you want. Xlib uses three predefined message types to report errors (strings and uppercase and lowercase matter):

XProtoError	The protocol error number is used as a string for the message argument.
XlibMessage	These are the message strings that are used internally by the library.
XRequest	The major request protocol number is used for the message argument. If no string is found in the error database, the default_string is returned to the buffer argument.

To report an error to the user when the requested display does not exist, use `XDisplayName`.

char **XDisplayName(*string*)
    char **string*;
string   Specifies the character string.

The `XDisplayName` function returns the name of the display that `XOpenDisplay` would attempt to use. If a NULL string is specified, `XDisplayName` looks in the environment for the display and returns the display name that XOpenDisplay would attempt to use. This makes it easier to report to the user precisely which display the program attempted to open when the initial connection attempt failed.

To handle fatal I/O errors, use XSetIOErrorHandler.

XSetIOErrorHandler(*handler*)
    int (*handler)(Display *);
handler   Specifies the program's supplied error handler.

The XSetIOErrorHandler sets the fatal I/O error handler. Xlib calls the program's supplied error handler if any sort of system call error occurs (for example, the connection to the server was lost). This is assumed to be a fatal condition, and the called routine should not return. If the I/O error handler does return, the client process exits.

Chapter 9
Predefined Property Functions

There are a number of predefined properties for information commonly associated with windows. The atoms for these predefined properties can be found in <X11/Xatom.h>, where the prefix XA_ is added to each atom name.

Xlib provides functions that you can use to perform operations on predefined properties. This chapter discusses how to:

• Communicate with window managers

• Manipulate standard colormaps

9.1 Communicating with Window Managers

This section discusses a set of properties and functions that are necessary for clients to communicate effectively with window managers. Some of these properties have complex structures. Because all the data in a single property on the server has to be of the same format (8-bit, 16-bit, or 32-bit) and because the C structures representing property types cannot be guaranteed to be uniform in the same way, Set and Get functions are provided for properties with complex structures.

These functions define but do not enforce minimal policy among window managers. Writers of window managers are urged to use the information in these properties rather than invent their own properties and types. A window manager writer, however, can define additional properties beyond this least-common denominator.

In addition to Set and Get functions for individual properties, Xlib includes one function, XSetStandardProperties, that sets all or portions of several properties. Applications are encouraged to provide the window manager more information than is possible with XSetStandard-Properties. To do so, they should call the Set functions for the additional or specific properties that they need.

To work well with most window managers, every application should specify the following information:

- Name of the application
- Name to be used in the icon
- Command used to invoke the application
- Size and window manager hints

Xlib does not set defaults for the properties described in this section. Thus, the default behavior is determined by the window manager and may be based on the presence or absence of certain properties. All the properties are considered to be hints to a window manager. When implementing window management policy, a window manager determines what to do with this information and can ignore it.

The supplied properties are:

Name	Type	Format	Description
WM_NAME	STRING	8	Name of the application.
WM_ICON_NAME	STRING	8	Name to be used in icon.
WM_NORMAL_HINTS	WM_SIZE_HINTS	32	Size hints for a window in its normal state. The C type of this property is XSizeHints.
WM_ZOOM_HINTS	WM_SIZE_HINTS	32	Size hints for a zoomed window. The C type of this property is XSizeHints.
WM_HINTS	WM_HINTS	32	Additional hints set by client for use by the window manager. The C type of this property is XWMHints.
WM_COMMAND	STRING	8	The command and arguments, separated by

Name	Type	Format	Description
			ASCII nulls, used to invoke the application.
WM_ICON_SIZE	WM_ICON_SIZE	32	The window manager may set this property on the root window to specify the icon sizes it supports. The C type of this property is `XIconSize`.
WM_CLASS	STRING	32	Set by application programs to allow window and session managers to obtain the application's resources from the resource database.
WM_TRANSIENT_FOR	WINDOW	32	Set by application programs to indicate to the window manager that a transient top-level window, such as a dialog box, is not really a normal application window.

The atom names stored in `<X11/Xatom.h>` are named XA_*PROPERTY_NAME*.

Xlib provides functions that you can use to set and get predefined properties. Note that calling the Set function for a property with complex structure redefines all members in that property, even though only some of those members may have a specified new value. Simple properties for which Xlib does not provide a Set or Get function can be set by using `XChange-Property`, and their values can be retrieved using `XGetWindowProperty`. The remainder of this section discusses how to:

- Set standard properties
- Set and get the name of a window
- Set and get the icon name of a window
- Set the command and arguments of the application
- Set and get window manager hints
- Set and get window size hints
- Set and get icon size hints

- Set and get the class of a window
- Set and get the transient property for a window

9.1.1   Setting Standard Properties

To specify a minimum set of properties describing the "quickie" application, use XSetStandardProperties. This function sets all or portions of the WM_NAME, WM_ICON_NAME, WM_HINTS, WM_COMMAND, and WM_NORMAL_HINTS properties.

XSetStandardProperties(*display, w, window_name, icon_name, icon_pixmap, argv,*
                    argc, hints)
          Display **display*;
          Window *w*;
          char **window_name*;
          char **icon_name*;
          Pixmap *icon_pixmap*;
          char ***argv*;
          int *argc*;
          XSizeHints **hints*;

display	Specifies the connection to the X server.
w	Specifies the window.
window_name	Specifies the window name, which should be a null-terminated string.
icon_name	Specifies the icon name, which should be a null-terminated string.
icon_pixmap	Specifies the bitmap that is to be used for the icon or None.
argv	Specifies the application's argument list.
argc	Specifies the number of arguments.
hints	Specifies a pointer to the size hints for the window in its normal state.

The XSetStandardProperties function provides a means by which simple applications set the most essential properties with a single call. XSetStandardProperties should be used to give a window manager some information about your program's preferences. It should not be used by applications that need to communicate more information than is possible with XSetStandardProperties. (Typically, argv is the argv array of your main program.)

    XSetStandardProperties can generate BadAlloc and BadWindow errors.

9.1.2 Setting and Getting Window Names

Xlib provides functions that you can use to set and read the name of a window. These functions set and read the WM_NAME property.

To assign a name to a window, use `XStoreName`.

XStoreName(*display, w, window_name*)
    Display **display*;
    Window *w*;
    char **window_name*;

display	Specifies the connection to the X server.
w	Specifies the window.
window_name	Specifies the window name, which should be a null-terminated string.

The `XStoreName` function assigns the name passed to window_name to the specified window. A window manager can display the window name in some prominent place, such as the title bar, to allow users to identify windows easily. Some window managers may display a window's name in the window's icon, although they are encouraged to use the window's icon name if one is provided by the application.

`XStoreName` can generate `BadAlloc` and `BadWindow` errors.

To get the name of a window, use `XFetchName`.

Status XFetchName(*display, w, window_name_return*)
    Display **display*;
    Window *w*;
    char ***window_name_return*;

display	Specifies the connection to the X server.
w	Specifies the window.
window_name_return	Returns a pointer to the window name, which is a null-terminated string.

The `XFetchName` function returns the name of the specified window. If it succeeds, it returns nonzero; otherwise, if no name has been set for the window, it returns zero. If the WM_NAME property has not been set for this window, `XFetchName` sets window_name_return to NULL. When finished with it, a client must free the window name string using `XFree`.

`XFetchName` can generate a `BadWindow` error.

9.1.3 Setting and Getting Icon Names

Xlib provides functions that you can use to set and read the name to be displayed in a window's icon. These functions set and read the WM_ICON_NAME property.

To set the name to be displayed in a window's icon, use XSetIconName.

XSetIconName(*display, w, icon_name*)
    Display **display*;
    Window *w*;
    char **icon_name*;

display   Specifies the connection to the X server.
w   Specifies the window.
icon_name   Specifies the icon name, which should be a null-terminated string.

XSetIconName can generate BadAlloc and BadWindow errors.

To get the name a window wants displayed in its icon, use XGetIconName.

Status XGetIconName(*display, w, icon_name_return*)
    Display **display*;
    Window *w*;
    char ***icon_name_return*;

display   Specifies the connection to the X server.
w   Specifies the window.
icon_name_return   Returns a pointer to the window's icon name, which is a null-terminated string.

The XGetIconName function returns the name to be displayed in the specified window's icon. If it succeeds, it returns nonzero; otherwise, if no icon name has been set for the window, it returns zero. If you never assigned a name to the window, XGetIconName sets icon_name_return to NULL. When finished with it, a client must free the icon name string using XFree.

    XGetIconName can generate a BadWindow error.

9.1.4 Setting the Command

To set the command property, use XSetCommand. This function sets the WM_COMMAND property.

XSetCommand(*display, w, argv, argc*)
    Display **display*;
    Window *w*;
    char ***argv*;
    int *argc*;
display   Specifies the connection to the X server.
w   Specifies the window.
argv   Specifies the application's argument list.
argc   Specifies the number of arguments.

The `XSetCommand` function sets the command and arguments used to invoke the application. (Typically, argv is the argv array of your main program.)

`XSetCommand` can generate `BadAlloc` and `BadWindow` errors.

9.1.5 Setting and Getting Window Manager Hints

The functions discussed in this section set and read the WM_HINTS property and use the flags and the `XWMHints` structure, as defined in the `<X11/Xutil.h>` header file:

```
/* Window manager hints mask bits */
#define InputHint              (1L << 0)
#define StateHint              (1L << 1)
#define IconPixmapHint         (1L << 2)
#define IconWindowHint         (1L << 3)
#define IconPositionHint       (1L << 4)
#define IconMaskHint           (1L << 5)
#define WindowGroupHint        (1L << 6)
#define AllHints (InputHint|StateHint|IconPixmapHint|IconWindowHint\
            IconPositionHint|IconMaskHint|WindowGroupHint)


/* Values */
typedef struct {
      long flags;              /* marks which fields in this structure are defined */
      Bool input;              /* does this application rely on the window
                                  manager to get keyboard input? */
      int initial_state;       /* see below */
      Pixmap icon_pixmap;      /* pixmap to be used as icon */
      Window icon_window;      /* window to be used as icon */
      int icon_x, icon_y;      /* initial position of icon */
```

```
Pixmap icon_mask;        /* pixmap to be used as mask for icon_pixmap */
XID window_group;        /* id of related window group */
/* this structure may be extended in the future */
} XWMHints;
```

The input member is used to communicate to the window manager the input focus model used by the application. Applications that expect input but never explicitly set focus to any of their subwindows (that is, use the push model of focus management), such as X10-style applications that use real-estate driven focus, should set this member to `True`. Similarly, applications that set input focus to their subwindows only when it is given to their top-level window by a window manager should also set this member to `True`. Applications that manage their own input focus by explicitly setting focus to one of their subwindows whenever they want keyboard input (that is, use the pull model of focus management) should set this member to `False`. Applications that never expect any keyboard input also should set this member to `False`.

Pull model window managers should make it possible for push model applications to get input by setting input focus to the top-level windows of applications whose input member is `True`. Push model window managers should make sure that pull model applications do not break them by resetting input focus to `PointerRoot` when it is appropriate (for example, whenever an application whose input member is `False` sets input focus to one of its subwindows).

The definitions for the initial_state flag are:

```
#define DontCareState    0    /* don't know or care */
#define NormalState      1    /* most applications start this way */
#define ZoomState        2    /* application wants to start zoomed */
#define IconicState      3    /* application wants to start as an icon */
#define InactiveState    4    /* application believes it is seldom used; some
                                  wm's may put it on inactive menu */
```

The icon_mask specifies which pixels of the icon_pixmap should be used as the icon. This allows for nonrectangular icons. Both the icon_pixmap and icon_mask must be bitmaps. The icon_window lets an application provide a window for use as an icon for window managers that support such use. The window_group lets you specify that this window belongs to a group of other windows. For example, if a single application manipulates multiple top-level windows, this allows you to provide enough information that a window manager can iconify all of the windows rather than just the one window.

To set the window manager hints for a window, use `XSetWMHints`.

XSetWMHints(*display, w, wmhints*)
    Display *display;
    Window *w*;
    XWMHints *wmhints;
display   Specifies the connection to the X server.
w   Specifies the window.
wmhints   Specifies a pointer to the window manager hints.

The `XSetWMHints` function sets the window manager hints that include icon information and location, the initial state of the window, and whether the application relies on the window manager to get keyboard input.

    `XSetWMHints` can generate `BadAlloc` and `BadWindow` errors.

To read the window manager hints for a window, use `XGetWMHints`.

XWMHints *XGetWMHints(*display, w*)
    Display *display;
    Window *w*;
display   Specifies the connection to the X server.
w   Specifies the window.

The `XGetWMHints` function reads the window manager hints and returns NULL if no WM_HINTS property was set on the window or a pointer to a `XWMHints` structure if it succeeds. When finished with the data, free the space used for it by calling `XFree`.

    `XGetWMHints` can generate a `BadWindow` error.

9.1.6   Setting and Getting Window Sizing Hints

Xlib provides functions that you can use to set or get window sizing hints.

    The functions discussed in this section use the flags and the `XSizeHints` structure, as defined in the `<X11/Xutil.h>` header file:

```
/* Size hints mask bits */
#define USPosition      (1L << 0)   /* user specified x, y */
#define USSize          (1L << 1)   /* user specified width, height */
#define PPosition       (1L << 2)   /* program specified position */
```

```
#define PSize      (1L << 3)  /* program specified size */
#define PMinSize   (1L << 4)  /* program specified minimum size */
#define PMaxSize   (1L << 5)  /* program specified maximum size */
#define PResizeInc (1L << 6)  /* program specified resize increments */
#define PAspect    (1L << 7)  /* program specified min and max
                                   aspect ratios */
#define PAllHints (PPosition|PSize|PMinSize|PMaxSize|\
                     PResizeInc|PAspect)
/* Values */
typedef struct {
    long flags;                    /* marks which fields in this structure are
                                       defined */

    int x, y;
    int width, height;
    int min_width, min_height;
    int max_width, max_height;
    int width_inc, height_inc;
    struct {
        int x;                     /* numerator */
        int y;                     /* denominator */
    } min_aspect, max_aspect;
} XSizeHints;
```

The x, y, width, and height members describe a desired position and size for the window. To indicate that this information was specified by the user, set the USPosition and USSize flags. To indicate that it was specified by the application without any user involvement, set PPosition and PSize. This lets a window manager know that the user specifically asked where the window should be placed or how the window should be sized and that the window manager does not have to rely on the program's opinion.

The min_width and min_height members specify the minimum window size that still allows the application to be useful. The max_width and max_height members specify the maximum window size. The width_inc and height_inc members define an arithmetic progression of sizes (minimum to maximum) into which the window prefers to be resized. The min_aspect and max_aspect members are expressed as ratios of x and y, and they allow an application to specify the range of aspect ratios it prefers.

The next two functions set and read the WM_NORMAL_HINTS property.

To set the size hints for a given window in its normal state, use
`XSetNormalHints`.

XSetNormalHints(*display, w, hints*)
    Display *display;
    Window *w*;
    XSizeHints *hints;
display   Specifies the connection to the X server.
w   Specifies the window.
hints   Specifies a pointer to the size hints for the window in its normal state.

The `XSetNormalHints` function sets the size hints structure for the specified window. Applications use `XSetNormalHints` to inform the window
manager of the size or position desirable for that window. In addition, an application that wants to move or resize itself should call `XSetNormalHints`
and specify its new desired location and size as well as making direct Xlib
calls to move or resize. This is because window managers may ignore redirected configure requests, but they pay attention to property changes.

To set size hints, an application not only must assign values to the appropriate members in the hints structure but also must set the flags member of
the structure to indicate which information is present and where it came
from. A call to `XSetNormalHints` is meaningless, unless the flags member
is set to indicate which members of the structure have been assigned values.

`XSetNormalHints` can generate `BadAlloc` and `BadWindow` errors.

To return the size hints for a window in its normal state, use
`XGetNormalHints`.

Status XGetNormalHints(*display, w, hints_return*)
    Display *display;
    Window *w*;
    XSizeHints *hints_return;
display   Specifies the connection to the X server.
w   Specifies the window.
hints_return   Returns the size hints for the window in its normal state.

The `XGetNormalHints` function returns the size hints for a window in its
normal state. It returns a nonzero status if it succeeds or zero if the application specified no normal size hints for this window.

`XGetNormalHints` can generate a `BadWindow` error.

The next two functions set and read the WM_ZOOM_HINTS property.

To set the zoom hints for a window, use `XSetZoomHints`.

XSetZoomHints(*display, w, zhints*)
    Display **display*;
    Window *w*;
    XSizeHints **zhints*;
display   Specifies the connection to the X server.
w   Specifies the window.
zhints   Specifies a pointer to the zoom hints.

Many window managers think of windows in one of three states: iconic, normal, or zoomed. The `XSetZoomHints` function provides the window manager with information for the window in the zoomed state.

    `XSetZoomHints` can generate `BadAlloc` and `BadWindow` errors.

To read the zoom hints for a window, use `XGetZoomHints`.

Status XGetZoomHints(*display, w, zhints_return*)
    Display **display*;
    Window *w*;
    XSizeHints **zhints_return*;
display   Specifies the connection to the X server.
w   Specifies the window.
zhints_return   Returns the zoom hints.

The `XGetZoomHints` function returns the size hints for a window in its zoomed state. It returns a nonzero status if it succeeds or zero if the application specified no zoom size hints for this window.

    `XGetZoomHints` can generate a `BadWindow` error.

To set the value of any property of type WM_SIZE_HINTS, use `XSetSizeHints`.

XSetSizeHints(*display, w, hints, property*)
    Display **display*;
    Window *w*;
    XSizeHints **hints*;
    Atom *property*;

> *display*   Specifies the connection to the X server.
> *w*   Specifies the window.
> *hints*   Specifies a pointer to the size hints.
> *property*   Specifies the property name.

The `XSetSizeHints` function sets the `XSizeHints` structure for the named property and the specified window. This is used by `XSetNormal-Hints` and `XSetZoomHints`, and can be used to set the value of any property of type WM_SIZE_HINTS. Thus, it may be useful if other properties of that type get defined.

   `XSetSizeHints` can generate `BadAlloc`, `BadAtom`, and `BadWindow` errors.

To read the value of any property of type WM_SIZE_HINTS, use `XGetSizeHints`.

Status XGetSizeHints(*display, w, hints_return, property*)
       Display **display*;
       Window *w*;
       XSizeHints **hints_return*;
       Atom *property*;
> *display*   Specifies the connection to the X server.
> *w*   Specifies the window.
> *hints_return* Returns the size hints.
> *property*   Specifies the property name.

`XGetSizeHints` returns the `XSizeHints` structure for the named property and the specified window. This is used by `XGetNormalHints` and `XGetZoomHints`. It also can be used to retrieve the value of any property of type WM_SIZE_HINTS. Thus, it may be useful if other properties of that type get defined. `XGetSizeHints` returns a nonzero status if a size hint was defined or zero otherwise.

   `XGetSizeHints` can generate `BadAtom` and `BadWindow` errors.

9.1.7   Setting and Getting Icon Size Hints

Applications can cooperate with window managers by providing icons in sizes supported by a window manager. To communicate the supported icon sizes to the applications, a window manager should set the icon size property on the root window of the screen. To find out what icon sizes a window manager supports, applications should read the icon size property from the root window of the screen.

The functions discussed in this section set or read the WM_ICON_SIZE property. In addition, they use the `XIconSize` structure, which is defined in `<X11/Xutil.h>` and contains:

```
typedef struct {
    int min_width, min_height;
    int max_width, max_height;
    int width_inc, height_inc;
} XIconSize;
```

The width_inc and height_inc members define an arithmetic progression of sizes (minimum to maximum) that represent the supported icon sizes.

To set the icon size hints for a window, use `XSetIconSizes`.

```
XSetIconSizes(display, w, size_list, count)
    Display *display;
    Window w;
    XIconSize *size_list;
    int count;
```

display   Specifies the connection to the X server.
w   Specifies the window.
size_list Specifies a pointer to the size list.
count   Specifies the number of items in the size list.

The `XSetIconSizes` function is used only by window managers to set the supported icon sizes.

`XSetIconSizes` can generate `BadAlloc` and `BadWindow` errors.

To return the icon sizes hints for a window, use `XGetIconSizes`.

```
Status XGetIconSizes(display, w, size_list_return, count_return)
    Display *display;
    Window w;
    XIconSize **size_list_return;
    int *count_return;
```

display   Specifies the connection to the X server.
w   Specifies the window.
size_list_return Returns a pointer to the size list.
count_return   Returns the number of items in the size list.

The XGetIconSizes function returns zero if a window manager has not set icon sizes or nonzero otherwise. XGetIconSizes should be called by an application that wants to find out what icon sizes would be most appreciated by the window manager under which the application is running. The application should then use XSetWMHints to supply the window manager with an icon pixmap or window in one of the supported sizes. To free the data allocated in size_list_return, use XFree.

XGetIconSizes can generate a BadWindow error.

9.1.8 Setting and Getting the Class of a Window

Xlib provides functions to set and get the class of a window. These functions set and read the WM_CLASS property. In addition, they use the XClassHint structure, which is defined in <X11/Xutil.h> and contains:

```
typedef struct {
    char *res_name;
    char *res_class;
} XClassHint;
```

The res_name member contains the application name, and the res_class member contains the application class. Note that the name set in this property may differ from the name set as WM_NAME. That is, WM_NAME specifies what should be displayed in the title bar and, therefore, can contain temporal information (for example, the name of a file currently in an editor's buffer). On the other hand, the name specified as part of WM_CLASS is the formal name of the application that should be used when retrieving the application's resources from the resource database.

To set the class of a window, use XSetClassHint.

```
XSetClassHint(display, w, class_hints)
    Display *display;
    Window w;
    XClassHint *class_hints;
```

display	Specifies the connection to the X server.
w	Specifies the window.
class_hints	Specifies a pointer to a XClassHint structure that is to be used.

The XSetClassHint function sets the class hint for the specified window.

XSetClassHint can generate BadAlloc and BadWindow errors.

To get the class of a window, use XGetClassHint.

Status XGetClassHint(*display, w, class_hints_return*)
  Display *display*;
  Window *w*;
  XClassHint *class_hints_return*;
display   Specifies the connection to the X server.
w   Specifies the window.
class_hints_return   Returns the XClassHint structure.

The XGetClassHint function returns the class of the specified window. To free res_name and res_class when finished with the strings, use XFree.

XGetClassHint can generate a BadWindow error.

9.1.9   Setting and Getting the Transient Property

An application may want to indicate to the window manager that a transient, top-level window (for example, a dialog box) is operating on behalf of (or is transient for) another window. To do so, the application would set the WM_TRANSIENT_FOR property of the dialog box to be the window ID of its main window. Some window managers use this information to unmap an application's dialog boxes (for example, when the main application window gets iconified).

The functions discussed in this section set and read the WM_TRANSIENT_FOR property.

To set the WM_TRANSIENT_FOR property for a window, use XSetTransientForHint.

XSetTransientForHint(*display, w, prop_window*)
  Display *display*;
  Window *w*;
  Window *prop_window*;
display   Specifies the connection to the X server.
w   Specifies the window.
prop_window   Specifies the window that the WM_TRANSIENT_FOR property is to be set to.

The `XSetTransientForHint` function sets the WM_TRANSIENT_FOR property of the specified window to the specified prop_window.

`XSetTransientForHint` can generate `BadAlloc` and `BadWindow` errors.

To get the WM_TRANSIENT_FOR value for a window, use `XGetTransientForHint`.

Status XGetTransientForHint(*display, w, prop_window_return*)
    Display **display*;
    Window *w*;
    Window **prop_window_return*;

display	Specifies the connection to the X server.
w	Specifies the window.
prop_window_return	Returns the WM_TRANSIENT_FOR property of the specified window.

`XGetTransientForHint` returns the WM_TRANSIENT_FOR property for the specified window.

`XGetTransientForHint` can generate a `BadWindow` error.

9.2   Manipulating Standard Colormaps

Applications with color palettes, smooth-shaded drawings, or digitized images demand large numbers of colors. In addition, these applications often require an efficient mapping from color triples to pixel values that display the appropriate colors.

As an example, consider a 3D display program that wants to draw a smoothly shaded sphere. At each pixel in the image of the sphere, the program computes the intensity and color of light reflected back to the viewer. The result of each computation is a triple of RGB coefficients in the range 0.0 to 1.0. To draw the sphere, the program needs a colormap that provides a large range of uniformly distributed colors. The colormap should be arranged so that the program can convert its RGB triples into pixel values very quickly, because drawing the entire sphere requires many such conversions.

On many current workstations, the display is limited to 256 or fewer colors. Applications must allocate colors carefully, not only to make sure they cover the entire range they need but also to make use of as many of the available colors as possible. On a typical X display, many applications are active at once. Most workstations have only one hardware look-up table for colors, so only one application colormap can be installed at a given time. The application using the installed colormap is displayed correctly, and the other applications "go technicolor" and are displayed with false colors.

As another example, consider a user who is running an image processing program to display earth-resources data. The image processing program needs a colormap set up with 8 reds, 8 greens, and 4 blues (a total of 256 colors). Because some colors are already in use in the default colormap, the image processing program allocates and installs a new colormap.

The user decides to alter some of the colors in the image. He invokes a color palette program to mix and choose colors. The color palette program also needs a colormap with 8 reds, 8 greens, and 4 blues, so just as the image-processing program, it must allocate and install a new colormap.

Because only one colormap can be installed at a time, the color palette may be displayed incorrectly whenever the image-processing program is active. Conversely, whenever the palette program is active, the image may be displayed incorrectly. The user can never match or compare colors in the palette and image. Contention for colormap resources can be reduced if applications with similar color needs share colormaps.

As another example, the image processing program and the color palette program could share the same colormap if there existed a convention that described how the colormap was set up. Whenever either program was active, both would be displayed correctly.

The standard colormap properties define a set of commonly used colormaps. Applications that share these colormaps and conventions display true colors more often and provide a better interface to the user.

9.2.1   Standard Colormaps

Standard colormaps allow applications to share commonly used color resources. This allows many applications to be displayed in true colors simultaneously, even when each application needs an entirely filled colormap.

Several standard colormaps are described in this section. Usually, a window manager creates these colormaps. Applications should use the standard colormaps if they already exist. If the standard colormaps do not exist, you should create them by opening a new connection, creating the properties, and setting the close-down mode of the connection to `RetainPermanent`.

The `XStandardColormap` structure contains:

```
typedef struct {
    Colormap colormap;
    unsigned long red_max;
    unsigned long red_mult;
    unsigned long green_max;
    unsigned long green_mult;
    unsigned long blue_max;
    unsigned long blue_mult;
    unsigned long base_pixel;
} XStandardColormap;
```

The colormap member is the colormap created by the `XCreateColormap` function. The red_max, green_max, and blue_max members give the maximum red, green, and blue values, respectively. Each color coefficient ranges from zero to its max, inclusive. For example, a common colormap allocation is 3/3/2 (3 planes for red, 3 planes for green, and 2 planes for blue). This colormap would have red_max = 7, green_max = 7, and blue_max = 3. An alternate allocation that uses only 216 colors is red_max = 5, green_max = 5, and blue_max = 5.

The red_mult, green_mult, and blue_mult members give the scale factors used to compose a full pixel value. (See the discussion of the base_pixel members for further information.) For a 3/3/2 allocation, red_mult might be 32, green_mult might be 4, and blue_mult might be 1. For a 6-colors-each allocation, red_mult might be 36, green_mult might be 6, and blue_mult might be 1.

The base_pixel member gives the base pixel value used to compose a full pixel value. Usually, the base_pixel is obtained from a call to the `XAllocColorPlanes` function. Given integer red, green, and blue coefficients in their appropriate ranges, one then can compute a corresponding pixel value by using the following expression:

r * red_mult + g * green_mult + b * blue_mult + base_pixel

For `GrayScale` colormaps, only the colormap, red_max, red_mult, and base_pixel members are defined. The other members are ignored.

To compute a `GrayScale` pixel value, use the following expression:

$$gray * red\_mult + base\_pixel$$

The properties containing the `XStandardColormap` information have the type RGB_COLOR_MAP.

9.2.2   Standard Colormap Properties and Atoms

Several standard colormaps are available. Each standard colormap is defined by a property, and each such property is identified by an atom. The following list names the atoms and describes the colormap associated with each one. The <`X11/Xatom.h`> header file contains the definitions for each of the following atoms, which are prefixed with XA_.

RGB_DEFAULT_MAP

This atom names a property. The value of the property is an `XStandard-Colormap`.

The property defines an RGB subset of the default colormap of the screen. Some applications only need a few RGB colors and may be able to allocate them from the system default colormap. This is the ideal situation because the fewer colormaps that are active in the system the more applications are displayed with correct colors at all times.

A typical allocation for the RGB_DEFAULT_MAP on 8-plane displays is 6 reds, 6 greens, and 6 blues. This gives 216 uniformly distributed colors (6 intensities of 36 different hues) and still leaves 40 elements of a 256-element colormap available for special-purpose colors for text, borders, and so on.

RGB_BEST_MAP

This atom names a property. The value of the property is an `XStandardColormap`.

The property defines the best RGB colormap available on the screen. (Of course, this is a subjective evaluation.) Many image processing and 3D applications need to use all available colormap cells and to distribute as many perceptually distinct colors as possible over those cells. This implies that there may be more green values available than red, as well as more green or red than blue.

On an 8-plane `PseudoColor` display, RGB_BEST_MAP should be a

3/3/2 allocation. On a 24-plane `DirectColor` display, RGB_BEST_MAP should be an 8/8/8 allocation. On other displays, the RGB_BEST_MAP allocation is purely up to the implementor of the display.

RGB_RED_MAP
RGB_GREEN_MAP
RGB_BLUE_MAP

These atoms name properties. The value of each property is an `XStandardColormap`.

The properties define all-red, all-green, and all-blue colormaps, respectively. These maps are used by applications that want to make color-separated images. For example, a user might generate a full-color image on an 8-plane display both by rendering an image three times (once with high color resolution in red, once with green, and once with blue) and by multiply-exposing a single frame in a camera.

RGB_GRAY_MAP

This atom names a property. The value of the property is an `XStandardColormap`.

The property describes the best `GrayScale` colormap available on the screen. As previously mentioned, only the colormap, red_max, red_mult, and base_pixel members of the `XStandardColormap` structure are used for `GrayScale` colormaps.

9.2.3 Getting and Setting an XStandardColormap Structure

To get the `XStandardColormap` structure associated with one of the described atoms, use `XGetStandardColormap`.

Status XGetStandardColormap(*display, w, colormap_return, property*)
    Display *display;
    Window *w*;
    XStandardColormap *colormap_return;
    Atom *property*;   /* RGB_BEST_MAP, etc */

display	Specifies the connection to the X server.
w	Specifies the window.
colormap_return	Returns the colormap associated with the specified atom.
property	Specifies the property name.

The XGetStandardColormap function returns the colormap definition associated with the atom supplied as the property argument. For example, to fetch the standard GrayScale colormap for a display, you use XGetStandardColormap with the following syntax:

XGetStandardColormap(dpy, DefaultRootWindow(dpy), &cmap, XA_RGB_GRAY_MAP);

Once you have fetched a standard colormap, you can use it to convert RGB values into pixel values. For example, given an XStandardColormap structure and floating-point RGB coefficients in the range 0.0 to 1.0, you can compose pixel values with the following C expression:

pixel = base_pixel
      + ((unsigned long) (0.5 + r * red_max)) * red_mult
      + ((unsigned long) (0.5 + g * green_max)) * green_mult
      + ((unsigned long) (0.5 + b * blue_max)) * blue_mult;

The use of addition rather than logical OR for composing pixel values permits allocations where the RGB value is not aligned to bit boundaries.

XGetStandardColormap can generate BadAtom and BadWindow errors.

To set a standard colormap, use XSetStandardColormap.

XSetStandardColormap(*display, w, colormap, property*)
    Display **display*;
    Window *w*;
    XStandardColormap **colormap*;
    Atom *property*;   /* RGB_BEST_MAP, etc. */

display   Specifies the connection to the X server.
w   Specifies the window.
colormap   Specifies the colormap.
property   Specifies the property name.

The XSetStandardColormap function usually is only used by window managers. To create a standard colormap, follow this procedure:

1. Open a new connection to the same server.
2. Grab the server.
3. See if the property is on the property list of the root window for the screen.
4. If the desired property is not present:
    — Create a colormap (not required for RGB_DEFAULT_MAP)

— Determine the color capabilities of the display.

— Call `XAllocColorPlanes` or `XAllocColorCells` to allocate cells in the colormap.

— Call `XStoreColors` to store appropriate color values in the colormap.

— Fill in the descriptive members in the `XStandardColormap` structure.

— Attach the property to the root window.

— Use `XSetCloseDownMode` to make the resource permanent.

5. Ungrab the server.

`XSetStandardColormap` can generate `BadAlloc`, `BadAtom`, and `Bad-Window` errors.

Chapter 10

Application Utility Functions

Once you have initialized the X system, you can use the Xlib utility functions to:

- Handle keyboard events
- Obtain the X environment defaults
- Parse window geometry strings
- Parse hardware color strings
- Generate regions
- Manipulate regions
- Use cut and paste buffers
- Determine the appropriate visual
- Manipulate images
- Manipulate bitmaps
- Use the resource manager
- Use the context manager

As a group, the functions discussed in this chapter provide the functionality that is frequently needed and that spans toolkits. Many of these functions do not generate actual protocol requests to the server.

10.1 Keyboard Utility Functions

This section discusses keyboard event functions and KeySym classification macros.

10.1.1 Keyboard Event Functions

The X server does not predefine the keyboard to be ASCII characters. It is often useful to know that the *a* key was just pressed or that it was just released. When a key is pressed or released, the X server sends keyboard events to client programs. The structures associated with keyboard events contain a keycode member that assigns a number to each physical key on the keyboard. For a discussion of keyboard event processing, see section 8.4.1. For information on how to manipulate the keyboard encoding, see section 7.9.

Because KeyCodes are completely arbitrary and may differ from server to server, client programs wanting to deal with ASCII text, for example, must explicitly convert the KeyCode value into ASCII. Therefore, Xlib provides functions to help you customize the keyboard layout. Keyboards differ dramatically, so writing code that presumes the existence of a particular key on the main keyboard creates portability problems.

Keyboard events are usually sent to the deepest viewable window underneath the pointer's position that is interested in that type of event. It is also possible to assign the keyboard input focus to a specific window. When the input focus is attached to a window, keyboard events go to the client that has selected input on that window rather than the window under the pointer.

The functions in this section handle the shift modifier computations suggested by the protocol. The KeySym table is internally modified to define the lowercase transformation of a–z by adding the lowercase KeySym to the first element of the KeySym list (used internally) defined for the KeyCode, when the list is of length 1. If you want the untransformed KeySyms defined for a key, you should only use the functions described in section 7.9.

To look up the KeySyms, use `XLookupKeysym`.

KeySym XLookupKeysym(*key_event, index*)
　　XKeyEvent *key_event*;
　　int *index*;

key_event   Specifies the `KeyPress` or `KeyRelease` event.

index   Specifies the index into the KeySyms list for the event's KeyCode.

The `XLookupKeysym` function uses a given keyboard event and the index you specified to return the KeySym from the list that corresponds to the KeyCode member in the `XKeyPressedEvent` or `XKeyReleasedEvent` structure. If no KeySym is defined for the KeyCode of the event, `XLookup-Keysym` returns `NoSymbol`.

To refresh the stored modifier and keymap information, use `XRefreshKeyboardMapping`.

XRefreshKeyboardMapping(*event_map*)
    XMappingEvent **event_map*;

event_map   Specifies the mapping event that is to be used.

The `XRefreshKeyboardMapping` function refreshes the stored modifier and keymap information. You usually call this function when a `Mapping-Notify` event with a request member of `MappingKeyboard` or `MappingModifier` occurs. The result is to update Xlib's knowledge of the keyboard.

To map a key event to an ISO Latin-1 string, use `XLookupString`.

int XLookupString(*event_struct, buffer_return, bytes_buffer, keysym_return,
                    status_in_out*)
    XKeyEvent **event_struct*;
    char **buffer_return*;
    int *bytes_buffer*;
    KeySym **keysym_return*;
    XComposeStatus **status_in_out*;

event_struct   Specifies the key event structure to be used. You can pass
                  `XKeyPressedEvent` or `XKeyReleasedEvent`.

buffer_return   Returns the translated characters.

bytes_buffer   Specifies the length of the buffer. No more than bytes_buffer of
                  translation are returned.

keysym_return   Returns the KeySym computed from the event if this argument is
                   not NULL.

status_in_out   Specifies or returns the `XComposeStatus` structure or NULL.

The `XLookupString` function is a convenience routine that maps a key event to an ISO Latin-1 string, using the modifier bits in the key event to deal with shift, lock, and control. It returns the translated string into the user's buffer. It also detects any rebound KeySyms (see `XRebindKeysym`) and returns the specified bytes. `XLookupString` returns the length of the string stored in the tag buffer. If the lock modifier has the caps lock KeySym associated with it, `XLookupString` interprets the lock modifier to perform caps lock processing.

If present (non-NULL), the `XComposeStatus` structure records the state, which is private to Xlib, that needs preservation across calls to `XLookupString` to implement compose processing.

To rebind the meaning of a KeySym for a client, use `XRebindKeysym`.

```
XRebindKeysym(display, keysym, list, mod_count, string, bytes_string)
      Display *display;
      KeySym keysym;
      KeySym list[];
      int mod_count;
      unsigned char *string;
      int bytes_string;
```

display	Specifies the connection to the X server.
keysym	Specifies the KeySym that is to be rebound.
list	Specifies the KeySyms to be used as modifiers.
mod_count	Specifies the number of modifiers in the modifier list.
string	Specifies a pointer to the string that is copied and will be returned by `XLookupString`.
bytes_string	Specifies the length of the string.

The `XRebindKeysym` function can be used to rebind the meaning of a KeySym for the client. It does not redefine any key in the X server but merely provides an easy way for long strings to be attached to keys. `XLookupString` returns this string when the appropriate set of modifier keys are pressed and when the KeySym would have been used for the translation. Note that you can rebind a KeySym that may not exist.

To convert the name of the KeySym to the KeySym code, use `XStringToKeysym`.

KeySym XStringToKeysym(*string*)
 char **string*;
string Specifies the name of the KeySym that is to be converted.

Valid KeySym names are listed in <X11/keysymdef.h> by removing the XK_ prefix from each name. If the specified string does not match a valid KeySym, XStringToKeysym returns NoSymbol.

To convert a KeySym code to the name of the KeySym, use XKeysymToString.

char *XKeysymToString(*keysym*)
 KeySym *keysym*;
keysym Specifies the KeySym that is to be converted.

The returned string is in a static area and must not be modified. If the specified KeySym is not defined, XKeysymToString returns a NULL.

To convert a key code to a defined KeySym, use XKeycodeToKeysym.

KeySym XKeycodeToKeysym(*display, keycode, index*)
 Display **display*;
 KeyCode *keycode*;
 int *index*;
display Specifies the connection to the X server.
keycode Specifies the KeyCode.
index Specifies the element of KeyCode vector.

XKeycodeToKeysym function uses internal Xlib tables and returns the KeySym defined for the specified KeyCode and the element of the KeyCode vector. If no symbol is defined, XKeycodeToKeysym returns NoSymbol.

To convert a KeySym to the appropriate KeyCode, use XKeysymToKeycode.

KeyCode XKeysymToKeycode(*display, keysym*)
 Display **display*;
 KeySym *keysym*;
display Specifies the connection to the X server.
keysym Specifies the KeySym that is to be searched for.

If the specified KeySym is not defined for any KeyCode, `XKeysym-ToKeycode` returns zero.

10.1.2 Keysym Classification Macros

You may want to test if a KeySym is, for example, on the keypad or on one of the function keys. You can use the KeySym macros to perform the following tests.

IsCursorKey(*keysym*)

Returns `True` if the specified KeySym is a cursor key.

IsFunctionKey(*keysym*)

Returns `True` if the specified KeySym is a function key.

IsKeypadKey(*keysym*)

Returns `True` if the specified KeySym is a keypad key.

IsMiscFunctionKey(*keysym*)

Returns `True` if the specified KeySym is a miscellaneous function key.

IsModifierKey(*keysym*)

Returns `True` if the specified KeySym is a modifier key.

IsPFKey(*keysym*)

Returns `True` if the specified KeySym is a PF key.

10.2 Obtaining the X Environment Defaults

A program often needs a variety of options in the X environment (for example, fonts, colors, mouse, background, text, and cursor). Specifying these options on the command line is inefficient and unmanageable because individual users have a variety of tastes with regard to window appearance.

XGetDefault makes it easy to find out the fonts, colors, and other environment defaults favored by a particular user. Defaults are usually loaded into the RESOURCE_MANAGER property on the root window at login. If no such property exists, a resource file in the user's home directory is loaded. On a UNIX-based system, this file is $HOME/.Xdefaults. After loading these defaults, XGetDefault merges additional defaults specified by the XENVIRONMENT environment variable. If XENVIRONMENT is defined, it contains a full path name for the additional resource file. If XENVIRONMENT is not defined, XGetDefault looks for $HOME/.Xdefaults-*name*, where *name* specifies the name of the machine on which the application is running. For details of the format of these files, see section 10.11.

The XGetDefault function provides a simple interface for clients not wishing to use the X toolkit or the more elaborate interfaces provided by the resource manager discussed in section 10.11.

char *XGetDefault(*display, program, option*)
    Display **display*;
    char **program*;
    char **option*;

display   Specifies the connection to the X server.
program   Specifies the program name for the Xlib defaults (usually argv[0] of the main program).
option   Specifies the option name.

The XGetDefault function returns the value NULL if the option name specified in this argument does not exist for the program. The strings returned by XGetDefault are owned by Xlib and should not be modified or freed by the client.

To obtain a pointer to the resource manager string of a display, use XResourceManagerString.

char * XResourceManagerString (*display*)
    Display **display*;
display   Specifies the connection to the X server.

The XResourceManagerString returns the RESOURCE_MANAGER property from the server's root window of screen zero, which was returned when the connection was opened using XOpenDisplay.

10.3   Parsing the Window Geometry

To parse standard window geometry strings, use `XParseGeometry`.

int XParseGeometry(*parsestring, x_return, y_return, width_return, height_return*)
    char **parsestring*;
    int **x_return, *y_return*;
    int **width_return, *height_return*;

parsestring	Specifies the string you want to parse.
x_return	
y_return	Return the x and y offsets.
width_return	
height_return	Return the width and height determined.

By convention, X applications use a standard string to indicate window size and placement. `XParseGeometry` makes it easier to conform to this standard because it allows you to parse the standard window geometry. Specifically, this function lets you parse strings of the form:

$$[=][<width>\text{x}<height>][\{+-\}<xoffset>\{+-\}<yoffset>]$$

The items in this form map into the arguments associated with this function. (Items enclosed in <> are integers, items in [] are optional, and items enclosed in {} indicate "choose one of." Note that the brackets should not appear in the actual string.)

The `XParseGeometry` function returns a bitmask that indicates which of the four values (width, height, xoffset, and yoffset) were actually found in the string and whether the x and y values are negative. By convention, -0 is not equal to $+0$, because the user needs to be able to say "position the window relative to the right or bottom edge." For each value found, the corresponding argument is updated. For each value not found, the argument is left unchanged. The bits are represented by `XValue`, `YValue`, `Width-Value`, `HeightValue`, `XNegative`, or `YNegative` and are defined in `<X11/Xutil.h>`. They will be set whenever one of the values is defined or one of the signs is set.

If the function returns either the `XValue` or `YValue` flag, you should place the window at the requested position.

To parse window geometry given a user-specified position and a default position, use `XGeometry`.

int XGeometry(*display, screen, position, default_position, bwidth, fwidth, fheight, xadder,*
          yadder, x_return, y_return, width_return, height_return)
    Display **display*;
    int *screen*;
    char **position, *default_position*;
    unsigned int *bwidth*;
    unsigned int *fwidth, fheight*;
    int *xadder, yadder*;
    int **x_return, *y_return*;
    int **width_return, *height_return*;

display	Specifies the connection to the X server.
screen	Specifies the screen.
position	
default_position	Specify the geometry specifications.
bwidth	Specifies the border width.
fheight	
fwidth	Specify the font height and width in pixels (increment size).
xadder	
yadder	Specify additional interior padding needed in the window.
x_return	
y_return	Return the x and y offsets.
width_return	
height_return	Return the width and height determined.

You pass in the border width (bwidth), size of the increments fwidth and fheight (typically font width and height), and any additional interior space (xadder and yadder) to make it easy to compute the resulting size. The XGeometry function returns the position the window should be placed given a position and a default position. XGeometry determines the placement of a window using a geometry specification as specified by XParseGeometry and the additional information about the window. Given a fully qualified default geometry specification and an incomplete geometry specification, XParseGeometry returns a bitmask value as defined above in the XParseGeometry call, by using the position argument.

The returned width and height will be the width and height specified by default_position as overridden by any user-specified position. They are not affected by fwidth, fheight, xadder, or yadder. The x and y coordinates are computed by using the border width, the screen width and height, padding as specified by xadder and yadder, and the fheight and fwidth times the width and height from the geometry specifications.

10.4   Parsing the Color Specifications

To parse color values, use XParseColor.

Status XParseColor(*display, colormap, spec, exact_def_return*)
    Display **display*;
    Colormap *colormap*;
    char **spec*;
    XColor **exact_def_return*;

display	Specifies the connection to the X server.
colormap	Specifies the colormap.
spec	Specifies the color name string. Case is ignored.
exact_def_return	Returns the exact color value for later use and sets the DoRed, DoGreen, and DoBlue flags.

The XParseColor function provides a simple way to create a standard user interface to color. It takes a string specification of a color, typically from a command line or XGetDefault option, and returns the corresponding red, green, and blue values that are suitable for a subsequent call to XAllocColor or XStoreColor. The color can be specified either as a color name (as in XAllocNamedColor) or as an initial sharp sign character followed by a numeric specification, in one of the following formats:

#RGB	(4 bits each)
#RRGGBB	(8 bits each)
#RRRGGGBBB	(12 bits each)
#RRRRGGGGBBBB	(16 bits each)

The R, G, and B represent single hexadecimal digits (both uppercase and lowercase). When fewer than 16 bits each are specified, they represent the most-significant bits of the value. For example, #3a7 is the same as #3000a0007000. The colormap is used only to determine which screen to look up the color on. For example, you can use the screen's default colormap.

If the initial character is a sharp sign but the string otherwise fails to fit the above formats or if the initial character is not a sharp sign and the named color does not exist in the server's database, XParseColor fails and returns zero.

XParseColor can generate a BadColor error.

10.5   Generating Regions

Regions are arbitrary sets of pixel locations. Xlib provides functions for manipulating regions. The opaque type `Region` is defined in <X11/Xutil.h>.

To generate a region from a polygon, use `XPolygonRegion`.

```
Region XPolygonRegion(points, n, fill_rule)
    XPoint points[ ];
    int n;
    int fill_rule;
```

points   Specifies an array of points.

n   Specifies the number of points in the polygon.

fill_rule   Specifies the fill-rule you want to set for the specified GC. You can pass `EvenOddRule` or `WindingRule`.

The `XPolygonRegion` function returns a region for the polygon defined by the points array. For an explanation of fill_rule, see `XCreateGC`.

To generate the smallest rectangle enclosing the region, use `XClipBox`.

```
XClipBox(r, rect_return)
    Region r;
    XRectangle *rect_return;
```

r   Specifies the region.

rect_return Returns the smallest enclosing rectangle.

The `XClipBox` function returns the smallest rectangle enclosing the specified region.

10.6   Manipulating Regions

Xlib provides functions that you can use to manipulate regions. This section discusses how to:

- Create, copy, or destroy regions
- Move or shrink regions
- Compute with regions
- Determine if regions are empty or equal
- Locate a point or rectangle in a region

10.6.1 Creating, Copying, or Destroying Regions

To create a new empty region, use `XCreateRegion`.

Region XCreateRegion()

To set the clip-mask of a GC to a region, use `XSetRegion`.

XSetRegion(*display, gc, r*)
     Display **display;
     GC *gc*;
     Region *r*;
display   Specifies the connection to the X server.
gc   Specifies the GC.
r   Specifies the region.

The `XSetRegion` function sets the clip-mask in the GC to the specified region. Once it is set in the GC, the region can be destroyed.

To deallocate the storage associated with a specified region, use `XDestroyRegion`.

XDestroyRegion(*r*)
     Region *r*;
r   Specifies the region.

10.6.2 Moving or Shrinking Regions

To move a region by a specified amount, use `XOffsetRegion`.

XOffsetRegion(*r, dx, dy*)
     Region *r*;
     int *dx, dy*;
r   Specifies the region.
dx
dy   Specify the x and y coordinates, which define the amount you want to move
        the specified region.

To reduce a region by a specified amount, use `XShrinkRegion`.

XShrinkRegion(*r*, *dx*, *dy*)
    Region *r*;
    int *dx*, *dy*;

r   Specifies the region.

dx

dy   Specify the x and y coordinates, which define the amount you want to shrink the specified region.

Positive values shrink the size of the region, and negative values expand the region.

10.6.3 Computing with Regions

To compute the intersection of two regions, use `XIntersectRegion`.

XIntersectRegion(*sra*, *srb*, *dr_return*)
    Region *sra*, *srb*, *dr_return*;

sra

srb   Specify the two regions with which you want to perform the computation.

dr_return   Returns the result of the computation.

To compute the union of two regions, use `XUnionRegion`.

XUnionRegion(*sra*, *srb*, *dr_return*)
    Region *sra*, *srb*, *dr_return*;

sra

srb   Specify the two regions with which you want to perform the computation.

dr_return   Returns the result of the computation.

To create a union of a source region and a rectangle, use `XUnionRectWithRegion`.

XUnionRectWithRegion(*rectangle*, *src_region*, *dest_region_return*)
    XRectangle **rectangle*;
    Region *src_region*;
    Region *dest_region_return*;

rectangle   Specifies the rectangle.

src_region   Specifies the source region to be used.

dest_region_return   Returns the destination region.

The `XUnionRectWithRegion` function updates the destination region from a union of the specified rectangle and the specified source region.

To subtract two regions, use `XSubtractRegion`.

XSubtractRegion(*sra, srb, dr_return*)
    Region *sra, srb, dr_return*;

sra
srb   Specify the two regions with which you want to perform the computation.
dr_return   Returns the result of the computation.

The `XSubtractRegion` function subtracts srb from sra and stores the results in dr_return.

To calculate the difference between the union and intersection of two regions, use `XXorRegion`.

XXorRegion(*sra, srb, dr_return*)
    Region *sra, srb, dr_return*;

sra
srb   Specify the two regions with which you want to perform the computation.
dr_return   Returns the result of the computation.

10.6.4   Determining if Regions Are Empty or Equal

To determine if the specified region is empty, use `XEmptyRegion`.

Bool XEmptyRegion(*r*)
    Region *r*;
r   Specifies the region.

The `XEmptyRegion` function returns `True` if the region is empty.

To determine if two regions have the same offset, size, and shape, use `XEqualRegion`.

Bool XEqualRegion(*r1, r2*)
    Region *r1, r2*;
r1
r2   Specify the two regions.

The XEqualRegion function returns True if the two regions have the same offset, size, and shape.

10.6.5   Locating a Point or a Rectangle in a Region

To determine if a specified point resides in a specified region, use XPointInRegion.

Bool XPointInRegion(*r, x, y*)
> Region *r*;
> int *x, y*;

r   Specifies the region.

x

y   Specify the x and y coordinates, which define the point.

The XPointInRegion function returns True if the point (x, y) is contained in the region r.

To determine if a specified rectangle is inside a region, use XRectInRegion.

int XRectInRegion(*r, x, y, width, height*)
> Region *r*;
> int *x, y*;
> unsigned int *width, height*;

r   Specifies the region.

x

y   Specify the x and y coordinates, which define the coordinates of the upper-left corner of the rectangle.

width

height   Specify the width and height, which define the rectangle .

The XRectInRegion function returns RectangleIn if the rectangle is entirely in the specified region, RectangleOut if the rectangle is entirely out of the specified region, and RectanglePart if the rectangle is partially in the specified region.

10.7   Using the Cut and Paste Buffers

Xlib provides functions that you can use to cut and paste buffers for programs using this form of communications. Selections are a more useful mechanism for interchanging data between clients because typed information can be exchanged. X provides property names for properties in which bytes can be stored for implementing cut and paste between windows (implemented by use of properties on the first root window of the display). It is up to applications to agree on how to represent the data in the buffers. The data is most often ISO Latin-1 text. The atoms for eight such buffer names are provided and can be accessed as a ring or as explicit buffers (numbered 0 through 7). New applications are encouraged to share data by using selections (see section 4.4).

To store data in cut buffer 0, use XStoreBytes.

XStoreBytes(*display, bytes, nbytes*)
    Display **display*;
    char **bytes*;
    int *nbytes*;
display   Specifies the connection to the X server.
bytes   Specifies the bytes, which are not necessarily ASCII or null-terminated.
nbytes   Specifies the number of bytes to be stored.

Note that the cut buffer's contents need not be text, so zero bytes are not special. The cut buffer's contents can be retrieved later by any client calling XFetchBytes.
    XStoreBytes can generate a BadAlloc error.

To store data in a specified cut buffer, use XStoreBuffer.

XStoreBuffer(*display, bytes, nbytes, buffer*)
    Display **display*;
    char **bytes*;
    int *nbytes*;
    int *buffer*;
display   Specifies the connection to the X server.
bytes   Specifies the bytes, which are not necessarily ASCII or null-terminated.
nbytes   Specifies the number of bytes to be stored.
buffer   Specifies the buffer in which you want to store the bytes.

If the property for the buffer has never been created, a BadAtom error results.
    XStoreBuffer can generate BadAlloc and BadAtom errors.

To return data from cut buffer 0, use `XFetchBytes`.

```
char *XFetchBytes(display, nbytes_return)
    Display *display;
    int *nbytes_return;
```

display	Specifies the connection to the X server.
nbytes_return	Returns the number of bytes in the buffer.

The `XFetchBytes` function returns the number of bytes in the nbytes_return argument, if the buffer contains data. Otherwise, the function returns NULL and sets nbytes to 0. The appropriate amount of storage is allocated and the pointer returned. The client must free this storage when finished with it by calling `XFree`. Note that the cut buffer does not necessarily contain text, so it may contain embedded zero bytes and may not terminate with a null byte.

To return data from a specified cut buffer, use `XFetchBuffer`.

```
char *XFetchBuffer(display, nbytes_return, buffer)
    Display *display;
    int *nbytes_return;
    int buffer;
```

display	Specifies the connection to the X server.
nbytes_return	Returns the number of bytes in the buffer.
buffer	Specifies the buffer from which you want the stored data returned.

The `XFetchBuffer` function returns zero to the nbytes_return argument if there is no data in the buffer.

`XFetchBuffer` can generate a `BadValue` error.

To rotate the cut buffers, use `XRotateBuffers`.

```
XRotateBuffers(display, rotate)
    Display *display;
    int rotate;
```

display	Specifies the connection to the X server.
rotate	Specifies how much to rotate the cut buffers.

The `XRotateBuffers` function rotates the cut buffers, such that buffer 0 becomes buffer n, buffer 1 becomes n + 1 mod 8, and so on. This cut buffer numbering is global to the display. Note that `XRotateBuffers` generates `BadMatch` errors if any of the eight buffers have not been created.

10.8 Determining the Appropriate Visual Type

A single display can support multiple screens. Each screen can have several different visual types supported at different depths. You can use the functions described in this section to determine which visual to use for your application.

The functions in this section use the visual information masks and the `XVisualInfo` structure, which is defined in `<X11/Xutil.h>` and contains:

```
/* Visual information mask bits */
#define VisualNoMask              0x0
#define VisualIDMask              0x1
#define VisualScreenMask          0x2
#define VisualDepthMask           0x4
#define VisualClassMask           0x8
#define VisualRedMaskMask         0x10
#define VisualGreenMaskMask       0x20
#define VisualBlueMaskMask        0x40
#define VisualColormapSizeMask    0x80
#define VisualBitsPerRGBMask      0x100
#define VisualAllMask             0x1FF
/* Values */
typedef struct {
    Visual *visual;
    VisualID visualid;
    int screen;
    unsigned int depth;
    int class;
    unsigned long red_mask;
    unsigned long green_mask;
    unsigned long blue_mask;
    int colormap_size;
    int bits_per_rgb;
} XVisualInfo;
```

To obtain a list of visual information structures that match a specified template, use `XGetVisualInfo`.

XVisualInfo *XGetVisualInfo(*display, vinfo_mask, vinfo_template, nitems_return*)
    Display **display*;
    long *vinfo_mask*;
    XVisualInfo **vinfo_template*;
    int **nitems_return*;

display	Specifies the connection to the X server.
vinfo_mask	Specifies the visual mask value.
vinfo_template	Specifies the visual attributes that are to be used in matching the visual structures.
nitems_return	Returns the number of matching visual structures.

The `XGetVisualInfo` function returns a list of visual structures that match the attributes specified by vinfo_template. If no visual structures match the template using the specified vinfo_mask, `XGetVisualInfo` returns a NULL. To free the data returned by this function, use `XFree`.

To obtain the visual information that matches the specified depth and class of the screen, use `XMatchVisualInfo`.

Status XMatchVisualInfo(*display, screen, depth, class, vinfo_return*)
    Display **display*;
    int *screen*;
    int *depth*;
    int *class*;
    XVisualInfo **vinfo_return*;

display	Specifies the connection to the X server.
screen	Specifies the screen.
depth	Specifies the depth of the screen.
class	Specifies the class of the screen.
vinfo_return	Returns the matched visual information.

The `XMatchVisualInfo` function returns the visual information for a visual that matches the specified depth and class for a screen. Because multiple visuals that match the specified depth and class can exist, the exact visual chosen is undefined. If a visual is found, `XMatchVisualInfo` returns nonzero and the information on the visual to vinfo_return. Otherwise, when a visual is not found, `XMatchVisualInfo` returns zero.

10.9 Manipulating Images

Xlib provides several functions that perform basic operations on images. All operations on images are defined using an XImage structure, as defined in <X11/Xlib.h>. Because the number of different types of image formats can be very large, this hides details of image storage properly from applications.

This section describes the functions for generic operations on images. Manufacturers can provide very fast implementations of these for the formats frequently encountered on their hardware. These functions are neither sufficient nor desirable to use for general image processing. Rather, they are here to provide minimal functions on screen format images. The basic operations for getting and putting images are XGetImage and XPutImage.

Note that no functions have been defined, as yet, to read and write images to and from disk files.

The XImage structure describes an image as it exists in the client's memory. The user can request that some of the members such as height, width, and xoffset be changed when the image is sent to the server. Note that bytes_per_line in concert with offset can be used to extract a subset of the image. Other members (for example, byte order, bitmap_unit, and so forth) are characteristics of both the image and the server. If these members differ between the image and the server, XPutImage makes the appropriate conversions. The first byte of the first line of plane n must be located at the address (data + (n * height * bytes_per_line)). For a description of the XImage structure, see section 6.7.

To allocate sufficient memory for an XImage structure, use XCreateImage.

XImage *XCreateImage(*display, visual, depth, format, offset, data, width, height, bitmap_pad, bytes_per_line*)

    Display **display;
    Visual **visual;
    unsigned int *depth*;
    int *format*;
    int *offset*;
    char **data;
    unsigned int *width*;

unsigned int *height*;
int *bitmap_pad*;
int *bytes_per_line*;

display	Specifies the connection to the X server.
visual	Specifies a pointer to the visual.
depth	Specifies the depth of the image.
format	Specifies the format for the image. You can pass `XYBitmap`, `XYPixmap` or `ZPixmap`.
offset	Specifies the number of pixels to ignore at the beginning of the scanline.
data	Specifies a pointer to the image data.
width	Specifies the width of the image, in pixels.
height	Specifies the height of the image, in pixels.
bitmap_pad	Specifies the quantum of a scanline (8, 16, or 32). In other words, the start of one scanline is separated in client memory from the start of the next scanline by an integer multiple of this many bits.
bytes_per_line	Specifies the number of bytes in the client image between the start of one scanline and the start of the next.

The `XCreateImage` function allocates the memory needed for an `XImage` structure for the specified display but does not allocate space for the image itself. Rather, it initializes the structure byte-order, bit-order, and bitmap-unit values from the display and returns a pointer to the `XImage` structure. The red, green, and blue mask values are defined for Z format images only and are derived from the `Visual` structure passed in. Other values also are passed in. The offset permits the rapid displaying of the image without requiring each scanline to be shifted into position. If you pass a zero value in bytes_per_line, Xlib assumes that the scanlines are contiguous in memory and calculates the value of bytes_per_line itself.

Note that when the image is created using `XCreateImage`, `XGetImage`, or `XSubImage`, the destroy procedure that the `XDestroyImage` function calls frees both the image structure and the data pointed to by the image structure.

The basic functions used to get a pixel, set a pixel, create a subimage, and add a constant offset to a Z format image are defined in the image object. The functions in this section are really macro invocations of the functions in the image object and are defined in <X11/Xutil.h>.

To obtain a pixel value in an image, use `XGetPixel`.

unsigned long XGetPixel(*ximage, x, y*)
    XImage **ximage*;
    int *x*;
    int *y*;
ximage   Specifies a pointer to the image.
x
y   Specify the x and y coordinates.

The `XGetPixel` function returns the specified pixel from the named image. The pixel value is returned in normalized format (that is, the least-significant byte of the long is the least-significant byte of the pixel). The image must contain the x and y coordinates.

To set a pixel value in an image, use `XPutPixel`.

int XPutPixel(*ximage, x, y, pixel*)
    XImage **ximage*;
    int *x*;
    int *y*;
    unsigned long *pixel*;
ximage   Specifies a pointer to the image.
x
y   Specify the x and y coordinates.
pixel   Specifies the new pixel value.

The `XPutPixel` function overwrites the pixel in the named image with the specified pixel value. The input pixel value must be in normalized format (that is, the least-significant byte of the long is the least-significant byte of the pixel). The image must contain the x and y coordinates.

To create a subimage, use `XSubImage`.

XImage *XSubImage(*ximage, x, y, subimage_width, subimage_height*)
    XImage **ximage*;
    int *x*;
    int *y*;
    unsigned int *subimage_width*;
    unsigned int *subimage_height*;
ximage   Specifies a pointer to the image.

x
y   Specify the x and y coordinates.
subimage_width   Specifies the width of the new subimage, in pixels.
subimage_height   Specifies the height of the new subimage, in pixels.

The XSubImage function creates a new image that is a subsection of an existing one. It allocates the memory necessary for the new XImage structure and returns a pointer to the new image. The data is copied from the source image, and the image must contain the rectangle defined by x, y, subimage_width, and subimage_height.

To increment each pixel in the pixmap by a constant value, use XAddPixel.

XAddPixel(*ximage, value*)
    XImage **ximage*;
    long *value*;
ximage   Specifies a pointer to the image.
value   Specifies the constant value that is to be added.

The XAddPixel function adds a constant value to every pixel in an image. It is useful when you have a base pixel value from allocating color resources and need to manipulate the image to that form.

To deallocate the memory allocated in a previous call to XCreateImage, use XDestroyImage.

int XDestroyImage(*ximage*)
    XImage **ximage*;
ximage   Specifies a pointer to the image.

The XDestroyImage function deallocates the memory associated with the XImage structure.

Note that when the image is created using XCreateImage, XGetImage, or XSubImage, the destroy procedure that this macro calls frees both the image structure and the data pointed to by the image structure.

10.10   Manipulating Bitmaps

Xlib provides functions that you can use to read a bitmap from a file, save a bitmap to a file, or create a bitmap. This section describes those functions that transfer bitmaps to and from the client's file system, thus allowing their reuse in a later connection (for example, from an entirely different client or to a different display or server).

The X version 11 bitmap file format is:

```
#define name_width width
#define name_height height
#define name_x_hot x
#define name_y_hot y
static char name_bits[] = { 0xNN, . . . }
```

The variables ending with _x_hot and _y_hot suffixes are optional because they are present only if a hotspot has been defined for this bitmap. The other variables are required. The _bits array must be large enough to contain the size bitmap. The bitmap unit is eight. The name is derived from the name of the file that you specified on the original command line by deleting the directory path and extension.

To read a bitmap from a file, use `XReadBitmapFile`.

```
int XReadBitmapFile(display, d, filename, width_return, height_return, bitmap_return,
                    x_hot_return, y_hot_return)
    Display *display;
    Drawable d;
    char *filename;
    unsigned int *width_return, *height_return;
    Pixmap *bitmap_return;
    int *x_hot_return, *y_hot_return;
```

display	Specifies the connection to the X server.
d	Specifies the drawable that indicates the screen.
filename	Specifies the file name to use. The format of the file name is operating-system dependent.
width_return	
height_return	Return the width and height values of the read in bitmap file.
bitmap_return	Returns the bitmap that is created.
x_hot_return	
y_hot_return	Return the hotspot coordinates.

The `XReadBitmapFile` function reads in a file containing a bitmap. The file can be either in the standard X version 10 format (that is, the format used by X version 10 bitmap program) or in the X version 11 bitmap format. If the file cannot be opened, `XReadBitmapFile` returns

BitmapOpenFailed. If the file can be opened but does not contain valid bitmap data, it returns BitmapFileInvalid. If insufficient working storage is allocated, it returns BitmapNoMemory. If the file is readable and valid, it returns BitmapSuccess.

XReadBitmapFile returns the bitmap's height and width, as read from the file, to width_return and height_return. It then creates a pixmap of the appropriate size, reads the bitmap data from the file into the pixmap, and assigns the pixmap to the caller's variable bitmap. The caller must free the bitmap using XFreePixmap when finished. If name_x_hot and name_y_hot exist, XReadBitmapFile returns them to x_hot_return and y_hot_return; otherwise, it returns −1, −1.

XReadBitmapFile can generate BadAlloc and BadDrawable errors.

To write out a bitmap to a file, use XWriteBitmapFile.

int XWriteBitmapFile(*display, filename, bitmap, width, height, x_hot, y_hot*)
    Display **display*;
    char **filename*;
    Pixmap *bitmap*;
    unsigned int *width, height*;
    int *x_hot, y_hot*;

display	Specifies the connection to the X server.
filename	Specifies the file name to use. The format of the file name is operating-system dependent.
bitmap	Specifies the bitmap.
width	
height	Specify the width and height.
x_hot	
y_hot	Specify where to place the hotspot coordinates (or −1, −1 if none are present) in the file.

The XWriteBitmapFile function writes a bitmap out to a file. While XReadBitmapFile can read in either X version 10 format or X version 11 format, XWriteBitmapFile always writes out X version 11 format. If the file cannot be opened for writing, it returns BitmapOpenFailed. If insufficient memory is allocated, XWriteBitmapFile returns BitmapNoMemory; otherwise, on no error, it returns BitmapSuccess. If x_hot and y_hot are not −1, −1, XWriteBitmapFile writes them out as the hotspot coordinates for the bitmap.

XWriteBitmapFile can generate BadDrawable and BadMatch errors.

To create a pixmap and then store bitmap-format data into it, use XCreatePixmapFromBitmapData.

Pixmap XCreatePixmapFromBitmapData(*display, d, data, width, height, fg, bg, depth*)
    Display *display;
    Drawable *d*;
    char *data;
    unsigned int *width, height*;
    unsigned long *fg, bg*;
    unsigned int *depth*;

display   Specifies the connection to the X server.
d   Specifies the drawable that indicates the screen.
data   Specifies the data in bitmap format.
width
height   Specify the width and height.
fg
bg   Specify the foreground and background pixel values to use.
depth   Specifies the depth of the pixmap.

XCreatePixmapFromBitmapData function creates a pixmap of the given depth and then does a bitmap-format XPutImage of the data into it. The depth must be supported by the screen of the specified drawable, or a BadMatch error results.

    XCreatePixmapFromBitmapData can generate BadAlloc and BadMatch errors.

To include a bitmap written out by XWriteBitmapFile in a program directly, as opposed to reading it in every time at run time, use XCreateBitmapFromData.

Pixmap XCreateBitmapFromData(*display, d, data, width, height*)
    Display *display;
    Drawable *d*;
    char *data;
    unsigned int *width, height*;

display   Specifies the connection to the X server.
d   Specifies the drawable that indicates the screen.

data   Specifies the location of the bitmap data.

width

height   Specify the width and height.

The XCreateBitmapFromData function allows you to include in your
C program (using #include) a bitmap file that was written out by
XWriteBitmapFile (X version 11 format only) without reading in the
bitmap file. The following example creates a gray bitmap:

#include "gray.bitmap"
Pixmap bitmap
bitmap = XCreateBitmapFromData(display, window, gray_bits, gray_width,
                                          gray_height);

If insufficient working storage was allocated, XCreateBitmapFromData
returns None. It is your responsibility to free the bitmap using XFree-
Pixmap when finished.

XCreateBitmapFromData can generate a BadAlloc error.

10.11   Using the Resource Manager

The resource manager is a database manager with a twist. In most database
systems, you perform a query using an imprecise specification, and you get
back a set of records. The resource manager, however, allows you to specify
a large set of values with an imprecise specification, to query the database
with a precise specification, and to get back only a single value. This should
be used by applications that need to know what the user prefers for colors,
fonts, and other resources. It is this use as a database for dealing with X resources that inspired the name "Resource Manager," although the resource
manager can be and is used in other ways.

For example, a user of your application may want to specify that all windows should have a blue background but that all mail-reading windows
should have a red background. Presuming that all applications use the resource manager, a user can define this information using only two lines of
specification. Your personal resource database usually is stored in a file and
is loaded onto a server property when you log in. This database is retrieved
automatically by Xlib when a connection is opened.

As an example of how the resource manager works, consider a mail-reading application called xmh. Assume that it is designed so that it uses a complex window hierarchy all the way down to individual command buttons, which may be actual small subwindows in some toolkits. These are often called objects or widgets. In such toolkit systems, each user interface object can be composed of other objects and can be assigned a name and a class. Fully qualified names or classes can have arbitrary numbers of component names, but a fully qualified name always has the same number of component names as a fully qualified class. This generally reflects the structure of the application as composed of these objects, starting with the application itself.

For example, the xmh mail program has a name "xmh" and is one of a class of "Mail" programs. By convention, the first character of class components is capitalized, and the first letter of name components is in lowercase. Each name and class finally has an attribute (for example "foreground" or "font"). If each window is properly assigned a name and class, it is easy for the user to specify attributes of any portion of the application.

At the top level, the application might consist of a paned window (that is, a window divided into several sections) named "toc". One pane of the paned window is a button box window named "buttons" and is filled with command buttons. One of these command buttons is used to retrieve (include) new mail and has the name "include". This window has a fully qualified name, "xmh.toc.buttons.include," and a fully qualified class, "Xmh.VPaned.Box. Command". Its fully qualified name is the name of its parent, "xmh.toc. buttons", followed by its name, "include". Its class is the class of its parent, "Xmh.VPaned.Box", followed by its particular class, "Command". The fully qualified name of a resource is the attribute's name appended to the object's fully qualified name, and the fully qualified class is its class appended to the object's class.

This include button needs the following resources:

- Title string
- Font
- Foreground color for its inactive state
- Background color for its inactive state
- Foreground color for its active state
- Background color for its active state

Each of the resources that this button needs are considered to be attributes of the button and, as such, have a name and a class. For example, the foreground color for the button in its active state might be named "active-Foreground", and its class would be "Foreground."

When an application looks up a resource (for example, a color), it passes the complete name and complete class of the resource to a look-up routine. After look up, the resource manager returns the resource value and the representation type.

The resource manager allows applications to store resources by an incomplete specification of name, class, and a representation type, as well as to retrieve them given a fully qualified name and class.

10.11.1 Resource Manager Matching Rules

The algorithm for determining which resource name or names match a given query is the heart of the database. Resources are stored with only partially specified names and classes, using pattern matching constructs. An asterisk (*) is used to represent any number of intervening components (including none). A period (.) is used to separate immediately adjacent components. All queries fully specify the name and class of the resource needed. A trailing period and asterisk are not removed. The library supports 100 components in a name or class. The look-up algorithm then searches the database for the name that most closely matches (is most specific) this full name and class. The rules for a match in order of precedence are:

1. The attribute of the name and class must match. For example, queries for:
   xterm.scrollbar.background   (name)
   XTerm.Scrollbar.Background   (class)
   will not match the following database entry:
   xterm.scrollbar:on
2. Database entries with name or class prefixed by a period (.) are more specific than those prefixed by an asterisk (*). For example, the entry xterm.geometry is more specific than the entry xterm*geometry.
3. Names are more specific than classes. For example, the entry "*scrollbar. background" is more specific than the entry "*Scrollbar.Background".
4. Specifying a name or class is more specific than omitting either. For example, the entry "Scrollbar*Background" is more specific than the entry "*Background".

5. Left components are more specific than right components. For example, "*vt100*background" is more specific than the entry "*scrollbar*background" for the query ".vt100.scrollbar.background".

6. If neither a period (.) nor an asterisk (*) is specified at the beginning, a period (.) is implicit. For example, "xterm.background" is identical to ".xterm. background".

Names and classes can be mixed. As an example of these rules, assume the following user preference specification:

xmh*background:	red
*command.font:	8x13
*command.background:	blue
*Command.Foreground:	green
xmh.toc*Command.activeForeground:	black

A query for the name "xmh.toc.messagefunctions.include. activeForeground" and class "Xmh.VPaned.Box.Command.Foreground" would match "xmh.toc*Command.activeForeground" and return "black". However, it also matches "*Command.Foreground".

Using the precedence algorithm described above, the resource manager would return the value specified by "xmh.toc*Command. activeForeground".

10.11.2 Basic Resource Manager Definitions

The definitions for the resource manager's use are contained in <X11/Xresource.h>. Xlib also uses the resource manager internally to allow for non-English language error messages.

Database values consist of a size, an address, and a representation type. The size is specified in bytes. The representation type is a way for you to store data tagged by some application-defined type (for example, "font" or "color"). It has nothing to do with the C data type or with its class. The XrmValue structure contains:

```
typedef struct {
    unsigned int size;
    caddr_t addr;
} XrmValue, *XrmValuePtr;
```

A resource database is an opaque type used by the look-up functions.

typedef struct _XrmHashBucketRec *XrmDatabase;

To initialize the resource manager, use `XrmInitialize`.

void XrmInitialize();

Most uses of the resource manager involve defining names, classes, and representation types as string constants. However, always referring to strings in the resource manager can be slow, because it is so heavily used in some toolkits. To solve this problem, a shorthand for a string is used in place of the string in many of the resource manager functions. Simple comparisons can be performed rather than string comparisons. The shorthand name for a string is called a quark and is the type `XrmQuark`. On some occasions, you may want to allocate a quark that has no string equivalent.

A quark is to a string what an atom is to a string in the server, but its use is entirely local to your application.

To allocate a new quark, use `XrmUniqueQuark`.

XrmQuark XrmUniqueQuark()

The `XrmUniqueQuark` function allocates a quark that is guaranteed not to represent any string that is known to the resource manager.

To allocate some memory you will never give back, use `Xpermalloc`.

char *Xpermalloc(*size*)
    unsigned int *size*;

The `Xpermalloc` function is used by some toolkits for permanently allocated storage and allows some performance and space savings over the completely general memory allocator.

Each name, class, and representation type is typedef'd as an `XrmQuark`.

```
typedef int XrmQuark, *XrmQuarkList;
typedef XrmQuark XrmName;
typedef XrmQuark XrmClass;
typedef XrmQuark XrmRepresentation;
```

Lists are represented as null-terminated arrays of quarks. The size of the array must be large enough for the number of components used.

```
typedef XrmQuarkList XrmNameList;
typedef XrmQuarkList XrmClassList;
```

To convert a string to a quark, use `XrmStringToQuark`.

```
#define XrmStringToName(string)              XrmStringToQuark(string)
#define XrmStringToClass(string)             XrmStringToQuark(string)
#define XrmStringToRepresentation(string)    XrmStringToQuark(string)
XrmQuark XrmStringToQuark(string)
     char *string;
```
string   Specifies the string for which a quark is to be allocated.

To convert a quark to a string, use `XrmQuarkToString`.

```
#define XrmNameToString(name)           XrmQuarkToSting(name)
#define XrmClassToString(class)         XrmQuarkToString(class)
#define XrmRepresentationToString(type) XrmQuarkToString(type)
char *XrmQuarkToString(quark)
     XrmQuark quark;
```
quark   Specifies the quark for which the equivalent string is desired.

These functions can be used to convert to and from quark representations. The string pointed to by the return value must not be modified or freed. If no string exists for that quark, `XrmQuarkToString` returns NULL.

To convert a string with one or more components to a quark list, use `XrmStringToQuarkList`.

```
#define XrmStringToNameList(str, name)   XrmStringToQuarkList((str), (name))
#define XrmStringToClassList(str,class)  XrmStringToQuarkList((str), (class))
void XrmStringToQuarkList(string, quarks_return)
     char *string;
     XrmQuarkList quarks_return;
```

string	Specifies the string for which a quark is to be allocated.
quarks_return	Returns the list of quarks.

The `XrmStringToQuarkList` function converts the null-terminated string (generally a fully qualified name) to a list of quarks. The components of the string are separated by a period or asterisk character.

A binding list is a list of type `XrmBindingList` and indicates if components of name or class lists are bound tightly or loosely (that is, if wildcarding of intermediate components is specified).

typedef enum {XrmBindTightly, XrmBindLoosely} XrmBinding, *XrmBindingList;

`XrmBindTightly` indicates that a period separates the components, and `XrmBindLoosely` indicates that an asterisk separates the components.

To convert a string with one or more components to a binding list and a quark list, use `XrmStringToBindingQuarkList`.

XrmStringToBindingQuarkList(*string, bindings_return, quarks_return*)
    char *string*;
    XrmBindingList *bindings_return*;
    XrmQuarkList *quarks_return*;

string	Specifies the string for which a quark is to be allocated.
bindings_return	Returns the binding list. The caller must allocate sufficient space for the binding list before calling `XrmStringToBinding-QuarkList`.
quarks_return	Returns the list of quarks. The caller must allocates sufficient space for the quarks list before calling `XrmStringToBinding-QuarkList`.

Component names in the list are separated by a period or an asterisk character. If the string does not start with a period or an asterisk, a period is assumed. For example, "*a.b*c" becomes:

quarks	a	b	c
bindings	loose	tight	loose

10.11.3 Resource Database Access

Xlib provides resource management functions that you can use to manipulate resource databases. The next sections discuss how to:

- Store and get resources
- Get database levels
- Merge two databases
- Retrieve and store databases

10.11.3.1 Storing Into a Resource Database

To store resources into the database, use `XrmPutResource` or `XrmQPutResource`. Both functions take a partial resource specification, a representation type, and a value. This value is copied into the specified database.

> void XrmPutResource(*database, specifier, type, value*)
>   XrmDatabase **database*;
>   char **specifier*;
>   char **type*;
>   XrmValue **value*;
>
> *database*   Specifies a pointer to the resource database.
> *specifier*   Specifies a complete or partial specification of the resource.
> *type*   Specifies the type of the resource.
> *value*   Specifies the value of the resource, which is specified as a string.

If database contains NULL, `XrmPutResource` creates a new database and returns a pointer to it. `XrmPutResource` is a convenience function that calls `XrmStringToBindingQuarkList` followed by:

XrmQPutResource(database, bindings, quarks, XrmStringToQuark(type), value)

> void XrmQPutResource(*database, bindings, quarks, type, value*)
>   XrmDatabase **database*;
>   XrmBindingList *bindings*;
>   XrmQuarkList *quarks*;
>   XrmRepresentation *type*;
>   XrmValue **value*;
>
> *database*   Specifies a pointer to the resource database.
> *bindings*   Specifies a list of bindings.
> *quarks*   Specifies the complete or partial name or the class list of the resource.
> *type*   Specifies the type of the resource.
> *value*   Specifies the value of the resource, which is specified as a string.

If database contains NULL, `XrmQPutResource` creates a new database and returns a pointer to it.

To add a resource that is specified as a string, use `XrmPutStringResource`.

void XrmPutStringResource(*database, specifier, value*)
    XrmDatabase *database;
    char *specifier;
    char *value;

database   Specifies a pointer to the resource database.
specifier   Specifies a complete or partial specification of the resource.
value   Specifies the value of the resource, which is specified as a string.

If database contains NULL, `XrmPutStringResource` creates a new database and returns a pointer to it. `XrmPutStringResource` adds a resource with the specified value to the specified database. `XrmPut-StringResource` is a convenience routine that takes both the resource and value as null-terminated strings, converts them to quarks, and then calls `XrmQPutResource`, using a "String" representation type.

To add a string resource using quarks as a specification, use `XrmQPutStringResource`.

void XrmQPutStringResource(*database, bindings, quarks, value*)
    XrmDatabase *database;
    XrmBindingList *bindings*;
    XrmQuarkList *quarks*;
    char *value;

database   Specifies a pointer to the resource database.
bindings   Specifies a list of bindings.
quarks   Specifies the complete or partial name or the class list of the resource.
value   Specifies the value of the resource, which is specified as a string.

If database contains NULL, `XrmQPutStringResource` creates a new database and returns a pointer to it. `XrmQPutStringResource` is a convenience routine that constructs an `XrmValue` for the value string (by calling strlen to compute the size) and then calls `XrmQPutResource`, using a "String" representation type.

To add a single resource entry that is specified as a string that contains both a name and a value, use `XrmPutLineResource`.

void XrmPutLineResource(*database, line*)
    XrmDatabase **database*;
    char **line*;
database   Specifies a pointer to the resource database.
line   Specifies the resource value pair as a single string. A single colon (:) separates the name from the value.

If database contains NULL, `XrmPutLineResource` creates a new database and returns a pointer to it. `XrmPutLineResource` adds a single resource entry to the specified database. Any white space before or after the name or colon in the line argument is ignored. The value is terminated by a new-line or a NULL character. To allow values to contain embedded new-line characters, a "\n" is recognized and replaced by a new-line character. For example, line might have the value "xterm*background:green\n". Null-terminated strings without a new line are also permitted.

10.11.3.2 Looking Up from a Resource Database

To retrieve a resource from a resource database, use `XrmGetResource` or `XrmQGetResource`.

Bool XrmGetResource(*database, str_name, str_class, str_type_return, value_return*)
    XrmDatabase *database*;
    char **str_name*;
    char **str_class*;
    char ***str_type_return*;
    XrmValue **value_return*;
database   Specifies the database that is to be used.
str_name   Specifies the fully qualified name of the value being retrieved (as a string).
str_class   Specifies the fully qualified class of the value being retrieved (as a string).
str_type_return   Returns a pointer to the representation type of the destination (as a string).
value_return   Returns the value in the database.

Bool XrmQGetResource(*database, quark_name, quark_class, quark_type_return, value_return*)
    XrmDatabase *database*;
    XrmNameList *quark_name*;
    XrmClassList *quark_class*;

XrmRepresentation *quark_type_return*;
XrmValue *value_return*;

database	Specifies the database that is to be used.
quark_name	Specifies the fully qualified name of the value being retrieved (as a quark).
quark_class	Specifies the fully qualified class of the value being retrieved (as a quark).
quark_type_return	Returns a pointer to the representation type of the destination (as a quark).
value_return	Returns the value in the database.

The `XrmGetResource` and `XrmQGetResource` functions retrieve a resource from the specified database. Both take a fully qualified name/class pair, a destination resource representation, and the address of a value (size/address pair). The value and returned type point into database memory; therefore, you must not modify the data.

The database only frees or overwrites entries on `XrmPutResource`, `XrmQPutResource`, or `XrmMergeDatabases`. A client that is not storing new values into the database or is not merging the database should be safe using the address passed back at any time until it exits. If a resource was found, both `XrmGetResource` and `XrmQGetResource` return `True`; otherwise, they return `False`.

10.11.3.3 Database Search Lists

Most applications and toolkits do not make random probes into a resource database to fetch resources. The X toolkit access pattern for a resource database is quite stylized. A series of from 1 to 20 probes are made with only the last name/class differing in each probe. The `XrmGetResource` function is at worst a 2^n algorithm, where n is the length of the name/class list. This can be improved upon by the application programmer by prefetching a list of database levels that might match the first part of a name/class list.

To return a list of database levels, use `XrmQGetSearchList`.

```
typedef XrmHashTable *XrmSearchList;

Bool XrmQGetSearchList(database, names, classes, list_return, list_length)
    XrmDatabase database;
    XrmNameList names;
    XrmClassList classes;
```

XrmSearchList *list_return*;
int *list_length*;

database	Specifies the database that is to be used.
names	Specifies a list of resource names.
classes	Specifies a list of resource classes.
list_return	Returns a search list for further use. The caller must allocate sufficient space for the list before calling `XrmQGetSearchList`.
list_length	Specifies the number of entries (not the byte size) allocated for list_return.

The `XrmQGetSearchList` function takes a list of names and classes and returns a list of database levels where a match might occur. The returned list is in best-to-worst order and uses the same algorithm as `XrmGetResource` for determining precedence. If list_return was large enough for the search list, `XrmQGetSearchList` returns `True`; otherwise, it returns `False`.

The size of the search list that the caller must allocate is dependent upon the number of levels and wildcards in the resource specifiers that are stored in the database. The worst case length is 3^n, where n is the number of name or class components in names or classes.

When using `XrmQGetSearchList` followed by multiple probes for resources with a common name and class prefix, only the common prefix should be specified in the name and class list to `XrmQGetSearchList`.

To search resource database levels for a given resource, use `XrmQ-GetSearchResource`.

Bool XrmQGetSearchResource(*list, name, class, type_return, value_return*)
    XrmSearchList *list*;
    XrmName *name*;
    XrmClass *class*;
    XrmRepresentation **type_return*;
    XrmValue **value_return*;

list	Specifies the search list returned by `XrmQGetSearchList`.
name	Specifies the resource name.
class	Specifies the resource class.
type_return	Returns data representation type.
value_return	Returns the value in the database.

The `XrmQGetSearchResource` function searches the specified database levels for the resource that is fully identified by the specified name and class.

The search stops with the first match. XrmQGetSearchResource returns True if the resource was found; otherwise, it returns False.

A call to XrmQGetSearchList with a name and class list containing all but the last component of a resource name followed by a call to XrmQGetSearchResource with the last component name and class returns the same database entry as XrmGetResource and XrmQGet-Resource with the fully qualified name and class.

10.11.3.4 Merging Resource Databases

To merge the contents of one database into another database, use XrmMergeDatabases.

void XrmMergeDatabases(*source_db, target_db*)
    XrmDatabase *source_db*, **target_db*;
source_db   Specifies the resource database that is to be merged into the target database.
target_db   Specifies a pointer to the resource database into which the source database is to be merged.

The XrmMergeDatabases function merges the contents of one database into another. It may overwrite entries in the destination database. This function is used to combine databases (for example, an application specific database of defaults and a database of user preferences). The merge is destructive; that is, the source database is destroyed.

10.11.3.5 Retrieving and Storing Databases

To retrieve a database from disk, use XrmGetFileDatabase.

XrmDatabase XrmGetFileDatabase(*filename*)
    char **filename*;
filename   Specifies the resource database file name.

The XrmGetFileDatabase function opens the specified file, creates a new resource database, and loads it with the specifications read in from the specified file. The specified file must contain lines in the format accepted by XrmPutLineResource. If it cannot open the specified file, XrmGet-FileDatabase returns NULL.

To store a copy of a database to disk, use `XrmPutFileDatabase`.

```
void XrmPutFileDatabase(database, stored_db)
      XrmDatabase database;
      char *stored_db;
```
database   Specifies the database that is to be used.
stored_db   Specifies the file name for the stored database.

The `XrmPutFileDatabase` function stores a copy of the specified database in the specified file. The file is an ASCII text file that contains lines in the format that is accepted by `XrmPutLineResource`.

To create a database from a string, use `XrmGetStringDatabase`.

```
XrmDatabase XrmGetStringDatabase(data)
      char *data;
```
data   Specifies the database contents using a string.

The `XrmGetStringDatabase` function creates a new database and stores the resources specified in the specified null-terminated string. `XrmGetStringDatabase` is similar to `XrmGetFileDatabase` except that it reads the information out of a string instead of out of a file. Each line is separated by a new-line character in the format accepted by `XrmPutLineResource`.

10.11.4 Parsing Command Line Options

The `XrmParseCommand` function can be used to parse the command line arguments to a program and modify a resource database with selected entries from the command line.

```
typedef enum {
      XrmoptionNoArg,        /* Value is specified in OptionDescRec.value */
      XrmoptionIsArg,        /* Value is the option string itself */
      XrmoptionStickyArg,    /* Value is characters immediately following option */
      XrmoptionSepArg,       /* Value is next argument in argv */
      XrmoptionResArg,       /* Resource and value in next argument in argv */
      XrmoptionSkipArg,      /* Ignore this option and the next argument in argv */
      XrmoptionSkipLine      /* Ignore this option and the rest of argv */
} XrmOptionKind;
```

```
typedef struct {
    char *option;          /* Option specification string in argv */
    char *specifier;       /* Binding and resource name (sans application
                              name) */
    XrmOptionKind argKind; /* Which style of option it is */
    caddr_t value;         /* Value to provide if XrmoptionNoArg */
} XrmOptionDescRec, *XrmOptionDescList;
```

To load a resource database from a C command line, use `XrmParse-Command`.

```
void XrmParseCommand(database, table, table_count, name, argc_in_out,
                     agrv_in_out)
    XrmDatabase *database;
    XrmOptionDescList table;
    int table_count;
    char *name;
    int *argc_in_out;
    char **argv_in_out;
```

database   Specifies a pointer to the resource database.
table   Specifies the table of command line arguments to be parsed.
table_count   Specifies the number of entries in the table.
name   Specifies the application name.
argc_in_out   Specifies the number of arguments and returns the number of
              remaining arguments.
argv_in_out   Specifies a pointer to the command line arguments and returns the
              remaining arguments.

The `XrmParseCommand` function parses an (argc, argv) pair according to the specified option table, loads recognized options into the specified database with type "String," and modifies the (argc, argv) pair to remove all recognized options.

The specified table is used to parse the command line. Recognized entries in the table are removed from argv, and entries are made in the specified resource database. The table entries contain information on the option string, the option name, the style of option, and a value to provide if the option kind is `XrmoptionNoArg`. The argc argument specifies the number of arguments in argv and is set to the remaining number of arguments that were not parsed. The name argument should be the name of your application for use in building the database entry. The name argument is prefixed to the resourceName in the option table before storing the specification. No separating (binding) character is inserted. The table must contain either a period (.) or an asterisk (*) as the first character in each resourceName entry. To specify a more completely qualified resource name, the resourceName entry can contain multiple components.

For example, the following is part of the standard option table from the X Toolkit `XtInitialize` function:

```
static XrmOptionDescRec opTable[] = {
{"−background",    "*background",                XrmoptionSepArg,  (caddr_t) NULL},
{"−bd",            "*borderColor",              XrmoptionSepArg,  (caddr_t) NULL},
{"−bg",            "*background",                XrmoptionSepArg,  (caddr_t) NULL},
{"−borderwidth",   "*TopLevelShell.borderWidth", XrmoptionSepArg,  (caddr_t) NULL},
{"−bordercolor",   "*borderColor",              XrmoptionSepArg,  (caddr_t) NULL},
{"−bw",            "*TopLevelShell.borderWidth", XrmoptionSepArg,  (caddr_t) NULL},
{"−display",       ".display",                   XrmoptionSepArg,  (caddr_t) NULL},
{"−fg",            "*foreground",                XrmoptionSepArg,  (caddr_t) NULL},
{"−fn",            "*font",                      XrmoptionSepArg,  (caddr_t) NULL},
{"−font",          "*font",                      XrmoptionSepArg,  (caddr_t) NULL},
{"−foreground",    "*foreground",                XrmoptionSepArg,  (caddr_t) NULL},
{"−geometry",      ".TopLevelShell.geometry",    XrmoptionSepArg,  (caddr_t) NULL},
{"−iconic",        ".TopLevelShell.iconic",      XrmoptionNoArg,   (caddr_t) "on"},
{"−name",          ".name",                      XrmoptionSepArg,  (caddr_t) NULL},
{"−reverse",       "*reverseVideo",              XrmoptionNoArg,   (caddr_t) "on"},
{"−rv",            "*reverseVideo",              XrmoptionNoArg,   (caddr_t) "on"},
{"−synchronous",   ".synchronous",               XrmoptionNoArg,   (caddr_t) "on"},
{"−title",         ".TopLevelShell.title",       XrmoptionSepArg,  (caddr_t) NULL},
{"−xrm",           NULL,                         XrmoptionResArg,  (caddr_t) NULL},
};
```

In this table, if the −background (or −bg) option is used to set background colors, the stored resource specifier matches all resources of attribute background. If the −borderwidth option is used, the stored resource specifier applies only to border width attributes of class TopLevelShell (that is, outermost windows, including pop-up windows). If the −title option is used to set a window name, only the topmost application windows receive the resource.

When parsing the command line, any unique unambiguous abbreviation for an option name in the table is considered a match for the option. Note that uppercase and lowercase matter.

10.12   Using the Context Manager

The context manager provides a way of associating data with a window in your program. Note that this is local to your program; the data is not stored in the server on a property list. Any amount of data in any number of pieces can be associated with a window, and each piece of data has a type associated with it. The context manager requires knowledge of the window and type to store or retrieve data.

Essentially, the context manager can be viewed as a two-dimensional, sparse array: one dimension is subscripted by the window and the other by a context type field. Each entry in the array contains a pointer to the data. Xlib provides context management functions with which you can save data values, get data values, delete entries, and create a unique context type. The symbols used are in <X11 / Xutil.h>.

To save a data value that corresponds to a window and context type, use XSaveContext.

int XSaveContext(*display, w, context, data*)
        Display *display*;
        Window *w*;
        XContext *context*;
        caddr_t *data*;

display   Specifies the connection to the X server.
w   Specifies the window with which the data is associated.
context   Specifies the context type to which the data belongs.
data   Specifies the data to be associated with the window and type.

If an entry with the specified window and type already exists, XSave-Context overrides it with the specified context. The XSaveContext function returns a nonzero error code if an error has occurred and zero otherwise. Possible errors are XCNOMEM (out of memory).

To get the data associated with a window and type, use XFindContext.

int XFindContext(*display, w, context, data_return*)
        Display *display*;
        Window *w*;
        XContext *context*;
        caddr_t *data_return*;

display	Specifies the connection to the X server.
w	Specifies the window with which the data is associated.
context	Specifies the context type to which the data belongs.
data_return	Returns a pointer to the data.

Because it is a return value, the data is a pointer. The XFindContext function returns a nonzero error code if an error has occurred and zero otherwise. Possible errors are XCNOENT (context-not-found).

To delete an entry for a given window and type, use XDeleteContext.

int XDeleteContext(*display, w, context*)
    Display **display*;
    Window *w*;
    XContext *context*;

display	Specifies the connection to the X server.
w	Specifies the window with which the data is associated.
context	Specifies the context type to which the data belongs.

The XDeleteContext function deletes the entry for the given window and type from the data structure. This function returns the same error codes that XFindContext returns if called with the same arguments. XDeleteContext does not free the data whose address was saved.

To create a unique context type that may be used in subsequent calls to XSaveContext and XFindContext, use XUniqueContext.

XContext XUniqueContext()

Part II. X Window System Protocol Version 11

Robert W. Scheifler

SECTION 1. PROTOCOL FORMATS

Request Format

Every request contains an 8-bit major opcode and a 16-bit length field expressed in units of four bytes. Every request consists of four bytes of a header (containing the major opcode, the length field, and a data byte) followed by zero or more additional bytes of data. The length field defines the total length of the request, including the header. The length field in a request must equal the minimum length required to contain the request. If the specified length is smaller or larger than the required length, an error is generated. Unused bytes in a request are not required to be zero. Major opcodes 128 through 255 are reserved for extensions. Extensions are intended to contain multiple requests, so extension requests typically have an additional minor opcode encoded in the "spare" data byte in the request header. However, the placement and interpretation of this minor opcode and of all other fields in extension requests are not defined by the core protocol. Every request on a given connection is implicitly assigned a sequence number, starting with one, that is used in replies, errors, and events.

Reply Format

Every reply contains a 32-bit length field expressed in units of four bytes. Every reply consists of 32 bytes followed by zero or more additional bytes of data, as specified in the length field. Unused bytes within a reply are not guaranteed to be zero. Every reply also contains the least-significant 16 bits of the sequence number of the corresponding request.

Error Format

Error reports are 32 bytes long. Every error includes an 8-bit error code. Error codes 128 through 255 are reserved for extensions. Every error also includes the major and minor opcodes of the failed request and the least-significant 16 bits of the sequence number of the request. For the following errors (see section 4), the failing resource ID is also returned: Colormap, Cursor, Drawable, Font, GContext, IDChoice, Pixmap, and Window. For Atom errors, the failing atom is returned: For Value errors, the failing value is returned. Other core errors return no additional data. Unused bytes within an error are not guaranteed to be zero.

Event Format

Events are 32 bytes long. Unused bytes within an event are not guaranteed to be zero. Every event contains an 8-bit type code. The most-significant bit in this code is set if the event was generated from a SendEvent request. Event codes 64 through 127 are reserved for extensions, although the core protocol does not define a mechanism for selecting interest in such events. Every core event (with the exception of KeymapNotify) also contains the least-significant 16 bits of the sequence number of the last request issued by the client that was (or is currently being) processed by the server.

SECTION 2. SYNTACTIC CONVENTIONS

Sections 3 through 12 use the following syntactic conventions.

- The syntax { ... } encloses a set of alternatives.
- The syntax [...] encloses a set of structure components.
- In general, TYPEs are in uppercase and AlternativeValues are capitalized.
- Requests in section 9 are described in the following format:

RequestName
   arg1: type1
     . . .
   argN: typeN
$\rightarrow$
   result1: type1
     . . .

resultM: typeM

Errors: kind1, . . ., kindK

Description

If no → is present in the description, then the request has no reply (it is asynchronous), although errors may still be reported. If →+ is used, then one or more replies can be generated for a single request.

- Events in section 11 are described in the following format:

EventName

value1: type1

   . . .

valueN: typeN

Description

SECTION 3. COMMON TYPES

LISTofFOO

A type name of the form LISTofFOO means a counted list of elements of type FOO. The size of the length field may vary (it is not necessarily the same size as a FOO), and in some cases, it may be implicit. It is fully specified in Appendix F. Except where explicitly noted, zero-length lists are legal.

BITMASK

LISTofVALUE

The types BITMASK and LISTofVALUE are somewhat special. Various requests contain arguments of the form:

value-mask: BITMASK

value-list: LISTofVALUE

These are used to allow the client to specify a subset of a heterogeneous collection of optional arguments. The value-mask specifies which arguments are to be provided; each such argument is assigned a unique bit position. The representation of the BITMASK will typically contain more bits than there are defined arguments. The unused bits in the value-mask must be zero (or the server generates a `Value` error). The value-list contains one value for each bit set to 1 in the mask, from least-significant to most-significant bit in the mask. Each value is represented with four bytes, but the actual value occupies only the least-significant bytes as required. The values of the unused bytes do not matter.

OR

A type of the form "T1 or . . . or Tn" means the union of the indicated types. A single-element type is given as the element without enclosing braces.

```
        WINDOW: 32-bit value (top three bits guaranteed to be zero)
        PIXMAP: 32-bit value (top three bits guaranteed to be zero)
        CURSOR: 32-bit value (top three bits guaranteed to be zero)
          FONT: 32-bit value (top three bits guaranteed to be zero)
      GCONTEXT: 32-bit value (top three bits guaranteed to be zero)
      COLORMAP: 32-bit value (top three bits guaranteed to be zero)
      DRAWABLE: WINDOW or PIXMAP
      FONTABLE: FONT or GCONTEXT
          ATOM: 32-bit value (top three bits guaranteed to be zero)
      VISUALID: 32-bit value (top three bits guaranteed to be zero)
         VALUE: 32-bit quantity (used only in LISTofVALUE)
          BYTE: 8-bit value
          INT8: 8-bit signed integer
         INT16: 16-bit signed integer
         INT32: 32-bit signed integer
         CARD8: 8-bit unsigned integer
        CARD16: 16-bit unsigned integer
        CARD32: 32-bit unsigned integer
     TIMESTAMP: CARD32
     BITGRAVITY: {Forget, Static, NorthWest, North, NorthEast, West,
                 Center, East, SouthWest, South, SouthEast}
    WINGRAVITY: {Unmap, Static, NorthWest, North, NorthEast, West,
                 Center, East, SouthWest, South, SouthEast}
          BOOL: {True, False}
         EVENT: {KeyPress, KeyRelease, OwnerGrabButton,
                 ButtonPress, ButtonRelease, EnterWindow,
                 LeaveWindow, PointerMotion, PointerMotionHint,
                 Button1Motion, Button2Motion, Button3Motion,
                 Button4Motion, Button5Motion, ButtonMotion,
                 Exposure, VisibilityChange, StructureNotify,
                 ResizeRedirect, SubstructureNotify,
                 SubstructureRedirect, FocusChange,
                 PropertyChange, ColormapChange, KeymapState}
```

POINTEREVENT: {ButtonPress, ButtonRelease, EnterWindow,
LeaveWindow, PointerMotion, PointerMotionHint,
Button1Motion, Button2Motion, Button3Motion,
Button4Motion, Button5Motion, ButtonMotion,
KeymapState}
DEVICEEVENT: {KeyPress, KeyRelease, ButtonPress, ButtonRelease,
PointerMotion, Button1Motion, Button2Motion,
Button3Motion, Button4Motion, Button5Motion,
ButtonMotion}
KEYSYM: 32-bit value (top three bits guaranteed to be zero)
KEYCODE: CARD8
BUTTON: CARD8
KEYMASK: {Shift, Lock, Control, Mod1, Mod2, Mod3, Mod4, Mod5}
BUTMASK: {Button1, Button2, Button3, Button4, Button5}
KEYBUTMASK: KEYMASK or BUTMASK

STRING8: LISTofCARD8
STRING16: LISTofCHAR2B
CHAR2B: [byte1, byte2: CARD8]
POINT: [x, y: INT16]
RECTANGLE: [x, y: INT16,
width, height: CARD16]
ARC: [x, y: INT16,
width, height: CARD16,
angle1, angle2: INT16]
HOST: [family: {Internet, DECnet, Chaos}
address: LISTofBYTE]

The [x,y] coordinates of a RECTANGLE specify the upper-left corner.

The primary interpretation of large characters in a STRING16 is that they are composed of two bytes used to index a 2-D matrix; hence, the use of CHAR2B rather than CARD16. This corresponds to the JIS/ISO method of indexing 2-byte characters. It is expected that most large fonts will be defined with 2-byte matrix indexing. For large fonts constructed with linear indexing, a CHAR2B can be interpreted as a 16-bit number by treating byte1 as the most-significant byte. This means that clients should always transmit such 16-bit character values most-significant byte first, as the server will never byte-swap CHAR2B quantities.

The length, format, and interpretation of a HOST address are specific to the family (see ChangeHosts request).

SECTION 4. ERRORS

In general, when a request terminates with an error, the request has no side effects (that is, there is no partial execution). The only requests for which this is not true are `ChangeWindowAttributes`, `ChangeGC`, `Poly-Text8`, `PolyText16`, `FreeColors`, `StoreColors`, and `Change-KeyboardControl`.

The following error codes result from various requests as follows:

Error	Description
Access	An attempt is made to grab a key/button combination already grabbed by another client.
	An attempt is made to free a colormap entry not allocated by the client.
	An attempt is made to store into a read-only or an unallocated colormap entry.
	An attempt is made to modify the access control list from other than the local host (or otherwise authorized client).
	An attempt is made to select an event type that only one client can select at a time when another client has already selected it.
Alloc	The server failed to allocate the requested resource. Note that the explicit listing of `Alloc` errors in requests only covers allocation errors at a very coarse level and is not intended to cover all cases of a server running out of allocation space in the middle of service. The semantics when a server runs out of allocation space are left unspecified, but a server may generate an `Alloc` error on any request for this reason, and clients should be prepared to receive such errors and handle or discard them.
Atom	A value for an ATOM argument does not name a defined ATOM.
Colormap	A value for a COLORMAP argument does not name a defined COLORMAP.
Cursor	A value for a CURSOR argument does not name a defined CURSOR.
Drawable	A value for a DRAWABLE argument does not name a defined WINDOW or PIXMAP.
Font	A value for a FONT argument does not name a defined FONT.

Error	Description
	A value for a FONTABLE argument does not name a defined FONT or a defined GCONTEXT.
GContext	A value for a GCONTEXT argument does not name a defined GCONTEXT.
IDChoice	The value chosen for a resource identifier either is not included in the range assigned to the client or is already in use.
Implementation	The server does not implement some aspect of the request. A server that generates this error for a core request is deficient. As such, this error is not listed for any of the requests, but clients should be prepared to receive such errors and handle or discard them.
Length	The length of a request is shorter or longer than that required to minimally contain the arguments. The length of a request exceeds the maximum length accepted by the server.
Match	An InputOnly window is used as a DRAWABLE. In a graphics request, the GCONTEXT argument does not have the same root and depth as the destination DRAWABLE argument. Some argument (or pair of arguments) has the correct type and range, but it fails to match in some other way required by the request.
Name	A font or color of the specified name does not exist.
Pixmap	A value for a PIXMAP argument does not name a defined PIXMAP.
Request	The major or minor opcode does not specify a valid request.
Value	Some numeric value falls outside the range of values accepted by the request. Unless a specific range is specified for an argument, the full range defined by the argument's type is accepted. Any argument defined as a set of alternatives typically can generate this error (due to the encoding).
Window	A value for a WINDOW argument does not name a defined WINDOW.

Note The Atom, Colormap, Cursor, Drawable, Font, GContext, Pixmap, and Window errors are also used when the argument type is extended by union with a set of fixed alternatives, for example, <WINDOW or PointerRoot or None>.

SECTION 5. KEYBOARDS

A KEYCODE represents a physical (or logical) key. Keycodes lie in the inclusive range [8,255]. A keycode value carries no intrinsic information, although server implementors may attempt to encode geometry information (for example, matrix) to be interpreted in a server-dependent fashion. The mapping between keys and keycodes cannot be changed using the protocol.

A KEYSYM is an encoding of a symbol on the cap of a key. The set of defined KEYSYMs include the character sets Latin 1, Latin 2, Latin 3, Latin 4, Kana, Arabic, Cryllic, Greek, Tech, Special, Publish, APL, and Hebrew as well as a set of symbols common on keyboards (Return, Help, Tab, and so on). KEYSYMs with the most-significant bit (of the 29 bits) set are reserved as vendor-specific.

A list of KEYSYMs is associated with each KEYCODE, and the length of the list can vary with each KEYCODE. The list is intended to convey the set of symbols on the corresponding key. By convention, if the list contains a single KEYSYM and that KEYSYM is alphabetic and case distinction is relevant for it, then it should be treated as equivalent to a two-element list of the lowercase and uppercase KEYSYMs. For example, if the list contains the single KEYSYM for uppercase *A*, then the client should treat it as if it were instead a pair with lowercase *a* as the first KEYSYM and uppercase *A* as the second KEYSYM.

For any KEYCODE, the first KEYSYM in the list normally should be chosen as the interpretation of a `KeyPress` when no modifier keys are down. The second KEYSYM in the list normally should be chosen when the Shift modifier is on or when the Lock modifier is on and Lock is interpreted as ShiftLock. When the Lock modifier is on and is interpreted as CapsLock, it is suggested that the Shift modifier first be applied to choose a KEYSYM. However, if that KEYSYM is lowercase alphabetic, the corresponding uppercase KEYSYM should be used instead. Other interpretations of CapsLock are possible. For example, it may be viewed as equivalent to ShiftLock, applying only when the first KEYSYM is lowercase alphabetic and the second KEYSYM is the corresponding uppercase alphabetic. No interpretation of KEYSYMs beyond the first two in a list is suggested here. No spatial geometry of the symbols on the key is defined by their order in the

KEYSYM list, although a geometry might be defined on a vendor-specific basis.

The mapping between KEYCODEs and KEYSYMs is not used directly by the server; it is merely stored for reading and writing by clients.

The KEYMASK modifier named Lock is intended to be mapped to either a CapsLock or a ShiftLock key, but which one is left as application-specific and/or user-specific. However, it is suggested that the determination be made according to the associated KEYSYM(s) of the corresponding KEYCODE.

SECTION 6. POINTERS

Buttons are always numbered starting with one.

SECTION 7. PREDEFINED ATOMS

Predefined atoms are not strictly necessary and may not be useful in all environments, but they will eliminate many `InternAtom` requests in most applications. Note that they are predefined only in the sense of having numeric values, not in the sense of having required semantics. The core protocol imposes no semantics on these names, except as they are used in FONTPROP structures (see `QueryFont` request).

The following names have predefined atom values. Note that uppercase and lowercase matter.

ARC	ITALIC_ANGLE	STRING
ATOM	MAX_SPACE	SUBSCRIPT_X
BITMAP	MIN_SPACE	SUBSCRIPT_Y
CAP_HEIGHT	NORM_SPACE	SUPERSCRIPT_X
CARDINAL	NOTICE	SUPERSCRIPT_Y
COLORMAP	PIXMAP	UNDERLINE_POSITION
COPYRIGHT	POINT	UNDERLINE_THICKNESS
CURSOR	POINT_SIZE	VISUALID
CUT_BUFFER0	PRIMARY	WEIGHT
CUT_BUFFER1	QUAD_WIDTH	WINDOW
CUT_BUFFER2	RECTANGLE	WM_CLASS
CUT_BUFFER3	RESOLUTION	WM_CLIENT_MACHINE
CUT_BUFFER4	RESOURCE_MANAGER	WM_COMMAND
CUT_BUFFER5	RGB_BEST_MAP	WM_HINTS

CUT_BUFFER6	RGB_BLUE_MAP	WM_ICON_NAME
CUT_BUFFER7	RGB_COLOR_MAP	WM_ICON_SIZE
DRAWABLE	RGB_DEFAULT_MAP	WM_NAME
END_SPACE	RGB_GRAY_MAP	WM_NORMAL_HINTS
FAMILY_NAME	RGB_GREEN_MAP	WM_SIZE_HINTS
FONT	RGB_RED_MAP	WM_TRANSIENT_FOR
FONT_NAME	SECONDARY	WM_ZOOM_HINTS
FULL_NAME	STRIKEOUT_ASCENT	X_HEIGHT
INTEGER		STRIKEOUT_DESCENT

To avoid conflicts with possible future names for which semantics might be imposed (either at the protocol level or in terms of higher level user interface models), names beginning with an underscore should be used for atoms that are private to a particular vendor or organization. To guarantee no conflicts between vendors and organizations, additional prefixes need to be used. However, the protocol does not define the mechanism for choosing such prefixes. For names private to a single application or end user but stored in globally accessible locations, it is suggested that two leading underscores be used to avoid conflicts with other names.

SECTION 8. CONNECTION SETUP

For remote clients, the X protocol can be built on top of any reliable byte stream.

The client must send an initial byte of data to identify the byte order to be employed. The value of the byte must be octal 102 or 154. The value 102 (ASCII uppercase B) means values are transmitted most-significant byte first, and value 154 (ASCII lowercase l) means values are transmitted least-significant byte first. Except where explicitly noted in the protocol, all 16-bit and 32-bit quantities sent by the client must be transmitted with this byte order, and all 16-bit and 32-bit quantities returned by the server will be transmitted with this byte order.

• Following the byte-order byte, the client sends the following information at connection setup:

protocol-major-version: CARD16
protocol-minor-version: CARD16
authorization-protocol-name: STRING8
authorization-protocol-data: STRING8

The version numbers indicate what version of the protocol the client expects the server to implement.

The authorization name indicates what authorization protocol the client expects the server to use, and the data is specific to that protocol. Specification of valid authorization mechanisms is not part of the core X protocol. It is hoped that eventually one authorization protocol will be agreed upon. In the meantime, a server that implements a different protocol than the client expects or that only implements the host-based mechanism may simply ignore this information. If both name and data strings are empty, this is to be interpreted as "no explicit authorization."

• The client receives the following information at connection setup:

   success: BOOL
   protocol-major-version: CARD16
   protocol-minor-version: CARD16
   length: CARD16

Length is the amount of additional data to follow, in units of four bytes. The version numbers are an escape hatch in case future revisions of the protocol are necessary. In general, the major version would increment for incompatible changes, and the minor version would increment for small upward compatible changes. Barring changes, the major version will be 11, and the minor version will be 0. The protocol version numbers returned indicate the protocol the server actually supports. This might not equal the version sent by the client. The server can (but need not) refuse connections from clients that offer a different version than the server supports. A server can (but need not) support more than one version simultaneously.

• The client receives the following additional data if authorization fails:

   reason: STRING8

• The client receives the following additional data if authorization is accepted:

   vendor: STRING8
   release-number: CARD32
   resource-id-base, resource-id-mask: CARD32
   image-byte-order: {LSBFirst, MSBFirst}
   bitmap-scanline-unit: {8, 16, 32}
   bitmap-scanline-pad: {8, 16, 32}

bitmap-bit-order: {LeastSignificant, MostSignificant}
pixmap-formats: LISTofFORMAT
roots: LISTofSCREEN
motion-buffer-size: CARD32
maximum-request-length: CARD16
min-keycode, max-keycode: KEYCODE

where:

    FORMAT: [depth: CARD8,
             bits-per-pixel: {1, 4, 8, 16, 24, 32}
             scanline-pad: {8, 16, 32}]
    SCREEN: [root: WINDOW
             width-in-pixels, height-in-pixels: CARD16
             width-in-millimeters, height-in-millimeters: CARD16
             allowed-depths: LISTofDEPTH
             root-depth: CARD8
             root-visual: VISUALID
             default-colormap: COLORMAP
             white-pixel, black-pixel: CARD32
             min-installed-maps, max-installed-maps: CARD16
             backing-stores: {Never, WhenMapped, Always}
             save-unders: BOOL
             current-input-masks: SETofEVENT]
    DEPTH: [depth: CARD8
             visuals: LISTofVISUALTYPE]
    VISUALTYPE: [visual-id: VISUALID
             class: {StaticGray, StaticColor, TrueColor, GrayScale,
                     PseudoColor, DirectColor}
             red-mask, green-mask, blue-mask: CARD32
             bits-per-rgb-value: CARD8
             colormap-entries: CARD16]

• The information that is global to the server is:

The vendor string gives some identification of the owner of the server implementation. The vendor controls the semantics of the release number.

The resource-id-mask contains a single contiguous set of bits (at least 18). The client allocates resource IDs for types WINDOW, PIXMAP, CURSOR, FONT, GCONTEXT, and COLORMAP by choosing a value with only some subset of these bits set and ORing it with resource-id-base. Only values constructed in this way can be used to name newly created resources over this connection. Resource IDs never have the top three bits set. The client is not restricted to linear or contiguous allocation of resource IDs. Once an ID has been freed, it can be reused, but this should not be necessary. An ID must be unique with respect to the IDs of all other resources, not just other resources of the same type. However, note that the value spaces of resource identifiers, atoms, visualids, and keysyms are distinguished by context, and as such, are not required to be disjoint; for example, a given numeric value might be both a valid window ID, a valid atom, and a valid keysym.

Although the server is in general responsible for byte-swapping data to match the client, images are always transmitted and received in formats (including byte order) specified by the server. The byte order for images is given by image-byte-order and applies to each scanline unit in XY format (bitmap format) and to each pixel value in Z format.

A bitmap is represented in scanline order. Each scanline is padded to a multiple of bits as given by bitmap-scanline-pad. The pad bits are of arbitrary value. The scanline is quantized in multiples of bits as given by the bitmap-scanline-unit. The bitmap-scanline-unit is always less than or equal to the bitmap-scanline-pad. Within each unit, the leftmost bit in the bitmap is either the least-significant or most-significant bit in the unit, as given by bitmap-bit-order. If a pixmap is represented in XY format, each plane is represented as a bitmap, and the planes appear from most-significant to least-significant in bit order with no padding between planes.

Pixmap-formats contains one entry for each depth value. The entry describes the Z format used to represent images of that depth. An entry for a depth is included if any screen supports that depth, and all screens supporting that depth must support only that Z format for that depth. In Z format, the pixels are in scanline order, left-to-right within a scanline.

The number of bits used to hold each pixel is given by bits-per-pixel. Bits-per-pixel may be larger than strictly required by the depth, in which case the least-significant bits are used to hold the pixmap data, and the values of the unused high-order bits are undefined. When the bits-per-pixel is 4, the order of nibbles in the byte is the same as the image byte-order. When the bits-per-pixel is 1, the format is identical for bitmap format. Each scanline is padded to a multiple of bits as given by scanline-pad. When bits-per-pixel is 1, this will be identical to bitmap-scanline-pad.

How a pointing device roams the screens is up to the server implementation and is transparent to the protocol. No geometry is defined among screens.

The server may retain the recent history of pointer motion and do so to a finer granularity than is reported by MotionNotify events. The Get-MotionEvents request makes such history available. The motion-buffer-size gives the approximate size of the history buffer.

Maximum-request-length specifies the maximum length of a request accepted by the server, in 4-byte units. That is, length is the maximum value that can appear in the length field of a request. Requests larger than this maximum generate a Length error, and the server will read and simply discard the entire request. Maximum-request-length will always be at least 4096 (that is, requests of length up to and including 16384 bytes will be accepted by all servers).

Min-keycode and max-keycode specify the smallest and largest keycode values transmitted by the server. Min-keycode is never less than 8, and max-keycode is never greater than 255. Not all keycodes in this range are required to have corresponding keys.

• The information that applies per screen is:

The allowed-depths specifies what pixmap and window depths are supported. Pixmaps are supported for each depth listed, and windows of that depth are supported if at least one visual type is listed for the depth. A pixmap depth of one is always supported and listed, but windows of depth one might not be supported. A depth of zero is never listed, but zero-depth InputOnly windows are always supported.

Root-depth and root-visual specify the depth and visual type of the root window. Width-in-pixels and height-in-pixels specify the size of the root window (which cannot be changed). The class of the root window is always InputOutput. Width-in-millimeters and height-in-millimeters can be used to determine the physical size and the aspect ratio.

The default-colormap is the one initially associated with the root window. Clients with minimal color requirements creating windows of the same depth as the root may want to allocate from this map by default.

Black-pixel and white-pixel can be used in implementing a monochrome application. These pixel values are for permanently allocated entries in the default-colormap. The actual RGB values may be settable on some screens and, in any case, may not actually be black and white. The names are intended to convey the expected relative intensity of the colors.

The border of the root window is initially a pixmap filled with the black-pixel. The initial background of the root window is a pixmap filled with some unspecified two-color pattern using black-pixel and white-pixel.

Min-installed-maps specifies the number of maps that can be guaranteed to be installed simultaneously (with `InstallColormap`), regardless of the number of entries allocated in each map. Max-installed-maps specifies the maximum number of maps that might possibly be installed simultaneously, depending on their allocations. Multiple static-visual colormaps with identical contents but differing in resource ID should be considered as a single map for the purposes of this number. For the typical case of a single hardware colormap, both values will be 1.

Backing-stores indicates when the server supports backing stores for this screen, although it may be storage limited in the number of windows it can support at once. If save-unders is `True`, the server can support the save-under mode in `CreateWindow` and `ChangeWindowAttributes`, although again it may be storage limited.

The current-input-events is what `GetWindowAttributes` would return for the all-event-masks for the root window.

- The information that applies per visual-type is:

A given visual type might be listed for more than one depth or for more than one screen.

For `PseudoColor`, a pixel value indexes a colormap to produce independent RGB values; the RGB values can be changed dynamically. `GrayScale` is treated in the same way as `PseudoColor` except which primary drives the screen is undefined; thus, the client should always store the same value for red, green, and blue in colormaps. For `DirectColor`, a pixel value is decomposed into separate RGB subfields, and each subfield separately indexes the colormap for the corresponding value. The RGB values can be changed dynamically. `TrueColor` is treated in the same way as `DirectColor` except the colormap has predefined read-only RGB values. These values are server-dependent but provide linear or near-linear increasing ramps in each primary. `StaticColor` is treated in the same way as `PseudoColor` except the colormap has predefined read-only RGB values, which are server-dependent. `StaticGray` is treated in the same way as `StaticColor` except the red, green, and blue values are equal for any single pixel value, resulting in shades of gray. `StaticGray` with a two-entry colormap can be thought of as monochrome.

The red-mask, green-mask, and blue-mask are only defined for `DirectColor` and `TrueColor`. Each has one contiguous set of bits set to 1 with no intersections. Usually each mask has the same number of bits set to 1.

The bits-per-rgb-value specifies the log base 2 of the number of distinct color intensity values (individually) of red, green, and blue. This number need not bear any relation to the number of colormap entries. Actual RGB values are always passed in the protocol within a 16-bit spectrum, with 0 being minimum intensity and 65535 being the maximum intensity. On hardware that provides a linear zero-based intensity ramp, the following relationship exists:

$$\text{hw-intensity} = \text{protocol-intensity} / (65536 / \text{total-hw-intensities})$$

Colormap entries are indexed from 0. The colormap-entries defines the number of available colormap entries in a newly created colormap. For `DirectColor` and `TrueColor`, this will usually be 2 to the power of the maximum number of bits set to 1 in red-mask, green-mask, and blue-mask.

SECTION 9: REQUESTS

CreateWindow

wid, parent: WINDOW
class: {`InputOutput`, `InputOnly`, `CopyFromParent`}
depth: CARD8
visual: VISUALID or `CopyFromParent`
x, y: INT16
width, height, border-width: CARD16
value-mask: BITMASK
value-list: LISTofVALUE

Errors: `IDChoice`, `Window`, `Pixmap`, `Colormap`, `Cursor`, `Match`, `Value`, `Alloc`

This request creates an unmapped window and assigns the identifier wid to it.

A class of CopyFromParent means the class is taken from the parent. A depth of zero for class InputOutput or CopyFromParent means the depth is taken from the parent. A visual of CopyFromParent means the visual type is taken from the parent. For class InputOutput, the visual type and depth must be a combination supported for the screen (or a Match error results). The depth need not be the same as the parent, but the parent must not be of class InputOnly (or a Match error results). For class InputOnly, the depth must be zero (or a Match error results), and the visual must be one supported for the screen (or a Match error results). However, the parent can have any depth and class.

The server essentially acts as if InputOnly windows do not exist for the purposes of graphics requests, exposure processing, and Visibility-Notify events. An InputOnly window cannot be used as a drawable (as a source or destination for graphics requests). InputOnly and Input-Output windows act identically in other respects—properties, grabs, input control, and so on.

The window is placed on top in the stacking order with respect to siblings. The x and y coordinates are relative to the parent's origin and specify the position of the upper-left outer corner of the window (not the origin). The width and height specify the inside size (not including the border) and must be nonzero (or a Value error results). The border-width for an InputOnly window must be zero (or a Match error results).

The value-mask and value-list specify attributes of the window that are to be explicitly initialized. The possible values are:

Attribute	*Type*
background-pixmap	PIXMAP or None or ParentRelative
background-pixel	CARD32
border-pixmap	PIXMAP or CopyFromParent
border-pixel	CARD32
bit-gravity	BITGRAVITY
win-gravity	WINGRAVITY
backing-store	{NotUseful, WhenMapped, Always}
backing-planes	CARD32

Attribute	Type
backing-pixel	CARD32
save-under	BOOL
event-mask	SETofEVENT
do-not-propagate-mask	SETofDEVICEEVENT
override-redirect	BOOL
colormap	COLORMAP or `CopyFromParent`
cursor	CURSOR or `None`

The default values when attributes are not explicitly initialized are:

Attribute	Default
background-pixmap	`None`
border-pixmap	`CopyFromParent`
bit-gravity	`Forget`
win-gravity	`NorthWest`
backing-store	`NotUseful`
backing-planes	all ones
backing-pixel	zero
save-under	`False`
event-mask	{ } (empty set)
do-not-propagate-mask	{ } (empty set)
override-redirect	`False`
colormap	`CopyFromParent`
cursor	`None`

Only the following attributes are defined for `InputOnly` windows:

- win-gravity
- event-mask
- do-not-propagate-mask
- override-redirect
- cursor

It is a `Match` error to specify any other attributes for `InputOnly` windows.

If background-pixmap is given, it overrides the default background-pixmap. The background pixmap and the window must have the same root and the same depth (or a `Match` error results). Any size pixmap can be used, although some sizes may be faster than others. If background `None` is specified, the window has no defined background. If background `ParentRelative` is specified, the parent's background is used, but the window must have the same depth as the parent (or a `Match` error results). If the parent has background `None`, then the window will also have background `None`. A copy of the parent's background is not made. The parent's background is reexamined each time the window background is required. If background-pixel is given, it overrides the default background-pixmap and any background-pixmap given explicitly, and a pixmap of undefined size filled with background-pixel is used for the background. Range checking is not performed on the background-pixel value; it is simply truncated to the appropriate number of bits. For a `ParentRelative` background, the background tile origin always aligns with the parent's background tile origin. Otherwise, the background tile origin is always the window origin.

When no valid contents are available for regions of a window and the regions are either visible or the server is maintaining backing store, the server automatically tiles the regions with the window's background unless the window has a background of `None`. If the background is `None`, the previus screen contents from other windows of the same depth as the window are simply left in place if the contents come from the parent of the window or an inferior of the parent; otherwise, the initial contents of the exposed regions are undefined. Exposure events are then generated for the regions, even if the background is `None`.

The border tile origin is always the same as the background tile origin. If border-pixmap is given, it overrides the default border-pixmap. The border pixmap and the window must have the same root and the same depth (or a `Match` error results). Any size pixmap can be used, although some sizes may be faster than others. If `CopyFromParent` is given, the parent's border pixmap is copied (subsequent changes to the parent's border attribute do not affect the child), but the window must have the same depth as the parent (or a `Match` error results). The pixmap might be copied by sharing the same pixmap object between the child and parent or by making a complete copy of the pixmap contents. If border-pixel is given, it overrides the default border-pixmap and any border-pixmap given explicitly, and a pixmap of undefined size filled with border-pixel is used for the border. Range checking is not performed on the border-pixel value; it is simply truncated to the appropriate number of bits.

Output to a window is always clipped to the inside of the window, so that the border is never affected.

The bit-gravity defines which region of the window should be retained if the window is resized, and win-gravity defines how the window should be repositioned if the parent is resized (see ConfigureWindow request).

A backing-store of WhenMapped advises the server that maintaining contents of obscured regions when the window is mapped would be beneficial. A backing-store of Always advises the server that maintaining contents even when the window is unmapped would be beneficial. In this case, the server may generate an exposure event when the window is created. A value of NotUseful advises the server that maintaining contents is unnecessary, although a server may still choose to maintain contents while the window is mapped. Note that if the server maintains contents, then the server should maintain complete contents not just the region within the parent boundaries, even if the window is larger than its parent. While the server maintains contents, exposure events will not normally be generated, but the server may stop maintaining contents at any time.

If save-under is True, the server is advised that when this window is mapped, saving the contents of windows it obscures would be beneficial.

When the contents of obscured regions of a window are being maintained, regions obscured by noninferior windows are included in the destination (and source, when the window is the source) of graphics requests, but regions obscured by inferior windows are not included.

The backing-planes indicates (with bits set to 1) which bit planes of the window hold dynamic data that must be preserved in backing-stores and during save-unders. The backing-pixel specifies what value to use in planes not covered by backing-planes. The server is free to save only the specified bit planes in the backing-store or save-under and regenerate the remaining planes with the specified pixel value. Any bits beyond the specified depth of the window in these values are simply ignored.

The event-mask defines which events the client is interested in for this window (or for some event types, inferiors of the window). The do-not-propagate-mask defines which events should not be propagated to ancestor windows when no client has the event type selected in this window.

The override-redirect specifies whether map and configure requests on this window should override a SubstructureRedirect on the parent, typically to inform a window manager not to tamper with the window.

The colormap specifies the colormap that best reflects the true colors of the window. Servers capable of supporting multiple hardware colormaps may use this information, and window managers may use it for `InstallColormap` requests. The colormap must have the same visual type as the window (or a `Match` error results). If `CopyFromParent` is specified, the parent's colormap is copied (subsequent changes to the parent's colormap attribute do not affect the child). However, the window must have the same visual type as the parent (or a `Match` error results), and the parent must not have a colormap of `None` (or a `Match` error results). For an explanation of `None`, see `FreeColormap` request. The colormap is copied by sharing the colormap object between the child and the parent, not by making a complete copy of the colormap contents.

If a cursor is specified, it will be used whenever the pointer is in the window. If `None` is specified, the parent's cursor will be used when the pointer is in the window, and any change in the parent's cursor will cause an immediate change in the displayed cursor.

This request generates a `CreateNotify` event.

The background and border pixmaps and the cursor may be freed immediately if no further explicit references to them are to be made.

Subsequent drawing into the background or border pixmap has an undefined effect on the window state. The server might or might not make a copy of the pixmap.

ChangeWindowAttributes

window: WINDOW
value-mask: BITMASK
value-list: LISTofVALUE

Errors: `Window`, `Pixmap`, `Colormap`, `Cursor`, `Match`, `Value`, `Access`

The value-mask and value-list specify which attributes are to be changed. The values and restrictions are the same as for `CreateWindow`.

Setting a new background, whether by background-pixmap or background-pixel, overrides any previous background. Setting a new border, whether by border-pixel or border-pixmap, overrides any previous border.

Changing the background does not cause the window contents to be changed. Setting the border or changing the background such that the border tile origin changes causes the border to be repainted. Changing the background of a root window to `None` or `ParentRelative` restores the default background pixmap. Changing the border of a root window to `CopyFromParent` restores the default border pixmap.

Changing the win-gravity does not affect the current position of the window.

Changing the backing-store of an obscured window to `WhenMapped` or `Always` or changing the backing-planes, backing-pixel, or save-under of a mapped window may have no immediate effect.

Multiple clients can select input on the same window; their event-masks are disjoint. When an event is generated, it will be reported to all interested clients. However, only one client at a time can select for `SubstructureRedirect`, only one client at a time can select for `ResizeRedirect`, and only one client at a time can select for `Button-Press`. An attempt to violate these restrictions results in an `Access` error.

There is only one do-not-propagate-mask for a window, not one per client.

Changing the colormap of a window (by defining a new map, not by changing the contents of the existing map) generates a `ColormapNotify` event. Changing the colormap of a visible window might have no immediate effect on the screen (see `InstallColormap` request).

Changing the cursor of a root window to `None` restores the default cursor.

The order in which attributes are verified and altered is server-dependent. If an error is generated, a subset of the attributes may have been altered.

GetWindowAttributes

    window: WINDOW

$\rightarrow$

    visual: VISUALID

    class: {`InputOutput`, `InputOnly`}

    bit-gravity: BITGRAVITY

    win-gravity: WINGRAVITY

    backing-store: {`NotUseful`, `WhenMapped`, `Always`}

    backing-planes: CARD32

    backing-pixel: CARD32

    save-under: BOOL

colormap: COLORMAP or `None`
map-is-installed: BOOL
map-state: {`Unmapped`, `Unviewable`, `Viewable`}
all-event-masks, your-event-mask: SETofEVENT
do-not-propagate-mask: SETofDEVICEEVENT
override-redirect: BOOL

Errors: `Window`

This request returns the current attributes of the window. A window is `Unviewable` if it is mapped but some ancestor is unmapped. All-event-masks is the inclusive-OR of all event masks selected on the window by clients. Your-event-mask is the event mask selected by the querying client.

DestroyWindow

window: WINDOW

Errors: `Window`

If the argument window is mapped, an `UnmapWindow` request is performed automatically. The window and all inferiors are then destroyed, and a `DestroyNotify` event is generated for each window. The ordering of the `DestroyNotify` events is such that for any given window, `Destroy-Notify` is generated on all inferiors of the window before being generated on the window itself. The ordering among siblings and across subhierarchies is not otherwise constrained.

Normal exposure processing on formerly obscured windows is performed.

If the window is a root window, this request has no effect.

DestroySubwindows

window: WINDOW

Errors: `Window`

This request performs a `DestroyWindow` request on all children of the window, in bottom-to-top stacking order.

ChangeSaveSet

window: WINDOW
mode: {`Insert`, `Delete`}

Errors: `Window`, `Match`, `Value`

This request adds or removes the specified window from the client's save-set. The window must have been created by some other client (or a `Match` error results). For further information about the use of the save-set, see section 10.

When windows are destroyed, the server automatically removes them from the save-set.

ReparentWindow

> *window, parent*: WINDOW
>
> *x, y:* INT16
>
> Errors: `Window`, `Match`

If the window is mapped, an `UnmapWindow` request is performed automatically first. The window is then removed from its current position in the hierarchy and is inserted as a child of the specified parent. The x and y coordinates are relative to the parent's origin and specify the new position of the upper-left outer corner of the window. The window is placed on top in the stacking order with respect to siblings. A `ReparentNotify` event is then generated. The override-redirect attribute of the window is passed on in this event; a value of `True` indicates that a window manager should not tamper with this window. Finally, if the window was originally mapped, a `MapWindow` request is performed automatically.

Normal exposure processing on formerly obscured windows is performed. The server might not generate exposure events for regions from the initial unmap that are immediately obscured by the final map.

A `Match` error is generated if:

- The new parent is not on the same screen as the old parent.
- The new parent is the window itself or an inferior of the window.
- The window has a `ParentRelative` background, and the new parent is not the same depth as the window.

MapWindow

> *window*: WINDOW
>
> Errors: `Window`

If the window is already mapped, this request has no effect.

If the override-redirect attribute of the window is `False` and some other client has selected `SubstructureRedirect` on the parent, then a `MapRequest` event is generated, but the window remains unmapped. Otherwise, the window is mapped, and a `MapNotify` event is generated.

If the window is now viewable and its contents have been discarded, the window is tiled with its background (if no background is defined, the existing screen contents are not altered), and zero or more exposure events are generated. If a backing-store has been maintained while the window was unmapped, no exposure events are generated. If a backing-store will now be maintained, a full-window exposure is always generated. Otherwise, only visible regions may be reported. Similar tiling and exposure take place for any newly viewable inferiors.

MapSubwindows

> *window*: WINDOW
>
> Errors: `Window`

This request performs a `MapWindow` request on all unmapped children of the window, in top-to-bottom stacking order.

UnmapWindow

> *window*: WINDOW
>
> Errors: `Window`

If the window is already unmapped, this request has no effect. Otherwise, the window is unmapped, and an `UnmapNotify` event is generated. Normal exposure processing on formerly obscured windows is performed.

UnmapSubwindows

> *window*: WINDOW
>
> Errors: `Window`

This request performs an `UnmapWindow` request on all mapped children of the window, in bottom-to-top stacking order.

ConfigureWindow

> *window*: WINDOW
>
> *value-mask*: BITMASK
>
> *value-list*: LISTofVALUE
>
> Errors: `Window, Match, Value`

This request changes the configuration of the window. The value-mask and value-list specify which values are to be given. The possible values are:

Attribute	Type
x	INT16
y	INT16
width	CARD16
height	CARD16
border-width	CARD16
sibling	WINDOW
stack-mode	{Above, Below, TopIf, BottomIf, Opposite}

The x and y coordinates are relative to the parent's origin and specify the position of the upper-left outer corner of the window. The width and height specify the inside size, not including the border, and must be nonzero (or a Value error results). Those values not specified are taken from the existing geometry of the window. Note that changing just the border-width leaves the outer-left corner of the window in a fixed position but moves the absolute position of the window's origin. It is a Match error to attempt to make the border-width of an InputOnly window nonzero.

If the override-redirect attribute of the window is False and some other client has selected SubstructureRedirect on the parent, a Configure-Request event is generated, and no further processing is performed. Otherwise, the following is performed:

If some other client has selected ResizeRedirect on the window and the inside width or height of the window is being changed, a ResizeRequest event is generated, and the current inside width and height are used instead. Note that the override-redirect attribute of the window has no effect on ResizeRedirect and that Substructure-Redirect on the parent has precedence over ResizeRedirect on the window.

The geometry of the window is changed as specified, the window is re-stacked among siblings, and a ConfigureNotify event is generated if the state of the window actually changes. If the inside width or height of the window has actually changed, then children of the window are affected, according to their win-gravity. Exposure processing is performed on formerly obscured windows (including the window itself and its inferiors if regions of

them were obscured but now are not). Exposure processing is also performed on any new regions of the window (as a result of increasing the width
or height) and on any regions where window contents are lost.

If the inside width or height of a window is not changed but the window
is moved or its border is changed, then the contents of the window are not
lost but move with the window. Changing the inside width or height of the
window causes its contents to be moved or lost, depending on the bit-gravity
of the window. It also causes children to be reconfigured, depending on
their win-gravity. For a change of width and height of W and H, we define
the [x, y] pairs as:

Direction	*Deltas*
NorthWest	$[0, 0]$
North	$[W/2, 0]$
NorthEast	$[W, 0]$
West	$[0, H/2]$
Center	$[W/2, H/2]$
East	$[W, H/2]$
SouthWest	$[0, H]$
South	$[W/2, H]$
SouthEast	$[W, H]$

When a window with one of these bit-gravities is resized, the corresponding
pair defines the change in position of each pixel in the window. When a window with one of these win-gravities has its parent window resized, the corresponding pair defines the change in position of the window within the parent. This repositioning generates a GravityNotify event. Gravity-
Notify events are generated after the ConfigureNotify event is generated.

A gravity of Static indicates that the contents or origin should not move
relative to the origin of the root window. If the change in size of the window
is coupled with a change in position of $[X, Y]$, then for bit-gravity the change
in position of each pixel is $[-X, -Y]$ and for win-gravity the change in position of a child when its parent is so resized is $[-X, -Y]$. Note that Static
gravity still only takes effect when the width or height of the window is
changed, not when the window is simply moved.

A bit-gravity of Forget indicates that the window contents are always discarded after a size change, even if backing-store or save-under has been requested. The window is tiled with its background (except, if no background is defined, the existing screen contents are not altered) and zero or more exposure events are generated. A server may also ignore the specified bit-gravity and use Forget instead.

A win-gravity of Unmap is like NorthWest, but the child is also unmapped when the parent is resized, and an UnmapNotify event is generated. UnmapNotify events are generated after the ConfigureNotify event is generated.

If a sibling and a stack-mode are specified, the window is restacked as follows:

Above	The window is placed just above the sibling.
Below	The window is placed just below the sibling.
TopIf	If the sibling occludes the window, then the window is placed at the top of the stack.
BottomIf	If the window occludes the sibling, then the window is placed at the bottom of the stack.
Opposite	If the sibling occludes the window, then the window is placed at the top of the stack. Otherwise, if the window occludes the sibling, then the window is placed at the bottom of the stack.

If a stack-mode is specified but no sibling is specified, the window is restacked as follows:

Above	The window is placed at the top of the stack.
Below	The window is placed at the bottom of the stack.
TopIf	If any sibling occludes the window, then the window is placed at the top of the stack.
BottomIf	If the window occludes any sibling, then the window is placed at the bottom of the stack.
Opposite	If any sibling occludes the window, then the window is placed at the top of the stack. Otherwise, if the window occludes any sibling, then the window is placed at the bottom of the stack.

It is a Match error if a sibling is specified without a stack-mode or if the window is not actually a sibling. Note that the computations for BottomIf, TopIf, and Opposite are performed with respect to the window's final geometry (as controlled by the other arguments to the request), not to its initial geometry.

Attempts to configure a root window have no effect.

CirculateWindow

window: WINDOW

direction: {RaiseLowest, LowerHighest}

Errors: Window, Value

If some other client has selected SubstructureRedirect on the window, then a CirculateRequest event is generated, and no further processing is performed. Otherwise, the following is performed, and then a CirculateNotify event is generated if the window is actually restacked.

For RaiseLowest, CirculateWindow raises the lowest mapped child (if any) that is occluded by another child to the top of the stack. For LowerHighest, CirculateWindow lowers the highest mapped child (if any) that occludes another child to the bottom of the stack. Exposure processing is performed on formerly obscured windows.

GetGeometry

drawable: DRAWABLE

$\rightarrow$

root: WINDOW

depth: CARD8

x, y: INT16

width, height, border-width: CARD16

Errors: Drawable

This request returns the root and current geometry of the drawable. The depth is the number of bits per pixel for the object. The x, y, and border-width will always be zero for pixmaps. For a window, the x and y coordinates specify the upper-left outer corner of the window relative to its parent's origin, and the width and height specify the inside size, not including the border.

It is legal to pass an InputOnly window as a drawable to this request.

QueryTree

window: WINDOW

$\rightarrow$

root: WINDOW

parent: WINDOW or None

children: LISTofWINDOW

Errors: Window

This request returns the root, the parent, and the children of the window. The children are listed in bottom-to-top stacking order.

InternAtom

name: STRING8

only-if-exists: BOOL

$\rightarrow$

atom: ATOM or None

Errors: Value, Alloc

This request returns the atom for the given name. If only-if-exists is False, then the atom is created if it does not exist. The string should use the ISO Latin-1 encoding. Uppercase and lowercase matter.

The lifetime of an atom is not tied to the interning client. Atoms remained defined until server reset (see section 10).

GetAtomName

atom: ATOM

$\rightarrow$

name: STRING8

Errors: Atom

This request returns the name for the given atom.

ChangeProperty

window: WINDOW

property, type: ATOM

format: {8, 16, 32}

mode: {Replace, Prepend, Append}

data: LISTofINT8 or LISTofINT16 or LISTofINT32

Errors: Window, Atom, Value, Match, Alloc

This request alters the property for the specified window. The type is uninterpreted by the server. The format specifies whether the data should be viewed as a list of 8-bit, 16-bit, or 32-bit quantities so that the server can correctly byte-swap as necessary.

If the mode is `Replace`, the previous property value is discarded. It the mode is `Prepend` or `Append`, then the type and format must match the existing property value (or a `Match` error results). If the property is undefined, it is treated as defined with the correct type and format with zero-length data. For `Prepend`, the data is tacked on to the beginning of the existing data, and for `Append`, it is tacked on to the end of the existing data.

This request generates a `PropertyNotify` event on the window.

The lifetime of a property is not tied to the storing client. Properties remain until explicitly deleted, until the window is destroyed, or until server reset (see section 10).

The maximum size of a property is server-dependent and may vary dynamically.

DeleteProperty

window: WINDOW

property: ATOM

Errors: `Window`, `Atom`

This request deletes the property from the specified window if the property exists and generates a `PropertyNotify` event on the window unless the property does not exist.

GetProperty

window: WINDOW

property: ATOM

type: ATOM or `AnyPropertyType`

long-offset, long-length: CARD32

delete: BOOL

$\rightarrow$

type: ATOM or `None`

format: {0, 8, 16, 32}

bytes-after: CARD32

value: LISTofINT8 or LISTofINT16 or LISTofINT32

Errors: `Window`, `Atom`, `Value`

If the specified property does not exist for the specified window, then the return type is `None`, the format and bytes-after are zero, and the value is empty. The delete argument is ignored in this case. If the specified property exists but its type does not match the specified type, then the return type is the actual type of the property, the format is the actual format of the property (never zero), the bytes-after is the length of the property in bytes (even if the format is 16 or 32), and the value is empty. The delete argument is ignored in this case. If the specified property exists and either `AnyPropertyType` is specified or the specified type matches the actual type of the property, then the return type is the actual type of the property, the format is the actual format of the property (never zero), and the bytes-after and value are as follows, given:

$$N = \text{actual length of the stored property in bytes (even if the format is 16 or 32)}$$
$$I = 4 * \text{long-offset}$$
$$T = N - I$$
$$L = \text{MINIMUM}(T, 4 * \text{long-length})$$
$$A = N - (I + L)$$

The returned value starts at byte index I in the property (indexing from 0), and its length in bytes is L. However, it is a `Value` error if long-offset is given such that L is negative. The value of bytes-after is A, giving the number of trailing unread bytes in the stored property. If delete is `True` and the bytes-after is zero, the property is also deleted from the window, and a `PropertyNotify` event is generated on the window.

RotateProperties

  window: WINDOW

  delta: INT16

  properties: LISTofATOM

  Errors: `Window`, `Atom`, `Match`

If the property names in the list are viewed as being numbered starting from zero, and there are N property names in the list, then the value associated with property name I becomes the value associated with property name (I + delta) mod N, for all I from zero to N − 1. The effect is to rotate the states by delta places around the virtual ring of property names (right for positive delta, left for negative delta).

If delta mod N is nonzero, a `PropertyNotify` event is generated for each property in the order listed.

If an atom occurs more than once in the list or no property with that name is defined for the window, a `Match` error is generated. If an `Atom` or `Match` error is generated, no properties are changed.

ListProperties

window: WINDOW

$\longrightarrow$

atoms: LISTofATOM

Errors: `Window`

This request returns the atoms of properties currently defined on the window.

SetSelectionOwner

selection: ATOM

owner: WINDOW or `None`

time: TIMESTAMP or `CurrentTime`

Errors: `Atom`, `Window`

This request changes the owner, owner window, and last-change time of the specified selection. This request has no effect if the specified time is earlier than the current last-change time of the specified selection or is later than the current server time. Otherwise, the last-change time is set to the specified time with `CurrentTime` replaced by the current server time. If the owner window is specified as `None`, then the owner of the selection becomes `None` (that is, no owner). Otherwise, the owner of the selection becomes the client executing the request. If the new owner (whether a client or `None`) is not the same as the current owner and the current owner is not `None`, then the current owner is sent a `SelectionClear` event.

If the client that is the owner of a selection is later terminated (that is, its connection is closed) or if the owner window it has specified in the request is later destroyed, then the owner of the selection automatically reverts to `None`, but the last-change time is not affected.

The selection atom is uninterpreted by the server. The owner window is returned by the `GetSelectionOwner` request and is reported in `SelectionRequest` and `SelectionClear` events.

Selections are global to the server.

GetSelectionOwner

    selection: ATOM

$\longrightarrow$

    owner: WINDOW or None

    Errors: Atom

This request returns the current owner window of the specified selection, if any. If None is returned, then there is no owner for the selection.

ConvertSelection

    selection, target: ATOM

    property: ATOM or None

    requestor: WINDOW

    time: TIMESTAMP or CurrentTime

    Errors: Atom, Window

If the specified selection has an owner, the server sends a Selection-Request event to that owner. If no owner for the specified selection exists, the server generates a SelectionNotify event to the requestor with property None. The arguments are passed on unchanged in either event.

SendEvent

    destination: WINDOW or PointerWindow or InputFocus

    propagate: BOOL

    event-mask: SETofEVENT

    event: <normal-event-format>

    Errors: Window, Value

If PointerWindow is specified, destination is replaced with the window that the pointer is in. If InputFocus is specified and the focus window contains the pointer, destination is replaced with the window that the pointer is in. Otherwise, destination is replaced with the focus window.

If the event-mask is the empty set, then the event is sent to the client that created the destination window. If that client no longer exists, no event is sent.

If propagate is False, then the event is sent to every client selecting on destination any of the event types in event-mask.

If propagate is True and no clients have selected on destination any of the event types in event-mask, then destination is replaced with the closest ancestor of destination for which some client has selected a type in event-mask and no intervening window has that type in its do-not-propagate-mask. If no such window exists or if the window is an ancestor of the focus window and InputFocus was originally specified as the destination, then the event is not sent to any clients. Otherwise, the event is reported to every client selecting on the final destination any of the types specified in event-mask.

The event code must be one of the core events or one of the events defined by an extension (or a Value error results) so that the server can correctly byte-swap the contents as necessary. The contents of the event are otherwise unaltered and unchecked by the server except to force on the most-significant bit of the event code and to set the sequence number in the event correctly.

Active grabs are ignored for this request.

GrabPointer

   grab-window: WINDOW

   owner-events: BOOL

   event-mask: SETofPOINTEREVENT

   pointer-mode, keyboard-mode: {Synchronous, Asynchronous}

   confine-to: WINDOW or None

   cursor: CURSOR or None

   time: TIMESTAMP or CurrentTime

   $\rightarrow$

   status: {Success, AlreadyGrabbed, Frozen, InvalidTime, NotViewable}

   Errors: Cursor, Window, Value

This request actively grabs control of the pointer. Further pointer events are only reported to the grabbing client. The request overrides any active pointer grab by this client.

If owner-events is False, all generated pointer events are reported with respect to grab-window and are only reported if selected by event-mask. If owner-events is True and a generated pointer event would normally be reported to this client, it is reported normally. Otherwise, the event is reported with respect to the grab-window and is only reported if selected by event-mask. For either value of owner-events, unreported events are simply discarded.

If pointer-mode is Asynchronous, pointer event processing continues normally. If the pointer is currently frozen by this client, then processing of pointer events is resumed. If pointer-mode is `Synchronous`, the state of the pointer (as seen by means of the protocol) appears to freeze, and no further pointer events are generated by the server until the grabbing client issues a releasing `AllowEvents` request or until the pointer grab is released. Actual pointer changes are not lost while the pointer is frozen. They are simply queued for later processing.

If keyboard-mode is `Asynchronous`, keyboard event processing is unaffected by activation of the grab. If keyboard-mode is `Synchronous`, the state of the keyboard (as seen by means of the protocol) appears to freeze, and no further keyboard events are generated by the server until the grabbing client issues a releasing `AllowEvents` request or until the pointer grab is released. Actual keyboard changes are not lost while the keyboard is frozen. They are simply queued for later processing.

If a cursor is specified, then it is displayed regardless of what window the pointer is in. If no cursor is specified, then when the pointer is in grab-window or one of its subwindows, the normal cursor for that window is displayed. Otherwise, the cursor for grab-window is displayed.

If a confine-to window is specified, then the pointer will be restricted to stay contained in that window. The confine-to window need have no relationship to the grab-window. If the pointer is not initially in the confine-to window, then it is warped automatically to the closest edge (and enter/leave events are generated normally) just before the grab activates. If the confine-to window is subsequently reconfigured, the pointer will be warped automatically as necessary to keep it contained in the window.

This request generates `EnterNotify` and `LeaveNotify` events.

The request fails with status `AlreadyGrabbed` if the pointer is actively grabbed by some other client. The request fails with status `Frozen` if the pointer is frozen by an active grab of another client. The request fails with status `NotViewable` if grab-window or confine-to window is not viewable or if the confine-to window lies completely outside the boundaries of the root window. The request fails with status `InvalidTime` if the specified time is earlier than the last-pointer-grab time or later than the current server time. Otherwise, the last-pointer-grab time is set to the specified time, with `CurrentTime` replaced by the current server time.

UngrabPointer

    time: TIMESTAMP or `CurrentTime`

This request releases the pointer if this client has it actively grabbed (from either `GrabPointer` or `GrabButton` or from a normal button press) and releases any queued events. The request has no effect if the specified time is earlier than the last-pointer-grab time or is later than the current server time.

    This request generates `EnterNotify` and `LeaveNotify` events.

    An `UngrabPointer` request is performed automatically if the event window or confine-to window for an active pointer grab becomes not viewable or if window reconfiguration causes the confine-to window to lie completely outside the boundaries of the root window.

GrabButton

    modifiers: SETofKEYMASK or `AnyModifier`

    button: BUTTON or `AnyButton`

    grab-window: WINDOW

    owner-events: BOOL

    event-mask: SETofPOINTEREVENT

    pointer-mode, keyboard-mode: {`Synchronous`, `Asynchronous`}

    confine-to: WINDOW or `None`

    cursor: CURSOR or `None`

    Errors: `Cursor`, `Window`, `Value`, `Access`

This request establishes a passive grab. In the future, the pointer is actively grabbed as described in `GrabPointer`, the last-pointer-grab time is set to the time at which the button was pressed (as transmitted in the `ButtonPress` event), and the `ButtonPress` event is reported if all of the following conditions are true:

- The pointer is not grabbed and the specified button is logically pressed when the specified modifier keys are logically down, and no other buttons or modifier keys are logically down.

- The grab-window contains the pointer.

- The confine-to window (if any) is viewable.

- A passive grab on the same button/key combination does not exist on any ancestor of grab-window.

The interpretation of the remaining arguments is the same as for GrabPointer. The active grab is terminated automatically when the logical state of the pointer has all buttons released, independent of the logical state of modifier keys. Note that the logical state of a device (as seen by means of the protocol) may lag the physical state if device event processing is frozen.

This request overrides all previous passive grabs by the same client on the same button/key combinations on the same window. A modifier of AnyModifier is equivalent to issuing the request for all possible modifier combinations (including the combination of no modifiers). It is not required that all specified modifiers have currently assigned keycodes. A button of AnyButton is equivalent to issuing the request for all possible buttons. Otherwise, it is not required that the button specified currently be assigned to a physical button.

An Access error is generated if some other client has already issued a GrabButton request with the same button/key combination on the same window. When using AnyModifier or AnyButton, the request fails completely (no grabs are established), and an Access error is generated if there is a conflicting grab for any combination. The request has no effect on an active grab.

UngrabButton

modifiers: SETofKEYMASK or AnyModifier

button: BUTTON or AnyButton

grab-window: WINDOW

Errors: Window, Value

This request releases the passive button/key combination on the specified window if it was grabbed by this client. A modifiers argument of Any-Modifier is equivalent to issuing the request for all possible modifier combinations (including the combination of no modifiers). A button of AnyButton is equivalent to issuing the request for all possible buttons. The request has no effect on an active grab.

ChangeActivePointerGrab

event-mask: SETofPOINTEREVENT

cursor: CURSOR or None

time: TIMESTAMP or CurrentTime

Errors: Cursor, Value

This request changes the specified dynamic parameters if the pointer is actively grabbed by the client and the specified time is no earlier than the last-pointer-grab time and no later than the current server time. The interpretation of event-mask and cursor are the same as in `GrabPointer`. This request has no effect on the parameters of any passive grabs established with `GrabButton`.

GrabKeyboard

grab-window: WINDOW
owner-events: BOOL
pointer-mode, keyboard-mode: {`Synchronous`, `Asynchronous`}
time: TIMESTAMP or `CurrentTime`

$\rightarrow$

status: {`Success`, `AlreadyGrabbed`, `Frozen`, `InvalidTime`,
    `NotViewable`}

Errors: `Window`, `Value`

This request actively grabs control of the keyboard. Further key events are reported only to the grabbing client. This request overrides any active keyboard grab by this client.

If owner-events is `False`, all generated key events are reported with respect to grab-window. If owner-events is `True` and if a generated key event would normally be reported to this client, it is reported normally. Otherwise, the event is reported with respect to the grab-window. Both `KeyPress` and `KeyRelease` events are always reported, independent of any event selection made by the client.

If keyboard-mode is `Asynchronous`, keyboard event processing continues normally. If the keyboard is currently frozen by this client, then processing of keyboard events is resumed. If keyboard-mode is `Synchronous`, the state of the keyboard (as seen by means of the protocol) appears to freeze. No further keyboard events are generated by the server until the grabbing client issues a releasing `AllowEvents` request or until the keyboard grab is released. Actual keyboard changes are not lost while the keyboard is frozen. They are simply queued for later processing.

If pointer-mode is `Asynchronous`, pointer event processing is unaffected by activation of the grab. If pointer-mode mode is `Synchronous`, the state of the pointer (as seen by means of the protocol) appears to freeze. No further pointer events are generated by the server until the grabbing client issues a releasing `AllowEvents` request or until the keyboard grab is released. Actual pointer changes are not lost while the pointer is frozen. They are simply queued for later processing.

This request generates `FocusIn` and `FocusOut` events.

The request fails with status `AlreadyGrabbed` if the keyboard is actively grabbed by some other client. The request fails with status `Frozen` if the keyboard is frozen by an active grab of another client. The request fails with status `NotViewable` if grab-window is not viewable. The request fails with status `InvalidTime` if the specified time is earlier than the last-keyboard-grab time or later than the current server time. Otherwise, the last-keyboard-grab time is set to the specified time with `CurrentTime` replaced by the current server time.

UngrabKeyboard

    time: TIMESTAMP or `CurrentTime`

This request releases the keyboard if this client has it actively grabbed (as a result of either `GrabKeyboard` or `GrabKey`) and releases any queued events. The request has no effect if the specified time is earlier than the last-keyboard-grab time or is later than the current server time.

This request generates `FocusIn` and `FocusOut` events.

An `UngrabKeyboard` is performed automatically if the event window for an active keyboard grab becomes not viewable.

GrabKey

    key: KEYCODE or `AnyKey`
    modifiers: SETofKEYMASK or `AnyModifier`
    grab-window: WINDOW
    owner-events: BOOL
    pointer-mode, keyboard-mode: {`Synchronous, Asynchronous`}
    Errors: `Window, Value, Access`

This request establishes a passive grab on the keyboard. In the future, the keyboard is actively grabbed as described in `GrabKeyboard`, the last-keyboard-grab time is set to the time at which the key was pressed (as transmitted in the `KeyPress` event), and the `KeyPress` event is reported if all of the following conditions are true:

- The keyboard is not grabbed and the specified key (which can itself be a modifier key) is logically pressed when the specified modifier keys are logically down, and no other modifier keys are logically down.
- Either the grab-window is an ancestor of (or is) the focus window, or the grab-window is a descendant of the focus window and contains the pointer.
- A passive grab on the same key combination does not exist on any ancestor of grab-window.

The interpretation of the remaining arguments is the same as for `GrabKeyboard`. The active grab is terminated automatically when the logical state of the keyboard has the specified key released, independent of the logical state of modifier keys. Note that the logical state of a device (as seen by means of the protocol) may lag the physical state if device event processing is frozen.

This request overrides all previous passive grabs by the same client on the same key combinations on the same window. A modifier of `AnyModifier` is equivalent to issuing the request for all possible modifier combinations (including the combination of no modifiers). It is not required that all modifiers specified have currently assigned keycodes. A key of `AnyKey` is equivalent to issuing the request for all possible keycodes. Otherwise, the key must be in the range specified by min-keycode and max-keycode in the connection setup (or a `Value` error results).

An `Access` error is generated if some other client has issued a `GrabKey` with the same key combination on the same window. When using `AnyModifier` or `AnyKey`, the request fails completely (no grabs are established), and an `Access` error is generated if there is a conflicting grab for any combination.

UngrabKey
> *key*: KEYCODE or `AnyKey`
> *modifiers*: SETofKEYMASK or `AnyModifier`
> *grab-window*: WINDOW
> Errors: `Window`, `Value`

This request releases the key combination on the specified window if it was grabbed by this client. A modifiers argument of `AnyModifier` is equivalent to issuing the request for all possible modifier combinations (including the combination of no modifiers). A key of `AnyKey` is equivalent to issuing the request for all possible keycodes. This request has no effect on an active grab.

AllowEvents

mode: {`AsyncPointer, SyncPointer, ReplayPointer,`
   `AsyncKeyboard, SyncKeyboard, ReplayKeyboard,`
   `AsyncBoth, SyncBoth`}

time: TIMESTAMP or `CurrentTime`

Errors: `Value`

This request releases some queued events if the client has caused a device to freeze. The request has no effect if the specified time is earlier than the last-grab time of the most recent active grab for the client or if the specified time is later than the current server time.

For `AsyncPointer`, if the pointer is frozen by the client, pointer event processing continues normally. If the pointer is frozen twice by the client on behalf of two separate grabs, `AsyncPointer` thaws for both. `AsyncPointer` has no effect if the pointer is not frozen by the client, but the pointer need not be grabbed by the client.

For `SyncPointer`, if the pointer is frozen and actively grabbed by the client, pointer event processing continues normally until the next `ButtonPress` or `ButtonRelease` event is reported to the client, at which time the pointer again appears to freeze. However, if the reported event causes the pointer grab to be released, then the pointer does not freeze. `SyncPointer` has no effect if the pointer is not frozen by the client or if the pointer is not grabbed by the client.

For `ReplayPointer`, if the pointer is actively grabbed by the client and is frozen as the result of an event having been sent to the client (either from the activation of a `GrabButton` or `AllowEvents` with mode `Sync-Pointer` but not from a `GrabPointer`), then the pointer grab is released and that event is completely reprocessed, this time ignoring any passive grabs at or above (towards the root) the grab-window of the grab just released. The request has no effect if the pointer is not grabbed by the client or if the pointer is not frozen as the result of an event.

For `AsyncKeyboard`, if the keyboard is frozen by the client, keyboard event processing continues normally. If the keyboard is frozen twice by the client on behalf of two separate grabs, `AsyncKeyboard` thaws for both. `AsyncKeyboard` has no effect if the keyboard is not frozen by the client, but the keyboard need not be grabbed by the client.

For `SyncKeyboard`, if the keyboard is frozen and actively grabbed by the client, keyboard event processing continues normally until the next `KeyPress` or `KeyRelease` event is reported to the client, at which time the keyboard again appears to freeze. However, if the reported event causes the keyboard grab to be released, then the keyboard does not freeze. `SyncKeyboard` has no effect if the keyboard is not frozen by the client or if the keyboard is not grabbed by the client.

For `ReplayKeyboard`, if the keyboard is actively grabbed by the client and is frozen as the result of an event having been sent to the client (either from the activation of a `GrabKey` or from a previous `AllowEvents` with mode `SyncKeyboard` but not from a `GrabKeyboard`), then the keyboard grab is released and that event is completely reprocessed, this time ignoring any passive grabs at or above (towards the root) the grab-window of the grab just released. The request has no effect if the keyboard is not grabbed by the client or if the keyboard is not frozen as the result of an event.

For `SyncBoth`, if both pointer and keyboard are frozen by the client, event processing (for both devices) continues normally until the next `ButtonPress`, `ButtonRelease`, `KeyPress`, or `KeyRelease` event is reported to the client for a grabbed device (button event for the pointer, key event for the keyboard), at which time the devices again appear to freeze. However, if the reported event causes the grab to be released, then the devices do not freeze (but if the other device is still grabbed, then a subsequent event for it will still cause both devices to freeze). `SyncBoth` has no effect unless both pointer and keyboard are frozen by the client. If the pointer or keyboard is frozen twice by the client on behalf of two separate grabs, `SyncBoth` thaws for both (but a subsequent freeze for `SyncBoth` will only freeze each device once).

For `AsyncBoth`, if the pointer and the keyboard are frozen by the client, event processing for both devices continues normally. If a device is frozen twice by the client on behalf of two separate grabs, `AsyncBoth` thaws for both. `AsyncBoth` has no effect unless both pointer and keyboard are frozen by the client.

AsyncPointer, SyncPointer, and ReplayPointer have no effect on processing of keyboard events. AsyncKeyboard, SyncKeyboard, and ReplayKeyboard have no effect on processing of pointer events.

It is possible for both a pointer grab and a keyboard grab to be active simultaneously (by the same or different clients). When a device is frozen on behalf of either grab, no event processing is performed for the device. It is possible for a single device to be frozen because of both grabs. In this case, the freeze must be released on behalf of both grabs before events can again be processed.

GrabServer

This request disables processing of requests and close-downs on all connections other than the one this request arrived on.

UngrabServer

This request restarts processing of requests and close-downs on other connections.

QueryPointer
   window: WINDOW
→
   root: WINDOW
   child: WINDOW or None
   same-screen: BOOL
   root-x, root-y, win-x, win-y: INT16
   mask: SETofKEYBUTMASK

   Errors: Window

The root window the pointer is logically on and the pointer coordinates relative to the root's origin are returned. If same-screen is False, then the pointer is not on the same screen as the argument window, child is None, and win-x and win-y are zero. If same-screen is True, then win-x and win-y are the pointer coordinates relative to the argument window's origin, and child is the child containing the pointer, if any. The current logical state of the modifier keys and the buttons are also returned. Note that the logical state of a device (as seen by means of the protocol) may lag the physical state if device event processing is frozen.

GetMotionEvents

start, stop: TIMESTAMP or `CurrentTime`

window: WINDOW

→

events: LISTofTIMECOORD

where:

TIMECOORD: [x, y: INT16

time: TIMESTAMP]

Errors: `Window`

This request returns all events in the motion history buffer that fall between the specified start and stop times (inclusive) and that have coordinates that lie within (including borders) the specified window at its present placement. The x and y coordinates are reported relative to the origin of the window.

If the start time is later than the stop time or if the start time is in the future, no events are returned. If the stop time is in the future, it is equivalent to specifying `CurrentTime`.

TranslateCoordinates

src-window, dst-window: WINDOW

src-x, src-y: INT16

→

same-screen: BOOL

child: WINDOW or `None`

dst-x, dst-y: INT16

Errors: `Window`

The src-x and src-y coordinates are taken relative to src-window's origin and are returned as dst-x and dst-y coordinates relative to dst-window's origin. If same-screen is `False`, then src-window and dst-window are on different screens, and dst-x and dst-y are zero. If the coordinates are contained in a mapped child of dst-window, then that child is returned.

WarpPointer

src-window: WINDOW or `None`

dst-window: WINDOW or `None`

src-x, src-y: INT16

src-width, src-height: CARD16

dst-x, dst-y: INT16

Errors: `Window`

If dst-window is `None`, this request moves the pointer by offsets [dst-x, dst-y] relative to the current position of the pointer. If dst-window is a window, this request moves the pointer to [dst-x, dst-y] relative to dst-window's origin. However, if src-window is not `None`, the move only takes place if src-window contains the pointer and the pointer is contained in the specified rectangle of src-window.

The src-x and src-y coordinates are relative to src-window's origin. If src-height is zero, it is replaced with the current height of src-window minus src-y. If src-width is zero, it is replaced with the current width of src-window minus src-x.

This request cannot be used to move the pointer outside the confine-to window of an active pointer grab. An attempt will only move the pointer as far as the closest edge of the confine-to window.

This request will generate events just as if the user had instantaneously moved the pointer.

SetInputFocus

focus: WINDOW or `PointerRoot` or `None`

revert-to: {`Parent`, `PointerRoot`, `None`}

time: TIMESTAMP or `CurrentTime`

Errors: `Window`, `Value`, `Match`

This request changes the input focus and the last-focus-change time. The request has no effect if the specified time is earlier than the current last-focus-change time or is later than the current server time. Otherwise, the last-focus-change time is set to the specified time with `CurrentTime` replaced by the current server time.

If `None` is specified as the focus, all keyboard events are discarded until a new focus window is set. In this case, the revert-to argument is ignored.

If a window is specified as the focus, it becomes the keyboard's focus window. If a generated keyboard event would normally be reported to this window or one of its inferiors, the event is reported normally. Otherwise, the event is reported with respect to the focus window.

If `PointerRoot` is specified as the focus, the focus window is dynamically taken to be the root window of whatever screen the pointer is on at each keyboard event. In this case, the revert-to argument is ignored.

This request generates `FocusIn` and `FocusOut` events.

The specified focus window must be viewable at the time of the request (or a `Match` error results). If the focus window later becomes not viewable, the new focus window depends on the revert-to argument. If revert-to is `Parent`, the focus reverts to the parent (or the closest viewable ancestor) and the new revert-to value is taken to be `None`. If revert-to is `PointerRoot` or `None`, the focus reverts to that value. When the focus reverts, `FocusIn` and `FocusOut` events are generated, but the last-focus-change time is not affected.

GetInputFocus
$\rightarrow$

focus: WINDOW or `PointerRoot` or `None`
revert-to: {`Parent`, `PointerRoot`, `None`}

This request returns the current focus state.

QueryKeymap
$\rightarrow$
keys: LISTofCARD8

This request returns a bit vector for the logical state of the keyboard. Each bit set to 1 indicates that the corresponding key is currently pressed. The vector is represented as 32 bytes. Byte N (from 0) contains the bits for keys 8N to 8N + 7 with the least-significant bit in the byte representing key 8N. Note that the logical state of a device (as seen by means of the protocol) may lag the physical state if device event processing is frozen.

OpenFont
fid: FONT
name: STRING8
Errors: `IDChoice`, `Name`, `Alloc`

This request loads the specified font, if necessary, and associates identifier fid with it. The font name should use the ISO Latin-1 encoding, and uppercase and lowercase do not matter.

Fonts are not associated with a particular screen and can be stored as a component of any graphics context.

CloseFont

>   *font*: FONT

>   Errors: Font

This request deletes the association between the resource ID and the font. The font itself will be freed when no other resource references it.

QueryFont

>   *font*: FONTABLE

$\rightarrow$

>   font-info: FONTINFO
>   char-infos: LISTofCHARINFO

where:

FONTINFO: [draw-direction: {LeftToRight, RightToLeft}
              min-char-or-byte2, max-char-or-byte2: CARD16
              min-byte1, max-byte1: CARD8
              all-chars-exist: BOOL
              default-char: CARD16
              min-bounds: CHARINFO
              max-bounds: CHARINFO
              font-ascent: INT16
              font-descent: INT16
              properties: LISTofFONTPROP]
FONTPROP: [name: ATOM
              value: <32-bit-value>]
CHARINFO: [left-side-bearing: INT16
              right-side-bearing: INT16
              character-width: INT16
              ascent: INT16
              descent: INT16
              attributes: CARD16]

>   Errors: Font

This request returns logical information about a font. If a gcontext is given for font, the currently contained font is used.

The draw-direction is just a hint and indicates whether most char-infos have a positive, `LeftToRight`, or a negative, `RightToLeft`, character-width metric. The core protocol defines no support for vertical text.

If min-byte1 and max-byte1 are both zero, then min-char-or-byte2 specifies the linear character index corresponding to the first element of char-infos, and max-char-or-byte2 specifies the linear character index of the last element. If either min-byte1 or max-byte1 are nonzero, then both min-char-or-byte2 and max-char-or-byte2 will be less than 256, and the 2-byte character index values corresponding to char-infos element N (counting from 0) are:

$$\text{byte1} = \text{N/D} + \text{min-byte1}$$
$$\text{byte2} = \text{N\textbackslash D} + \text{min-char-or-byte2}$$

where:

$$\text{D} = \text{max-char-or-byte2} - \text{min-char-or-byte2} + 1$$
$$/ = \text{integer division}$$
$$\textbackslash = \text{integer modulus}$$

If char-infos has length zero, then min-bounds and max-bounds will be identical, and the effective char-infos is one filled with this char-info, of length:

$$\text{L} = \text{D} * (\text{max-byte1} - \text{min-byte1} + 1)$$

That is, all glyphs in the specified linear or matrix range have the same information, as given by min-bounds (and max-bounds). If all-chars-exist is `True`, then all characters in char-infos have nonzero bounding boxes.

The default-char specifies the character that will be used when an undefined or nonexistent character is used. Note that default-char is a CARD16, not CHAR2B. For a font using 2-byte matrix format, the default-char has byte1 in the most-significant byte and byte2 in the least-significant byte. If the default-char itself specifies an undefined or nonexistent character, then no printing is performed for an undefined or nonexistent character.

The min-bounds and max-bounds contain the minimum and maximum values of each individual CHARINFO component over all char-infos (ignoring nonexistent characters). The bounding box of the font (that is, the smallest rectangle enclosing the shape obtained by superimposing all characters at the same origin [x,y]) has its upper-left coordinate at:

$$[x + min\text{-}bounds.left\text{-}side\text{-}bearing, \; y - max\text{-}bounds.ascent]$$

with a width of:

$$max\text{-}bounds.right\text{-}side\text{-}bearing - min\text{-}bounds.left\text{-}side\text{-}bearing$$

and a height of:

$$max\text{-}bounds.ascent + max\text{-}bounds.descent$$

The font-ascent is the logical extent of the font above the baseline and is used for determining line spacing. Specific characters may extend beyond this. The font-descent is the logical extent of the font at or below the baseline and is used for determining line spacing. Specific characters may extend beyond this. If the baseline is at Y-coordinate y, then the logical extent of the font is inclusive between the Y-coordinate values (y − font-ascent) and (y + font-descent − 1).

A font is not guaranteed to have any properties. The interpretation of the property value (for example, INT32, CARD32) must be derived from *a priori* knowledge of the property. When possible, fonts should have at least the following properties (note that uppercase and lowercase matter).

Property	Type	Description
MIN_SPACE	CARD32	The minimum interword spacing, in pixels.
NORM_SPACE	CARD32	The normal interword spacing, in pixels.
MAX_SPACE	CARD32	The maximum interword spacing, in pixels.
END_SPACE	CARD32	The additional spacing at the end of sentences, in pixels.
SUPERSCRIPT_X SUPERSCRIPT_Y	INT32	Offsets from the character origin where superscripts should begin, in pixels. If the origin is at [x,y], then superscripts should begin at [x + SUPERSCRIPT_X, y − SUPERSCRIPT_Y].

Property	*Type*	*Description*
SUBSCRIPT_X SUBSCRIPT_Y	INT32	Offsets from the character origin where subscripts should begin, in pixels. If the origin is at [x,y], then subscripts should begin at [x + SUBSCRIPT_X, y + SUBSCRIPT_Y].
UNDERLINE_POSITION	INT32	Y offset from the baseline to the top of an underline, in pixels. If the baseline is Y-coordinate y, then the top of the underline is at (y + UNDERLINE_POSITION).
UNDERLINE_THICKNESS	CARD32	Thickness of the underline, in pixels.
STRIKEOUT_ASCENT STRIKEOUT_DESCENT	INT32	Vertical extents for boxing or voiding characters, in pixels. If the baseline is at Y-coordinate y, then the top of the strikeout box is at (y − STRIKEOUT_ASCENT) and the height of the box is (STRIKEOUT_ASCENT + STRIKEOUT_DESCENT).
ITALIC_ANGLE	INT32	The angle of the dominant staffs of characters in the font, in degrees scaled by 64, relative to the three-o'clock position from the character origin, with positive indicating counterclockwise motion (as in Arc requests).
X _HEIGHT	INT32	1 ex as in TeX, but expressed in units of pixels. Often the height of lowercase x.
QUAD_WIDTH	INT32	1 em as in TeX, but expressed in units of pixels. Often the width of the digits 0–9.
CAP_HEIGHT	INT32	Y offset from the baseline to the top of the capital letters, ignoring accents, in pixels. If the baseline is at Y-coordinate y,

Property	Type	Description
		then the top of the capitals is at (y − CAP_HEIGHT).
WEIGHT	CARD32	The weight or boldness of the font, expressed as a value between 0 and 1000.
POINT_SIZE	CARD32	The point size, expressed in 1/10, of this font at the ideal resolution.
RESOLUTION	CARD32	The number of pixels per point, expressed in 1/100, at which this font was created.

For a character origin at [x,y], the bounding box of a character (that is, the smallest rectangle enclosing the character's shape), described in terms of CHARINFO components, is a rectangle with its upper-left corner at:

$$[x + \text{left-side-bearing}, y - \text{ascent}]$$

with a width of:

$$\text{right-side-bearing} - \text{left-side-bearing}$$

and a height of:

$$\text{ascent} + \text{descent}$$

and the origin for the next character is defined to be:

$$[x + \text{character-width}, y]$$

Note that the baseline is logically viewed as being just below nondescending characters (when descent is zero, only pixels with Y-coordinates less than y are drawn) and that the origin is logically viewed as being coincident with the left edge of a nonkerned character (when left-side-bearing is zero, no pixels with X-coordinate less than x are drawn).

Note that CHARINFO metric values can be negative.

A nonexistent character is represented with all CHARINFO components zero.

The interpretation of the per-character attributes field is server-dependent.

QueryTextExtents
   font: FONTABLE
   string: STRING16
$\rightarrow$

   draw-direction: {LeftToRight, RightToLeft}
   font-ascent: INT16
   font-descent: INT16
   overall-ascent: INT16
   overall-descent: INT16
   overall-width: INT32
   overall-left: INT32
   overall-right: INT32

   Errors: Font

This request returns the logical extents of the specified string of characters
in the specified font. If a gcontext is given for font, the currently contained
font is used. The draw-direction, font-ascent, and font-descent are the same
as described in QueryFont. The overall-ascent is the maximum of the ascent metrics of all characters in the string, and the overall-descent is the
maximum of the descent metrics. The overall-width is the sum of the
character-width metrics of all characters in the string. For each character in
the string, let W be the sum of the character-width metrics of all characters
preceding it in the string, let L be the left-side-bearing metric of the character plus W, and let R be the right-side-bearing metric of the character plus
W. The overall-left is the minimum L of all characters in the string, and the
overall-right is the maximum R.

   For fonts defined with linear indexing rather than 2-byte matrix indexing,
the server will interpret each CHAR2B as a 16-bit number that has been
transmitted most-significant byte first (that is, byte1 of the CHAR2B is taken
as the most-significant byte).

   If the font has no defined default-char, then undefined characters in the
string are taken to have all zero metrics.

ListFonts
   pattern: STRING8
   max-names: CARD16
$\rightarrow$

   names: LISTofSTRING8

This request returns a list of available font names (as controlled by the font search path; see SetFontPath request) that match the pattern. At most, max-names names will be returned. The pattern should use the ISO Latin-1 encoding, and uppercase and lowercase do not matter. In the pattern, the "?" character (octal value 77) will match any single character, and the "*" character (octal value 52) will match any number of characters. The returned names are in lowercase.

ListFontsWithInfo

>   *pattern*: STRING8

>   *max-names*: CARD16

→+

>   name: STRING8

>   info: FONTINFO

>   replies-hint: CARD32

where:

FONTINFO: ‹same type definition as in QueryFont›

This request is similar to ListFonts, but it also returns information about each font. The information returned for each font is identical to what QueryFont would return except that the per-character metrics are not returned. Note that this request can generate multiple replies. With each reply, replies-hint may provide an indication of how many more fonts will be returned. This number is a hint only and may be larger or smaller than the number of fonts actually returned. A zero value does not guarantee that no more fonts will be returned. After the font replies, a reply with a zero-length name is sent to indicate the end of the reply sequence.

SetFontPath

>   *path*: LISTofSTRING8

>   Errors: Value

This request defines the search path for font lookup. There is only one search path per server, not one per client. The interpretation of the strings is operating-system-dependent, but the strings are intended to specify directories to be searched in the order listed.

Setting the path to the empty list restores the default path defined for the server.

As a side effect of executing this request, the server is guaranteed to flush all cached information about fonts for which there currently are no explicit resource IDs allocated.

The meaning of an error from this request is system specific.

GetFontPath

path: LISTofSTRING8

This request returns the current search path for fonts.

CreatePixmap

pid: PIXMAP
drawable: DRAWABLE
depth: CARD8
width, height: CARD16
Errors: IDChoice, Drawable, Value, Alloc

This request creates a pixmap and assigns the identifier pid to it. The width and height must be nonzero (or a Value error results). The depth must be one of the depths supported by the root of the specified drawable (or a Value error results). The initial contents of the pixmap are undefined.

It is legal to pass an InputOnly window as a drawable to this request.

FreePixmap

pixmap: PIXMAP
Errors: Pixmap

This request deletes the association between the resource ID and the pixmap. The pixmap storage will be freed when no other resource references it.

CreateGC

cid: GCONTEXT
drawable: DRAWABLE
value-mask: BITMASK
value-list: LISTofVALUE

Errors: IDChoice, Drawable, Pixmap, Font, Match, Value,
   Alloc

This request creates a graphics context and assigns the identifier cid to it.
The gcontext can be used with any destination drawable having the same
root and depth as the specified drawable; use with other drawables results in
a Match error.

The value-mask and value-list specify which components are to be explicitly initialized. The context components are:

Component	Type
function	{Clear, And, AndReverse, Copy, AndInverted, NoOp, Xor, Or, Nor, Equiv, Invert, OrReverse, CopyInverted, OrInverted, Nand, Set}
plane-mask	CARD32
foreground	CARD32
background	CARD32
line-width	CARD16
line-style	{Solid, OnOffDash, DoubleDash}
cap-style	{NotLast, Butt, Round, Projecting}
join-style	{Miter, Round, Bevel}
fill-style	{Solid, Tiled, OpaqueStippled, Stippled}
fill-rule	{EvenOdd, Winding}
arc-mode	{Chord, PieSlice}
tile	PIXMAP
stipple	PIXMAP
tile-stipple-x-origin	INT16
tile-stipple-y-origin	INT16
font	FONT
subwindow-mode	{ClipByChildren, IncludeInferiors}
graphics-exposures	BOOL
clip-x-origin	INT16
clip-y-origin	INT16
clip-mask	PIXMAP or None
dash-offset	CARD16
dashes	CARD8

In graphics operations, given a source and destination pixel, the result is
computed bitwise on corresponding bits of the pixels; that is, a Boolean

operation is performed in each bit plane. The plane-mask restricts the operation to a subset of planes, so the result is:

((src FUNC dst) AND plane-mask) OR (dst AND (NOT plane-mask))

Range checking is not performed on the values for foreground, background, or plane-mask. They are simply truncated to the appropriate number of bits.

The meanings of the functions are:

Function	Operation
Clear	0
And	src AND dst
AndReverse	src AND (NOT dst)
Copy	src
AndInverted	(NOT src) AND dst
NoOp	dst
Xor	src XOR dst
Or	src OR dst
Nor	(NOT src) AND (NOT dst)
Equiv	(NOT src) XOR dst
Invert	NOT dst
OrReverse	src OR (NOT dst)
CopyInverted	NOT src
OrInverted	(NOT src) OR dst
Nand	(NOT src) OR (NOT dst)
Set	1

The line-width is measured in pixels and can be greater than or equal to one, a wide line, or the special value zero, a thin line.

Wide lines are drawn centered on the path described by the graphics request. Unless otherwise specified by the join or cap style, the bounding box of a wide line with endpoints $[x1, y1]$, $[x2, y2]$ and width w is a rectangle with vertices at the following real coordinates:

$$[x1 - (w*sn/2), \ y1 + (w*cs/2)], \ [x1 + (w*sn/2), \ y1 - (w*cs/2)],$$
$$[x2 - (w*sn/2), \ y2 + (w*cs/2)], \ [x2 + (w*sn/2), \ y2 - (w*cs/2)]$$

The sn is the sine of the angle of the line and cs is the cosine of the angle of the line. A pixel is part of the line (and hence drawn) if the center of the pixel is fully inside the bounding box, which is viewed as having infinitely thin edges. If the center of the pixel is exactly on the bounding box, it is part of the line if and only if the interior is immediately to its right (x increasing direction). Pixels with centers on a horizontal edge are a special case and are part of the line if and only if the interior or the boundary is immediately below (y increasing direction) and if the interior or the boundary is immediately to the right (x increasing direction). Note that this description is a mathematical model describing the pixels that are drawn for a wide line and does not imply that trigonometry is required to implement such a model. Real or fixed point arithmetic is recommended for computing the corners of the line endpoints for lines greater than one pixel in width.

Thin lines (zero line-width) are "one pixel wide" lines drawn using an unspecified, device-dependent algorithm. There are only two constraints on this algorithm. First, if a line is drawn unclipped from $[x1,y1]$ to $[x2,y2]$ and another line is drawn unclipped from $[x1+dx,y1+dy]$ to $[x2+dx,y2+dy]$, then a point $[x,y]$ is touched by drawing the first line if and only if the point $[x+dx,y+dy]$ is touched by drawing the second line. Second, the effective set of points comprising a line cannot be affected by clipping. Thus, a point is touched in a clipped line if and only if the point lies inside the clipping region and the point would be touched by the line when drawn unclipped.

Note that a wide line drawn from $[x1,y1]$ to $[x2,y2]$ always draws the same pixels as a wide line drawn from $[x2,y2]$ to $[x1,y1]$, not counting cap-style and join-style. Implementors are encouraged to make this property true for thin lines, but it is not required. A line-width of zero may differ from a line-width of one in which pixels are drawn. In general, drawing a thin line will be faster than drawing a wide line of width one, but thin lines may not mix well aesthetically with wide lines because of the different drawing algorithms. If it is desirable to obtain precise and uniform results across all displays, a client should always use a line-width of one, rather than a line-width of zero.

The line-style defines which sections of a line are drawn:

Solid	The full path of the line is drawn.
DoubleDash	The full path of the line is drawn, but the even dashes are filled differently than the odd dashes (see fill-style), with Butt cap-style used where even and odd dashes meet.

OnOffDash   Only the even dashes are drawn, and cap-style applies to all internal ends of the individual dashes (except NotLast is treated as Butt).

The cap-style defines how the endpoints of a path are drawn:

NotLast   The result is equivalent to Butt, except that for a line-width of zero the final endpoint is not drawn.

Butt   The result is square at the endpoint (perpendicular to the slope of the line) with no projection beyond.

Round   The result is a circular arc with its diameter equal to the line-width, centered on the endpoint; it is equivalent to Butt for line-width zero.

Projecting   The result is square at the end, but the path continues beyond the endpoint for a distance equal to half the line-width; it is equivalent to Butt for line-width zero.

The join-style defines how corners are drawn for wide lines:

Miter   The outer edges of the two lines extend to meet at an angle. However, if the angle is less than 11 degrees, a Bevel join-style is used instead.

Round   The result is a circular arc with a diameter equal to the line-width, centered on the joinpoint.

Bevel   The result is Butt endpoint styles, and then the triangular "notch" is filled.

For a line with coincident endpoints ($x1 = x2$, $y1 = y2$), when the cap-style is applied to both endpoints, the semantics depends on the line-width and the cap-style:

NotLast   thin   This is device-dependent, but the desired effect is that nothing is drawn.

Butt   thin   This is device-dependent, but the desired effect is that a single pixel is drawn.

Round   thin   This is the same as Butt/thin.

Projecting   thin   This is the same as Butt/thin.

Butt   wide   Nothing is drawn.

Round   wide   The closed path is a circle, centered at the endpoint and with a diameter equal to the line-width.

Projecting	wide	The closed path is a square, aligned with the coordinate axes, centered at the endpoint and with sides equal to the line-width.

For a line with coincident endpoints (x1 = x2, y1 = y2), when the join-style is applied at one or both endpoints, the effect is as if the line was removed from the overall path. However, if the total path consists of (or is reduced to) a single point joined with itself, the effect is the same as when the cap-style is applied at both endpoints.

The tile/stipple and clip origins are interpreted relative to the origin of whatever destination drawable is specified in a graphics request.

The tile pixmap must have the same root and depth as the gcontext (or a Match error results). The stipple pixmap must have depth 1 and must have the same root as the gcontext (or a Match error results). For fill-style Stippled (but not fill-style OpaqueStippled), the stipple pattern is tiled in a single plane and acts as an additional clip mask to be ANDed with the clip-mask. Any size pixmap can be used for tiling or stippling, although some sizes may be faster to use than others.

The fill-style defines the contents of the source for line, text, and fill requests. For all text and fill requests (for example, PolyText8, PolyText16, PolyFillRectangle, FillPoly, and PolyFillArc) as well as for line requests with line-style Solid (for example, PolyLine, PolySegment, PolyRectangle, PolyArc), and for the even dashes for line requests with line-style OnOffDash or DoubleDash:

Solid	Foreground
Tiled	Tile
OpaqueStippled	A tile with the same width and height as stipple but with background everywhere stipple has a zero and with foreground everywhere stipple has a one
Stippled	Foreground masked by stipple

For the odd dashes for line requests with line-style DoubleDash:

Solid	Background
Tiled	Same as for even dashes
OpaqueStippled	Same as for even dashes
Stippled	Background masked by stipple

The dashes value allowed here is actually a simplified form of the more general patterns that can be set with `SetDashes`. Specifying a value of N here is equivalent to specifying the two element list [N, N] in `SetDashes`. The value must be nonzero (or a `Value` error results). The meaning of dash-offset and dashes are explained in the `SetDashes` request.

The clip-mask restricts writes to the destination drawable. Only pixels where the clip-mask has bits set to 1 are drawn. Pixels are not drawn outside the area covered by the clip-mask or where the clip-mask has bits set to 0. The clip-mask affects all graphics requests, but it does not clip sources. The clip-mask origin is interpreted relative to the origin of whatever destination drawable is specified in a graphics request. If a pixmap is specified as the clip-mask, it must have depth 1 and have the same root as the gcontext (or a `Match` error results). If clip-mask is `None`, then pixels are always drawn, regardless of the clip origin. The clip-mask can also be set with the `SetClipRectangles` request.

For `ClipByChildren`, both source and destination windows are additionally clipped by all viewable `InputOutput` children. For `Include-Inferiors`, neither source nor destination window is clipped by inferiors. This will result in including subwindow contents in the source and drawing through subwindow boundaries of the destination. The use of `Include-Inferiors` with a source or destination window of one depth with mapped inferiors of differing depth is not illegal, but the semantics is undefined by the core protocol.

The fill-rule defines what pixels are inside (that is, are drawn) for paths given in `FillPoly` requests. `EvenOdd` means a point is inside if an infinite ray with the point as origin crosses the path an odd number of times. For `Winding`, a point is inside if an infinite ray with the point as origin crosses an unequal number of clockwise and counterclockwise directed path segments. A clockwise directed path segment is one that crosses the ray from left to right as observed from the point. A counterclockwise segment is one that crosses the ray from right to left as observed from the point. The case where a directed line segment is coincident with the ray is uninteresting because one can simply choose a different ray that is not coincident with a segment.

For both fill rules, a point is infinitely small and the path is an infinitely thin line. A pixel is inside if the center point of the pixel is inside and the center point is not on the boundary. If the center point is on the boundary, the pixel is inside if and only if the polygon interior is immediately to its right (x increasing direction). Pixels with centers along a horizontal edge are a special case and are inside if and only if the polygon interior is immediately below (y increasing direction).

The arc-mode controls filling in the `PolyFillArc` request.

The graphics-exposures flag controls `GraphicsExposure` event generation for `CopyArea` and `CopyPlane` requests (and any similar requests defined by extensions).

The default component values are:

Component	Default
function	Copy
plane-mask	all ones
foreground	0
background	1
line-width	0
line-style	Solid
cap-style	Butt
join-style	Miter
fill-style	Solid
fill-rule	EvenOdd
arc-mode	PieSlice
tile	Pixmap of unspecified size filled with foreground pixel (that is, client specified pixel if any, else 0) (subsequent changes to foreground do not affect this pixmap)
stipple	Pixmap of unspecified size filled with ones
tile-stipple-x-origin	0
tile-stipple-y-origin	0
font	\<server-dependent-font\>
subwindow-mode	ClipByChildren
graphics-exposures	True
clip-x-origin	0
clip-y-origin	0
clip-mask	None
dash-offset	0
dashes	4 (that is, the list [4, 4])

Storing a pixmap in a gcontext might or might not result in a copy being made. If the pixmap is later used as the destination for a graphics request, the change might or might not be reflected in the gcontext. If the pixmap is used simultaneously in a graphics request as both a destination and as a tile or stipple, the results are not defined.

It is quite likely that some amount of gcontext information will be cached in display hardware and that such hardware can only cache a small number of gcontexts. Given the number and complexity of components, clients should view switching between gcontexts with nearly identical state as significantly more expensive than making minor changes to a single gcontext.

ChangeGC

   gc: GCONTEXT

   value-mask: BITMASK

   value-list: LISTofVALUE

   Errors: `GContext`, `Pixmap`, `Font`, `Match`, `Value`, `Alloc`

This request changes components in gc. The value-mask and value-list specify which components are to be changed. The values and restrictions are the same as for `CreateGC`.

Changing the clip-mask also overrides any previous `SetClip-Rectangles` request on the context. Changing dash-offset or dashes overrides any previous `SetDashes` request on the context.

The order in which components are verified and altered is server-dependent. If an error is generated, a subset of the components may have been altered.

CopyGC

   src-gc, dst-gc: GCONTEXT

   value-mask: BITMASK

   Errors: `GContext`, `Value`, `Match`, `Alloc`

This request copies components from src-gc to dst-gc. The value-mask specifies which components to copy, as for `CreateGC`. The two gcontexts must have the same root and the same depth (or a `Match` error results).

SetDashes

> *gc*: GCONTEXT
>
> *dash-offset*: CARD16
>
> *dashes*: LISTofCARD8
>
> Errors: GContext, Value, Alloc

This request sets dash-offset and dashes in gc for dashed line styles. Dashes cannot be empty (or a Value error results). Specifying an odd-length list is equivalent to specifying the same list concatenated with itself to produce an even-length list. The initial and alternating elements of dashes are the even dashes; the others are the odd dashes. Each element specifies a dash length in pixels. All of the elements must be nonzero (or a Value error results). The dash-offset defines the phase of the pattern, specifying how many pixels into dashes the pattern should actually begin in any single graphics request. Dashing is continuous through path elements combined with a join-style, but it is reset to the dash-offset each time a cap-style is applied at a line endpoint.

The unit of measure for dashes is the same as in the ordinary coordinate system. Ideally, a dash length is measured along the slope of the line, but implementations are only required to match this ideal for horizontal and vertical lines. Failing the ideal semantics, it is suggested that the length be measured along the major axis of the line. The major axis is defined as the x axis for lines drawn at an angle of between -45 and $+45$ degrees or between 315 and 225 degrees from the x axis. For all other lines, the major axis is the y axis.

SetClipRectangles

> *gc*: GCONTEXT
>
> *clip-x-origin, clip-y-origin*: INT16
>
> *rectangles*: LISTofRECTANGLE
>
> *ordering*: {UnSorted, YSorted, YXSorted, YXBanded}
>
> Errors: GContext, Value, Alloc, Match

This request changes clip-mask in gc to the specified list of rectangles and sets the clip origin. Output will be clipped to remain contained within the rectangles. The clip origin is interpreted relative to the origin of whatever destination drawable is specified in a graphics request. The rectangle coordinates are interpreted relative to the clip origin. The rectangles should be nonintersecting, or graphics results will be undefined. Note that the list of rectangles can be empty, which effectively disables output. This is the opposite of passing None as the clip-mask in CreateGC and ChangeGC.

If known by the client, ordering relations on the rectangles can be specified with the ordering argument. This may provide faster operation by the server. If an incorrect ordering is specified, the server may generate a Match error, but it is not required to do so. If no error is generated, the graphics results are undefined. UnSorted means that the rectangles are in arbitrary order. YSorted means that the rectangles are nondecreasing in their Y origin. YXSorted additionally constrains YSorted order in that all rectangles with an equal Y origin are nondecreasing in their X origin. YXBanded additionally constrains YXSorted by requiring that, for every possible Y scanline, all rectangles that include that scanline have identical Y origins and Y extents.

FreeGC

gc: GCONTEXT

Errors: GContext

This request deletes the association between the resource ID and the gcontext and destroys the gcontext.

ClearArea

window: WINDOW

x, y: INT16

width, height: CARD16

exposures: BOOL

Errors: Window, Value, Match

The x and y coordinates are relative to the window's origin and specify the upper-left corner of the rectangle. If width is zero, it is replaced with the current width of the window minus x. If height is zero, it is replaced with the current height of the window minus y. If the window has a defined background tile, the rectangle tangle is tiled with a plane-mask of all ones and function of Copy and a subwindow-mode of ClipByChildren. If the window has background None, the contents of the window are not changed. In either case, if exposures is True, then one or more exposure events are generated for regions of the rectangle that are either visible or are being retained in a backing store.

It is a `Match` error to use an `InputOnly` window in this request.

CopyArea

src-drawable, dst-drawable: DRAWABLE
gc: GCONTEXT
src-x, src-y: INT16
width, height: CARD16
dst-x, dst-y: INT16

Errors: `Drawable`, `GContext`, `Match`

This request combines the specified rectangle of src-drawable with the specified rectangle of dst-drawable. The src-x and src-y coordinates are relative to src-drawable's origin. The dst-x and dst-y are relative to dst-drawable's origin, each pair specifying the upper-left corner of the rectangle. The src-drawable must have the same root and the same depth as dst-drawable (or a `Match` error results).

If regions of the source rectangle are obscured and have not been retained in backing store or if regions outside the boundaries of the source drawable are specified, then those regions are not copied, but the following occurs on all corresponding destination regions that are either visible or are retained in backing-store. If the dst-drawable is a window with a background other than `None`, these corresponding destination regions are tiled (with plane-mask of all ones and function `Copy`) with that background. Regardless of tiling and whether the destination is a window or a pixmap, if graphics-exposures in gc is `True`, then `GraphicsExposure` events for all corresponding destination regions are generated.

If graphics-exposures is `True` but no `GraphicsExposure` events are generated, then a `NoExposure` event is generated.

GC components: function, plane-mask, subwindow-mode, graphics-exposures, clip-x-origin, clip-y-origin, clip-mask

CopyPlane

src-drawable, dst-drawable: DRAWABLE
gc: GCONTEXT
src-x, src-y: INT16
width, height: CARD16

dst-x, dst-y: INT16

bit-plane: CARD32

Errors: `Drawable, GContext, Value, Match`

The src-drawable must have the same root as dst-drawable (or a `Match` error results), but it need not have the same depth. The bit-plane must have exactly one bit set to 1 and the value of bit-plane must be less than 2^N where N is the depth of src-drawable (or a `Value` error results). Effectively, a pixmap of the same depth as dst-drawable and with size specified by the source region is formed using the foreground/background pixels in gc (foreground everywhere the bit-plane in src-drawable contains a bit set to 1, background everywhere the bit-plane contains a bit set to 0), and the equivalent of a `CopyArea` is performed, with all the same exposure semantics. This can also be thought of as using the specified region of the source bit-plane as a stipple with a fill-style of `OpaqueStippled` for filling a rectangular area of the destination.

GC components: function, plane-mask, foreground, background, subwindow-mode, graphics-exposures, clip-x-origin, clip-y-origin, clip-mask

PolyPoint

drawable: DRAWABLE

gc: GCONTEXT

coordinate-mode: {`Origin, Previous`}

points: LISTofPOINT

Errors: `Drawable, GContext, Value, Match`

This request combines the foreground pixel in gc with the pixel at each point in the drawable. The points are drawn in the order listed.

The first point is always relative to the drawable's origin. The rest are relative either to that origin or the previous point, depending on the coordinate-mode.

GC components: function, plane-mask, foreground, subwindow-mode, clip-x-origin, clip-y-origin, clip-mask

PolyLine

drawable: DRAWABLE

gc: GCONTEXT

coordinate-mode: {`Origin, Previous`}

points: LISTofPOINT

Errors: `Drawable`, `GContext`, `Value`, `Match`

This request draws lines between each pair of points (point[i], point[i + 1]). The lines are drawn in the order listed. The lines join correctly at all intermediate points, and if the first and last points coincide, the first and last lines also join correctly.

For any given line, no pixel is drawn more than once. If thin (zero linewidth) lines intersect, the intersecting pixels are drawn multiple times. If wide lines intersect, the intersecting pixels are drawn only once, as though the entire `PolyLine` were a single filled shape.

The first point is always relative to the drawable's origin. The rest are relative either to that origin or the previous point, depending on the coordinate-mode.

GC components: function, plane-mask, line-width, line-style, cap-style, join-style, fill-style, subwindow-mode, clip-x-origin, clip-y-origin, clip-mask

GC mode-dependent components: foreground, background, tile, stipple, tile-stipple-x-origin, tile-stipple-y-origin, dash-offset, dashes

PolySegment

drawable: DRAWABLE

gc: GCONTEXT

segments: LISTofSEGMENT

where:

SEGMENT: [x1, y1, x2, y2: INT16]

Errors: `Drawable`, `GContext`, `Match`

For each segment, this request draws a line between [x1, y1] and [x2, y2]. The lines are drawn in the order listed. No joining is performed at coincident endpoints. For any given line, no pixel is drawn more than once. If lines intersect, the intersecting pixels are drawn multiple times.

GC components: function, plane-mask, line-width, line-style, cap-style, fill-style, subwindow-mode, clip-x-origin, clip-y-origin, clip-mask

GC mode-dependent components: foreground, background, tile, stipple, tile-stipple-x-origin, tile-stipple-y-origin, dash-offset, dashes

PolyRectangle

drawable: DRAWABLE

gc: GCONTEXT

rectangles: LISTofRECTANGLE

Errors: `Drawable`, `GContext`, `Match`

This request draws the outlines of the specified rectangles, as if a five-point `PolyLine` were specified for each rectangle:

$$[x,y]\ [x+width,y]\ [x+width,y+height]\ [x,y+height]\ [x,y]$$

The x and y coordinates of each rectangle are relative to the drawable's origin and define the upper-left corner of the rectangle.

The rectangles are drawn in the order listed. For any given rectangle, no pixel is drawn more than once. If rectangles intersect, the intersecting pixels are drawn multiple times.

GC components: function, plane-mask, line-width, line-style, join-style, fill-style, subwindow-mode, clip-x-origin, clip-y-origin, clip-mask

GC mode-dependent components: foreground, background, tile, stipple, tile-stipple-x-origin, tile-stipple-y-origin, dash-offset, dashes

PolyArc

drawable: DRAWABLE

gc: GCONTEXT

arcs: LISTofARC

Errors: `Drawable`, `GContext`, `Match`

This request draws circular or elliptical arcs. Each arc is specified by a rectangle and two angles. The angles are signed integers in degrees scaled by 64, with positive indicating counterclockwise motion and negative indicating clockwise motion. The start of the arc is specified by angle1 relative to the three-o'clock position from the center of the rectangle, and the path and extent of the arc is specified by angle2 relative to the start of the arc. If the magnitude of angle2 is greater than 360 degrees, it is truncated to 360 degrees. The x and y coordinates of the rectangle are relative to the origin of the drawable. For an arc specified as [x,y,w,h,a1,a2], the origin of the major and minor axes is at $[x+(w/2),y+(h/2)]$, and the infinitely thin path describing the entire circle/ellipse intersects the horizontal axis at $[x,y+(h/2)]$ and [x + w,y + (h/2)] and intersects the vertical axis at [x + (w/2),y] and [x + (w/2), y + h]. These coordinates can be fractional; that is, they are not truncated to discrete coordinates. The path should be defined by the ideal mathematical path. For a wide line with line-width lw, the bounding outlines for filling are given by the two infinitely thin paths consisting of all points whose perpendicular distance from the path of the circle/ellipse is equal to lw/2 (which may be a fractional value). The cap-style and join-style are applied the same as for a line corresponding to the tangent of the circle/ellipse at the endpoint.

For an arc specified as [x,y,w,h,a1,a2], the angles must be specified in the effectively skewed coordinate system of the ellipse (for a circle, the angles and coordinate systems are identical). The relationship between these angles and angles expressed in the normal coordinate system of the screen (as measured with a protractor) is as follows:

$$skewed\text{-}angle = atan(tan(normal\text{-}angle) * w/h) + adjust$$

The skewed-angle and normal-angle are expressed in radians (rather than in degrees scaled by 64) in the range [0,2*PI). The atan returns a value in the range [− PI/2,PI/2]. The adjust is:

0	for normal-angle in the range [0,PI/2)
PI	for normal-angle in the range [PI/2,(3*PI)/2)
2*PI	for normal-angle in the range [(3*PI)/2,2*PI)

The arcs are drawn in the order listed. If the last point in one arc coincides with the first point in the following arc, the two arcs will join correctly. If the first point in the first arc coincides with the last point in the last arc, the two arcs will join correctly. For any given arc, no pixel is drawn more than once. If two arcs join correctly and the line-width is greater than zero and the arcs intersect, no pixel is drawn more than once. Otherwise, the intersecting pixels of intersecting arcs are drawn multiple times. Specifying an arc with one endpoint and a clockwise extent draws the same pixels as specifying the other endpoint and an equivalent counterclockwise extent, except as it affects joins.

By specifying one axis to be zero, a horizontal or vertical line can be drawn.

Angles are computed based solely on the coordinate system, ignoring the aspect ratio.

GC components: function, plane-mask, line-width, line-style, cap-style, join-style, fill-style, subwindow-mode, clip-x-origin, clip-y-origin, clip-mask

GC mode-dependent components: foreground, background, tile, stipple, tile-stipple-x-origin, tile-stipple-y-origin, dash-offset, dashes

FillPoly

drawable: DRAWABLE

gc: GCONTEXT

shape: {Complex, Nonconvex, Convex}

coordinate-mode: {Origin, Previous}

points: LISTofPOINT

Errors: Drawable, GContext, Match, Value

This request fills the region closed by the specified path. The path is closed automatically if the last point in the list does not coincide with the first point. No pixel of the region is drawn more than once.

The first point is always relative to the drawable's origin. The rest are relative either to that origin or the previous point, depending on the coordinate-mode.

The shape parameter may be used by the server to improve performance. Complex means the path may self-intersect.

Nonconvex means the path does not self-intersect, but the shape is not wholly convex. If known by the client, specifying Nonconvex over Complex may improve performance. If Nonconvex is specified for a self-intersecting path, the graphics results are undefined.

Convex means the path is wholly convex. If known by the client, specifying Convex can improve performance. If Convex is specified for a path that is not convex, the graphics results are undefined.

GC components: function, plane-mask, fill-style, fill-rule, subwindow-mode, clip-x-origin, clip-y-origin, clip-mask

GC mode-dependent components: foreground, background, tile, stipple, tile-stipple-x-origin, tile-stipple-y-origin

PolyFillRectangle

drawable: DRAWABLE

gc: GCONTEXT

rectangles: LISTofRECTANGLE

Errors: Drawable, GContext, Match

This request fills the specified rectangles, as if a four-point `FillPoly` were specified for each rectangle:

$$[x,y]\ [x+width,y]\ [x+width,y+height]\ [x,y+height]$$

The x and y coordinates of each rectangle are relative to the drawable's origin and define the upper-left corner of the rectangle.

The rectangles are drawn in the order listed. For any given rectangle, no pixel is drawn more than once. If rectangles intersect, the intersecting pixels are drawn multiple times.

GC components: function, plane-mask, fill-style, subwindow-mode, clip-x-origin, clip-y-origin, clip-mask

GC mode-dependent components: foreground, background, tile, stipple, tile-stipple-x-origin, tile-stipple-y-origin

PolyFillArc

   drawable: DRAWABLE

   gc: GCONTEXT

   arcs: LISTofARC

   Errors: `Drawable`, `GContext`, `Match`

For each arc, this request fills the region closed by the infinitely thin path described by the specified arc and one or two line segments, depending on the arc-mode. For `Chord`, the single line segment joining the endpoints of the arc is used. For `PieSlice`, the two line segments joining the endpoints of the arc with the center point are used. The arcs are as specified in the `PolyArc` request.

The arcs are filled in the order listed. For any given arc, no pixel is drawn more than once. If regions intersect, the intersecting pixels are drawn multiple times.

GC components: function, plane-mask, fill-style, arc-mode, subwindow-mode, clip-x-origin, clip-y-origin, clip-mask

GC mode-dependent components: foreground, background, tile, stipple, tile-stipple-x-origin, tile-stipple-y-origin

PutImage

   drawable: DRAWABLE

   gc: GCONTEXT

   depth: CARD8

width, height: CARD16

dst-x, dst-y: INT16

left-pad: CARD8

format: {`Bitmap`, `XYPixmap`, `ZPixmap`}

data: LISTofBYTE

Errors: `Drawable`, `GContext`, `Match`, `Value`

This request combines an image with a rectangle of the drawable. The dst-x and dst-y coordinates are relative to the drawable's origin.

If `Bitmap` format is used, then depth must be one (or a `Match` error results), and the image must be in XY format. The foreground pixel in gc defines the source for bits set to 1 in the image, and the background pixel defines the source for the bits set to 0.

For `XYPixmap` and `ZPixmap`, the depth must match the depth of the drawable (or a `Match` error results). For `XYPixmap`, the image must be sent in XY format. For `ZPixmap`, the image must be sent in the Z format defined for the given depth.

The left-pad must be zero for `ZPixmap` format (or a `Match` error results). For `Bitmap` and `XYPixmap` format, left-pad must be less than bitmap-scanline-pad as given in the server connection setup information (or a `Match` error results). The first left-pad bits in every scanline are to be ignored by the server. The actual image begins that many bits into the data. The width argument defines the width of the actual image and does not include left-pad.

GC components: function, plane-mask, subwindow-mode, clip-x-origin, clip-y-origin, clip-mask

GC mode-dependent components: foreground, background

GetImage

drawable: DRAWABLE

x, y: INT16

width, height: CARD16

plane-mask: CARD32

format: {`XYPixmap`, `ZPixmap`}

→

depth: CARD8

visual: VISUALID or None

data: LISTofBYTE

Errors: Drawable, Value, Match

This request returns the contents of the given rectangle of the drawable in the given format. The x and y coordinates are relative to the drawable's origin and define the upper-left corner of the rectangle. If XYPixmap is specified, only the bit planes specified in plane-mask are transmitted, with the planes appearing from most-significant to least-significant in bit order. If ZPixmap is specified, then bits in all planes not specified in plane-mask are transmitted as zero. Range checking is not performed on plane-mask; extraneous bits are simply ignored. The returned depth is as specified when the drawable was created and is the same as a depth component in a FORMAT structure (in the connection setup), not a bits-per-pixel component. If the drawable is a window, its visual type is returned. If the drawable is a pixmap, the visual is None.

If the drawable is a pixmap, then the given rectangle must be wholly contained within the pixmap (or a Match error results). If the drawable is a window, the window must be viewable, and it must be the case that, if there were no inferiors or overlapping windows, the specified rectangle of the window would be fully visible on the screen and wholly contained within the outside edges of the window (or a Match error results). Note that the borders of the window can be included and read with this request. If the window has a backing store, then the backing-store contents are returned for regions of the window that are obscured by noninferior windows; otherwise, the returned contents of such obscured regions are undefined. Also undefined are the returned contents of visible regions of inferiors of different depth than the specified window. The pointer cursor image is not included in the contents returned.

This request is not general-purpose in the same sense as other graphics-related requests. It is intended specifically for rudimentary hardcopy support.

PolyText8

drawable: DRAWABLE

gc: GCONTEXT

x, y: INT16

items: LISTofTEXTITEM8

where:

TEXTITEM8: TEXTELT8 or FONT
  TEXTELT8: [delta: INT8
          string: STRING8]

  Errors: `Drawable`, `GContext`, `Match`, `Font`

The x and y coordinates are relative to the drawable's origin and specify the baseline starting position (the initial character origin). Each text item is processed in turn. A font item causes the font to be stored in gc and to be used for subsequent text. Switching among fonts does not affect the next character origin. A text element delta specifies an additional change in the position along the x axis before the string is drawn; the delta is always added to the character origin. Each character image, as defined by the font in gc, is treated as an additional mask for a fill operation on the drawable.

All contained FONTs are always transmitted most-significant byte first.

If a `Font` error is generated for an item, the previous items may have been drawn.

For fonts defined with 2-byte matrix indexing, each STRING8 byte is interpreted as a byte2 value of a CHAR2B with a byte1 value of zero.

GC components: function, plane-mask, fill-style, font, subwindow-mode, clip-x-origin, clip-y-origin, clip-mask

GC mode-dependent components: foreground, background, tile, stipple, tile-stipple-x-origin, tile-stipple-y-origin

PolyText16

  drawable: DRAWABLE
  gc: GCONTEXT
  x, y: INT16
  items: LISTofTEXTITEM16

where:

TEXTITEM16: TEXTELT16 or FONT
  TEXTELT16: [delta: INT8
           string: STRING16]

  Errors: `Drawable`, `GContext`, `Match`, `Font`

This request is similar to `PolyText8`, except 2-byte (or 16-bit) characters are used. For fonts defined with linear indexing rather than 2-byte matrix indexing, the server will interpret each CHAR2B as a 16-bit number that has been transmitted most-significant byte first (that is, byte1 of the CHAR2B is taken as the most-significant byte).

ImageText8

drawable: DRAWABLE
gc: GCONTEXT
x, y: INT16
string: STRING8

Errors: `Drawable`, `GContext`, `Match`

The x and y coordinates are relative to the drawable's origin and specify the baseline starting position (the initial character origin). The effect is first to fill a destination rectangle with the background pixel defined in gc and then to paint the text with the foreground pixel. The upper-left corner of the filled rectangle is at:

$$[x, y - \text{font-ascent}]$$

the width is:

$$\text{overall-width}$$

and the height is:

$$\text{font-ascent} + \text{font-descent}$$

The overall-width, font-ascent, and font-descent are as they would be returned by a `QueryTextExtents` call using gc and string.

The function and fill-style defined in gc are ignored for this request. The effective function is `Copy`, and the effective fill-style `Solid`.

For fonts defined with 2-byte matrix indexing, each STRING8 byte is interpreted as a byte2 value of a CHAR2B with a byte1 value of zero.

GC components: plane-mask, foreground, background, font, subwindow-mode, clip-x-origin, clip-y-origin, clip-mask

ImageText16

drawable: DRAWABLE
gc: GCONTEXT

x, y: INT16

string: STRING16

Errors: `Drawable`, `GContext`, `Match`

This request is similar to `ImageText8`, except 2-byte (or 16-bit) characters are used. For fonts defined with linear indexing rather than 2-byte matrix indexing, the server will interpret each CHAR2B as a 16-bit number that has been transmitted most-significant byte first (that is, byte1 of the CHAR2B is taken as the most-significant byte).

CreateColormap

mid: COLORMAP

visual: VISUALID

window: WINDOW

alloc: {`None`, `All`}

Errors: `IDChoice`, `Window`, `Value`, `Match`, `Alloc`

This request creates a colormap of the specified visual type for the screen on which the window resides and associates the identifier mid with it. The visual type must be one supported by the screen (or a `Match` error results). The initial values of the colormap entries are undefined for classes `GrayScale`, `PseudoColor`, and `DirectColor`. For `StaticGray`, `StaticColor`, and `TrueColor`, the entries will have defined values, but those values are specific to the visual and are not defined by the core protocol. For `StaticGray`, `StaticColor`, and `TrueColor`, alloc must be specified as `None` (or a `Match` error results). For the other classes, if alloc is `None`, the colormap initially has no allocated entries, and clients can allocate entries.

If alloc is `All`, then the entire colormap is "allocated" writable. The initial values of all allocated entries are undefined. For `GrayScale` and `PseudoColor`, the effect is as if an `AllocColorCells` request returned all pixel values from zero to N − 1, where N is the colormap-entries value in the specified visual. For `DirectColor`, the effect is as if an `AllocColorPlanes` request returned a pixel value of zero and red-mask, green-mask, and blue-mask values containing the same bits as the corresponding masks in the specified visual. However, in all cases, none of these entries can be freed with `FreeColors`.

FreeColormap

> *cmap*: COLORMAP
>
> Errors: `Colormap`

This request deletes the association between the resource ID and the colormap and frees the colormap storage. If the colormap is an installed map for a screen, it is uninstalled (see `UninstallColormap` request). If the colormap is defined as the colormap for a window (by means of `CreateWindow` or `ChangeWindowAttributes`), the colormap for the window is changed to `None`, and a `ColormapNotify` event is generated. The protocol does not define the colors displayed for a window with a colormap of `None`.

This request has no effect on a default colormap for a screen.

CopyColormapAndFree

> *mid, src-cmap*: COLORMAP
>
> Errors: `IDChoice`, `Colormap`, `Alloc`

This request creates a colormap of the same visual type and for the same screen as src-cmap, and it associates identifier mid with it. It also moves all of the client's existing allocations from src-cmap to the new colormap with their color values intact and their read-only or writable characteristics intact, and it frees those entries in src-cmap. Color values in other entries in the new colormap are undefined. If src-cmap was created by the client with alloc `All` (see `CreateColormap` request), then the new colormap is also created with alloc `All`, all color values for all entries are copied from src-cmap, and then all entries in src-cmap are freed. If src-cmap was not created by the client with alloc `All`, then the allocations to be moved are all those pixels and planes that have been allocated by the client using either `AllocColor`, `AllocNamedColor`, `AllocColorCells`, or `AllocColorPlanes` and that have not been freed since they were allocated.

InstallColormap

> *cmap*: COLORMAP
>
> Errors: `Colormap`

This request makes this colormap an installed map for its screen. All windows associated with this colormap immediately display with true colors. As a side effect, additional colormaps might be implicitly installed or uninstalled by the server. Which other colormaps get installed or uninstalled is server-dependent except that the required list must remain installed.

If cmap is not already an installed map, a `ColormapNotify` event is generated on every window having cmap as an attribute. In addition, for every other colormap that is installed or uninstalled as a result of the request, a `ColormapNotify` event is generated on every window having that colormap as an attribute.

At any time, there is a subset of the installed maps that are viewed as an ordered list and are called the required list. The length of the required list is at most M, where M is the min-installed-maps specified for the screen in the connection setup. The required list is maintained as follows. When a colormap is an explicit argument to `InstallColormap`, it is added to the head of the list; the list is truncated at the tail, if necessary, to keep the length of the list to at most M. When a colormap is an explicit argument to `UninstallColormap` and it is in the required list, it is removed from the list. A colormap is not added to the required list when it is installed implicitly by the server, and the server cannot implicitly uninstall a colormap that is in the required list.

Initially the default colormap for a screen is installed (but is not in the required list).

UninstallColormap

cmap: COLORMAP

Errors: `Colormap`

If cmap is on the required list for its screen (see `InstallColormap` request), it is removed from the list. As a side effect, cmap might be uninstalled, and additional colormaps might be implicitly installed or uninstalled. Which colormaps get installed or uninstalled is server-dependent except that the required list must remain installed.

If cmap becomes uninstalled, a `ColormapNotify` event is generated on every window having cmap as an attribute. In addition, for every other colormap that is installed or uninstalled as a result of the request, a `ColormapNotify` event is generated on every window having that colormap as an attribute.

ListInstalledColormaps
   window: WINDOW
→
   cmaps: LISTofCOLORMAP
   Errors: `Window`

This request returns a list of the currently installed colormaps for the screen of the specified window. The order of colormaps is not significant, and there is no explicit indication of the required list (see `InstallColormap` request).

AllocColor
   cmap: COLORMAP
   red, green, blue: CARD16
→
   pixel: CARD32
   red, green, blue: CARD16
   Errors: `Colormap`, `Alloc`

This request allocates a read-only colormap entry corresponding to the closest RGB values provided by the hardware. It also returns the pixel and the RGB values actually used.

AllocNamedColor
   cmap: COLORMAP
   name: STRING8
→
   pixel: CARD32
   exact-red, exact-green, exact-blue: CARD16
   visual-red, visual-green, visual-blue: CARD16
   Errors: `Colormap`, `Name`, `Alloc`

This request looks up the named color with respect to the screen associated with the colormap. Then, it does an `AllocColor` on cmap. The name should use the ISO Latin-1 encoding, and uppercase and lowercase do not matter. The exact RGB values specify the true values for the color, and the visual values specify the values actually used in the colormap.

AllocColorCells

   cmap: COLORMAP

   colors, planes: CARD16

   contiguous: BOOL

$\rightarrow$

   pixels, masks: LISTofCARD32

   Errors: `Colormap`, `Value`, `Alloc`

The number of colors must be positive, and the number of planes must be nonnegative (or a `Value` error results). If C colors and P planes are requested, then C pixels and P masks are returned. No mask will have any bits in common with any other mask or with any of the pixels. By ORing together masks and pixels, $C*2^P$ distinct pixels can be produced; all of these are allocated writable by the request. For `GrayScale` or `PseudoColor`, each mask will have exactly one bit set to 1; for `DirectColor`, each will have exactly three bits set to 1. If contiguous is `True` and if all masks are ORed together, a single contiguous set of bits will be formed for `GrayScale` or `PseudoColor`, and three contiguous sets of bits (one within each pixel subfield) for `DirectColor`. The RGB values of the allocated entries are undefined.

AllocColorPlanes

   cmap: COLORMAP

   colors, reds, greens, blues: CARD16

   contiguous: BOOL

$\rightarrow$

   pixels: LISTofCARD32

   red-mask, green-mask, blue-mask: CARD32

   Errors: `Colormap`, `Value`, `Alloc`

The number of colors must be positive, and the reds, greens, and blues must be nonnegative (or a `Value` error results). If C colors, R reds, G greens, and B blues are requested, then C pixels are returned, and the masks have R, G, and B bits set, respectively. If contiguous is `True`, then each mask will have a contiguous set of bits. No mask will have any bits in common with any other mask or with any of the pixels. For `DirectColor`, each mask will lie within the corresponding pixel subfield. By ORing together subsets of masks with pixels, $C*2^{R+G+B}$ distinct pixels can be produced; all of these are allocated by the request. The initial RGB values of the allocated entries are undefined. In the colormap, there are only $C*2^R$ independent red entries, $C*2^G$ independent green entries, and $C*2^B$ independent blue entries. This is true even for PseudoColor. When the colormap entry for a pixel value is changed using StoreColors or StoreNamedColor, the pixel is decomposed according to the masks and the corresponding independent entries are updated.

FreeColors

    cmap: COLORMAP

    pixels: LISTofCARD32

    plane-mask: CARD32

    Errors: Colormap, Access, Value

The plane-mask should not have any bits in common with any of the pixels. The set of all pixels is produced by ORing together subsets of plane-mask with the pixels. The request frees all of these pixels that were allocated by the client (using AllocColor, AllocNamedColor, AllocColorCells, and AllocColorPlanes). Note that freeing an individual pixel obtained from AllocColorPlanes may not actually allow it to be reused until all of its related pixels are also freed.

All specified pixels that are allocated by the client in cmap are freed, even if one or more pixels produce an error. A Value error is generated if a specified pixel is not a valid index into cmap, and an Access error is generated if a specified pixel is not allocated by the client (that is, is unallocated or is only allocated by another client). If more than one pixel is in error, it is arbitrary as to which pixel is reported.

StoreColors

    cmap: COLORMAP

    items: LISTofCOLORITEM

where:

COLORITEM: [pixel: CARD32

               do-red, do-green, do-blue: BOOL

               red, green, blue: CARD16]

Errors: `Colormap`, `Access`, `Value`

This request changes the colormap entries of the specified pixels. The do-red, do-green, and do-blue fields indicate which components should actually be changed. If the colormap is an installed map for its screen, the changes are visible immediately.

All specified pixels that are allocated writable in cmap (by any client) are changed, even if one or more pixels produce an error. A `Value` error is generated if a specified pixel is not a valid index into cmap, and an `Access` error is generated if a specified pixel is unallocated or is allocated read-only. If more than one pixel is in error, it is arbitrary as to which pixel is reported.

StoreNamedColor

    cmap: COLORMAP

    pixel: CARD32

    name: STRING8

    do-red, do-green, do-blue: BOOL

    Errors: `Colormap`, `Name`, `Access`, `Value`

This request looks up the named color with respect to the screen associated with cmap and then does a `StoreColors` in cmap. The name should use the ISO Latin-1 encoding, and uppercase and lowercase do not matter. The `Access` and `Value` errors are the same as in `StoreColors`.

QueryColors

    cmap: COLORMAP

    pixels: LISTofCARD32

$\rightarrow$

    colors: LISTofRGB

where:

  RGB: [red, green, blue: CARD16]

  Errors: `Colormap`, `Value`

This request returns the color values stored in cmap for the specified pixels. The values returned for an unallocated entry are undefined. A `Value` error is generated if a pixel is not a valid index into cmap. If more than one pixel is in error, it is arbitrary as to which pixel is reported.

LookupColor

 cmap: COLORMAP

 name: STRING8

→

 exact-red, exact-green, exact-blue: CARD16

 visual-red, visual-green, visual-blue: CARD16

 Errors: `Colormap`, `Name`

This request looks up the string name of a color with respect to the screen associated with cmap and returns both the exact color values and the closest values provided by the hardware with respect to the visual type of cmap. The name should use the ISO Latin-1 encoding, and uppercase and lowercase do not matter.

CreateCursor

 cid: CURSOR

 source: PIXMAP

 mask: PIXMAP or `None`

 fore-red, fore-green, fore-blue: CARD16

 back-red, back-green, back-blue: CARD16

 x, y: CARD16

 Errors: `IDChoice`, `Pixmap`, `Match`, `Alloc`

This request creates a cursor and associates identifier cid with it. The foreground and background RGB values must be specified, even if the server only has a `StaticGray` or `GrayScale` screen. The foreground is used for the bits set to 1 in the source, and the background is used for the bits set to 0. Both source and mask (if specified) must have depth one (or a `Match` error results), but they can have any root. The mask pixmap defines the shape of the cursor. That is, the bits set to 1 in the mask define which source pixels will be displayed, and where the mask has bits set to 0, the corresponding bits of the source pixmap are ignored. If no mask is given, all pixels of the source are displayed. The mask, if present, must be the same size as the source (or a `Match` error results). The x and y coordinates define the hotspot relative to the source's origin and must be a point within the source (or a `Match` error results).

The components of the cursor may be transformed arbitrarily to meet display limitations.

The pixmaps can be freed immediately if no further explicit references to them are to be made.

Subsequent drawing in the source or mask pixmap has an undefined effect on the cursor. The server might or might not make a copy of the pixmap.

CreateGlyphCursor

    cid: CURSOR

    source-font: FONT

    mask-font: FONT or `None`

    source-char, mask-char: CARD16

    fore-red, fore-green, fore-blue: CARD16

    back-red, back-green, back-blue: CARD16

    Errors: `IDChoice`, `Font`, `Value`, `Alloc`

This request is similar to `CreateCursor`, except the source and mask bitmaps are obtained from the specified font glyphs. The source-char must be a defined glyph in source-font, and if mask-font is given, mask-char must be a defined glyph in mask-font (or a `Value` error results). The mask font and character are optional. The origins of the source and mask (if it is defined) glyphs are positioned coincidently and define the hotspot. The source and mask need not have the same bounding box metrics, and there is no restriction on the placement of the hotspot relative to the bounding boxes. If no mask is given, all pixels of the source are displayed. Note that source-char and mask-char are CARD16, not CHAR2B. For 2-byte matrix fonts, the 16-bit value should be formed with byte1 in the most-significant byte and byte2 in the least-significant byte.

The components of the cursor may be transformed arbitrarily to meet display limitations.

The fonts can be freed immediately if no further explicit references to them are to be made.

FreeCursor

cursor: CURSOR

Errors: `Cursor`

This request deletes the association between the resource ID and the cursor. The cursor storage will be freed when no other resource references it.

RecolorCursor

cursor: CURSOR

fore-red, fore-green, fore-blue: CARD16

back-red, back-green, back-blue: CARD16

Errors: `Cursor`

This request changes the color of a cursor. If the cursor is being displayed on a screen, the change is visible immediately.

QueryBestSize

class: {`Cursor`, `Tile`, `Stipple`}

drawable: DRAWABLE

width, height: CARD16

→

width, height: CARD16

Errors: `Drawable`, `Value`, `Match`

This request returns the best size that is closest to the argument size. For `Cursor`, this is the largest size that can be fully displayed. For `Tile`, this is the size that can be tiled fastest. For `Stipple`, this is the size that can be stippled fastest.

For `Cursor`, the drawable indicates the desired screen. For `Tile` and `Stipple`, the drawable indicates the screen and also possibly the window class and depth. An `InputOnly` window cannot be used as the drawable for `Tile` or `Stipple` (or a `Match` error results).

QueryExtension

name: STRING8

→

present: BOOL

major-opcode: CARD8

first-event: CARD8

first-error: CARD8

This request determines if the named extension is present. If so, the major opcode for the extension is returned, if it has one. Otherwise, zero is returned. Any minor opcode and the request formats are specific to the extension. If the extension involves additional event types, the base event type code is returned. Otherwise, zero is returned. The format of the events is specific to the extension. If the extension involves additional error codes, the base error code is returned. Otherwise, zero is returned. The format of additional data in the errors is specific to the extension.

The extension name should use the ISO Latin-1 encoding, and uppercase and lowercase matter.

ListExtensions
→

names: LISTofSTRING8

This request returns a list of all extensions supported by the server.

SetModifierMapping
  keycodes-per-modifier: CARD8
  keycodes: LISTofKEYCODE
→

status: {Success, Busy, Failed}

Errors: Value, Alloc

This request specifies the keycodes (if any) of the keys to be used as modifiers. The number of keycodes in the list must be 8*keycodes-per-modifier (or a Length error results). The keycodes are divided into eight sets, with each set containing keycodes-per-modifier elements. The sets are assigned to the modifiers Shift, Lock, Control, Mod1, Mod2, Mod3, Mod4, and Mod5, in order. Only nonzero keycode values are used within each set; zero values are ignored. All of the nonzero keycodes must be in the range specified by min-keycode and max-keycode in the connection setup (or a Value error results). The order of keycodes within a set does not matter. If no nonzero values are specified in a set, the use of the corresponding modifier is disabled, and the modifier bit will always be zero. Otherwise, the modifier bit will be one whenever at least one of the keys in the corresponding set is in the down position.

A server can impose restrictions on how modifiers can be changed (for example, if certain keys do not generate up transitions in hardware, if auto-repeat cannot be disabled on certain keys, or if multiple keys per modifier are not supported). The status reply is `Failed` if some such restriction is violated, and none of the modifiers is changed.

If the new nonzero keycodes specified for a modifier differ from those currently defined and any (current or new) keys for that modifier are logically in the down state, then the status reply is `Busy`, and none of the modifiers is changed.

This request generates a `MappingNotify` event on a `Success` status.

GetModifierMapping
$\rightarrow$

> keycodes-per-modifier: CARD8
> keycodes: LISTofKEYCODE

This request returns the keycodes of the keys being used as modifiers. The number of keycodes in the list is 8*keycodes-per-modifier. The keycodes are divided into eight sets, with each set containing keycodes-per-modifier elements. The sets are assigned to the modifiers `Shift`, `Lock`, `Control`, `Mod1`, `Mod2`, `Mod3`, `Mod4`, and `Mod5`, in order. The keycodes-per-modifier value is chosen arbitrarily by the server; zeroes are used to fill in unused elements within each set. If only zero values are given in a set, the use of the corresponding modifier has been disabled. The order of keycodes within each set is chosen arbitrarily by the server.

ChangeKeyboardMapping

> *first-keycode*: KEYCODE
> *keysyms-per-keycode*: CARD8
> *keysyms*: LISTofKEYSYM
> Errors: `Value`, `Alloc`

This request defines the symbols for the specified number of keycodes, starting with the specified keycode. The symbols for keycodes outside this range remained unchanged. The number of elements in the keysyms list must be a multiple of keysyms-per-keycode (or a `Length` error results). The first-keycode must be greater than or equal to min-keycode as returned in the connection setup (or a `Value` error results) and:

$$\text{first-keycode} + (\text{keysyms-length} / \text{keysyms-per-keycode}) - 1$$

must be less than or equal to max-keycode as returned in the connection setup (or else a `Value` error results). KEYSYM number N (counting from zero) for keycode K has an index (counting from zero) of:

$$(K - \text{first-keycode}) * \text{keysyms-per-keycode} + N$$

in keysyms. The keysyms-per-keycode can be chosen arbitrarily by the client to be large enough to hold all desired symbols. A special KEYSYM value of `NoSymbol` should be used to fill in unused elements for individual keycodes. It is legal for `NoSymbol` to appear in nontrailing positions of the effective list for a keycode.

This request generates a `MappingNotify` event.

There is no requirement that the server interpret this mapping; it is merely stored for reading and writing by clients (see section 5).

GetKeyboardMapping
   first-keycode: KEYCODE
   count: CARD8
$\rightarrow$

   keysyms-per-keycode: CARD8
   keysyms: LISTofKEYSYM

   Errors: `Value`

This request returns the symbols for the specified number of keycodes, starting with the specified keycode. The first-keycode must be greater than or equal to min-keycode as returned in the connection setup (or a `Value` error results), and:

$$\text{first-keycode} + \text{count} - 1$$

must be less than or equal to max-keycode as returned in the connection setup (or a `Value` error results). The number of elements in the keysyms list is:

$$\text{count} * \text{keysyms-per-keycode}$$

and KEYSYM number N (counting from zero) for keycode K has an index (counting from zero) of:

$$(K - \text{first-keycode}) * \text{keysyms-per-keycode} + N$$

in keysyms. The keysyms-per-keycode value is chosen arbitrarily by the server to be large enough to report all requested symbols. A special KEYSYM value of `NoSymbol` is used to fill in unused elements for individual keycodes.

ChangeKeyboardControl

> *value-mask*: BITMASK
>
> *value-list*: LISTofVALUE
>
> Errors: `Match`, `Value`

This request controls various aspects of the keyboard. The value-mask and value-list specify which controls are to be changed. The possible values are:

Control	Type
key-click-percent	INT8
bell-percent	INT8
bell-pitch	INT16
bell-duration	INT16
led	CARD8
led-mode	{On, Off}
key	KEYCODE
auto-repeat-mode	{On, Off, Default}

The key-click-percent sets the volume for key clicks between 0 (off) and 100 (loud) inclusive, if possible. Setting to -1 restores the default. Other negative values generate a `Value` error.

The bell-percent sets the base volume for the bell between 0 (off) and 100 (loud) inclusive, if possible. Setting to -1 restores the default. Other negative values generate a `Value` error.

The bell-pitch sets the pitch (specified in Hz) of the bell, if possible. Setting to -1 restores the default. Other negative values generate a `Value` error.

The bell-duration sets the duration of the bell (specified in milliseconds), if possible. Setting to -1 restores the default. Other negative values generate a Value error.

If both led-mode and led are specified, then the state of that LED is changed, if possible. If only led-mode is specified, then the state of all LEDs are changed, if possible. At most 32 LEDs, numbered from one, are supported. No standard interpretation of LEDs is defined. It is a Match error if an led is specified without an led-mode.

If both auto-repeat-mode and key are specified, then the auto-repeat mode of that key is changed, if possible. If only auto-repeat-mode is specified, then the global auto-repeat mode for the entire keyboard is changed, if possible, without affecting the per-key settings. It is a Match error if a key is specified without an auto-repeat-mode. Each key has an individual mode of whether or not it should auto-repeat and a default setting for that mode. In addition, there is a global mode of whether auto-repeat should be enabled or not and a default setting for that mode. When the global mode is On, keys should obey their individual auto-repeat modes. When the global mode is Off, no keys should auto-repeat. An auto-repeating key generates alternating KeyPress and KeyRelease events. When a key is used as a modifier, it is desirable for the key not to auto-repeat, regardless of the auto-repeat setting for that key.

A bell generator connected with the console but not directly on the keyboard is treated as if it were part of the keyboard.

The order in which controls are verified and altered is server-dependent. If an error is generated, a subset of the controls may have been altered.

GetKeyboardControl

$\rightarrow$

    key-click-percent: CARD8
    bell-percent: CARD8
    bell-pitch: CARD16
    bell-duration: CARD16
    led-mask: CARD32
    global-auto-repeat: {On, Off}
    auto-repeats: LISTofCARD8

This request returns the current control values for the keyboard. For the LEDs, the least-significant bit of led-mask corresponds to LED one, and each one bit in led-mask indicates an LED that is lit. The auto-repeats is a bit vector; each one bit indicates that auto-repeat is enabled for the corresponding key. The vector is represented as 32 bytes. Byte N (from 0) contains the bits for keys 8N to 8N + 7, with the least-significant bit in the byte representing key 8N.

Bell

  percent: INT8

  Errors: `Value`

This request rings the bell on the keyboard at a volume relative to the base volume for the keyboard, if possible. Percent can range from − 100 to 100 inclusive (or a `Value` error results). The volume at which the bell is rung when percent is nonnegative is:

$$\text{base} - [(\text{base} * \text{percent}) / 100] + \text{percent}$$

When percent is negative, it is:

$$\text{base} + [(\text{base} * \text{percent}) / 100]$$

SetPointerMapping

  map: LISTofCARD8

→

  status: {`Success`, `Busy`}

  Errors: `Value`

This request sets the mapping of the pointer. Elements of the list are indexed starting from one. The length of the list must be the same as `GetPointerMapping` would return (or a `Value` error results). The index is a core button number, and the element of the list defines the effective number.

A zero element disables a button. Elements are not restricted in value by the number of physical buttons, but no two elements can have the same nonzero value (or a `Value` error results).

If any of the buttons to be altered are logically in the down state, the status reply is `Busy`, and the mapping is not changed.

This request generates a `MappingNotify` event on a `Success` status.

GetPointerMapping

$\rightarrow$

  map: LISTofCARD8

This request returns the current mapping of the pointer. Elements of the list are indexed starting from one. The length of the list indicates the number of physical buttons.

  The nominal mapping for a pointer is the identity mapping: map [i]=i.

ChangePointerControl

  do-acceleration, do-threshold: BOOL
  acceleration-numerator, acceleration-denominator: INT16
  threshold: INT16

  Errors: `Value`

This request defines how the pointer moves. The acceleration is a multiplier for movement expressed as a fraction. For example, specifying 3/1 means the pointer moves three times as fast as normal. The fraction can be rounded arbitrarily by the server. Acceleration only takes effect if the pointer moves more than threshold number of pixels at once and only applies to the amount beyond the threshold. Setting a value to -1 restores the default. Other negative values generate a `Value` error, as does a zero value for acceleration-denominator.

GetPointerControl

$\rightarrow$

  acceleration-numerator, acceleration-denominator: CARD16
  threshold: CARD16

This request returns the current acceleration and threshold for the pointer.

SetScreenSaver

  timeout, interval: INT16
  prefer-blanking: {`Yes`, `No`, `Default`}
  allow-exposures: {`Yes`, `No`, `Default`}

  Errors: `Value`

The timeout and interval are specified in seconds; setting a value to -1 restores the default. Other negative values generate a Value error. If the timeout value is zero, screen-saver is disabled. If the timeout value is nonzero, screen-saver is enabled. Once screen-saver is enabled, if no input from the keyboard or pointer is generated for timeout seconds, screen-saver is activated. For each screen, if blanking is preferred and the hardware supports video blanking, the screen will simply go blank. Otherwise, if either exposures are allowed or the screen can be regenerated without sending exposure events to clients, the screen is changed in a server-dependent fashion to avoid phosphor burn. Otherwise, the state of the screens does not change, and screen-saver is not activated. At the next keyboard or pointer input or at the next ForceScreenSaver with mode Reset, screen-saver is deactivated, and all screen states are restored.

If the server-dependent screen-saver method is amenable to periodic change, interval serves as a hint about how long the change period should be, with zero hinting that no periodic change should be made. Examples of ways to change the screen include scrambling the color map periodically, moving an icon image about the screen periodically, or tiling the screen with the root window background tile, randomly reorigined periodically.

GetScreenSaver

$\rightarrow$

timeout, interval: CARD16
prefer-blanking: {Yes, No}
allow-exposures: {Yes, No}

This request returns the current screen-saver control values.

ForceScreenSaver

mode: {Activate, Reset}
Errors: Value

If the mode is Activate and screen-saver is currently deactivated, then screen-saver is activated (even if screen-saver has been disabled with a timeout value of zero). If the mode is Reset and screen-saver is currently enabled, then screen-saver is deactivated (if it was activated), and the activation timer is reset to its initial state as if device input had just been received.

ChangeHosts
mode: {Insert, Delete}
host: HOST
Errors: Access, Value

This request adds or removes the specified host from the access control list. When the access control mechanism is enabled and a host attempts to establish a connection to the server, the host must be in this list, or the server will refuse the connection.

The client must reside on the same host as the server and/or have been granted permission by a server-dependent method to execute this request (or an Access error results).

An initial access control list can usually be specified, typically by naming a file that the server reads at startup and reset.

The following address families are defined. A server is not required to support these families and may support families not listed here. Use of an unsupported family, an improper address format, or an improper address length within a supported family results in a Value error.

For the Internet family, the address must be four bytes long. The address bytes are in standard IP order; the server performs no automatic swapping on the address bytes. For a Class A address, the network number is the first byte in the address, and the host number is the remaining three bytes, most-significant byte first. For a Class B address, the network number is the first two bytes and the host number is the last two bytes, each most-significant byte first. For a Class C address, the network number is the first three bytes, most-significant byte first, and the last byte is the host number.

For the DECnet family, the server performs no automatic swapping on the address bytes. A Phase IV address is two bytes long: the first byte contains the least-significant eight bits of the node number, and the second byte contains the most-significant two bits of the node number in the least-significant two bits of the byte and the area in the most-significant six bits of the byte.

For the Chaos family, the address must be two bytes long. The host number is always the first byte in the address, and the subnet number is always the second byte. The server performs no automatic swapping on the address bytes.

ListHosts

$\rightarrow$

   mode: {Enabled, Disabled}
   hosts: LISTofHOST

This request returns the hosts on the access control list and whether use of the list at connection setup is currently enabled or disabled.

   Each HOST is padded to a multiple of four bytes.

SetAccessControl

   mode: {Enable, Disable}
   Errors: Value, Access

This request enables or disables the use of the access control list at connection setups.

   The client must reside on the same host as the server and/or have been granted permission by a server-dependent method to execute this request (or an Access error results).

SetCloseDownMode

   mode: {Destroy, RetainPermanent, RetainTemporary}
   Errors: Value

This request defines what will happen to the client's resources at connection close. A connection starts in Destroy mode. The meaning of the close-down mode is described in section 10.

KillClient

   resource: CARD32 or AllTemporary
   Errors: Value

If a valid resource is specified, KillClient forces a close-down of the client that created the resource. If the client has already terminated in either RetainPermanent or RetainTemporary mode, all of the client's resources are destroyed (see section 10). If AllTemporary is specified, then the resources of all clients that have terminated in RetainTemporary are destroyed.

NoOperation

This request has no arguments and no results, but the request length field can be nonzero, which allows the request to be any multiple of four bytes in length. The bytes contained in the request are uninterpreted by the server.

This request can be used in its minimum four byte form as padding where necessary by client libraries that find it convenient to force requests to begin on 64-bit boundaries.

SECTION 10. CONNECTION CLOSE

At connection close, all event selections made by the client are discarded. If the client has the pointer actively grabbed, an `UngrabPointer` is performed. If the client has the keyboard actively grabbed, an `UngrabKeyboard` is performed. All passive grabs by the client are released. If the client has the server grabbed, an `UngrabServer` is performed. All selections (see `SetSelectionOwner` request) owned by the client are disowned. If close-down mode (see `SetCloseDownMode` request) is `RetainPermanent` or `RetainTemporary`, then all resources (including colormap entries) allocated by the client are marked as permanent or temporary, respectively (but this does not prevent other clients from explicitly destroying them). If the mode is `Destroy`, all of the client's resources are destroyed.

When a client's resources are destroyed, for each window in the client's save-set, if the window is an inferior of a window created by the client, the save-set window is reparented to the closest ancestor such that the save-set window is not an inferior of a window created by the client. If the save-set window is unmapped, a `MapWindow` request is performed on it (even if it was not an inferior of a window created by the client). The reparenting leaves unchanged the absolute coordinates (with respect to the root window) of the upper-left outer corner of the save-set window. After save-set processing, all windows created by the client are destroyed. For each nonwindow resource created by the client, the appropriate `Free` request is performed. All colors and colormap entries allocated by the client are freed.

A server goes through a cycle of having no connections and having some connections. At every transition to the state of having no connections as a result of a connection closing with a `Destroy` close-down mode, the server resets its state as if it had just been started. This starts by destroying all lingering resources from clients that have terminated in `RetainPermanent` or `RetainTemporary` mode. It additionally includes deleting all but the predefined atom identifiers, deleting all properties on all root windows, resetting all device maps and attributes (key click, bell volume, acceleration), resetting the access control list, restoring the standard root tiles and cursors, restoring the default font path, and restoring the input focus to state `PointerRoot`.

Note that closing a connection with a close-down mode of `RetainPermanent` or `RetainTemporary` will not cause the server to reset.

SECTION 11. EVENTS

When a button press is processed with the pointer in some window W and no active pointer grab is in progress, the ancestors of W are searched from the root down, looking for a passive grab to activate. If no matching passive grab on the button exists, then an active grab is started automatically for the client receiving the event, and the last-pointer-grab time is set to the current server time. The effect is essentially equivalent to a `GrabButton` with arguments:

Argument	Value
event-window	Event window
event-mask	Client's selected pointer events on the event window
pointer-mode and keyboard-mode	`Asynchronous`
owner-events	`True` if the client has `OwnerGrabButton` selected on the event window, otherwise `False`
confine-to	`None`
cursor	`None`

The grab is terminated automatically when the logical state of the pointer has all buttons released. `UngrabPointer` and `ChangeActiveGrab` can both be used to modify the active grab.

KeyPress
KeyRelease
ButtonPress
ButtonRelease
MotionNotify

> *root, event*: WINDOW
> *child*: WINDOW or None
> *same-screen*: BOOL
> *root-x, root-y, event-x, event-y*: INT16
> *detail*: <see below>
> *state*: SETofKEYBUTMASK
> *time*: TIMESTAMP

These events are generated either when a key or button logically changes
state or when the pointer logically moves. The generation of these logical
changes may lag the physical changes if device event processing is frozen.
Note that KeyPress and KeyRelease are generated for all keys, even
those mapped to modifier bits. The source of the event is the window the
pointer is in. The window the event is reported with respect to is called the
event window. The event window is found by starting with the source window and looking up the hierarchy for the first window on which any client
has selected interest in the event (provided no intervening window prohibits
event generation by including the event type in its do-not-propagate-mask).
The actual window used for reporting can be modified by active grabs and,
in the case of keyboard events, can be modified by the focus window.

The root is the root window of the source window, and root-x and root-y
are the pointer coordinates relative to root's origin at the time of the event.
Event is the event window. If the event window is on the same screen as root,
then event-x and event-y are the pointer coordinates relative to the event
window's origin. Otherwise, event-x and event-y are zero. If the source window is an inferior of the event window, then child is set to the child of the
event window that is an ancestor of (or is) the source window. Otherwise, it
is set to None. The state component gives the logical state of the buttons and
modifier keys just before the event. The detail component type varies with
the event type:

Event	Component
KeyPress, KeyRelease	KEYCODE
ButtonPress, ButtonRelease	BUTTON
MotionNotify	{Normal, Hint}

MotionNotify events are only generated when the motion begins and ends in the window. The granularity of motion events is not guaranteed, but a client selecting for motion events is guaranteed to get at least one event when the pointer moves and comes to rest. Selecting PointerMotion receives events independent of the state of the pointer buttons. By selecting some subset of Button[1-5]Motion instead, MotionNotify events will only be received when one or more of the specified buttons are pressed. By selecting ButtonMotion, MotionNotify events will be received only when at least one button is pressed. The events are always of type MotionNotify, independent of the selection. If PointerMotionHint is selected, the server is free to send only one MotionNotify event (with detail Hint) to the client for the event window until either the key or button state changes, the pointer leaves the event window, or the client issues a QueryPointer or GetMotionEvents request.

EnterNotify
LeaveNotify
    root, event: WINDOW
    child: WINDOW or None
    same-screen: BOOL
    root-x, root-y, event-x, event-y: INT16
    mode: {Normal, Grab, Ungrab}
    detail: {Ancestor, Virtual, Inferior, Nonlinear,
        NonlinearVirtual}
    focus: BOOL
    state: SETofKEYBUTMASK
    time: TIMESTAMP

If pointer motion or window hierarchy change causes the pointer to be in a different window than before, EnterNotify and LeaveNotify events are generated instead of a MotionNotify event. Only clients selecting EnterWindow on a window receive EnterNotify events, and only clients selecting `LeaveNotify` receive `LeaveNotify` events. The pointer position reported in the event is always the final position, not the initial position of the pointer. The root is the root window for this position, and root-x and root-y are the pointer coordinates relative to root's origin at the time of the event. Event is the event window. If the event window is on the same screen as root, then event-x and event-y are the pointer coordinates relative to the event window's origin. Otherwise, event-x and event-y are zero. In a `LeaveNotify` event, if a child of the event window contains the initial position of the pointer, then the child component is set to that child. Otherwise, it is `None`. For an `EnterNotify` event, if a child of the event window contains the final pointer position, then the child component is set to that child. Otherwise, it is `None`. If the event window is the focus window or an inferior of the focus window, then focus is `True`. Otherwise, focus is `False`.

Normal pointer motion events have mode `Normal`. Pseudo-motion events when a grab activates have mode `Grab`, and pseudo-motion events when a grab deactivates have mode `Ungrab`.

All `EnterNotify` and `LeaveNotify` events caused by a hierarchy change are generated after any hierarchy event caused by that change (that is, `UnmapNotify`, `MapNotify`, `ConfigureNotify`, `GravityNotify`, `CirculateNotify`), but the ordering of `EnterNotify` and `Leave-Notify` events with respect to `FocusOut`, `VisibilityNotify`, and `Expose` events is not constrained.

Normal events are generated as follows:

When the pointer moves from window A to window B and A is an inferior of B:

- `LeaveNotify` with detail `Ancestor` is generated on A.
- `LeaveNotify` with detail `Virtual` is generated on each window between A and B exclusive (in that order).
- `EnterNotify` with detail `Inferior` is generated on B.

When the pointer moves from window A to window B and B is an inferior of A:

- `LeaveNotify` with detail `Inferior` is generated on A.
- `EnterNotify` with detail `Virtual` is generated on each window between A and B exclusive (in that order).
- `EnterNotify` with detail `Ancestor` is generated on B.

When the pointer moves from window A to window B and window C is their least common ancestor:

- LeaveNotify with detail Nonlinear is generated on A.
- LeaveNotify with detail NonlinearVirtual is generated on each window between A and C exclusive (in that order).
- EnterNotify with detail NonlinearVirtual is generated on each window between C and B exclusive (in that order).
- EnterNotify with detail Nonlinear is generated on B.

When the pointer moves from window A to window B on different screens:

- LeaveNotify with detail Nonlinear is generated on A.
- If A is not a root window, LeaveNotify with detail NonlinearVirtual is generated on each window above A up to and including its root (in order).
- If B is not a root window, EnterNotify with detail NonlinearVirtual is generated on each window from B's root down to but not including B (in order).
- EnterNotify with detail Nonlinear is generated on B.

When a pointer grab activates (but after any initial warp into a confine-to window and before generating any actual ButtonPress event that activates the grab), G is the grab-window for the grab, and P is the window the pointer is in:

- EnterNotify and LeaveNotify events with mode Grab are generated (as for Normal above) as if the pointer were to suddenly warp from its current position in P to some position in G. However, the pointer does not warp, and the pointer position is used as both the initial and final positions for the events.

When a pointer grab deactivates (but after generating any actual ButtonRelease event that deactivates the grab), G is the grab-window for the grab, and P is the window the pointer is in:

- EnterNotify and LeaveNotify events with mode Ungrab are generated (as for Normal above) as if the pointer were to suddenly warp from some position in G to its current position in P. However, the pointer does not warp, and the current pointer position is used as both the initial and final positions for the events.

FocusIn

FocusOut

> *event*: WINDOW
>
> *mode*: {Normal, WhileGrabbed, Grab, Ungrab}
>
> *detail*: {Ancestor, Virtual, Inferior, Nonlinear,
>   NonlinearVirtual, Pointer, PointerRoot, None}

These events are generated when the input focus changes and are reported to clients selecting FocusChange on the window. Events generated by SetInputFocus when the keyboard is not grabbed have mode Normal. Events generated by SetInputFocus when the keyboard is grabbed have mode WhileGrabbed. Events generated when a keyboard grab activates have mode Grab, and events generated when a keyboard grab deactivates have mode Ungrab.

All FocusOut events caused by a window unmap are generated after any UnmapNotify event, but the ordering of FocusOut with respect to generated EnterNotify, LeaveNotify, VisibilityNotify, and Expose events is not constrained.

Normal and WhileGrabbed events are generated as follows:

When the focus moves from window A to window B, A is an inferior of B, and the pointer is in window P:

- FocusOut with detail Ancestor is generated on A.
- FocusOut with detail Virtual is generated on each window between A and B exclusive (in order).
- FocusIn with detail Inferior is generated on B.
- If P is an inferior of B but P is not A or an inferior of A or an ancestor of A, FocusIn with detail Pointer is generated on each window below B down to and including P (in order).

When the focus moves from window A to window B, B is an inferior of A, and the pointer is in window P:

- If P is an inferior of A but P is not an inferior of B or an ancestor of B, FocusOut with detail Pointer is generated on each window from P up to but not including A (in order).
- FocusOut with detail Inferior is generated on A.

- FocusIn with detail `Virtual` is generated on each window between A and B exclusive (in order).
- FocusIn with detail `Ancestor` is generated on B.

When the focus moves from window A to window B, window C is their least common ancestor, and the pointer is in window P:

- If P is an inferior of A, FocusOut with detail `Pointer` is generated on each window from P up to but not including A (in order).
- FocusOut with detail `Nonlinear` is generated on A.
- FocusOut with detail `NonlinearVirtual` is generated on each window between A and C exclusive (in order).
- FocusIn with detail `NonlinearVirtual` is generated on each window between C and B exclusive (in order).
- FocusIn with detail `Nonlinear` is generated on B.
- If P is an inferior of B, FocusIn with detail `Pointer` is generated on each window below B down to and including P (in order).

When the focus moves from window A to window B on different screens and the pointer is in window P:

- If P is an inferior of A, FocusOut with detail `Pointer` is generated on each window from P up to but not including A (in order).
- FocusOut with detail `Nonlinear` is generated on A.
- If A is not a root window, FocusOut with detail `NonlinearVirtual` is generated on each window above A up to and including its root (in order).
- If B is not a root window, FocusIn with detail `NonlinearVirtual` is generated on each window from B's root down to but not including B (in order).
- FocusIn with detail `Nonlinear` is generated on B.
- If P is an inferior of B, FocusIn with detail `Pointer` is generated on each window below B down to and including P (in order).

When the focus moves from window A to `PointerRoot` (or `None`) and the pointer is in window P:

- If P is an inferior of A, FocusOut with detail `Pointer` is generated on each window from P up to but not including A (in order).
- FocusOut with detail `Nonlinear` is generated on A.

- If A is not a root window, FocusOut with detail NonlinearVirtual is generated on each window above A up to and including its root (in order).
- FocusIn with detail PointerRoot (or None) is generated on all root windows.
- If the new focus is PointerRoot, FocusIn with detail Pointer is generated on each window from P's root down to and including P (in order).

When the focus moves from PointerRoot (or None) to window A and the pointer is in window P:

- If the old focus is PointerRoot, FocusOut with detail Pointer is generated on each window from P up to and including P's root (in order).
- FocusOut with detail PointerRoot (or None) is generated on all root windows.
- If A is not a root window, FocusIn with detail NonlinearVirtual is generated on each window from A's root down to but not including A (in order).
- FocusIn with detail Nonlinear is generated on A.
- If P is an inferior of A, FocusIn with detail Pointer is generated on each window below A down to and including P (in order).

When the focus moves from PointerRoot to None (or vice versa) and the pointer is in window P:

- If the old focus is PointerRoot, FocusOut with detail Pointer is generated on each window from P up to and including P's root (in order).
- FocusOut with detail PointerRoot (or None) is generated on all root windows.
- FocusIn with detail None (or PointerRoot) is generated on all root windows.
- If the new focus is PointerRoot, FocusIn with detail Pointer is generated on each window from P's root down to and including P (in order).

When a keyboard grab activates (but before generating any actual KeyPress event that activates the grab), G is the grab-window for the grab, and F is the current focus:

- FocusIn and FocusOut events with mode Grab are generated (as for Normal above) as if the focus were to change from F to G.

When a keyboard grab deactivates (but after generating any actual KeyRelease event that deactivates the grab), G is the grab-window for the grab, and F is the current focus:

- FocusIn and FocusOut events with mode Ungrab are generated (as for Normal above) as if the focus were to change from G to F.

KeymapNotify

> *keys*: LISTofCARD8

The value is a bit vector as described in QueryKeymap. This event is reported to clients selecting KeymapState on a window and is generated immediately after every EnterNotify and FocusIn.

Expose

> *window*: WINDOW
> *x, y, width, height*: CARD16
> *count*: CARD16

This event is reported to clients selecting Exposure on the window. It is generated when no valid contents are available for regions of a window, and either the regions are visible, the regions are viewable and the server is (perhaps newly) maintaining backing store on the window, or the window is not viewable but the server is (perhaps newly) honoring window's backing-store attribute of Always or WhenMapped. The regions are decomposed into an arbitrary set of rectangles, and an Expose event is generated for each rectangle.

For a given action causing exposure events, the set of events for a given window are guaranteed to be reported contiguously. If count is zero, then no more Expose events for this window follow. If count is nonzero, then at least that many more Expose events for this window follow (and possibly more).

The x and y coordinates are relative to window's origin and specify the upper-left corner of a rectangle. The width and height specify the extent of the rectangle.

Expose events are never generated on InputOnly windows.

All Expose events caused by a hierarchy change are generated after any hierarchy event caused by that change (for example, UnmapNotify, MapNotify, ConfigureNotify, GravityNotify, CirculateNotify). All Expose events on a given window are generated after any VisibilityNotify event on that window, but it is not required that all Expose events on all windows be generated after all Visibility events on all windows. The ordering of Expose events with respect to FocusOut, EnterNotify, and LeaveNotify events is not constrained.

GraphicsExposure

drawable: DRAWABLE

x, y, width, height: CARD16

count: CARD16

major-opcode: CARD8

minor-opcode: CARD16

This event is reported to clients selecting graphics-exposures in a graphics context and is generated when a destination region could not be computed due to an obscured or out-of-bounds source region. All of the regions exposed by a given graphics request are guaranteed to be reported contiguously. If count is zero then no more `GraphicsExposure` events for this window follow. If count is nonzero, then at least that many more `GraphicsExposure` events for this window follow (and possibly more).

The x and y coordinates are relative to drawable's origin and specify the upper-left corner of a rectangle. The width and height specify the extent of the rectangle.

The major and minor opcodes identify the graphics request used. For the core protocol, major-opcode is always `CopyArea` or `CopyPlane`, and minor-opcode is always zero.

NoExposure

drawable: DRAWABLE

major-opcode: CARD8

minor-opcode: CARD16

This event is reported to clients selecting graphics-exposures in a graphics context and is generated when a graphics request that might produce `GraphicsExposure` events does not produce any. The drawable specifies the destination used for the graphics request.

The major and minor opcodes identify the graphics request used. For the core protocol, major-opcode is always `CopyArea` or `CopyPlane`, and the minor-opcode is always zero.

VisibilityNotify

window: WINDOW

state: {`Unobscured`, `PartiallyObscured`, `FullyObscured`}

This event is reported to clients selecting `VisibilityChange` on the window. In the following, the state of the window is calculated ignoring all of the window's subwindows. When a window changes state from partially or fully obscured or not viewable to viewable and completely unobscured, an event with `Unobscured` is generated. When a window changes state from viewable and completely unobscured or not viewable, to viewable and partially obscured, an event with `PartiallyObscured` is generated. When a window changes state from viewable and completely unobscured, from viewable and partially obscured, or from not viewable to viewable and fully obscured, an event with `FullyObscured` is generated.

`VisibilityNotify` events are never generated on `InputOnly` windows.

All `VisibilityNotify` events caused by a hierarchy change are generated after any hierarchy event caused by that change (for example, `UnmapNotify`, `MapNotify`, `ConfigureNotify`, `GravityNotify`, `CirculateNotify`). Any `VisibilityNotify` event on a given window is generated before any `Expose` events on that window, but it is not required that all `VisibilityNotify` events on all windows be generated before all `Expose` events on all windows. The ordering of `VisibilityNotify` events with respect to `FocusOut`, `EnterNotify`, and `LeaveNotify` events is not constrained.

CreateNotify

parent, window: WINDOW
x, y: INT16
width, height, border-width: CARD16
override-redirect: BOOL

This event is reported to clients selecting `SubstructureNotify` on the parent and is generated when the window is created. The arguments are as in the `CreateWindow` request.

DestroyNotify

event, window: WINDOW

This event is reported to clients selecting `StructureNotify` on the window and to clients selecting `SubstructureNotify` on the parent. It is generated when the window is destroyed. The event is the window on which the event was generated, and the window is the window that is destroyed.

The ordering of the `DestroyNotify` events is such that for any given window, `DestroyNotify` is generated on all inferiors of the window before being generated on the window itself. The ordering among siblings and across subhierarchies is not otherwise constrained.

UnmapNotify

event, window: WINDOW

from-configure: BOOL

This event is reported to clients selecting `StructureNotify` on the window and to clients selecting `SubstructureNotify` on the parent. It is generated when the window changes state from mapped to unmapped. The event is the window on which the event was generated, and the window is the window that is unmapped. The from-configure flag is `True` if the event was generated as a result of the window's parent being resized when the window itself had a win-gravity of `Unmap`.

MapNotify

event, window: WINDOW

override-redirect: BOOL

This event is reported to clients selecting `StructureNotify` on the window and to clients selecting `SubstructureNotify` on the parent. It is generated when the window changes state from unmapped to mapped. The event is the window on which the event was generated, and the window is the window that is mapped. The override-redirect flag is from the window's attribute.

MapRequest

parent, window: WINDOW

This event is reported to the client selecting `SubstructureRedirect` on the parent and is generated when a `MapWindow` request is issued on an unmapped window with an override-redirect attribute of `False`.

ReparentNotify

event, window, parent: WINDOW

x, y: INT16

override-redirect: BOOL

This event is reported to clients selecting `SubstructureNotify` on either the old or the new parent and to clients selecting `StructureNotify` on the window. It is generated when the window is reparented. The event is the window on which the event was generated. The window is the window that has been rerooted. The parent specifies the new parent. The x and y coordinates are relative to the new parent's origin and specify the position of the upper-left outer corner of the window. The override-redirect flag is from the window's attribute.

ConfigureNotify

event, window: WINDOW
x, y: INT16
width, height, border-width: CARD16
above-sibling: WINDOW or `None`
override-redirect: BOOL

This event is reported to clients selecting `StructureNotify` on the window and to clients selecting `SubstructureNotify` on the parent. It is generated when a `ConfigureWindow` request actually changes the state of the window. The event is the window on which the event was generated, and the window is the window that is changed. The x and y coordinates are relative to the new parent's origin and specify the position of the upper-left outer corner of the window. The width and height specify the inside size, not including the border. If above-sibling is `None`, then the window is on the bottom of the stack with respect to siblings. Otherwise, the window is immediately on top of the specified sibling. The override-redirect flag is from the window's attribute.

GravityNotify

event, window: WINDOW
x, y: INT16

This event is reported to clients selecting `SubstructureNotify` on the parent and to clients selecting `StructureNotify` on the window. It is generated when a window is moved because of a change in size of the parent. The event is the window on which the event was generated, and the window is the window that is moved. The x and y coordinates are relative to the new parent's origin and specify the position of the upper-left outer corner of the window.

ResizeRequest
  window: WINDOW
  width, height: CARD16

This event is reported to the client selecting `ResizeRedirect` on the window and is generated when a `ConfigureWindow` request by some other client on the window attempts to change the size of the window. The width and height are the inside size, not including the border.

ConfigureRequest
  parent, window: WINDOW
  x, y: INT16
  width, height, border-width: CARD16
  sibling: WINDOW or `None`
  stack-mode: {`Above`, `Below`, `TopIf`, `BottomIf`, `Opposite`}
  value-mask: BITMASK

This event is reported to the client selecting `SubstructureRedirect` on the parent and is generated when a `ConfigureWindow` request is issued on the window by some other client. The value-mask indicates which components were specified in the request. The value-mask and the corresponding values are reported as given in the request. The remaining values are filled in from the current geometry of the window, except in the case of sibling and stack-mode, which are reported as `None` and `Above` (respectively) if not given in the request.

CirculateNotify
  event, window: WINDOW
  place: {`Top`, `Bottom`}

This event is reported to clients selecting `StructureNotify` on the window and to clients selecting `SubstructureNotify` on the parent. It is generated when the window is actually restacked from a `CirculateWindow` request. The event is the window on which the event was generated, and the window is the window that is restacked. If place is `Top`, the window is now on top of all siblings. Otherwise, it is below all siblings.

CirculateRequest

> *parent, window*: WINDOW
> *place*: {Top, Bottom}

This event is reported to the client selecting `SubstructureRedirect` on the parent and is generated when a `CirculateWindow` request is issued on the parent and a window actually needs to be restacked. The window specifies the window to be restacked, and the place specifies what the new position in the stacking order should be.

PropertyNotify

> *window*: WINDOW
> *atom*: ATOM
> *state*: {NewValue, Deleted}
> *time*: TIMESTAMP

This event is reported to clients selecting `PropertyChange` on the window and is generated with state `NewValue` when a property of the window is changed using `ChangeProperty` or `RotateProperties`, even when adding zero-length data using `ChangeProperty` and when replacing all or part of a property with identical data using `ChangeProperty` or `RotateProperties`. It is generated with state `Deleted` when a property of the window is deleted using request `DeleteProperty` or `Get-Property`. The timestamp indicates the server time when the property was changed.

SelectionClear

> *owner*: WINDOW
> *selection*: ATOM
> *time*: TIMESTAMP

This event is reported to the current owner of a selection and is generated when a new owner is being defined by means of `SetSelectionOwner`. The timestamp is the last-change time recorded for the selection. The owner argument is the window that was specified by the current owner in its `SetSelectionOwner` request.

SelectionRequest

> *owner*: WINDOW
> *selection*: ATOM

target: ATOM
property: ATOM or `None`
requestor: WINDOW
time: TIMESTAMP or `CurrentTime`

This event is reported to the owner of a selection and is generated when a client issues a `ConvertSelection` request. The owner argument is the window that was specified in the `SetSelectionOwner` request. The remaining arguments are as in the `ConvertSelection` request.

The owner should convert the selection based on the specified target type. If a property is specified, the owner should store the result as that property on the requestor window and then send a `SelectionNotify` event to the requestor using `SendEvent` with an empty event-mask (that is, the event should be sent to the creator of the requestor window). If `None` is specified as the property, the owner should choose a property name, store the result as that property on the requestor window, and then send a `SelectionNotify` giving that actual property name. If the selection cannot be converted as requested, the owner should send a `SelectionNotify` with the property set to `None`.

SelectionNotify

requestor: WINDOW
selection, target: ATOM
property: ATOM or `None`
time: TIMESTAMP or `CurrentTime`

This event is generated by the server in response to a `ConvertSelection` request when there is no owner for the selection. When there is an owner, it should be generated by the owner using `SendEvent`. The owner of a selection should send this event to a requestor either when a selection has been converted and stored as a property or when a selection conversion could not be performed (indicated with property `None`).

ColormapNotify

window: WINDOW
colormap: COLORMAP or `None`
new: BOOL
state: {`Installed`, `Uninstalled`}

This event is reported to clients selecting `ColormapChange` on the window. It is generated with value `True` for new when the colormap attribute of the window is changed and is generated with value `False` for new when the colormap of a window is installed or uninstalled. In either case, the state indicates whether the colormap is currently installed.

MappingNotify
request: {`Modifier`, `Keyboard`, `Pointer`}
first-keycode, count: CARD8

This event is sent to all clients. There is no mechanism to express disinterest in this event. The detail indicates the kind of change that occurred: `Modifiers` for a successful `SetModifierMapping`, `Keyboard` for a successful `ChangeKeyboardMapping`, and `Pointer` for a successful `Set-PointerMapping`. If the detail is `Keyboard`, then first-keycode and count indicate the range of altered keycodes.

ClientMessage
window: WINDOW
type: ATOM
format: {8, 16, 32}
data: LISTofINT8 or LISTofINT16 or LISTofINT32

This event is only generated by clients using `SendEvent`. The type specifies how the data is to be interpreted by the receiving client; the server places no interpretation on the type or the data. The format specifies whether the data should be viewed as a list of 8-bit, 16-bit, or 32-bit quantities, so that the server can correctly byte-swap, as necessary. The data always consists of either twenty 8-bit values or ten 16-bit values or five 32-bit values, although particular message types might not make use of all of these values.

SECTION 12. FLOW CONTROL AND CONCURRENCY

Whenever the server is writing to a given connection, it is permissible for the server to stop reading from that connection (but if the writing would block, it must continue to service other connections). The server is not required to buffer more than a single request per connection at one time. For a given connection to the server, a client can block while reading from the connection but should undertake to read (events and errors) when writing would block. Failure on the part of a client to obey this rule could result in a deadlocked connection, although deadlock is probably unlikely unless either the transport layer has very little buffering or the client attempts to send large numbers of requests without ever reading replies or checking for errors and events.

If a server is implemented with internal concurrency, the overall effect must be as if individual requests are executed to completion in some serial order, and requests from a given connection must be executed in delivery order (that is, the total execution order is a shuffle of the individual streams). The execution of a request includes validating all arguments, collecting all data for any reply, and generating and queueing all required events. However, it does not include the actual transmission of the reply and the events. In addition, the effect of any other cause that can generate multiple events (for example, activation of a grab or pointer motion) must effectively generate and queue all required events indivisibly with respect to all other causes and requests. For a request from a given client, any events destined for that client that are caused by executing the request must be sent to the client before any reply or error is sent.

Appendix A

Xlib Functions and Protocol Requests

This appendix provides two tables that relate to Xlib functions and the X protocol. The following table lists each Xlib function (in alphabetical order) and the corresponding protocol request that it generates.

Xlib Function	Protocol Request
XActivateScreenSaver	ForceScreenSaver
XAddHost	ChangeHosts
XAddHosts	ChangeHosts
XAddToSaveSet	ChangeSaveSet
XAllocColor	AllocColor
XAllocColorCells	AllocColorCells
XAllocColorPlanes	AllocColorPlanes
XAllocNamedColor	AllocNamedColor
XAllowEvents	AllowEvents
XAutoRepeatOff	ChangeKeyboardControl
XAutoRepeatOn	ChangeKeyboardControl
XBell	Bell
XChangeActivePointerGrab	ChangeActivePointerGrab
XChangeGC	ChangeGC
XChangeKeyboardControl	ChangeKeyboardControl
XChangeKeyboardMapping	ChangeKeyboardMapping
XChangePointerControl	ChangePointerControl
XChangeProperty	ChangeProperty
XChangeSaveSet	ChangeSaveSet

Xlib Function	Protocol Request
XChangeWindowAttributes	ChangeWindowAttributes
XCirculateSubwindows	CirculateWindow
XCirculateSubwindowsDown	CirculateWindow
XCirculateSubwindowsUp	CirculateWindow
XClearArea	ClearArea
XClearWindow	ClearArea
XConfigureWindow	ConfigureWindow
XConvertSelection	ConvertSelection
XCopyArea	CopyArea
XCopyColormapAndFree	CopyColormapAndFree
XCopyGC	CopyGC
XCopyPlane	CopyPlane
XCreateBitmapFromData	CreateGC
	CreatePixmap
	FreeGC
	PutImage
XCreateColormap	CreateColormap
XCreateFontCursor	CreateGlyphCursor
XCreateGC	CreateGC
XCreateGlyphCursor	CreateGlyphCursor
XCreatePixmap	CreatePixmap
XCreatePixmapCursor	CreateCursor
XCreatePixmapFromData	CreateGC
	CreatePixmap
	FreeGC
	PutImage
XCreateSimpleWindow	CreateWindow
XCreateWindow	CreateWindow
XDefineCursor	ChangeWindowAttributes
XDeleteProperty	DeleteProperty
XDestroySubwindows	DestroySubwindows
XDestroyWindow	DestroyWindow
XDisableAccessControl	SetAccessControl
XDrawArc	PolyArc
XDrawArcs	PolyArc
XDrawImageString	ImageText8
XDrawImageString16	ImageText16
XDrawLine	PolySegment
XDrawLines	PolyLine
XDrawPoint	PolyPoint

Xlib Function	Protocol Request
XDrawPoints	PolyPoint
XDrawRectangle	PolyRectangle
XDrawRectangles	PolyRectangle
XDrawSegments	PolySegment
XDrawString	PolyText8
XDrawString16	PolyText16
XDrawText	PolyText8
XDrawText16	PolyText16
XEnableAccessControl	SetAccessControl
XFetchBytes	GetProperty
XFetchName	GetProperty
XFillArc	PolyFillArc
XFillArcs	PolyFillArc
XFillPolygon	FillPoly
XFillRectangle	PolyFillRectangle
XFillRectangles	PolyFillRectangle
XForceScreenSaver	ForceScreenSaver
XFreeColormap	FreeColormap
XFreeColors	FreeColors
XFreeCursor	FreeCursor
XFreeFont	CloseFont
XFreeGC	FreeGC
XFreePixmap	FreePixmap
XGetAtomName	GetAtomName
XGetFontPath	GetFontPath
XGetGeometry	GetGeometry
XGetIconSizes	GetProperty
XGetImage	GetImage
XGetInputFocus	GetInputFocus
XGetKeyboardControl	GetKeyboardControl
XGetKeyboardMapping	GetKeyboardMapping
XGetMotionEvents	GetMotionEvents
XGetModifierMapping	GetModifierMapping
XGetNormalHints	GetProperty
XGetPointerControl	GetPointerControl
XGetPointerMapping	GetPointerMapping
XGetScreenSaver	GetScreenSaver
XGetSelectionOwner	GetSelectionOwner
XGetSizeHints	GetProperty
XGetWMHints	GetProperty

Xlib Function	Protocol Request
XGetWindowAttributes	GetWindowAttributes
	GetGeometry
XGetWindowProperty	GetProperty
XGetZoomHints	GetProperty
XGrabButton	GrabButton
XGrabKey	GrabKey
XGrabKeyboard	GrabKeyboard
XGrabPointer	GrabPointer
XGrabServer	GrabServer
XInitExtension	QueryExtension
XInstallColormap	InstallColormap
XInternAtom	InternAtom
XKillClient	KillClient
XListExtensions	ListExtensions
XListFonts	ListFonts
XListFontsWithInfo	ListFontsWithInfo
XListHosts	ListHosts
XListInstalledColormaps	ListInstalledColormaps
XListProperties	ListProperties
XLoadFont	OpenFont
XLoadQueryFont	OpenFont
	QueryFont
XLookupColor	LookupColor
XLowerWindow	ConfigureWindow
XMapRaised	ConfigureWindow
	MapWindow
XMapSubwindows	MapSubwindows
XMapWindow	MapWindow
XMoveResizeWindow	ConfigureWindow
XMoveWindow	ConfigureWindow
XNoOp	NoOperation
XOpenDisplay	CreateGC
XParseColor	LookupColor
XPutImage	PutImage
XQueryBestCursor	QueryBestSize
XQueryBestSize	QueryBestSize
XQueryBestStipple	QueryBestSize
XQueryBestTile	QueryBestSize
XQueryColor	QueryColors
XQueryColors	QueryColors

Xlib Function	Protocol Request
XQueryExtension	QueryExtension
XQueryFont	QueryFont
XQueryKeymap	QueryKeymap
XQueryPointer	QueryPointer
XQueryTextExtents	QueryTextExtents
XQueryTextExtents16	QueryTextExtents
XQueryTree	QueryTree
XRaiseWindow	ConfigureWindow
XReadBitmapFile	CreateGC
	CreatePixmap
	FreeGC
	PutImage
XRecolorCursor	RecolorCursor
XRemoveFromSaveSet	ChangeSaveSet
XRemoveHost	ChangeHosts
XRemoveHosts	ChangeHosts
XReparentWindow	ReparentWindow
XResetScreenSaver	ForceScreenSaver
XResizeWindow	ConfigureWindow
XRestackWindows	ConfigureWindow
XRotateBuffers	RotateProperties
XRotateWindowProperties	RotateProperties
XSelectInput	ChangeWindowAttributes
XSendEvent	SendEvent
XSetAccessControl	SetAccessControl
XSetArcMode	ChangeGC
XSetBackground	ChangeGC
XSetClipMask	ChangeGC
XSetClipOrigin	ChangeGC
XSetClipRectangles	SetClipRectangles
XSetCloseDownMode	SetCloseDownMode
XSetCommand	ChangeProperty
XSetDashes	SetDashes
XSetFillRule	ChangeGC
XSetFillStyle	ChangeGC
XSetFont	ChangeGC
XSetFontPath	SetFontPath
XSetForeground	ChangeGC
XSetFunction	ChangeGC
XSetGraphicsExposures	ChangeGC

Xlib Function	*Protocol Request*
XSetIconName	ChangeProperty
XSetIconSizes	ChangeProperty
XSetInputFocus	SetInputFocus
XSetLineAttributes	ChangeGC
XSetModifierMapping	SetModifierMapping
XSetNormalHints	ChangeProperty
XSetPlaneMask	ChangeGC
XSetPointerMapping	SetPointerMapping
XSetScreenSaver	SetScreenSaver
XSetSelectionOwner	SetSelectionOwner
XSetSizeHints	ChangeProperty
XSetStandardProperties	ChangeProperty
XSetState	ChangeGC
XSetStipple	ChangeGC
XSetSubwindowMode	ChangeGC
XSetTile	ChangeGC
XSetTSOrigin	ChangeGC
XSetWMHints	ChangeProperty
XSetWindowBackground	ChangeWindowAttributes
XSetWindowBackgroundPixmap	ChangeWindowAttributes
XSetWindowBorder	ChangeWindowAttributes
XSetWindowBorderPixmap	ChangeWindowAttributes
XSetWindowBorderWidth	ConfigureWindow
XSetWindowColormap	ChangeWindowAttributes
XSetZoomHints	ChangeProperty
XStoreBuffer	ChangeProperty
XStoreBytes	ChangeProperty
XStoreColor	StoreColors
XStoreColors	StoreColors
XStoreName	ChangeProperty
XStoreNamedColor	StoreNamedColor
XSync	GetInputFocus
XTranslateCoordinates	TranslateCoordinates
XUndefineCursor	ChangeWindowAttributes
XUngrabButton	UngrabButton
XUngrabKey	UngrabKey
XUngrabKeyboard	UngrabKeyboard
XUngrabPointer	UngrabPointer

Xlib Function	Protocol Request
XUngrabServer	UngrabServer
XUninstallColormap	UninstallColormap
XUnloadFont	CloseFont
XUnmapSubwindows	UnmapSubwindows
XUnmapWindow	UnmapWindow
XWarpPointer	WarpPointer

The following table lists each X protocol request (in alphabetical order) and the Xlib functions that reference it.

Protocol Request	Xlib Function
AllocColor	XAllocColor
AllocColorCells	XAllocColorCells
AllocColorPlanes	XAllocColorPlanes
AllocNamedColor	XAllocNamedColor
AllowEvents	XAllowEvents
Bell	XBell
SetAccessControl	XDisableAccessControl
	XEnableAccessControl
	XSetAccessControl
ChangeActivePointerGrab	XChangeActivePointerGrab
SetCloseDownMode	XSetCloseDownMode
ChangeGC	XChangeGC
	XSetArcMode
	XSetBackground
	XSetClipMask
	XSetClipOrigin
	XSetFillRule
	XSetFillStyle
	XSetFont
	XSetForeground
	XSetFunction
	XSetGraphicsExposures
	XSetLineAttributes
	XSetPlaneMask
	XSetState
	XSetStipple
	XSetSubwindowMode

Protocol Request	Xlib Function
	XSetTile
	XSetTSOrigin
ChangeHosts	XAddHost
	XAddHosts
	XRemoveHost
	XRemoveHosts
ChangeKeyboardControl	XAutoRepeatOff
	XAutoRepeatOn
	XChangeKeyboardControl
ChangeKeyboardMapping	XChangeKeyboardMapping
ChangePointerControl	XChangePointerControl
ChangeProperty	XChangeProperty
	XSetCommand
	XSetIconName
	XSetIconSizes
	XSetNormalHints
	XSetSizeHints
	XSetStandardProperties
	XSetWMHints
	XSetZoomHints
	XStoreBuffer
	XStoreBytes
	XStoreName
ChangeSaveSet	XAddToSaveSet
	XChangeSaveSet
	XRemoveFromSaveSet
ChangeWindowAttributes	XChangeWindowAttributes
	XDefineCursor
	XSelectInput
	XSetWindowBackground
	XSetWindowBackgroundPixmap
	XSetWindowBorder
	XSetWindowBorderPixmap
	XSetWindowColormap
	XUndefineCursor
CirculateWindow	XCirculateSubwindowsDown
	XCirculateSubwindowsUp
	XCirculateSubwindows
ClearArea	XClearArea
	XClearWindow

Protocol Request	Xlib Function
CloseFont	XFreeFont
	XUnloadFont
ConfigureWindow	XConfigureWindow
	XLowerWindow
	XMapRaised
	XMoveResizeWindow
	XMoveWindow
	XRaiseWindow
	XResizeWindow
	XRestackWindows
	XSetWindowBorderWidth
ConvertSelection	XConvertSelection
CopyArea	XCopyArea
CopyColormapAndFree	XCopyColormapAndFree
CopyGC	XCopyGC
CopyPlane	XCopyPlane
CreateColormap	XCreateColormap
CreateCursor	XCreatePixmapCursor
CreateGC	XCreateGC
	XCreateBitmapFromData
	XCreatePixmapFromData
	XOpenDisplay
	XReadBitmapFile
CreateGlyphCursor	XCreateFontCursor
	XCreateGlyphCursor
CreatePixmap	XCreatePixmap
	XCreateBitmapFromData
	XCreatePixmapFromData
	XReadBitmapFile
CreateWindow	XCreateSimpleWindow
	XCreateWindow
DeleteProperty	XDeleteProperty
DestroySubwindows	XDestroySubwindows
DestroyWindow	XDestroyWindow
FillPoly	XFillPolygon
ForceScreenSaver	XActivateScreenSaver
	XForceScreenSaver
	XResetScreenSaver
FreeColormap	XFreeColormap
FreeColors	XFreeColors

Protocol Request	Xlib Function
FreeCursor	XFreeCursor
FreeGC	XFreeGC
	XCreateBitmapFromData
	XCreatePixmapFromData
	XReadBitmapFile
FreePixmap	XFreePixmap
GetAtomName	XGetAtomName
GetFontPath	XGetFontPath
GetGeometry	XGetGeometry
	XGetWindowAttributes
GetImage	XGetImage
GetInputFocus	XGetInputFocus
	XSync
GetKeyboardControl	XGetKeyboardControl
GetKeyboardMapping	XGetKeyboardMapping
GetModifierMapping	XGetModifierMapping
GetMotionEvents	XGetMotionEvents
GetPointerControl	XGetPointerControl
GetPointerMapping	XGetPointerMapping
GetProperty	XFetchBytes
	XFetchName
	XGetIconSizes
	XGetNormalHints
	XGetSizeHints
	XGetWMHints
	XGetWindowProperty
	XGetZoomHints
GetSelectionOwner	XGetSelectionOwner
GetWindowAttributes	XGetWindowAttributes
GrabButton	XGrabButton
GrabKey	XGrabKey
GrabKeyboard	XGrabKeyboard
GrabPointer	XGrabPointer
GrabServer	XGrabServer
ImageText16	XDrawImageString16
ImageText8	XDrawImageString
InstallColormap	XInstallColormap
InternAtom	XInternAtom
KillClient	XKillClient
ListExtensions	XListExtensions

Protocol Request	*Xlib Function*
ListFonts	XListFonts
ListFontsWithInfo	XListFontsWithInfo
ListHosts	XListHosts
ListInstalledColormaps	XListInstalledColormaps
ListProperties	XListProperties
LookupColor	XLookupColor
	XParseColor
MapSubwindows	XMapSubwindows
MapWindow	XMapRaised
	XMapWindow
NoOperation	XNoOp
OpenFont	XLoadFont
	XLoadQueryFont
PolyArc	XDrawArc
	XDrawArcs
PolyFillArc	XFillArc
	XFillArcs
PolyFillRectangle	XFillRectangle
	XFillRectangles
PolyLine	XDrawLines
PolyPoint	XDrawPoint
	XDrawPoints
PolyRectangle	XDrawRectangle
	XDrawRectangles
PolySegment	XDrawLine
	XDrawSegments
PolyText16	XDrawString16
	XDrawText16
PolyText8	XDrawString
	XDrawText
PutImage	XPutImage
	XCreateBitmapFromData
	XCreatePixmapFromData
	XReadBitmapFile
QueryBestSize	XQueryBestCursor
	XQueryBestSize
	XQueryBestStipple
	XQueryBestTile
QueryColors	XQueryColor
	XQueryColors

Protocol Request	Xlib Function
QueryExtension	XInitExtension
	XQueryExtension
QueryFont	XLoadQueryFont
	XQueryFont
QueryKeymap	XQueryKeymap
QueryPointer	XQueryPointer
QueryTextExtents	XQueryTextExtents
	XQueryTextExtents16
QueryTree	XQueryTree
RecolorCursor	XRecolorCursor
ReparentWindow	XReparentWindow
RotateProperties	XRotateBuffers
	XRotateWindowProperties
SendEvent	XSendEvent
SetClipRectangles	XSetClipRectangles
SetCloseDownMode	XSetCloseDownMode
SetDashes	XSetDashes
SetFontPath	XSetFontPath
SetInputFocus	XSetInputFocus
SetModifierMapping	XSetModifierMapping
SetPointerMapping	XSetPointerMapping
SetScreenSaver	XGetScreenSaver
	XSetScreenSaver
SetSelectionOwner	XSetSelectionOwner
StoreColors	XStoreColor
	XStoreColors
StoreNamedColor	XStoreNamedColor
TranslateCoordinates	XTranslateCoordinates
UngrabButton	XUngrabButton
UngrabKey	XUngrabKey
UngrabKeyboard	XUngrabKeyboard
UngrabPointer	XUngrabPointer
UngrabServer	XUngrabServer
UninstallColormap	XUninstallColormap
UnmapSubwindows	XUnmapSubWindows
UnmapWindow	XUnmapWindow
WarpPointer	XWarpPointer

Appendix B

X Font Cursors

The following are the available cursors that can be used with XCreate-FontCursor.

✕	XC_X_cursor		XC_clock
↗	XC_arrow		XC_coffee_mug
⊤	XC_based_arrow_down		XC_cross
⊥	XC_based_arrow_up		XC_cross_reverse
⇀	XC_boat	+	XC_crosshair
#	XC_bogosity		XC_diamond_cross
⌐	XC_bottom_left_corner	●	XC_dot
⌐	XC_bottom_right_corner	⊡	XC_dot_box_mask
↓	XC_bottom_side	↕	XC_double_arrow
⊥	XC_bottom_tee	↗	XC_draft_large
▣	XC_box_spiral	↗	XC_draft_small
↑	XC_center_ptr		XC_draped_box
○	XC_circle		XC_exchange

XC_fleur

XC_gobbler

XC_gumby

XC_hand

XC_hand1_mask

XC_heart

XC_icon

XC_iron_cross

XC_left_ptr

XC_left_side

XC_left_tee

XC_leftbutton

XC_ll_angle

XC_lr_angle

XC_man

XC_middlebutton

XC_mouse

XC_pencil

XC_pirate

XC_plus

XC_question_arrow

XC_right_ptr

XC_right_side

XC_right_tee

XC_rightbutton

XC_rtl_logo

XC_sailboat

XC_sb_down_arrow

XC_sb_h_double_arrow

XC_sb_left_arrow

XC_sb_right_arrow

XC_sb_up_arrow

XC_sb_v_double_arrow

XC_shuttle

XC_sizing

XC_spider

XC_spraycan

XC_star

XC_target

XC_tcross

XC_top_left_arrow

XC_top_left_corner

XC_top_right_corner

XC_top_side

XC_top_tee

XC_trek

XC_ul_angle

XC_umbrella

XC_ur_angle

XC_watch

XC_xterm

Appendix C

Extensions

Because X can evolve by extensions to the core protocol, it is important that extensions not be perceived as second class citizens. At some point, your favorite extensions may be adopted as additional parts of the X Standard.

Therefore, there should be little to distinguish the use of an extension from that of the core protocol. To avoid having to initialize extensions explicitly in application programs, it is also important that extensions perform "lazy evaluations" and automatically initialize themselves when called for the first time.

This appendix describes techniques for writing extensions to Xlib that will run at essentially the same performance as the core protocol requests.

Note   It is expected that a given extension to X consists of multiple requests. Defining ten new features as ten separate extensions is a bad practice. Rather, they should be packaged into a single extension and should use minor opcodes to distinguish the requests.

The symbols and macros used for writing stubs to Xlib are listed in <X11/Xlibint.h>.

Basic Protocol Support Routines

The basic protocol requests for extensions are XQueryExtension and XListExtensions.

Bool XQueryExtension(*display, name, major_opcode_return, first_event_return,*
                     first_error_return)
    Display **display*;
    char **name*;
    int **major_opcode_return*;
    int **first_event_return*;
    int **first_error_return*;

XQueryExtension determines if the named extension is present. If so, the
major opcode for the extension is returned (if it has one); otherwise, False
is returned. Any minor opcode and the request formats are specific to the
extension. If the extension involves additional event types, the base event
type code is returned; otherwise, False is returned. The format of the
events is specific to the extension. If the extension involves additional error
codes, the base error code is returned; otherwise, False is returned. The
format of additional data in the errors is specific to the extension.

The extension name should be in the ISO Latin-1 encoding, and uppercase and lowercase do matter.

char **XListExtensions(*display, nextensions_return*)
    Display **display*;
    int **nextensions_return*;

XListExtensions returns a list of all extensions supported by the
server.

XFreeExtensionList(*list*)
    char ***list*;

XFreeExtensionList frees the memory allocated by XList-
Extensions.

Hooking into Xlib

These functions allow you to hook into the library. They are not normally
used by application programmers but are used by people who need to extend the core X protocol and the X library interface. The functions, which
generate protocol requests for X, are typically called stubs.

In extensions, stubs first should check to see if they have initialized themselves on a connection. If they have not, they then should call XInitExtension to attempt to initialize themselves on the connection.

If the extension needs to be informed of GC/font allocation or deallocation or if the extension defines new event types, the functions described here allow the extension to be called when these events occur.

The XExtCodes structure returns the information from XInit-Extension and is defined in <X11/Xlib.h>:

```
typedef struct _XExtCodes {    /* public to extension, cannot be changed */
    int extension;             /* extension number */
    int major_opcode;          /* major op-code assigned by server */
    int first_event;           /* first event number for the extension */
    int first_error;           /* first error number for the extension */
} XExtCodes;

XExtCodes *XInitExtension(display, name)
    Display *display;
    char *name;
```

XInitExtension determines if the extension exists. Then, it allocates storage for maintaining the information about the extension on the connection, chains this onto the extension list for the connection, and returns the information the stub implementor will need to access the extension. If the extension does not exist, XInitExtension returns NULL.

In particular, the extension number in the XExtCodes structure is needed in the other calls that follow. This extension number is unique only to a single connection.

```
XExtCodes *XAddExtension (display)
    Display *display;
```

For local Xlib extensions, XAddExtension allocates the XExtCodes structure, bumps the extension number count, and chains the extension onto the extension list. (This permits extensions to Xlib without requiring server extensions.)

Hooks into the Library

These functions allow you to define procedures that are to be called when various circumstances occur. The procedures include the creation of a new

GC for a connection, the copying of a GC, the freeing a GC, the creating and freeing of fonts, the conversion of events defined by extensions to and from wire format, and the handling of errors.

All of these functions return the previous routine defined for this extension.

```
int (*XESetCloseDisplay(display, extension, proc))()
     Display *display;     /* display */
     int extension;        /* extension number */
     int (*proc)();        /* routine to call when display closed */
```

You use this procedure to define a procedure to be called whenever XCloseDisplay is called. This procedure returns any previously defined procedure, usually NULL.

When XCloseDisplay is called, your routine is called with these arguments:

```
(*proc)(display, codes)
     Display *display;
     XExtCodes *codes;
```

```
int (*XESetCreateGC(display, extension, proc))()
     Display *display;     /* display */
     int extension;        /* extension number */
     int (*proc)();        /* routine to call when GC created */
```

You use this procedure to define a procedure to be called whenever a new GC is created. This procedure returns any previously defined procedure, usually NULL.

When a GC is created, your routine is called with these arguments:

```
(*proc)(display, gc, codes)
     Display *display;
     GC gc;
     XExtCodes *codes;
```

```
int (*XESetCopyGC(display, extension, proc))()
     Display *display;     /* display */
     int extension;        /* extension number */
     int (*proc)();        /* routine to call when GC copied */
```

You use this procedure to define a procedure to be called whenever a GC is copied. This procedure returns any previously defined procedure, usually NULL.

When a GC is copied, your routine is called with these arguments:

```
(*proc)(display, gc, codes)
    Display *display;
    GC gc;
    XExtCodes *codes;
```

```
int (*XESetFreeGC(display, extension, proc))()
    Display *display;     /* display */
    int extension;        /* extension number */
    int (*proc)();        /* routine to call when GC freed */
```

You use this procedure to define a procedure to be called whenever a GC is freed. This procedure returns any previously defined procedure, usually NULL.

When a GC is freed, your routine is called with these arguments:

```
(*proc)(display, gc, codes)
    Display *display;
    GC gc;
    XExtCodes *codes;
```

```
int (*XESetCreateFont(display, extension, proc))()
    Display *display;     /* display */
    int extension;        /* extension number */
    int (*proc)();        /* routine to call when font created */
```

You use this procedure to define a procedure to be called whenever `XLoadQueryFont` and `XQueryFont` are called. This procedure returns any previously defined procedure, usually NULL.

When `XLoadQueryFont` or `XQueryFont` is called, your routine is called with these arguments:

```
(*proc)(display, fs, codes)
    Display *display;
    XFontStruct *fs;
    XExtCodes *codes;
```

int (*XESetFreeFont(*display, extension, proc*))()
    Display **display*;   /* display */
    int *extension*;   /* extension number */
    int (**proc*)();   /* routine to call when font freed */

You use this procedure to define a procedure to be called whenever `XFreeFont` is called. This procedure returns any previously defined procedure, usually NULL.

When `XFreeFont` is called, your routine is called with these arguments:

(*proc)(*display, fs, codes*)
    Display **display*;
    XFontStruct **fs*;
    XExtCodes **codes*;

The next two functions allow you to define new events to the library.

Note   There is an implementation limit such that your host event structure size cannot be bigger than the size of the `XEvent` union of structures. There also is no way to guarantee that more than 24 elements or 96 characters in the structure will be fully portable between machines.

int (*XESetWireToEvent(*display, event_number, proc*))()
    Display **display*;   /* display */
    int *event_number*; /* event routine to replace */
    Bool (**proc*)();   /* routine to call when converting event */

You use this procedure to define a procedure to be called when an event needs to be converted from wire format (`xEvent`) to host format (`XEvent`). The event number defines which protocol event number to install a conversion routine for. This procedure returns any previously defined procedure.

Note   You can replace a core event conversion routine with one of your own, although this is not encouraged. It would, however, allow you to intercept a core event and modify it before being placed in the queue or otherwise examined.

When Xlib needs to convert an event from wire format to host format, your routine is called with these arguments:

```
Status (*proc)(display, re, event)
    Display *display;
    XEvent *re;
    xEvent *event;
```

Your routine must return status to indicate if the conversion succeeded. The re argument is a pointer to where the host format event should be stored, and the event argument is the 32-byte wire event structure. In the XEvent structure you are creating, type must be the first member and window must be the second member. You should fill in the type member with the type specified for the xEvent structure. You should copy all other members from the xEvent structure (wire format) to the XEvent structure (host format). Your conversion routine should return True if the event should be placed in the queue or False if it should not be placed in the queue.

```
Status (*XESetEventToWire(display, event_number, proc))()
    Display *display;        /* display */
    int event_number;        /* event routine to replace */
    int (*proc)();           /* routine to call when converting event */
```

You use this procedure to define a procedure to be called when an event needs to be converted from host format (XEvent) to wire format (xEvent) form. The event number defines which protocol event number to install a conversion routine for. This procedure returns any previously defined procedure. It returns zero if the conversion fails or nonzero otherwise.

Note   You can replace a core event conversion routine with one of your own, although this is not encouraged. It would, however, allow you to intercept a core event and modify it before being sent to another client.

When Xlib needs to convert an event from wire format to host format, your routine is called with these arguments:

```
(*proc)(display, re, event)
    Display *display;
    XEvent *re;
    xEvent *event;
```

The re argument is a pointer to the host format event, and the event argument is a pointer to where the 32-byte wire event structure should be stored. In the XEvent structure that you are forming, you must have "type" as the first member and "window" as the second. You then should fill in the type with the type from the xEvent structure. All other members then should be copied from the wire format to the XEvent structure.

```
int (*XESetError(display, extension, proc))()
    Display *display;      /* display */
    int extension;         /* extension number */
    int (*proc)();         /* routine to call when X error happens */
```

Inside Xlib, there are times that you may want to suppress the calling of the external error handling when an error occurs. This allows status to be returned on a call at the cost of the call being synchronous (though most such routines are query operations, in any case, and are typically programmed to be synchronous).

When Xlib detects a protocol error in _XReply, it calls your procedure with these arguments:

```
int (*proc)(display, err, codes, ret_code)
    Display *display;
    xError *err;
    XExtCodes *codes;
    int *ret_code;
```

The err argument is a pointer to the 32-byte wire format error. The codes argument is a pointer to the extension codes structure. The ret_code argument is the return code you may want _XReply returned to.

If your routine returns a zero value, the error is not suppressed, and the client's error handler is called. (For further information, see section 8.12.2.) If your routine returns nonzero, the error is suppressed, and _XReply returns the value of ret_code.

```
char *(*XESetErrorString(display, extension, proc))()
    Display *display;      /* display */
    int extension;         /* extension number */
    char *(*proc)():       /* routine to call to obtain an error string*/
```

The XGetErrorText function returns a string to the user for an error. XESetErrorString allows you to define a routine to be called that should return a pointer to the error message. The following is an example.

```
char *(*proc)(display, code, codes, buffer, nbytes)
    Display *display;
    int code;
    XExtCodes *codes;
    char *buffer;
    int nbytes;
```

Your procedure is called with the error code for every error detected. You should copy nbytes of a null-terminated string containing the error message to buffer.

```
int (*XESetFlushGC(display, extension, proc))()
    Display *display;      /* display */
    int extension;         /* extension number */
    char *(*proc)();       /* routine to call when I/O error happens */
```

The XESetFlushGC procedure is identical to XESetCopyGC except that XESetFlushGC is called when a GC cache needs to be updated in the server.

Hooks onto Xlib Data Structures

Various Xlib data structures have provisions for extension routines to chain extension supplied data onto a list. These structures are GC, Visual, Screen, ScreenFormat, Display, and XFontStruct. Because the list pointer is always the first member in the structure, a single set of routines can be used to manipulate the data on these lists.

The following structure is used in the routines in this section and is defined in <X11/Xlib.h>:

```
typedef struct _XExtData {
    int number;                  /* number returned by XInitExtension */
    struct _XExtData *next;      /* next item on list of data for structure */
    int (*free)();               /* if defined, called to free private */
    char *private;               /* data private to this extension. */
} XExtData;
```

When any of the data structures listed above are freed, the list is walked, and the structure's free routine (if any) is called. If free is NULL, then the library frees both the data pointed to by the private member and the structure itself.

```
union { Display *display;
      GC gc;
      Visual *visual
      Screen *screen
      ScreenFormat *pixmap_format;
      XFontStruct *font } XEDataObject;
```

```
XExtData **XEHeadOfExtensionList(object)
      XEDataObject object;
```

`XEHeadOfExtensionList` returns a pointer to the list of extension structures attached to the specified object. In concert with `XAddTo-ExtensionList`, `XEHeadOfExtensionList` allows an extension to attach arbitrary data to any of the structures of types contained in `XEDataObject`.

```
XAddToExtensionList(structure, ext_data)
      struct _XExtData **structure;   /* pointer to structure to add */
      XExtData *ext_data;             /* extension data structure to add */
```

The structure argument is a pointer to one of the data structures enumerated above. You must initialize ext_data→number with the extension number before calling this routine.

```
XExtData *XFindOnExtensionList(structure, number)
      struct _XExtData **structure;
      int number;                     /* extension number from XInitExtension */
```

`XFindOnExtensionList` returns the first extension data structure for the extension numbered number. It is expected that an extension will add at most one extension data structure to any single data structure's extension data list. There is no way to find additional structures.

The `XAllocID` macro, which allocates and returns a resource ID, is defined in `<Xll/Xlib.h>`.

XAllocID(*display*)
    Display **display*;

This macro is a call through the `Display` structure to the internal resource ID allocator. It returns a resource ID that you can use when creating new resources.

GC Caching

GCs are cached by the library to allow merging of independent change requests to the same GC into single protocol requests. This is typically called a write back cache. Any extension routine whose behavior depends on the contents of a GC must flush the GC cache to make sure the server has up-to-date contents in its GC.

The `FlushGC` macro checks the dirty bits in the library's GC structure and calls `_XFlushGCCache` if any elements have changed. The `FlushGC` macro is defined as follows:

FlushGC(*display, gc*)
    Display **display*;
    GC *gc*;

Note that if you extend the GC to add additional resource ID components, you should ensure that the library stub sends the change request immediately. This is because a client can free a resource immediately after using it, so if you only stored the value in the cache without forcing a protocol request, the resource might be destroyed before being set into the GC. You can use the `_XFlushGCCache` procedure to force the cache to be flushed. The `_XFlushGCCache` procedure is defined as follows:

_XFlushGCCache(*display, gc*)
    Display **display*;
    GC *gc*;

Graphics Batching

If you extend X to add more poly graphics primitives, you may be able to take advantage of facilities in the library to allow back-to-back single calls to be transformed into poly requests. This may dramatically improve perfor-

mance of programs that are not written using poly requests. A pointer to an
xReq, called last_req in the display structure, is the last request being processed. By checking that the last request type, drawable, gc, and other options are the same as the new one and that there is enough space left in the
buffer, you may be able to just extend the previous graphics request by ex-
tending the length field of the request and appending the data to the buffer.
This can improve performance by five times or more in naive programs. For
example, here is the source for the XDrawPoint stub. (Writing extension
stubs is discussed in the next section.)

```
#include "copyright.h"
#include "Xlibint.h"
/* precompute the maximum size of batching request allowed */
static int size = sizeof(xPolyPointReq) + EPERBATCH * sizeof(xPoint);
XDrawPoint(dpy, d, gc, x, y)
    register Display *dpy;
    Drawable d;
    GC gc;
    int x, y; /* INT16 */
{
    xPoint *point;
    LockDisplay(dpy);
    FlushGC(dpy, gc);
    {
    register xPolyPointReq *req = (xPolyPointReq *) dpy→last_req;
    /* if same as previous request, with same drawable, batch requests */
    if (
            (req→reqType == X_PolyPoint)
        && (req→drawable == d)
        && (req→gc == gc→gid)
        && (req→coordMode == CoordModeOrigin)
        && ((dpy→bufptr + sizeof (xPoint)) <= dpy→bufmax)
        && (((char *)dpy→bufptr − (char *)req) < size)) {
            point = (xPoint *) dpy→bufptr;
            req→length += sizeof (xPoint) >> 2;
        dpy→bufptr += sizeof (xPoint);
    }
```

```
else {
  GetReqExtra(PolyPoint, 4, req); /* 1 point = 4 bytes */
  req→drawable = d;
  req→gc = gc→gid;
  req→coordMode = CoordModeOrigin;
  point = (xPoint *) (req + 1);
  }
point→x = x;
point→y = y;
}
UnlockDisplay(dpy);
SyncHandle();}
```

To keep clients from generating very long requests that may monopolize the server, there is a symbol defined in <X11/Xlibint.h> of EPERBATCH on the number of requests batched. Most of the performance benefit occurs in the first few merged requests. Note that FlushGC is called *before* picking up the value of last_req, because it may modify this field.

Writing Extension Stubs

All X requests always contain the length of the request, expressed as a 16-bit quantity of 32 bits. This means that a single request can be no more than 256K bytes in length. Some servers may not support single requests of such a length. The value of dpy→max_request_size contains the maximum length as defined by the server implementation. For further information, see part B, "X Window System Protocol."

Requests, Replies, and Xproto.h

The <X11/Xproto.h> file contains three sets of definitions that are of interest to the stub implementor: request names, request structures, and reply structures.

You need to generate a file equivalent to <X11/Xproto.h> for your extension and need to include it in your stub routine. Each stub routine also must include <X11/Xlibint.h>.

The identifiers are deliberately chosen in such a way that, if the request is called X_DoSomething, then its request structure is xDoSomethingReq, and its reply is xDoSomethingReply. The GetReq family of macros, defined in <X11/Xlibint.h>, takes advantage of this naming scheme.

For each X request, there is a definition in <X11/Xproto.h> that looks similar to this:

#define X_DoSomething   42

In your extension header file, this will be a minor opcode, instead of a major opcode.

Request Format

Every request contains an 8-bit major opcode and a 16-bit length field expressed in units of four bytes. Every request consists of four bytes of header (containing the major opcode, the length field, and a data byte) followed by zero or more additional bytes of data. The length field defines the total length of the request, including the header. The length field in a request must equal the minimum length required to contain the request. If the specified length is smaller or larger than the required length, the server should generate a BadLength error. Unused bytes in a request are not required to be zero.

long XMaxRequestSize(*display*)
    Display **display*;

XMaxRequestSize returns the maximum request size (in 4-byte units) supported by the server. Single protocol requests to the server can be no longer than this size. Extensions should be designed in such a way that long protocol requests can be split up into smaller requests. The protocol guarantees the size to be no smaller than 4096 unit (16384 bytes).

Major opcodes 128 through 255 are reserved for extensions. Extensions are intended to contain multiple requests, so extension requests typically have an additional minor opcode encoded in the "spare" data byte in the request header, but the placement and interpretation of this minor opcode as well as all other fields in extension requests are not defined by the core protocol. Every request is implicitly assigned a sequence number (starting with one) used in replies, errors, and events.

To help but not cure portability problems to certain machines, the B16 and B32 macros have been defined so that they can become bitfield specifications on some machines. For example, on a Cray, these should be used for all 16-bit and 32-bit quantities, as discussed below.

Most protocol requests have a corresponding structure typedef in `<X11/Xproto.h>`, which looks like:

```
typedef struct _DoSomethingReq {
    CARD8 reqType;              /* X_DoSomething */
    CARD8 someDatum;            /* used differently in different requests */
    CARD16 length B16;          /* total # of bytes in request, divided by 4 */
    . . .
    /* request-specific data */
    . . .
} xDoSomethingReq;
```

If a core protocol request has a single 32-bit argument, you need not declare a request structure in your extension header file. Instead, such requests use `<X11/Xproto.h>`'s xResourceReq structure. This structure is used for any request whose single argument is a `Window`, `Pixmap`, `Drawable`, `GContext`, `Font`, `Cursor`, `Colormap`, `Atom`, or `VisualID`.

```
typedef struct _ResourceReq {
    CARD8 reqType;              /* the request type, e.g.
                                    X_DoSomething */
    BYTE pad;                   /* not used */
    CARD16 length B16;          /* 2 (= total # of bytes in request,
                                    divided by 4) */
    CARD32 id B32;              /* the Window, Drawable, Font,
                                    GContext, etc. */
} xResourceReq;
```

If convenient, you can do something similar in your extension header file.

In both of these structures, the reqType field identifies the type of the request (for example, X_MapWindow or X_CreatePixmap). The length field tells how long the request is in units of 4-byte longwords. This length includes both the request structure itself and any variable length data, such as strings or lists, that follow the request structure. Request structures come in different sizes, but all requests are padded to be multiples of four bytes long.

A few protocol requests take no arguments at all. Instead, they use `<X11/Xproto.h>`'s xReq structure, which contains only a reqType and a length (and a pad byte).

If the protocol request requires a reply, then <X11/Xproto.h> also contains a reply structure typedef:

```
typedef struct _DoSomethingReply {
    BYTE type;                       /* always X_Reply */
    BYTE someDatum;                  /* used differently in different requests */
    CARD16 sequenceNumber B16;       /* # of requests sent so far */
    CARD32 length B32;               /* # of additional bytes, divided by 4 */
    . . .
    /* request-specific data */
    . . .
} xDoSomethingReply;
```

Most of these reply structures are 32 bytes long. If there are not that many reply values, then they contain a sufficient number of pad fields to bring them up to 32 bytes. The length field is the total number of bytes in the request minus 32, divided by 4. This length will be nonzero only if:

- The reply structure is followed by variable length data such as a list or string.
- The reply structure is longer than 32 bytes.

Only `GetWindowAttributes`, `QueryFont`, `QueryKeymap`, and `GetKeyboardControl` have reply structures longer than 32 bytes in the core protocol.

A few protocol requests return replies that contain no data. <X11/Xproto.h> does not define reply structures for these. Instead, they use the `xGenericReply` structure, which contains only a type, length, and sequence number (and sufficient padding to make it 32 bytes long).

Starting to Write a Stub Routine

An Xlib stub routine should always start like this:

```
#include "Xlibint.h"
XDoSomething (arguments,...)
/* argument declarations */
{
    register XDoSomethingReq *req;
```

If the protocol request has a reply, then the variable declarations should include the reply structure for the request. The following is an example:

```
xDoSomethingReply rep;
```

Locking Data Structures

To lock the display structure for systems that want to support multithreaded access to a single display connection, each stub will need to lock its critical section. Generally, this section is the point from just before the appropriate GetReq call until all arguments to the call have been stored into the buffer. The precise instructions needed for this locking depend upon the machine architecture. Two calls, which are generally implemented as macros, have been provided.

LockDisplay(*display*)
    Display **display*;

UnlockDisplay(*display*)
    Display **display*;

Sending the Protocol Request and Arguments

After the variable declarations, a stub routine should call one of four macros defined in `<X11/Xlibint.h>`: `GetReq`, `GetReqExtra`, `GetResReq`, or `GetEmptyReq`. All of these macros take, as their first argument, the name of the protocol request as declared in `<X11/Xproto.h>` except with X_ removed. The macro then appends the request structure to the output buffer, fills in its type and length field, and sets req to point to it.

If the protocol request has no arguments (for instance, X_GrabServer), then use `GetEmptyReq`.

```
GetEmptyReq (DoSomething);
```

If the protocol request has a single 32-bit argument (such as a `Pixmap`, `Window`, `Drawable`, `Atom`, and so on), then use `GetResReq`. The second argument to the macro is the 32-bit object. `_MapWindow` is a good example.

```
GetResReq (DoSomething, rid);
```

The rid argument is the `Pixmap`, `Window`, or other resource ID.

If the protocol request takes any other argument list, then call `GetReq`. After the `GetReq`, you need to set all the other fields in the request structure, usually from arguments to the stub routine.

```
GetReq (DoSomething);
/* fill in arguments here */
req→arg1 = arg1;
req→arg2 = arg2;
```

A few stub routines (such as `XCreateGC` and `XCreatePixmap`) return a resource ID to the caller but pass a resource ID as an argument to the protocol request. Such routines use the macro `XAllocID` to allocate a resource ID from the range of IDs that were assigned to this client when it opened the connection.

```
rid = req→rid = XAllocID();
return (rid);
```

Finally, some stub routines transmit a fixed amount of variable length data after the request. Typically, these routines (such as `XMoveWindow` and `XSetBackground`) are special cases of more general functions like `XMoveResizeWindow` and `XChangeGC`. These special case routines use `GetReqExtra`, which is the same as `GetReq` except that it takes an additional argument (the number of extra bytes to allocate in the output buffer after the request structure). This number should always be a multiple of four.

Variable Length Arguments

Some protocol requests take additional variable length data that follow the `xDoSomethingReq` structure. The format of this data varies from request to request. Some requests require a sequence of 8-bit bytes, others a sequence of 16-bit or 32-bit entities, and still others a sequence of structures.

It is necessary to add the length of any variable length data to the length field of the request structure. That length field is in units of 32-bit longwords. If the data is a string or other sequence of 8-bit bytes, then you must round the length up and shift it before adding:

```
req→length += (nbytes+3)>>2;
```

To transmit variable length data, use the `Data` macro. If the data fits into the output buffer, then this macro copies it to the buffer. If it does not fit, however, the `Data` macro calls `_XSend`, which transmits first the contents of the buffer and then your data. The `Data` macro takes three arguments: the Display, a pointer to the beginning of the data, and the number of bytes to be sent.

```
Data(display, (char *) data, nbytes);
```

If the data are 16-bit entities, then use the `PackData` macro instead. It takes the same arguments and does the same things, but it does the right thing on machines where a short is 32 bits instead of the usual 16.

Data (*display*, (char *) *data*, *nbytes*)
Data16 (*display*, (short *) *data*, *nbytes*)
Data32 (*display*, (long *) *data*, *nbytes*)

`Data`, `Data16`, and `Data32` are macros that may use their last argument more than once, so that argument should be a variable rather than an expression such as "nitems*sizeof(item)." You should do that kind of computation in a separate statement before calling them. Use the appropriate macro when sending byte, short, or long data.

If the protocol request requires a reply, then call the procedure `_XSend` instead of the `Data` macro. `_XSend` takes the same arguments, but because it sends your data immediately instead of copying it into the output buffer (which would later be flushed anyway by the following call on `_XReply`), it is faster.

Replies

If the protocol request has a reply, then call `_XReply` after you have finished dealing with all the fixed and variable length arguments. `_XReply` flushes the output buffer and waits for an `xReply` packet to arrive. If any events arrive in the meantime, `_XReply` places them in the queue for later use.

Status _XReply(*display, rep, extra, discard*)
    Display **display*;
    xReply **rep*;
    int *extra*;   /* number of 32-bit words expected after the reply */
    Bool *discard*;   /* should I discard data following "extra" words? */

_XReply waits for a reply packet and copies its contents into the specified rep. _XReply handles error and event packets that occur before the reply is received. _XReply takes four arguments:

- A Display structure
- A pointer to a reply structure (which must be cast to an xReply *)
- The number of additional bytes (beyond sizeof(xReply) = 32 bytes) in the reply structure
- A Boolean that indicates whether _XReply is to discard any additional bytes beyond those it was told to read

Because most reply structures are 32 bytes long, the third argument is usually 0. The only core protocol exceptions are the replies to Get-WindowAttributes, QueryFont, QueryKeymap, and GetKeyboard-Control, which have longer replies.

    The last argument should be False if the reply structure is followed by additional variable length data (such as a list or string). It should be True if there is not any variable length data.

Note   This last argument is provided for upward-compatibility reasons to allow a client to communicate properly with a hypothetical later version of the server that sends more data than the client expected. For example, some later version of GetWindowAttributes might use a larger, but compatible, xGetWindowAttributesReply that contains additional attribute data at the end.

    _XReply returns True if it received a reply successfully or False if it received any sort of error.

    For a request with a reply that is not followed by variable length data, you write something like:

```
_XReply(display, (xReply *) &rep, 0, True);
*ret1 = rep.ret1;
*ret2 = rep.ret2;
*ret3 = rep.ret3;
UnlockDisplay(dpy);
SyncHandle();
return (rep.ret4);
}
```

If there is variable length data after the reply, change the True to False, and use the appropriate _XRead function to read the variable length data.

_XRead (*display, data, nbytes*)
    Display **display*;
    char **data*;
    long *nbytes*;

_XRead reads the specified number of bytes into data.

_XRead16 (*display, data, nbytes*)
    Display **display*;
    short **data*;
    long *nbytes*;

_XRead16 reads the specified number of bytes, unpacking them as 16-bit quantities, into the specified array as shorts.

_XRead32 (*display, data, nbytes*)
    Display **display*;
    long **data*;
    long *nbytes*;

_XRead32 reads the specified number of bytes, unpacking them as 32-bit quantities, into the specified array as longs.

_XRead16Pad (*display, data, nbytes*)
    Display **display*;
    short **data*;
    long *nbytes*;

_XRead16Pad reads the specified number of bytes, unpacking them as 16-bit quantities, into the specified array as shorts. If the number of bytes is not a multiple of four, _XRead16Pad reads up to three additional pad bytes.

_XReadPad (*display, data, nbytes*)
    Display **display*;
    char **data*;
    long *nbytes*;

_XReadPad reads the specified number of bytes into data. If the number of bytes is not a multiple of four, _XReadPad reads up to three additional pad bytes.

Each protocol request is a little different. For further information, see the Xlib sources for examples.

Synchronous Calling

To ease debugging, each routine should have a call, just before returning to the user, to a routine called SyncHandle. This routine generally is implemented as a macro. If synchronous mode is enabled (see XSynchronize), the request is sent immediately. The library, however, waits until any error the routine could generate at the server has been handled.

Allocating and Deallocating Memory

To support the possible reentry of these routines, you must observe several conventions when allocating and deallocating memory, most often done when returning data to the user from the window system of a size the caller could not know in advance (for example, a list of fonts or a list of extensions). The standard C library routines on many systems are not protected against signals or other multithreaded uses. The following analogies to standard I/O library routines have been defined:

Xmalloc()   Replaces malloc()
Xfree()   Replaces free()
Xcalloc()   Replaces calloc()

These should be used in place of any calls you would make to the normal C library routines.

If you need a single scratch buffer inside a critical section (for example, to pack and unpack data to and from the wire protocol), the general memory allocators may be too expensive to use (particularly in output routines, which are performance critical). The routine below returns a scratch buffer for your use:

```
char *_XAllocScratch(display, nbytes)
    Display *display;
    unsigned long nbytes;
```

This storage must only be used inside of the critical section of your stub.

Portability Considerations

Many machine architectures, including many of the more recent RISC architectures, do not correctly access data at unaligned locations; their compilers pad out structures to preserve this characteristic. Many other machines capable of unaligned references pad inside of structures as well to preserve alignment, because accessing aligned data is usually much faster. Because the library and the server use structures to access data at arbitrary points in a byte stream, all data in request and reply packets *must* be naturally aligned; that is, 16-bit data starts on 16-bit boundaries in the request and 32-bit data on 32-bit boundaries. All requests must be a multiple of 32 bits in length to preserve the natural alignment in the data stream. You must pad structures out to 32-bit boundaries. Pad information does not have to be zeroed unless you want to preserve such fields for future use in your protocol requests. Floating point varies radically between machines and should be avoided completely if at all possible.

This code may run on machines with 16-bit ints. So, if any integer argument, variable, or return value either can take only nonnegative values or is declared as a CARD16 in the protocol, be sure to declare it as unsigned int and not as int. (This, of course, does not apply to Booleans or enumerations.)

Similarly, if any integer argument or return value is declared CARD32 in the protocol, declare it as an unsigned long and not as int or long. This also goes for any internal variables that may take on values larger than the maximum 16-bit unsigned int.

The library currently assumes that a char is 8 bits, a short is 16 bits, an int is 16 or 32 bits, and a long is 32 bits. The `PackData` macro is a half-hearted attempt to deal with the possibility of 32-bit shorts. However, much more work is needed to make this work properly.

Deriving the Correct Extension Opcode

The remaining problem a writer of an extension stub routine faces that the core protocol does not face is to map from the call to the proper major and minor opcodes. While there are a number of strategies, the simplest and fastest is outlined below.

1. Declare an array of pointers, _NFILE long (this is normally found in <`stdio.h`> and is the number of file descriptors supported on the system) of type `XExtCodes`. Make sure these are all initialized to NULL.

2. When your stub is entered, your initialization test is just to use the display pointer passed in to access the file descriptor and an index into the array. If the entry is NULL, then this is the first time you are entering the routine for this display. Call your initialization routine and pass it to the display pointer.

3. Once in your initialization routine, call `XInitExtension`; if it succeeds, store the pointer returned into this array. Make sure to establish a close display handler to allow you to zero the entry. Do whatever other initialization your extension requires. (For example, install event handlers and so on). Your initialization routine would normally return a pointer to the `XExtCodes` structure for this extension, which is what would normally be found in your array of pointers.

4. After returning from your initialization routine, the stub can now continue normally, because it has its major opcode safely in its hand in the `XExtCodes` structure.

Appendix D

Version 10 Compatibility Functions

Drawing and Filling Polygons and Curves

Xlib provides functions that you can use to draw or fill arbitrary polygons or curves. These functions are provided mainly for compatibility with X10 and have no server support. That is, they call other Xlib functions, not the server directly. Thus, if you just have straight lines to draw, using XDrawLines or XDrawSegments is much faster.

The functions discussed here provide all the functionality of the X10 functions XDraw, XDrawFilled, XDrawPatterned, XDrawDashed, and XDrawTiled. They are as compatible as possible given X11's new line drawing functions. One thing to note, however, is that VertexDrawLastPoint is no longer supported. Also, the error status returned is the opposite of what it was under X10 (this is the X11 standard error status). XAppend-Vertex and XClearVertexFlag from X10 also are not supported.

Just how the graphics context you use is set up actually determines whether you get dashes or not, and so on. Lines are properly joined if they connect and include the closing of a closed figure (see XDrawLines). The functions discussed here fail (return zero) only if they run out of memory or are passed a Vertex list that has a Vertex with VertexStartClosed set that is not followed by a Vertex with VertexEndClosed set.

To achieve the effects of the X10 `XDraw`, `XDrawDashed`, and `XDrawPatterned`, use `XDraw`.

```
#include <X11/X10.h>
Status XDraw(display, d, gc, vlist, vcount)
      Display *display;
      Drawable d;
      GC gc;
      Vertex *vlist;
      int vcount;
```

display   Specifies the connection to the X server.
d   Specifies the drawable.
gc   Specifies the GC.
vlist   Specifies a pointer to the list of vertices that indicate what to draw.
vcount   Specifies how many vertices are in vlist.

`XDraw` draws an arbitrary polygon or curve. The figure drawn is defined by the specified list of vertices (vlist). The points are connected by lines as specified in the flags in the vertex structure.

Each Vertex, as defined in `<X11/X10.h>`, is a structure with the following members:

```
typedef struct _Vertex {
      short x,y;
      unsigned short flags;
} Vertex;
```

The x and y members are the coordinates of the vertex that are relative to either the upper-left inside corner of the drawable (if `VertexRelative` is zero) or the previous vertex (if `VertexRelative` is one).

The flags, as defined in `<X11/X10.h>`, are as follows:

```
VertexRelative        0x0001      /* else absolute */
VertexDontDraw        0x0002      /* else draw */
VertexCurved          0x0004      /* else straight */
VertexStartClosed     0x0008      /* else not */
VertexEndClosed       0x0010      /* else not */
```

- If `VertexRelative` is not set, the coordinates are absolute (that is, relative to the drawable's origin). The first vertex must be an absolute vertex.

- If `VertexDontDraw` is one, no line or curve is drawn from the previous vertex to this one. This is analogous to picking up the pen and moving to another place before drawing another line.

- If `VertexCurved` is one, a spline algorithm is used to draw a smooth curve from the previous vertex through this one to the next vertex. Otherwise, a straight line is drawn from the previous vertex to this one. It makes sense to set `Vertex-Curved` to one only if a previous and next vertex are both defined (either explicitly in the array or through the definition of a closed curve).

- It is permissible for `VertexDontDraw` bits and `VertexCurved` bits to both be one. This is useful if you want to define the previous point for the smooth curve but do not want an actual curve drawing to start until this point.

- If `VertexStartClosed` is one, then this point marks the beginning of a closed curve. This vertex must be followed later in the array by another vertex whose effective coordinates are identical and that has a `VertexEndClosed` bit of one. The points in between form a cycle to determine predecessor and successor vertices for the spline algorithm.

This function uses these GC components: function, plane-mask, line-width, line-style, cap-style, join-style, fill-style, subwindow-mode, clip-x-origin, clip-y-origin, and clip-mask. It also uses these GC mode-dependent components: foreground, background, tile, stipple, tile-stipple-x-origin, tile-stipple-y-origin, dash-offset, and dash-list.

To achieve the effects of the X10 `XDrawTiled` and `XDrawFilled`, use `XDrawFilled`.

```
#include <X11/X10.h>
```

Status XDrawFilled(*display, d, gc, vlist, vcount*)
    Display **display*;
    Drawable *d*;
    GC *gc*;
    Vertex **vlist*;
    int *vcount*;

display   Specifies the connection to the X server.
d   Specifies the drawable.
gc   Specifies the GC.
vlist   Specifies a pointer to the list of vertices that indicate what to draw.
vcount   Specifies how many vertices are in vlist.

XDrawFilled draws arbitrary polygons or curves and then fills them.

This function uses these GC components: function, plane-mask, line-width, line-style, cap-style, join-style, fill-style, subwindow-mode, clip-x-origin, clip-y-origin, and clip-mask. It also uses these GC mode-dependent components: foreground, background, tile, stipple, tile-stipple-x-origin, tile-stipple-y-origin, dash-offset, dash-list, fill-style, and fill-rule.

Associating User Data with a Value

These functions have been superseded by the context management functions (see section 10.12). It is often necessary to associate arbitrary information with resource IDs. Xlib provides the XAssocTable functions that you can use to make such an association. Application programs often need to be able to easily refer to their own data structures when an event arrives. The XAssocTable system provides users of the X library with a method for associating their own data structures with X resources (Pixmaps, Fonts, Windows, and so on).

An XAssocTable can be used to type X resources. For example, the user may want to have three or four types of windows, each with different properties. This can be accomplished by associating each X window ID with a pointer to a window property data structure defined by the user. A generic type has been defined in the X library for resource IDs. It is called an XID.

There are a few guidelines that should be observed when using an XAssocTable:

- All XIDs are relative to the specified display.
- Because of the hashing scheme used by the association mechanism, the following rules for determining the size of a XAssocTable should be followed. Associations will be made and looked up more efficiently if the table size (number of buckets in the hashing system) is a power of two and if there are not more than 8 XIDs per bucket.

To return a pointer to a new XAssocTable, use XCreateAssocTable.

XAssocTable *XCreateAssocTable(*size*)
      int *size*;
size   Specifies the number of buckets in the hash system of XAssocTable.

The size argument specifies the number of buckets in the hash system of XAssocTable. For reasons of efficiency the number of buckets should be a power of two. Some size suggestions might be: use 32 buckets per 100 objects, and a reasonable maximum number of objects per buckets is 8. If an error allocating memory for the XAssocTable occurs, a NULL pointer is returned.

To create an entry in a given XAssocTable, use XMakeAssoc.

XMakeAssoc(*display, table, x_id, data*)
    Display **display*;
    XAssocTable **table*;
    XID *x_id*;
    char **data*;

display   Specifies the connection to the X server.
table   Specifies the assoc table.
x_id   Specifies the X resource ID.
data   Specifies the data to be associated with the X resource ID.

XMakeAssoc inserts data into an XAssocTable keyed on an XID. Data is inserted into the table only once. Redundant inserts are ignored. The queue in each association bucket is sorted from the lowest XID to the highest XID.

To obtain data from a given XAssocTable, use XLookUpAssoc.

char *XLookUpAssoc(*display, table, x_id*)
    Display **display*;
    XAssocTable **table*;
    XID *x_id*;

display   Specifies the connection to the X server.
table   Specifies the assoc table.
x_id   Specifies the X resource ID.

XLookUpAssoc retrieves the data stored in an XAssocTable by its XID. If an appropriately matching XID can be found in the table, XLookUpAssoc returns the data associated with it. If the x_id cannot be found in the table, it returns NULL.

To delete an entry from a given XAssocTable, use XDeleteAssoc.

XDeleteAssoc(*display, table, x_id*)
    Display **display*;
    XAssocTable **table*;
    XID *x_id;*
display   Specifies the connection to the X server.
table   Specifies the assoc table.
x_id   Specifies the X resource ID.

XDeleteAssoc deletes an association in an XAssocTable keyed on its XID. Redundant deletes (and deletes of nonexistent XIDs) are ignored. Deleting associations in no way impairs the performance of an XAssocTable.

To free the memory associated with a given XAssocTable, use XDestroyAssocTable.

XDestroyAssocTable(*table*)
    XAssocTable **table*;
table   Specifies the assoc table.

Appendix E

KEYSYM Encoding

For convenience, KEYSYM values are viewed as split into four bytes:

- Byte 1 (for the purposes of this encoding) is the most-significant 5 bits (because of the 29-bit effective values)
- Byte 2 is the next most-significant 8 bits
- Byte 3 is the next most-significant 8 bits
- Byte 4 is the least-significant 8 bits

The standard KEYSYM values all have the zero values for bytes 1 and 2. Byte 3 indicates a character code set, and byte 4 indicates a particular character within that set.

Byte 3	Byte 4
0	Latin 1
1	Latin 2
2	Latin 3
3	Latin 4
4	Kana
5	Arabic
6	Cyrillic
7	Greek
8	Technical
9	Special
10	Publishing
11	APL
12	Hebrew
255	Keyboard

Each character set contains gaps where codes have been removed that were duplicates with codes in previous character sets (that is, character sets with lesser byte 3 value).

The 94 and 96 character code sets have been moved to occupy the right-hand quadrant (decimal 129 through 256), so the ASCII subset has a unique encoding across byte 4, which corresponds to the ASCII character code. However, this cannot be guaranteed with future registrations and does not apply to all of the Keyboard set.

To the best of our knowledge, the Latin, Kana, Arabic, Cyrillic, Greek, APL, and Hebrew sets are from the appropriate ISO and/or ECMA international standards. There are no Technical, Special, or Publishing international standards, so these sets are based on Digital Equipment Corporation standards.

The ordering between the sets (byte 3) is essentially arbitrary. Although the national and international standards bodies are commencing deliberations regarding international 2-byte and 4-byte character sets, we do not know of any proposed layouts.

The order may be arbitrary, but it is important in dealing with duplicate coding. As far as possible, KEYSYM values are the same as the character code. In the Latin-1 to Latin-4 sets, all duplicate glyphs occupy the same code position. However, duplicates between Greek and Technical do not occupy the same code position. Thus, applications wishing to use the technical character set must transform the keysym by means of an array.

There is a difference between European and US usage of the names Pilcrow, Paragraph, and Section, as follows:

US name	*European name*	*code position in Latin-1*
Section sign	Paragraph sign	10/07
Paragraph sign	Pilcrow sign	11/06

We have adopted the names used by both the ISO and ECMA standards. Thus, 11/06 is the Pilcrow sign, and 10/07 is the Paragraph sign (Section sign). This favors the European usage.

The Keyboard set is a miscellaneous collection of commonly occuring keys on keyboards. Within this set, the keypad symbols are generally duplicates of symbols found on keys on the main part of the keyboard, but they are distinguished here because they often have a distinguishable semantics associated with them.

Keyboards tend to be comparatively standard with respect to the alphanumeric keys, but they differ radically on the miscellaneous function keys. Many function keys are left over from early timesharing days or are designed for a specific application. Keyboard layouts from large manufacturers tend to have lots of keys for every conceivable purpose, whereas small workstation manufacturers often add keys that are solely for support of some of their unique functionality. There are two ways of thinking about how to define keysyms for such a world:

- The Engraving approach
- The Common approach

The Engraving approach is to create a keysym for every unique key engraving. This is effectively taking the union of all key engravings on all keyboards. For example, some keyboards label function keys across the top as F1 through Fn, and others label them as PF1 through PFn. These would be different keys under the Engraving approach. Likewise, Lock would differ from Shift Lock, which is different from the up-arrow symbol that has the effect of changing lowercase to uppercase. There are lots of other aliases such as Del, DEL, Delete, Remove, and so forth. The Engraving approach makes it easy to decide if a new entry should be added to the keysym set: if it does not exactly match an existing one, then a new one is created. One estimate is that there would be on the order of 300–500 Keyboard keysyms using this approach, without counting foreign translations and variations.

The Common approach tries to capture all of the keys present on an interesting number of keyboards, folding likely aliases into the same keysym. For example, Del, DEL, and Delete are all merged into a single keysym. Vendors would be expected to augment the keysym set (using the vendor-specific encoding space) to include all of their unique keys that were not included in the standard set. Each vendor decides which of its keys map into the standard keysyms, which presumable can be overridden by a user. It is more difficult to implement this approach, because judgment is required about when a sufficient set of keyboards implements an engraving to justify making it a keysym in the standard set and about which engravings should be merged into a single keysym. Under this scheme there are an estimated 100–150 keysyms.

Although neither scheme is perfect or elegant, the Common approach has been selected because it makes it easier to write a portable application. Having the Delete functionality merged into a single keysym allows an application to implement a deletion function and expect reasonable bindings on a wide set of workstations. Under the Common approach, application writers are still free to look for and interpret vendor-specific keysyms, but because they are in the extended set, the application developer is more conscious that they are writing the application in a nonportable fashion.

In the listings starting on the next page, Code Pos is a representation of byte 4 of the KEYSYM value, expressed as most-significant/least significant 4-bit values. The Code Pos numbers are for reference only and do not affect the KEYSYM value. In all cases, the KEYSYM value is:

byte3 * 256 + byte4

Latin-1 KEYSYM Set

Byte 3	Byte 4	Code Pos	Character	Name
000	032	02/00		SPACE
000	033	02/01	!	EXCLAMATION POINT
000	034	02/02	"	QUOTATION MARK
000	035	02/03	#	NUMBER SIGN
000	036	02/04	$	DOLLAR SIGN
000	037	02/05	%	PERCENT SIGN
000	038	02/06	&	AMPERSAND
000	039	02/07	'	APOSTROPHE
000	040	02/08	(	LEFT PARENTHESIS
000	041	02/09	)	RIGHT PARENTHESIS
000	042	02/10	*	ASTERISK
000	043	02/11	+	PLUS SIGN
000	044	02/12	,	COMMA
000	045	02/13	-	HYPHEN, MINUS SIGN
000	046	02/14	.	FULL STOP
000	047	02/15	/	SOLIDUS
000	048	03/00	0	DIGIT ZERO
000	049	03/01	1	DIGIT ONE
000	050	03/02	2	DIGIT TWO
000	051	03/03	3	DIGIT THREE
000	052	03/04	4	DIGIT FOUR
000	053	03/05	5	DIGIT FIVE
000	054	03/06	6	DIGIT SIX
000	055	03/07	7	DIGIT SEVEN
000	056	03/08	8	DIGIT EIGHT
000	057	03/09	9	DIGIT NINE
000	058	03/10	:	COLON
000	059	03/11	;	SEMICOLON

000	060	03/12	<	LESS THAN SIGN
000	061	03/13	=	EQUALS SIGN
000	062	03/14	>	GREATER THAN SIGN
000	063	03/15	?	QUESTION MARK
000	064	04/00	@	COMMERCIAL AT
000	065	04/01	A	LATIN CAPITAL LETTER A
000	066	04/02	B	LATIN CAPITAL LETTER B
000	067	04/03	C	LATIN CAPITAL LETTER C
000	068	04/04	D	LATIN CAPITAL LETTER D
000	069	04/05	E	LATIN CAPITAL LETTER E
000	070	04/06	F	LATIN CAPITAL LETTER F
000	071	04/07	G	LATIN CAPITAL LETTER G
000	072	04/08	H	LATIN CAPITAL LETTER H
000	073	04/09	I	LATIN CAPITAL LETTER I
000	074	04/10	J	LATIN CAPITAL LETTER J
000	075	04/11	K	LATIN CAPITAL LETTER K
000	076	04/12	L	LATIN CAPITAL LETTER L
000	077	04/13	M	LATIN CAPITAL LETTER M
000	078	04/14	N	LATIN CAPITAL LETTER N
000	079	04/15	O	LATIN CAPITAL LETTER O
000	080	05/00	P	LATIN CAPITAL LETTER P
000	081	05/01	Q	LATIN CAPITAL LETTER Q
000	082	05/02	R	LATIN CAPITAL LETTER R
000	083	05/03	S	LATIN CAPITAL LETTER S
000	084	05/04	T	LATIN CAPITAL LETTER T
000	085	05/05	U	LATIN CAPITAL LETTER U
000	086	05/06	V	LATIN CAPITAL LETTER V
000	087	05/07	W	LATIN CAPITAL LETTER W
000	088	05/08	X	LATIN CAPITAL LETTER X
000	089	05/09	Y	LATIN CAPITAL LETTER Y
000	090	05/10	Z	LATIN CAPITAL LETTER Z
000	091	05/11	[	LEFT SQUARE BRACKET

Byte 3	Byte 4	Code Pos	Character	Name
000	092	05/12	\	REVERSE SOLIDUS
000	093	05/13	]	RIGHT SQUARE BRACKET
000	094	05/14	^	CIRCUMFLEX ACCENT
000	095	05/15	_	LOW LINE
000	096	06/00	`	GRAVE ACCENT
000	097	06/01	a	LATIN SMALL LETTER a
000	098	06/02	b	LATIN SMALL LETTER b
000	099	06/03	c	LATIN SMALL LETTER c
000	100	06/04	d	LATIN SMALL LETTER d
000	101	06/05	e	LATIN SMALL LETTER e
000	102	06/06	f	LATIN SMALL LETTER f
000	103	06/07	g	LATIN SMALL LETTER g
000	104	06/08	h	LATIN SMALL LETTER h
000	105	06/09	i	LATIN SMALL LETTER i
000	106	06/10	j	LATIN SMALL LETTER j
000	107	06/11	k	LATIN SMALL LETTER k
000	108	06/12	l	LATIN SMALL LETTER l
000	109	06/13	m	LATIN SMALL LETTER m
000	110	06/14	n	LATIN SMALL LETTER n
000	111	06/15	o	LATIN SMALL LETTER o
000	112	07/00	p	LATIN SMALL LETTER p
000	113	07/01	q	LATIN SMALL LETTER q
000	114	07/02	r	LATIN SMALL LETTER r
000	115	07/03	s	LATIN SMALL LETTER s
000	116	07/04	t	LATIN SMALL LETTER t
000	117	07/05	u	LATIN SMALL LETTER u
000	118	07/06	v	LATIN SMALL LETTER v
000	119	07/07	w	LATIN SMALL LETTER w
000	120	07/08	x	LATIN SMALL LETTER x

000	121	07/09	y	LATIN SMALL LETTER y
000	122	07/10	z	LATIN SMALL LETTER z
000	123	07/11	{	LEFT CURLY BRACKET
000	124	07/12	|	VERTICAL LINE
000	125	07/13	}	RIGHT CURLY BRACKET
000	126	07/14	~	TILDE
000	160	10/00		NO-BREAK SPACE
000	161	10/01	¡	INVERTED EXCLAMATION MARK
000	162	10/02	¢	CENT SIGN
000	163	10/03	£	POUND SIGN
000	164	10/04	¤	CURRENCY SIGN
000	165	10/05	¥	YEN SIGN
000	166	10/06	¦	BROKEN VERTICAL BAR
000	167	10/07	§	PARAGRAPH SIGN, SECTION SIGN
000	168	10/08	¨	DIAERESIS
000	169	10/09	©	COPYRIGHT SIGN
000	170	10/10	ª	FEMININE ORDINAL INDICATOR
000	171	10/11	«	LEFT ANGLE QUOTATION MARK
000	172	10/12	¬	NOT SIGN
000	174	10/14	®	REGISTERED TRADEMARK SIGN
000	175	10/15	¯	MACRON
000	176	11/00	°	DEGREE SIGN, RING ABOVE
000	177	11/01	±	PLUS-MINUS SIGN
000	178	11/02	²	SUPERSCRIPT TWO
000	179	11/03	³	SUPERSCRIPT THREE
000	180	11/04	´	ACUTE ACCENT
000	181	11/05	µ	MICRO SIGN
000	182	11/06	¶	PILCROW SIGN
000	183	11/07	·	MIDDLE DOT
000	184	11/08	¸	CEDILLA
000	185	11/09	¹	SUPERSCRIPT ONE
000	186	11/10	º	MASCULINE ORDINAL INDICATOR

Byte 3	Byte 4	Code Pos	Character	Name
000	187	11/11	»	RIGHT ANGLE QUOTATION MARK
000	188	11/12	¼	VULGAR FRACTION ONE QUARTER
000	189	11/13	½	VULGAR FRACTION ONE HALF
000	190	11/14	¾	VULGAR FRACTION THREE QUARTERS
000	191	11/15	¿	INVERTED QUESTION MARK
000	192	12/00	À	LATIN CAPITAL LETTER A WITH GRAVE ACCENT
000	193	12/01	Á	LATIN CAPITAL LETTER A WITH ACUTE ACCENT
000	194	12/02	Â	LATIN CAPITAL LETTER A WITH CIRCUMFLEX ACCENT
000	195	12/03	Ã	LATIN CAPITAL LETTER A WITH TILDE
000	196	12/04	Ä	LATIN CAPITAL LETTER A WITH DIAERESIS
000	197	12/05	Å	LATIN CAPITAL LETTER A WITH RING ABOVE
000	198	12/06	Æ	LATIN CAPITAL DIPHTHONG AE
000	199	12/07	Ç	LATIN CAPITAL LETTER C WITH CEDILLA
000	200	12/08	È	LATIN CAPITAL LETTER E WITH GRAVE ACCENT
000	201	12/09	É	LATIN CAPITAL LETTER E WITH ACUTE ACCENT
000	202	12/10	Ê	LATIN CAPITAL LETTER E WITH CIRCUMFLEX ACCENT
000	203	12/11	Ë	LATIN CAPITAL LETTER E WITH DIAERESIS
000	204	12/12	Ì	LATIN CAPITAL LETTER I WITH GRAVE ACCENT
000	205	12/13	Í	LATIN CAPITAL LETTER I WITH ACUTE ACCENT
000	206	12/14	Î	LATIN CAPITAL LETTER I WITH CIRCUMFLEX ACCENT
000	207	12/15	Ï	LATIN CAPITAL LETTER I WITH DIAERESIS
000	208	13/00	Ð	ICELANDIC CAPITAL LETTER ETH
000	209	13/01	Ñ	LATIN CAPITAL LETTER N WITH TILDE
000	210	13/02	Ò	LATIN CAPITAL LETTER O WITH GRAVE ACCENT
000	211	13/03	Ó	LATIN CAPITAL LETTER O WITH ACUTE ACCENT
000	212	13/04	Ô	LATIN CAPITAL LETTER O WITH CIRCUMFLEX ACCENT
000	213	13/05	Õ	LATIN CAPITAL LETTER O WITH TILDE
000	214	13/06	Ö	LATIN CAPITAL LETTER O WITH DIAERESIS
000	215	13/07	×	MULTIPLICATION SIGN

000	13/08	216	ø	LATIN CAPITAL LETTER O WITH OBLIQUE STROKE
000	13/09	217	Ù	LATIN CAPITAL LETTER U WITH GRAVE ACCENT
000	13/10	218	Ú	LATIN CAPITAL LETTER U WITH ACUTE ACCENT
000	13/11	219	Û	LATIN CAPITAL LETTER U WITH CIRCUMFLEX ACCENT
000	13/12	220	Ü	LATIN CAPITAL LETTER U WITH DIAERESIS
000	13/13	221	Ý	LATIN CAPITAL LETTER Y WITH ACUTE ACCENT
000	13/14	222	Þ	ICELANDIC CAPITAL LETTER THORN
000	13/15	223	ß	GERMAN SMALL LETTER SHARP s
000	14/00	224	à	LATIN SMALL LETTER a WITH GRAVE ACCENT
000	14/01	225	á	LATIN SMALL LETTER a WITH ACUTE ACCENT
000	14/02	226	â	LATIN SMALL LETTER a WITH CIRCUMFLEX ACCENT
000	14/03	227	ã	LATIN SMALL LETTER a WITH TILDE
000	14/04	228	ä	LATIN SMALL LETTER a WITH DIAERESIS
000	14/05	229	å	LATIN SMALL LETTER a WITH RING ABOVE
000	14/06	230	æ	LATIN SMALL DIPHTHONG ae
000	14/07	231	ç	LATIN SMALL LETTER c WITH CEDILLA
000	14/08	232	è	LATIN SMALL LETTER e WITH GRAVE ACCENT
000	14/09	233	é	LATIN SMALL LETTER e WITH ACUTE ACCENT
000	14/10	234	ê	LATIN SMALL LETTER e WITH CIRCUMFLEX ACCENT
000	14/11	235	ë	LATIN SMALL LETTER e WITH DIAERESIS
000	14/12	236	ì	LATIN SMALL LETTER i WITH GRAVE ACCENT
000	14/13	237	í	LATIN SMALL LETTER i WITH ACUTE ACCENT
000	14/14	238	î	LATIN SMALL LETTER i WITH CIRCUMFLEX ACCENT
000	14/15	239	ï	LATIN SMALL LETTER i WITH DIAERESIS
000	15/00	240	ð	ICELANDIC SMALL LETTER ETH
000	15/01	241	ñ	LATIN SMALL LETTER n WITH TILDE
000	15/02	242	ò	LATIN SMALL LETTER o WITH GRAVE ACCENT
000	15/03	243	ó	LATIN SMALL LETTER o WITH ACUTE ACCENT
000	15/04	244	ô	LATIN SMALL LETTER o WITH CIRCUMFLEX ACCENT
000	15/05	245	õ	LATIN SMALL LETTER o WITH TILDE
000	15/06	246	ö	LATIN SMALL LETTER o WITH DIAERESIS
000	15/07	247	÷	DIVISION SIGN

Byte 3	Byte 4	Code Pos	Character	Name
000	248	15/08	ø	LATIN SMALL LETTER o WITH OBLIQUE STROKE
000	249	15/09	ù	LATIN SMALL LETTER u WITH GRAVE ACCENT
000	250	15/10	ú	LATIN SMALL LETTER u WITH ACUTE ACCENT
000	251	15/11	û	LATIN SMALL LETTER u WITH CIRCUMFLEX ACCENT
000	252	15/12	ü	LATIN SMALL LETTER u WITH DIAERESIS
000	253	15/13	ý	LATIN SMALL LETTER y WITH ACUTE ACCENT
000	254	15/14	þ	ICELANDIC SMALL LETTER THORN
000	255	15/15	ÿ	LATIN SMALL LETTER y WITH DIAERESIS

Latin-2 KEYSYM Set

Byte 3	Byte 4	Code Pos	Character	Name
001	161	10/01	Ą	LATIN CAPITAL LETTER A WITH OGONEK
001	162	10/02	˘	BREVE
001	163	10/03	Ł	LATIN CAPITAL LETTER L WITH STROKE
001	165	10/05	Ľ	LATIN CAPITAL LETTER L WITH CARON
001	166	10/06	Ś	LATIN CAPITAL LETTER S WITH ACUTE ACCENT
001	169	10/09	Š	LATIN CAPITAL LETTER S WITH CARON
001	170	10/10	Ş	LATIN CAPITAL LETTER S WITH CEDILLA
001	171	10/11	Ť	LATIN CAPITAL LETTER T WITH CARON
001	172	10/12	Ź	LATIN CAPITAL LETTER Z WITH ACUTE ACCENT
001	174	10/14	Ž	LATIN CAPITAL LETTER Z WITH CARON
001	175	10/15	Ż	LATIN CAPITAL LETTER Z WITH DOT ABOVE
001	177	11/01	ą	LATIN SMALL LETTER a WITH OGONEK
001	178	11/02	˛	OGONEK
001	179	11/03	ł	LATIN SMALL LETTER l WITH STROKE
001	181	11/05	ľ	LATIN SMALL LETTER l WITH CARON
001	182	11/06	ś	LATIN SMALL LETTER s WITH ACUTE ACCENT
001	183	11/07	ˇ	CARON
001	185	11/09	š	LATIN SMALL LETTER s WITH CARON
001	186	11/10	ş	LATIN SMALL LETTER s WITH CEDILLA

001	187	11/11	ť	LATIN SMALL LETTER t WITH CARON
001	188	11/12	ź	LATIN SMALL LETTER z WITH ACUTE ACCENT
001	189	11/13	˝	DOUBLE ACUTE ACCENT
001	190	11/14	ž	LATIN SMALL LETTER z WITH CARON
001	191	11/15	ż	LATIN SMALL LETTER z WITH DOT ABOVE
001	192	12/00	Ŕ	LATIN CAPITAL LETTER R WITH ACUTE ACCENT
001	195	12/03	Ă	LATIN CAPITAL LETTER A WITH BREVE
001	197	12/05	Ĺ	LATIN CAPITAL LETTER L WITH ACUTE ACCENT
001	198	12/06	Ć	LATIN CAPITAL LETTER C WITH ACUTE ACCENT
001	200	12/08	Č	LATIN CAPITAL LETTER C WITH CARON
001	202	12/10	Ę	LATIN CAPITAL LETTER E WITH OGONEK
001	204	12/12	Ě	LATIN CAPITAL LETTER E WITH CARON
001	207	12/15	Ď	LATIN CAPITAL LETTER D WITH CARON
001	208	13/00	Đ	LATIN CAPITAL LETTER D WITH STROKE
001	209	13/01	Ń	LATIN CAPITAL LETTER N WITH ACUTE ACCENT
001	210	13/02	Ň	LATIN CAPITAL LETTER N WITH CARON
001	213	13/05	Ő	LATIN CAPITAL LETTER O WITH DOUBLE ACUTE ACCENT
001	216	13/08	Ř	LATIN CAPITAL LETTER R WITH CARON
001	217	13/09	Ů	LATIN CAPITAL LETTER U WITH RING ABOVE
001	219	13/11	Ű	LATIN CAPITAL LETTER U WITH DOUBLE ACUTE ACCENT
001	222	13/14	Ţ	LATIN CAPITAL LETTER T WITH CEDILLA
001	224	14/00	ŕ	LATIN SMALL LETTER r WITH ACUTE ACCENT
001	227	14/03	ă	LATIN SMALL LETTER a WITH BREVE
001	229	14/05	ĺ	LATIN SMALL LETTER l WITH ACUTE ACCENT
001	230	14/06	ć	LATIN SMALL LETTER c WITH ACUTE ACCENT
001	232	14/08	č	LATIN SMALL LETTER c WITH CARON
001	234	14/10	ę	LATIN SMALL LETTER e WITH OGONEK
001	236	14/12	ě	LATIN SMALL LETTER e WITH CARON
001	239	14/15	ď	LATIN SMALL LETTER d WITH CARON
001	240	15/00	đ	LATIN SMALL LETTER d WITH STROKE
001	241	15/01	ń	LATIN SMALL LETTER n WITH ACUTE ACCENT
001	242	15/02	ň	LATIN SMALL LETTER n WITH CARON

Byte 3	Byte 4	Code Pos	Character	Name
001	245	15/05	ő	LATIN SMALL LETTER o WITH DOUBLE ACUTE ACCENT
001	248	15/08	ř	LATIN SMALL LETTER r WITH CARON
001	249	15/09	ů	LATIN SMALL LETTER u WITH RING ABOVE
001	251	15/11	ű	LATIN SMALL LETTER u WITH DOUBLE ACUTE ACCENT
001	254	15/14	ţ	LATIN SMALL LETTER t WITH CEDILLA
001	255	15/15	·	DOT ABOVE

Latin-3 KEYSYM Set

Byte 3	Byte 4	Code Pos	Character	Name
002	161	10/01	Ħ	LATIN CAPITAL LETTER H WITH STROKE
002	166	10/06	Ĥ	LATIN CAPITAL LETTER H WITH CIRCUMFLEX ACCENT
002	169	10/09	İ	LATIN CAPITAL LETTER I WITH DOT ABOVE
002	171	10/11	Ğ	LATIN CAPITAL LETTER G WITH BREVE
002	172	10/12	Ĵ	LATIN CAPITAL LETTER J WITH CIRCUMFLEX ACCENT
002	177	11/01	ħ	LATIN SMALL LETTER h WITH STROKE
002	182	11/06	ĥ	LATIN SMALL LETTER h WITH CIRCUMFLEX ACCENT
002	185	11/09	ı	SMALL DOTLESS LETTER i
002	187	11/11	ğ	LATIN SMALL LETTER g WITH BREVE
002	188	11/12	ĵ	LATIN SMALL LETTER j WITH CIRCUMFLEX ACCENT
002	197	12/05	Ċ	LATIN CAPITAL LETTER C WITH DOT ABOVE
002	198	12/06	Ĉ	LATIN CAPITAL LETTER C WITH CIRCUMFLEX ACCENT
002	213	13/05	Ġ	LATIN CAPITAL LETTER G WITH DOT ABOVE
002	216	13/08	Ĝ	LATIN CAPITAL LETTER G WITH CIRCUMFLEX ACCENT
002	221	13/13	Ŭ	LATIN CAPITAL LETTER U WITH BREVE
002	222	13/14	Ŝ	LATIN CAPITAL LETTER S WITH CIRCUMFLEX ACCENT
002	229	14/05	ċ	LATIN SMALL LETTER c WITH DOT ABOVE
002	230	14/06	ĉ	LATIN SMALL LETTER c WITH CIRCUMFLEX ACCENT
002	245	15/05	ġ	LATIN SMALL LETTER g WITH DOT ABOVE
002	248	15/08	ĝ	LATIN SMALL LETTER g WITH CIRCUMFLEX ACCENT

002	253	15/13	ŭ	LATIN SMALL LETTER u WITH BREVE
002	254	15/14	ŝ	LATIN SMALL LETTER s WITH CIRCUMFLEX ACCENT

Latin-4 KEYSYM Set

003	162	10/02	ĸ	LATIN SMALL LETTER KAPPA
003	163	10/03	Ŗ	LATIN CAPITAL LETTER R WITH CEDILLA
003	165	10/05	Ĩ	LATIN CAPITAL LETTER I WITH TILDE
003	166	10/06	Ļ	LATIN CAPITAL LETTER L WITH CEDILLA
003	170	10/10	Ē	LATIN CAPITAL LETTER E WITH MACRON
003	171	10/11	Ģ	LATIN CAPITAL LETTER G WITH CEDILLA
003	172	10/12	Ŧ	LATIN CAPITAL LETTER T WITH OBLIQUE STROKE
003	179	11/03	ŗ	LATIN SMALL LETTER r WITH CEDILLA
003	181	11/05	ĩ	LATIN SMALL LETTER i WITH TILDE
003	182	11/06	ļ	LATIN SMALL LETTER l WITH CEDILLA
003	186	11/10	ē	LATIN SMALL LETTER e WITH MACRON
003	187	11/11	ǵ	LATIN SMALL LETTER g WITH ACUTE ACCENT
003	188	11/12	ŧ	LATIN SMALL LETTER t WITH OBLIQUE STROKE
003	189	11/13	Ŋ	LAPPISH CAPITAL LETTER ENG
003	191	11/15	ŋ	LAPPISH SMALL LETTER ENG
003	192	12/00	Ā	LATIN CAPITAL LETTER A WITH MACRON
003	199	12/07	Į	LATIN CAPITAL LETTER I WITH OGONEK
003	204	12/12	Ė	LATIN CAPITAL LETTER E WITH DOT ABOVE
003	207	12/15	Ī	LATIN CAPITAL LETTER I WITH MACRON
003	209	13/01	Ņ	LATIN CAPITAL LETTER N WITH CEDILLA
003	210	13/02	Ō	LATIN CAPITAL LETTER O WITH MACRON
003	211	13/03	Ķ	LATIN CAPITAL LETTER K WITH CEDILLA
003	217	13/09	Ų	LATIN CAPITAL LETTER U WITH OGONEK
003	221	13/13	Ũ	LATIN CAPITAL LETTER U WITH TILDE
003	222	13/14	Ū	LATIN CAPITAL LETTER U WITH MACRON
003	224	14/00	ā	LATIN SMALL LETTER a WITH MACRON
003	231	14/07	į	LATIN SMALL LETTER i WITH OGONEK
003	236	14/12	ė	LATIN SMALL LETTER e WITH DOT ABOVE

Byte 3	Byte 4	Code Pos	Character	Name
003	239	14/15	ī	LATIN SMALL LETTER i WITH MACRON
003	241	15/01	ņ	LATIN SMALL LETTER n WITH CEDILLA
003	242	15/02	ō	LATIN SMALL LETTER o WITH MACRON
003	243	15/03	ķ	LATIN SMALL LETTER k WITH CEDILLA
003	249	15/09	ų	LATIN SMALL LETTER u WITH OGONEK
003	253	15/13	ũ	LATIN SMALL LETTER u WITH TILDE
003	254	15/14	ū	LATIN SMALL LETTER u WITH MACRON

Kana KEYSYM Set

Byte 3	Byte 4	Code Pos	Character	Name
004	126	07/14	‾	OVERLINE
004	161	10/01	｡	KANA FULL STOP
004	162	10/02	｢	KANA OPENING BRACKET
004	163	10/03	｣	KANA CLOSING BRACKET
004	164	10/04	､	KANA COMMA
004	165	10/05	･	KANA MIDDLE DOT
004	166	10/06	ｦ	KANA LETTER WO
004	167	10/07	ｧ	KANA LETTER SMALL A
004	168	10/08	ｨ	KANA LETTER SMALL I
004	169	10/09	ｩ	KANA LETTER SMALL U
004	170	10/10	ｪ	KANA LETTER SMALL E
004	171	10/11	ｫ	KANA LETTER SMALL O
004	172	10/12	ｬ	KANA LETTER SMALL YA
004	173	10/13	ｭ	KANA LETTER SMALL YU
004	174	10/14	ｮ	KANA LETTER SMALL YO
004	175	10/15	ｯ	KANA LETTER SMALL TU
004	176	11/00	ｰ	PROLONGED SOUND SYMBOL
004	177	11/01	ｱ	KANA LETTER A
004	178	11/02	ｲ	KANA LETTER I
004	179	11/03	ｳ	KANA LETTER U

004	180	11/04	エ	KANA LETTER E
004	181	11/05	オ	KANA LETTER O
004	182	11/06	カ	KANA LETTER KA
004	183	11/07	キ	KANA LETTER KI
004	184	11/08	ク	KANA LETTER KU
004	185	11/09	ケ	KANA LETTER KE
004	186	11/10	コ	KANA LETTER KO
004	187	11/11	サ	KANA LETTER SA
004	188	11/12	シ	KANA LETTER SHI
004	189	11/13	ス	KANA LETTER SU
004	190	11/14	セ	KANA LETTER SE
004	191	11/15	ソ	KANA LETTER SO
004	192	12/00	タ	KANA LETTER TA
004	193	12/01	チ	KANA LETTER TI
004	194	12/02	ツ	KANA LETTER TU
004	195	12/03	テ	KANA LETTER TE
004	196	12/04	ト	KANA LETTER TO
004	197	12/05	ナ	KANA LETTER NA
004	198	12/06	ニ	KANA LETTER NI
004	199	12/07	ヌ	KANA LETTER NU
004	200	12/08	ネ	KANA LETTER NE
004	201	12/09	ノ	KANA LETTER NO
004	202	12/10	ハ	KANA LETTER HA
004	203	12/11	ヒ	KANA LETTER HI
004	204	12/12	フ	KANA LETTER HU
004	205	12/13	ヘ	KANA LETTER HE
004	206	12/14	ホ	KANA LETTER HO
004	207	12/15	マ	KANA LETTER MA
004	208	13/00	ミ	KANA LETTER MI
004	209	13/01	ム	KANA LETTER MU
004	210	13/02	メ	KANA LETTER ME
004	211	13/03	モ	KANA LETTER MO

Byte 3	Byte 4	Code Pos	Character	Name
004	212	13/04	ヰ	KANA LETTER YA
004	213	13/05	ユ	KANA LETTER YU
004	214	13/06	ヨ	KANA LETTER YO
004	215	13/07	ラ	KANA LETTER RA
004	216	13/08	リ	KANA LETTER RI
004	217	13/09	ル	KANA LETTER RU
004	218	13/10	レ	KANA LETTER RE
004	219	13/11	ロ	KANA LETTER RO
004	220	13/12	ワ	KANA LETTER WA
004	221	13/13	ン	KANA LETTER N
004	222	13/14	゛	VOICED SOUND SYMBOL
004	223	13/15	゜	SEMIVOICED SOUND SYMBOL

Arabic KEYSYM Set

Byte 3	Byte 4	Code Pos	Character	Name
005	172	10/12	،	ARABIC COMMA
005	187	11/11	؛	ARABIC SEMICOLON
005	191	11/15	؟	ARABIC QUESTION MARK
005	193	12/01	ء	ARABIC LETTER HAMZA
005	194	12/02	آ	ARABIC LETTER MADDA ON ALEF
005	195	12/03	أ	ARABIC LETTER HAMZA ON ALEF
005	196	12/04	ؤ	ARABIC LETTER HAMZA ON WAW
005	197	12/05	إ	ARABIC LETTER HAMZA UNDER ALEF
005	198	12/06	ئ	ARABIC LETTER HAMZA ON YEH
005	199	12/07	ا	ARABIC LETTER ALEF
005	200	12/08	ب	ARABIC LETTER BEH
005	201	12/09	ة	ARABIC LETTER TEH MARBUTA
005	202	12/10	ت	ARABIC LETTER TEH
005	203	12/11	ث	ARABIC LETTER THEH
005	204	12/12	ج	ARABIC LETTER JEEM

005	12/13	205	ن·ט	ARABIC LETTER HAH
005	12/14	206		ARABIC LETTER KHAH
005	12/15	207		ARABIC LETTER DAL
005	13/00	208		ARABIC LETTER THAL
005	13/01	209		ARABIC LETTER RA
005	13/02	210		ARABIC LETTER ZAIN
005	13/03	211		ARABIC LETTER SEEN
005	13/04	212		ARABIC LETTER SHEEN
005	13/05	213		ARABIC LETTER SAD
005	13/06	214		ARABIC LETTER DAD
005	13/07	215		ARABIC LETTER TAH
005	13/08	216		ARABIC LETTER ZAH
005	13/09	217		ARABIC LETTER AIN
005	13/10	218		ARABIC LETTER GHAIN
005	14/00	224		ARABIC LETTER TATWEEL
005	14/01	225		ARABIC LETTER FEH
005	14/02	226		ARABIC LETTER QAF
005	14/03	227		ARABIC LETTER KAF
005	14/04	228		ARABIC LETTER LAM
005	14/05	229		ARABIC LETTER MEEM
005	14/06	230		ARABIC LETTER NOON
005	14/07	231		ARABIC LETTER HEH
005	14/08	232		ARABIC LETTER WAW
005	14/09	233		ARABIC LETTER ALEF MAKSURA
005	14/10	234		ARABIC LETTER YEH
005	14/11	235		ARABIC LETTER FATHATAN
005	14/12	236		ARABIC LETTER DAMMATAN
005	14/13	237		ARABIC LETTER KASRATAN
005	14/14	238		ARABIC LETTER FATHA
005	14/15	239		ARABIC LETTER DAMMA
005	15/00	240		ARABIC LETTER KASRA
005	15/01	241		ARABIC LETTER SHADDA
005	15/02	242		ARABIC LETTER SUKUN

Cyrillic KEYSYM Set

Byte 3	Byte 4	Code Pos	Character	Name
006	161	10/01	ђ	SERBIAN SMALL LETTER DJE
006	162	10/02	ѓ	MACEDONIA SMALL LETTER GJE
006	163	10/03	ё	CYRILLIC SMALL LETTER IO
006	164	10/04	є	UKRAINIAN SMALL LETTER JE
006	165	10/05	ѕ	MACEDONIA SMALL LETTER DSE
006	166	10/06	і	UKRAINIAN SMALL LETTER I
006	167	10/07	ї	UKRAINIAN SMALL LETTER YI
006	168	10/08	ј	SERBIAN SMALL LETTER JE
006	169	10/09	љ	SERBIAN SMALL LETTER LJE
006	170	10/10	њ	SERBIAN SMALL LETTER NJE
006	171	10/11	ќ	SERBIAN SMALL LETTER TSHE
006	172	10/12	ћ	MACEDONIA SMALL LETTER KJE
006	174	10/14	ў	BYELORUSSIAN SMALL LETTER SHORT U
006	175	10/15	џ	SERBIAN SMALL LETTER DZE
006	176	11/00	№	NUMERO SIGN
006	177	11/01	Ђ	SERBIAN CAPITAL LETTER DJE
006	178	11/02	Ѓ	MACEDONIA CAPITAL LETTER GJE
006	179	11/03	Ё	CYRILLIC CAPITAL LETTER IO
006	180	11/04	Є	UKRAINIAN CAPITAL LETTER JE
006	181	11/05	Ѕ	MACEDONIA CAPITAL LETTER DSE
006	182	11/06	І	UKRAINIAN CAPITAL LETTER I
006	183	11/07	Ї	UKRAINIAN CAPITAL LETTER YI
006	184	11/08	Ј	SERBIAN CAPITAL LETTER JE
006	185	11/09	Љ	SERBIAN CAPITAL LETTER LJE
006	186	11/10	Њ	SERBIAN CAPITAL LETTER NJE
006	187	11/11	Ћ	SERBIAN CAPITAL LETTER TSHE
006	188	11/12	Ќ	MACEDONIA CAPITAL LETTER KJE
006	190	11/14	Ў	BYELORUSSIAN CAPITAL LETTER SHORT U

006				
006	191	11/15	џ	SERBIAN CAPITAL LETTER DZE
006	192	12/00	ю	CYRILLIC SMALL LETTER YU
006	193	12/01	а	CYRILLIC SMALL LETTER A
006	194	12/02	б	CYRILLIC SMALL LETTER BE
006	195	12/03	ц	CYRILLIC SMALL LETTER TSE
006	196	12/04	д	CYRILLIC SMALL LETTER DE
006	197	12/05	е	CYRILLIC SMALL LETTER IE
006	198	12/06	ф	CYRILLIC SMALL LETTER EF
006	199	12/07	г	CYRILLIC SMALL LETTER GHE
006	200	12/08	х	CYRILLIC SMALL LETTER HA
006	201	12/09	и	CYRILLIC SMALL LETTER I
006	202	12/10	й	CYRILLIC SMALL LETTER SHORT I
006	203	12/11	к	CYRILLIC SMALL LETTER KA
006	204	12/12	л	CYRILLIC SMALL LETTER EL
006	205	12/13	м	CYRILLIC SMALL LETTER EM
006	206	12/14	н	CYRILLIC SMALL LETTER EN
006	207	12/15	о	CYRILLIC SMALL LETTER O
006	208	13/00	п	CYRILLIC SMALL LETTER PE
006	209	13/01	я	CYRILLIC SMALL LETTER YA
006	210	13/02	р	CYRILLIC SMALL LETTER ER
006	211	13/03	с	CYRILLIC SMALL LETTER ES
006	212	13/04	т	CYRILLIC SMALL LETTER TE
006	213	13/05	у	CYRILLIC SMALL LETTER U
006	214	13/06	ж	CYRILLIC SMALL LETTER ZHE
006	215	13/07	в	CYRILLIC SMALL LETTER VE
006	216	13/08	ь	CYRILLIC SMALL SOFT SIGN
006	217	13/09	ы	CYRILLIC SMALL LETTER YERU
006	218	13/10	з	CYRILLIC SMALL LETTER ZE
006	219	13/11	ш	CYRILLIC SMALL LETTER SHA
006	220	13/12	э	CYRILLIC SMALL LETTER E
006	221	13/13	щ	CYRILLIC SMALL LETTER SHCHA
006	222	13/14	ч	CYRILLIC SMALL LETTER CHE

Byte 3	Byte 4	Code Pos	Character	Name
006	223	13/15	ъ	CYRILLIC SMALL HARD SIGN
006	224	14/00	ю	CYRILLIC CAPITAL LETTER YU
006	225	14/01	А	CYRILLIC CAPITAL LETTER A
006	226	14/02	Б	CYRILLIC CAPITAL LETTER BE
006	227	14/03	Ц	CYRILLIC CAPITAL LETTER TSE
006	228	14/04	Д	CYRILLIC CAPITAL LETTER DE
006	229	14/05	Е	CYRILLIC CAPITAL LETTER IE
006	230	14/06	Ф	CYRILLIC CAPITAL LETTER EF
006	231	14/07	Г	CYRILLIC CAPITAL LETTER GHE
006	232	14/08	Х	CYRILLIC CAPITAL LETTER HA
006	233	14/09	И	CYRILLIC CAPITAL LETTER I
006	234	14/10	Й	CYRILLIC CAPITAL LETTER SHORT I
006	235	14/11	К	CYRILLIC CAPITAL LETTER KA
006	236	14/12	Л	CYRILLIC CAPITAL LETTER EL
006	237	14/13	М	CYRILLIC CAPITAL LETTER EM
006	238	14/14	Н	CYRILLIC CAPITAL LETTER EN
006	239	14/15	О	CYRILLIC CAPITAL LETTER O
006	240	15/00	П	CYRILLIC CAPITAL LETTER PE
006	241	15/01	Я	CYRILLIC CAPITAL LETTER YA
006	242	15/02	Р	CYRILLIC CAPITAL LETTER ER
006	243	15/03	С	CYRILLIC CAPITAL LETTER ES
006	244	15/04	Т	CYRILLIC CAPITAL LETTER TE
006	245	15/05	У	CYRILLIC CAPITAL LETTER U
006	246	15/06	Ж	CYRILLIC CAPITAL LETTER ZHE
006	247	15/07	В	CYRILLIC CAPITAL LETTER VE
006	248	15/08	Ь	CYRILLIC CAPITAL SOFT SIGN
006	249	15/09	Ы	CYRILLIC CAPITAL LETTER YERU
006	250	15/10	З	CYRILLIC CAPITAL LETTER ZE
006	251	15/11	Ш	CYRILLIC CAPITAL LETTER SHA

006	252	15/12	Э	CYRILLIC CAPITAL LETTER E
006	253	15/13	Щ	CYRILLIC CAPITAL LETTER SHCHA
006	254	15/14	Ч	CYRILLIC CAPITAL LETTER CHE
006	255	15/15	Ъ	CYRILLIC CAPITAL LETTER HARD SIGN

Greek KEYSYM Set

007	161	10/01	Ά	GREEK CAPITAL LETTER ALPHA WITH ACCENT
007	162	10/02	Έ	GREEK CAPITAL LETTER EPSILON WITH ACCENT
007	163	10/03	Ή	GREEK CAPITAL LETTER ETA WITH ACCENT
007	164	10/04	Ί	GREEK CAPITAL LETTER IOTA WITH ACCENT
007	165	10/05	Ϊ	GREEK CAPITAL LETTER IOTA WITH DIAERESIS
007	166	10/06	Ἵ	GREEK CAPITAL LETTER IOTA WITH ACCENT + DIAERESIS
007	167	10/07	Ό	GREEK CAPITAL LETTER OMICRON WITH ACCENT
007	168	10/08	Ύ	GREEK CAPITAL LETTER UPSILON WITH ACCENT
007	169	10/09	Ϋ	GREEK CAPITAL LETTER UPSILON WITH DIAERESIS
007	170	10/10	Ὕ	GREEK CAPITAL LETTER UPSILON WITH ACCENT + DIAERESIS
007	171	10/11	Ώ	GREEK CAPITAL LETTER OMEGA WITH ACCENT
007	177	11/01	ά	GREEK SMALL LETTER ALPHA WITH ACCENT
007	178	11/02	έ	GREEK SMALL LETTER EPSILON WITH ACCENT
007	179	11/03	ή	GREEK SMALL LETTER ETA WITH ACCENT
007	180	11/04	ί	GREEK SMALL LETTER IOTA WITH ACCENT
007	181	11/05	ϊ	GREEK SMALL LETTER IOTA WITH DIAERESIS
007	182	11/06	ΐ	GREEK SMALL LETTER IOTA WITH ACCENT + DIAERESIS
007	183	11/07	ό	GREEK SMALL LETTER OMICRON WITH ACCENT
007	184	11/08	ύ	GREEK SMALL LETTER UPSILON WITH ACCENT
007	185	11/09	ϋ	GREEK SMALL LETTER UPSILON WITH DIAERESIS
007	186	11/10	ΰ	GREEK SMALL LETTER UPSILON WITH ACCENT + DIAERESIS
007	187	11/11	ώ	GREEK SMALL LETTER OMEGA WITH ACCENT
007	193	12/01	Α	GREEK CAPITAL LETTER ALPHA
007	194	12/02	Β	GREEK CAPITAL LETTER BETA
007	195	12/03	Γ	GREEK CAPITAL LETTER GAMMA
007	196	12/04	Δ	GREEK CAPITAL LETTER DELTA

Byte 3	Byte 4	Code Pos	Character	Name
007	197	12/05	Ε	GREEK CAPITAL LETTER EPSILON
007	198	12/06	Ζ	GREEK CAPITAL LETTER ZETA
007	199	12/07	Η	GREEK CAPITAL LETTER ETA
007	200	12/08	Θ	GREEK CAPITAL LETTER THETA
007	201	12/09	Ι	GREEK CAPITAL LETTER IOTA
007	202	12/10	Κ	GREEK CAPITAL LETTER KAPPA
007	203	12/11	Λ	GREEK CAPITAL LETTER LAMBDA
007	204	12/12	Μ	GREEK CAPITAL LETTER MU
007	205	12/13	Ν	GREEK CAPITAL LETTER NU
007	206	12/14	Ξ	GREEK CAPITAL LETTER XI
007	207	12/15	Ο	GREEK CAPITAL LETTER OMICRON
007	208	13/00	Π	GREEK CAPITAL LETTER PI
007	209	13/01	Ρ	GREEK CAPITAL LETTER RHO
007	210	13/02	Σ	GREEK CAPITAL LETTER SIGMA
007	212	13/04	Τ	GREEK CAPITAL LETTER TAU
007	213	13/05	Υ	GREEK CAPITAL LETTER UPSILON
007	214	13/06	Φ	GREEK CAPITAL LETTER PHI
007	215	13/07	Χ	GREEK CAPITAL LETTER CHI
007	216	13/08	Ψ	GREEK CAPITAL LETTER PSI
007	217	13/09	Ω	GREEK CAPITAL LETTER OMEGA
007	225	14/01	α	GREEK SMALL LETTER ALPHA
007	226	14/02	β	GREEK SMALL LETTER BETA
007	227	14/03	γ	GREEK SMALL LETTER GAMMA
007	228	14/04	δ	GREEK SMALL LETTER DELTA
007	229	14/05	ε	GREEK SMALL LETTER EPSILON
007	230	14/06	ζ	GREEK SMALL LETTER ZETA
007	231	14/07	η	GREEK SMALL LETTER ETA
007	232	14/08	θ	GREEK SMALL LETTER THETA
007	233	14/09	ι	GREEK SMALL LETTER IOTA

007	234	14/10	κ	GREEK SMALL LETTER KAPPA
007	235	14/11	λ	GREEK SMALL LETTER LAMBDA
007	236	14/12	μ	GREEK SMALL LETTER MU
007	237	14/13	ν	GREEK SMALL LETTER NU
007	238	14/14	ξ	GREEK SMALL LETTER XI
007	239	14/15	o	GREEK SMALL LETTER OMICRON
007	240	15/00	π	GREEK SMALL LETTER PI
007	241	15/01	ρ	GREEK SMALL LETTER RHO
007	242	15/02	σ	GREEK SMALL LETTER SIGMA
007	243	15/03	ς	GREEK SMALL LETTER FINAL SMALL SIGMA
007	244	15/04	τ	GREEK SMALL LETTER TAU
007	245	15/05	υ	GREEK SMALL LETTER UPSILON
007	246	15/06	φ	GREEK SMALL LETTER PHI
007	247	15/07	χ	GREEK SMALL LETTER CHI
007	248	15/08	ψ	GREEK SMALL LETTER PSI
007	249	15/09	ω	GREEK SMALL LETTER OMEGA

Technical KEYSYM Set

008	161	10/01	⌐	LEFT RADICAL
008	162	10/02	⌐	TOP LEFT RADICAL
008	163	10/03			HORIZONTAL CONNECTOR
008	164	10/04	⌐	TOP INTEGRAL
008	165	10/05	⌐	BOTTOM INTEGRAL
008	166	10/06	—	VERTICAL CONNECTOR
008	167	10/07	⌐	TOP LEFT SQUARE BRACKET
008	168	10/08	⌐	BOTTOM LEFT SQUARE BRACKET
008	169	10/09	⌐	TOP RIGHT SQUARE BRACKET
008	170	10/10	⌐	BOTTOM RIGHT SQUARE BRACKET
008	171	10/11	⌐	TOP LEFT PARENTHESIS
008	172	10/12	⌐	BOTTOM LEFT PARENTHESIS
008	173	10/13	⌐	TOP RIGHT PARENTHESIS
008	174	10/14	⌐	BOTTOM RIGHT PARENTHESIS

Byte 3	Byte 4	Code Pos	Character	Name
008	175	10/15		LEFT MIDDLE CURLY BRACE
008	176	11/00		RIGHT MIDDLE CURLY BRACE
008	177	11/01		TOP LEFT SUMMATION
008	178	11/02		BOTTOM LEFT SUMMATION
008	179	11/03		TOP VERTICAL SUMMATION CONNECTOR
008	180	11/04		BOTTOM VERTICAL SUMMATION CONNECTOR
008	181	11/05		TOP RIGHT SUMMATION
008	182	11/06		BOTTOM RIGHT SUMMATION
008	183	11/07		RIGHT MIDDLE SUMMATION
008	188	11/12		LESS THAN OR EQUAL SIGN
008	189	11/13		NOT EQUAL SIGN
008	190	11/14		GREATER THAN OR EQUAL SIGN
008	191	11/15		INTEGRAL
008	192	12/00		THEREFORE
008	193	12/01		VARIATION, PROPORTIONAL TO
008	194	12/02		INFINITY
008	197	12/05		NABLA, DEL
008	200	12/08		IS APPROXIMATE TO
008	201	12/09		SIMILAR OR EQUAL TO
008	205	12/13		IF AND ONLY IF
008	206	12/14		IMPLIES
008	207	12/15		IDENTICAL TO
008	214	13/06		RADICAL
008	218	13/10		IS INCLUDED IN
008	219	13/11		INCLUDES
008	220	13/12		INTERSECTION
008	221	13/13		UNION
008	222	13/14		LOGICAL AND
008	223	13/15		LOGICAL OR

008	14/15	239	∂	PARTIAL DERIVATIVE
008	15/06	246	f	FUNCTION
008	15/11	251	↓	LEFT ARROW
008	15/12	252	↑	UPWARD ARROW
008	15/13	253	↑	RIGHT ARROW
008	15/14	254	→	DOWNWARD ARROW

Special KEYSYM Set

009	13/15	223	(BLANK)	BLANK
009	14/00	224	◆	SOLID DIAMOND
009	14/01	225	▩	CHECKERBOARD
009	14/02	226		"HT"
009	14/03	227		"FF"
009	14/04	228		"CR"
009	14/05	229		"LF"
009	14/08	232		"NL"
009	14/09	233		"VT"
009	14/10	234	⌐	LOWER-RIGHT CORNER
009	14/11	235	⌐	UPPER-RIGHT CORNER
009	14/12	236	⌐	UPPER-LEFT CORNER
009	14/13	237	⌐	LOWER-LEFT CORNER
009	14/14	238	+	CROSSING-LINES
009	14/15	239	SCAN 1	HORIZONTAL LINE, SCAN 1
009	15/00	240	SCAN 3	HORIZONTAL LINE, SCAN 3
009	15/01	241	SCAN 5	HORIZONTAL LINE, SCAN 5
009	15/02	242	SCAN 7	HORIZONTAL LINE, SCAN 7
009	15/03	243	SCAN 9	HORIZONTAL LINE, SCAN 9
009	15/04	244	⊢	LEFT "T"
009	15/05	245	⊣	RIGHT "T"
009	15/06	246	⊥	BOTTOM "T"
009	15/07	247	⊤	TOP "T"
009	15/08	248		VERTICAL BAR

Publish KEYSYM Set

Byte 3	Byte 4	Code Pos	Character	Name
010	161	10/01		EM SPACE
010	162	10/02		EN SPACE
010	163	10/03		3/EM SPACE
010	164	10/04		4/EM SPACE
010	165	10/05		DIGIT SPACE
010	166	10/06		PUNCTUATION SPACE
010	167	10/07		THIN SPACE
010	168	10/08		HAIR SPACE
010	169	10/09		EM DASH
010	170	10/10	—	EN DASH
010	172	10/12	]	SIGNIFICANT BLANK SYMBOL
010	174	10/14	∴	ELLIPSIS
010	175	10/15	∷	DOUBLE BASELINE DOT
010	176	11/00	⅓	VULGAR FRACTION ONE THIRD
010	177	11/01	⅔	VULGAR FRACTION TWO THIRDS
010	178	11/02	⅕	VULGAR FRACTION ONE FIFTH
010	179	11/03	⅖	VULGAR FRACTION TWO FIFTHS
010	180	11/04	⅗	VULGAR FRACTION THREE FIFTHS
010	181	11/05	⅘	VULGAR FRACTION FOUR FIFTHS
010	182	11/06	⅙	VULGAR FRACTION ONE SIXTH
010	183	11/07	⅚	VULGAR FRACTION FIVE SIXTHS
010	184	11/08	℅	CARE OF
010	187	11/11	–	FIGURE DASH
010	188	11/12	⟨	LEFT ANGLE BRACKET
010	189	11/13	·	DECIMAL POINT
010	190	11/14	⟩	RIGHT ANGLE BRACKET
010	191	11/15	■	MARKER
010	195	12/03	⅛	VULGAR FRACTION ONE EIGHTH

010	196	12/04	⅜	VULGAR FRACTION THREE EIGHTHS
010	197	12/05	⅝	VULGAR FRACTION FIVE EIGHTHS
010	198	12/06	⅞	VULGAR FRACTION SEVEN EIGHTHS
010	201	12/09	™	TRADEMARK SIGN
010	202	12/10	℠	SIGNATURE MARK
010	203	12/11	Ⓜ	TRADEMARK SIGN IN CIRCLE
010	204	12/12	▽	LEFT OPEN TRIANGLE
010	205	12/13	△	RIGHT OPEN TRIANGLE
010	206	12/14	○	EM OPEN CIRCLE
010	207	12/15	□	EM OPEN RECTANGLE
010	208	13/00	'	LEFT SINGLE QUOTATION MARK
010	209	13/01	'	RIGHT SINGLE QUOTATION MARK
010	210	13/02	"	LEFT DOUBLE QUOTATION MARK
010	211	13/03	"	RIGHT DOUBLE QUOTATION MARK
010	212	13/04	℞	PRESCRIPTION, TAKE, RECIPE
010	214	13/06	′	MINUTES
010	215	13/07	″	SECONDS
010	217	13/09	†	LATIN CROSS
010	218	13/10	✡	HEXAGRAM
010	219	13/11	■	FILLED RECTANGLE BULLET
010	220	13/12	▼	FILLED LEFT TRIANGLE BULLET
010	221	13/13	▲	FILLED RIGHT TRIANGLE BULLET
010	222	13/14	●	EM FILLED CIRCLE
010	223	13/15	■	EM FILLED RECTANGLE
010	224	14/00	○	EN OPEN CIRCLE BULLET
010	225	14/01	□	EN OPEN SQUARE BULLET
010	226	14/02	▯	OPEN RECTANGULAR BULLET
010	227	14/03	◁	OPEN TRIANGULAR BULLET UP
010	228	14/04	▷	OPEN TRIANGULAR BULLET DOWN
010	229	14/05	☆	OPEN STAR
010	230	14/06	●	EN FILLED CIRCLE BULLET
010	231	14/07	■	EN FILLED SQUARE BULLET

Byte 3	Byte 4	Code Pos	Character	Name
010	232	14/08	◀	FILLED TRIANGULAR BULLET UP
010	233	14/09	▶	FILLED TRIANGULAR BULLET DOWN
010	234	14/10	◖	LEFT POINTER
010	235	14/11	◗	RIGHT POINTER
010	236	14/12	♣	CLUB
010	237	14/13	♦	DIAMOND
010	238	14/14	♥	HEART
010	240	15/00	✠	MALTESE CROSS
010	241	15/01	†	DAGGER
010	242	15/02	‡	DOUBLE DAGGER
010	243	15/03	✓	CHECK MARK, TICK
010	244	15/04	✗	BALLOT CROSS
010	245	15/05	♯	MUSICAL SHARP
010	246	15/06	♭	MUSICAL FLAT
010	247	15/07	♂	MALE SYMBOL
010	248	15/08	♀	FEMALE SYMBOL
010	249	15/09	℡	TELEPHONE SYMBOL
010	250	15/10	℺	TELEPHONE RECORDER SYMBOL
010	251	15/11	℗	PHONOGRAPH COPYRIGHT SIGN
010	252	15/12	‸	CARET
010	253	15/13	‚	SINGLE LOW QUOTATION MARK
010	254	15/14	„	DOUBLE LOW QUOTATION MARK
010	255	15/15	□	CURSOR

APL KEYSYM Set

Byte 3	Byte 4	Code Pos	Character	Name
011	163	10/03	⋁	LEFT CARET
011	166	10/06	⋀	RIGHT CARET
011	168	10/08	⋁	DOWN CARET
011	169	10/09	⋀	UP CARET

011	192	12/00	‾	OVERBAR
011	194	12/02	⊥	DOWN TACK
011	195	12/03	∪	UP SHOE (CAP)
011	196	12/04	⌊	DOWN STILE
011	198	12/06			UNDERBAR
011	202	12/10	∘	JOT
011	204	12/12	□	QUAD
011	206	12/14	⊤	UP TACK
011	207	12/15	∘	CIRCLE
011	211	13/03	⌈	UP STILE
011	214	13/06	∩	DOWN SHOE (CUP)
011	216	13/08	⊃	RIGHT SHOE
011	218	13/10	⊂	LEFT SHOE
011	220	13/12	⊢	LEFT TACK
011	252	15/12	⊣	RIGHT TACK

Hebrew KEYSYM Set

012	224	14/00	א	HEBREW LETTER ALEPH
012	225	14/01	ב	HEBREW LETTER BETH
012	226	14/02	ג	HEBREW LETTER GIMMEL
012	227	14/03	ד	HEBREW LETTER DALETH
012	228	14/04	ה	HEBREW LETTER HE
012	229	14/05	ו	HEBREW LETTER WAW
012	230	14/06	ז	HEBREW LETTER ZAYIN
012	231	14/07	ח	HEBREW LETTER HET
012	232	14/08	ט	HEBREW LETTER TETH
012	233	14/09	י	HEBREW LETTER YOD
012	234	14/10	ך	HEBREW LETTER FINAL KAPH
012	235	14/11	כ	HEBREW LETTER KAPH
012	236	14/12	ל	HEBREW LETTER LAMED
012	237	14/13	ם	HEBREW LETTER FINAL MEM
012	238	14/14	מ	HEBREW LETTER MEM

Byte 3	Byte 4	Code Pos	Character	Name
012	239	14/15	ן	HEBREW LETTER FINAL NUN
012	240	15/00	נ	HEBREW LETTER NUN
012	241	15/01	ס	HEBREW LETTER SAMEKH
012	242	15/02	ע	HEBREW LETTER AYIN
012	243	15/03	ף	HEBREW LETTER FINAL PE
012	244	15/04	פ	HEBREW LETTER PE
012	245	15/05	ץ	HEBREW LETTER FINAL ZADI
012	246	15/06	צ	HEBREW LETTER ZADI
012	247	15/07	ק	HEBREW KUF
012	248	15/08	ר	HEBREW RESH
012	249	15/09	ש	HEBREW SHIN
012	250	15/10	ת	HEBREW TAF

KEYBOARD KEYSYM Set

Byte 3	Byte 4	Code Pos	Character	Name
255	008	00/08		BACKSPACE, BACK SPACE, BACK CHAR
255	009	00/09		TAB
255	010	00/10		LINEFEED, LF
255	011	00/11		CLEAR
255	013	00/13		RETURN, ENTER
255	019	01/03		PAUSE, HOLD, SCROLL LOCK
255	027	01/11		ESCAPE
255	032	02/00		MULTI-KEY CHARACTER PREFACE
255	033	02/01		KANJI, KANJI CONVERT
255	080	05/00		HOME
255	081	05/01		LEFT, MOVE LEFT, LEFT ARROW
255	082	05/02		UP, MOVE UP, UP ARROW
255	083	05/03		RIGHT, MOVE RIGHT, RIGHT ARROW
255	084	05/04		DOWN, MOVE DOWN, DOWN ARROW
255	085	05/05		PRIOR, PREVIOUS

255	086	05/06	NEXT
255	087	05/07	END, EOL
255	088	05/08	BEGIN, BOL
255	096	06/00	SELECT, MARK
255	097	06/01	PRINT
255	098	06/02	EXECUTE, RUN, DO
255	099	06/03	INSERT, INSERT HERE
255	101	06/05	UNDO, OOPS
255	102	06/06	REDO, AGAIN
255	103	06/07	MENU
255	104	06/08	FIND, SEARCH
255	105	06/09	CANCEL, STOP, ABORT, EXIT
255	106	06/10	HELP, QUESTION MARK
255	107	06/11	BREAK
255	126	07/14	MODE SWITCH, SCRIPT SWITCH, CHARACTER SET SWITCH
255	127	07/15	NUM LOCK
255	128	08/00	KEYPAD SPACE
255	137	08/09	KEYPAD TAB
255	141	08/13	KEYPAD ENTER
255	145	09/01	KEYPAD F1, PF1, A
255	146	09/02	KEYPAD F2, PF2, B
255	147	09/03	KEYPAD F3, PF3, C
255	148	09/04	KEYPAD F4, PF4, D
255	170	10/10	KEYPAD MULTIPLICATION SIGN, ASTERISK
255	171	10/11	KEYPAD PLUS SIGN
255	172	10/12	KEYPAD SEPARATOR, COMMA
255	173	10/13	KEYPAD MINUS SIGN, HYPHEN
255	174	10/14	KEYPAD DECIMAL POINT, FULL STOP
255	175	10/15	KEYPAD DIVISION SIGN, SOLIDUS
255	176	11/00	KEYPAD DIGIT ZERO
255	177	11/01	KEYPAD DIGIT ONE
255	178	11/02	KEYPAD DIGIT TWO

Byte 3	Byte 4	Code Pos	Character	Name
255	179	11/03		KEYPAD DIGIT THREE
255	180	11/04		KEYPAD DIGIT FOUR
255	181	11/05		KEYPAD DIGIT FIVE
255	182	11/06		KEYPAD DIGIT SIX
255	183	11/07		KEYPAD DIGIT SEVEN
255	184	11/08		KEYPAD DIGIT EIGHT
255	185	11/09		KEYPAD DIGIT NINE
255	189	11/13		KEYPAD EQUALS SIGN
255	190	11/14		F1
255	191	11/15		F2
255	192	12/00		F3
255	193	12/01		F4
255	194	12/02		F5
255	195	12/03		F6
255	196	12/04		F7
255	197	12/05		F8
255	198	12/06		F9
255	199	12/07		F10
255	200	12/08		F11, L1
255	201	12/09		F12, L2
255	202	12/10		F13, L3
255	203	12/11		F14, L4
255	204	12/12		F15, L5
255	205	12/13		F16, L6
255	206	12/14		F17, L7
255	207	12/15		F18, L8
255	208	13/00		F19, L9
255	209	13/01		F20, L10
255	210	13/02		F21, R1

255	211	13/03	F22, R2
255	212	13/04	F23, R3
255	213	13/05	F24, R4
255	214	13/06	F25, R5
255	215	13/07	F26, R6
255	216	13/08	F27, R7
255	217	13/09	F28, R8
255	218	13/10	F29, R9
255	219	13/11	F30, R10
255	220	13/12	F31, R11
255	221	13/13	F32, R12
255	222	13/14	F33, R13
255	223	13/15	F34, R14
255	224	14/00	F35, R15
255	225	14/01	LEFT SHIFT
255	226	14/02	RIGHT SHIFT
255	227	14/03	LEFT CONTROL
255	228	14/04	RIGHT CONTROL
255	229	14/05	CAPS LOCK
255	230	14/06	SHIFT LOCK
255	231	14/07	LEFT META
255	232	14/08	RIGHT META
255	233	14/09	LEFT ALT
255	234	14/10	RIGHT ALT
255	235	14/11	LEFT SUPER
255	236	14/12	RIGHT SUPER
255	237	14/13	LEFT HYPER
255	238	14/14	RIGHT HYPER
255	255	15/15	DELETE, RUBOUT

Appendix F

Protocol Encoding

Syntactic Conventions

All numbers are in decimal, unless prefixed with #x, in which case they are in hexadecimal (base 16).

The general syntax used to describe requests, replies, errors, events, and compound types is:

NameofThing
encode-form

. . .

encode-form

Each encode-form describes a single component.

For components described in the protocol as:

name: TYPE

the encode-form is:

N   TYPE   name

N is the number of bytes occupied in the data stream, and TYPE is the interpretation of those bytes. For example,

depth: CARD8

becomes:

1   CARD8   depth

For components with a static numeric value the encode-form is:

N   value   name

The value is always interpreted as an N-byte unsigned integer. For example, the first two bytes of a `Window` error are always zero (indicating an error in general) and three (indicating the `Window` error in particular):

1   0   Error
1   3   code

For components described in the protocol as:

name: {Name1,...,NameI}

the encode-form is:

N   name
        value1   Name1
        . . .
        valueI   NameI

The value is always interpreted as an N-byte unsigned integer. Note that the size of N is sometimes larger than that strictly required to encode the values. For example:

class: {InputOutput, InputOnly, CopyFromParent}

becomes:

2   class
        0   CopyFromParent
        1   InputOutput
        2   InputOnly

For components described in the protocol as:

NAME: TYPE or Alternative1...or AlternativeI

the encode-form is:

N   TYPE   NAME
        value1   Alternative1
        . . .
        valueI   AlternativeI

The alternative values are guaranteed not to conflict with the encoding of TYPE. For example:

destination: WINDOW or `PointerWindow` or `InputFocus`

becomes:

```
4       WINDOW                                      destination
    0   PointerWindow
    1   InputFocus
```

For components described in the protocol as:

value-mask: BITMASK

the encode-form is:

```
N       BITMASK                                     value-mask
    mask1    mask-name1
      . . .
    maskI    mask-nameI
```

The individual bits in the mask are specified and named, and N is 2 or 4. The most-significant bit in a BITMASK is reserved for use in defining chained (multiword) bitmasks, as extensions augment existing core requests. The precise interpretation of this bit is not yet defined here, although a probable mechanism is that a 1-bit indicates that another N bytes of bitmask follow, with bits within the overall mask still interpreted from least-significant to most-significant with an N-byte unit, with N-byte units interpreted in stream order, and with the overall mask being byte-swapped in individual N-byte units.

For LISTofVALUE encodings, the request is followed by a section of the form:

VALUEs
encode-form

. . .

encode-form

listing an encode-form for each VALUE. The NAME in each encode-form keys to the corresponding BITMASK bit. The encoding of a VALUE always occupies four bytes, but the number of bytes specified in the encoding-form indicates how many of the least-significant bytes are actually used; the remaining bytes are unused and their values do not matter.

In various cases, the number of bytes occupied by a component will be specified by a lowercase single-letter variable name instead of a specific numeric value, and often some other component will have its value specified as a simple numeric expression involving these variables. Components specified with such expressions are always interpreted as unsigned integers. The scope of such variables is always just the enclosing request, reply, error, event, or compound type structure. For example:

| 2 | 3+n | request length |
| 4n | LISTofPOINT | points |

For unused bytes (the values of the bytes are undefined and do not matter), the encode-form is:

| N | | unused |

If the number of unused bytes is variable, the encode-form typically is:

| p | | unused, p=pad(E) |

where E is some expression, and pad(E) is the number of bytes needed to round E up to a multiple of four.

$$\text{pad}(E) = (4 - (E \bmod 4)) \bmod 4$$

Common Types

LISTofFOO

In this document the LISTof notation strictly means some number of repetitions of the FOO encoding; the actual length of the list is encoded elsewhere.

SETofFOO

A set is always represented by a bitmask, with a 1-bit indicating presence in the set.

BITMASK: CARD32
WINDOW: CARD32
PIXMAP: CARD32
CURSOR: CARD32
FONT: CARD32

GCONTEXT: CARD32
COLORMAP: CARD32
DRAWABLE: CARD32
FONTABLE: CARD32
ATOM: CARD32
VISUALID: CARD32
BYTE: 8-bit value
INT8: 8-bit signed integer
INT16: 16-bit signed integer
INT32: 32-bit signed integer
CARD8: 8-bit unsigned integer
CARD16: 16-bit unsigned integer
CARD32: 32-bit unsigned integer
TIMESTAMP: CARD32

BITGRAVITY

0	Forget
1	NorthWest
2	North
3	NorthEast
4	West
5	Center
6	East
7	SouthWest
8	South
9	SouthEast
10	Static

WINGRAVITY

0	Unmap
1	NorthWest
2	North
3	NorthEast
4	West
5	Center
6	East
7	SouthWest
8	South
9	SouthEast
10	Static

BOOL

0	False
1	True

SETofEVENT

#x00000001	KeyPress
#x00000002	KeyRelease
#x00000004	ButtonPress
#x00000008	ButtonRelease
#x00000010	EnterWindow
#x00000020	LeaveWindow
#x00000040	PointerMotion
#x00000080	PointerMotionHint
#x00000100	Button1Motion
#x00000200	Button2Motion
#x00000400	Button3Motion
#x00000800	Button4Motion
#x00001000	Button5Motion
#x00002000	ButtonMotion
#x00004000	KeymapState
#x00008000	Exposure
#x00010000	VisibilityChange
#x00020000	StructureNotify
#x00040000	ResizeRedirect
#x00080000	SubstructureNotify
#x00100000	SubstructureRedirect
#x00200000	FocusChange
#x00400000	PropertyChange
#x00800000	ColormapChange
#x01000000	OwnerGrabButton
#xfe000000	unused but must be zero

SETofPOINTEREVENT
encodings are the same as for SETofEVENT, except with

#xffff8003	unused but must be zero

SETofDEVICEEVENT
encodings are the same as for SETofEVENT, except with

#xffffc0b0	unused but must be zero

KEYSYM: CARD32
KEYCODE: CARD8
BUTTON: CARD8
SETofKEYBUTMASK

#x0001	Shift
#x0002	Lock
#x0004	Control
#x0008	Mod1
#x0010	Mod2
#x0020	Mod3
#x0040	Mod4
#x0080	Mod5
#x0100	Button1
#x0200	Button2
#x0400	Button3
#x0800	Button4
#x1000	Button5
#xc000	unused but must be zero

SETofKEYMASK

encodings are the same as for SETofKEYBUTMASK, except with

#xff00	unused but must be zero

STRING8: LISTofCARD8
STRING16: LISTofCHAR2B
CHAR2B

1	CARD8	byte1
1	CARD8	byte2

POINT

2	INT16	x
2	INT16	y

RECTANGLE

2	INT16	x
2	INT16	y
2	CARD16	width
2	CARD16	height

ARC

2	INT16	x
2	INT16	y
2	CARD16	width
2	CARD16	height
2	INT16	angle1
2	INT16	angle2

HOST

1		family
	0 Internet	
	1 DECnet	
	2 Chaos	
1		unused
2	n	length of address
n	LISTofBYTE	address
p		unused, p = pad(n)

STR

1	n	length of name in bytes
n	STRING8	name

Errors

Request

1	0	Error
1	1	code
2	CARD16	sequence number
4		unused
2	CARD16	minor opcode
1	CARD8	major opcode
21		unused

Value

1	0	Error
1	2	code
2	CARD16	sequence number
4	<32-bits>	bad value

2	CARD16	minor opcode
1	CARD8	major opcode
21		unused

Window

1	0	Error
1	3	code
2	CARD16	sequence number
4	CARD32	bad resource id
2	CARD16	minor opcode
1	CARD8	major opcode
21		unused

Pixmap

1	0	Error
1	4	code
2	CARD16	sequence number
4	CARD32	bad resource id
2	CARD16	minor opcode
1	CARD8	major opcode
21		unused

Atom

1	0	Error
1	5	code
2	CARD16	sequence number
4	CARD32	bad atom id
2	CARD16	minor opcode
1	CARD8	major opcode
21		unused

Cursor

1	0	Error
1	6	code
2	CARD16	sequence number
4	CARD32	bad resource id
2	CARD16	minor opcode
1	CARD8	Major opcode
21		unused

Font

1	0	Error
1	7	code
2	CARD16	sequence number
4	CARD32	bad resource id
2	CARD16	minor opcode
1	CARD8	major opcode
21		unused

Match

1	0	Error
1	8	code
2	CARD16	sequence number
4		unused
2	CARD16	minor opcode
1	CARD8	major opcode
21		unused

Drawable

1	0	Error
1	9	code
2	CARD16	sequence number
4	CARD32	bad resource id
2	CARD16	minor opcode
1	CARD8	major opcode
21		unused

Access

1	0	Error
1	10	code
2	CARD16	sequence number
4		unused
2	CARD16	minor opcode
1	CARD8	major opcode
21		unused

Alloc

1	0	Error
1	11	code

2	CARD16	sequence number
4		unused
2	CARD16	minor opcode
1	CARD8	major opcode
21		unused

Colormap

1	0	Error
1	12	code
2	CARD16	sequence number
4	CARD32	bad resource id
2	CARD16	minor opcode
1	CARD8	major opcode
21		unused

GContext

1	0	Error
1	13	code
2	CARD16	sequence number
4	CARD32	bad resource id
2	CARD16	minor opcode
1	CARD8	major opcode
21		unused

IDChoice

1	0	Error
1	14	code
2	CARD16	sequence number
4	CARD32	bad resource id
2	CARD16	minor opcode
1	CARD8	major opcode
21		unused

Name

1	0	Error
1	15	code
2	CARD16	sequence number
4		unused
2	CARD16	minor opcode

1	CARD8	major opcode
21		unused

Length

1	0	Error
1	16	code
2	CARD16	sequence number
4		unused
2	CARD16	minor opcode
1	CARD8	major opcode
21		unused

Implementation

1	0	Error
1	17	code
2	CARD16	sequence number
4		unused
2	CARD16	minor opcode
1	CARD8	major opcode
21		unused

Keyboards

KEYCODE values are always greater than 7 (and less than 256).

KEYSYM values with the bit #x10000000 set are reserved as vendor-specific.

The names and encodings of the standard KEYSYM values are contained in appendix E.

Pointers

BUTTON values are numbered starting with one.

Predefined Atoms

PRIMARY	1
SECONDARY	2
ARC	3
ATOM	4
BITMAP	5

CARDINAL	6
COLORMAP	7
CURSOR	8
CUT_BUFFER0	9
CUT_BUFFER1	10
CUT_BUFFER2	11
CUT_BUFFER3	12
CUT_BUFFER4	13
CUT_BUFFER5	14
CUT_BUFFER6	15
CUT_BUFFER7	16
DRAWABLE	17
FONT	18
INTEGER	19
PIXMAP	20
POINT	21
RECTANGLE	22
RESOURCE_MANAGER	23
RGB_COLOR_MAP	24
RGB_BEST_MAP	25
RGB_BLUE_MAP	26
RGB_DEFAULT_MAP	27
RGB_GRAY_MAP	28
RGB_GREEN_MAP	29
RGB_RED_MAP	30
STRING	31
VISUALID	32
WINDOW	33
WM_COMMAND	34
WM_HINTS	35
WM_CLIENT_MACHINE	36
WM_ICON_NAME	37
WM_ICON_SIZE	38
WM_NAME	39
WM_NORMAL_HINTS	40
WM_SIZE_HINTS	41
WM_ZOOM_HINTS	42
MIN_SPACE	43
NORM_SPACE	44
MAX_SPACE	45
END_SPACE	46
SUPERSCRIPT_X	47

SUPERSCRIPT_Y	48	
SUBSCRIPT_X	49	
SUBSCRIPT_Y	50	
UNDERLINE_POSITION	51	
UNDERLINE_THICKNESS	52	
STRIKEOUT_ASCENT	53	
STRIKEOUT_DESCENT	54	
ITALIC_ANGLE	55	
X_HEIGHT	56	
QUAD_WIDTH	57	
WEIGHT	58	
POINT_SIZE	59	
RESOLUTION	60	
COPYRIGHT	61	
NOTICE	62	
FONT_NAME	63	
FAMILY_NAME	64	
FULL_NAME	65	
CAP_HEIGHT	66	
WM_CLASS	67	
WM_TRANSIENT_FOR	68	

Connection Setup

For TCP connections, displays on a given host are numbered starting from 0, and the server for display N listens and accepts connections on port 6000 + N. For DECnet connections, displays on a given host are numbered starting from 0, and the server for display N listens and accepts connections on the object name obtained by concatenating "X\$X" with the decimal representation for N. for example, X\$X0 and X\$X1.

Information sent by the client at connection setup:

1		byte-order
	#x42	MSB first
	#x6C	LSB first
1		unused
2	CARD16	protocol-major-version
2	CARD16	protocol-minor-version
2	n	length of authorization-protocol-name

2	d	length of authorization-protocol-data
2		unused
n	STRING8	authorization-protocol-name
p		unused, p = pad(n)
d	STRING8	authorization-protocol-data
q		unused, q = pad(d)

Except where explicitly noted in the protocol, all 16-bit and 32-bit quantities sent by the client must be transmitted with the specified byte order, and all 16-bit and 32-bit quantities returned by the server will be transmitted with this byte order.

Information received by the client if authorization fails:

1	0	failed
1	n	length of reason in bytes
2	CARD16	protocol-major-version
2	CARD16	protocol-minor-version
2	$(n+p)/4$	length in 4-byte units of "additional data"
n	STRING8	reason
p		unused, p = pad(n)

Information received by the client if authorization is accepted:

1	1	success
1		unused
2	CARD16	protocol-major-version
2	CARD16	protocol-minor-version
2	$8+2n+(v+p+m)/4$	length in 4-byte units of "additional data"
4	CARD32	release-number
4	CARD32	resource-id-base
4	CARD32	resource-id-mask
4	CARD32	motion-buffer-size
2	v	length of vendor
2	CARD16	maximum-request-length
1	CARD8	number of SCREENs in roots
1	n	number for FORMATs in pixmap-formats
1		image-byte-order
	0 LSBFirst	
	1 MSBFirst	

1		bitmap-format-bit-order
	0 LeastSignificant	
	1 MostSignificant	
1	CARD8	bitmap-format-scanline-unit
1	CARD8	bitmap-format-scanline-pad
1	KEYCODE	min-keycode
1	KEYCODE	max-keycode
4		unused
v	STRING8	vendor
p		unused, p = pad(v)
8n	LISTofFORMAT	pixmap-formats
m	LISTofSCREEN	roots (m is always a multiple of 4)

FORMAT

1	CARD8	depth
1	CARD8	bits-per-pixel
1	CARD8	scanline-pad
5		unused

SCREEN

4	WINDOW	root
4	COLORMAP	default-colormap
4	CARD32	white-pixel
4	CARD32	black-pixel
4	SETofEVENT	current-input-masks
2	CARD16	width-in-pixels
2	CARD16	height-in-pixels
2	CARD16	width-in-millimeters
2	CARD16	height-in-millimeters
2	CARD16	min-installed-maps
2	CARD16	max-installed-maps
4	VISUALID	root-visual
1		backing-stores
	0 Never	
	1 WhenMapped	
	2 Always	
1	BOOL	save-unders
1	CARD8	root-depth

| 1 | CARD8 | number of DEPTHs in allowed-depths |
| n | LISTofDEPTH | allowed-depths (n is always a multiple of 4) |

DEPTH

1	CARD8	depth
1		unused
2	n	number of VISUALTYPES in visuals
4		unused
24n	LISTofVISUALTYPE	visuals

VISUALTYPE

4	VISUALID	visual-id
1		class
	0 StaticGray	
	1 GrayScale	
	2 StaticColor	
	3 PseudoColor	
	4 TrueColor	
	5 DirectColor	
1	CARD8	bits-per-rgb-value
2	CARD16	colormap-entries
4	CARD32	red-mask
4	CARD32	green-mask
4	CARD32	blue-mask
4		unused

Requests
CreateWindow

1	1	opcode
1	CARD8	depth
2	8+n	request length
4	WINDOW	wid
4	WINDOW	parent
2	INT16	x
2	INT16	y
2	CARD16	width

2	CARD16		height
2	CARD16		border-width
2			class
	0	CopyFromParent	
	1	InputOutput	
	2	InputOnly	
4	VISUALID		visual
	0	CopyFromParent	
4	BITMASK		value-mask (has n bits set to 1)
	#x00000001	background-pixmap	
	#x00000002	background-pixel	
	#x00000004	border-pixmap	
	#x00000008	border-pixel	
	#x00000010	bit-gravity	
	#x00000020	win-gravity	
	#x00000040	backing-store	
	#x00000080	backing-planes	
	#x00000100	backing-pixel	
	#x00000200	override-redirect	
	#x00000400	save-under	
	#x00000800	event-mask	
	#x00001000	do-not-propagate-mask	
	#x00002000	colormap	
	#x00004000	cursor	
4n	LISTofVALUE		value-list

VALUEs

4	PIXMAP		background-pixmap
	0	None	
	1	ParentRelative	
4	CARD32		background-pixel
4	PIXMAP		border-pixmap
	0	CopyFromParent	
4	CARD32		border-pixel
1	BITGRAVITY		bit-gravity
1	WINGRAVITY		win-gravity
1			backing-store
	0	NotUseful	
	1	WhenMapped	
	2	Always	
4	CARD32		backing-planes
4	CARD32		backing-pixel

1	BOOL	override-redirect
1	BOOL	save-under
4	SETofEVENT	event-mask
4	SETofDEVICEEVENT	do-not-propagate-mask
4	COLORMAP	colormap
	0 CopyFromParent	
4	CURSOR	cursor
	0 None	

ChangeWindowAttributes

1	2	opcode
1		unused
2	3+n	request length
4	WINDOW	window
4	BITMASK	value-mask (has n bits set to 1)
	encodings are the same as for CreateWindow	
4n	LISTofVALUE	value-list
	encodings are the same as for CreateWindow	

GetWindowAttributes

1	3	opcode
1		unused
2	2	request length
4	WINDOW	window
→		
1	1	Reply
1		backing-store
	0 NotUseful	
	1 WhenMapped	
	2 Always	
2	CARD16	sequence number
4	3	reply length
4	VISUALID	visual
2		class
	1 InputOutput	
	2 InputOnly	
1	BITGRAVITY	bit-gravity
1	WINGRAVITY	win-gravity

4	CARD32	backing-planes
4	CARD32	backing-pixel
1	BOOL	save-under
1	BOOL	map-is-installed
1		map-state

	0	Unmapped
	1	Unviewable
	2	Viewable

1	BOOL	override-redirect
4	COLORMAP	colormap

	0	None

4	SETofEVENT	all-event-masks
4	SETofEVENT	your-event-mask
2	SETofDEVICEEVENT	do-not-propagate-mask
2		unused

DestroyWindow

1	4	opcode
1		unused
2	2	request length
4	WINDOW	window

DestroySubwindows

1	5	opcode
1		unused
2	2	request length
4	WINDOW	window

ChangeSaveSet

1	6	opcode
1		mode

	0	Insert
	1	Delete

2	2	request length
4	WINDOW	window

ReparentWindow

1	7	opcode
1		unused

2	4	request length
4	WINDOW	window
4	WINDOW	parent
2	INT16	x
2	INT16	y

MapWindow

1	8	opcode
1		unused
2	2	request length
4	WINDOW	window

MapSubwindows

1	9	opcode
1		unused
2	2	request length
4	WINDOW	window

UnmapWindow

1	10	opcode
1		unused
2	2	request length
4	WINDOW	window

UnmapSubwindows

1	11	opcode
1		unused
2	2	request length
4	WINDOW	window

ConfigureWindow

1	12		opcode
1			unused
2	3 + n		request length
4	WINDOW		window
2	BITMASK		value-mask (has n bits set to 1)
	#x0001	x	
	#x0002	y	
	#x0004	width	

		#x0008	height	
		#x0010	border-width	
		#x0020	sibling	
		#x0040	stack-mode	
2				unused
4n	LISTofVALUE			value-list

VALUEs

2	INT16			x
2	INT16			y
2	CARD16			width
2	CARD16			height
2	CARD16			border-width
4	WINDOW			sibling
1				stack-mode
		0	Above	
		1	Below	
		2	TopIf	
		3	BottomIf	
		4	Opposite	

CirculateWindow

1	13			opcode
1				direction
		0	RaiseLowest	
		1	LowerHighest	
2	2			request length
4	WINDOW				window

GetGeometry

1	14		opcode
1			unused
2	2		request length
4	DRAWABLE		drawable
→			
1	1		Reply
1	CARD8		depth
2	CARD16		sequence number
4	0		reply length
4	WINDOW		root

2	INT16	x
2	INT16	y
2	CARD16	width
2	CARD16	height
2	CARD16	border-width
10		unused

QueryTree

1	15	opcode
1		unused
2	2	request length
4	WINDOW	window
→		
1	1	Reply
1		unused
2	CARD16	sequence number
4	n	reply length
4	WINDOW	root
4	WINDOW	parent
	0 None	
2	n	number of WINDOWs in children
14		unused
4n	LISTofWINDOW	children

InternAtom

1	16	opcode
1	BOOL	only-if-exists
2	$2 + (n+p)/4$	request length
2	n	length of name
2		unused
n	STRING8	name
p		unused, $p = pad(n)$
→		
1	1	Reply
1		unused
2	CARD16	sequence number
4	0	reply length
4	ATOM	atom
	0 None	
20		unused

GetAtomName

1	17	opcode
1		unused
2	2	request length
4	ATOM	atom

→

1	1	Reply
1		unused
2	CARD16	sequence number
4	(n+p)/4	reply length
2	n	length of name
22		unused
n	String8	name
p		unused, p=pad(n)

ChangeProperty

1	18	opcode
1		mode
	0 Replace	
	1 Prepend	
	2 Append	
2	6+(n+p)/4	request length
4	WINDOW	window
4	ATOM	property
4	ATOM	type
1	CARD8	format
3		unused
4	CARD32	length of data in format units
		(= n for format = 8)
		(= n/2 for format = 16)
		(= n/4 for format = 32)
n	LISTofBYTE	data
		(n is a multiple of 2 for
		format = 16)
		(n is a multiple of 4 for
		format = 32)
p		unused, p=pad(n)

DeleteProperty

1	19	opcode
1		unused

2	3	request length
4	WINDOW	window
4	ATOM	property

GetProperty

1	20	opcode
1	BOOL	delete
2	6	request length
4	WINDOW	window
4	ATOM	property
4	ATOM	type
	0 AnyPropertyType	
4	CARD32	long-offset
4	CARD32	long-length

$\rightarrow$

1	1	Reply
1	CARD8	format
2	CARD16	sequence number
4	(n + p)/4	reply length
4	ATOM	type
	0 None	
4	CARD32	bytes-after
4	CARD32	length of value in format units

(= 0 for format = 0)
(= n for format = 8)
(= n/2 for format = 16)
(= n/4 for format = 32)

12		unused
n	LISTofBYTE	value

(n is zero for format = 0)
(n is a multiple of 2 for
format = 16)
(n is a multiple of 4 for
format = 32)
unused, p = pad(n)

p		

ListProperties

1	21	opcode
1		unused
2	2	request length

4	WINDOW	window
→		
1	1	Reply
1		unused
2	CARD16	sequence number
4	n	reply length
2	n	number of ATOMs in atoms
22		unused
4n	LISTofATOM	atoms

SetSelectionOwner

1	22	opcode
1		unused
2	4	request length
4	WINDOW	owner
	0 None	
4	ATOM	selection
4	TIMESTAMP	time
	0 CurrentTime	

GetSelectionOwner

1	23	opcode
1		unused
2	2	request length
4	ATOM	selection
→		
1	1	Reply
1		unused
2	CARD16	sequence number
4	0	reply length
4	WINDOW	owner
	0 None	
20		unused

ConvertSelection

1	24	opcode
1		unused
2	6	request length
4	WINDOW	requestor
4	ATOM	selection

4	ATOM	target
4	ATOM	property
	0 None	
4	TIMESTAMP	time
	0 CurrentTime	

SendEvent

1	25	opcode
1	BOOL	propagate
2	11	request length
4	WINDOW	destination
	0 PointerWindow	
	1 InputFocus	
4	SETofEVENT	event-mask
32	standard event format (see the Events section)	event

GrabPointer

1	26	opcode
1	BOOL	owner-events
2	6	request length
4	WINDOW	grab-window
2	SETofPOINTEREVENT	event-mask
1		pointer-mode
	0 Synchronous	
	1 Asynchronous	
1		keyboard-mode
	0 Synchronous	
	1 Asynchronous	
4	WINDOW	confine-to
	0 None	
4	CURSOR	cursor
	0 None	
4	TIMESTAMP	time
	0 CurrentTime	
→		
1	1	Reply
1		status
	0 Success	
	1 AlreadyGrabbed	
	2 InvalidTime	

	3	NotViewable	
	4	Frozen	
2	CARD16		sequence number
4	0		reply length
24			unused

UngrabPointer

1	27		opcode
1			unused
2	2		request length
4	TIMESTAMP		time
	0	CurrentTime	

GrabButton

1	28		opcode
1	BOOL		owner-events
2	6		request length
4	WINDOW		grab-window
2	SETofPOINTEREVENT		event-mask
1			pointer-mode
	0	Synchronous	
	1	Asynchronous	
1			keyboard-mode
	0	Synchronous	
	1	Asynchronous	
4	WINDOW		confine-to
	0	None	
4	CURSOR		cursor
	0	None	
1	BUTTON		button
	0	AnyButton	
1			unused
2	SETofKEYMASK		modifiers
	#x8000	AnyModifier	

UngrabButton

1	29		opcode
1	BUTTON		button
	0	AnyButton	
2	3		request length
4	WINDOW		grab-window

2	SETofKEYMASK	modifiers
	#x8000 AnyModifier	
2		unused

ChangeActivePointerGrab

1	30	opcode
1		unused
2	4	request length
4	CURSOR	cursor
	0 None	
4	TIMESTAMP	time
	0 CurrentTime	
2	SETofPOINTEREVENT	event-mask
2		unused

GrabKeyboard

1	31	opcode
1	BOOL	owner-events
2	4	request length
4	WINDOW	grab-window
4	TIMESTAMP	time
	0 CurrentTime	
1		pointer-mode
	0 Synchronous	
	1 Asynchronous	
1		keyboard-mode
	0 Synchronous	
	1 Asynchronous	
2		unused
→		
1	1	Reply
1		status
	0 Success	
	1 AlreadyGrabbed	
	2 InvalidTime	
	3 NotViewable	
	4 Frozen	
2	CARD16	sequence number
4	0	reply length
24		unused

UngrabKeyboard

1	32	opcode
1		unused
2	2	request length
4	TIMESTAMP	time
	0 `CurrentTime`	

GrabKey

1	33	opcode
1	BOOL	owner-events
2	4	request length
4	WINDOW	grab-window
2	SETofKEYMASK	modifiers
	#x8000 `AnyModifier`	
1	KEYCODE	key
	0 `AnyKey`	
1		pointer-mode
	0 `Synchronous`	
	1 `Asynchronous`	
1		keyboard-mode
	0 `Synchronous`	
	1 `Asynchronous`	
3		unused

UngrabKey

1	34	opcode
1	KEYCODE	key
	0 `AnyKey`	
2	3	request length
4	WINDOW	grab-window
2	SETofKEYMASK	modifiers
	#x8000 `AnyModifier`	
2		unused

AllowEvents

1	35	opcode
1		mode
	0 `AsyncPointer`	
	1 `SyncPointer`	

	2	ReplayPointer
	3	AsyncKeyboard
	4	SyncKeyboard
	5	ReplayKeyboard
	6	AsyncBoth
	7	SyncBoth

2	2		request length
4	TIMESTAMP		time
	0	CurrentTime	

GrabServer

1	36	opcode
1		unused
2	1	request length

UngrabServer

1	37	opcode
1		unused
2	1	request length

QueryPointer

1	38	opcode
1		unused
2	2	request length
4	WINDOW	window

→

1	1	Reply
1	BOOL	same-screen
2	CARD16	sequence number
4	0	reply length
4	WINDOW	root
4	WINDOW	child
	0 None	
2	INT16	root-x
2	INT16	root-y
2	INT16	win-x
2	INT16	win-y
2	SETofKEYBUTMASK	mask
6		unused

GetMotionEvents

1	39	opcode
1		unused
2	4	request length
4	WINDOW	window
4	TIMESTAMP	start
	0 CurrentTime	
4	TIMESTAMP	stop
	0 CurrentTime	
→		
1	1	Reply
1		unused
2	CARD16	sequence number
4	2n	reply length
4	n	number of TIMECOORDs in events
20		unused
8n	LISTofTIMECOORD	events

TIMECOORD

4	TIMESTAMP	time
2	CARD16	x
2	CARD16	y

TranslateCoordinates

1	40	opcode
1		unused
2	4	request length
4	WINDOW	src-window
4	WINDOW	dst-window
2	INT16	src-x
2	INT16	src-y
→		
1	1	Reply
1	BOOL	same-screen
2	CARD16	sequence number
4	0	reply length
4	WINDOW	child
	0 None	

2	INT16		dst-x
2	INT16		dst-y
16			unused

WarpPointer

1	41		opcode
1			unused
2	6		request length
4	WINDOW		src-window
	0	None	
4	WINDOW		dst-window
	0	None	
2	INT16		src-x
2	INT16		src-y
2	CARD16		src-width
2	CARD16		src-height
2	INT16		dst-x
2	INT16		dst-y

SetInputFocus

1	42		opcode
1			revert-to
	0	None	
	1	PointerRoot	
	2	Parent	
2	3		request length
4	WINDOW		focus
	0	None	
	1	PointerRoot	
4	TIMESTAMP		time
	0	CurrentTime	

GetInputFocus

1	43		opcode
1			unused
2	1		request length
→			
1	1		Reply
1			revert-to

	0 None	
	1 PointerRoot	
	2 Parent	
2	CARD16	sequence number
4	0	reply length
4	WINDOW	focus
	0 None	
	1 PointerRoot	
20		unused

QueryKeymap

1	44	opcode
1		unused
2	1	request length
→		
1	1	Reply
1		unused
2	CARD16	sequence number
4	2	reply length
32	LISTofCARD8	keys

OpenFont

1	45	opcode
1		unused
2	$3+(n+p)/4$	request length
4	FONT	fid
2	n	length of name
2		unused
n	STRING8	name
p		unused, $p = pad(n)$

CloseFont

1	46	opcode
1		unused
2	2	request length
4	FONT	font

QueryFont

1	47	opcode
1		unused

2	2	request length
4	FONTABLE	font
$\rightarrow$		
1	1	Reply
1		unused
2	CARD16	sequence number
4	$7 + 2n + 3m$	reply length
12	CHARINFO	min-bounds
4		unused
12	CHARINFO	max-bounds
4		unused
2	CARD16	min-char-or-byte2
2	CARD16	max-char-or-byte2
2	CARD16	default-char
2	n	number of FONTPROPs in properties
1		draw-direction
	0 LeftToRight	
	1 RightToLeft	
1	CARD8	min-byte1
1	CARD8	max-byte1
1	BOOL	all-chars-exist
2	INT16	font-ascent
2	INT16	font-descent
4	m	number of CHARINFOs in char-infos
8n	LISTofFONTPROP	properties
12m	LISTofCHARINFO	char-infos

FONTPROP

4	ATOM	name
4	<32-bits>	value

CHARINFO

2	INT16	left-side-bearing
2	INT16	right-side-bearing
2	INT16	character-width
2	INT16	ascent
2	INT16	descent
2	CARD16	attributes

QueryTextExtents

1	48	opcode
1	BOOL	odd length, True if p = 2
2	2 + (2n + p)/4	request length
4	FONTABLE	font
2n	STRING16	string
p		unused, p = pad(2n)
→		
1	1	Reply
1		draw-direction
	0 LeftToRight	
	1 RightToLeft	
2	CARD16	sequence number
4	0	reply length
2	INT16	font-ascent
2	INT16	font-descent
2	INT16	overall-ascent
2	INT16	overall-descent
4	INT32	overall-width
4	INT32	overall-left
4	INT32	overall-right
4		unused

ListFonts

1	49	opcode
1		unused
2	2 + (n + p)/4	request length
2	CARD16	max-names
2	n	length of pattern
n	STRING8	pattern
p		unused, p = pad(n)
→		
1	1	Reply
1		unused
2	CARD16	sequence number
4	(n + p)/4	reply length
2	CARD16	number of STRs in names
22		unused
n	LISTofSTR	names
p		unused, p = pad(n)

ListFontsWithInfo

1	50	opcode
1		unused
2	$2 + (n + p)/4$	request length
2	CARD16	max-names
2	n	length of pattern
n	STRING8	pattern
p		unused, $p = pad(n)$

→ (except for last in series)

1	1	Reply
1	n	length of name in bytes
2	CARD16	sequence number
4	$7 + 2m + (n + p)/4$	reply length
12	CHARINFO	min-bounds
4		unused
12	CHARINFO	max-bounds
4		unused
2	CARD16	min-char-or-byte2
2	CARD16	max-char-or-byte2
2	CARD16	default-char
2	m	number of FONTPROPs in properties
1		draw-direction
	0 LeftToRight	
	1 RightToLeft	
1	CARD8	min-byte1
1	CARD8	max-byte1
1	BOOL	all-chars-exist
2	INT16	font-ascent
2	INT16	font-descent
4	CARD32	replies-hint
8m	LISTofFONTPROP	properties
n	STRING8	name
p		unused, $p = pad(n)$

FONTPROP
encodings are the same as
for `QueryFont`

CHARINFO
encodings are the same as
for `QueryFont`

→ (last in series)

1	1	Reply
1	0	last-reply indicator
2	CARD16	sequence number
4	7	reply length
52		unused

SetFontPath

1	51	opcode
1		unused
2	2+(n+p)/4	request length
2	CARD16	number of STRs in path
2		unused
n	LISTofSTR	path
p		unused, p=pad(n)

GetFontPath

1	52	opcode
1		unused
2	1	request list

→

1	1	Reply
1		unused
2	CARD16	sequence number
4	(n+p)/4	reply length
2	CARD16	number of STRs in path
22		unused
n	LISTofSTR	path
p		unused, p=pad(n)

CreatePixmap

1	53	opcode
1	CARD8	depth
2	4	request length
4	PIXMAP	pid
4	DRAWABLE	drawable
2	CARD16	width
2	CARD16	height

FreePixmap

1	54	opcode
1		unused
2	2	request length
4	PIXMAP	pixmap

CreateGC

1	55	opcode
1		unused
2	4 + n	request length
4	GCONTEXT	cid
4	DRAWABLE	drawable
4	BITMASK	value-mask
		(has n bits set to 1)
	#x00000001	function
	#x00000002	plane-mask
	#x00000004	foreground
	#x00000008	background
	#x00000010	line-width
	#x00000020	line-style
	#x00000040	cap-style
	#x00000080	join-style
	#x00000100	fill-style
	#x00000200	fill-rule
	#x00000400	tile
	#x00000800	stipple
	#x00001000	tile-stipple-x-origin
	#x00002000	tile-stipple-y-origin
	#x00004000	font
	#x00008000	subwindow-mode
	#x00010000	graphics-exposures
	#x00020000	clip-x-origin
	#x00040000	clip-y-origin
	#x00080000	clip-mask
	#x00100000	dash-offset
	#x00200000	dashes
	#x00400000	arc-mode
4n	LISTofVALUE	value-list

VALUEs

1			function
	0	Clear	
	1	And	
	2	AndReverse	
	3	Copy	
	4	AndInverted	
	5	NoOp	
	6	Xor	
	7	Or	
	8	Nor	
	9	Equiv	
	10	Invert	
	11	OrReverse	
	12	CopyInverted	
	13	OrInverted	
	14	Nand	
	15	Set	
4		CARD32	plane-mask
4		CARD32	foreground
4		CARD32	background
2		CARD16	line-width
1			line-style
	0	Solid	
	1	OnOffDash	
	2	DoubleDash	
1			cap-style
	0	NotLast	
	1	Butt	
	2	Round	
	3	Projecting	
1			join-style
	0	Miter	
	1	Round	
	2	Bevel	
1			fill-style
	0	Solid	
	1	Tiled	
	2	Stippled	
	3	OpaqueStippled	
1			fill-rule

	0 EvenOdd	
	1 Winding	
4	PIXMAP	tile
4	PIXMAP	stipple
2	INT16	tile-stipple-x-origin
2	INT16	tile-stipple-y-origin
4	FONT	font
1		subwindow-mode
	0 ClipByChildren	
	1 IncludeInferiors	
1	BOOL	graphics-exposures
2	INT16	clip-x-origin
2	INT16	clip-y-origin
4	PIXMAP	clip-mask
	0 None	
2	CARD16	dash-offset
1	CARD8	dashes
1		arc-mode
	0 Chord	
	1 PieSlice	

ChangeGC

1	56	opcode
1		unused
2	3+n	request length
4	GCONTEXT	gc
4	BITMASK	value-mask
		(has n bits set to 1)
	encodings are the same as for CreateGC	
4n	LISTofVALUE	value-list
	encodings are the same as for CreateGC	

CopyGC

1	57	opcode
1		unused
2	4	request length
4	GCONTEXT	src-gc

4	GCONTEXT	dst-gc
4	BITMASK	value-mask
	encodings are the same	
	as for `CreateGC`	

SetDashes

1	58	opcode
1		unused
2	$3 + (n + p)/4$	request length
4	GCONTEXT	gc
2	CARD16	dash-offset
2	n	length of dashes
n	LISTofCARD8	dashes
p		unused, $p = pad(n)$

SetClipRectangles

1	59	opcode
1		ordering
	0 UnSorted	
	1 YSorted	
	2 YXSorted	
	3 YXBanded	
2	$3 + 2n$	request length
4	GCONTEXT	gc
2	INT16	clip-x-origin
2	INT16	clip-y-origin
8n	LISTofRECTANGLE	rectangles

FreeGC

1	60	opcode
1		unused
2	2	request length
4	GCONTEXT	gc

ClearArea

1	61	opcode
1	BOOL	exposures
2	4	request length
4	WINDOW	window

2	INT16	x
2	INT16	y
2	CARD16	width
2	CARD16	height

CopyArea

1	62	opcode
1		unused
2	7	request length
4	DRAWABLE	src-drawable
4	DRAWABLE	dst-drawable
4	GCONTEXT	gc
2	INT16	src-x
2	INT16	src-y
2	INT16	dst-x
2	INT16	dst-y
2	CARD16	width
2	CARD16	height

CopyPlane

1	63	opcode
1		unused
2	8	request length
4	DRAWABLE	src-drawable
4	DRAWABLE	dst-drawable
4	GCONTEXT	gc
2	INT16	src-x
2	INT16	src-y
2	INT16	dst-x
2	INT16	dst-y
2	CARD16	width
2	CARD16	height
4	CARD32	bit-plane

PolyPoint

1	64		opcode
1			coordinate-mode
	0	Origin	
	1	Previous	
2	3+n		request length

4	DRAWABLE	drawable
4	GCONTEXT	gc
4n	LISTofPOINT	points

PolyLine

1	65	opcode
1		coordinate-mode
	0 Origin	
	1 Previous	
2	3 + n	request length
4	DRAWABLE	drawable
4	GCONTEXT	gc
4n	LISTofPOINT	points

PolySegment

1	66	opcode
1		unused
2	3 + 2n	request length
4	DRAWABLE	drawable
4	GCONTEXT	gc
8n	LISTofSEGMENT	segments

SEGMENT

2	INT16	x1
2	INT16	y1
2	INT16	x2
2	INT16	y2

PolyRectangle

1	67	opcode
1		unused
2	3 + 2n	request length
4	DRAWABLE	drawable
4	GCONTEXT	gc
8n	LISTofRECTANGLE	rectangles

PolyArc

| 1 | 68 | opcode |
| 1 | | unused |

2	3 + 3n	request length
4	DRAWABLE	drawable
4	GCONTEXT	gc
12n	LISTofARC	arcs

FillPoly

1	69	opcode
1		unused
2	4 + n	request length
4	DRAWABLE	drawable
4	GCONTEXT	gc
1		shape
	0 Complex	
	1 Nonconvex	
	2 Convex	
1		coordinate-mode
	0 Origin	
	1 Previous	
2		unused
4n	LISTofPOINT	points

PolyFillRectangle

1	70	opcode
1		unused
2	3 + 2n	request length
4	DRAWABLE	drawable
4	GCONTEXT	gc
8n	LISTofRECTANGLE	rectangles

PolyFillArc

1	71	opcode
1		unused
2	3 + 3n	request length
4	DRAWABLE	drawable
4	GCONTEXT	gc
12n	LISTofARC	arcs

PutImage

| 1 | 72 | opcode |
| 1 | | format |

	0	`Bitmap`	
	1	`XYPixmap`	
	2	`ZPixmap`	
2	$6+(n+p)/4$		request length
4	DRAWABLE		drawable
4	GCONTEXT		gc
2	CARD16		width
2	CARD16		height
2	INT16		dst-x
2	INT16		dst-y
1	CARD8		left-pad
1	CARD8		depth
2			unused
n	LISTofBYTE		data
p			unused, $p=pad(n)$

GetImage

1	73		opcode
1			format
	1	`XYPixmap`	
	2	`ZPixmap`	
2	5		request length
4	DRAWABLE		drawable
2	INT16		x
2	INT16		y
2	CARD16		width
2	CARD16		height
4	CARD32		plane-mask
$\rightarrow$			
1	1		Reply
1	CARD8		depth
2	CARD16		sequence number
4	$(n+p)/4$		reply length
4	VISUALID		visual
	0	`None`	
20			unused
n	LISTofBYTE		data
p			unused, $p=pad(n)$

PolyText8

1	74		opcode
1			unused

2	4 + (n + p)/4	request length
4	DRAWABLE	drawable
4	GCONTEXT	gc
2	INT16	x
2	INT16	y
n	LISTofTEXTITEM8	items
p		unused, p = pad(n)
		(p is always 0 or 1)

TEXTITEM8

1	m	length of string
		(cannot be 255)
1	INT8	delta
m	STRING8	string
or		
1	255	font-shift indicator
1		font byte 3
		(most-significant)
1		font byte 2
1		font byte 1
1		font byte 0
		(least-significant)

PolyText16

1	75	opcode
1		unused
2	4 + (n + p)/4	request length
4	DRAWABLE	drawable
4	GCONTEXT	gc
2	INT16	x
2	INT16	y
n	LISTofTEXTITEM16	items
p		unused, p = pad(n)
		(p is always 0 or 1)

TEXTITEM16

1	m	number of CHAR2Bs
		in string (cannot)
		by 255)
1	INT8	delta

m	STRING16		string
or			
1	255		font-shift indicator
1			font byte 3
			(most-significant)
1			font byte 2
1			font byte 1
1			font byte 0
			(least-significant)

ImageText8

1	76	opcode
1	n	length of string
2	4 + (n + p)/4	request length
4	DRAWABLE	drawable
4	GCONTEXT	gc
2	INT16	x
2	INT16	y
n	STRING8	string
p		unused, p = pad(n)

ImageText16

1	77	opcode
1	n	number of CHAR2Bs
		in string
2	4 + (2n + p)/4	request length
4	DRAWABLE	drawable
4	GCONTEXT	gc
2	INT16	x
2	INT16	y
2n	STRING16	string
p		unused, p = pad(2n)

CreateColormap

1	78		opcode
1			alloc
	0	None	
	1	All	
2	4		request length

4	COLORMAP	mid
4	WINDOW	window
4	VISUALID	visual

FreeColormap

1	79	opcode
1		unused
2	2	request length
4	COLORMAP	cmap

CopyColormapAndFree

1	80	opcode
1		unused
2	3	request length
4	COLORMAP	mid
4	COLORMAP	src-cmap

InstallColormap

1	81	opcode
1		unused
2	2	request length
4	COLORMAP	cmap

UninstallColormap

1	82	opcode
1		unused
2	2	request length
4	COLORMAP	cmap

ListInstalledColormaps

1	83	opcode
1		unused
2	2	request length
4	WINDOW	window

→

1	1	Reply
1		unused
2	CARD16	sequence number
4	n	reply length

2	n	number of COLORMAPs in cmaps
22		unused
4n	LISTofCOLORMAP	cmaps

AllocColor

1	84	opcode
1		unused
2	4	request length
4	COLORMAP	cmap
2	CARD16	red
2	CARD16	green
2	CARD16	blue
2		unused
→		
1	1	Reply
1		unused
2	CARD16	sequence number
4	0	reply length
2	CARD16	red
2	CARD16	green
2	CARD16	blue
2		unused
4	CARD32	pixel
12		unused

AllocNamedColor

1	85	opcode
1		unused
2	3 + (n + p)/4	request length
4	COLORMAP	cmap
2	n	length of name
2		unused
n	STRING8	name
p		unused, p = pad(n)
→		
1	1	Reply
1		unused
2	CARD16	sequence number
4	0	reply length
4	CARD32	pixel

2	CARD16	exact-red
2	CARD16	exact-green
2	CARD16	exact-blue
2	CARD16	visual-red
2	CARD16	visual-green
2	CARD16	visual-blue
8		unused

AllocColorCells

1	86	opcode
1	BOOL	contiguous
2	3	request length
4	COLORMAP	cmap
2	CARD16	colors
2	CARD16	planes
→		
1	1	Reply
1		unused
2	CARD16	sequence number
4	n+m	reply length
2	n	number of CARD32s in pixels
2	m	number of CARD32s in masks
20		unused
4n	LISTofCARD32	pixels
4m	LISTofCARD32	masks

AllocColorPlanes

1	87	opcode
1	BOOL	contiguous
2	4	request length
4	COLORMAP	cmap
2	CARD16	colors
2	CARD16	reds
2	CARD16	greens
2	CARD16	blues
→		
1	1	Reply
1		unused
2	CARD16	sequence number

4	n	reply length
2	n	number of CARD32s in pixels
2		unused
4	CARD32	red-mask
4	CARD32	green-mask
4	CARD32	blue-mask
8		unused
4n	LISTofCARD32	pixels

FreeColors

1	88	opcode
1		unused
2	3 + n	request length
4	COLORMAP	cmap
4	CARD32	plane-mask
4n	LISTofCARD32	pixels

StoreColors

1	89	opcode
1		unused
2	2 + 3n	request length
4	COLORMAP	cmap
12n	LISTofCOLORITEM	items

COLORITEM

4	CARD32	pixel
2	CARD16	red
2	CARD16	green
2	CARD16	blue
1		do-red, do-green, do-blue
	#x01	do-red (1 is True, 0 is False)
	#x02	do-green (1 is True, 0 is False)
	#x04	do-blue (1 is True, 0 is False)
	#xf8	unused
1		unused

StoreNamedColor

1	90	opcode
1		do-red, do-green, do-blue

	#x01	do-red (1 is True, 0 is False)
	#x02	do-green (1 is True, 0 is False)
	#x04	do-blue (1 is True, 0 is False)
	#xf8	unused

2	4 + (n + p)/4	request length
4	COLORMAP	cmap
4	CARD32	pixel
2	n	length of name
2		unused
n	STRING8	name
p		unused, p = pad(n)

QueryColors

1	91	opcode
1		unused
2	2 + n	request length
4	COLORMAP	cmap
4n	LISTofCARD32	pixels
→		
1	1	Reply
1		unused
2	CARD16	sequence number
4	2n	reply length
2	n	number of RGBs in colors
22		unused
8n	LISTofRGB	colors

RGB

2	CARD16	red
2	CARD16	green
2	CARD16	blue
2		unused

LookupColor

1	92	opcode
1		unused
2	3 + (n + p)/4	request length
4	COLORMAP	cmap
2	n	length of name
2		unused

n	STRING8	name
p		unused, p = pad(n)
→		
1	1	Reply
1		unused
2	CARD16	sequence number
4	0	reply length
2	CARD16	exact-red
2	CARD16	exact-green
2	CARD16	exact-blue
2	CARD16	visual-red
2	CARD16	visual-green
2	CARD16	visual-blue
12		unused

CreateCursor

1	93	opcode
1		unused
2	8	request length
4	CURSOR	cid
4	PIXMAP	source
4	PIXMAP	mask
	0 None	
2	CARD16	fore-red
2	CARD16	fore-green
2	CARD16	fore-blue
2	CARD16	back-red
2	CARD16	back-green
2	CARD16	back-blue
2	CARD16	x
2	CARD16	y

CreateGlyphCursor

1	94	CreateGlyphCursor
1		unused
2	8	request length
4	CURSOR	cid
4	FONT	source-font
4	FONT	mask-font
	0 None	
2	CARD16	source-char

2	CARD16	mask-char
2	CARD16	fore-red
2	CARD16	fore-green
2	CARD16	fore-blue
2	CARD16	back-red
2	CARD16	back-green
2	CARD16	back-blue

FreeCursor

1	95	opcode
1		unused
2	2	request length
4	CURSOR	cursor

RecolorCursor

1	96	opcode
1		unused
2	5	request length
4	CURSOR	cursor
2	CARD16	fore-red
2	CARD16	fore-green
2	CARD16	fore-blue
2	CARD16	back-red
2	CARD16	back-green
2	CARD16	back-blue

QueryBestSize

1	97		opcode
1			class
	0	Cursor	
	1	Tile	
	2	Stipple	
2	3		request length
4	DRAWABLE		drawable
2	CARD16		width
2	CARD16		height
→			
1	1		Reply
1			unused
2	CARD16		sequence number
4	0		reply length

2	CARD16	width
2	CARD16	height
20		unused

QueryExtension

1	98	opcode
1		unused
2	2+(n+p)/4	request length
2	n	length of name
2		unused
n	STRING8	name
p		unused, p=pad(n)
→		
1	1	Reply
1		unused
2	CARD16	sequence number
4	0	reply length
1	BOOL	present
1	CARD8	major-opcode
1	CARD8	first-event
1	CARD8	first-error
20		unused

ListExtensions

1	99	opcode
1		unused
2	1	request length
→		
1	1	Reply
1	CARD8	number of STRs in names
2	CARD16	sequence number
4	(n+p)/4	reply length
24		unused
n	LISTofSTR	names
p		unused, p=pad(n)

ChangeKeyboardMapping

1	100	opcode
1	n	keycode-count
2	2+nm	request length

1	KEYCODE	first-keycode
1	m	keysyms-per-keycode
2		unused
4nm	LISTofKEYSYM	keysyms

GetKeyboardMapping

1	101	opcode
1		unused
2	2	request length
1	KEYCODE	first-keycode
1	CARD8	count
2		unused

→

1	1	Reply
1	n	keysyms-per-keycode
2	CARD16	sequence number
4	nm	reply length (m = count field from the request)
24		unused
4nm	LISTofKEYSYM	keysyms

ChangeKeyboardControl

1	102	opcode
1		unused
2	2+n	request length
4	BITMASK	value-mask (has n bits set to 1)

	#x0001	key-click-percent
	#x0002	bell-percent
	#x0004	bell-pitch
	#x0008	bell-duration
	#x0010	led
	#x0020	led-mode
	#x0040	key
	#x0080	auto-repeat-mode

| 4n | LISTofVALUE | value-list |

VALUEs

| 1 | INT8 | key-click-percent |
| 1 | INT8 | bell-percent |

2	INT16	bell-pitch
2	INT16	bell-duration
1	CARD8	led
1		led-mode

> 0 Off
> 1 On

1	KEYCODE	key
1		auto-repeat-mode

> 0 Off
> 1 On
> 2 Default

GetKeyboardControl

1	103	opcode
1		unused
2	1	request length
→		
1	1	Reply
1		global-auto-repeat

> 0 Off
> 1 On

2	CARD16	sequence number
4	5	reply length
4	CARD32	led-mask
1	CARD8	key-click-percent
1	CARD8	bell-percent
2	CARD16	bell-pitch
2	CARD16	bell-duration
2		unused
32	LISTofCARD8	auto-repeats

Bell

1	104	opcode
1	INT8	percent
2	1	request length

ChangePointerControl

1	105	opcode
1		unused
2	3	request length

2	INT16		acceleration-numerator
2	INT16		acceleration-denominator
2	INT16		threshold
1	BOOL		do-acceleration
1	BOOL		do-threshold

GetPointerControl

1	106		opcode
1			unused
2	1		request length

→

1	1		Reply
1			unused
2	CARD16		sequence number
4	0		reply length
2	CARD16		acceleration-numerator
2	CARD16		acceleration-denominator
2	CARD16		threshold
18			unused

SetScreenSaver

1	107		opcode
1			unused
2	3		request length
2	INT16		timeout
2	INT16		interval
1			prefer-blanking
	0	No	
	1	Yes	
	2	Default	
1			allow-exposures
	0	No	
	1	Yes	
	2	Default	
2			unused

GetScreenSaver

1	108		opcode
1			unused
2	1		request length

→

1	1	Reply
1		unused
2	CARD16	sequence number
4	0	reply length
2	CARD16	timeout
2	CARD16	interval
1		prefer-blanking
	0 No	
	1 Yes	
1		allow-exposures
	0 No	
	1 Yes	
18		unused

ChangeHosts

1	109	opcode
1		mode
	0 Insert	
	1 Delete	
2	2+(n+p)/4	request length
1		family
	0 Internet	
	1 DECnet	
	2 Chaos	
1		unused
2	CARD16	length of address
n	LISTofCARD8	address
p		unused, p = pad(n)

ListHosts

1	110	opcode
1		unused
2	1	request length
→		
1	1	Reply
1		mode
	0 Disabled	
	1 Enabled	
2	CARD16	sequence number
4	n/4	reply length

2	CARD16	number of HOSTs in hosts
22		unused
n	LISTofHOST	hosts (n always a multiple of 4)

SetAccessControl

1	111	opcode
1		mode
	0 Disable	
	1 Enable	
2	1	request length

SetCloseDownMode

1	112	opcode
1		mode
	0 Destroy	
	1 RetainPermanent	
	2 RetainTemporary	
2	1	request length

KillClient

1	113	opcode
1		unused
2	2	request length
4	CARD32	resource
	0 AllTemporary	

RotateProperties

1	114	opcode
1		unused
2	3+n	request length
4	WINDOW	window
2	n	number of properties
2	INT16	delta
4n	LISTofATOM	properties

ForceScreenSaver

| 1 | 115 | opcode |
| 1 | | mode |

	0 Reset	
	1 Activate	
2	1	request length

SetPointerMapping

1	116	opcode
1	n	length of map
2	1 + (n + p)/4	request length
n	LISTofCARD8	map
p		unused, p = pad(n)
→		
1	1	Reply
1		status
	0 Success	
	1 Busy	
2	CARD16	sequence number
4	0	reply length
24		unused

GetPointerMapping

1	117	opcode
1		unused
2	1	request length
→		
1	1	Reply
1	n	length of map
2	CARD16	sequence number
4	(n + p)/4	reply length
24		unused
n	LISTofCARD8	map
p		unused, p = pad(n)

SetModifierMapping

1	118	opcode
1	n	keycodes-per-modifier
2	1 + 2n	request length
8n	LISTofKEYCODE	keycodes
→		
1	1	Reply
1		status

	0	Success
	1	Busy
	2	Failed
2	CARD16	sequence number
4	0	reply length
24		unused

GetModifierMapping

1	119	opcode
1		unused
2	1	request length
→		
1	1	Reply
1	n	keycodes-per-modifier
2	CARD16	sequence number
4	2n	reply length
24		unused
8n	LISTofKEYCODE	keycodes

NoOperation

1	127	opcode
1		unused
2	1	request length

Events
KeyPress

1	2	code
1	KEYCODE	detail
2	CARD16	sequence number
4	TIMESTAMP	time
4	WINDOW	root
4	WINDOW	event
4	WINDOW	child
	0 None	
2	INT16	root-x
2	INT16	root-y
2	INT16	event-x
2	INT16	event-y
2	SETofKEYBUTMASK	state

1	BOOL	same-screen
1		unused

KeyRelease

1	3	code
1	KEYCODE	detail
2	CARD16	sequence number
4	TIMESTAMP	time
4	WINDOW	root
4	WINDOW	event
4	WINDOW	child
	0 None	
2	INT16	root-x
2	INT16	root-y
2	INT16	event-x
2	INT16	event-y
2	SETofKEYBUTMASK	state
1	BOOL	same-screen
1		unused

ButtonPress

1	4	code
1	BUTTON	detail
2	CARD16	sequence number
4	TIMESTAMP	time
4	WINDOW	root
4	WINDOW	event
4	WINDOW	child
	0 None	
2	INT16	root-x
2	INT16	root-y
2	INT16	event-x
2	INT16	event-y
2	SETofKEYBUTMASK	state
1	BOOL	same-screen
1		unused

ButtonRelease

1	5	code
1	BUTTON	detail
2	CARD16	sequence number

4	TIMESTAMP		time
4	WINDOW		root
4	WINDOW		event
4	WINDOW		child
	0	None	
2	INT16		root-x
2	INT16		root-y
2	INT16		event-x
2	INT16		event-y
2	SETofKEYBUTMASK		state
1	BOOL		same-screen
1			unused

MotionNotify

1	6		code
1			detail
	0	Normal	
	1	Hint	
2	CARD16		sequence number
4	TIMESTAMP		time
4	WINDOW		root
4	WINDOW		event
4	WINDOW		child
	0	None	
2	INT16		root-x
2	INT16		root-y
2	INT16		event-x
2	INT16		event-y
2	SETofKEYBUTMASK		state
1	BOOL		same-screen
1			unused

EnterNotify

1	7		code
1			detail
	0	Ancestor	
	1	Virtual	
	2	Inferior	
	3	Nonlinear	
	4	NonlinearVirtual	

2	CARD16	sequence number
4	TIMESTAMP	time
4	WINDOW	root
4	WINDOW	event
4	WINDOW	child
	0 None	
2	INT16	root-x
2	INT16	root-y
2	INT16	event-x
2	INT16	event-y
2	SETofKEYBUTMASK	state
1		mode
	0 Normal	
	1 Grab	
	2 Ungrab	
1		same-screen, focus
	#x01 focus (1 is True, 0 is False)	
	#x02 same-screen (1 is True, 0 is False)	
	#xfc unused	

LeaveNotify

1	8	code
1		detail
	0 Ancestor	
	1 Virtual	
	2 Inferior	
	3 Nonlinear	
	4 NonlinearVirtual	
2	CARD16	sequence number
4	TIMESTAMP	time
4	WINDOW	root
4	WINDOW	event
4	WINDOW	child
	0 None	
2	INT16	root-x
2	INT16	root-y
2	INT16	event-x
2	INT16	event-y
2	SETofKEYBUTMASK	state
1		mode

	0 Normal	
	1 Grab	
	2 Ungrab	
1		same-screen, focus
	#x01 focus (1 is True, 0 is False)	
	#x02 same-screen (1 is True, 0 is False)	
	#xfc unused	

FocusIn

1	9	code
1		detail
	0 Ancestor	
	1 Virtual	
	2 Inferior	
	3 Nonlinear	
	4 NonlinearVirtual	
	5 Pointer	
	6 PointerRoot	
	7 None	
2	CARD16	sequence number
4	WINDOW	event
1		mode
	0 Normal	
	1 Grab	
	2 Ungrab	
	3 WhileGrabbed	
23		unused

FocusOut

1	10	code
1		detail
	0 Ancestor	
	1 Virtual	
	2 Inferior	
	3 Nonlinear	
	4 NonlinearVirtual	
	5 Pointer	
	6 PointerRoot	
	7 None	

2	CARD16	sequence number
4	WINDOW	event
1		mode

```
0  Normal
1  Grab
2  Ungrab
3  WhileGrabbed
```

23		unused

KeymapNotify

1	11	code
31	LISTofCARD8	keys (byte for keycodes 0–7 is omitted)

Expose

1	12	code
1		unused
2	CARD16	sequence number
4	WINDOW	window
2	CARD16	x
2	CARD16	y
2	CARD16	width
2	CARD16	height
2	CARD16	count
14		unused

GraphicsExposure

1	13	code
1		unused
2	CARD16	sequence number
4	DRAWABLE	drawable
2	CARD16	x
2	CARD16	y
2	CARD16	width
2	CARD16	height
2	CARD16	minor-opcode
2	CARD16	count
1	CARD8	major-opcode
11		unused

NoExposure

1	14	code
1		unused
2	CARD16	sequence number
4	DRAWABLE	drawable
2	CARD16	minor-opcode
1	CARD8	major-opcode
21		unused

VisibilityNotify

1	15	code
1		unused
2	CARD16	sequence number
4	WINDOW	window
1		state

	0	Unobscured
	1	PartiallyObscured
	2	FullyObscured

23		unused

CreateNotify

1	16	code
1		unused
2	CARD16	sequence number
4	WINDOW	parent
4	WINDOW	window
2	INT16	x
2	INT16	y
2	CARD16	width
2	CARD16	height
2	CARD16	border-width
1	BOOL	override-redirect
9		unused

DestroyNotify

1	17	code
1		unused
2	CARD16	sequence number
4	WINDOW	event

| 4 | WINDOW | window |
| 20 | | unused |

UnmapNotify

1	18	code
1		unused
2	CARD16	sequence number
4	WINDOW	event
4	WINDOW	window
1	BOOL	from-configure
19		unused

MapNotify

1	19	code
1		unused
2	CARD16	sequence number
4	WINDOW	event
4	WINDOW	window
1	BOOL	override-redirect
19		unused

MapRequest

1	20	code
1		unused
2	CARD16	sequence number
4	WINDOW	parent
4	WINDOW	window
20		unused

ReparentNotify

1	21	code
1		unused
2	CARD16	sequence number
4	WINDOW	event
4	WINDOW	window
4	WINDOW	parent
2	INT16	x
2	INT16	y
1	BOOL	override-redirect
11		unused

ConfigureNotify

1	22		code
1			unused
2	CARD16		sequence number
4	WINDOW		event
4	WINDOW		window
4	WINDOW		above-sibling
	0	None	
2	INT16		x
2	INT16		y
2	CARD16		width
2	CARD16		height
2	CARD16		border-width
1	BOOL		override-redirect
5			unused

ConfigureRequest

1	23		code
1			stack-mode
	0	Above	
	1	Below	
	2	TopIf	
	3	BottomIf	
	4	Opposite	
2	CARD16		sequence number
4	WINDOW		parent
4	WINDOW		window
4	WINDOW		sibling
	0	None	
2	INT16		x
2	INT16		y
2	CARD16		width
2	CARD16		height
2	CARD16		border-width
2	BITMASK		value-mask
	#x0001	x	
	#x0002	y	
	#x0004	width	
	#x0008	height	
	#x0010	border-width	

```
       #x0020   sibling
       #x0040   stack-mode
4                                                  unused
```

GravityNotify

```
1     24                                           code
1                                                  unused
2     CARD16                                       sequence number
4     WINDOW                                       event
4     WINDOW                                       window
2     INT16                                        x
2     INT16                                        y
16                                                 unused
```

ResizeRequest

```
1     25                                           code
1                                                  unused
2     CARD16                                       sequence number
4     WINDOW                                       window
2     CARD16                                       width
2     CARD16                                       height
20                                                 unused
```

CirculateNotify

```
1     26                                           code
1                                                  unused
2     CARD16                                       sequence number
4     WINDOW                                       event
4     WINDOW                                       window
4     WINDOW                                       unused
1                                                  place
      0    Top
      1    Bottom
15                                                 unused
```

CirculateRequest

```
1     27                                           code
1                                                  unused
2     CARD16                                       sequence number
4     WINDOW                                       parent
```

4	WINDOW		window
4			unused
1			place
	0	Top	
	1	Bottom	
15			unused

PropertyNotify

1	28		code
1			unused
2	CARD16		sequence number
4	WINDOW		window
4	ATOM		atom
4	TIMESTAMP		time
1			state
	0	NewValue	
	1	Deleted	
15			unused

SelectionClear

1	29		code
1			unused
2	CARD16		sequence number
4	TIMESTAMP		time
4	WINDOW		owner
4	ATOM		selection
16			unused

SelectionRequest

1	30		code
1			unused
2	CARD16		sequence number
4	TIMESTAMP		time
	0	CurrentTime	
4	WINDOW		owner
4	WINDOW		requestor
4	ATOM		selection
4	ATOM		target

4	ATOM	property
	0 None	
4		unused

SelectionNotify

1	31	code
1		unused
2	CARD16	sequence number
4	TIMESTAMP	time
	0 CurrentTime	
4	WINDOW	requestor
4	ATOM	selection
4	ATOM	target
4	ATOM	property
	0 None	
8		unused

ColormapNotify

1	32	code
1		unused
2	CARD16	sequence number
4	WINDOW	window
4	COLORMAP	colormap
	0 None	
1	BOOL	new
1		state
	0 Uninstalled	
	1 Installed	
18		unused

ClientMessage

1	33	code
1	CARD8	format
2	CARD16	sequence number
4	WINDOW	window
4	ATOM	type
20		data

MappingNotify

1	34	code
1		unused
2	CARD16	sequence number
1		request
	0 Modifier	
	1 Keyboard	
	2 Pointer	
1	KEYCODE	first-keycode
1	CARD8	count
25		unused

Glossary

Access control list X maintains a list of hosts from which client programs can be run. By default, only programs on the local host and hosts specified in an initial list read by the server can use the display. This access control list can be changed by clients on the local host. Some server implementations can also implement other authorization mechanisms in addition to or in place of this mechanism. The action of this mechanism can be conditional based on the authorization protocol name and data received by the server at connection setup.

Active grab A grab is active when the pointer or keyboard is actually owned by the single grabbing client.

Ancestors If W is an inferior of Á, then A is an ancestor of W.

Atom An atom is a unique ID corresponding to a string name. Atoms are used to identify properties, types, and selections.

Background An InputOutput window can have a background, which is defined as a pixmap. When regions of the window have their contents lost or invalidated, the server automatically tiles those regions with the background.

Backing store When a server maintains the contents of a window, the pixels saved off-screen are known as a backing store.

Bit gravity When a window is resized, the contents of the window are not necessarily discarded. It is possible to request that the server relocate the previous contents to some region of the window (though no guarantees are made). This attraction of window contents for some location of a window is known as bit gravity.

Bit plane   When a pixmap or window is thought of as a stack of bitmaps, each bitmap is called a bit plane or plane.

Bitmap   A bitmap is a pixmap of depth one.

Border   An `InputOutput` window can have a border of equal thickness on all four sides of the window. The contents of the border are defined by a pixmap, and the server automatically maintains the contents of the border. Exposure events are never generated for border regions.

Button grabbing   Buttons on the pointer can be passively grabbed by a client. When the button is pressed, the pointer is then actively grabbed by the client.

Byte order   For image (pixmap/bitmap) data, the server defines the byte order, and clients with different native byte ordering must swap bytes as necessary. For all other parts of the protocol, the client defines the byte order, and the server swaps bytes as necessary.

Children   The children of a window are its first-level subwindows.

Class   Windows can be of different classes or types. See the entries for `InputOnly` and `InputOutput` windows for further information about valid window types.

Client   An application program connects to the window system server by some interprocess communication (IPC) path, such as a TCP connection or a shared memory buffer. This program is referred to as a client of the window system server. More precisely, the client is the IPC path itself. A program with multiple paths open to the server is viewed as multiple clients by the protocol. Resource lifetimes are controlled by connection lifetimes, not by program lifetimes.

Clipping region   In a graphics context, a bitmap or list of rectangles can be specified to restrict output to a particular region of the window. The image defined by the bitmap or rectangles is called a clipping region.

Colormap   A colormap consists of a set of entries defining color values. The colormap associated with a window is used to display the contents of the window; each pixel value indexes the colormap to produce RGB values that drive the guns of a monitor. Depending on hardware limitations, one or more colormaps can be installed at one time so that windows associated with those maps display with true colors.

Connection   The IPC path between the server and client program is known as a connection. A client program typically (but not necessarily) has one connection to the server over which requests and events are sent.

Containment   A window contains the pointer if the window is viewable and the hotspot of the cursor is within a visible region of the window or a visible region of one of its inferiors. The border of the window is included as part of the window for containment. The pointer is in a window if the window contains the pointer but no inferior contains the pointer.

Coordinate system   The coordinate system has X horizontal and Y vertical, with the origin [0, 0] at the upper left. Coordinates are discrete and are in terms of pixels. Each window and pixmap has its own coordinate system. For a window, the origin is inside the border at the inside upper-left corner.

Cursor   A cursor is the visible shape of the pointer on a screen. It consists of a hotspot, a source bitmap, a shape bitmap, and a pair of colors. The cursor defined for a window controls the visible appearance when the pointer is in that window.

Depth   The depth of a window or pixmap is the number of bits per pixel it has. The depth of a graphics context is the depth of the drawables it can be used in conjunction with graphics output.

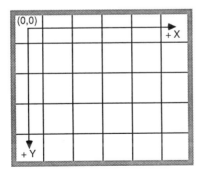

Coordinates Are Pixel Centers

Figure G.1.   Coordinate system

Device   Keyboards, mice, tablets, track-balls, button boxes, and so on are all collectively known as input devices. Pointers can have one or more buttons (the most common number is three). The core protocol only deals with two devices: the keyboard and the pointer.

DirectColor   `DirectColor` is a class of colormap in which a pixel value is decomposed into three separate subfields for indexing. The first subfield indexes an array to produce red intensity values. The second subfield indexes a second array to produce blue intensity values. The third subfield indexes a third array to produce green intensity values. The RGB (red, green, and blue) values in the colormap entry can be changed dynamically.

Display   A server, together with its screens and input devices, is called a display. The Xlib `Display` structure contains all information about the particular display and its screens as well as the state that Xlib needs to communicate with the display over a particular connection.

Drawable   Both windows and pixmaps can be used as sources and destinations in graphics operations. These windows and pixmaps are collectively known as drawables. However, an `InputOnly` window cannot be used as a source or destination in a graphics operation.

Event   Clients are informed of information asynchronously by means of events. These events can be either asynchronously generated from devices or generated as side effects of client requests. Events are grouped into types. The server never sends an event to a client unless the client has specifically asked to be informed of that type of event. However, clients can force events to be sent to other clients. Events are typically reported relative to a window.

Event mask   Events are requested relative to a window. The set of event types a client requests relative to a window is described by using an event mask.

Event propagation   Device-related events propagate from the source window to ancestor windows until some client has expressed interest in handling that type of event or until the event is discarded explicitly.

Event source   The deepest viewable window that the pointer is in is called the source of a device-related event.

Event synchronization There are certain race conditions possible when demultiplexing device events to clients (in particular, deciding where pointer and keyboard events should be sent when in the middle of window management operations). The event synchronization mechanism allows synchronous processing of device events.

Exposure event Servers do not guarantee to preserve the contents of windows when windows are obscured or reconfigured. Exposure events are sent to clients to inform them when contents of regions of windows have been lost.

Extension Named extensions to the core protocol can be defined to extend the system. Extensions to output requests, resources, and event types are all possible, and expected.

Font A font is an array of glyphs (typically characters). The protocol does no translation or interpretation of character sets. The client simply indicates values used to index the glyph array. A font contains additional metric information to determine interglyph and interline spacing.

Frozen events Clients can freeze event processing during keyboard and pointer grabs.

GC GC is an abbreviation for graphics context. See *Graphics context.*

Glyph A glyph is an image in a font, typically of a character.

Grab Keyboard keys, the keyboard, pointer buttons, the pointer, and the server can be grabbed for exclusive use by a client. In general, these facilities are not intended to be used by normal applications but are intended for various input and window managers to implement various styles of user interfaces.

Graphics context Various information for graphics output is stored in a graphics context (GC), such as foreground pixel, background pixel, line width, clipping region, and so on. A graphics context can only be used with drawables that have the same root and the same depth as the graphics context.

Gravity The contents of windows and windows themselves have a gravity, which determines how the contents move when a window is resized. See *Bit gravity* and *Window gravity.*

GrayScale GrayScale can be viewed as a degenerate case of Pseudo-Color, in which the red, green, and blue values in any given colormap entry are equal and thus produce shades of gray. The gray values can be changed dynamically.

Hotspot A cursor has an associated hotspot, which defines the point in the cursor corresponding to the coordinates reported for the pointer.

Identifier An identifier is a unique value associated with a resource that clients use to name that resource. The identifier can be used over any connection to name the resource.

Inferiors The inferiors of a window are all of the subwindows nested below it: the children, the children's children, and so on.

Input focus The input focus is usually a window defining the scope for processing of keyboard input. If a generated keyboard event usually would be reported to this window or one of its inferiors, the event is reported as usual. Otherwise, the event is reported with respect to the focus window. The input focus also can be set such that all keyboard events are discarded and such that the focus window is dynamically taken to be the root window of whatever screen the pointer is on at each keyboard event.

Input manager Control over keyboard input is typically provided by an input manager client, which usually is part of a window manager.

InputOnly window An InputOnly window is a window that cannot be used for graphics requests. InputOnly windows are invisible and are used to control such things as cursors, input event generation, and grabbing. InputOnly windows cannot have InputOutput windows as inferiors.

InputOutput window An InputOutput window is the normal kind of window that is used for both input and output. InputOutput windows can have both InputOutput and InputOnly windows as inferiors.

Key grabbing Keys on the keyboard can be passively grabbed by a client. When the key is pressed, the keyboard is then actively grabbed by the client.

Keyboard grabbing A client can actively grab control of the keyboard, and key events will be sent to that client rather than the client the events would normally have been sent to.

Keysym   An encoding of a symbol on a keycap on a keyboard.

Mapped   A window is said to be mapped if a map call has been performed on it. Unmapped windows and their inferiors are never viewable or visible.

Modifier keys   Shift, Control, Meta, Super, Hyper, Alt, Compose, Apple, CapsLock, ShiftLock, and similar keys are called modifier keys.

Monochrome   Monochrome is a special case of `StaticGray` in which there are only two colormap entries.

Obscure   A window is obscured if some other window obscures it. A window can be partially obscured and so still have visible regions. Window A obscures window B if both are viewable `InputOutput` windows, if A is higher in the global stacking order, and if the rectangle defined by the outside edges of A intersects the rectangle defined by the outside edges of B. Note the distinction between obscures and occludes. Also note that window borders are included in the calculation.

Occlude   A window is occluded if some other window occludes it. Window A occludes window B if both are mapped, if A is higher in the global stacking order, and if the rectangle defined by the outside edges of A intersects the rectangle defined by the outside edges of B. Note the distinction between occludes and obscures. Also note that window borders are included in the calculation and that `InputOnly` windows never obscure other windows but can occlude other windows.

Padding   Some padding bytes are inserted in the data stream to maintain alignment of the protocol requests on natural boundaries. This increases ease of portability to some machine architectures.

Parent window   If C is a child of P, then P is the parent of C.

Passive grab   Grabbing a key or button is a passive grab. The grab activates when the key or button is actually pressed.

Pixel value   A pixel is an N-bit value, where N is the number of bit planes used in a particular window or pixmap (that is, is the depth of the window or pixmap). A pixel in a window indexes a colormap to derive an actual color to be displayed.

Pixmap   A pixmap is a three-dimensional array of bits. A pixmap is normally thought of as a two-dimensional array of pixels, where each pixel can be a value from 0 to $2^N - 1$, and where N is the depth (z axis) of the pixmap. A pixmap can also be thought of as a stack of N bitmaps. A pixmap can only be used on the screen that it was created in.

Plane   When a pixmap or window is thought of as a stack of bitmaps, each bitmap is called a plane or bit plane.

Plane mask   Graphics operations can be restricted to only affect a subset of bit planes of a destination. A plane mask is a bit mask describing which planes are to be modified. The plane mask is stored in a graphics context.

Pointer   The pointer is the pointing device currently attached to the cursor and tracked on the screens.

Pointer grabbing   A client can actively grab control of the pointer. Then button and motion events will be sent to that client rather than the client the events would normally have been sent to.

Pointing device   A pointing device is typically a mouse, tablet, or some other device with effective dimensional motion. The core protocol defines only one visible cursor, which tracks whatever pointing device is attached as the pointer.

Property   Windows can have associated properties that consist of a name, a type, a data format, and some data. The protocol places no interpretation on properties. They are intended as a general-purpose naming mechanism for clients. For example, clients might use properties to share information such as resize hints, program names, and icon formats with a window manager.

Property list   The property list of a window is the list of properties that have been defined for the window.

PseudoColor   PseudoColor is a class of colormap in which a pixel value indexes the colormap entry to produce independent RGB values; that is, the colormap is viewed as an array of triples (RGB values). The RGB values can be changed dynamically.

Rectangle   A rectangle specified by [x,y,w,h] has an infinitely thin outline path with corners at [x,y], [x+w,y], [x+w,y+h], and [x, y+h]. When a rectangle is filled, the lower-right edges are not drawn. For example, if w=h=0, nothing would be drawn. For w=h=1, a single pixel would be drawn.

Redirecting control Window managers (or client programs) may enforce window layout policy in various ways. When a client attempts to change the size or position of a window, the operation may be redirected to a specified client rather than the operation actually being performed.

Reply Information requested by a client program using the X protocol is sent back to the client with a reply. Both events and replies are multiplexed on the same connection. Most requests do not generate replies, but some requests generate multiple replies.

Request A command to the server is called a request. It is a single block of data sent over a connection.

Resource Windows, pixmaps, cursors, fonts, graphics contexts, and colormaps are known as resources. They all have unique identifiers associated with them for naming purposes. The lifetime of a resource usually is bounded by the lifetime of the connection over which the resource was created.

RGB values RGB values are the red, green, and blue intensity values that are used to define a color. These values are always represented as 16-bit, unsigned numbers, with 0 the minimum intensity and 65535 the maximum intensity. The X server scales these values to match the display hardware.

Root The root of a pixmap or graphics context is the same as the root of whatever drawable was used when the pixmap or GC was created. The root of a window is the root window under which the window was created.

Root window Each screen has a root window covering it. The root window cannot be reconfigured or unmapped, but otherwise it acts as a full-fledged window. A root window has no parent.

Save-set The save-set of a client is a list of other clients' windows that, if they are inferiors of one of the clients' windows at connection close, should not be destroyed and that should be remapped if currently unmapped. Save-sets are typically used by window managers to avoid lost windows if the manager should terminate abnormally.

Scanline A scanline is a list of pixel or bit values viewed as a horizontal row (all values having the same y coordinate) of an image, with the values ordered by increasing the x coordinate.

Scanline order   An image represented in scanline order contains scanlines ordered by increasing the y coordinate.

Screen   A server can provide several independent screens, which typically have physically independent monitors. This would be the expected configuration when there is only a single keyboard and pointer shared among the screens. A `Screen` structure contains the information about that screen and is linked to the `Display` structure.

Selection   A selection can be thought of as an indirect property with dynamic type. That is, rather than having the property stored in the X server, it is maintained by some client (the owner). A selection is global and is thought of as belonging to the user and being maintained by clients, rather than being private to a particular window subhierarchy or a particular set of clients. When a client asks for the contents of a selection, it specifies a selection target type, which can be used to control the transmitted representation of the contents. For example, if the selection is "the last thing the user clicked on," and that is currently an image, then the target type might specify whether the contents of the image should be sent in XY format or Z format.

The target type can also be used to control the class of contents transmitted; for example, asking for the "looks" (fonts, line spacing, indentation, and so forth) of a paragraph selection, rather than the text of the paragraph. The target type can also be used for other purposes. The protocol does not constrain the semantics.

Server   The server, which is also referred to as the X server, provides the basic windowing mechanism. It handles IPC connections from clients, demultiplexes graphics requests onto the screens, and multiplexes input back to the appropriate clients.

Server grabbing   The server can be grabbed by a single client for exclusive use. This prevents processing of any requests from other client connections until the grab is completed. This is typically only a transient state for such things as rubber-banding, pop-up menus, or executing requests indivisibly.

Sibling   Children of the same parent window are known as sibling windows.

Stacking order   Sibling windows, similar to sheets of paper on a desk, can stack on top of each other. Windows above both obscure and occlude lower windows. The relationship between sibling windows is known as the stacking order.

StaticColor   `StaticColor` can be viewed as a degenerate case of `PseudoColor` in which the RGB values are predefined and read-only.

StaticGray   `StaticGray` can be viewed as a degenerate case of `Gray-Scale` in which the gray values are predefined and read-only. The values are typically linear or near-linear increasing ramps.

Status   Many Xlib functions return a success status. If the function does not succeed, however, its arguments are not disturbed.

Stipple   A stipple pattern is a bitmap that is used to tile a region to serve as an additional clip mask for a fill operation with the foreground color.

Tile   A pixmap can be replicated in two dimensions to tile a region. The pixmap itself is also known as a tile.

Timestamp   A timestamp is a time value expressed in milliseconds. It is typically the time since the last server reset. Timestamp values wrap around (after about 49.7 days). The server, given its current time is represented by timestamp T, always interprets timestamps from clients by treating half of the timestamp space as being earlier in time than T and half of the timestamp space as being later in time than T. One timestamp value, represented by the constant `CurrentTime`, is never generated by the server. This value is reserved for use in requests to represent the current server time.

TrueColor   `TrueColor` can be viewed as a degenerate case of `DirectColor` in which the subfields in the pixel value directly encode the corresponding RGB values. That is, the colormap has predefined read-only RGB values. The values are typically linear or near-linear increasing ramps.

Type   A type is an arbitrary atom used to identify the interpretation of property data. Types are completely uninterpreted by the server. They are solely for the benefit of clients. X predefines type atoms for many frequently used types, and clients also can define new types.

Viewable   A window is viewable if it and all of its ancestors are mapped. This does not imply that any portion of the window is actually visible. Graphics requests can be performed on a window when it is not viewable, but output will not be retained unless the server is maintaining backing store.

Visible   A region of a window is visible if someone looking at the screen can actually see it; that is, the window is viewable and the region is not occluded by any other window.

Window gravity   When windows are resized, subwindows may be repositioned automatically relative to some position in the window. This attraction of a subwindow to some part of its parent is known as window gravity.

Window manager   Manipulation of windows on the screen and much of the user interface (policy) is typically provided by a window manager client.

XY format   The data for a pixmap is said to be in XY format if it is organized as a set of bitmaps representing individual bit planes with the planes appearing from most-significant to least-significant bit order.

Z format   The data for a pixmap is said to be in Z format if it is organized as a set of pixel values in scanline order.

Index

Expose event,
  as side effect of restacking window, 6
  can be generated if background-pixmap `None`, 34
  checked before mapping to avoid repainting, 46
  formal description of protocol event, 450
  generated,
    by `XMapWindow` unless backing store present, 31
    if `XDestroyWindow` called on mapped window, 43
    if window resized with `ForgetGravity`, 36
    on specified window in `XDestroy-Subwindows`, 44
    with certain settings of backing store, 37
    if `XCirculateSubwindows` exposes obscured windows, 55
    if `XLowerWindow` exposes obscured windows, 54
    if `XRaiseWindow` exposes obscured windows, 54
    if moving window,
      causes loss of contents, 51, 53
      exposes obscured windows, 51, 53
    if resizing window
      causes loss of contents, 52, 53
      exposes obscured windows, 52, 53
    on obscured windows uncovered with unmap, 47
  protocol encoding, 607
  sent to allow repainting of hidden window, 5
exposing,
  events, discussion and related Xlib structures, 234
  `VisibilityNotify` event, discussion and related Xlib structures, 245
  due to graphic requests, `GraphicsExposure` protocol event, 451
  graphics requests did not generate exposure, `NoExposure` protocol event, 451
  windows, generate `Expose` protocol event, 450
Exposure,
  as AlternativeValue for EVENT, 348
Exposure event,
  if part of mapped window becomes visible, 44
exposure,
  event, glossary entry, 619
  events, and preservation and regeneration of window contents, 234
  processing, if window is reconfigured with `XWindowChanges`, 49
  setting flag of given GC using `XSet-GraphicsExposures`, 117
extensions,
  adding extension using `XAddExtension`, 478
  allocating storage for information about extensions using `XInitExtension`, 478

  of argument type using OR, 348
  chaining additional data onto certain Xlib data structures, 484
  complete list of those supported by server using `XListExtensions`, 477
  defining procedures to be called when various circumstances occur, 478
  error codes reserved for extensions in error format, 346
  general discussion of role of extensions in X Standard, 475
  glossary entry, 619
  opcodes reserved for extensions in requests, 345
  presence checked using `XQueryExtension`, 477
  querying for,
    list of extensions using `ListExtensions` protocol request, 431
    presence of extension, using `Query-Extension` protocol request, 430
extents,
  See Also widths
  computing logical string, discussion and related Xlib functions, 147
  querying for character strings, discussion and related Xlib functions, 149
external symbols,
  represented in mixed case by Xlib, 7

False,
  Boolean defined in Xlib, 9
family,
  as element in type description of HOST, 349
FAMILY_NAME,
  listed as a built-in font property type, 70
  in list of atoms with predefined values, 354
fatal,
  setting fatal I/O error handler, using `XSetIO-ErrorHandler`, 274
feel,
  of interaction with pointer, controlling with `XChangePointerControl`, 196
fetching,
  data from,
    cut buffer 0 using `XFetchBytes`, 314
    specified cut buffer using `XFetchBuffer`, 314
files,
  bitmap file format definitions, discussion and related Xlib functions, 321
  connection number is file descriptor on UNIX-based system, 13
  reading bitmap from file using `XReadBitmap-File`, 321
  retrieving resource databases from disk files using `XrmGetFileDatabase`, 336

WINDOW

Ordering Information

Use the form below to order additional copies of this book. Or for quicker service, call toll-free:

1-800-343-8321

Digital Press
Digital Equipment Corporation
12 Crosby Drive
Bedford, MA 01730

Order No.	Title	Qty.	Price*	Total
EY-6737E-DP	X Window System		$55.00	

subtotal	
tax	
total	

Method of payment
Include payment with order to get FREE shipping.

_____ Check enclosed, payable   _____ MasterCard
to Digital Equipment   _____ VISA
Corporation
_____ Purchase order (please   Card no. _____
enclose)
P.O. no. _____   Expiration date _____
Signature _____

Ship/bill to:

Name _____

Address _____

_____

City _____ State _____ Zip _____

---

*__Important!__ Price is subject to change without notice. Taxes and shipping, if applicable, are not included in the price. Price and terms are U.S. only.

Please address inquiries regarding discounts on multiple-copy orders to: Sales Manager, Digital Press, BUO-E94, 12 Crosby Drive, Bedford, MA 01730.